a **GET FUZZY** treasury by darby conley

THE POTPOURRIFIC GREAT BIG GRAB BAG OF GET FUZZY

Andrews McMeel
Publishing, LLC

Kansas City

Get Fuzzy is distributed internationally by United Feature Syndicate, Inc.

08 09 10 11 12 BAM 10 9 8 7 6 5 4 3 2 1

ISBN-13: 978-0-7407-7367-9
ISBN-10: 0-7407-7367-4

Library of Congress Control Number: 2008926293

www.andrewsmcmeel.com

Get Fuzzy can be viewed on the Internet at
www.comics.com.

THE POTPOURRIFIC GREAT BIG GRAB BAG OF GET FUZZY

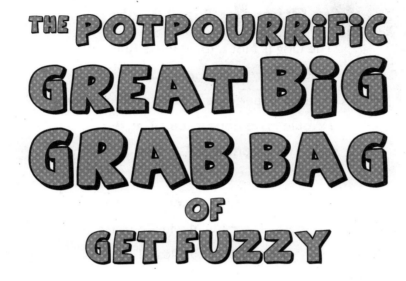

Other *Get Fuzzy* Books

The Dog Is Not a Toy (House Rule #4)

Fuzzy Logic: Get Fuzzy 2

The Get Fuzzy Experience: Are You Bucksperienced

I Would Have Bought You a Cat, But . . .

Blueprint for Disaster

Say Cheesy

Scrum Bums

I'm Ready for My Movie Contract

Take Our Cat, Please!

Treasuries

Groovitude: A Get Fuzzy Treasury

Bucky Katt's Big Book of Fun

Loserpalooza

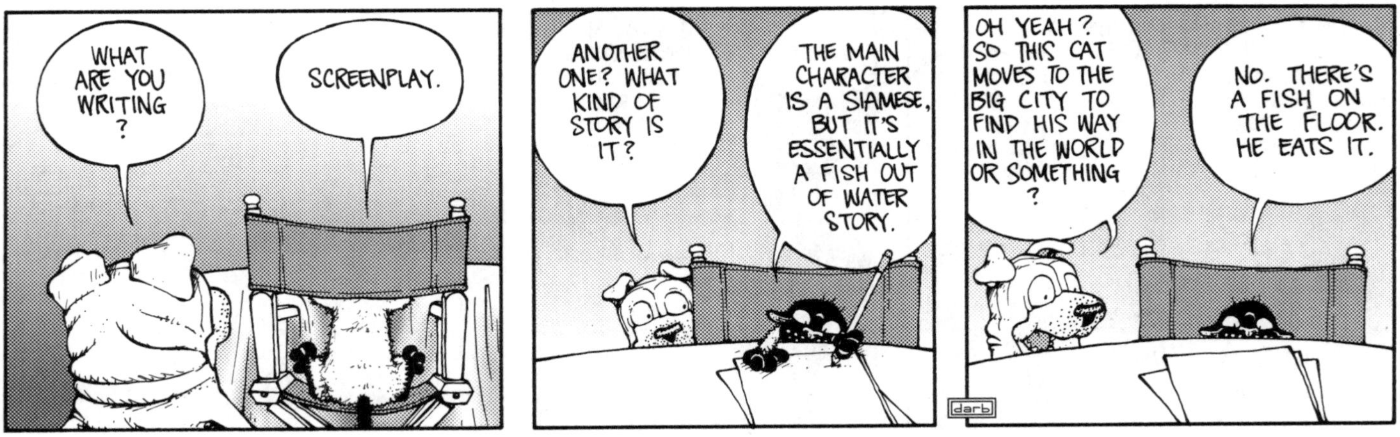
WHAT ARE YOU WRITING ?
SCREENPLAY.
ANOTHER ONE? WHAT KIND OF STORY IS IT?
THE MAIN CHARACTER IS A SIAMESE, BUT IT'S ESSENTIALLY A FISH OUT OF WATER STORY.
OH YEAH? SO THIS CAT MOVES TO THE BIG CITY TO FIND HIS WAY IN THE WORLD OR SOMETHING ?
NO. THERE'S A FISH ON THE FLOOR. HE EATS IT.
darb

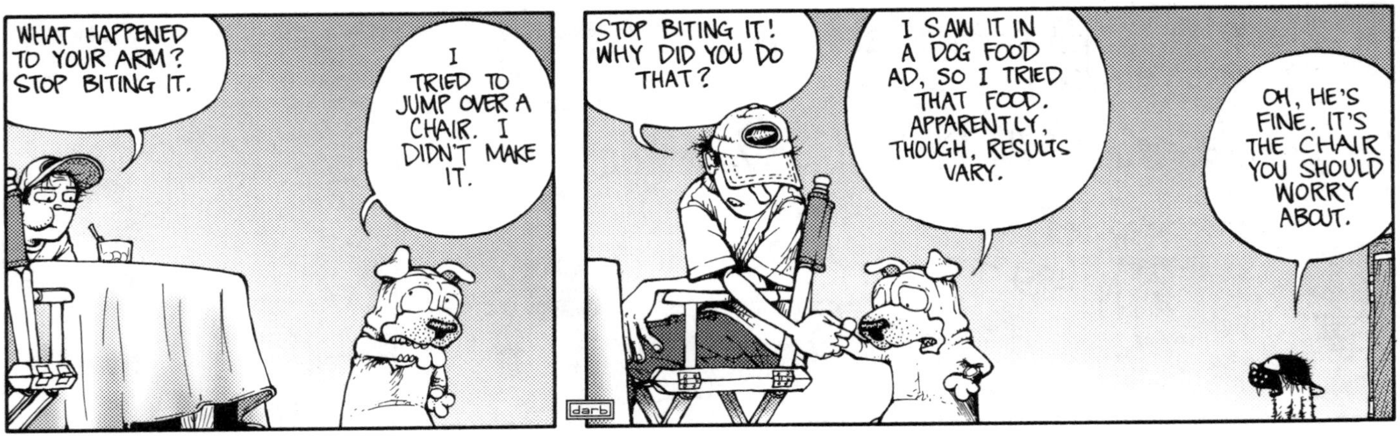
WHAT HAPPENED TO YOUR ARM? STOP BITING IT.
I TRIED TO JUMP OVER A CHAIR. I DIDN'T MAKE IT.
darb
STOP BITING IT! WHY DID YOU DO THAT?
I SAW IT IN A DOG FOOD AD, SO I TRIED THAT FOOD. APPARENTLY, THOUGH, RESULTS VARY.
OH, HE'S FINE. IT'S THE CHAIR YOU SHOULD WORRY ABOUT.

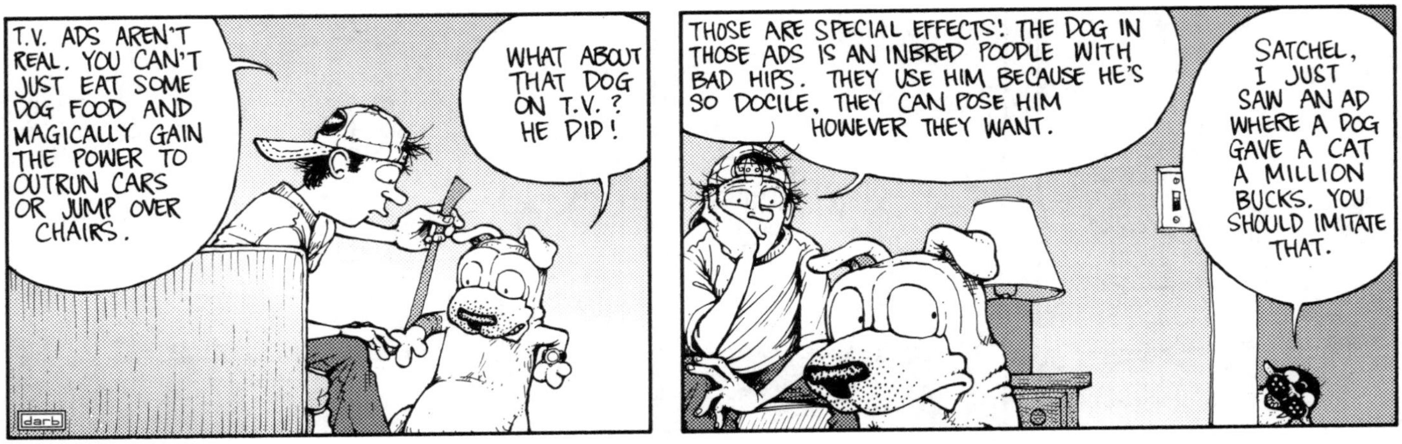
T.V. ADS AREN'T REAL. YOU CAN'T JUST EAT SOME DOG FOOD AND MAGICALLY GAIN THE POWER TO OUTRUN CARS OR JUMP OVER CHAIRS.
WHAT ABOUT THAT DOG ON T.V.? HE DID!
darb
THOSE ARE SPECIAL EFFECTS! THE DOG IN THOSE ADS IS AN INBRED POODLE WITH BAD HIPS. THEY USE HIM BECAUSE HE'S SO DOCILE, THEY CAN POSE HIM HOWEVER THEY WANT.
SATCHEL, I JUST SAW AN AD WHERE A DOG GAVE A CAT A MILLION BUCKS. YOU SHOULD IMITATE THAT.

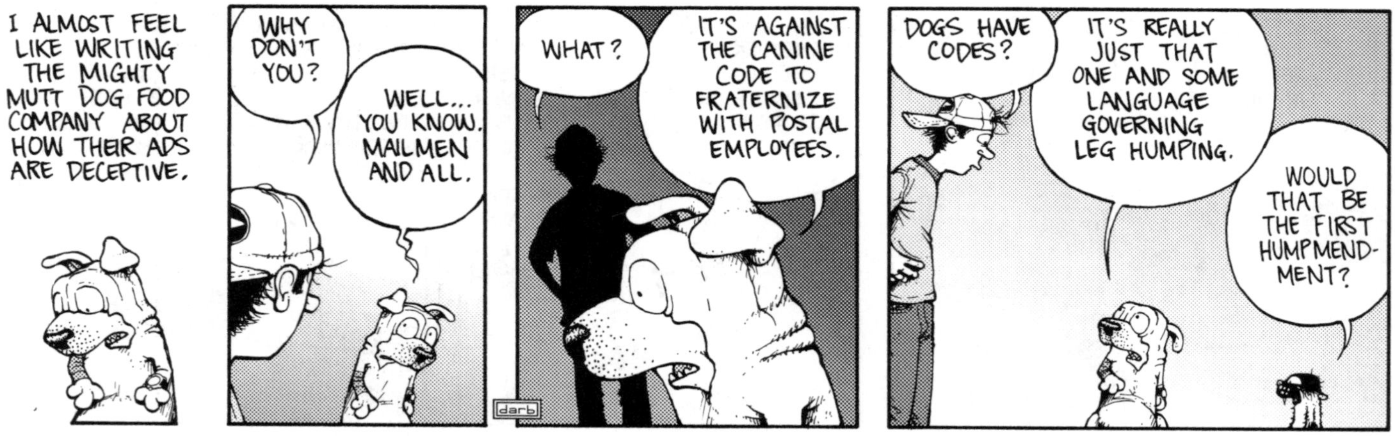
I ALMOST FEEL LIKE WRITING THE MIGHTY MUTT DOG FOOD COMPANY ABOUT HOW THEIR ADS ARE DECEPTIVE.
WHY DON'T YOU?
WELL... YOU KNOW. MAILMEN AND ALL.
WHAT?
IT'S AGAINST THE CANINE CODE TO FRATERNIZE WITH POSTAL EMPLOYEES.
darb
DOGS HAVE CODES?
IT'S REALLY JUST THAT ONE AND SOME LANGUAGE GOVERNING LEG HUMPING.
WOULD THAT BE THE FIRST HUMPMEND-MENT?

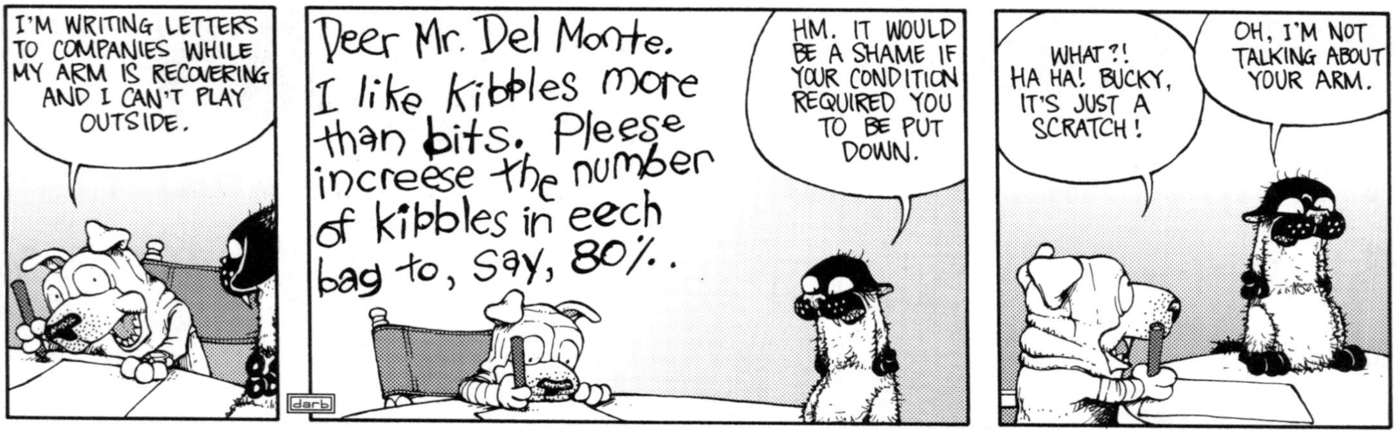
I'M WRITING LETTERS TO COMPANIES WHILE MY ARM IS RECOVERING AND I CAN'T PLAY OUTSIDE.
Deer Mr. Del Monte. I like kibbles more than bits. Pleese increese the number of kibbles in eech bag to, say, 80%..
HM. IT WOULD BE A SHAME IF YOUR CONDITION REQUIRED YOU TO BE PUT DOWN.
darb
WHAT?! HA HA! BUCKY, IT'S JUST A SCRATCH!
OH, I'M NOT TALKING ABOUT YOUR ARM.

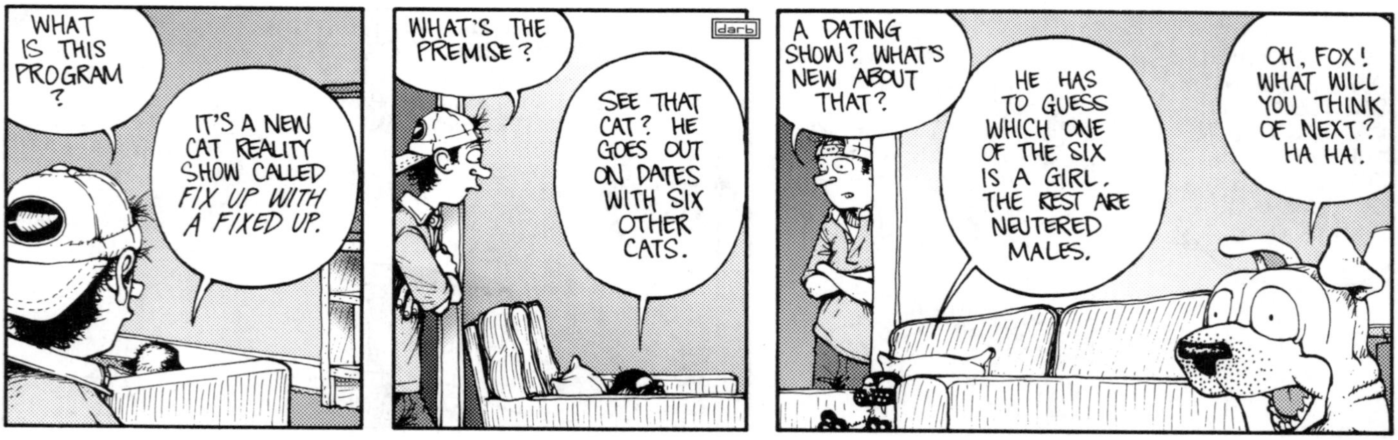
WHAT IS THIS PROGRAM?
IT'S A NEW CAT REALITY SHOW CALLED *FIX UP WITH A FIXED UP.*
WHAT'S THE PREMISE?
SEE THAT CAT? HE GOES OUT ON DATES WITH SIX OTHER CATS.
darb
A DATING SHOW? WHAT'S NEW ABOUT THAT?
HE HAS TO GUESS WHICH ONE OF THE SIX IS A GIRL. THE REST ARE NEUTERED MALES.
OH, FOX! WHAT WILL YOU THINK OF NEXT? HA HA!

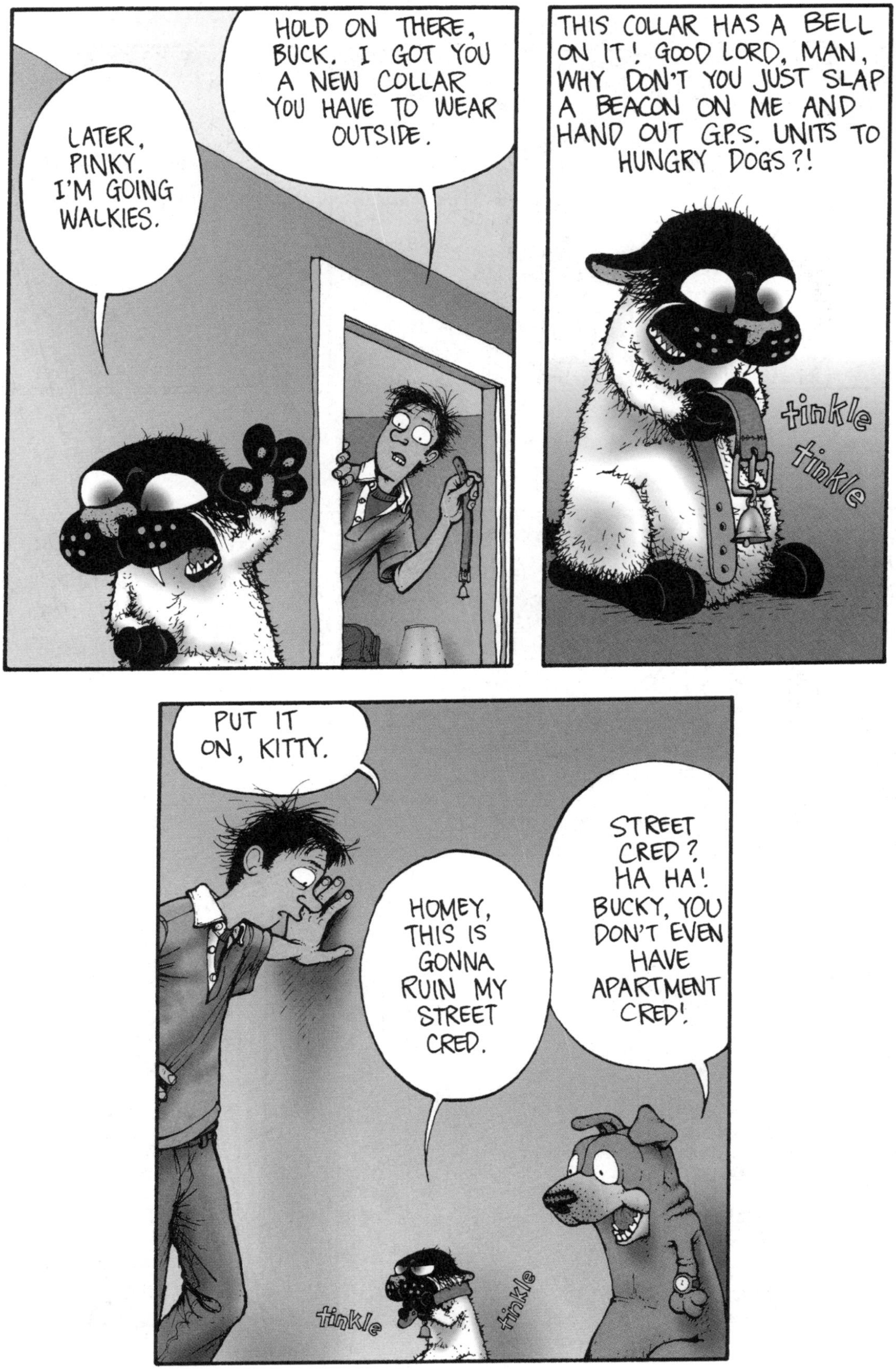
LATER, PINKY. I'M GOING WALKIES.
HOLD ON THERE, BUCK. I GOT YOU A NEW COLLAR YOU HAVE TO WEAR OUTSIDE.
THIS COLLAR HAS A BELL ON IT! GOOD LORD, MAN, WHY DON'T YOU JUST SLAP A BEACON ON ME AND HAND OUT G.P.S. UNITS TO HUNGRY DOGS?!
tinkle
tinkle
PUT IT ON, KITTY.
HOMEY, THIS IS GONNA RUIN MY STREET CRED.
STREET CRED? HA HA! BUCKY, YOU DON'T EVEN HAVE APARTMENT CRED!
tinkle
tinkle

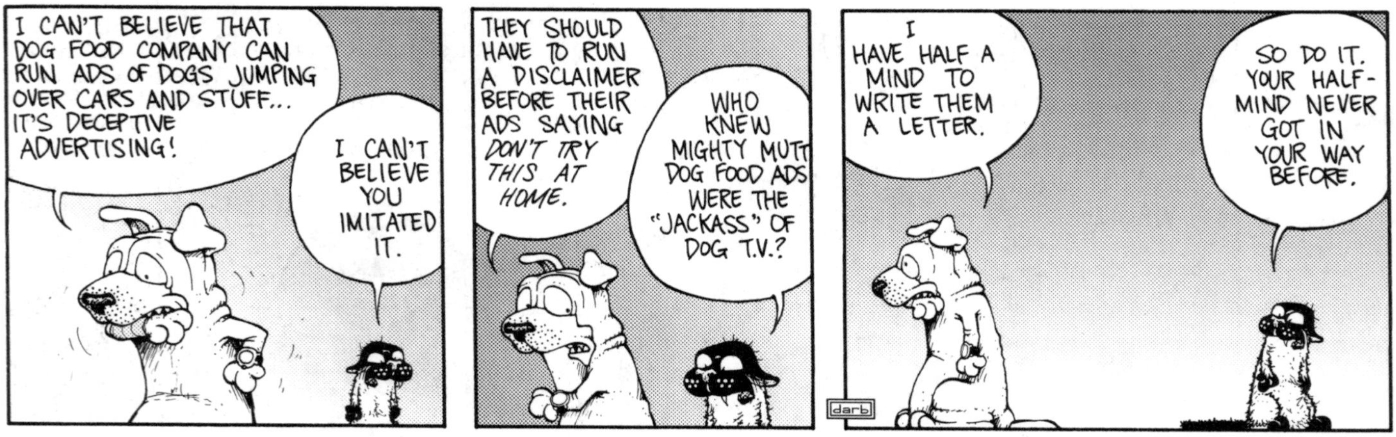
I CAN'T BELIEVE THAT DOG FOOD COMPANY CAN RUN ADS OF DOGS JUMPING OVER CARS AND STUFF... IT'S DECEPTIVE ADVERTISING!
I CAN'T BELIEVE YOU IMITATED IT.
THEY SHOULD HAVE TO RUN A DISCLAIMER BEFORE THEIR ADS SAYING *DON'T TRY THIS AT HOME.*
WHO KNEW MIGHTY MUTT DOG FOOD ADS WERE THE "JACKASS" OF DOG T.V.?
I HAVE HALF A MIND TO WRITE THEM A LETTER.
SO DO IT. YOUR HALF-MIND NEVER GOT IN YOUR WAY BEFORE.

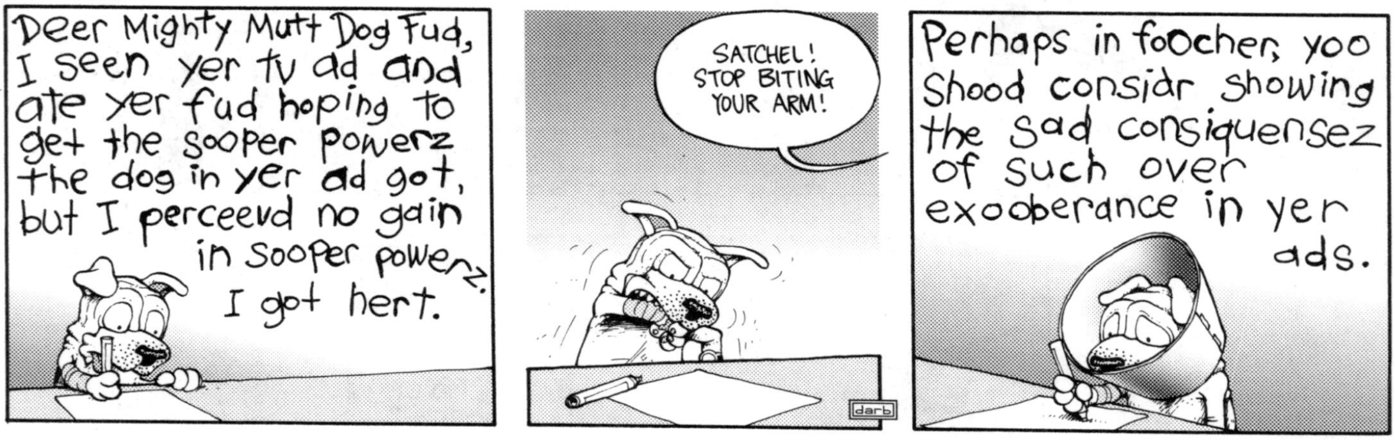
Deer Mighty Mutt Dog Fud, I seen yer tv ad and ate yer fud hoping to get the sooper powerz the dog in yer ad got, but I perceevd no gain in sooper powerz. I got hert.
SATCHEL! STOP BITING YOUR ARM!
Perhaps in foocher, yoo shood considr showing the sad consiquensez of such over exooberance in yer ads.

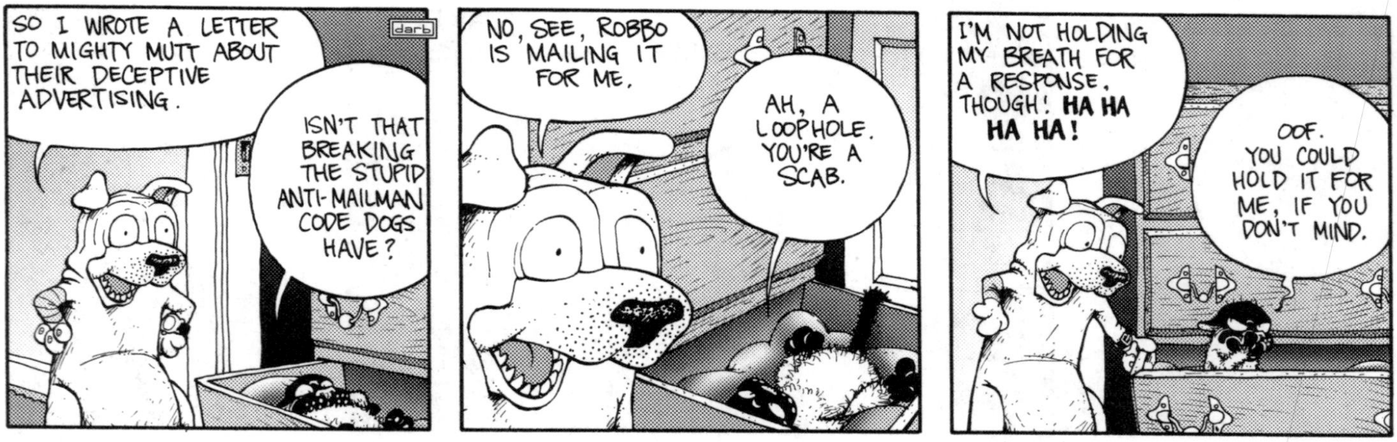
SO I WROTE A LETTER TO MIGHTY MUTT ABOUT THEIR DECEPTIVE ADVERTISING.
ISN'T THAT BREAKING THE STUPID ANTI-MAILMAN CODE DOGS HAVE?
NO, SEE, ROBBO IS MAILING IT FOR ME.
AH, A LOOPHOLE. YOU'RE A SCAB.
I'M NOT HOLDING MY BREATH FOR A RESPONSE, THOUGH! **HA HA HA HA!**
OOF. YOU COULD HOLD IT FOR ME, IF YOU DON'T MIND.

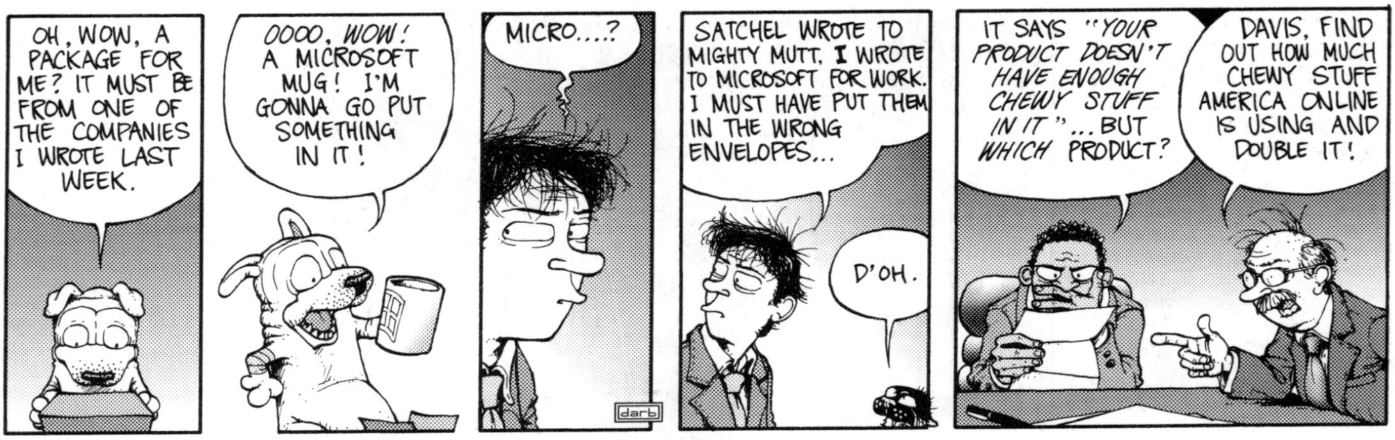
OH, WOW, A PACKAGE FOR ME? IT MUST BE FROM ONE OF THE COMPANIES I WROTE LAST WEEK.
OOOO, WOW! A MICROSOFT MUG! I'M GONNA GO PUT SOMETHING IN IT!
MICRO....?
darb
SATCHEL WROTE TO MIGHTY MUTT. I WROTE TO MICROSOFT FOR WORK. I MUST HAVE PUT THEM IN THE WRONG ENVELOPES...
D'OH.
IT SAYS "YOUR PRODUCT DOESN'T HAVE ENOUGH CHEWY STUFF IN IT"... BUT WHICH PRODUCT?
DAVIS, FIND OUT HOW MUCH CHEWY STUFF AMERICA ONLINE IS USING AND DOUBLE IT!

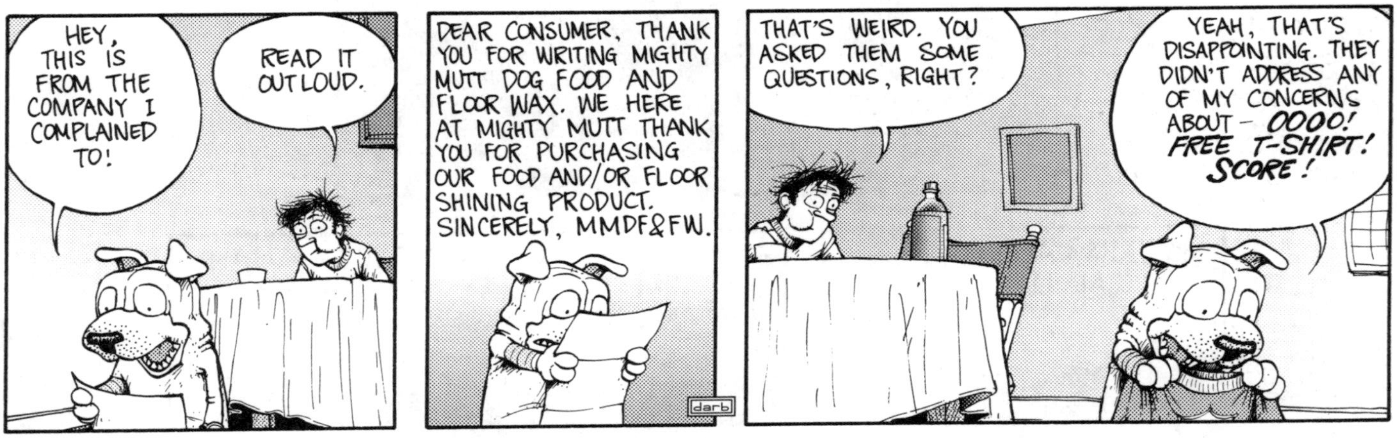
HEY, THIS IS FROM THE COMPANY I COMPLAINED TO!
READ IT OUTLOUD.
DEAR CONSUMER, THANK YOU FOR WRITING MIGHTY MUTT DOG FOOD AND FLOOR WAX. WE HERE AT MIGHTY MUTT THANK YOU FOR PURCHASING OUR FOOD AND/OR FLOOR SHINING PRODUCT. SINCERELY, MMDF&FW.
darb
THAT'S WEIRD. YOU ASKED THEM SOME QUESTIONS, RIGHT?
YEAH, THAT'S DISAPPOINTING. THEY DIDN'T ADDRESS ANY OF MY CONCERNS ABOUT – OOOO! FREE T-SHIRT! SCORE!

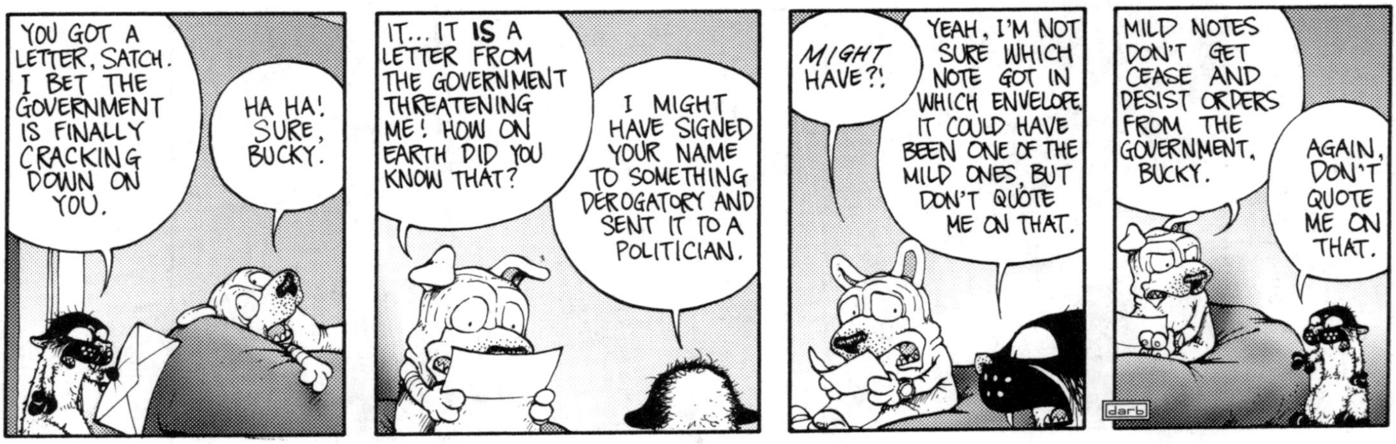
YOU GOT A LETTER, SATCH. I BET THE GOVERNMENT IS FINALLY CRACKING DOWN ON YOU.
HA HA! SURE, BUCKY.
IT... IT IS A LETTER FROM THE GOVERNMENT THREATENING ME! HOW ON EARTH DID YOU KNOW THAT?
I MIGHT HAVE SIGNED YOUR NAME TO SOMETHING DEROGATORY AND SENT IT TO A POLITICIAN.
MIGHT HAVE?!
YEAH, I'M NOT SURE WHICH NOTE GOT IN WHICH ENVELOPE. IT COULD HAVE BEEN ONE OF THE MILD ONES, BUT DON'T QUOTE ME ON THAT.
MILD NOTES DON'T GET CEASE AND DESIST ORDERS FROM THE GOVERNMENT, BUCKY.
AGAIN, DON'T QUOTE ME ON THAT.
darb

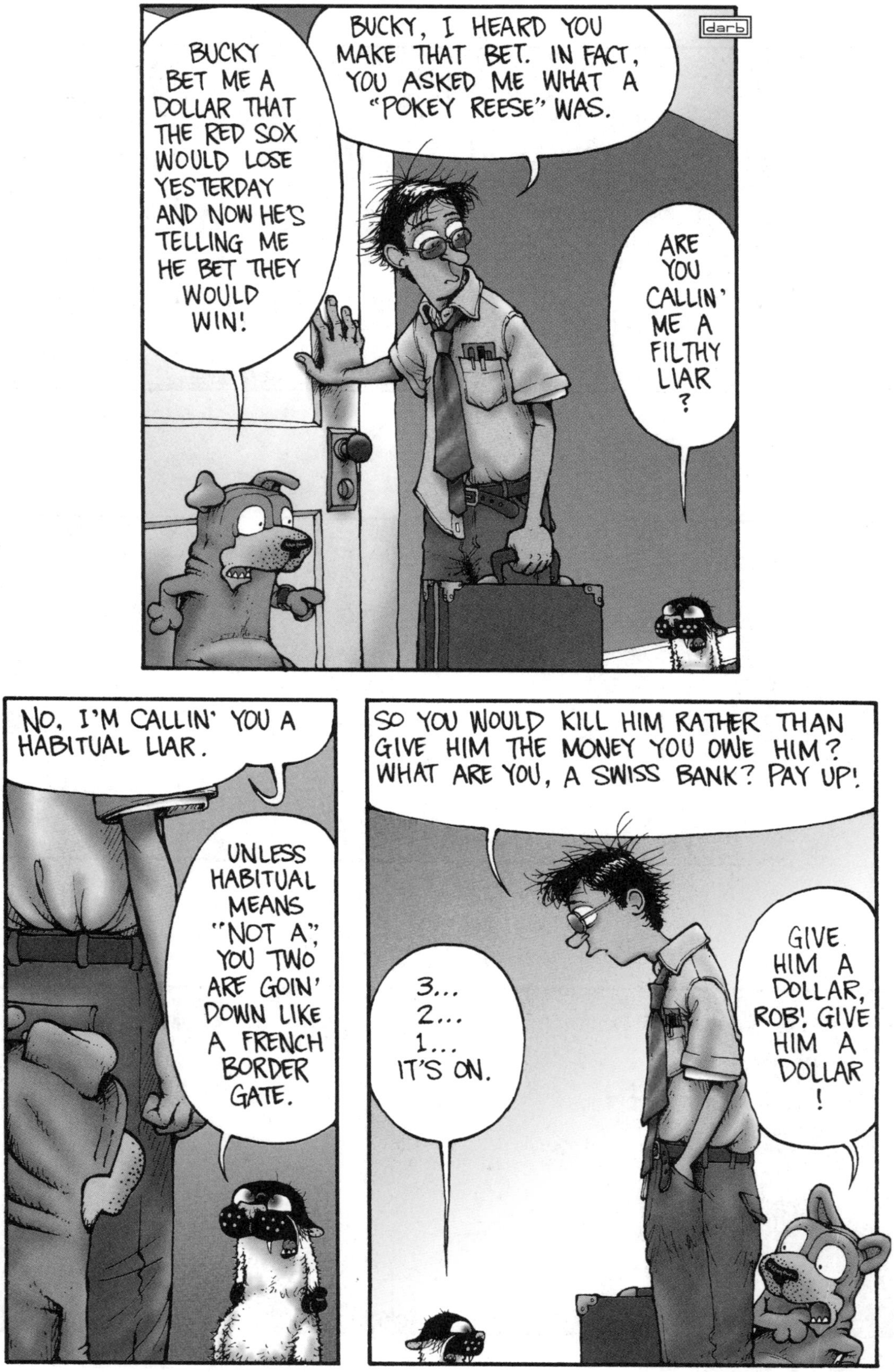
BUCKY BET ME A DOLLAR THAT THE RED SOX WOULD LOSE YESTERDAY AND NOW HE'S TELLING ME HE BET THEY WOULD WIN!
BUCKY, I HEARD YOU MAKE THAT BET. IN FACT, YOU ASKED ME WHAT A "POKEY REESE" WAS.
ARE YOU CALLIN' ME A FILTHY LIAR?
NO, I'M CALLIN' YOU A HABITUAL LIAR.
UNLESS HABITUAL MEANS "NOT A", YOU TWO ARE GOIN' DOWN LIKE A FRENCH BORDER GATE.
SO YOU WOULD KILL HIM RATHER THAN GIVE HIM THE MONEY YOU OWE HIM? WHAT ARE YOU, A SWISS BANK? PAY UP!
3... 2... 1... IT'S ON.
GIVE HIM A DOLLAR, ROB! GIVE HIM A DOLLAR!

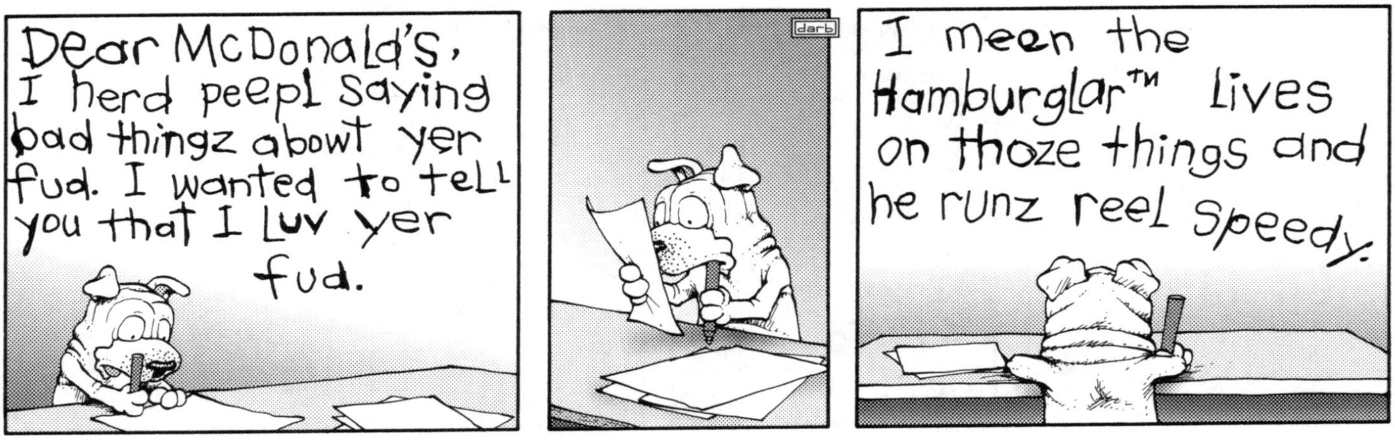
Dear McDonald's,
I herd peepl saying bad thingz abowt yer fud. I wanted to tell you that I Luv yer fud.
darb
I meen the Hamburglar™ Lives on thoze things and he runz reel speedy.

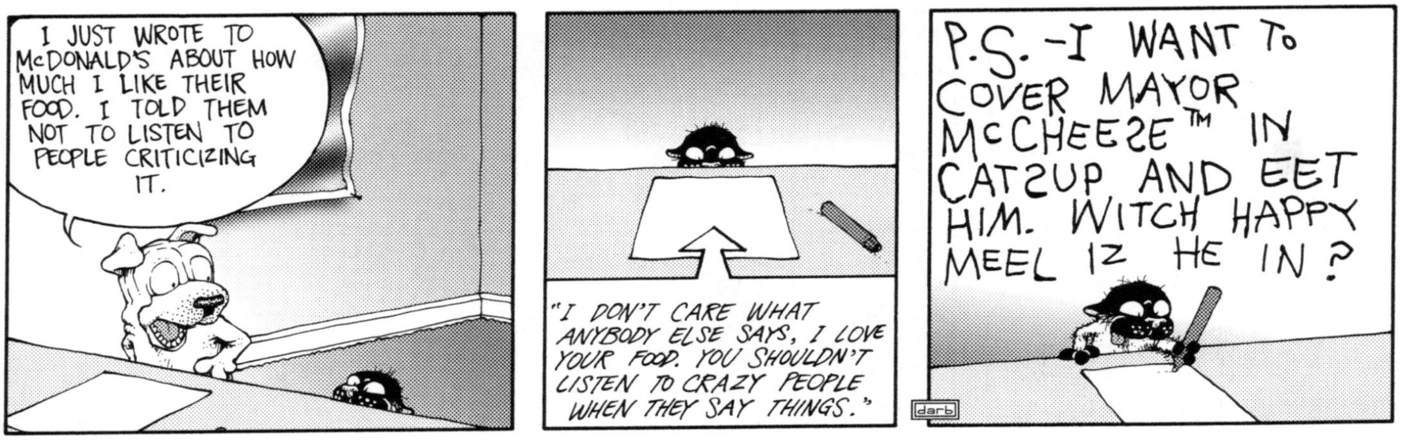
I JUST WROTE TO McDONALD'S ABOUT HOW MUCH I LIKE THEIR FOOD. I TOLD THEM NOT TO LISTEN TO PEOPLE CRITICIZING IT.
"I DON'T CARE WHAT ANYBODY ELSE SAYS, I LOVE YOUR FOOD. YOU SHOULDN'T LISTEN TO CRAZY PEOPLE WHEN THEY SAY THINGS."
darb
P.S. -I WANT TO COVER MAYOR McCHEEZE™ IN CATZUP AND EET HIM. WITCH HAPPY MEEL IZ HE IN?

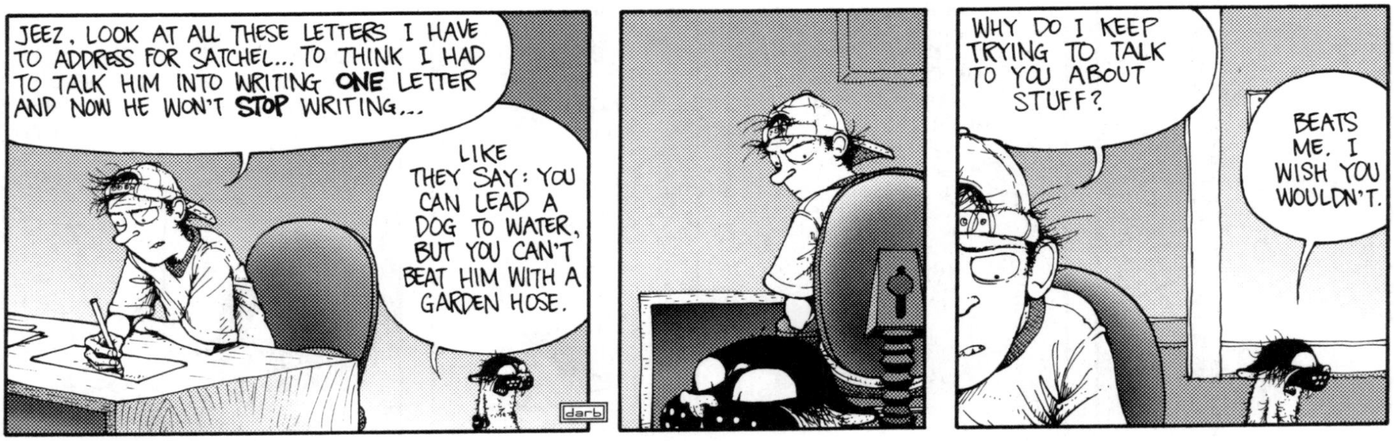
JEEZ, LOOK AT ALL THESE LETTERS I HAVE TO ADDRESS FOR SATCHEL... TO THINK I HAD TO TALK HIM INTO WRITING ONE LETTER AND NOW HE WON'T STOP WRITING...
LIKE THEY SAY: YOU CAN LEAD A DOG TO WATER, BUT YOU CAN'T BEAT HIM WITH A GARDEN HOSE.
darb
WHY DO I KEEP TRYING TO TALK TO YOU ABOUT STUFF?
BEATS ME. I WISH YOU WOULDN'T.

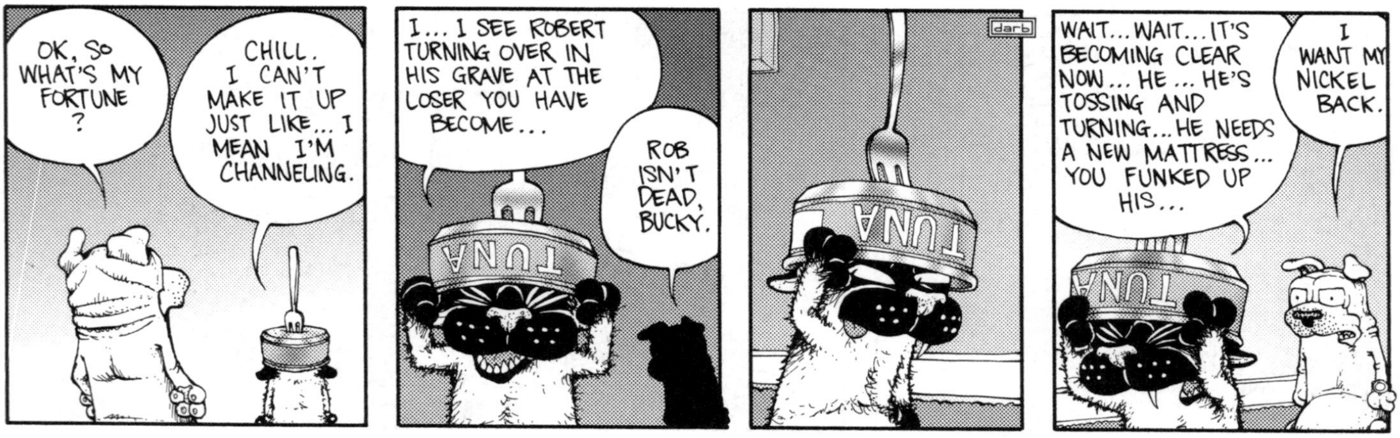
OK, SO WHAT'S MY FORTUNE ?
CHILL. I CAN'T MAKE IT UP JUST LIKE... I MEAN I'M CHANNELING.
I... I SEE ROBERT TURNING OVER IN HIS GRAVE AT THE LOSER YOU HAVE BECOME...
TUNA
ROB ISN'T DEAD, BUCKY.
darb
TUNA
WAIT... WAIT... IT'S BECOMING CLEAR NOW... HE... HE'S TOSSING AND TURNING... HE NEEDS A NEW MATTRESS... YOU FUNKED UP HIS...
I WANT MY NICKEL BACK.
TUNA

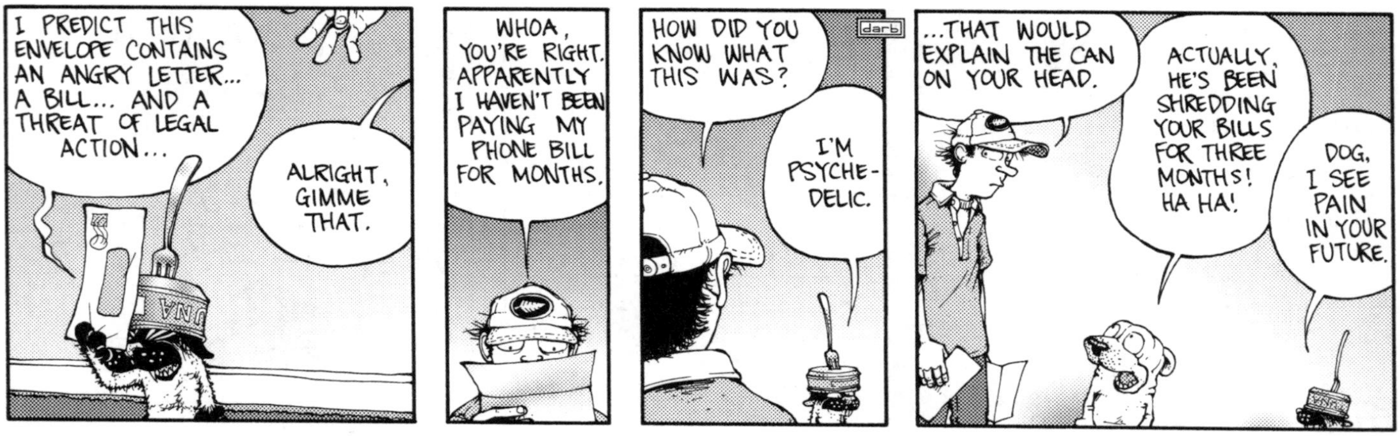
I PREDICT THIS ENVELOPE CONTAINS AN ANGRY LETTER... A BILL... AND A THREAT OF LEGAL ACTION...
ALRIGHT, GIMME THAT.
TUNA
WHOA, YOU'RE RIGHT. APPARENTLY I HAVEN'T BEEN PAYING MY PHONE BILL FOR MONTHS.
HOW DID YOU KNOW WHAT THIS WAS?
darb
I'M PSYCHE-DELIC.
...THAT WOULD EXPLAIN THE CAN ON YOUR HEAD.
ACTUALLY, HE'S BEEN SHREDDING YOUR BILLS FOR THREE MONTHS! HA HA!
DOG, I SEE PAIN IN YOUR FUTURE.

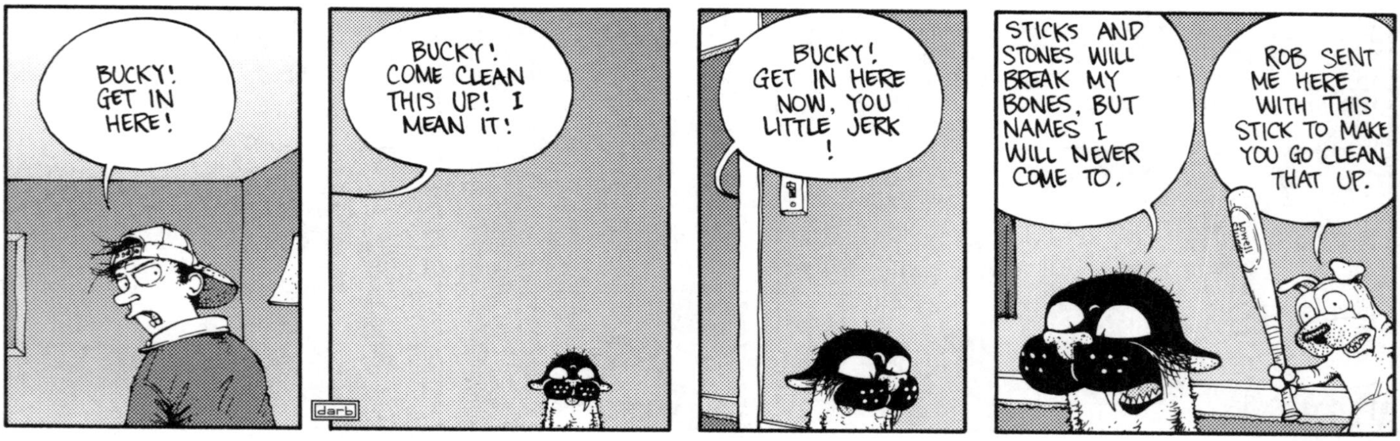
BUCKY! GET IN HERE!
darb
BUCKY! COME CLEAN THIS UP! I MEAN IT!
BUCKY! GET IN HERE NOW, YOU LITTLE JERK !
STICKS AND STONES WILL BREAK MY BONES, BUT NAMES I WILL NEVER COME TO.
ROB SENT ME HERE WITH THIS STICK TO MAKE YOU GO CLEAN THAT UP.

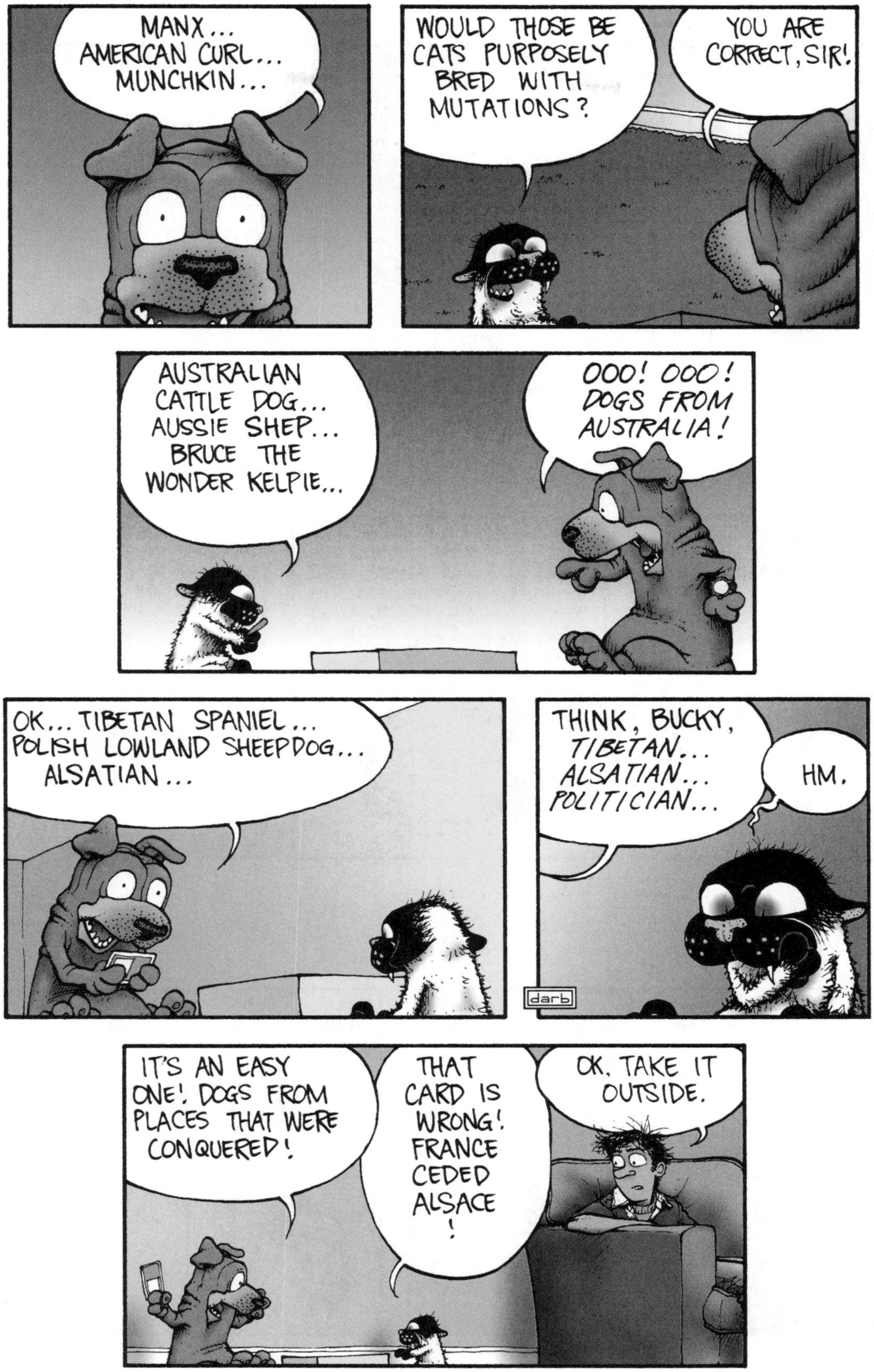

MANX... AMERICAN CURL... MUNCHKIN...
WOULD THOSE BE CATS PURPOSELY BRED WITH MUTATIONS?
YOU ARE CORRECT, SIR!
AUSTRALIAN CATTLE DOG... AUSSIE SHEP... BRUCE THE WONDER KELPIE...
OOO! OOO! DOGS FROM AUSTRALIA!
OK... TIBETAN SPANIEL... POLISH LOWLAND SHEEPDOG... ALSATIAN...
THINK, BUCKY, TIBETAN... ALSATIAN... POLITICIAN...
HM.
darb
IT'S AN EASY ONE! DOGS FROM PLACES THAT WERE CONQUERED!
THAT CARD IS WRONG! FRANCE CEDED ALSACE!
OK, TAKE IT OUTSIDE.

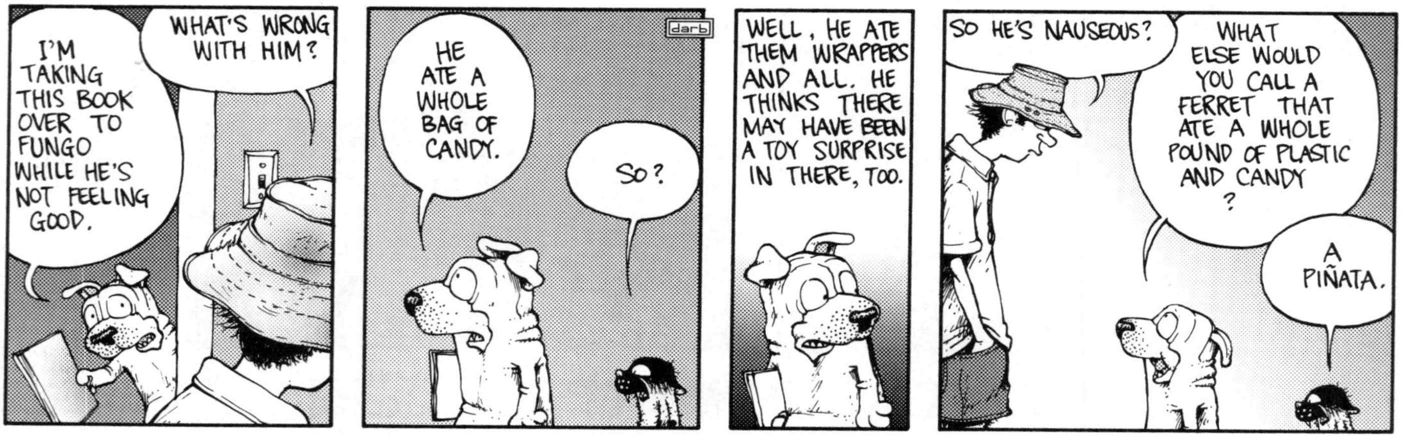
I'M TAKING THIS BOOK OVER TO FUNGO WHILE HE'S NOT FEELING GOOD.
WHAT'S WRONG WITH HIM?
HE ATE A WHOLE BAG OF CANDY.
SO?
WELL, HE ATE THEM WRAPPERS AND ALL. HE THINKS THERE MAY HAVE BEEN A TOY SURPRISE IN THERE, TOO.
SO HE'S NAUSEOUS?
WHAT ELSE WOULD YOU CALL A FERRET THAT ATE A WHOLE POUND OF PLASTIC AND CANDY?
A PIÑATA.

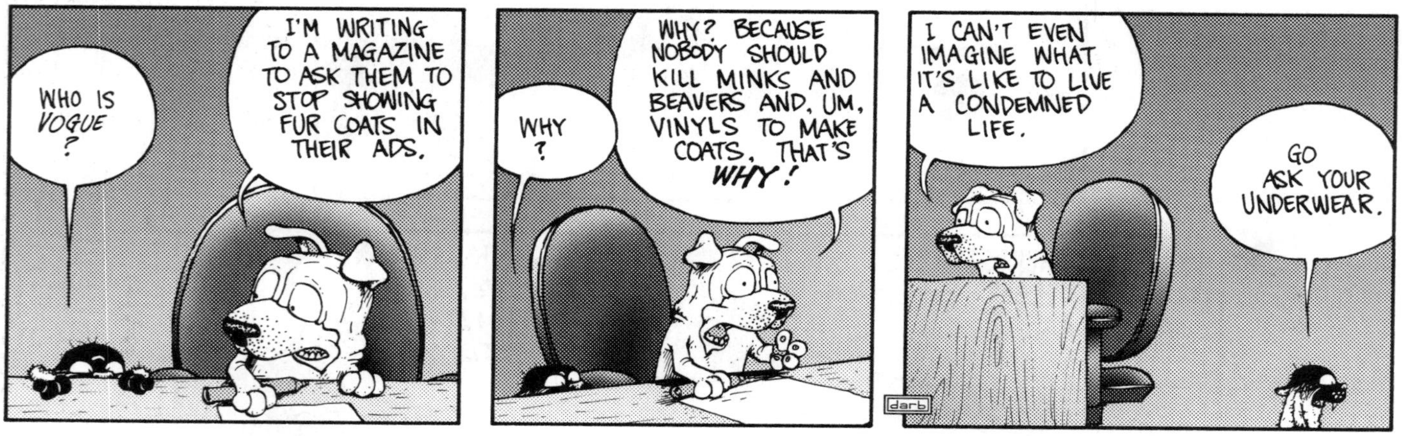
WHO IS *VOGUE*?
I'M WRITING TO A MAGAZINE TO ASK THEM TO STOP SHOWING FUR COATS IN THEIR ADS.
WHY?
WHY? BECAUSE NOBODY SHOULD KILL MINKS AND BEAVERS AND, UM, VINYLS TO MAKE COATS. THAT'S ***WHY!***
I CAN'T EVEN IMAGINE WHAT IT'S LIKE TO LIVE A CONDEMNED LIFE.
GO ASK YOUR UNDERWEAR.

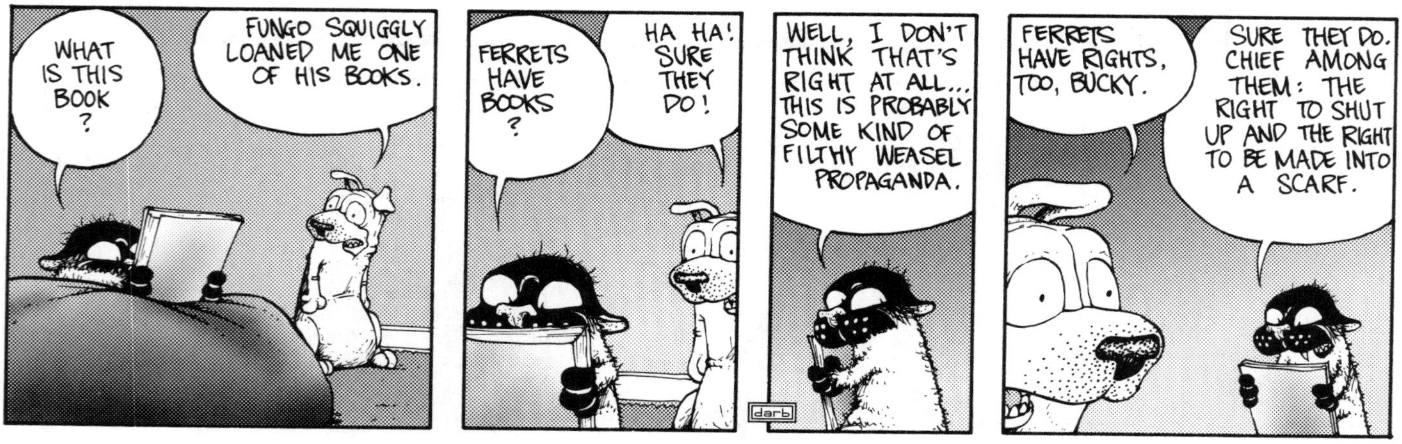
WHAT IS THIS BOOK?
FUNGO SQUIGGLY LOANED ME ONE OF HIS BOOKS.
FERRETS HAVE BOOKS?
HA HA! SURE THEY DO!
WELL, I DON'T THINK THAT'S RIGHT AT ALL... THIS IS PROBABLY SOME KIND OF FILTHY WEASEL PROPAGANDA.
FERRETS HAVE RIGHTS, TOO, BUCKY.
SURE THEY DO. CHIEF AMONG THEM: THE RIGHT TO SHUT UP AND THE RIGHT TO BE MADE INTO A SCARF.

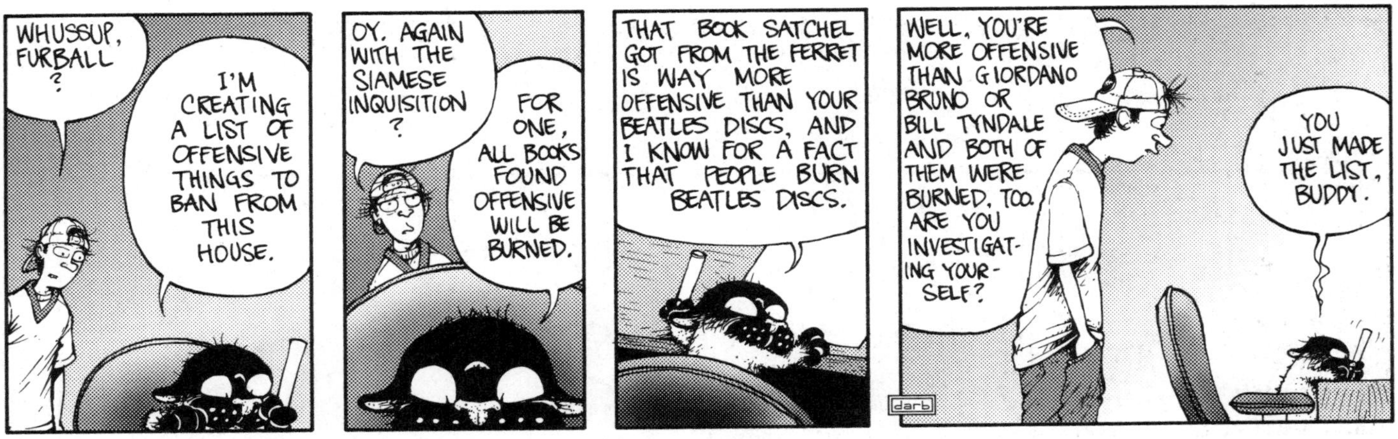
WHUSSUP, FURBALL ?
I'M CREATING A LIST OF OFFENSIVE THINGS TO BAN FROM THIS HOUSE.
OY. AGAIN WITH THE SIAMESE INQUISITION ?
FOR ONE, ALL BOOKS FOUND OFFENSIVE WILL BE BURNED.
THAT BOOK SATCHEL GOT FROM THE FERRET IS WAY MORE OFFENSIVE THAN YOUR BEATLES DISCS, AND I KNOW FOR A FACT THAT PEOPLE BURN BEATLES DISCS.
WELL, YOU'RE MORE OFFENSIVE THAN GIORDANO BRUNO OR BILL TYNDALE AND BOTH OF THEM WERE BURNED, TOO. ARE YOU INVESTIGATING YOURSELF?
YOU JUST MADE THE LIST, BUDDY.
darb

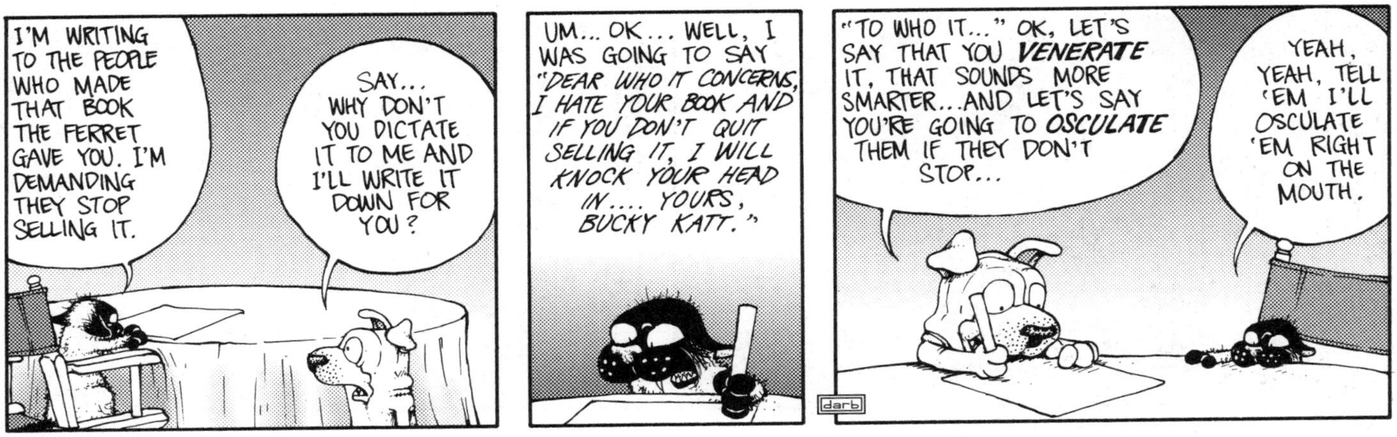
I'M WRITING TO THE PEOPLE WHO MADE THAT BOOK THE FERRET GAVE YOU. I'M DEMANDING THEY STOP SELLING IT.
SAY... WHY DON'T YOU DICTATE IT TO ME AND I'LL WRITE IT DOWN FOR YOU?
UM... OK... WELL, I WAS GOING TO SAY "DEAR WHO IT CONCERNS, I HATE YOUR BOOK AND IF YOU DON'T QUIT SELLING IT, I WILL KNOCK YOUR HEAD IN.... YOURS, BUCKY KATT."
"TO WHO IT..." OK, LET'S SAY THAT YOU **VENERATE** IT, THAT SOUNDS MORE SMARTER...AND LET'S SAY YOU'RE GOING TO **OSCULATE** THEM IF THEY DON'T STOP...
YEAH, YEAH, TELL 'EM I'LL OSCULATE 'EM RIGHT ON THE MOUTH.
darb

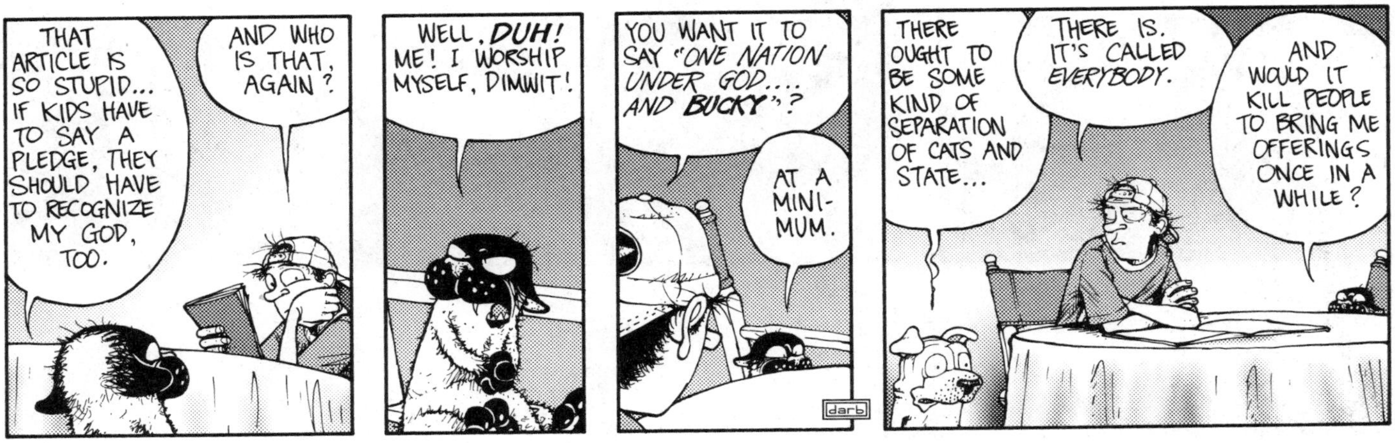
THAT ARTICLE IS SO STUPID... IF KIDS HAVE TO SAY A PLEDGE, THEY SHOULD HAVE TO RECOGNIZE MY GOD, TOO.
AND WHO IS THAT, AGAIN?
WELL, **DUH!** ME! I WORSHIP MYSELF, DIMWIT!
YOU WANT IT TO SAY "ONE NATION UNDER GOD.... AND **BUCKY**"?
AT A MINIMUM.
darb
THERE OUGHT TO BE SOME KIND OF SEPARATION OF CATS AND STATE...
THERE IS. IT'S CALLED EVERYBODY.
AND WOULD IT KILL PEOPLE TO BRING ME OFFERINGS ONCE IN A WHILE?

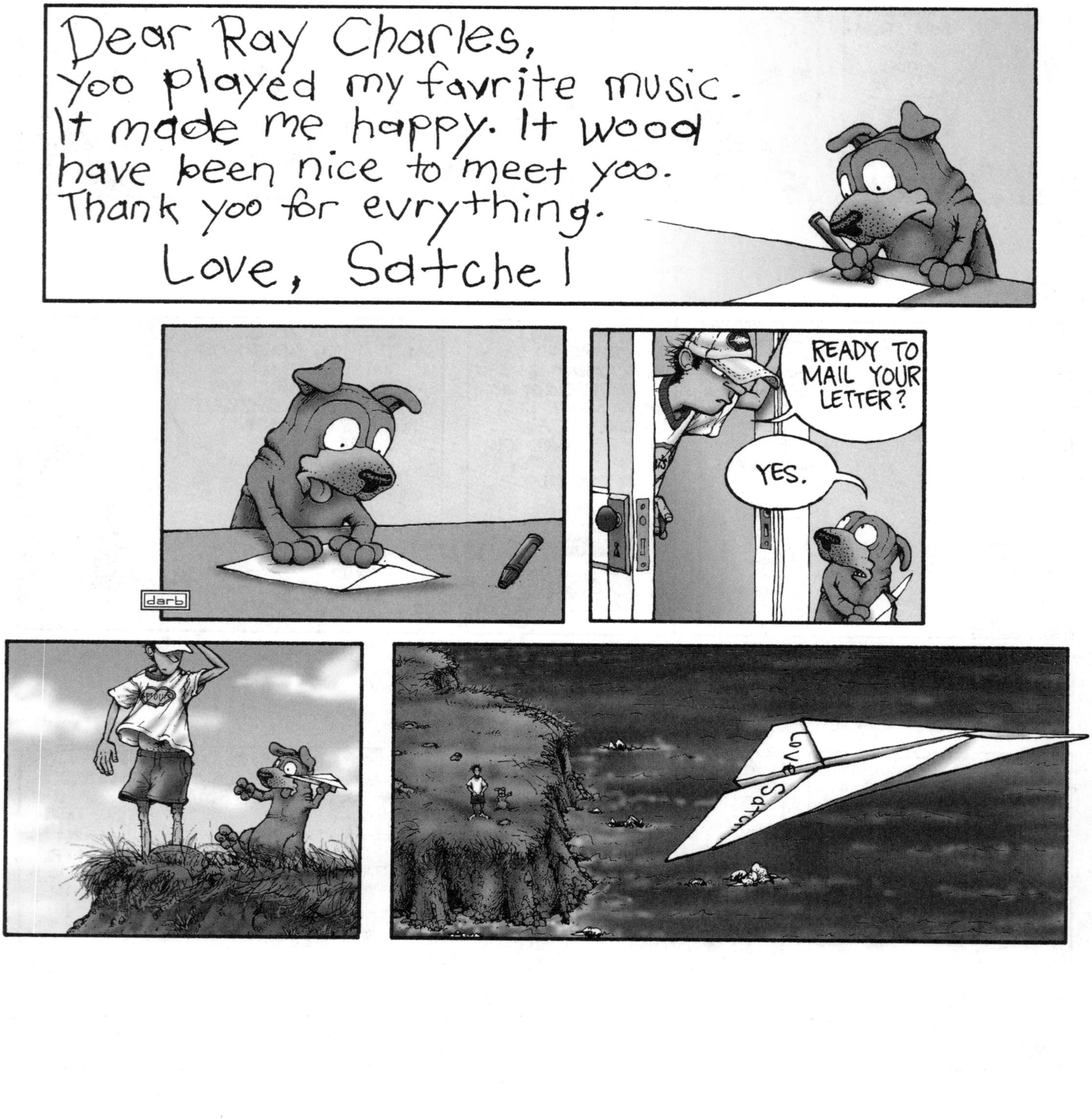
Dear Ray Charles,
Yoo played my favrite music.
It made me happy. It wood
have been nice to meet yoo.
Thank yoo for evrything.
Love, Satchel
READY TO MAIL YOUR LETTER?
YES.

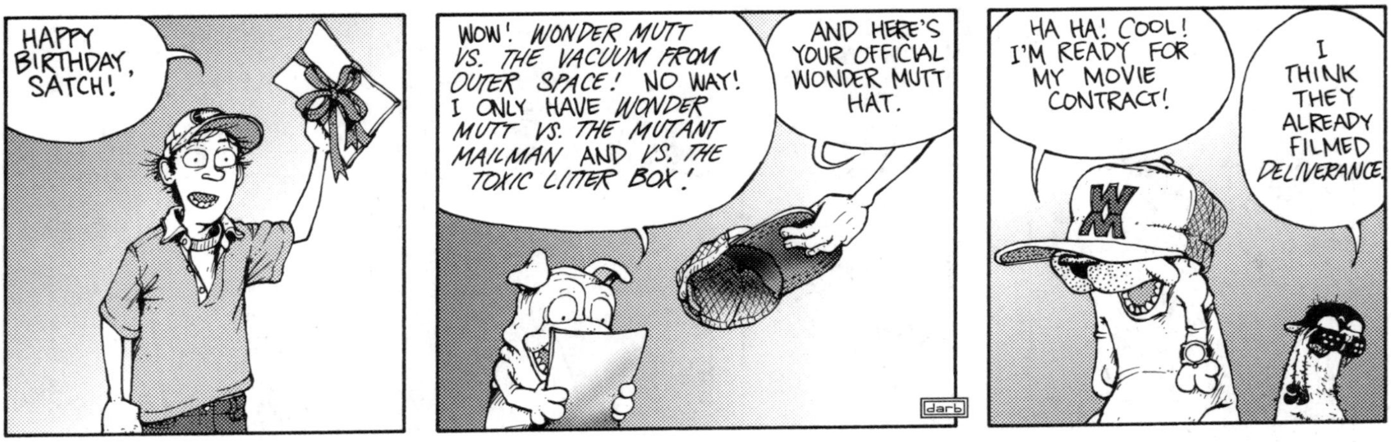
HAPPY BIRTHDAY, SATCH!
WOW! WONDER MUTT VS. THE VACUUM FROM OUTER SPACE! NO WAY! I ONLY HAVE WONDER MUTT VS. THE MUTANT MAILMAN AND VS. THE TOXIC LITTER BOX!
AND HERE'S YOUR OFFICIAL WONDER MUTT HAT.
HA HA! COOL! I'M READY FOR MY MOVIE CONTRACT!
I THINK THEY ALREADY FILMED DELIVERANCE.

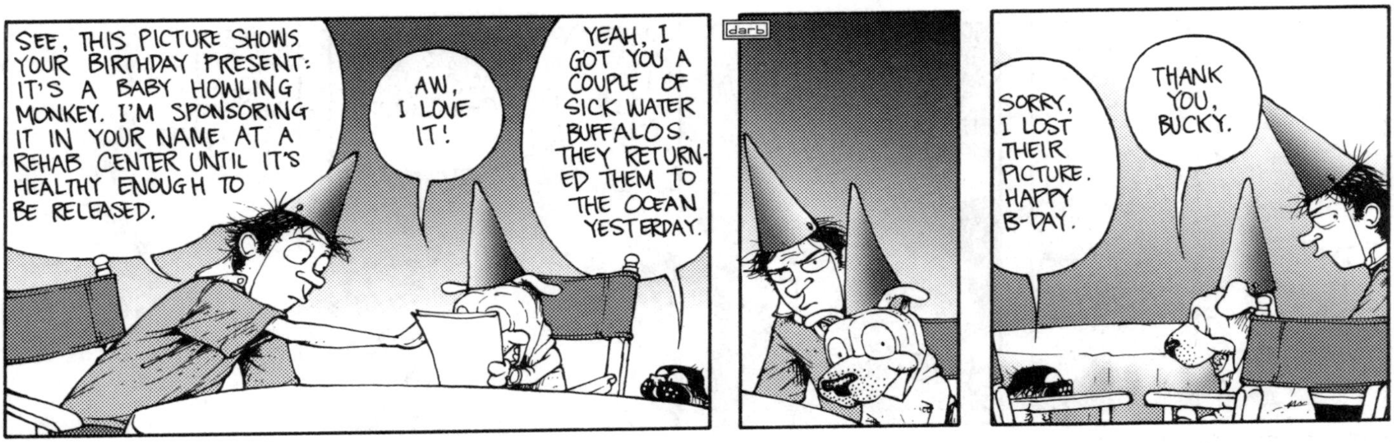
SEE, THIS PICTURE SHOWS YOUR BIRTHDAY PRESENT: IT'S A BABY HOWLING MONKEY. I'M SPONSORING IT IN YOUR NAME AT A REHAB CENTER UNTIL IT'S HEALTHY ENOUGH TO BE RELEASED.
AW, I LOVE IT!
YEAH, I GOT YOU A COUPLE OF SICK WATER BUFFALOS. THEY RETURNED THEM TO THE OCEAN YESTERDAY.
SORRY, I LOST THEIR PICTURE. HAPPY B-DAY.
THANK YOU, BUCKY.

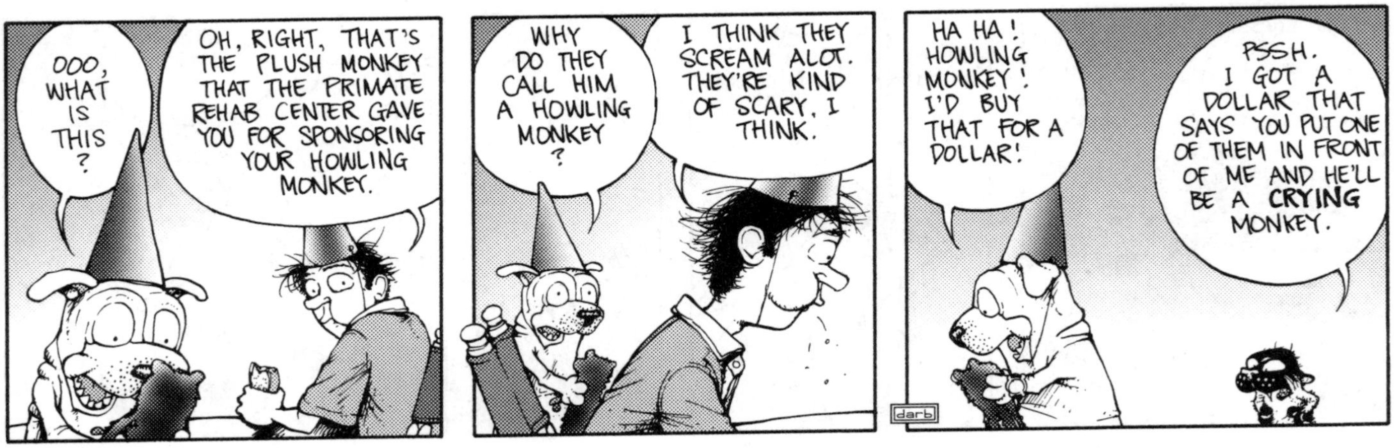
OOO, WHAT IS THIS?
OH, RIGHT, THAT'S THE PLUSH MONKEY THAT THE PRIMATE REHAB CENTER GAVE YOU FOR SPONSORING YOUR HOWLING MONKEY.
WHY DO THEY CALL HIM A HOWLING MONKEY?
I THINK THEY SCREAM ALOT. THEY'RE KIND OF SCARY, I THINK.
HA HA! HOWLING MONKEY! I'D BUY THAT FOR A DOLLAR!
PSSH. I GOT A DOLLAR THAT SAYS YOU PUT ONE OF THEM IN FRONT OF ME AND HE'LL BE A CRYING MONKEY.

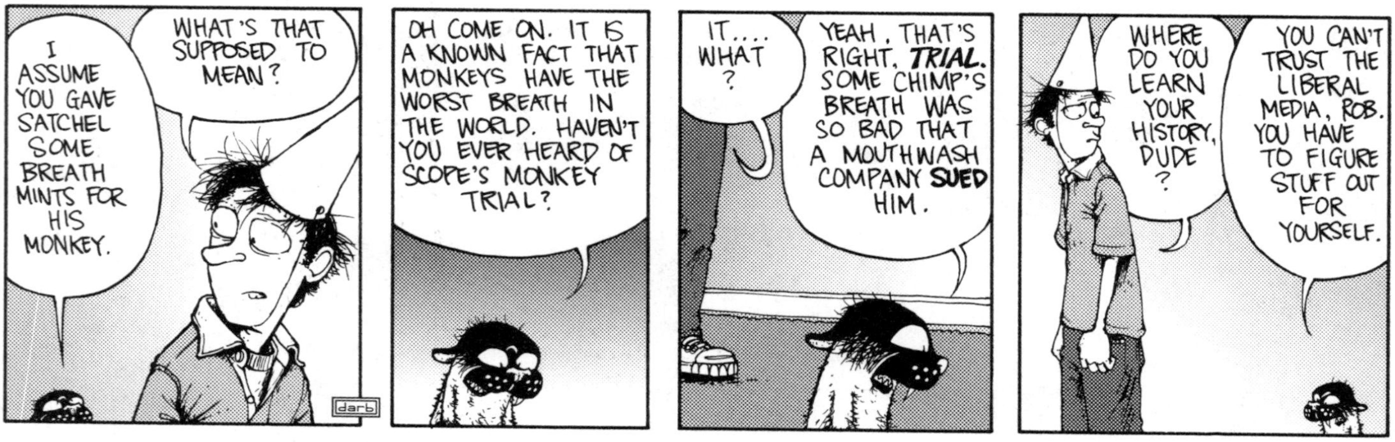
I ASSUME YOU GAVE SATCHEL SOME BREATH MINTS FOR HIS MONKEY.
WHAT'S THAT SUPPOSED TO MEAN?
OH COME ON. IT IS A KNOWN FACT THAT MONKEYS HAVE THE WORST BREATH IN THE WORLD. HAVEN'T YOU EVER HEARD OF SCOPE'S MONKEY TRIAL?
IT.... WHAT?
YEAH, THAT'S RIGHT, **TRIAL.** SOME CHIMP'S BREATH WAS SO BAD THAT A MOUTHWASH COMPANY **SUED** HIM.
WHERE DO YOU LEARN YOUR HISTORY, DUDE?
YOU CAN'T TRUST THE LIBERAL MEDIA, ROB. YOU HAVE TO FIGURE STUFF OUT FOR YOURSELF.

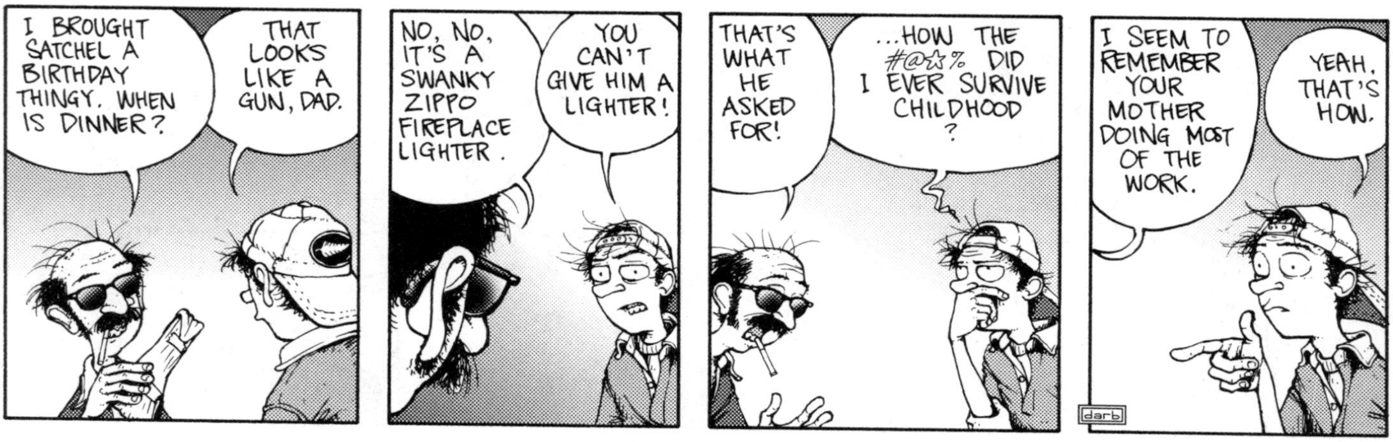
I BROUGHT SATCHEL A BIRTHDAY THINGY. WHEN IS DINNER?
THAT LOOKS LIKE A GUN, DAD.
NO, NO, IT'S A SWANKY ZIPPO FIREPLACE LIGHTER.
YOU CAN'T GIVE HIM A LIGHTER!
THAT'S WHAT HE ASKED FOR!
...HOW THE #@☆% DID I EVER SURVIVE CHILDHOOD?
I SEEM TO REMEMBER YOUR MOTHER DOING MOST OF THE WORK.
YEAH, THAT'S HOW.

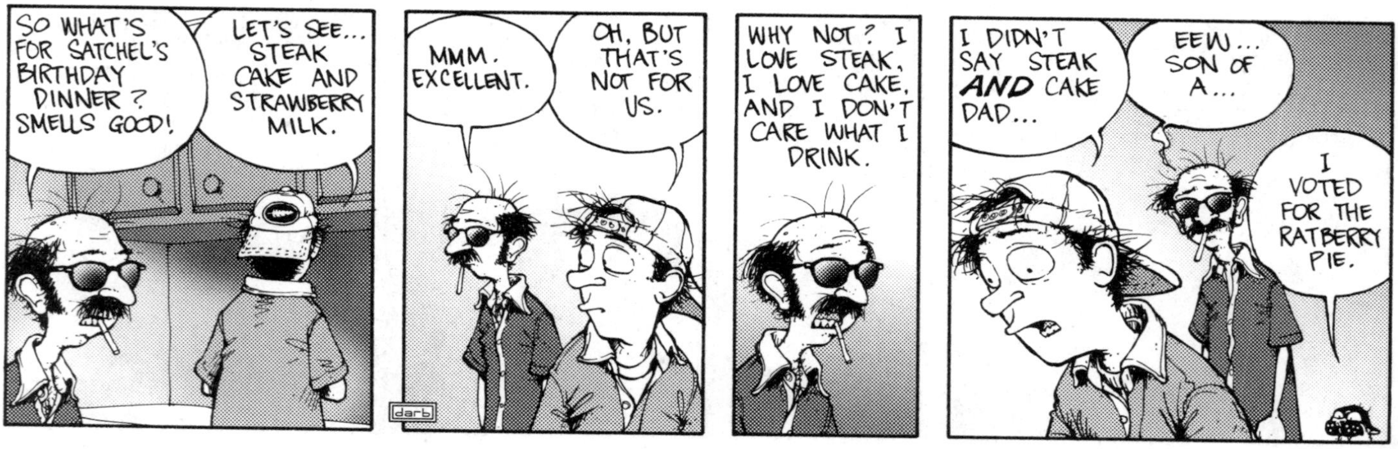
SO WHAT'S FOR SATCHEL'S BIRTHDAY DINNER? SMELLS GOOD!
LET'S SEE... STEAK CAKE AND STRAWBERRY MILK.
MMM. EXCELLENT.
OH, BUT THAT'S NOT FOR US.
WHY NOT? I LOVE STEAK, I LOVE CAKE, AND I DON'T CARE WHAT I DRINK.
I DIDN'T SAY STEAK ***AND*** CAKE DAD...
EEW... SON OF A...
I VOTED FOR THE RATBERRY PIE.

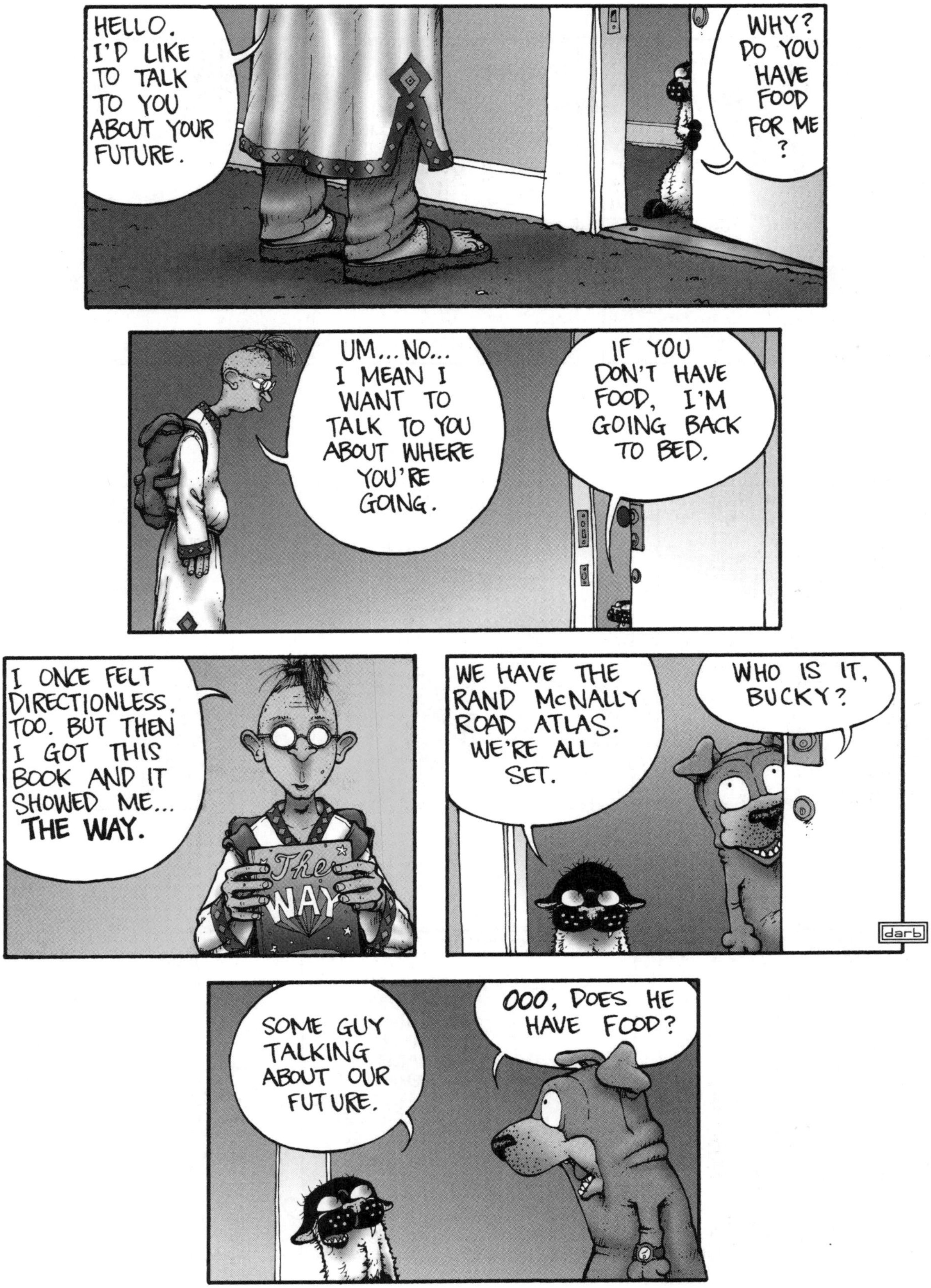
HELLO. I'D LIKE TO TALK TO YOU ABOUT YOUR FUTURE.
WHY? DO YOU HAVE FOOD FOR ME ?
UM... NO... I MEAN I WANT TO TALK TO YOU ABOUT WHERE YOU'RE GOING.
IF YOU DON'T HAVE FOOD, I'M GOING BACK TO BED.
I ONCE FELT DIRECTIONLESS, TOO. BUT THEN I GOT THIS BOOK AND IT SHOWED ME... **THE WAY.**
The WAY
WE HAVE THE RAND McNALLY ROAD ATLAS. WE'RE ALL SET.
WHO IS IT, BUCKY?
darb
SOME GUY TALKING ABOUT OUR FUTURE.
OOO, DOES HE HAVE FOOD?

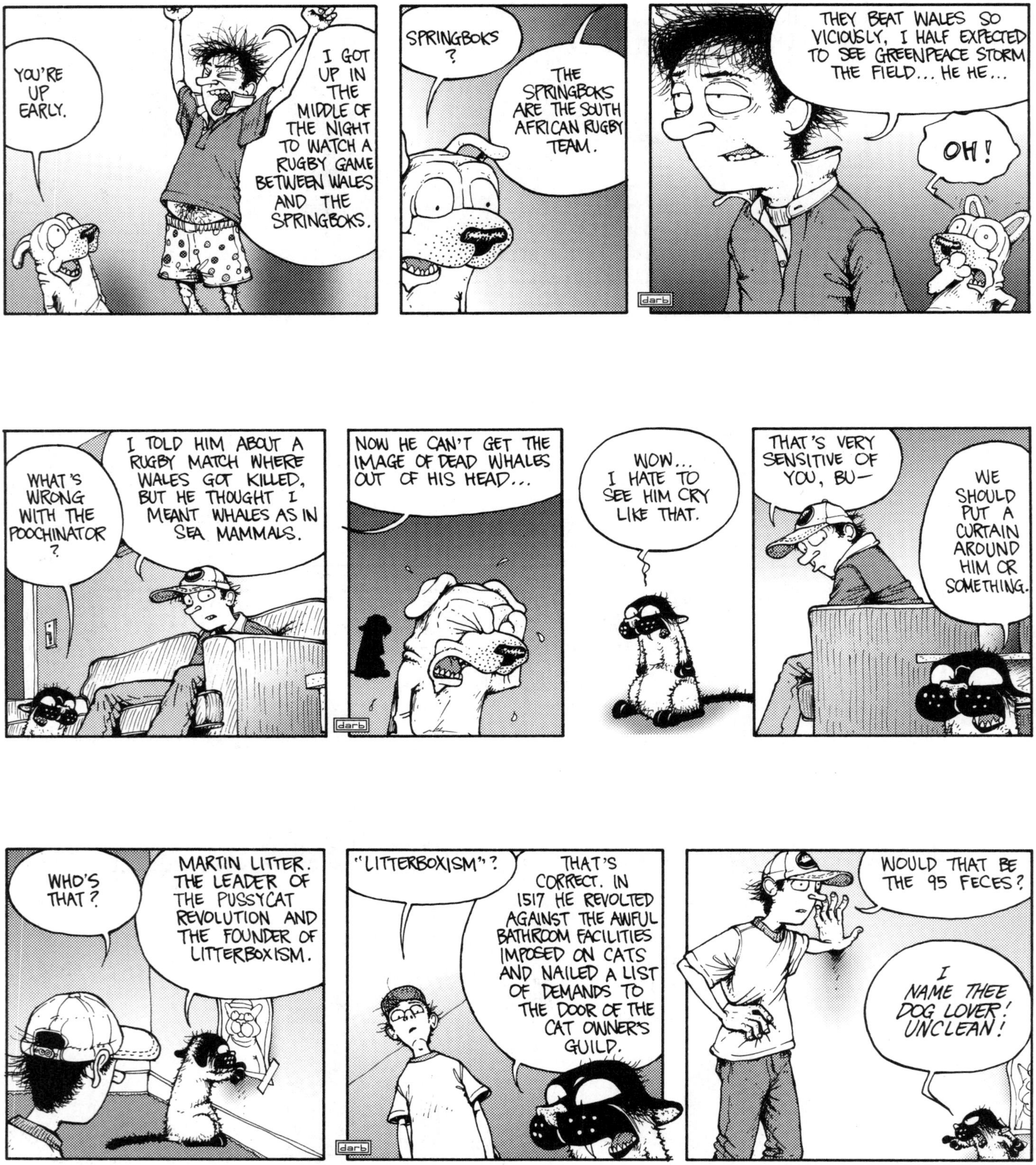
YOU'RE UP EARLY.
I GOT UP IN THE MIDDLE OF THE NIGHT TO WATCH A RUGBY GAME BETWEEN WALES AND THE SPRINGBOKS.
SPRINGBOKS?
THE SPRINGBOKS ARE THE SOUTH AFRICAN RUGBY TEAM.
THEY BEAT WALES SO VICIOUSLY, I HALF EXPECTED TO SEE GREENPEACE STORM THE FIELD... HE HE...
OH!
darb
WHAT'S WRONG WITH THE POOCHINATOR?
I TOLD HIM ABOUT A RUGBY MATCH WHERE WALES GOT KILLED, BUT HE THOUGHT I MEANT WHALES AS IN SEA MAMMALS.
NOW HE CAN'T GET THE IMAGE OF DEAD WHALES OUT OF HIS HEAD...
WOW... I HATE TO SEE HIM CRY LIKE THAT.
THAT'S VERY SENSITIVE OF YOU, BU—
WE SHOULD PUT A CURTAIN AROUND HIM OR SOMETHING.
darb
WHO'S THAT?
MARTIN LITTER. THE LEADER OF THE PUSSYCAT REVOLUTION AND THE FOUNDER OF LITTERBOXISM.
"LITTERBOXISM"?
THAT'S CORRECT. IN 1517 HE REVOLTED AGAINST THE AWFUL BATHROOM FACILITIES IMPOSED ON CATS AND NAILED A LIST OF DEMANDS TO THE DOOR OF THE CAT OWNER'S GUILD.
WOULD THAT BE THE 95 FECES?
I NAME THEE DOG LOVER! UNCLEAN!
darb

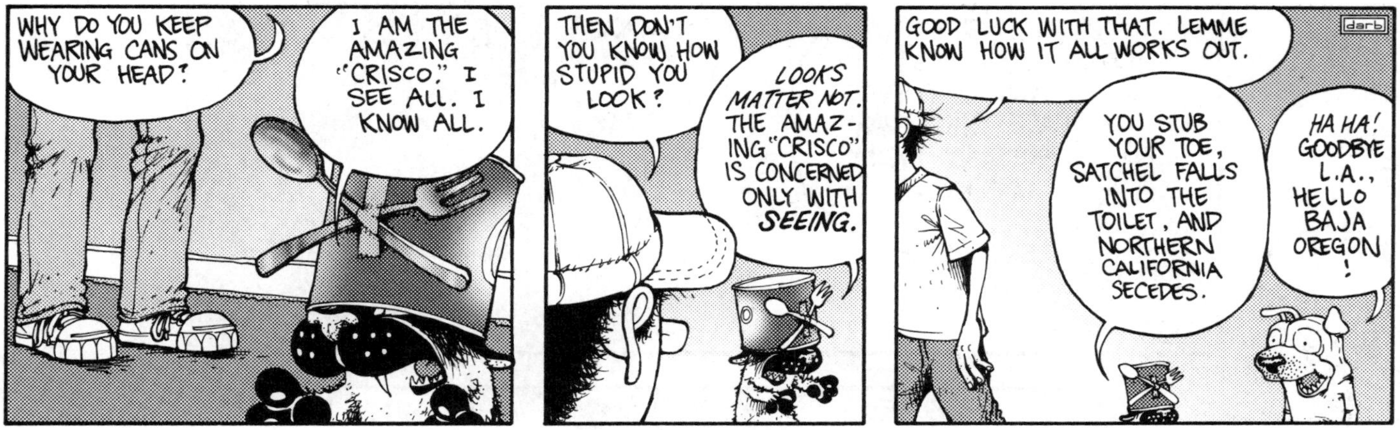
WHY DO YOU KEEP WEARING CANS ON YOUR HEAD?
I AM THE AMAZING "CRISCO." I SEE ALL. I KNOW ALL.
THEN DON'T YOU KNOW HOW STUPID YOU LOOK?
LOOKS MATTER NOT. THE AMAZ-ING "CRISCO" IS CONCERNED ONLY WITH SEEING.
GOOD LUCK WITH THAT. LEMME KNOW HOW IT ALL WORKS OUT.
YOU STUB YOUR TOE, SATCHEL FALLS INTO THE TOILET, AND NORTHERN CALIFORNIA SECEDES.
HA HA! GOODBYE L.A., HELLO BAJA OREGON!
darb

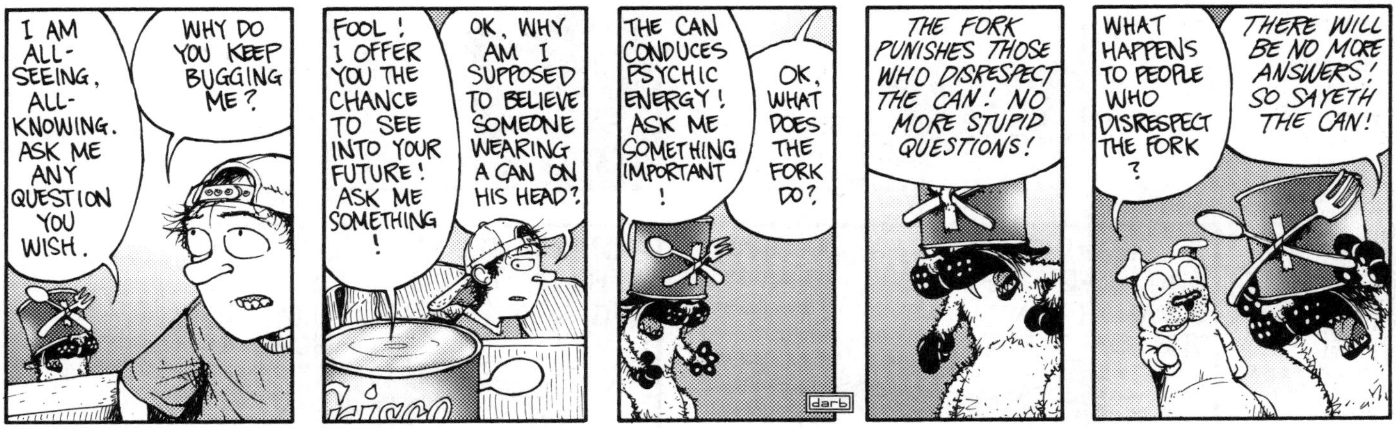
I AM ALL-SEEING, ALL-KNOWING. ASK ME ANY QUESTION YOU WISH.
WHY DO YOU KEEP BUGGING ME?
FOOL! I OFFER YOU THE CHANCE TO SEE INTO YOUR FUTURE! ASK ME SOMETHING!
OK, WHY AM I SUPPOSED TO BELIEVE SOMEONE WEARING A CAN ON HIS HEAD?
THE CAN CONDUCES PSYCHIC ENERGY! ASK ME SOMETHING IMPORTANT!
OK, WHAT DOES THE FORK DO?
darb
THE FORK PUNISHES THOSE WHO DISRESPECT THE CAN! NO MORE STUPID QUESTIONS!
WHAT HAPPENS TO PEOPLE WHO DISRESPECT THE FORK?
THERE WILL BE NO MORE ANSWERS! SO SAYETH THE CAN!

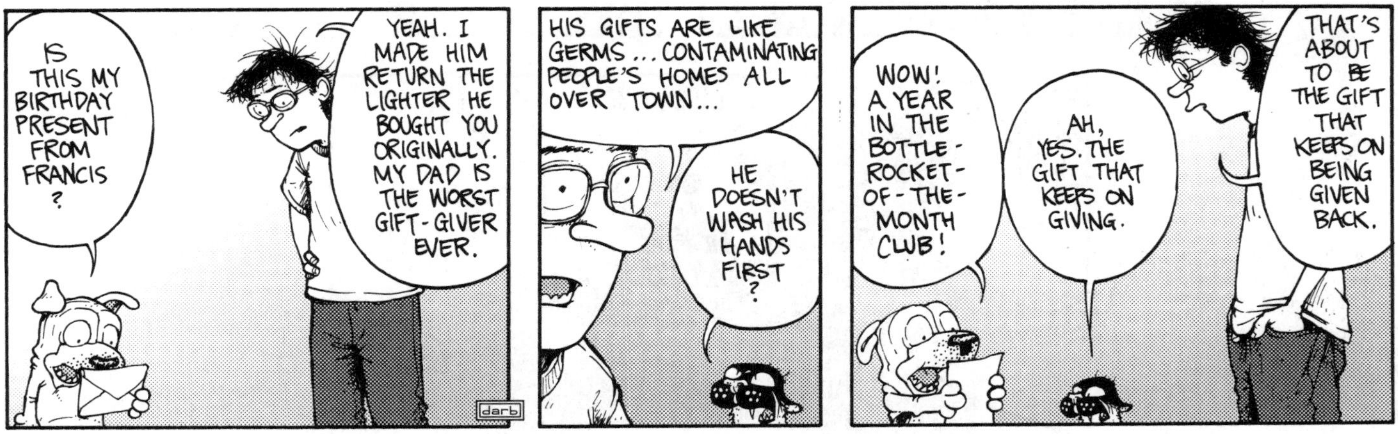
IS THIS MY BIRTHDAY PRESENT FROM FRANCIS?
YEAH. I MADE HIM RETURN THE LIGHTER HE BOUGHT YOU ORIGINALLY. MY DAD IS THE WORST GIFT-GIVER EVER.
darb
HIS GIFTS ARE LIKE GERMS... CONTAMINATING PEOPLE'S HOMES ALL OVER TOWN...
HE DOESN'T WASH HIS HANDS FIRST?
WOW! A YEAR IN THE BOTTLE-ROCKET-OF-THE-MONTH CLUB!
AH, YES. THE GIFT THAT KEEPS ON GIVING.
THAT'S ABOUT TO BE THE GIFT THAT KEEPS ON BEING GIVEN BACK.

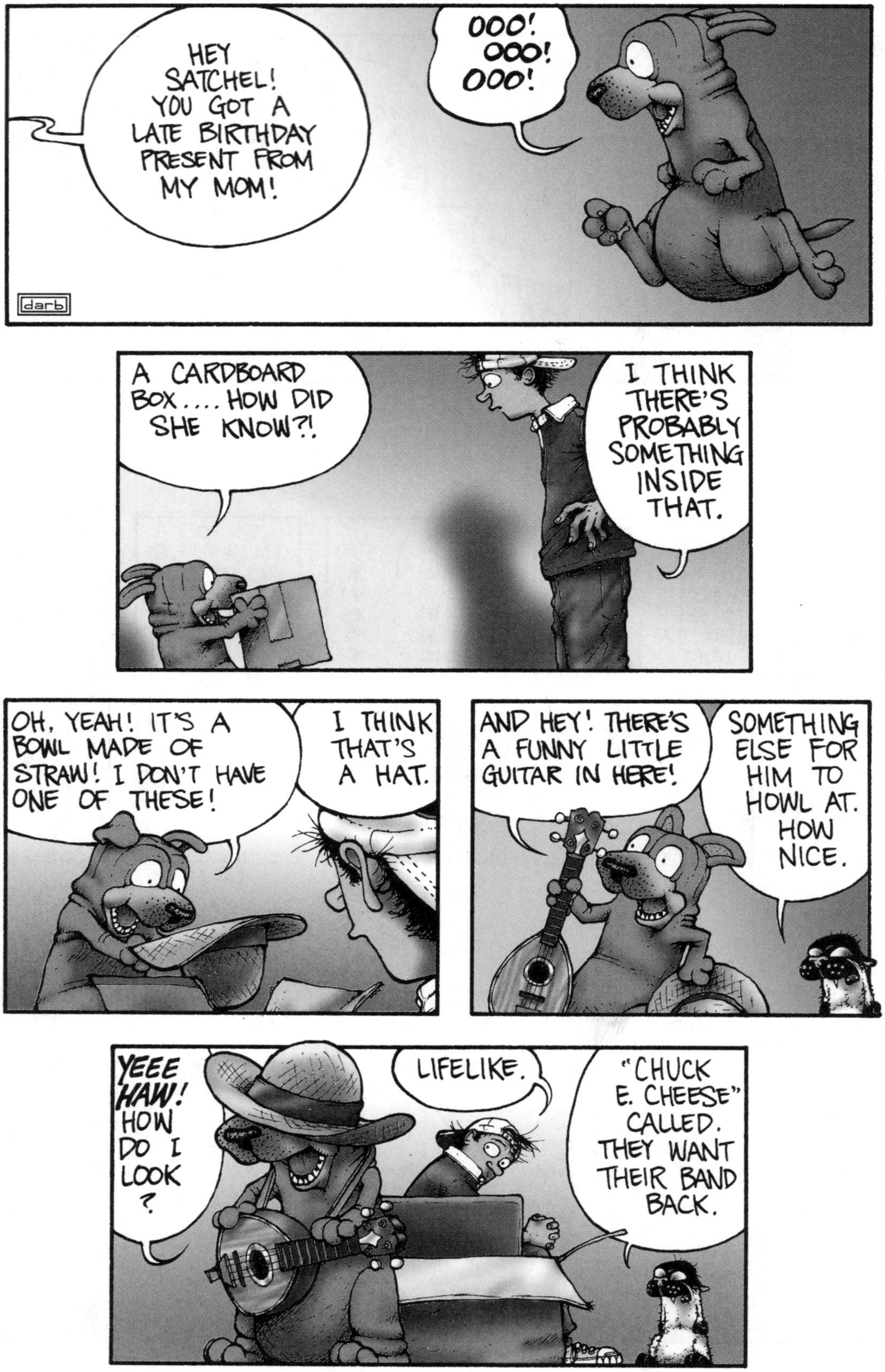
HEY SATCHEL! YOU GOT A LATE BIRTHDAY PRESENT FROM MY MOM!
OOO! OOO! OOO!
darb
A CARDBOARD BOX.... HOW DID SHE KNOW?!
I THINK THERE'S PROBABLY SOMETHING INSIDE THAT.
OH, YEAH! IT'S A BOWL MADE OF STRAW! I DON'T HAVE ONE OF THESE!
I THINK THAT'S A HAT.
AND HEY! THERE'S A FUNNY LITTLE GUITAR IN HERE!
SOMETHING ELSE FOR HIM TO HOWL AT. HOW NICE.
YEEE HAW! HOW DO I LOOK?
LIFELIKE.
"CHUCK E. CHEESE" CALLED. THEY WANT THEIR BAND BACK.

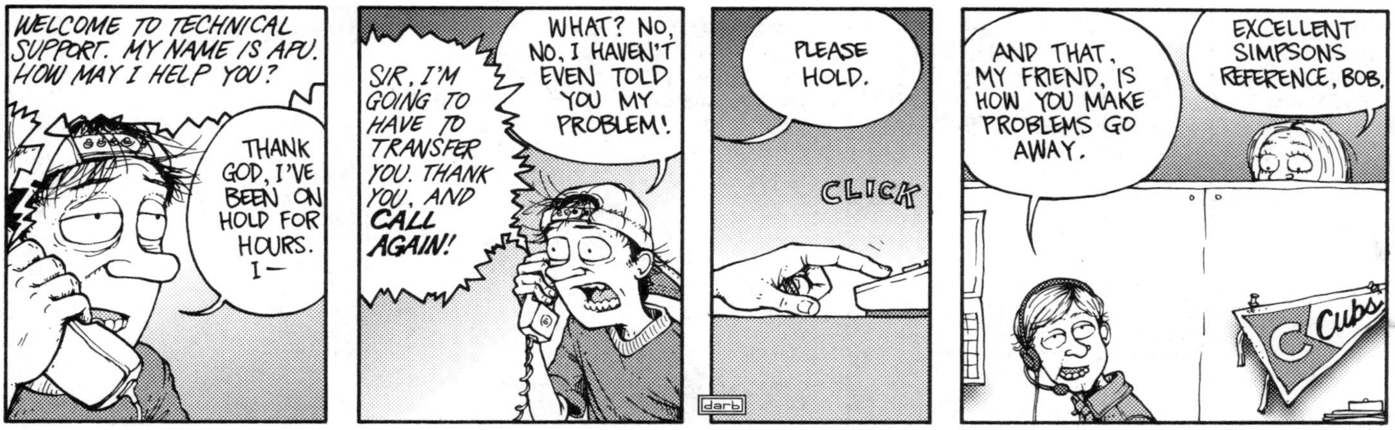
WELCOME TO TECHNICAL SUPPORT. MY NAME IS APU. HOW MAY I HELP YOU?
THANK GOD, I'VE BEEN ON HOLD FOR HOURS. I—
SIR, I'M GOING TO HAVE TO TRANSFER YOU. THANK YOU, AND CALL AGAIN!
WHAT? NO, NO, I HAVEN'T EVEN TOLD YOU MY PROBLEM!
PLEASE HOLD.
CLICK
darb
AND THAT, MY FRIEND, IS HOW YOU MAKE PROBLEMS GO AWAY.
EXCELLENT SIMPSONS REFERENCE, BOB.
Cubs

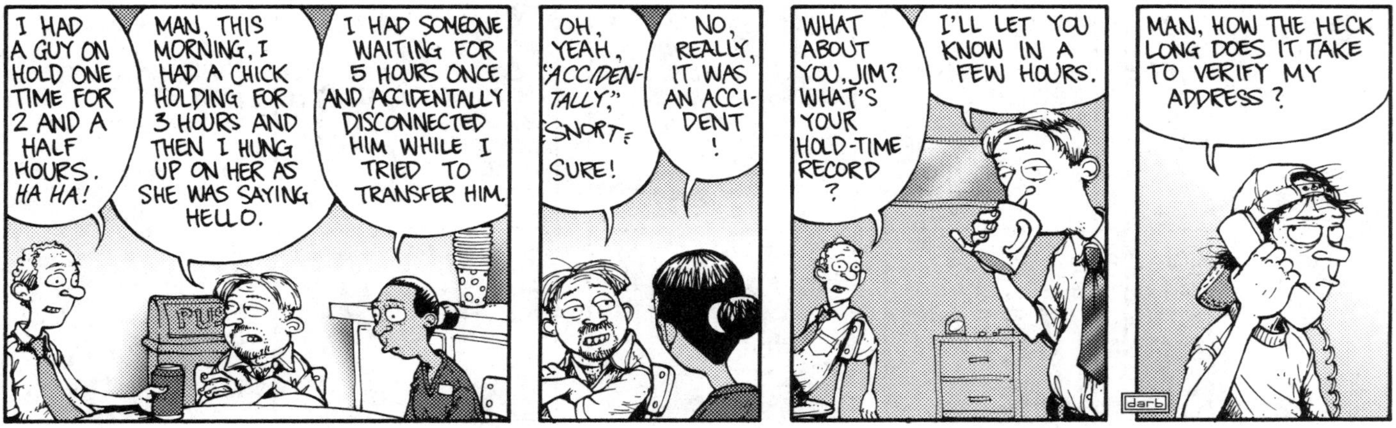
I HAD A GUY ON HOLD ONE TIME FOR 2 AND A HALF HOURS. HA HA!
MAN, THIS MORNING, I HAD A CHICK HOLDING FOR 3 HOURS AND THEN I HUNG UP ON HER AS SHE WAS SAYING HELLO.
I HAD SOMEONE WAITING FOR 5 HOURS ONCE AND ACCIDENTALLY DISCONNECTED HIM WHILE I TRIED TO TRANSFER HIM.
OH, YEAH, "ACCIDENTALLY," SNORT SURE!
NO, REALLY, IT WAS AN ACCIDENT!
WHAT ABOUT YOU, JIM? WHAT'S YOUR HOLD-TIME RECORD?
I'LL LET YOU KNOW IN A FEW HOURS.
MAN, HOW THE HECK LONG DOES IT TAKE TO VERIFY MY ADDRESS?
darb

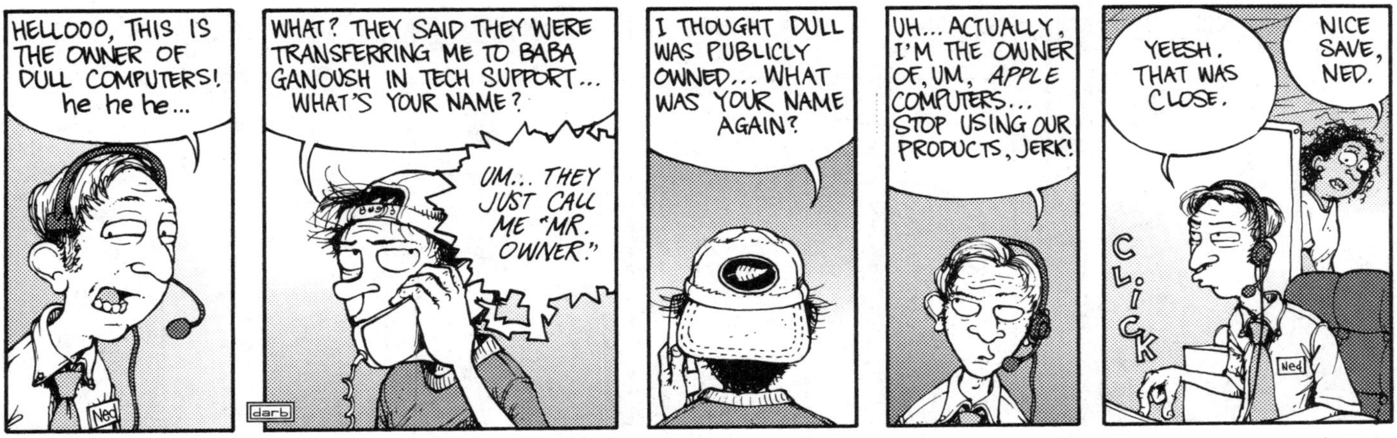
HELLOOO, THIS IS THE OWNER OF DULL COMPUTERS! he he he...
Ned
darb
WHAT? THEY SAID THEY WERE TRANSFERRING ME TO BABA GANOUSH IN TECH SUPPORT... WHAT'S YOUR NAME?
UM... THEY JUST CALL ME "MR. OWNER."
I THOUGHT DULL WAS PUBLICLY OWNED... WHAT WAS YOUR NAME AGAIN?
UH... ACTUALLY, I'M THE OWNER OF, UM, APPLE COMPUTERS... STOP USING OUR PRODUCTS, JERK!
YEESH. THAT WAS CLOSE.
NICE SAVE, NED.
CLICK
Ned

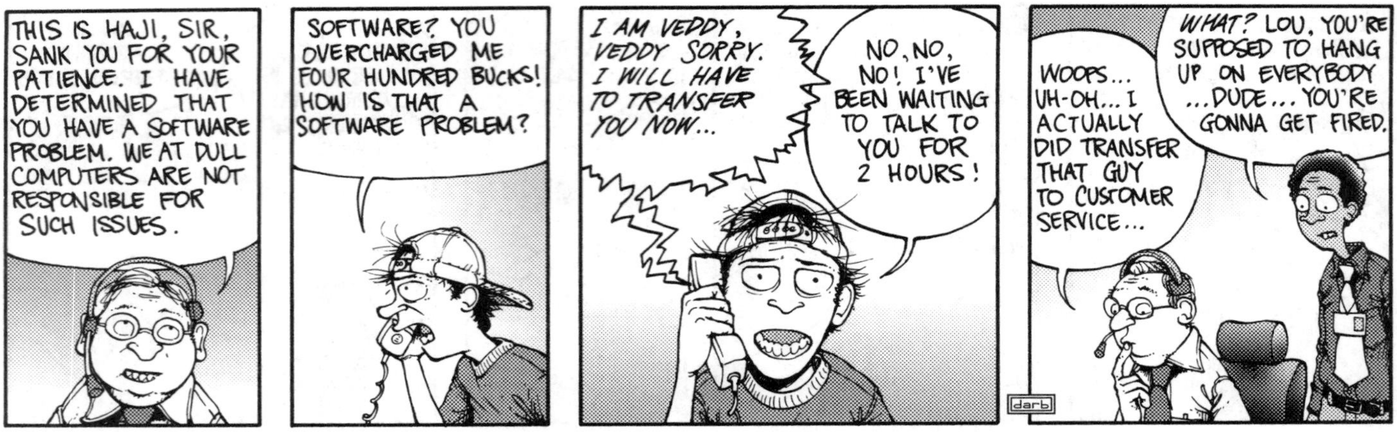
THIS IS HAJI, SIR, SANK YOU FOR YOUR PATIENCE. I HAVE DETERMINED THAT YOU HAVE A SOFTWARE PROBLEM. WE AT DULL COMPUTERS ARE NOT RESPONSIBLE FOR SUCH ISSUES.
SOFTWARE? YOU OVERCHARGED ME FOUR HUNDRED BUCKS! HOW IS THAT A SOFTWARE PROBLEM?
I AM VEDDY, VEDDY SORRY. I WILL HAVE TO TRANSFER YOU NOW...
NO, NO, NO! I'VE BEEN WAITING TO TALK TO YOU FOR 2 HOURS!
WHAT? LOU, YOU'RE SUPPOSED TO HANG UP ON EVERYBODY ...DUDE... YOU'RE GONNA GET FIRED.
WOOPS... UH-OH... I ACTUALLY DID TRANSFER THAT GUY TO CUSTOMER SERVICE...
darb

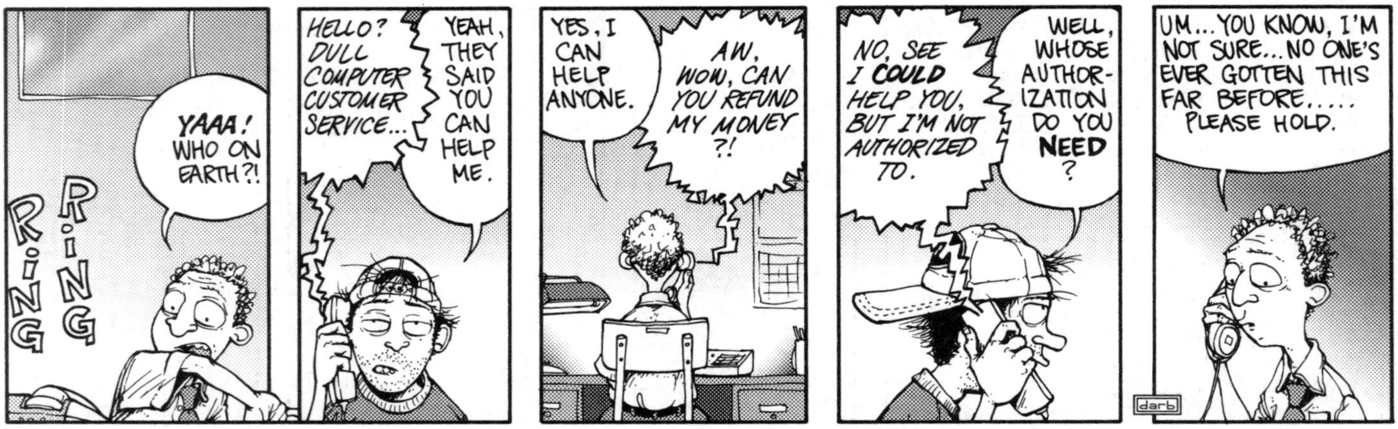
RING RING
YAAA! WHO ON EARTH?!
HELLO? DULL COMPUTER CUSTOMER SERVICE...
YEAH, THEY SAID YOU CAN HELP ME.
YES, I CAN HELP ANYONE.
AW, WOW, CAN YOU REFUND MY MONEY?!
NO, SEE I COULD HELP YOU, BUT I'M NOT AUTHORIZED TO.
WELL, WHOSE AUTHORIZATION DO YOU NEED?
UM... YOU KNOW, I'M NOT SURE... NO ONE'S EVER GOTTEN THIS FAR BEFORE..... PLEASE HOLD.
darb

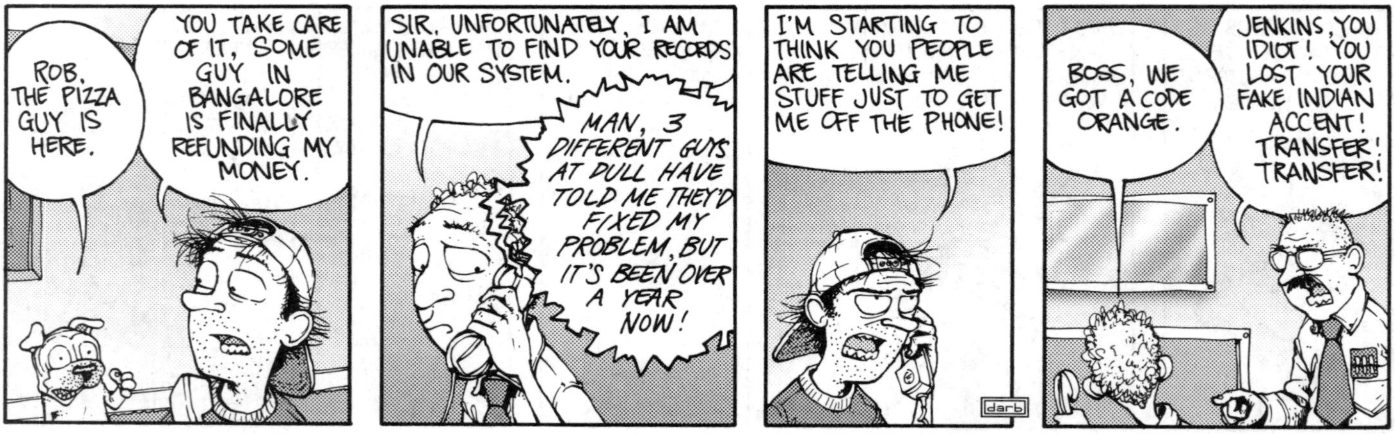
ROB, THE PIZZA GUY IS HERE.
YOU TAKE CARE OF IT, SOME GUY IN BANGALORE IS FINALLY REFUNDING MY MONEY.
SIR, UNFORTUNATELY, I AM UNABLE TO FIND YOUR RECORDS IN OUR SYSTEM.
MAN, 3 DIFFERENT GUYS AT DULL HAVE TOLD ME THEY'D FIXED MY PROBLEM, BUT IT'S BEEN OVER A YEAR NOW!
I'M STARTING TO THINK YOU PEOPLE ARE TELLING ME STUFF JUST TO GET ME OFF THE PHONE!
darb
BOSS, WE GOT A CODE ORANGE.
JENKINS, YOU IDIOT! YOU LOST YOUR FAKE INDIAN ACCENT! TRANSFER! TRANSFER!

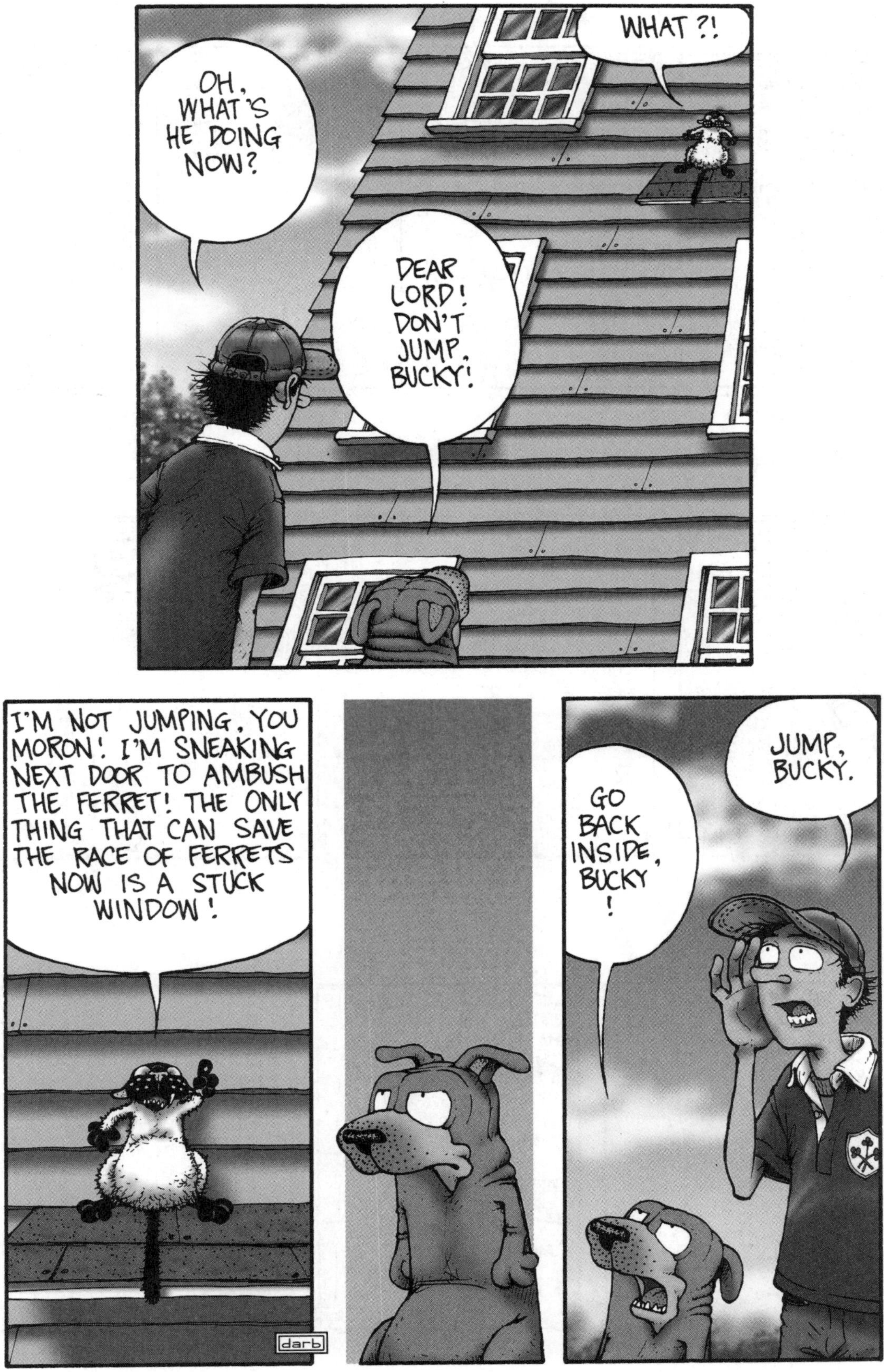

OH, WHAT'S HE DOING NOW?
WHAT?!
DEAR LORD! DON'T JUMP, BUCKY!
I'M NOT JUMPING, YOU MORON! I'M SNEAKING NEXT DOOR TO AMBUSH THE FERRET! THE ONLY THING THAT CAN SAVE THE RACE OF FERRETS NOW IS A STUCK WINDOW!
darb
JUMP, BUCKY.
GO BACK INSIDE, BUCKY!

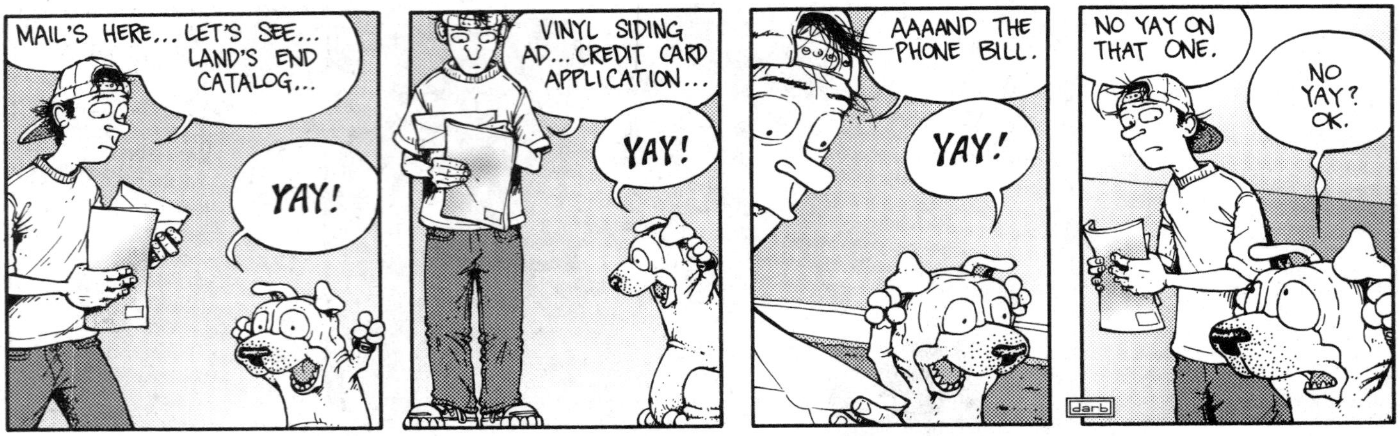
MAIL'S HERE... LET'S SEE... LAND'S END CATALOG...
YAY!
VINYL SIDING AD... CREDIT CARD APPLICATION...
YAY!
AAAAND THE PHONE BILL.
YAY!
NO YAY ON THAT ONE.
NO YAY? OK.
darb

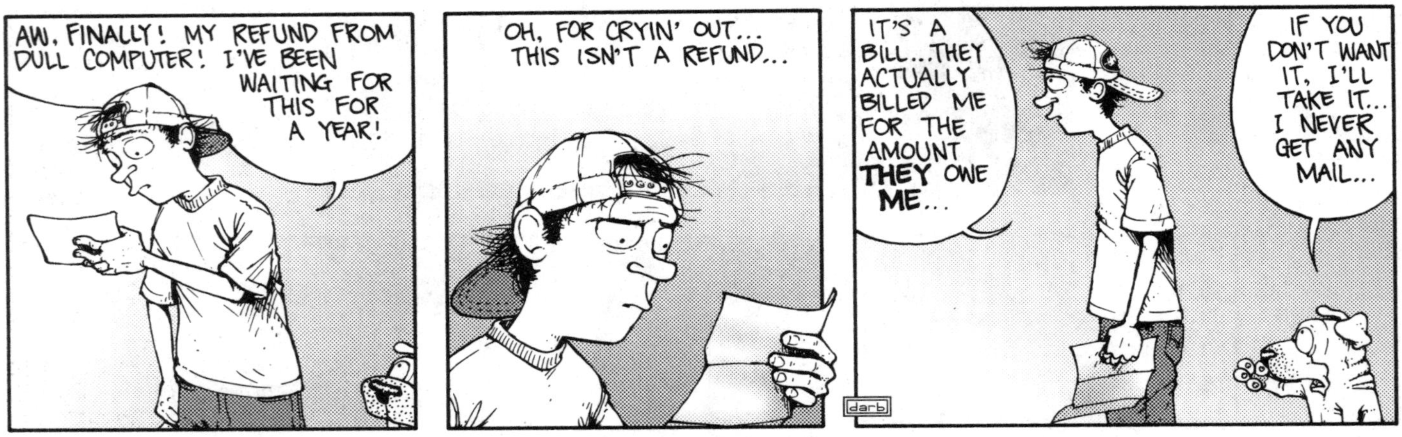
AW, FINALLY! MY REFUND FROM DULL COMPUTER! I'VE BEEN WAITING FOR THIS FOR A YEAR!
OH, FOR CRYIN' OUT... THIS ISN'T A REFUND...
darb
IT'S A BILL... THEY ACTUALLY BILLED ME FOR THE AMOUNT **THEY** OWE **ME**...
IF YOU DON'T WANT IT, I'LL TAKE IT... I NEVER GET ANY MAIL...

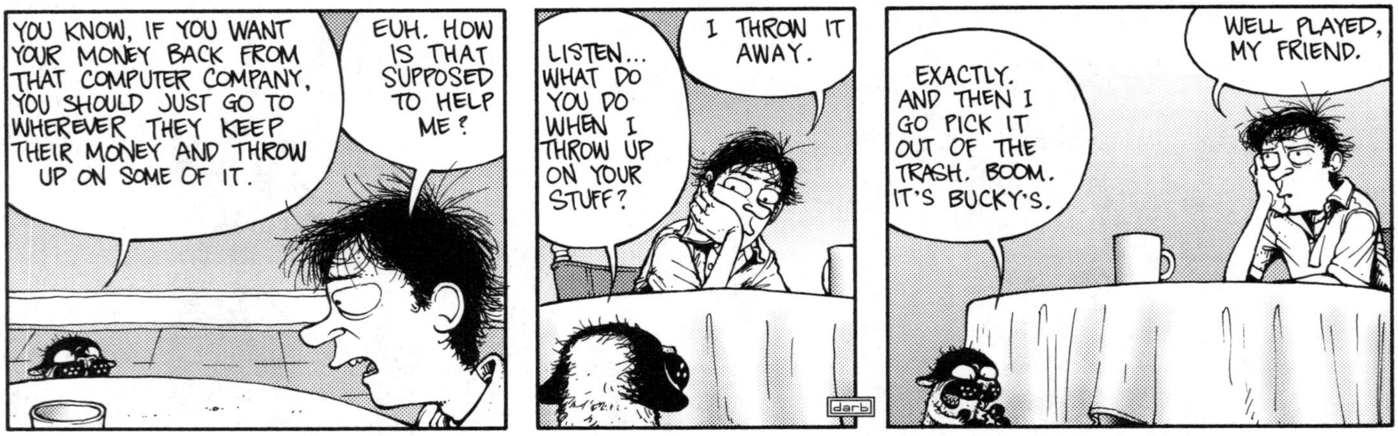
YOU KNOW, IF YOU WANT YOUR MONEY BACK FROM THAT COMPUTER COMPANY, YOU SHOULD JUST GO TO WHEREVER THEY KEEP THEIR MONEY AND THROW UP ON SOME OF IT.
EUH. HOW IS THAT SUPPOSED TO HELP ME?
LISTEN... WHAT DO YOU DO WHEN I THROW UP ON YOUR STUFF?
I THROW IT AWAY.
darb
EXACTLY. AND THEN I GO PICK IT OUT OF THE TRASH. BOOM. IT'S BUCKY'S.
WELL PLAYED, MY FRIEND.

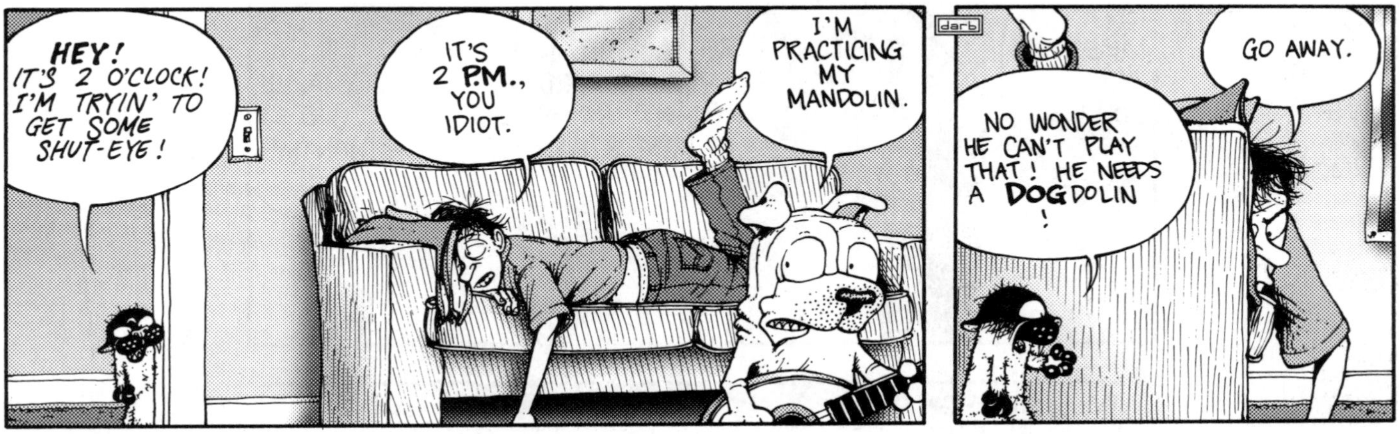
HEY! IT'S 2 O'CLOCK! I'M TRYIN' TO GET SOME SHUT-EYE!
IT'S 2 P.M., YOU IDIOT.
I'M PRACTICING MY MANDOLIN.
GO AWAY.
NO WONDER HE CAN'T PLAY THAT! HE NEEDS A DOGDOLIN!
darb

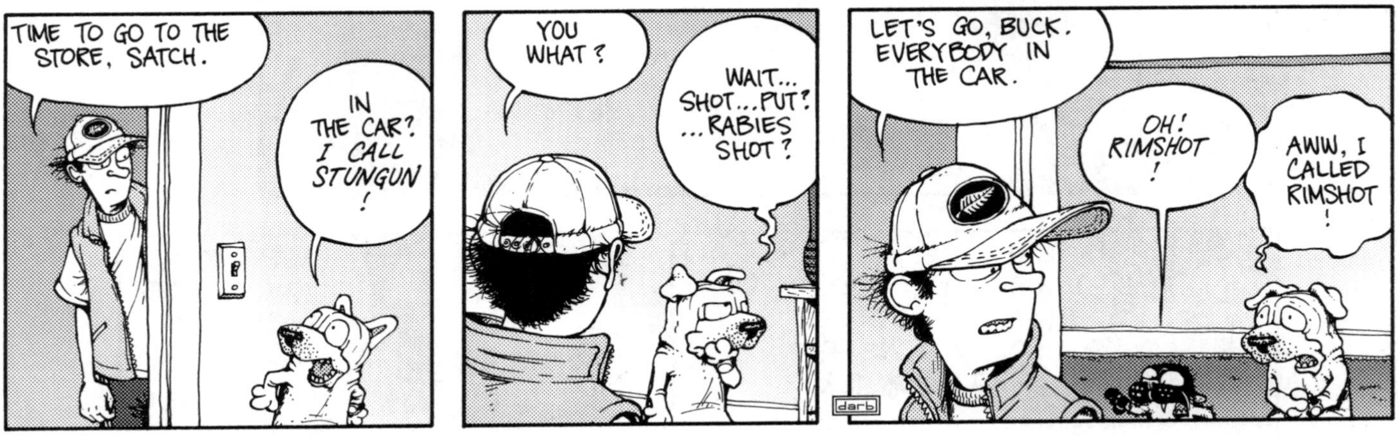
TIME TO GO TO THE STORE, SATCH.
IN THE CAR? I CALL STUNGUN!
YOU WHAT?
WAIT... SHOT...PUT? ...RABIES SHOT?
LET'S GO, BUCK. EVERYBODY IN THE CAR.
OH! RIMSHOT!
AWW, I CALLED RIMSHOT!
darb

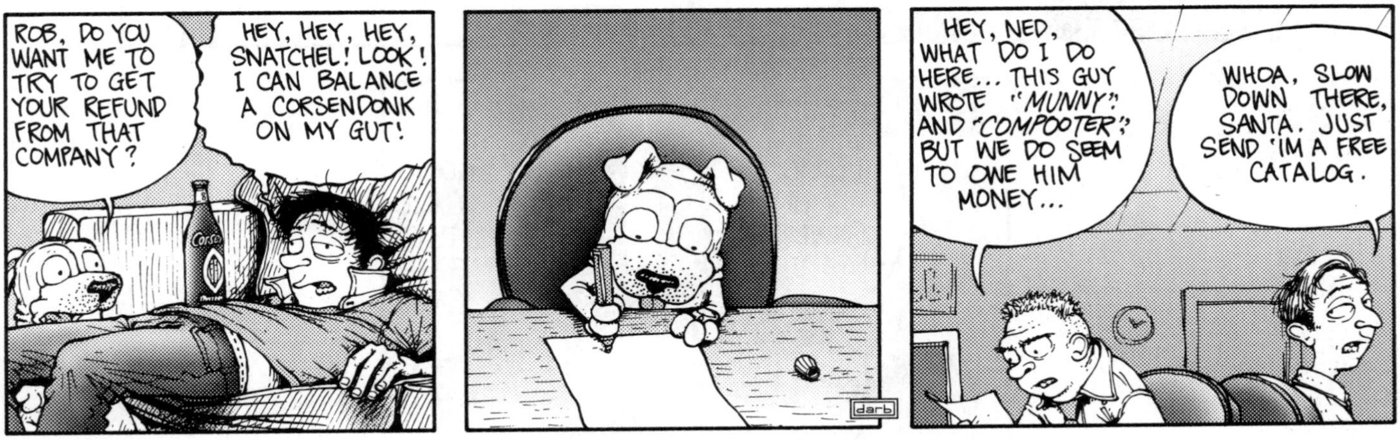
ROB, DO YOU WANT ME TO TRY TO GET YOUR REFUND FROM THAT COMPANY?
HEY, HEY, HEY, SNATCHEL! LOOK! I CAN BALANCE A CORSENDONK ON MY GUT!
darb
HEY, NED, WHAT DO I DO HERE... THIS GUY WROTE "MUNNY" AND "COMPOOTER," BUT WE DO SEEM TO OWE HIM MONEY...
WHOA, SLOW DOWN THERE, SANTA. JUST SEND 'IM A FREE CATALOG.

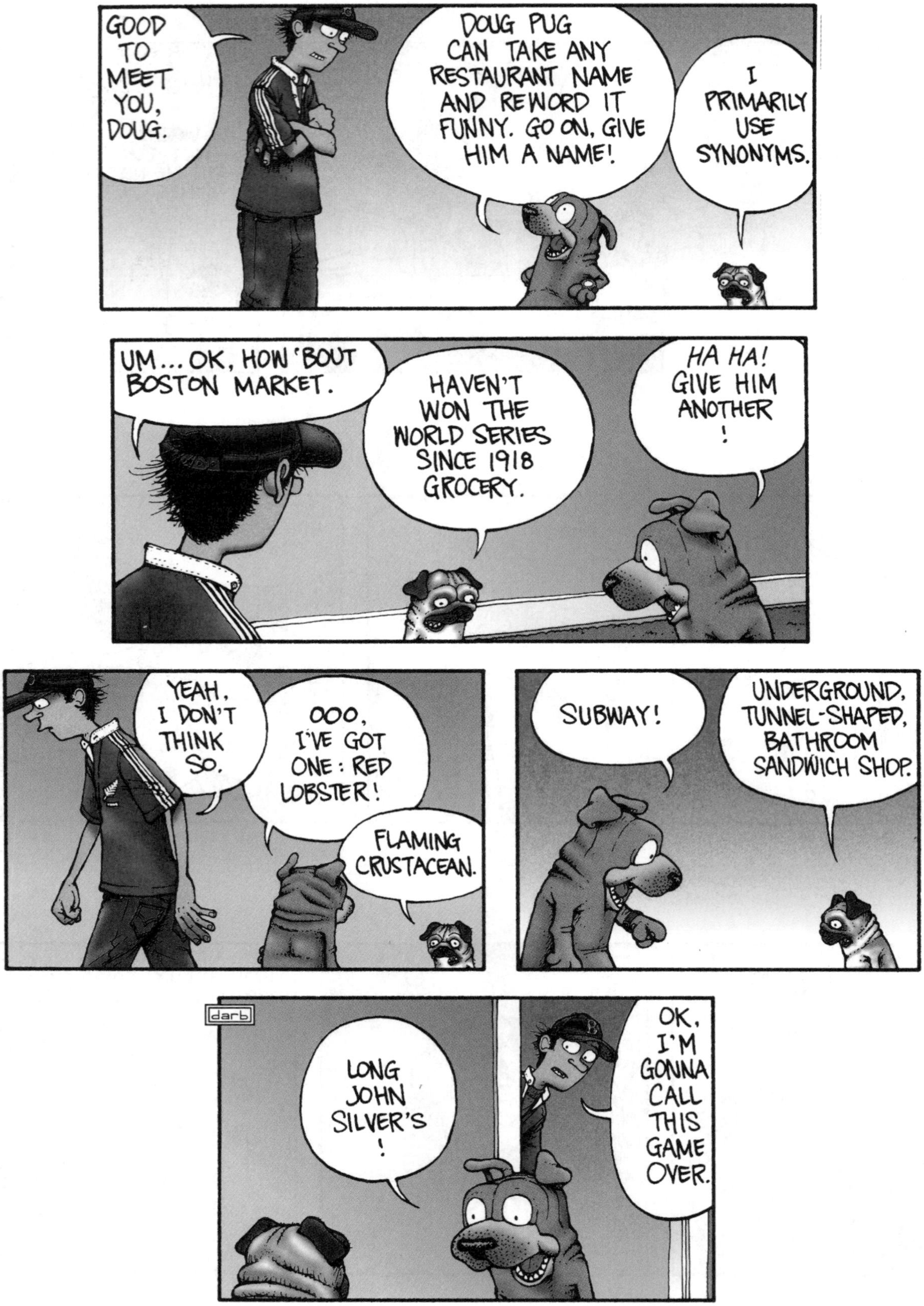
GOOD TO MEET YOU, DOUG.
DOUG PUG CAN TAKE ANY RESTAURANT NAME AND REWORD IT FUNNY. GO ON, GIVE HIM A NAME!
I PRIMARILY USE SYNONYMS.
UM... OK, HOW 'BOUT BOSTON MARKET.
HAVEN'T WON THE WORLD SERIES SINCE 1918 GROCERY.
HA HA! GIVE HIM ANOTHER!
YEAH, I DON'T THINK SO.
OOO, I'VE GOT ONE: RED LOBSTER!
FLAMING CRUSTACEAN.
SUBWAY!
UNDERGROUND, TUNNEL-SHAPED, BATHROOM SANDWICH SHOP.
darb
LONG JOHN SILVER'S!
OK, I'M GONNA CALL THIS GAME OVER.

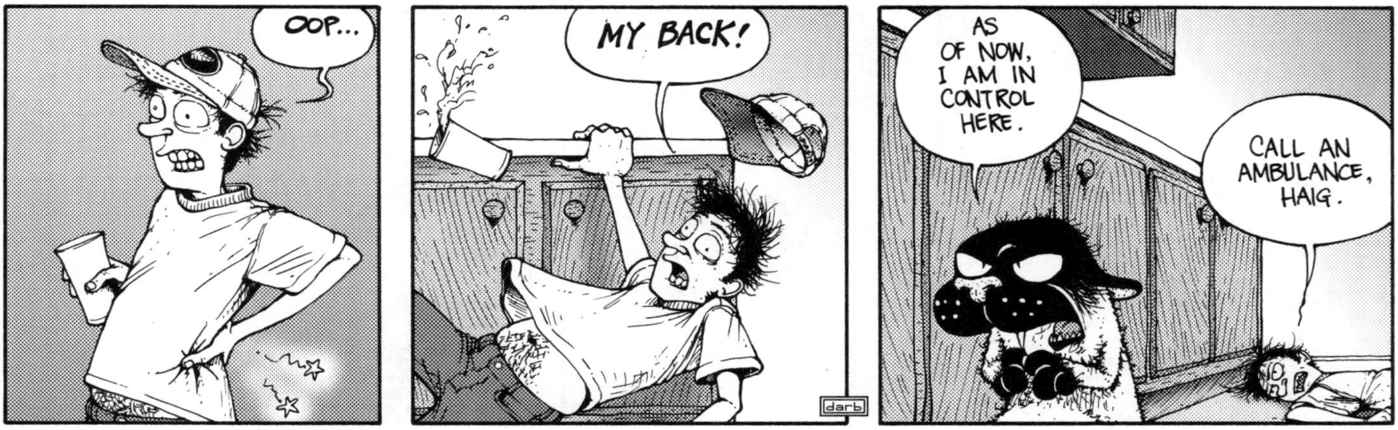
OOP...
MY BACK!
AS OF NOW, I AM IN CONTROL HERE.
CALL AN AMBULANCE, HAIG.

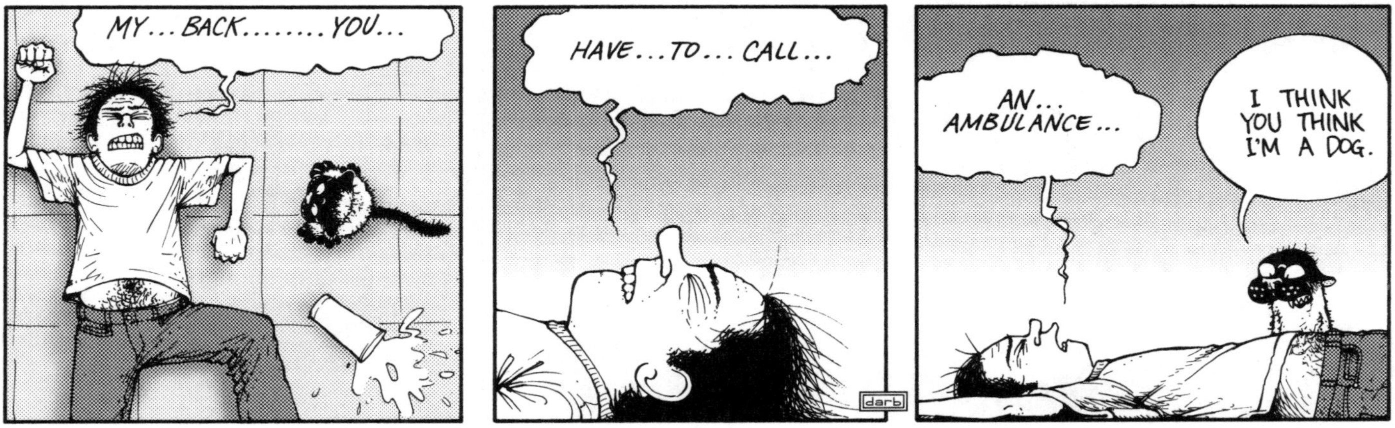
MY... BACK........ YOU...
HAVE... TO... CALL...
AN... AMBULANCE...
I THINK YOU THINK I'M A DOG.

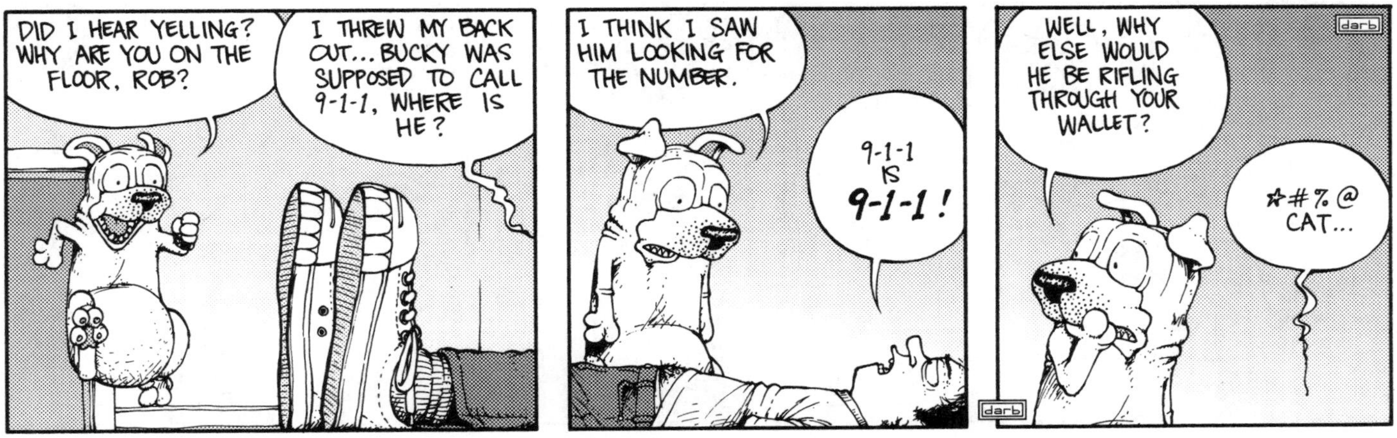
DID I HEAR YELLING? WHY ARE YOU ON THE FLOOR, ROB?
I THREW MY BACK OUT... BUCKY WAS SUPPOSED TO CALL 9-1-1, WHERE IS HE?
I THINK I SAW HIM LOOKING FOR THE NUMBER.
9-1-1 IS 9-1-1!
WELL, WHY ELSE WOULD HE BE RIFLING THROUGH YOUR WALLET?
☆#%@ CAT...

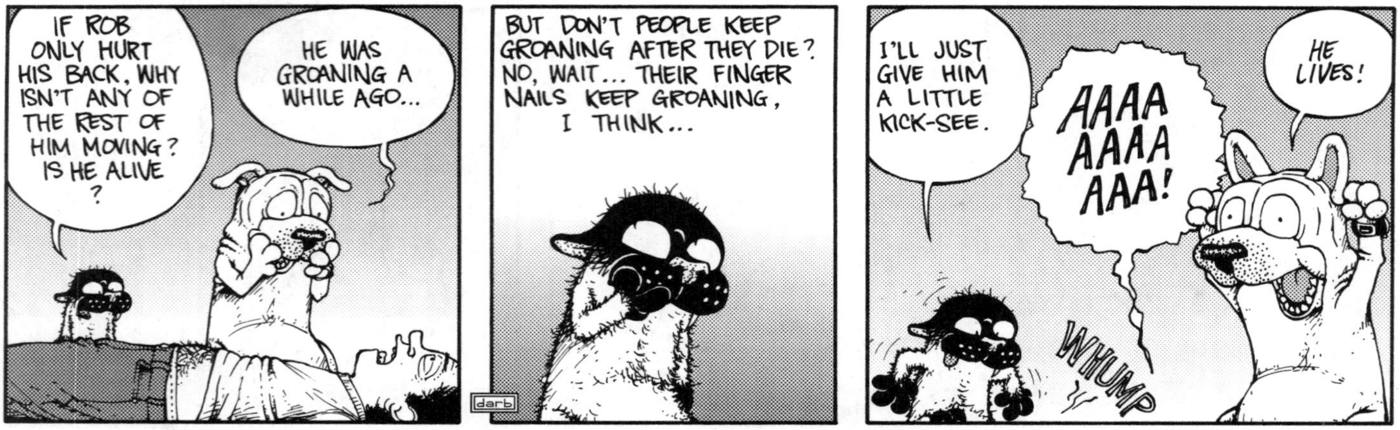
IF ROB ONLY HURT HIS BACK, WHY ISN'T ANY OF THE REST OF HIM MOVING? IS HE ALIVE ?
HE WAS GROANING A WHILE AGO...
darb
BUT DON'T PEOPLE KEEP GROANING AFTER THEY DIE? NO, WAIT... THEIR FINGER NAILS KEEP GROANING, I THINK...
I'LL JUST GIVE HIM A LITTLE KICK-SEE.
AAAA AAAA AAA!
HE LIVES!
WHUMP

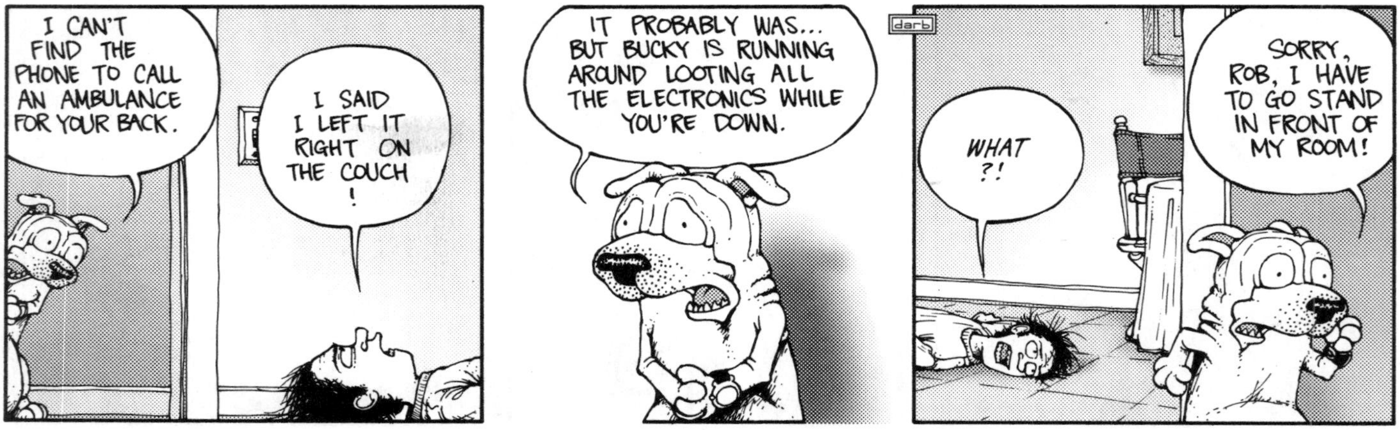
I CAN'T FIND THE PHONE TO CALL AN AMBULANCE FOR YOUR BACK.
I SAID I LEFT IT RIGHT ON THE COUCH !
IT PROBABLY WAS... BUT BUCKY IS RUNNING AROUND LOOTING ALL THE ELECTRONICS WHILE YOU'RE DOWN.
darb
WHAT ?!
SORRY, ROB, I HAVE TO GO STAND IN FRONT OF MY ROOM!

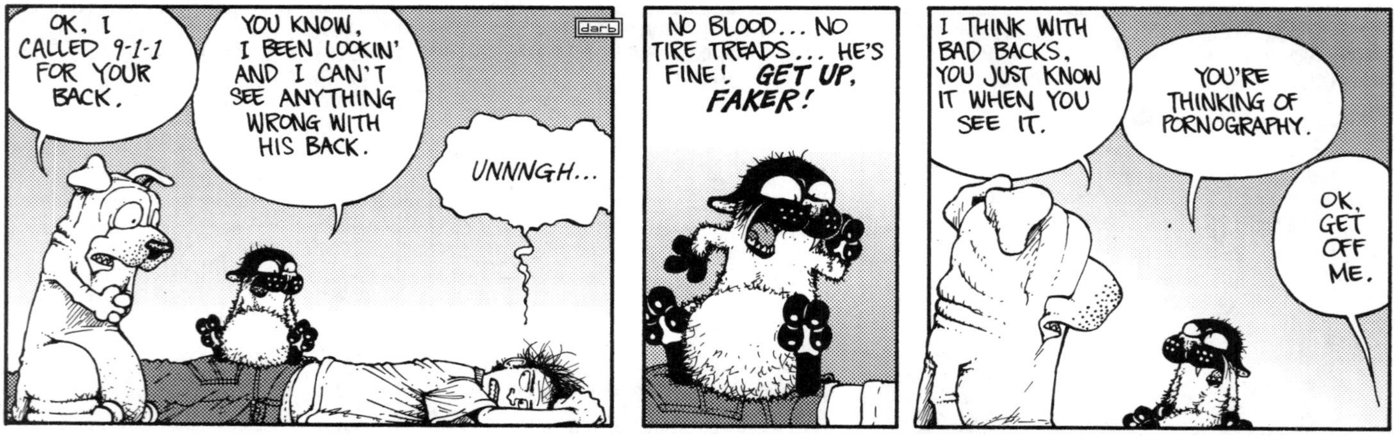
OK, I CALLED 9-1-1 FOR YOUR BACK.
YOU KNOW, I BEEN LOOKIN' AND I CAN'T SEE ANYTHING WRONG WITH HIS BACK.
darb
UNNNGH...
NO BLOOD... NO TIRE TREADS... HE'S FINE! GET UP, FAKER!
I THINK WITH BAD BACKS, YOU JUST KNOW IT WHEN YOU SEE IT.
YOU'RE THINKING OF PORNOGRAPHY.
OK, GET OFF ME.

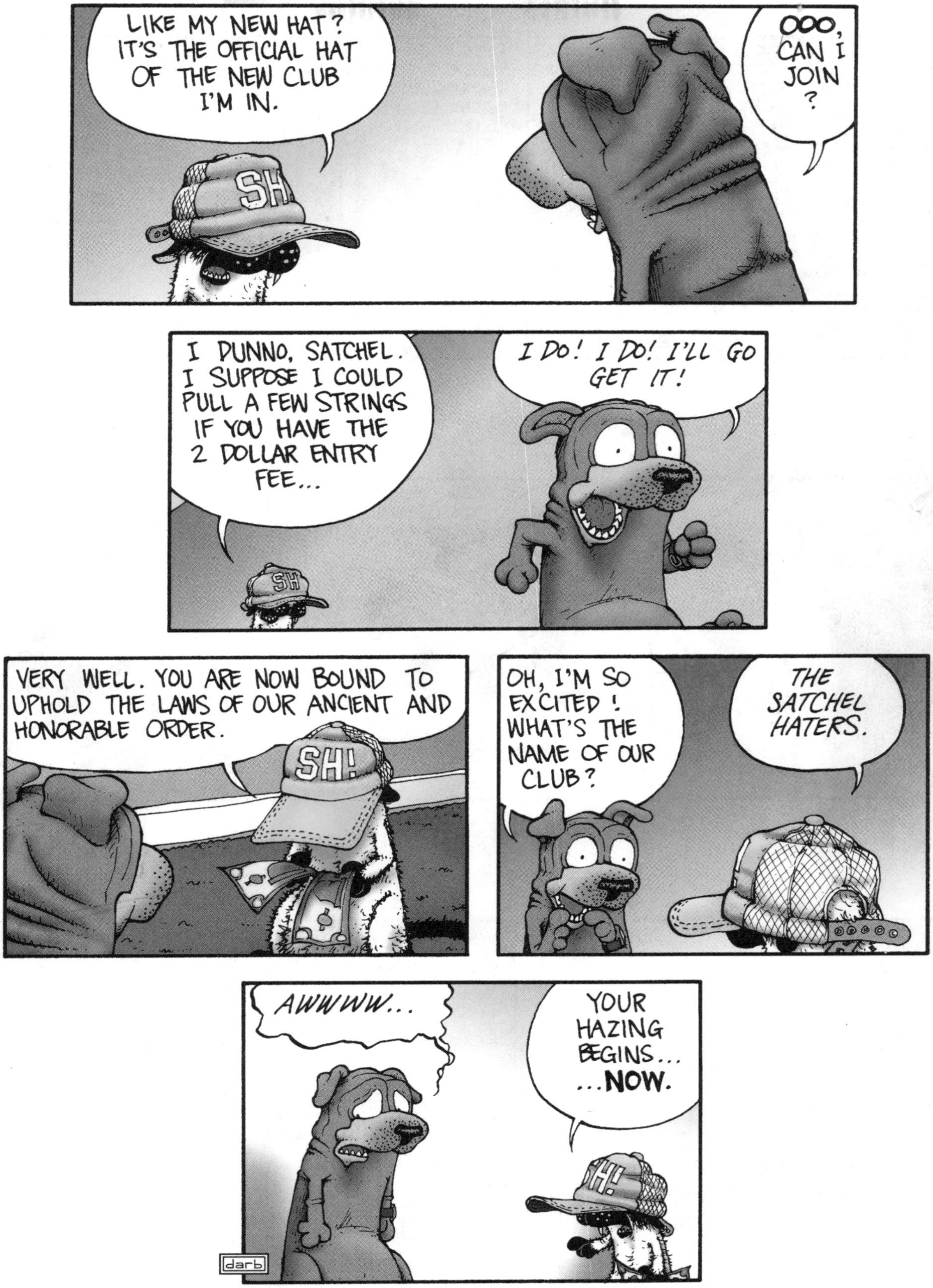
LIKE MY NEW HAT? IT'S THE OFFICIAL HAT OF THE NEW CLUB I'M IN.
OOO, CAN I JOIN?
I DUNNO, SATCHEL. I SUPPOSE I COULD PULL A FEW STRINGS IF YOU HAVE THE 2 DOLLAR ENTRY FEE...
I DO! I DO! I'LL GO GET IT!
VERY WELL. YOU ARE NOW BOUND TO UPHOLD THE LAWS OF OUR ANCIENT AND HONORABLE ORDER.
SH!
OH, I'M SO EXCITED! WHAT'S THE NAME OF OUR CLUB?
THE SATCHEL HATERS.
AWWWW...
YOUR HAZING BEGINS... ...NOW.
darb

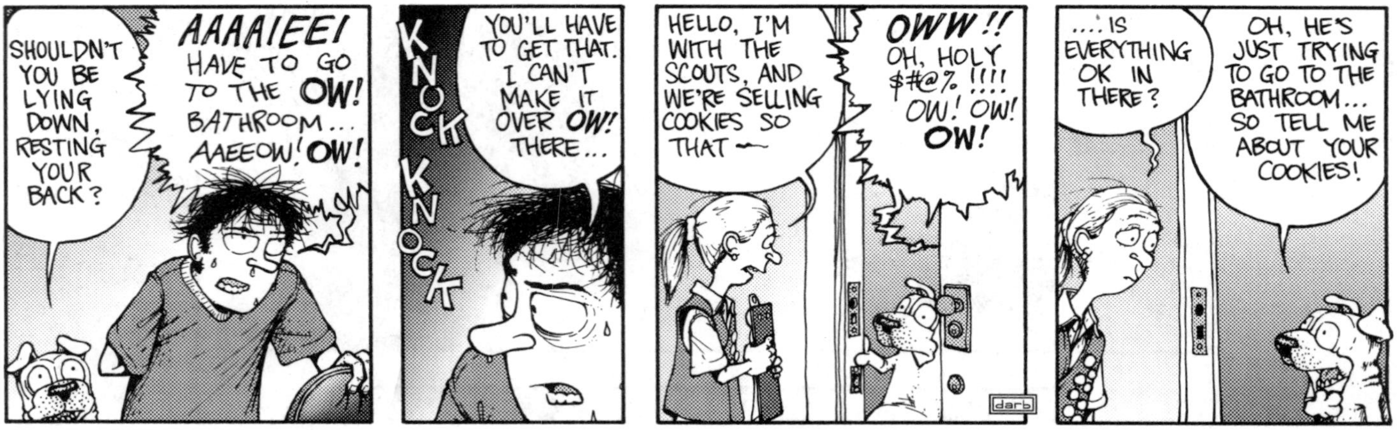
SHOULDN'T YOU BE LYING DOWN, RESTING YOUR BACK?
AAAAIEE! HAVE TO GO TO THE OW! BATHROOM... AAEEOW! OW!
KNOCK KNOCK
YOU'LL HAVE TO GET THAT. I CAN'T MAKE IT OVER OW! THERE...
HELLO, I'M WITH THE SCOUTS, AND WE'RE SELLING COOKIES SO THAT—
OWW!! OH, HOLY $#@%!!!! OW! OW! OW!
...IS EVERYTHING OK IN THERE?
OH, HE'S JUST TRYING TO GO TO THE BATHROOM... SO TELL ME ABOUT YOUR COOKIES!

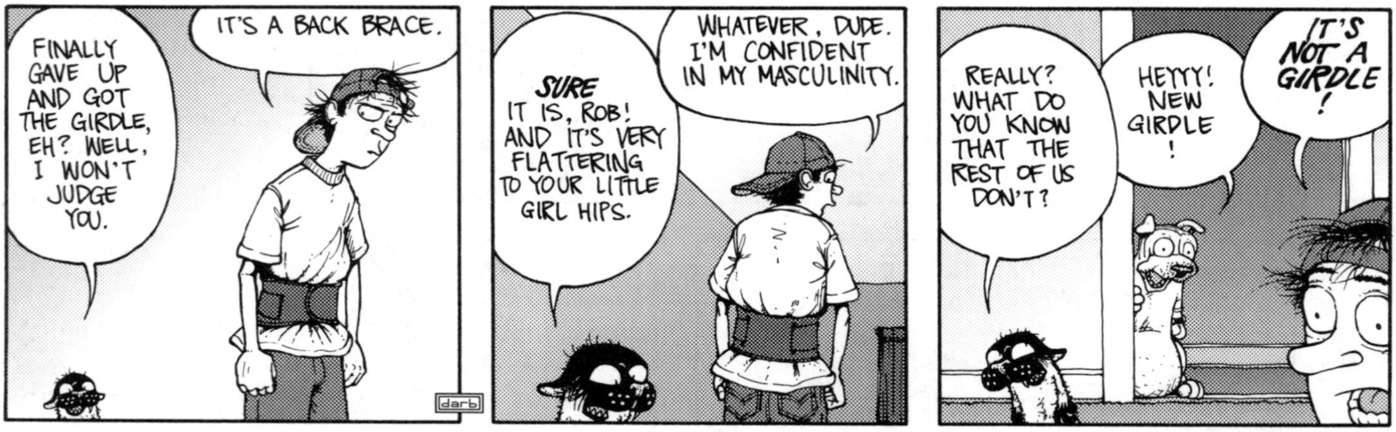
FINALLY GAVE UP AND GOT THE GIRDLE, EH? WELL, I WON'T JUDGE YOU.
IT'S A BACK BRACE.
SURE IT IS, ROB! AND IT'S VERY FLATTERING TO YOUR LITTLE GIRL HIPS.
WHATEVER, DUDE. I'M CONFIDENT IN MY MASCULINITY.
REALLY? WHAT DO YOU KNOW THAT THE REST OF US DON'T?
HEYYY! NEW GIRDLE!
IT'S NOT A GIRDLE!

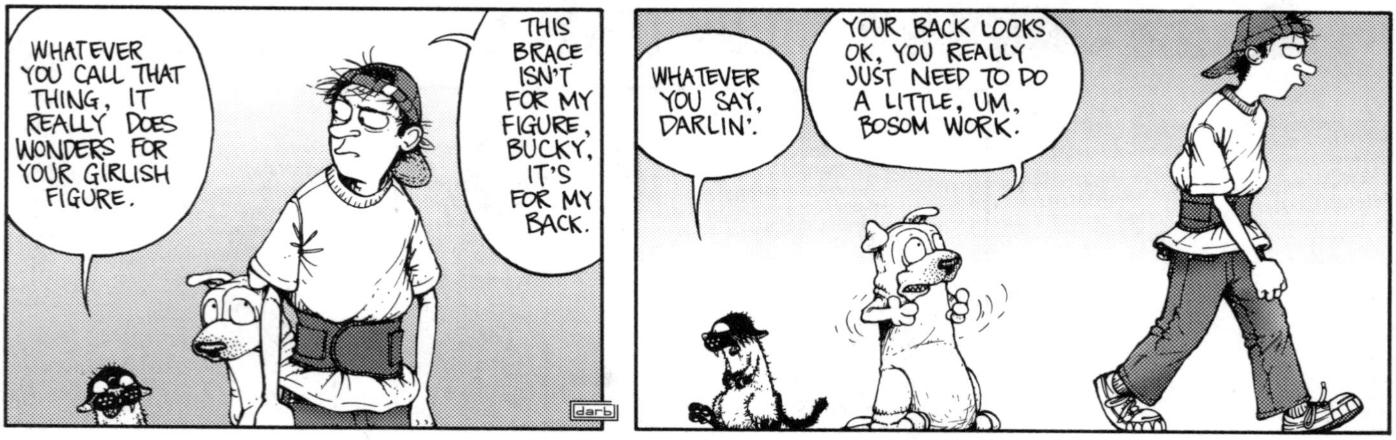
WHATEVER YOU CALL THAT THING, IT REALLY DOES WONDERS FOR YOUR GIRLISH FIGURE.
THIS BRACE ISN'T FOR MY FIGURE, BUCKY, IT'S FOR MY BACK.
WHATEVER YOU SAY, DARLIN'.
YOUR BACK LOOKS OK, YOU REALLY JUST NEED TO DO A LITTLE, UM, BOSOM WORK.

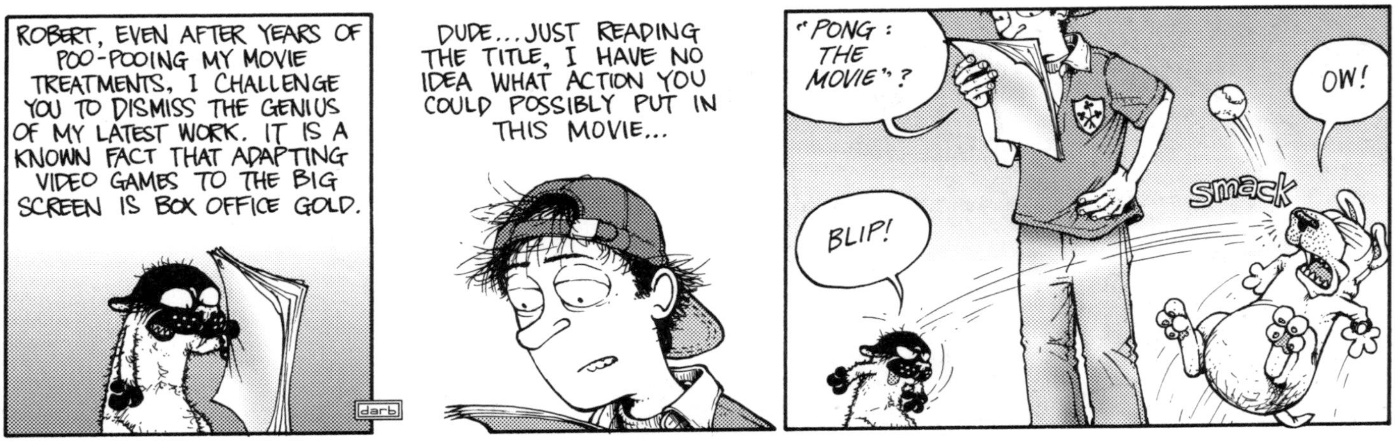
ROBERT, EVEN AFTER YEARS OF POO-POOING MY MOVIE TREATMENTS, I CHALLENGE YOU TO DISMISS THE GENIUS OF MY LATEST WORK. IT IS A KNOWN FACT THAT ADAPTING VIDEO GAMES TO THE BIG SCREEN IS BOX OFFICE GOLD.
darb
DUDE... JUST READING THE TITLE, I HAVE NO IDEA WHAT ACTION YOU COULD POSSIBLY PUT IN THIS MOVIE...
"PONG: THE MOVIE"?
BLIP!
OW!
smack

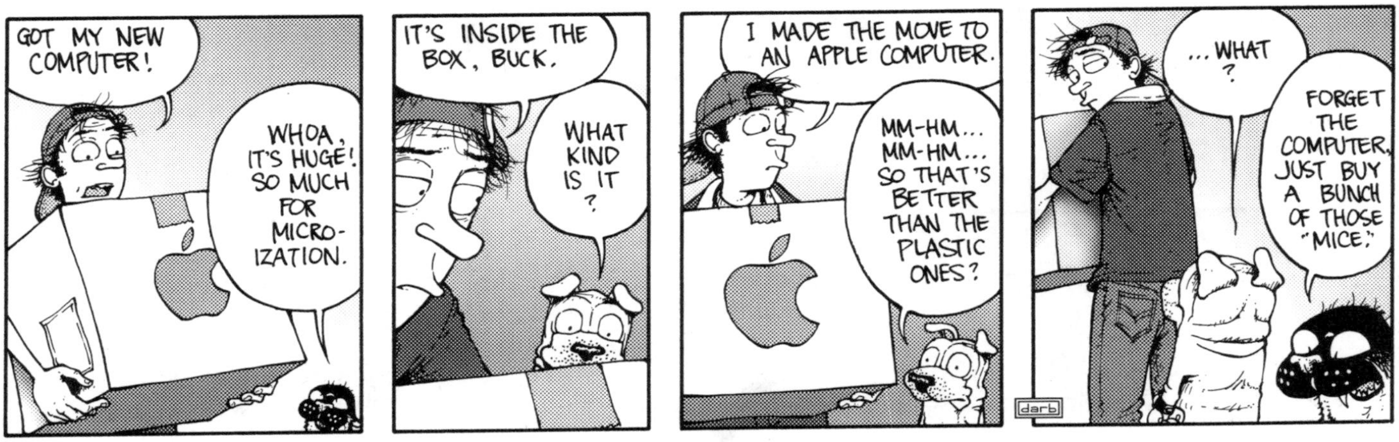
GOT MY NEW COMPUTER!
WHOA, IT'S HUGE! SO MUCH FOR MICRO-IZATION.
IT'S INSIDE THE BOX, BUCK.
WHAT KIND IS IT?
I MADE THE MOVE TO AN APPLE COMPUTER.
MM-HM... MM-HM... SO THAT'S BETTER THAN THE PLASTIC ONES?
darb
...WHAT?
FORGET THE COMPUTER, JUST BUY A BUNCH OF THOSE "MICE."

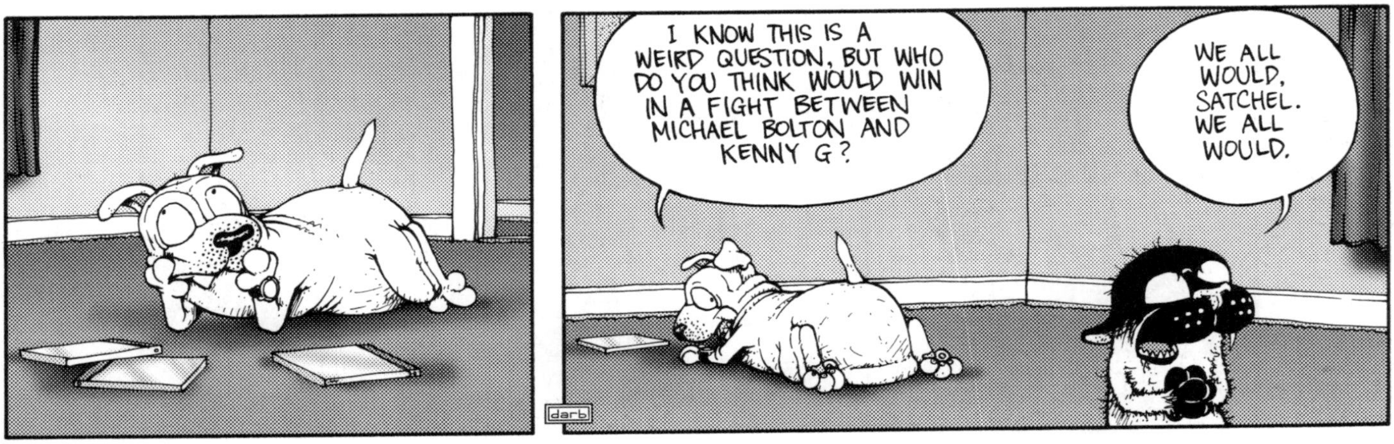
darb
I KNOW THIS IS A WEIRD QUESTION, BUT WHO DO YOU THINK WOULD WIN IN A FIGHT BETWEEN MICHAEL BOLTON AND KENNY G?
WE ALL WOULD, SATCHEL. WE ALL WOULD.

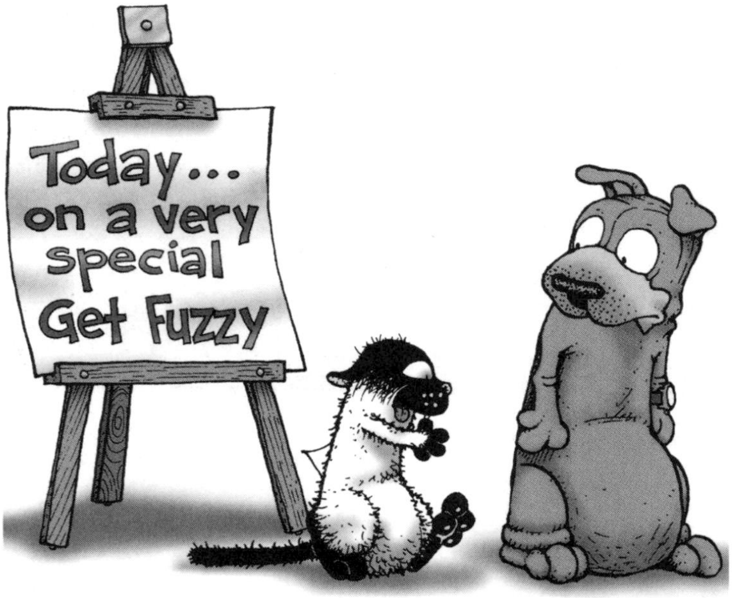
Today... on a very special Get Fuzzy

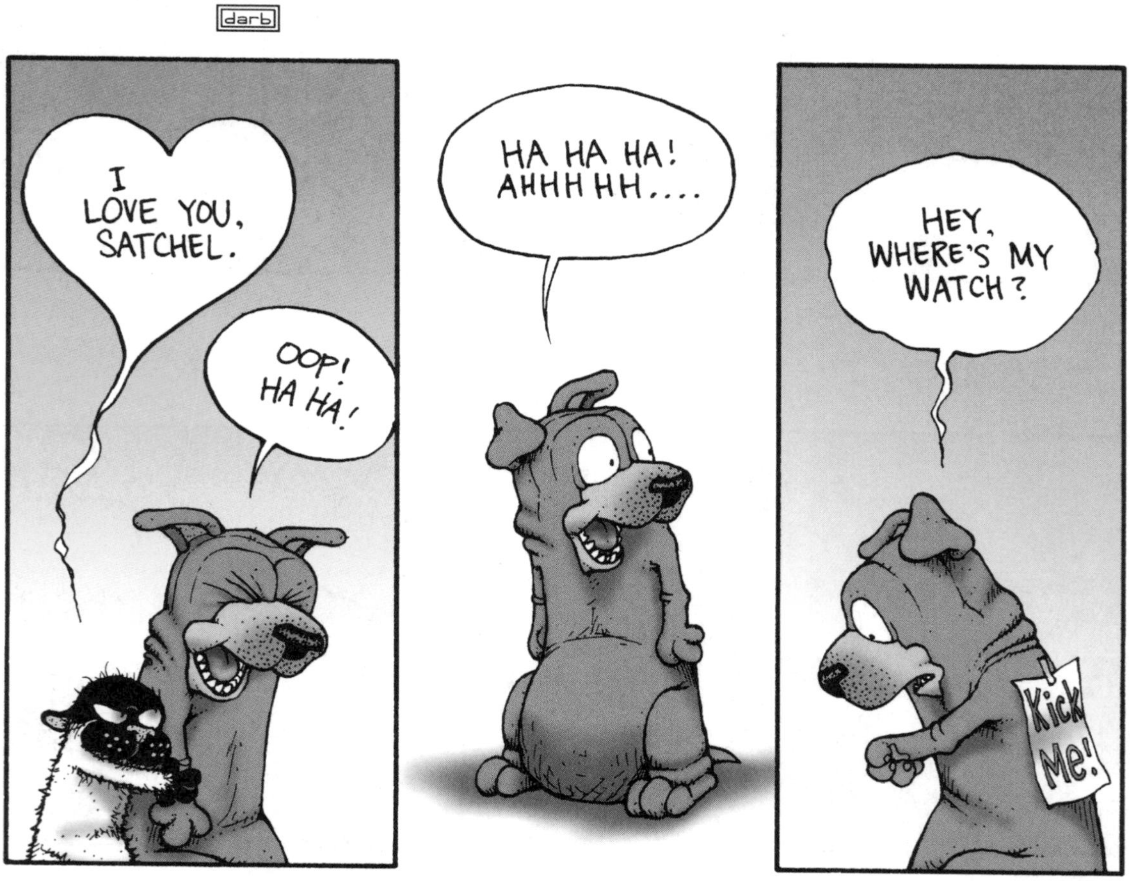
darb
I LOVE YOU, SATCHEL.
OOP! HA HA!
HA HA HA! AHHHHH....
HEY, WHERE'S MY WATCH?
Kick Me!

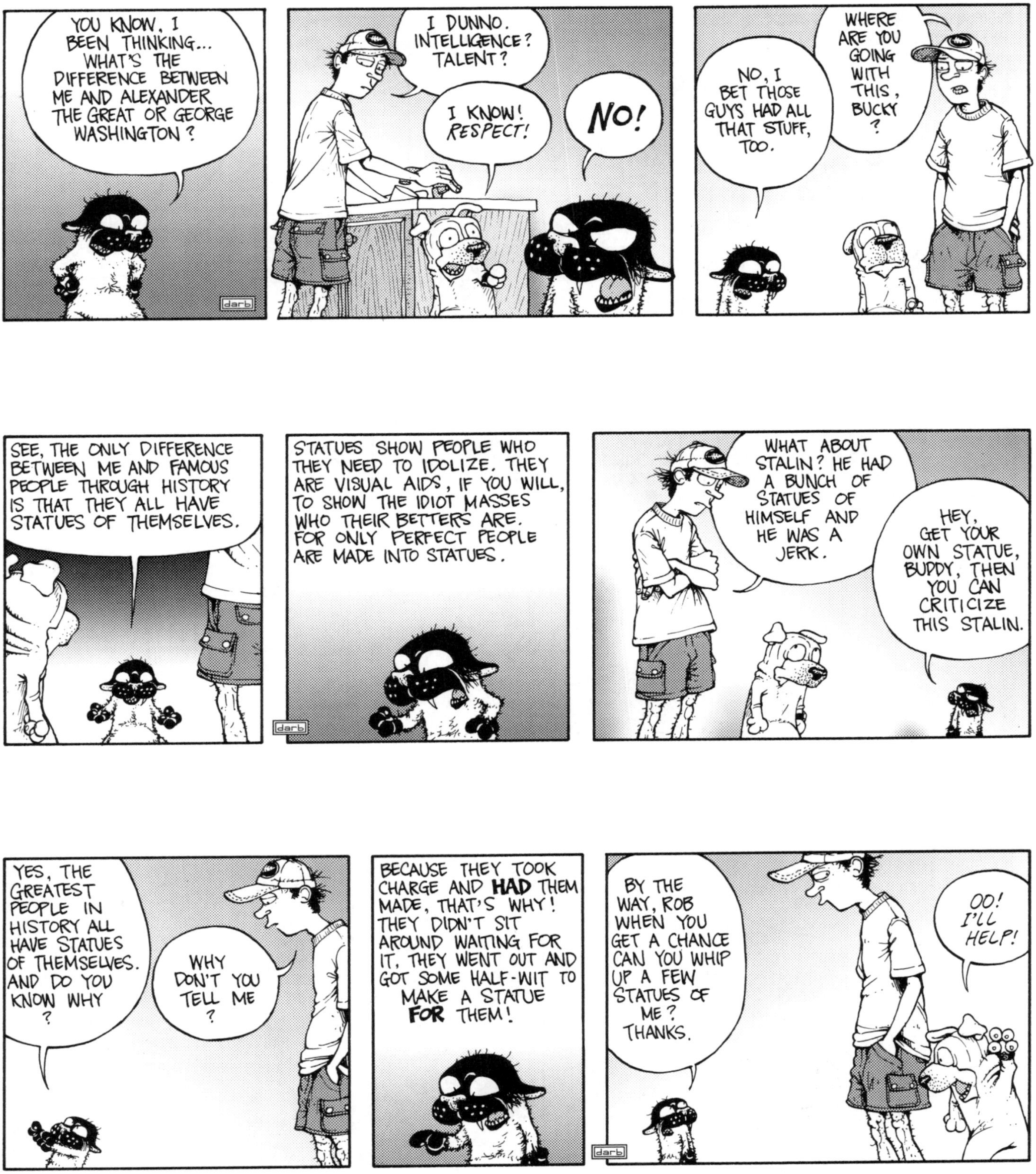
YOU KNOW, I BEEN THINKING... WHAT'S THE DIFFERENCE BETWEEN ME AND ALEXANDER THE GREAT OR GEORGE WASHINGTON?
darb
I DUNNO. INTELLIGENCE? TALENT?
I KNOW! RESPECT!
NO!
NO, I BET THOSE GUYS HAD ALL THAT STUFF, TOO.
WHERE ARE YOU GOING WITH THIS, BUCKY?
SEE, THE ONLY DIFFERENCE BETWEEN ME AND FAMOUS PEOPLE THROUGH HISTORY IS THAT THEY ALL HAVE STATUES OF THEMSELVES.
STATUES SHOW PEOPLE WHO THEY NEED TO IDOLIZE. THEY ARE VISUAL AIDS, IF YOU WILL, TO SHOW THE IDIOT MASSES WHO THEIR BETTERS ARE. FOR ONLY PERFECT PEOPLE ARE MADE INTO STATUES.
darb
WHAT ABOUT STALIN? HE HAD A BUNCH OF STATUES OF HIMSELF AND HE WAS A JERK.
HEY, GET YOUR OWN STATUE, BUDDY, THEN YOU CAN CRITICIZE THIS STALIN.
YES, THE GREATEST PEOPLE IN HISTORY ALL HAVE STATUES OF THEMSELVES. AND DO YOU KNOW WHY?
WHY DON'T YOU TELL ME?
BECAUSE THEY TOOK CHARGE AND HAD THEM MADE, THAT'S WHY! THEY DIDN'T SIT AROUND WAITING FOR IT, THEY WENT OUT AND GOT SOME HALF-WIT TO MAKE A STATUE FOR THEM!
BY THE WAY, ROB WHEN YOU GET A CHANCE CAN YOU WHIP UP A FEW STATUES OF ME? THANKS.
OO! I'LL HELP!
darb

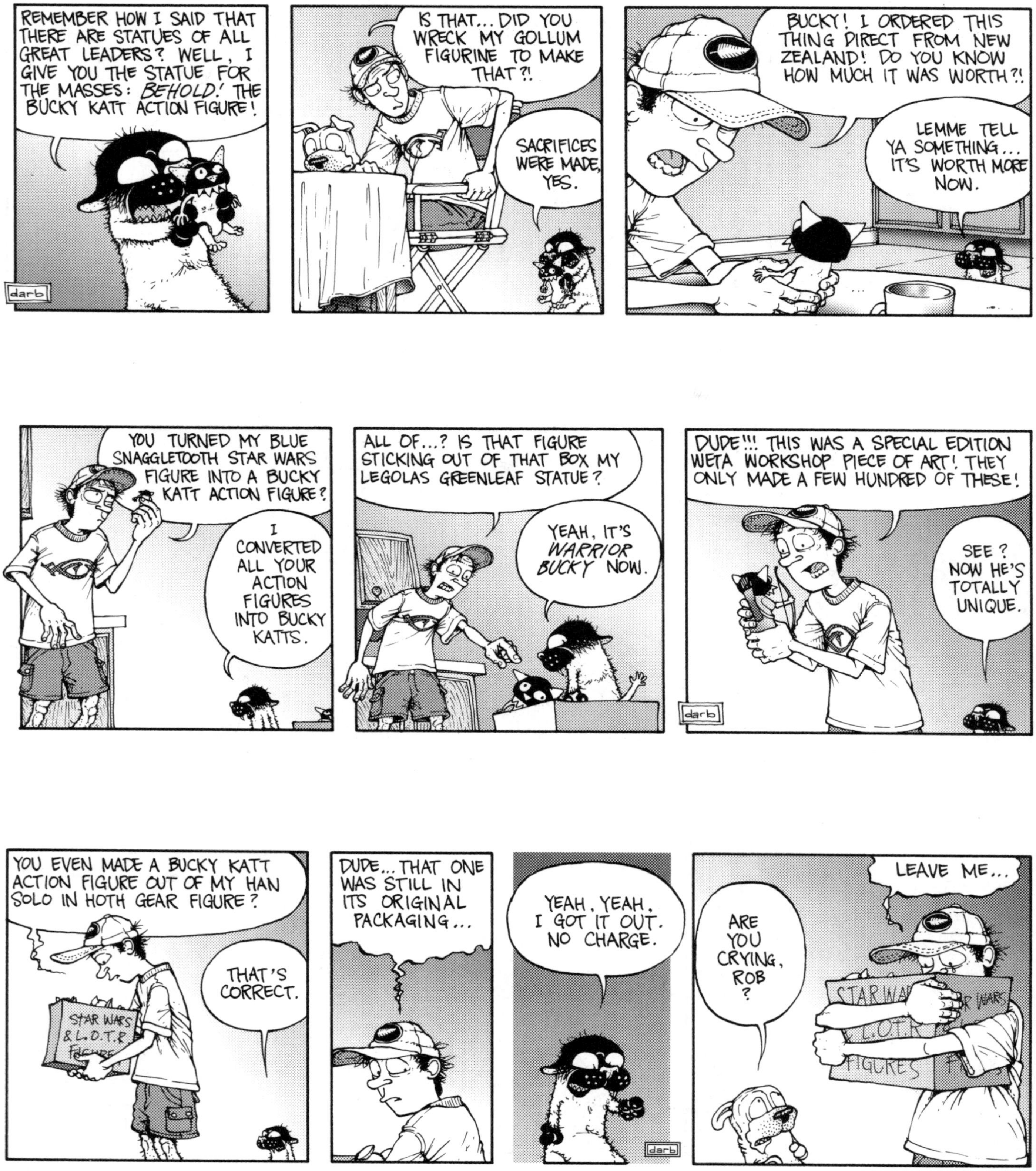
REMEMBER HOW I SAID THAT THERE ARE STATUES OF ALL GREAT LEADERS? WELL, I GIVE YOU THE STATUE FOR THE MASSES: *BEHOLD!* THE BUCKY KATT ACTION FIGURE!
darb
IS THAT... DID YOU WRECK MY GOLLUM FIGURINE TO MAKE THAT?!
SACRIFICES WERE MADE, YES.
BUCKY! I ORDERED THIS THING DIRECT FROM NEW ZEALAND! DO YOU KNOW HOW MUCH IT WAS WORTH?!
LEMME TELL YA SOMETHING... IT'S WORTH MORE NOW.
YOU TURNED MY BLUE SNAGGLETOOTH STAR WARS FIGURE INTO A BUCKY KATT ACTION FIGURE?
I CONVERTED ALL YOUR ACTION FIGURES INTO BUCKY KATTS.
ALL OF...? IS THAT FIGURE STICKING OUT OF THAT BOX MY LEGOLAS GREENLEAF STATUE?
YEAH, IT'S *WARRIOR BUCKY* NOW.
DUDE!!! THIS WAS A SPECIAL EDITION WETA WORKSHOP PIECE OF ART! THEY ONLY MADE A FEW HUNDRED OF THESE!
SEE? NOW HE'S TOTALLY UNIQUE.
darb
YOU EVEN MADE A BUCKY KATT ACTION FIGURE OUT OF MY HAN SOLO IN HOTH GEAR FIGURE?
STAR WARS & L.O.T.R
THAT'S CORRECT.
DUDE... THAT ONE WAS STILL IN ITS ORIGINAL PACKAGING...
YEAH, YEAH. I GOT IT OUT. NO CHARGE.
darb
LEAVE ME...
ARE YOU CRYING, ROB?
STAR WARS
L.O.T.R
FIGURES

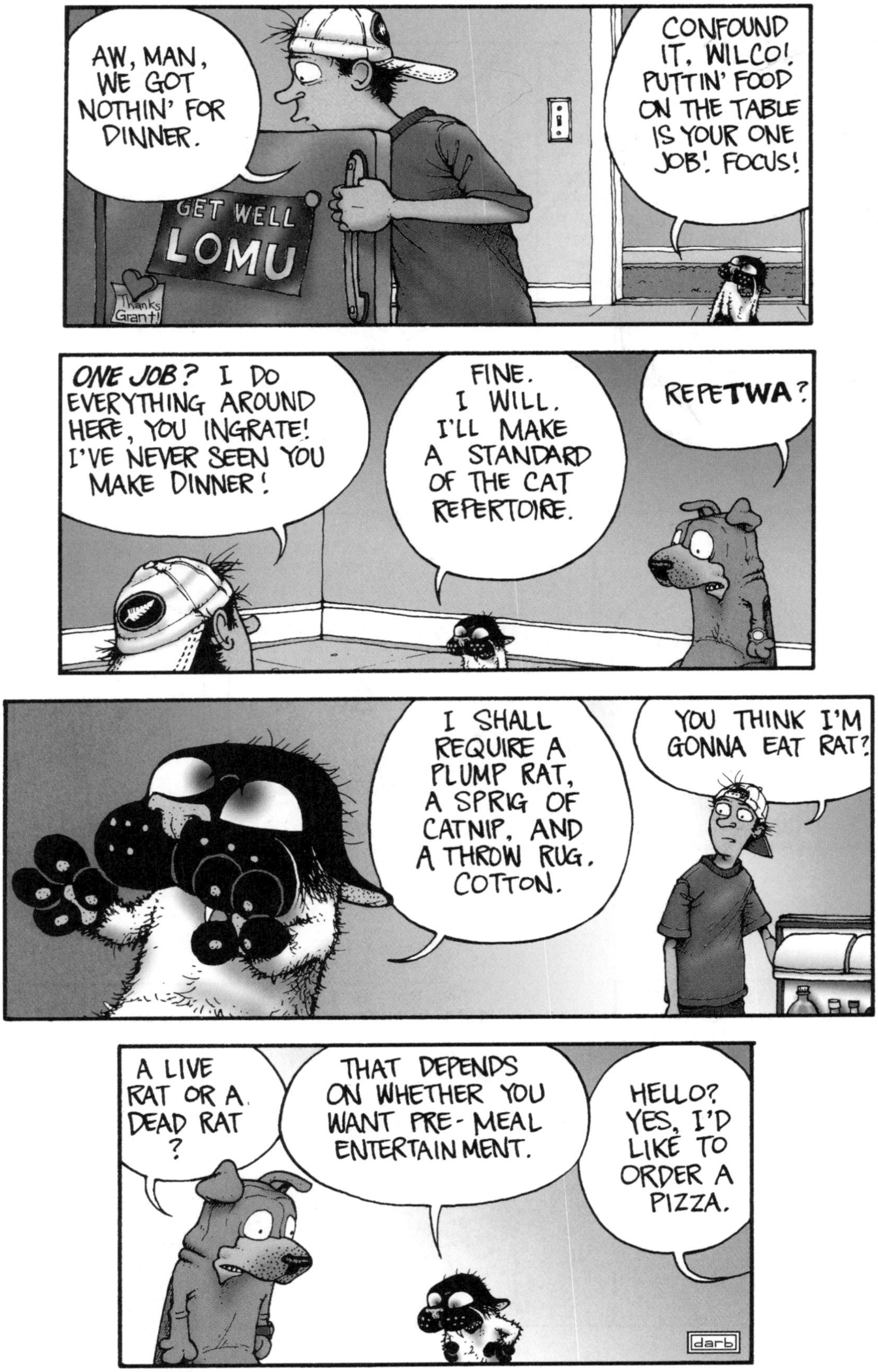
AW, MAN, WE GOT NOTHIN' FOR DINNER.
CONFOUND IT, WILCO! PUTTIN' FOOD ON THE TABLE IS YOUR ONE JOB! FOCUS!
GET WELL LOMU
Thanks Grant!
ONE JOB? I DO EVERYTHING AROUND HERE, YOU INGRATE! I'VE NEVER SEEN YOU MAKE DINNER!
FINE. I WILL. I'LL MAKE A STANDARD OF THE CAT REPERTOIRE.
REPETWA?
I SHALL REQUIRE A PLUMP RAT, A SPRIG OF CATNIP, AND A THROW RUG. COTTON.
YOU THINK I'M GONNA EAT RAT?
A LIVE RAT OR A DEAD RAT?
THAT DEPENDS ON WHETHER YOU WANT PRE-MEAL ENTERTAINMENT.
HELLO? YES, I'D LIKE TO ORDER A PIZZA.
darb

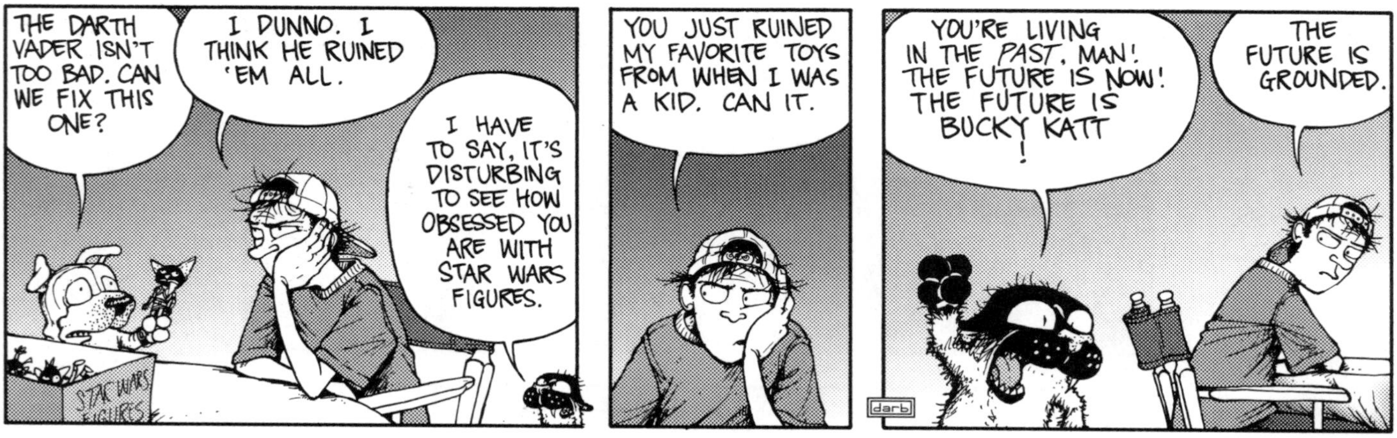
THE DARTH VADER ISN'T TOO BAD. CAN WE FIX THIS ONE?
I DUNNO. I THINK HE RUINED 'EM ALL.
I HAVE TO SAY, IT'S DISTURBING TO SEE HOW OBSESSED YOU ARE WITH STAR WARS FIGURES.
STAR WARS FIGURES
YOU JUST RUINED MY FAVORITE TOYS FROM WHEN I WAS A KID. CAN IT.
YOU'RE LIVING IN THE *PAST*, MAN! THE FUTURE IS NOW! THE FUTURE IS BUCKY KATT!
THE FUTURE IS GROUNDED.
darb

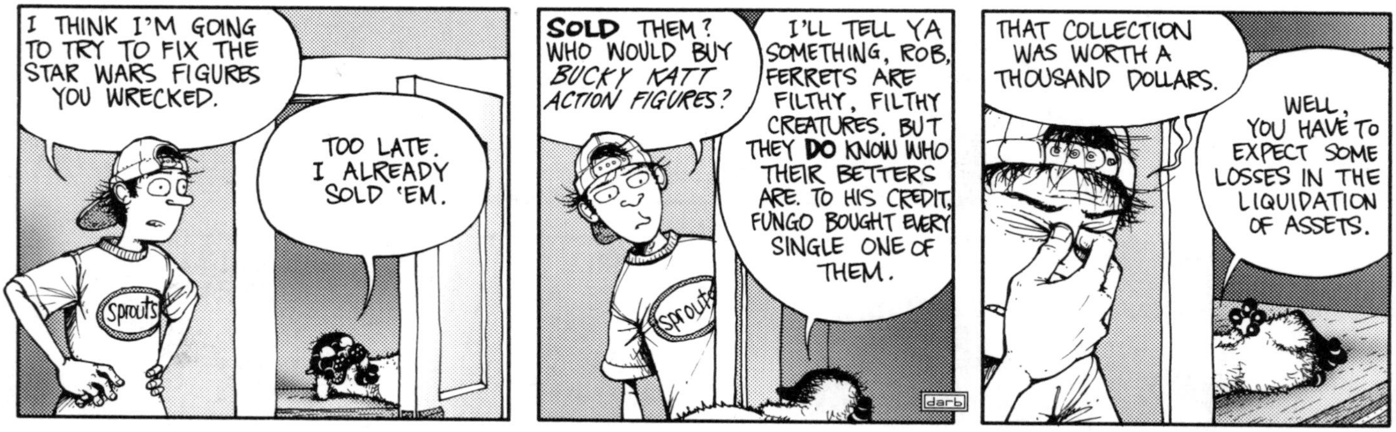
I THINK I'M GOING TO TRY TO FIX THE STAR WARS FIGURES YOU WRECKED.
TOO LATE. I ALREADY SOLD 'EM.
sprouts
SOLD THEM? WHO WOULD BUY *BUCKY KATT ACTION FIGURES?*
I'LL TELL YA SOMETHING, ROB, FERRETS ARE FILTHY, FILTHY CREATURES. BUT THEY **DO** KNOW WHO THEIR BETTERS ARE. TO HIS CREDIT, FUNGO BOUGHT EVERY SINGLE ONE OF THEM.
darb
THAT COLLECTION WAS WORTH A THOUSAND DOLLARS.
WELL, YOU HAVE TO EXPECT SOME LOSSES IN THE LIQUIDATION OF ASSETS.

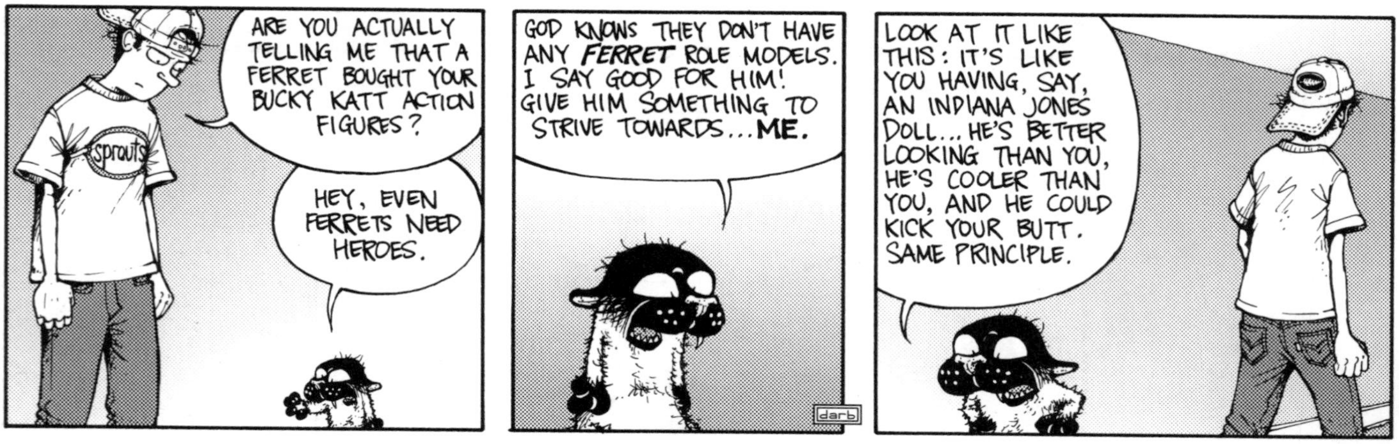
ARE YOU ACTUALLY TELLING ME THAT A FERRET BOUGHT YOUR BUCKY KATT ACTION FIGURES?
HEY, EVEN FERRETS NEED HEROES.
sprouts
GOD KNOWS THEY DON'T HAVE ANY ***FERRET*** ROLE MODELS. I SAY GOOD FOR HIM! GIVE HIM SOMETHING TO STRIVE TOWARDS... **ME.**
darb
LOOK AT IT LIKE THIS: IT'S LIKE YOU HAVING, SAY, AN INDIANA JONES DOLL... HE'S BETTER LOOKING THAN YOU, HE'S COOLER THAN YOU, AND HE COULD KICK YOUR BUTT. SAME PRINCIPLE.

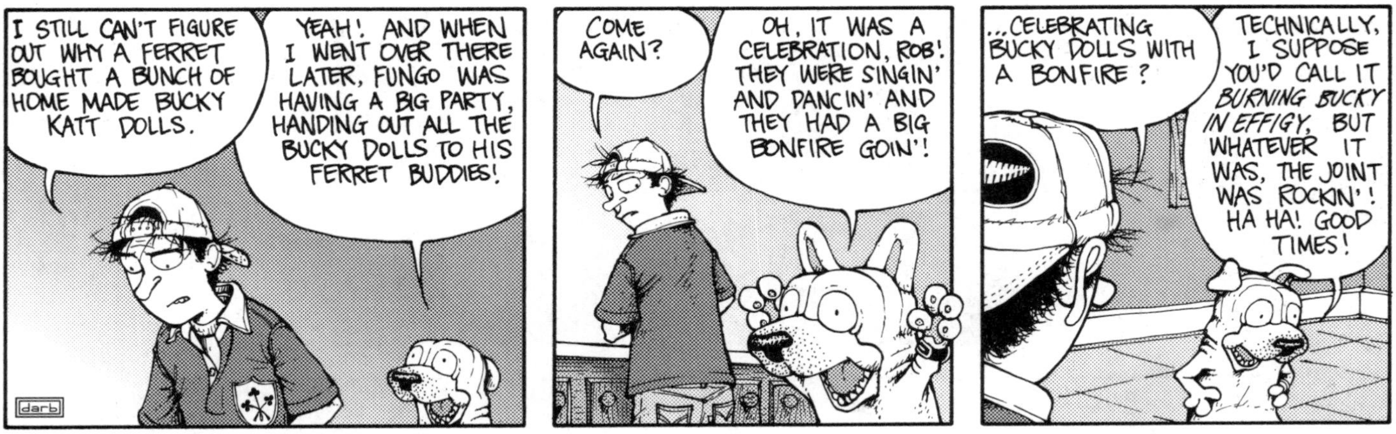
I STILL CAN'T FIGURE OUT WHY A FERRET BOUGHT A BUNCH OF HOME MADE BUCKY KATT DOLLS.
YEAH! AND WHEN I WENT OVER THERE LATER, FUNGO WAS HAVING A BIG PARTY, HANDING OUT ALL THE BUCKY DOLLS TO HIS FERRET BUDDIES!
darb
COME AGAIN?
OH, IT WAS A CELEBRATION, ROB! THEY WERE SINGIN' AND DANCIN' AND THEY HAD A BIG BONFIRE GOIN'!
...CELEBRATING BUCKY DOLLS WITH A BONFIRE?
TECHNICALLY, I SUPPOSE YOU'D CALL IT *BURNING BUCKY IN EFFIGY*, BUT WHATEVER IT WAS, THE JOINT WAS ROCKIN'! HA HA! GOOD TIMES!

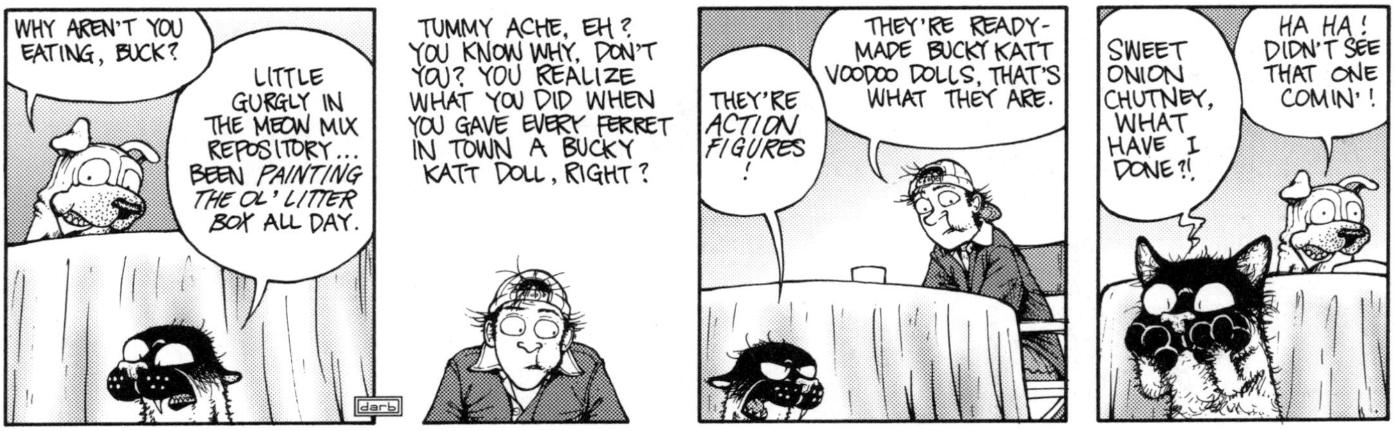
WHY AREN'T YOU EATING, BUCK?
LITTLE GURGLY IN THE MEOW MIX REPOSITORY... BEEN *PAINTING THE OL' LITTER BOX* ALL DAY.
darb
TUMMY ACHE, EH? YOU KNOW WHY, DON'T YOU? YOU REALIZE WHAT YOU DID WHEN YOU GAVE EVERY FERRET IN TOWN A BUCKY KATT DOLL, RIGHT?
THEY'RE *ACTION FIGURES*!
THEY'RE READY-MADE BUCKY KATT VOODOO DOLLS, THAT'S WHAT THEY ARE.
SWEET ONION CHUTNEY, WHAT HAVE I DONE?!
HA HA! DIDN'T SEE THAT ONE COMIN'!

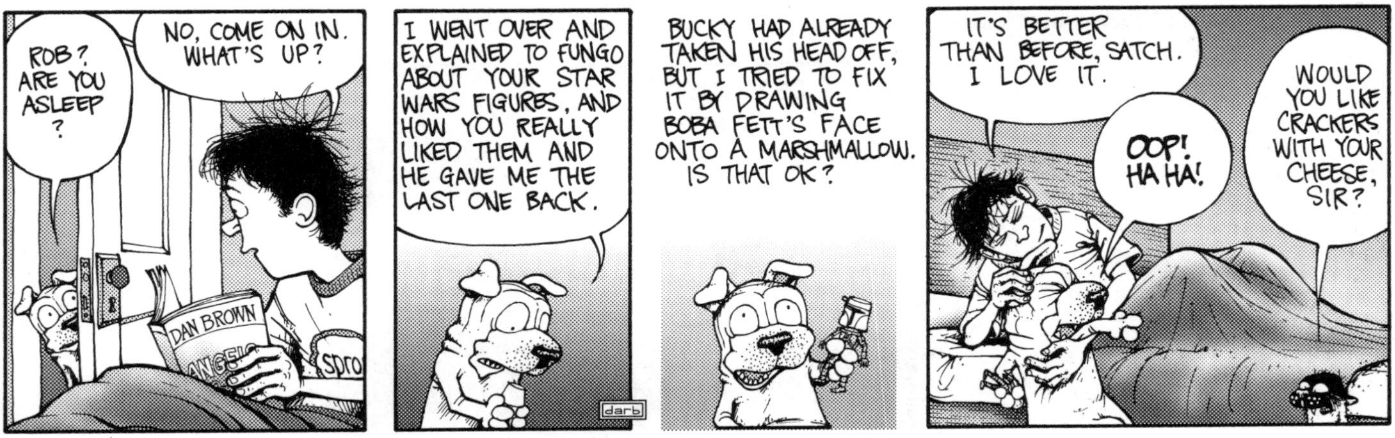
ROB? ARE YOU ASLEEP?
NO, COME ON IN. WHAT'S UP?
DAN BROWN
I WENT OVER AND EXPLAINED TO FUNGO ABOUT YOUR STAR WARS FIGURES, AND HOW YOU REALLY LIKED THEM AND HE GAVE ME THE LAST ONE BACK.
darb
BUCKY HAD ALREADY TAKEN HIS HEAD OFF, BUT I TRIED TO FIX IT BY DRAWING BOBA FETT'S FACE ONTO A MARSHMALLOW. IS THAT OK?
IT'S BETTER THAN BEFORE, SATCH. I LOVE IT.
OOP! HA HA!
WOULD YOU LIKE CRACKERS WITH YOUR CHEESE, SIR?

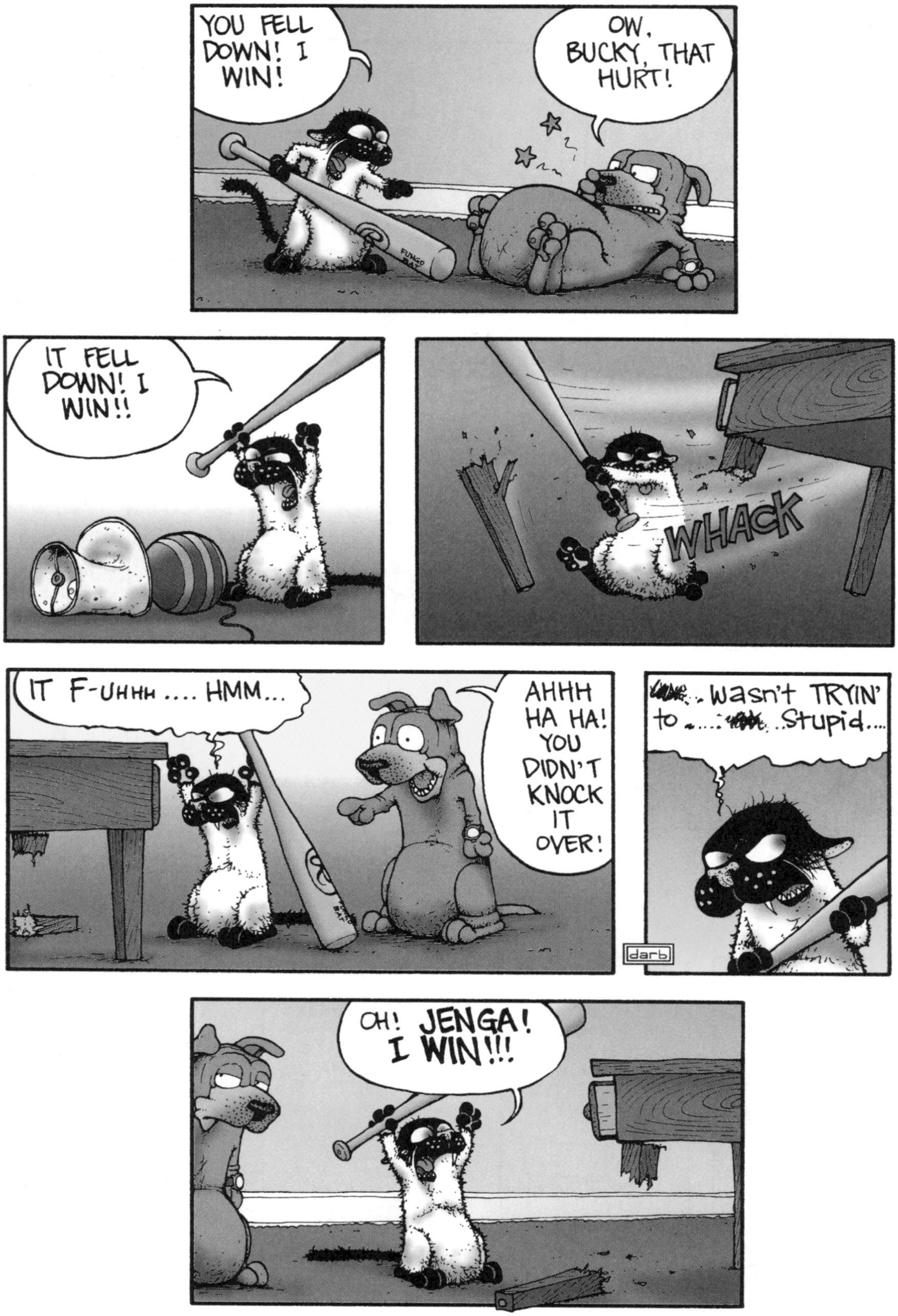
YOU FELL DOWN! I WIN!
OW. BUCKY, THAT HURT!
FUNGO BAT
IT FELL DOWN! I WIN!!
WHACK
IT F-UHHH .... HMM...
AHHH HA HA! YOU DIDN'T KNOCK IT OVER!
..wasn't TRYIN' to ....Stupid....
darb
OH! JENGA! I WIN!!!

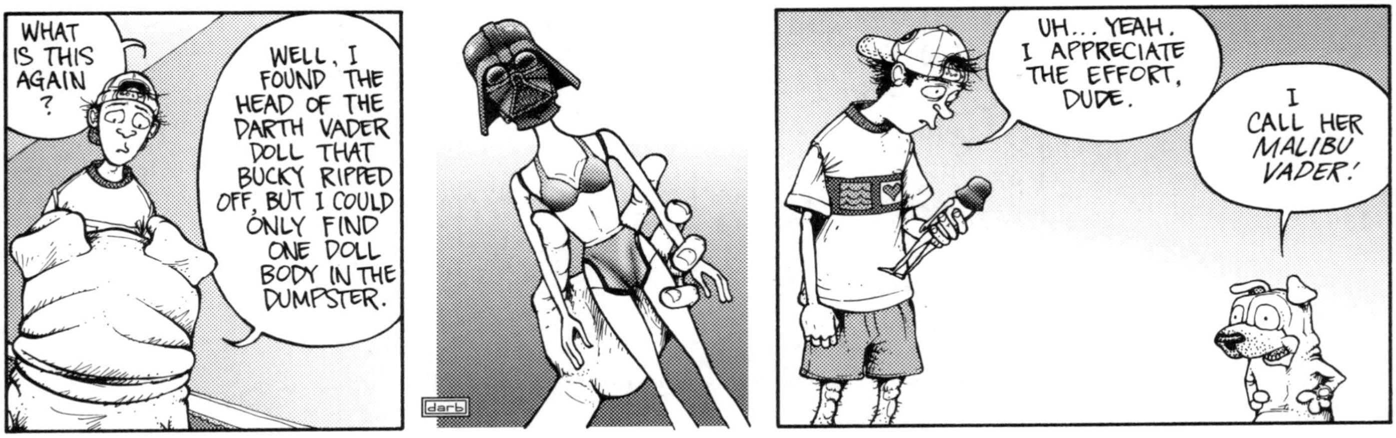
WHAT IS THIS AGAIN?
WELL, I FOUND THE HEAD OF THE DARTH VADER DOLL THAT BUCKY RIPPED OFF, BUT I COULD ONLY FIND ONE DOLL BODY IN THE DUMPSTER.
UH... YEAH. I APPRECIATE THE EFFORT, DUDE.
I CALL HER *MALIBU VADER!*

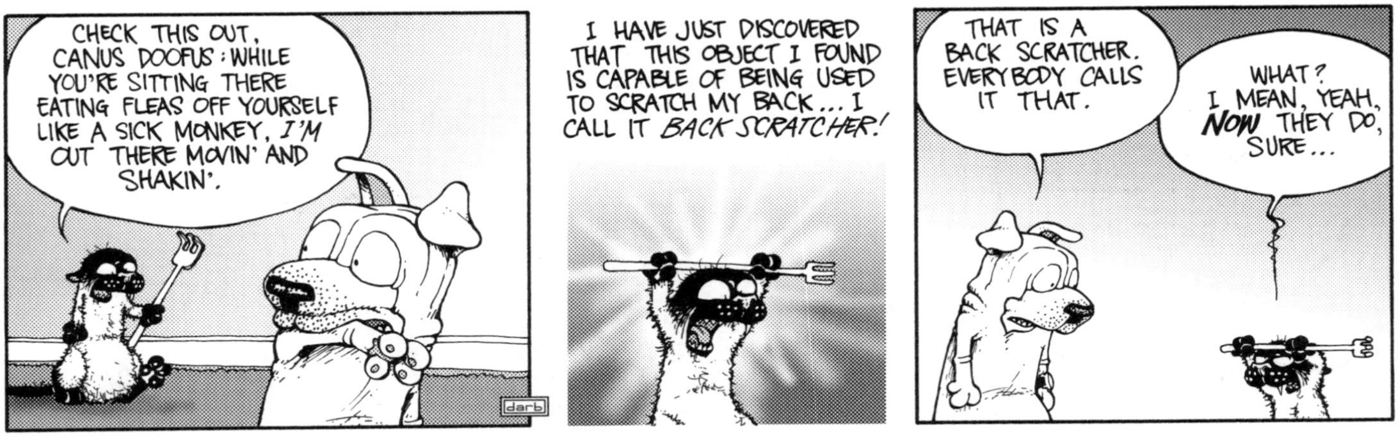
CHECK THIS OUT, CANUS DOOFUS: WHILE YOU'RE SITTING THERE EATING FLEAS OFF YOURSELF LIKE A SICK MONKEY, *I'M* OUT THERE MOVIN' AND SHAKIN'.
I HAVE JUST DISCOVERED THAT THIS OBJECT I FOUND IS CAPABLE OF BEING USED TO SCRATCH MY BACK... I CALL IT *BACK SCRATCHER!*
THAT IS A BACK SCRATCHER. EVERYBODY CALLS IT THAT.
WHAT? I MEAN, YEAH, **NOW** THEY DO, SURE...

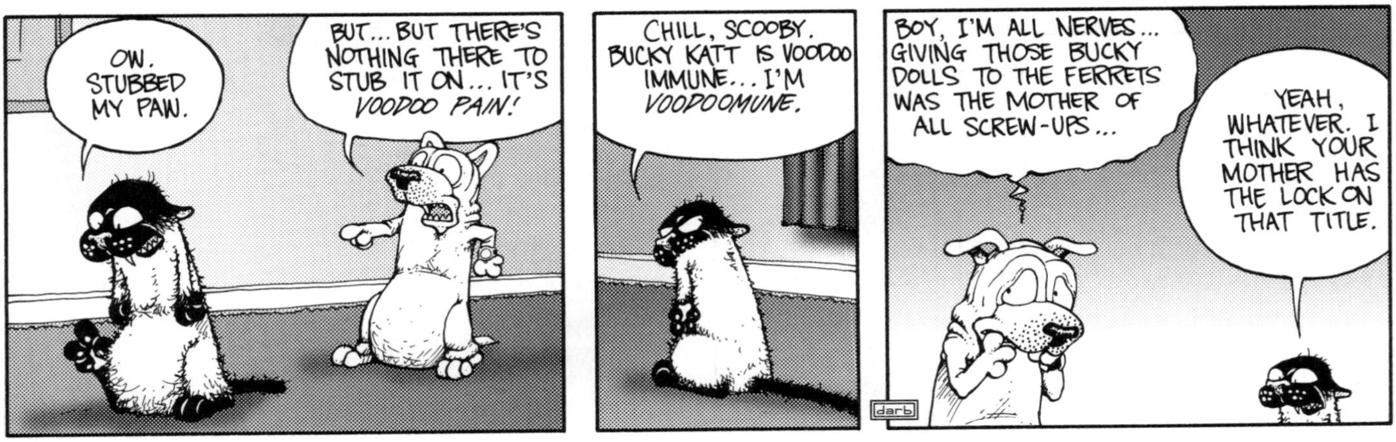
OW. STUBBED MY PAW.
BUT... BUT THERE'S NOTHING THERE TO STUB IT ON... IT'S *VOODOO PAIN!*
CHILL, SCOOBY. BUCKY KATT IS VOODOO IMMUNE... I'M *VOODOOMUNE.*
BOY, I'M ALL NERVES... GIVING THOSE BUCKY DOLLS TO THE FERRETS WAS THE MOTHER OF ALL SCREW-UPS...
YEAH, WHATEVER. I THINK YOUR MOTHER HAS THE LOCK ON THAT TITLE.

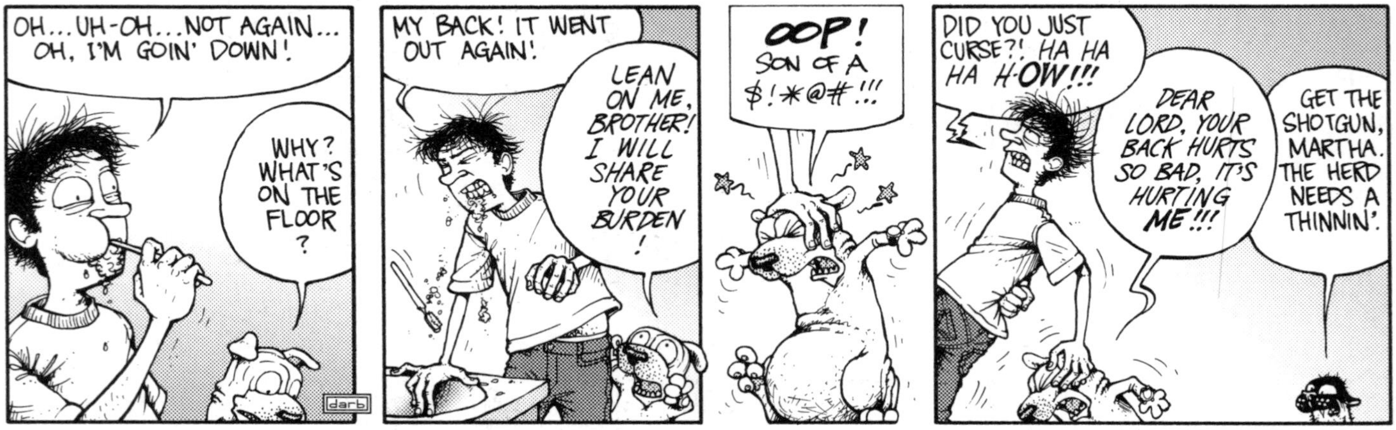
OH... UH-OH... NOT AGAIN... OH, I'M GOIN' DOWN!
WHY? WHAT'S ON THE FLOOR?
darb
MY BACK! IT WENT OUT AGAIN!
LEAN ON ME, BROTHER! I WILL SHARE YOUR BURDEN!
OOP! SON OF A $!*@#!!!
DID YOU JUST CURSE?! HA HA HA H-OW!!!
DEAR LORD, YOUR BACK HURTS SO BAD, IT'S HURTING ME!!!
GET THE SHOTGUN, MARTHA. THE HERD NEEDS A THINNIN'.

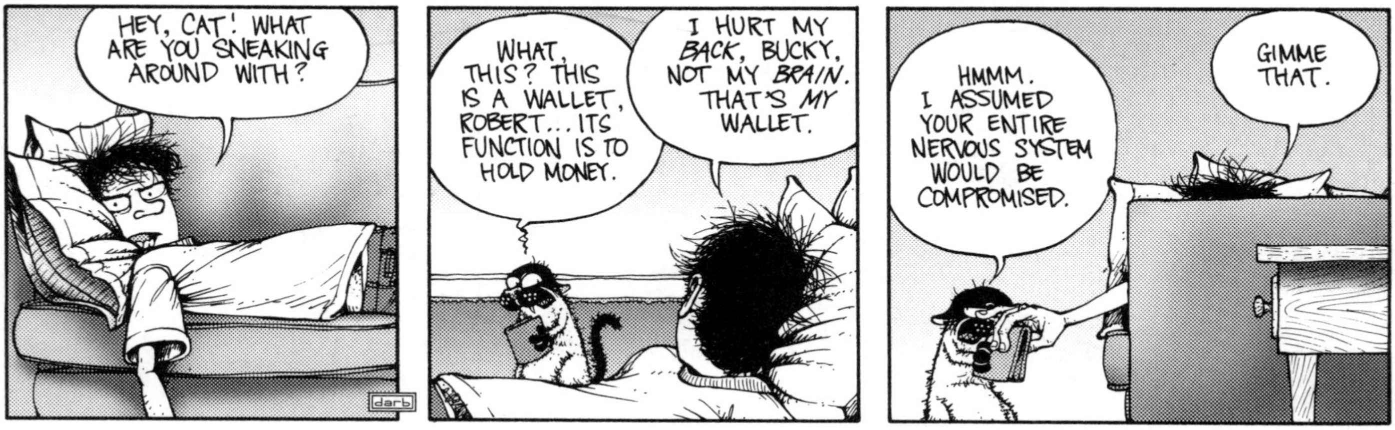
HEY, CAT! WHAT ARE YOU SNEAKING AROUND WITH?
darb
WHAT, THIS? THIS IS A WALLET, ROBERT... ITS FUNCTION IS TO HOLD MONEY.
I HURT MY BACK, BUCKY, NOT MY BRAIN. THAT'S MY WALLET.
HMMM. I ASSUMED YOUR ENTIRE NERVOUS SYSTEM WOULD BE COMPROMISED.
GIMME THAT.

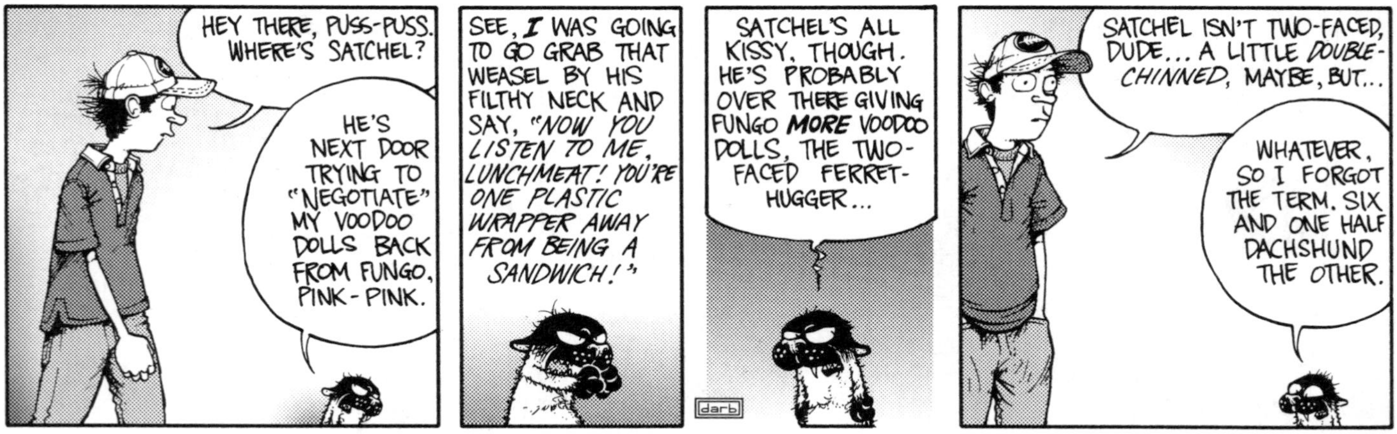
HEY THERE, PUSS-PUSS. WHERE'S SATCHEL?
HE'S NEXT DOOR TRYING TO "NEGOTIATE" MY VOODOO DOLLS BACK FROM FUNGO, PINK-PINK.
SEE, I WAS GOING TO GO GRAB THAT WEASEL BY HIS FILTHY NECK AND SAY, "NOW YOU LISTEN TO ME, LUNCHMEAT! YOU'RE ONE PLASTIC WRAPPER AWAY FROM BEING A SANDWICH!"
darb
SATCHEL'S ALL KISSY, THOUGH. HE'S PROBABLY OVER THERE GIVING FUNGO MORE VOODOO DOLLS, THE TWO-FACED FERRET-HUGGER...
SATCHEL ISN'T TWO-FACED, DUDE... A LITTLE DOUBLE-CHINNED, MAYBE, BUT...
WHATEVER, SO I FORGOT THE TERM. SIX AND ONE HALF DACHSHUND THE OTHER.

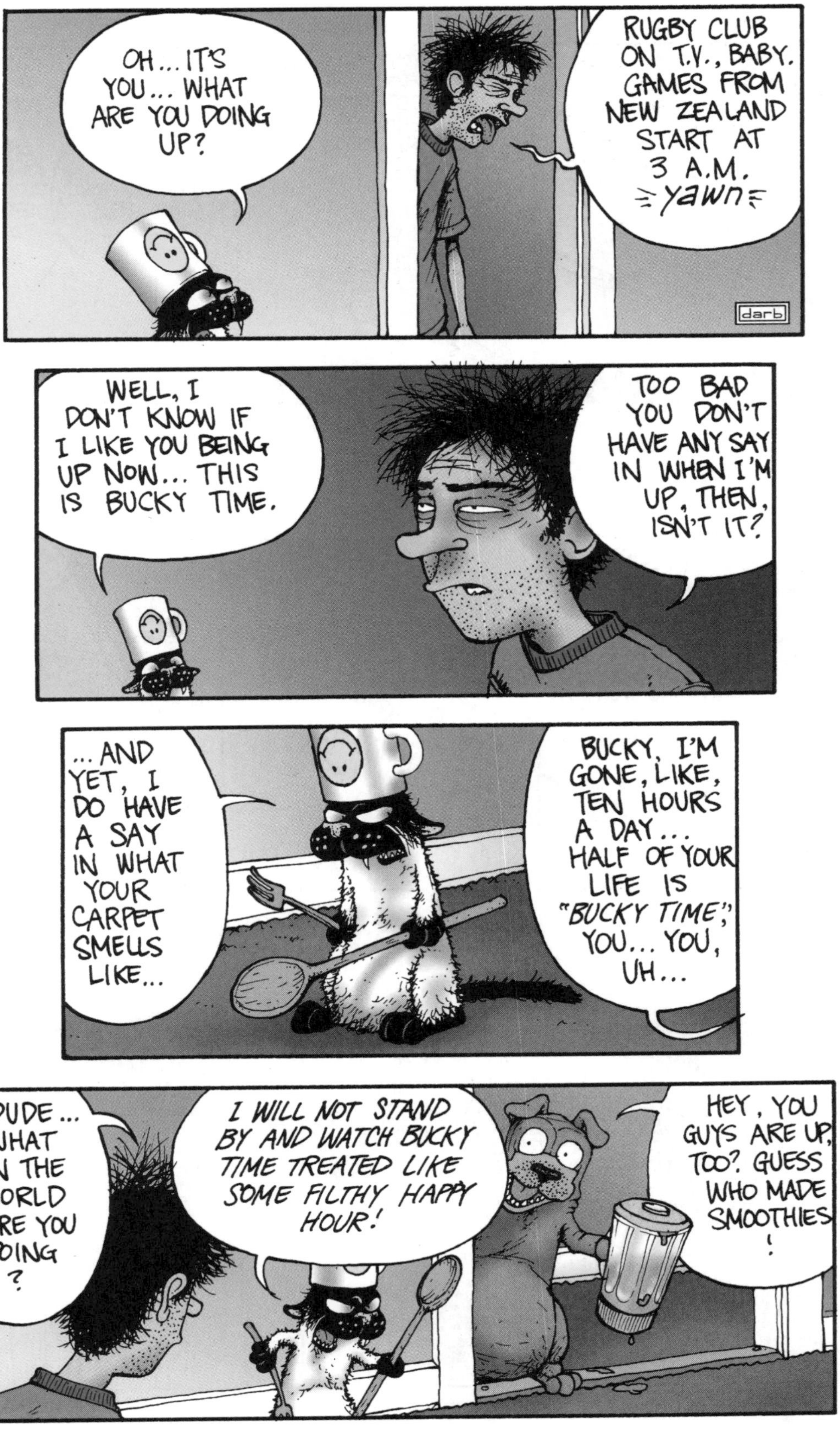
OH... IT'S YOU... WHAT ARE YOU DOING UP?
RUGBY CLUB ON T.V., BABY. GAMES FROM NEW ZEALAND START AT 3 A.M. yawn
darb
WELL, I DON'T KNOW IF I LIKE YOU BEING UP NOW... THIS IS BUCKY TIME.
TOO BAD YOU DON'T HAVE ANY SAY IN WHEN I'M UP, THEN, ISN'T IT?
...AND YET, I DO HAVE A SAY IN WHAT YOUR CARPET SMELLS LIKE...
BUCKY, I'M GONE, LIKE, TEN HOURS A DAY... HALF OF YOUR LIFE IS "BUCKY TIME," YOU... YOU, UH...
DUDE... WHAT IN THE WORLD ARE YOU DOING?
I WILL NOT STAND BY AND WATCH BUCKY TIME TREATED LIKE SOME FILTHY HAPPY HOUR!
HEY, YOU GUYS ARE UP, TOO? GUESS WHO MADE SMOOTHIES!

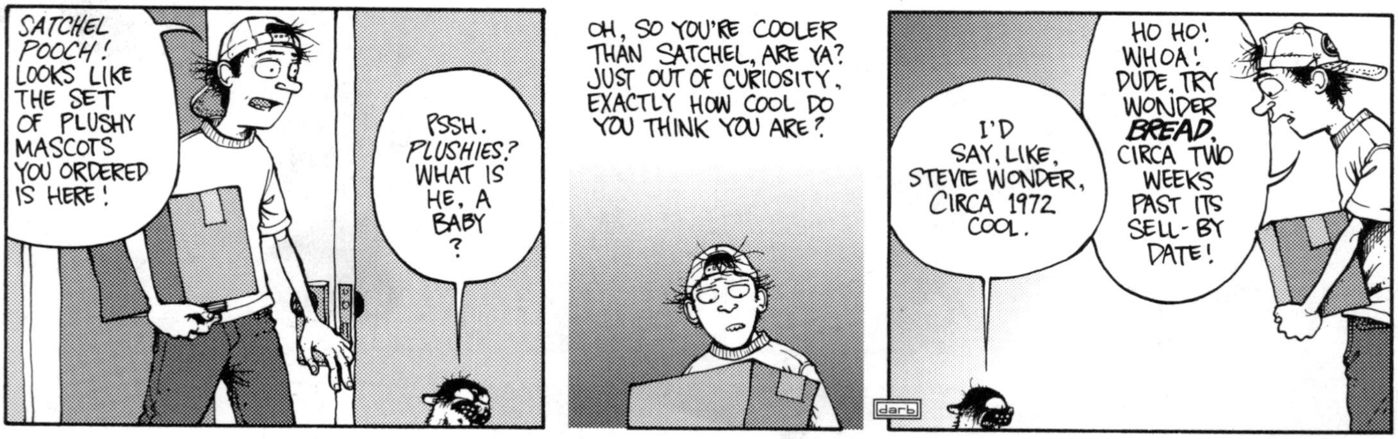
SATCHEL POOCH! LOOKS LIKE THE SET OF PLUSHY MASCOTS YOU ORDERED IS HERE!
PSSH. PLUSHIES? WHAT IS HE, A BABY?
OH, SO YOU'RE COOLER THAN SATCHEL, ARE YA? JUST OUT OF CURIOSITY, EXACTLY HOW COOL DO YOU THINK YOU ARE?
I'D SAY, LIKE, STEVIE WONDER, CIRCA 1972 COOL.
HO HO! WHOA! DUDE, TRY WONDER BREAD, CIRCA TWO WEEKS PAST ITS SELL-BY DATE!

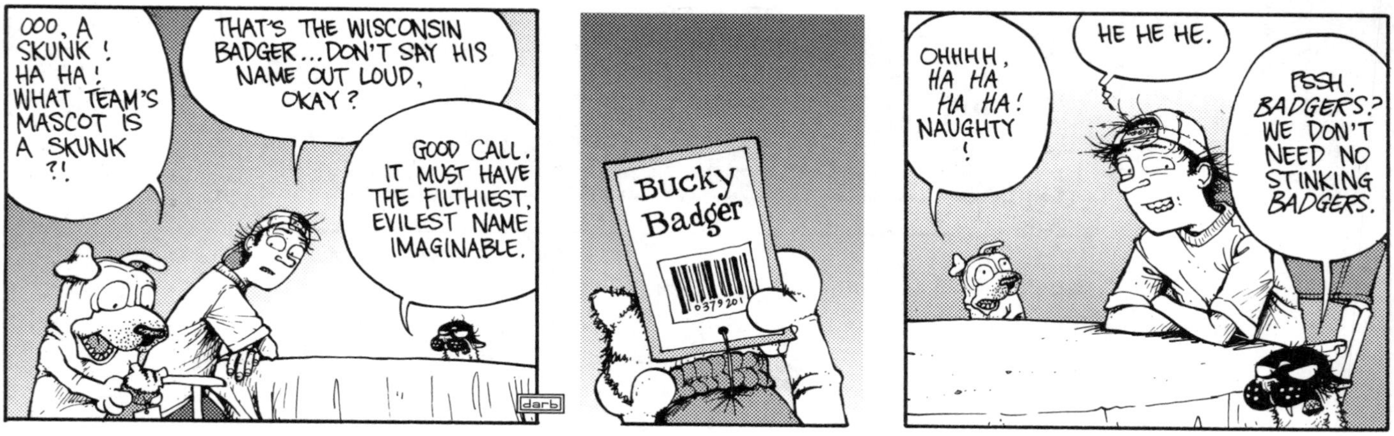
OOO, A SKUNK! HA HA! WHAT TEAM'S MASCOT IS A SKUNK?!
THAT'S THE WISCONSIN BADGER... DON'T SAY HIS NAME OUT LOUD, OKAY?
GOOD CALL. IT MUST HAVE THE FILTHIEST, EVILEST NAME IMAGINABLE.
Bucky Badger
OHHHH, HA HA HA HA! NAUGHTY!
HE HE HE.
PSSH. BADGERS? WE DON'T NEED NO STINKING BADGERS.

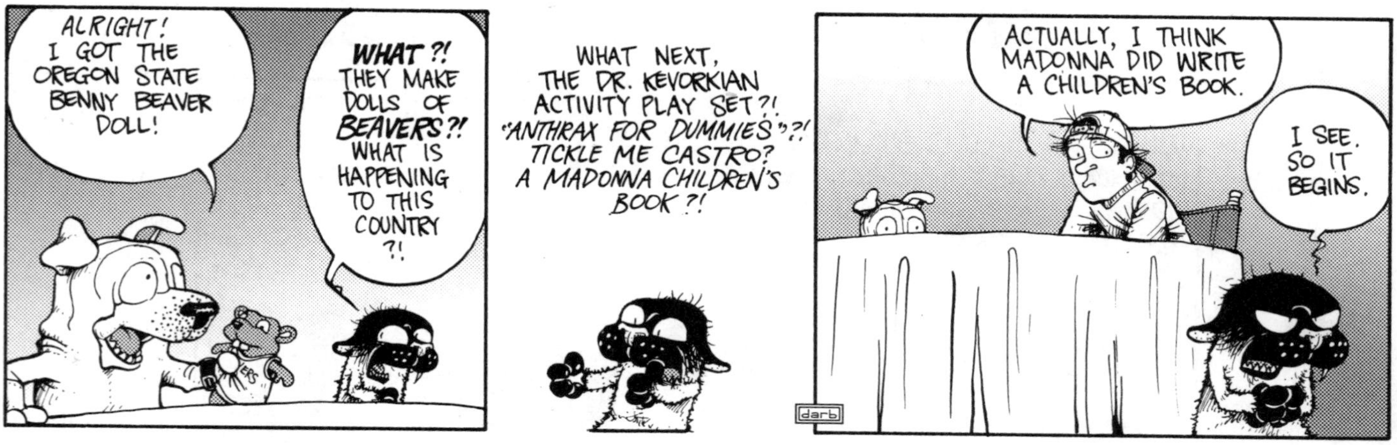
ALRIGHT! I GOT THE OREGON STATE BENNY BEAVER DOLL!
WHAT?! THEY MAKE DOLLS OF BEAVERS?! WHAT IS HAPPENING TO THIS COUNTRY?!
WHAT NEXT, THE DR. KEVORKIAN ACTIVITY PLAY SET?! "ANTHRAX FOR DUMMIES"?! TICKLE ME CASTRO? A MADONNA CHILDREN'S BOOK?!
ACTUALLY, I THINK MADONNA DID WRITE A CHILDREN'S BOOK.
I SEE. SO IT BEGINS.

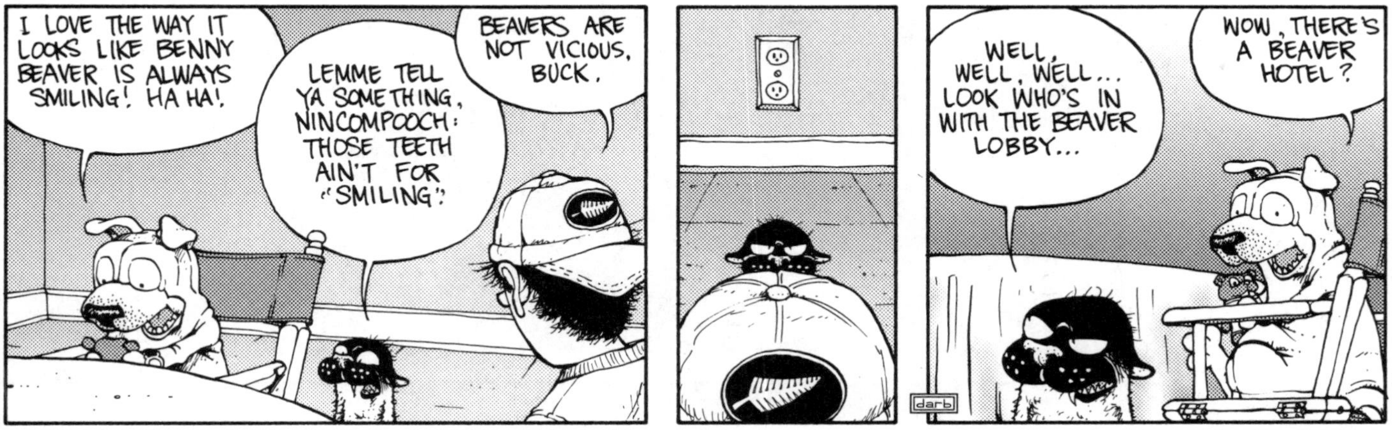
I LOVE THE WAY IT LOOKS LIKE BENNY BEAVER IS ALWAYS SMILING! HA HA!
LEMME TELL YA SOMETHING, NINCOMPOOCH: THOSE TEETH AIN'T FOR "SMILING."
BEAVERS ARE NOT VICIOUS, BUCK.
WELL, WELL, WELL... LOOK WHO'S IN WITH THE BEAVER LOBBY...
WOW, THERE'S A BEAVER HOTEL?
darb

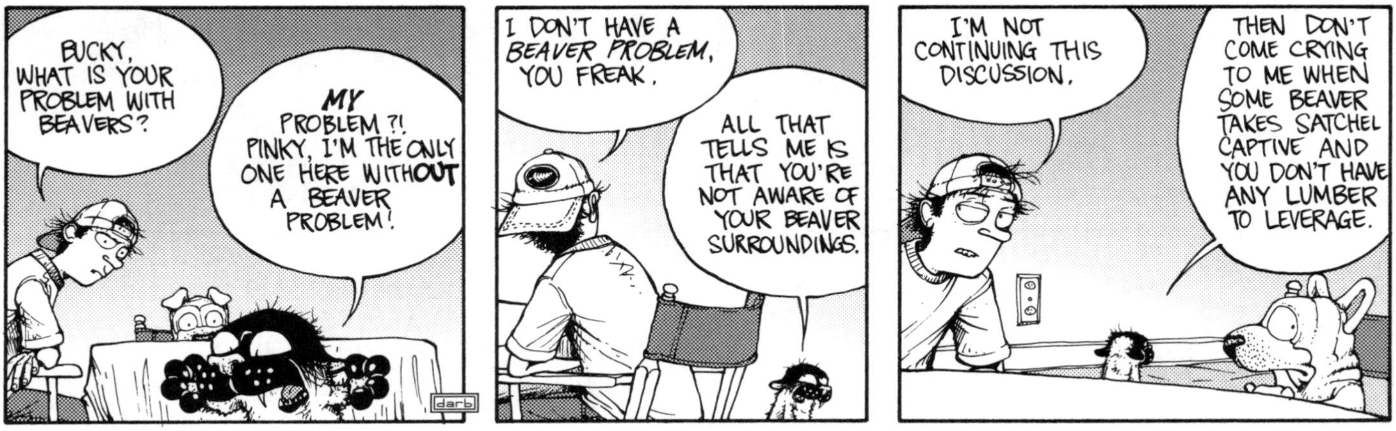
BUCKY, WHAT IS YOUR PROBLEM WITH BEAVERS?
MY PROBLEM?! PINKY, I'M THE ONLY ONE HERE WITHOUT A BEAVER PROBLEM!
darb
I DON'T HAVE A BEAVER PROBLEM, YOU FREAK.
ALL THAT TELLS ME IS THAT YOU'RE NOT AWARE OF YOUR BEAVER SURROUNDINGS.
I'M NOT CONTINUING THIS DISCUSSION.
THEN DON'T COME CRYING TO ME WHEN SOME BEAVER TAKES SATCHEL CAPTIVE AND YOU DON'T HAVE ANY LUMBER TO LEVERAGE.

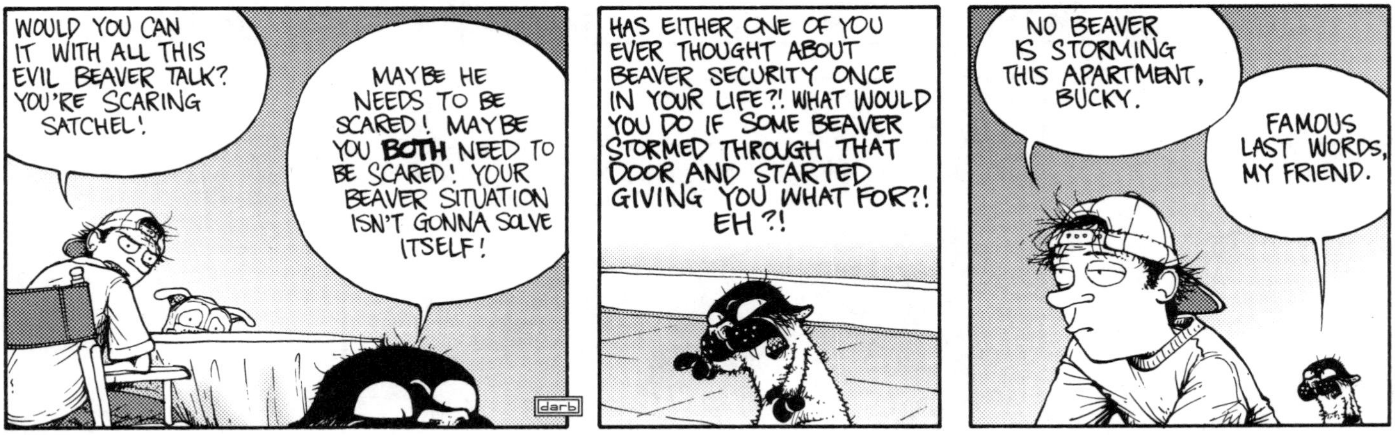
WOULD YOU CAN IT WITH ALL THIS EVIL BEAVER TALK? YOU'RE SCARING SATCHEL!
MAYBE HE NEEDS TO BE SCARED! MAYBE YOU BOTH NEED TO BE SCARED! YOUR BEAVER SITUATION ISN'T GONNA SOLVE ITSELF!
darb
HAS EITHER ONE OF YOU EVER THOUGHT ABOUT BEAVER SECURITY ONCE IN YOUR LIFE?! WHAT WOULD YOU DO IF SOME BEAVER STORMED THROUGH THAT DOOR AND STARTED GIVING YOU WHAT FOR?! EH?!
NO BEAVER IS STORMING THIS APARTMENT, BUCKY.
FAMOUS LAST WORDS, MY FRIEND.

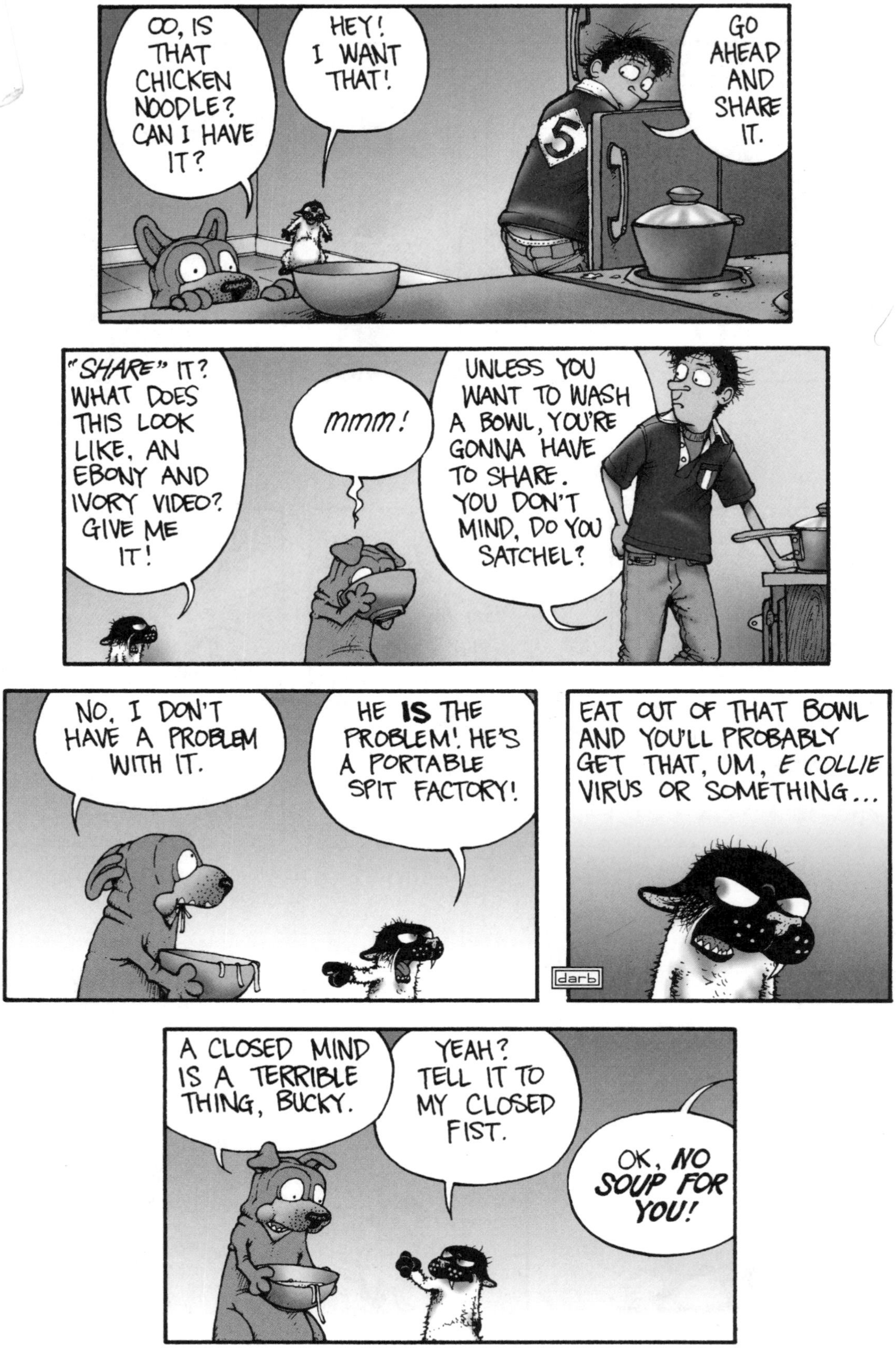
OO, IS THAT CHICKEN NOODLE? CAN I HAVE IT?
HEY! I WANT THAT!
GO AHEAD AND SHARE IT.
"SHARE" IT? WHAT DOES THIS LOOK LIKE, AN EBONY AND IVORY VIDEO? GIVE ME IT!
mmm!
UNLESS YOU WANT TO WASH A BOWL, YOU'RE GONNA HAVE TO SHARE. YOU DON'T MIND, DO YOU SATCHEL?
NO. I DON'T HAVE A PROBLEM WITH IT.
HE IS THE PROBLEM! HE'S A PORTABLE SPIT FACTORY!
EAT OUT OF THAT BOWL AND YOU'LL PROBABLY GET THAT, UM, E COLLIE VIRUS OR SOMETHING...
darb
A CLOSED MIND IS A TERRIBLE THING, BUCKY.
YEAH? TELL IT TO MY CLOSED FIST.
OK, NO SOUP FOR YOU!

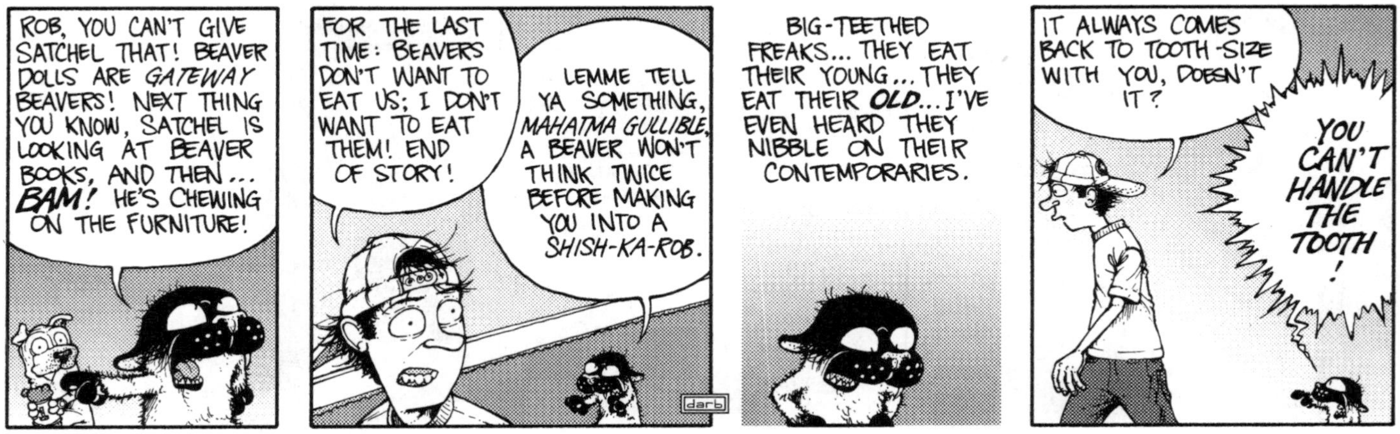
ROB, YOU CAN'T GIVE SATCHEL THAT! BEAVER DOLLS ARE GATEWAY BEAVERS! NEXT THING YOU KNOW, SATCHEL IS LOOKING AT BEAVER BOOKS, AND THEN... BAM! HE'S CHEWING ON THE FURNITURE!
FOR THE LAST TIME: BEAVERS DON'T WANT TO EAT US; I DON'T WANT TO EAT THEM! END OF STORY!
LEMME TELL YA SOMETHING, MAHATMA GULLIBLE, A BEAVER WON'T THINK TWICE BEFORE MAKING YOU INTO A SHISH-KA-ROB.
BIG-TEETHED FREAKS... THEY EAT THEIR YOUNG... THEY EAT THEIR OLD... I'VE EVEN HEARD THEY NIBBLE ON THEIR CONTEMPORARIES.
IT ALWAYS COMES BACK TO TOOTH-SIZE WITH YOU, DOESN'T IT?
YOU CAN'T HANDLE THE TOOTH!

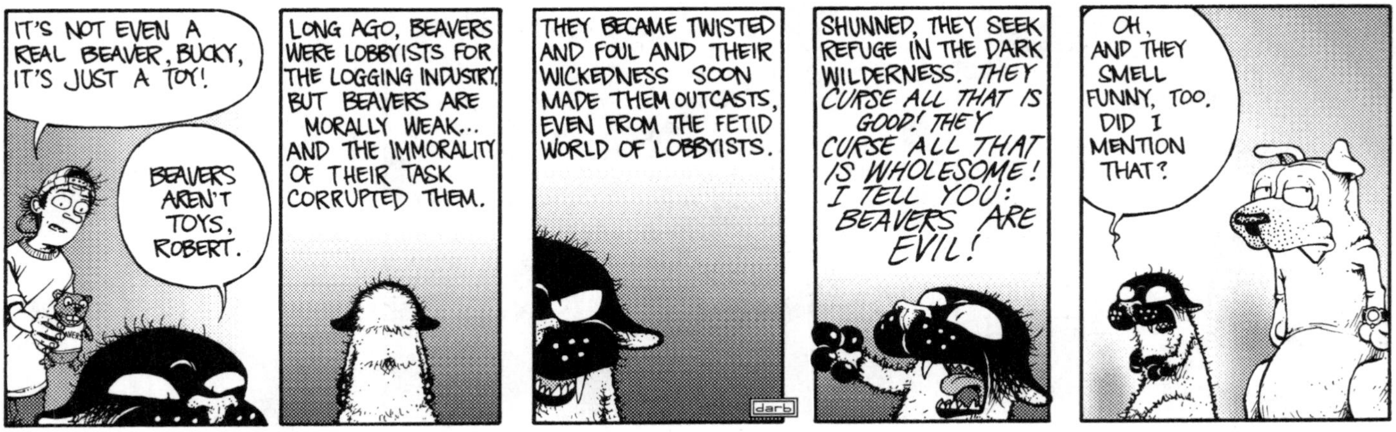
IT'S NOT EVEN A REAL BEAVER, BUCKY, IT'S JUST A TOY!
BEAVERS AREN'T TOYS, ROBERT.
LONG AGO, BEAVERS WERE LOBBYISTS FOR THE LOGGING INDUSTRY. BUT BEAVERS ARE MORALLY WEAK... AND THE IMMORALITY OF THEIR TASK CORRUPTED THEM.
THEY BECAME TWISTED AND FOUL AND THEIR WICKEDNESS SOON MADE THEM OUTCASTS, EVEN FROM THE FETID WORLD OF LOBBYISTS.
SHUNNED, THEY SEEK REFUGE IN THE DARK WILDERNESS. THEY CURSE ALL THAT IS GOOD! THEY CURSE ALL THAT IS WHOLESOME! I TELL YOU: BEAVERS ARE EVIL!
OH, AND THEY SMELL FUNNY, TOO. DID I MENTION THAT?

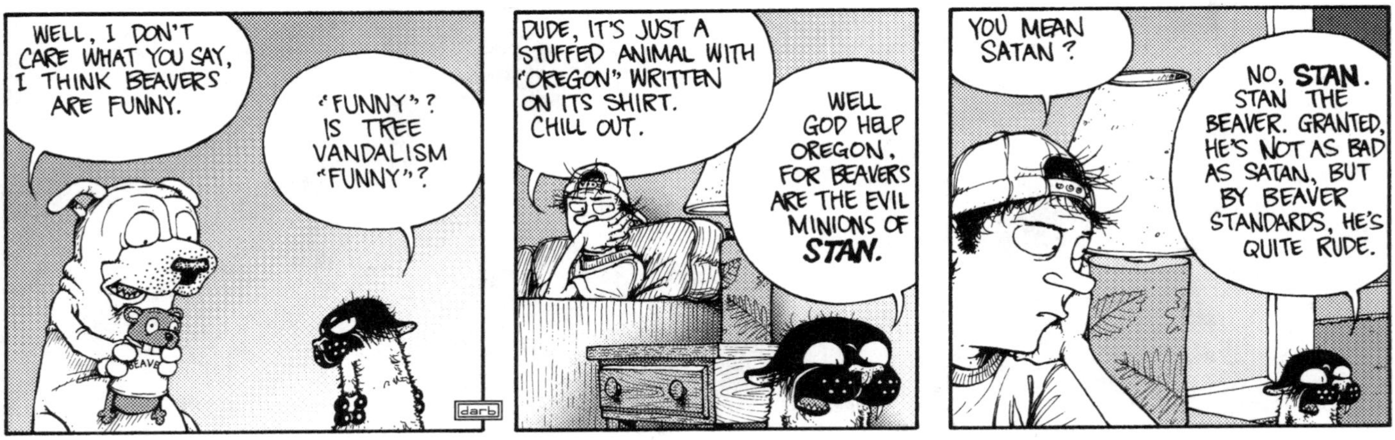
WELL, I DON'T CARE WHAT YOU SAY, I THINK BEAVERS ARE FUNNY.
"FUNNY"? IS TREE VANDALISM "FUNNY"?
DUDE, IT'S JUST A STUFFED ANIMAL WITH "OREGON" WRITTEN ON ITS SHIRT. CHILL OUT.
WELL GOD HELP OREGON, FOR BEAVERS ARE THE EVIL MINIONS OF STAN.
YOU MEAN SATAN?
NO, STAN. STAN THE BEAVER. GRANTED, HE'S NOT AS BAD AS SATAN, BUT BY BEAVER STANDARDS, HE'S QUITE RUDE.

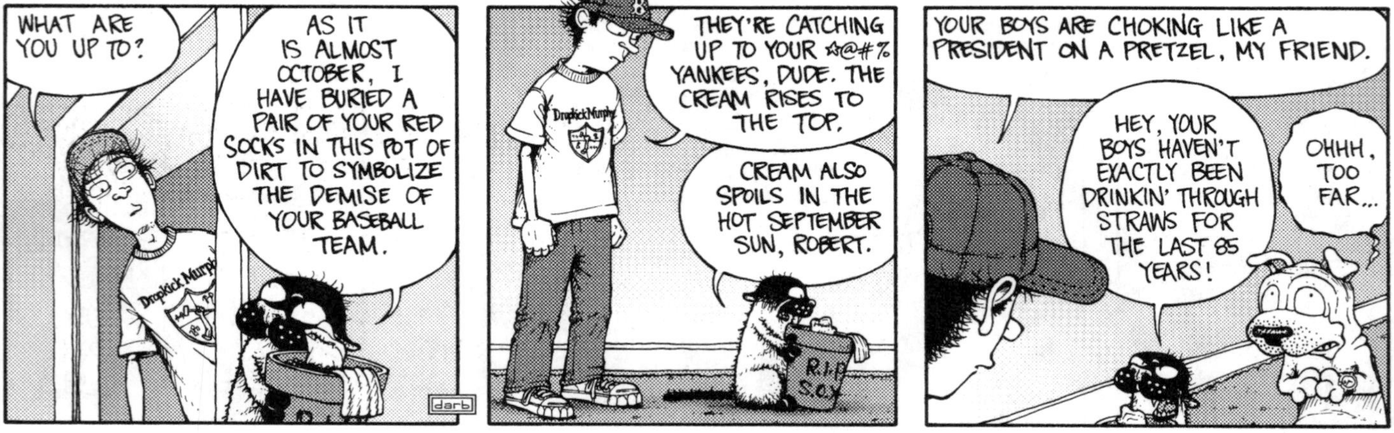
WHAT ARE YOU UP TO?
AS IT IS ALMOST OCTOBER, I HAVE BURIED A PAIR OF YOUR RED SOCKS IN THIS POT OF DIRT TO SYMBOLIZE THE DEMISE OF YOUR BASEBALL TEAM.
THEY'RE CATCHING UP TO YOUR ☆@#% YANKEES, DUDE. THE CREAM RISES TO THE TOP.
CREAM ALSO SPOILS IN THE HOT SEPTEMBER SUN, ROBERT.
R.I.P. S.O.X
YOUR BOYS ARE CHOKING LIKE A PRESIDENT ON A PRETZEL, MY FRIEND.
HEY, YOUR BOYS HAVEN'T EXACTLY BEEN DRINKIN' THROUGH STRAWS FOR THE LAST 85 YEARS!
OHHH, TOO FAR...
darb

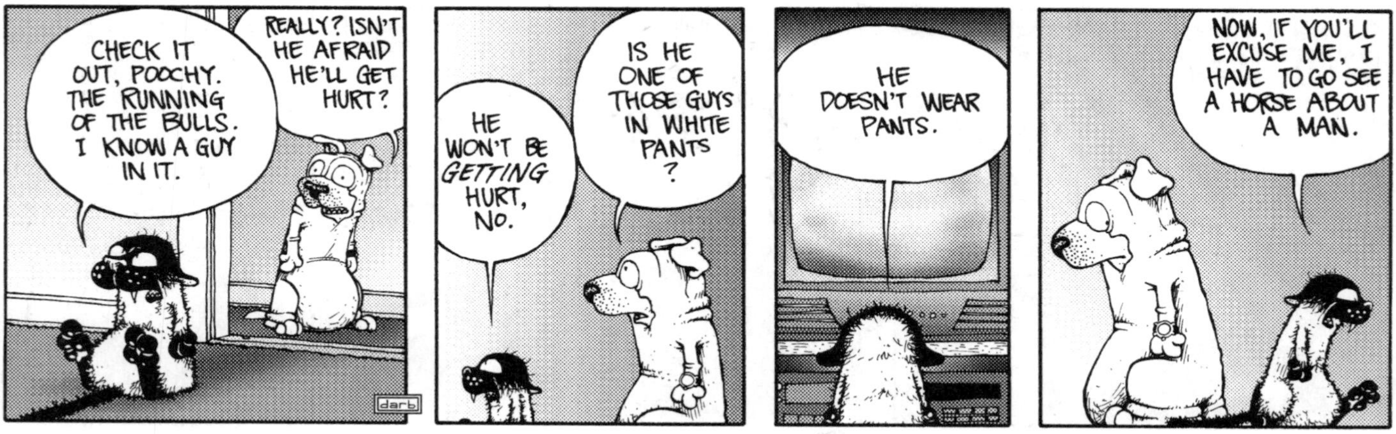
CHECK IT OUT, POOCHY. THE RUNNING OF THE BULLS. I KNOW A GUY IN IT.
REALLY? ISN'T HE AFRAID HE'LL GET HURT?
IS HE ONE OF THOSE GUYS IN WHITE PANTS?
HE WON'T BE *GETTING* HURT, NO.
HE DOESN'T WEAR PANTS.
NOW, IF YOU'LL EXCUSE ME, I HAVE TO GO SEE A HORSE ABOUT A MAN.
darb

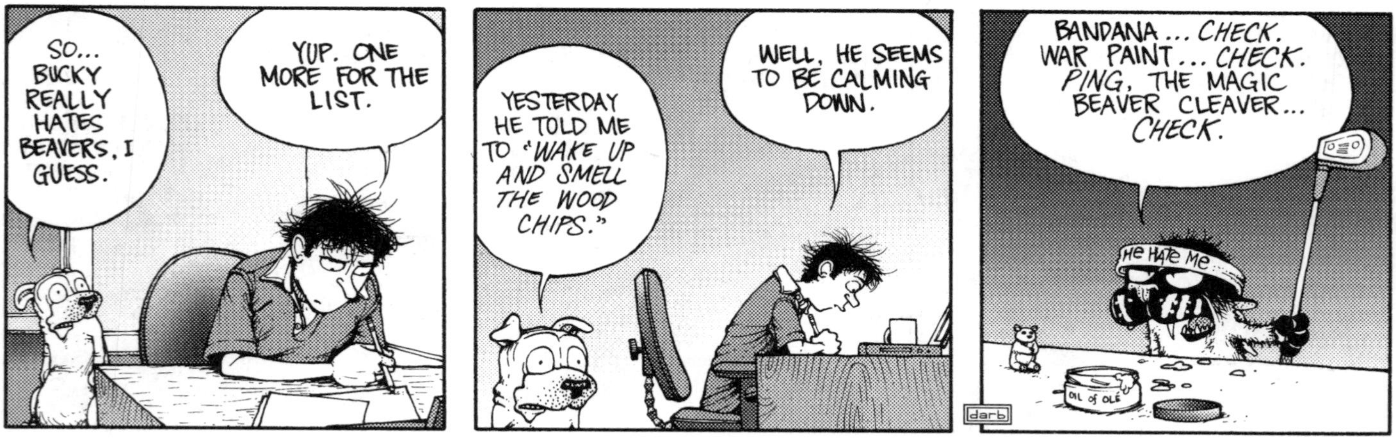
SO... BUCKY REALLY HATES BEAVERS, I GUESS.
YUP. ONE MORE FOR THE LIST.
WELL, HE SEEMS TO BE CALMING DOWN.
YESTERDAY HE TOLD ME TO "*WAKE UP AND SMELL THE WOOD CHIPS.*"
BANDANA... *CHECK.* WAR PAINT... *CHECK.* *PING*, THE MAGIC BEAVER CLEAVER... *CHECK.*
He Hate Me
OIL of OLÉ
darb

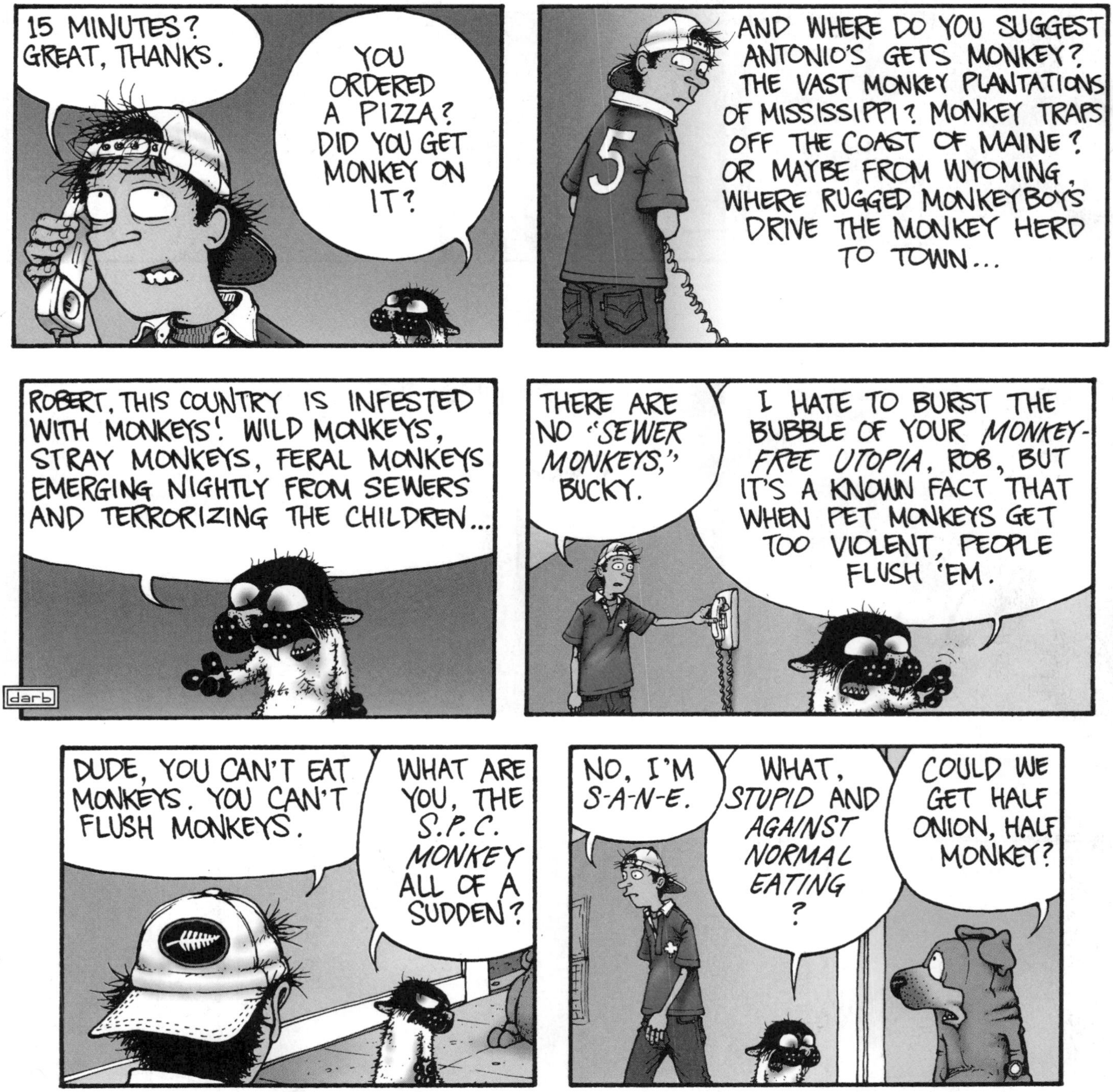
15 MINUTES? GREAT, THANKS.
YOU ORDERED A PIZZA? DID YOU GET MONKEY ON IT?
AND WHERE DO YOU SUGGEST ANTONIO'S GETS MONKEY? THE VAST MONKEY PLANTATIONS OF MISSISSIPPI? MONKEY TRAPS OFF THE COAST OF MAINE? OR MAYBE FROM WYOMING, WHERE RUGGED MONKEYBOYS DRIVE THE MONKEY HERD TO TOWN...
ROBERT, THIS COUNTRY IS INFESTED WITH MONKEYS! WILD MONKEYS, STRAY MONKEYS, FERAL MONKEYS EMERGING NIGHTLY FROM SEWERS AND TERRORIZING THE CHILDREN...
darb
THERE ARE NO "*SEWER MONKEYS*," BUCKY.
I HATE TO BURST THE BUBBLE OF YOUR *MONKEY-FREE UTOPIA*, ROB, BUT IT'S A KNOWN FACT THAT WHEN PET MONKEYS GET TOO VIOLENT, PEOPLE FLUSH 'EM.
DUDE, YOU CAN'T EAT MONKEYS. YOU CAN'T FLUSH MONKEYS.
WHAT ARE YOU, THE *S.P.C. MONKEY* ALL OF A SUDDEN?
NO, I'M *S-A-N-E.*
WHAT, *STUPID* AND *AGAINST NORMAL EATING*?
COULD WE GET HALF ONION, HALF MONKEY?

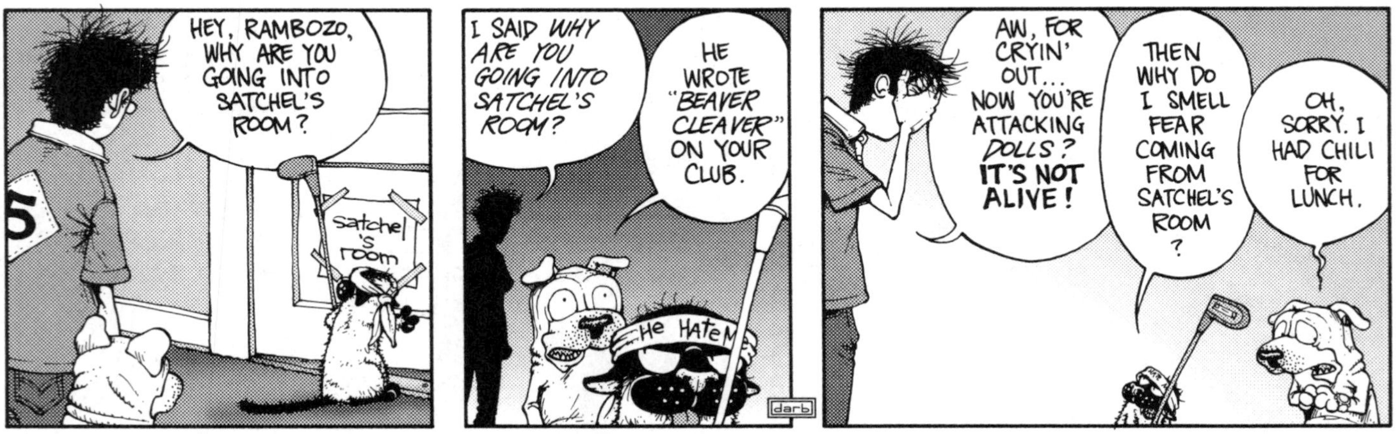
HEY, RAMBOZO, WHY ARE YOU GOING INTO SATCHEL'S ROOM?
satchel 's room
I SAID *WHY ARE YOU GOING INTO SATCHEL'S ROOM?*
HE WROTE "*BEAVER CLEAVER*" ON YOUR CLUB.
HE HATE M
AW, FOR CRYIN' OUT... NOW YOU'RE ATTACKING *DOLLS?* **IT'S NOT ALIVE!**
THEN WHY DO I SMELL FEAR COMING FROM SATCHEL'S ROOM ?
OH, SORRY. I HAD CHILI FOR LUNCH.
darb

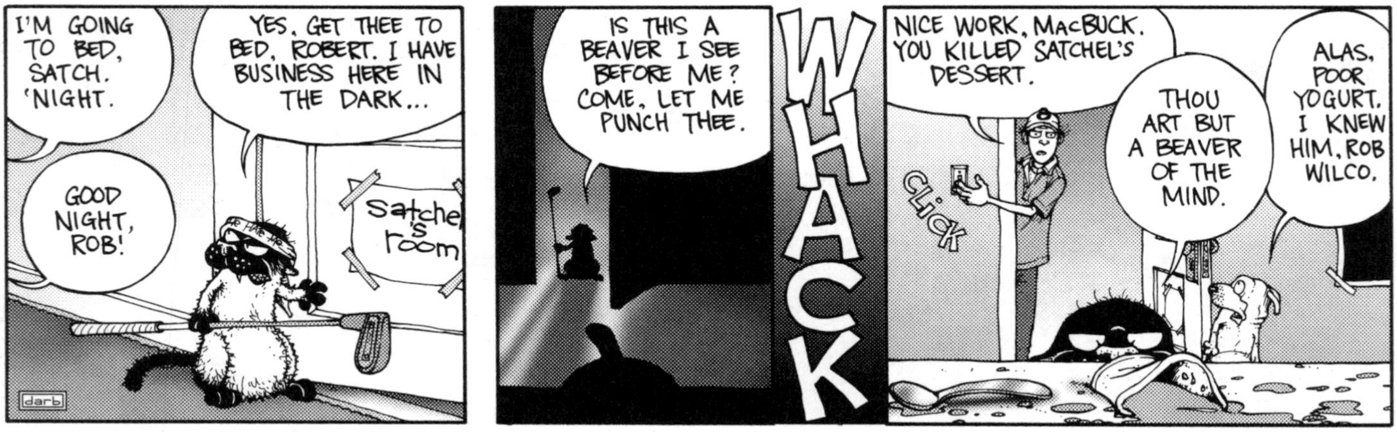
I'M GOING TO BED, SATCH. 'NIGHT.
YES, GET THEE TO BED, ROBERT. I HAVE BUSINESS HERE IN THE DARK...
GOOD NIGHT, ROB!
satchel 's room
darb
IS THIS A BEAVER I SEE BEFORE ME? COME, LET ME PUNCH THEE.
WHACK
NICE WORK, MACBUCK. YOU KILLED SATCHEL'S DESSERT.
CLICK
THOU ART BUT A BEAVER OF THE MIND.
ALAS, POOR YOGURT. I KNEW HIM, ROB WILCO.

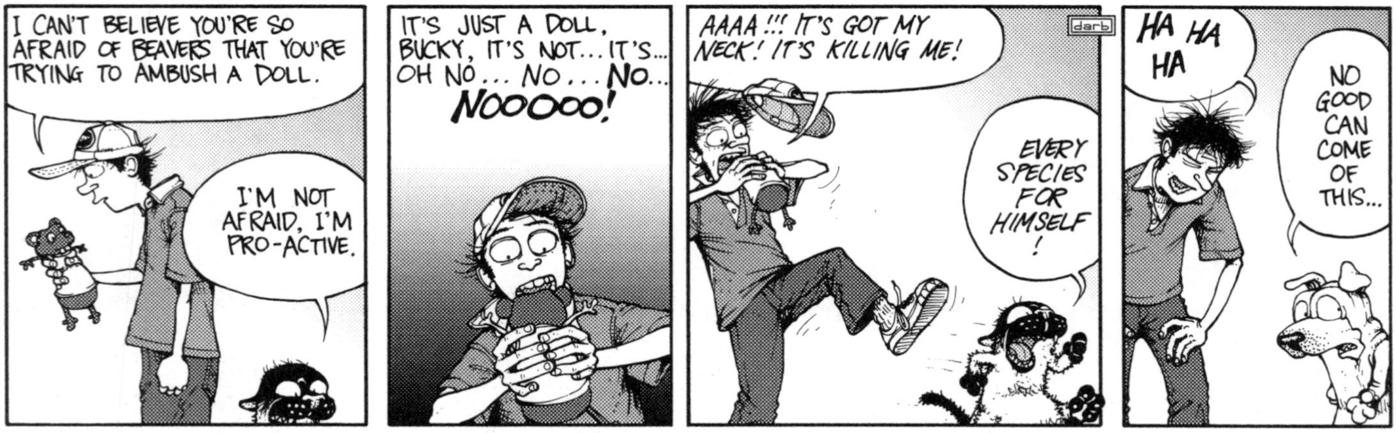
I CAN'T BELIEVE YOU'RE SO AFRAID OF BEAVERS THAT YOU'RE TRYING TO AMBUSH A DOLL.
I'M NOT AFRAID, I'M PRO-ACTIVE.
IT'S JUST A DOLL, BUCKY, IT'S NOT... IT'S... OH NO... NO... NO...
NOOOOO!
AAAA!!! IT'S GOT MY NECK! IT'S KILLING ME!
darb
EVERY SPECIES FOR HIMSELF!
HA HA HA
NO GOOD CAN COME OF THIS...

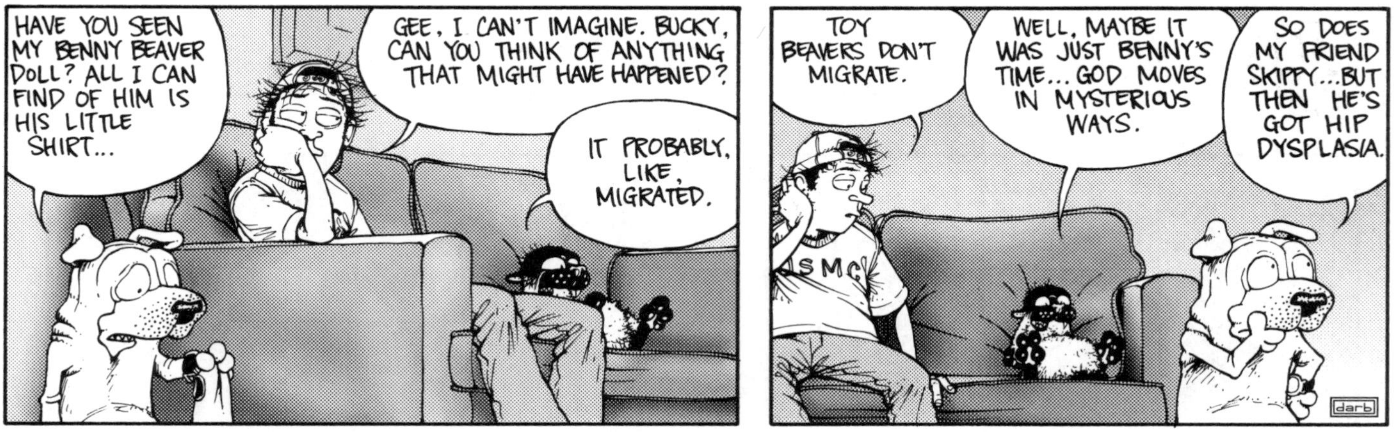
HAVE YOU SEEN MY BENNY BEAVER DOLL? ALL I CAN FIND OF HIM IS HIS LITTLE SHIRT...
GEE, I CAN'T IMAGINE. BUCKY, CAN YOU THINK OF ANYTHING THAT MIGHT HAVE HAPPENED?
IT PROBABLY, LIKE, MIGRATED.
TOY BEAVERS DON'T MIGRATE.
WELL, MAYBE IT WAS JUST BENNY'S TIME... GOD MOVES IN MYSTERIOUS WAYS.
SO DOES MY FRIEND SKIPPY...BUT THEN HE'S GOT HIP DYSPLASIA.
darb

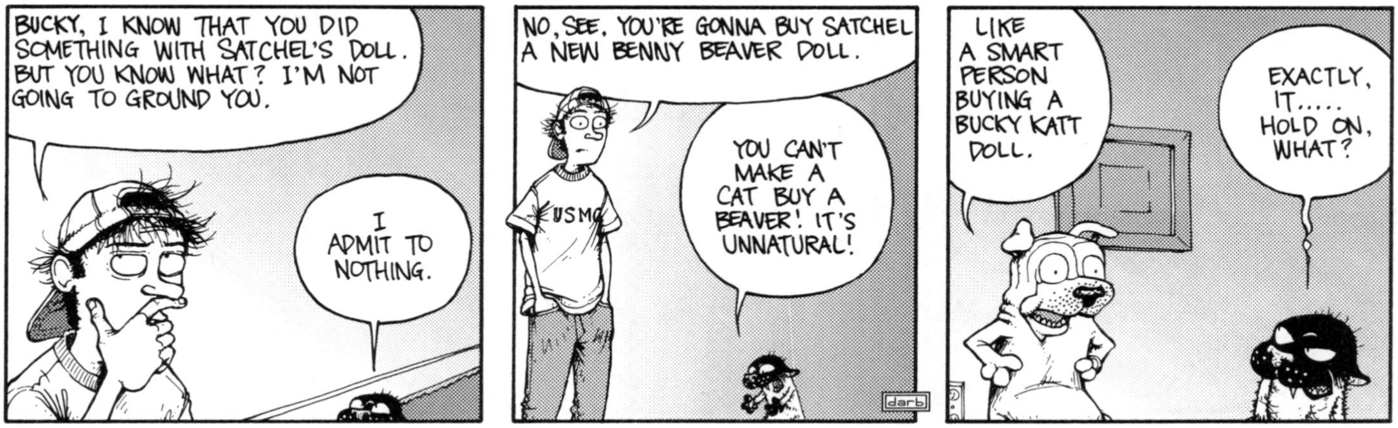
BUCKY, I KNOW THAT YOU DID SOMETHING WITH SATCHEL'S DOLL. BUT YOU KNOW WHAT? I'M NOT GOING TO GROUND YOU.
I ADMIT TO NOTHING.
NO, SEE. YOU'RE GONNA BUY SATCHEL A NEW BENNY BEAVER DOLL.
YOU CAN'T MAKE A CAT BUY A BEAVER! IT'S UNNATURAL!
darb
LIKE A SMART PERSON BUYING A BUCKY KATT DOLL.
EXACTLY, IT..... HOLD ON, WHAT?

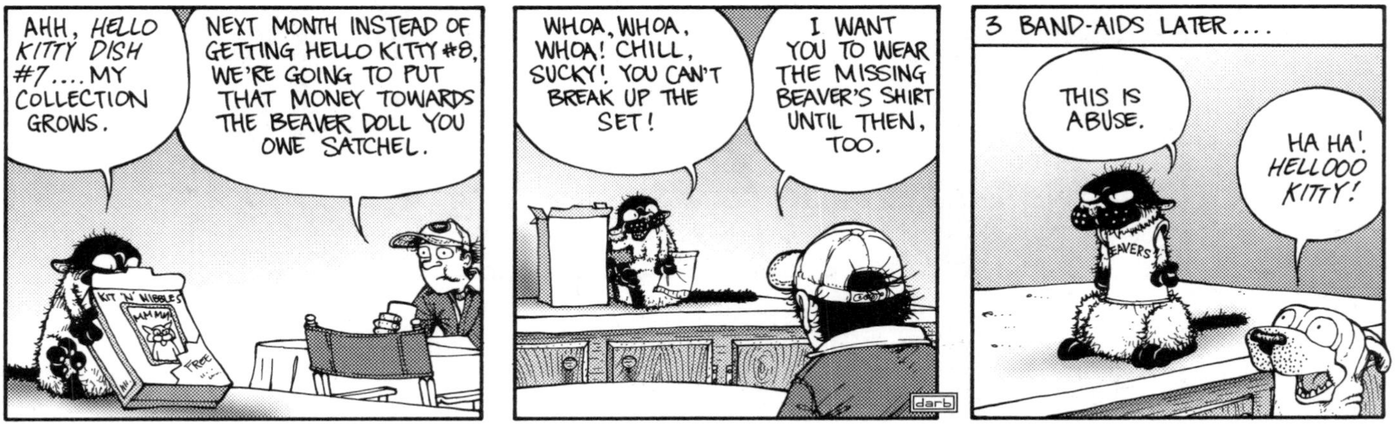
AHH, *HELLO KITTY DISH* #7.... MY COLLECTION GROWS.
NEXT MONTH INSTEAD OF GETTING HELLO KITTY #8, WE'RE GOING TO PUT THAT MONEY TOWARDS THE BEAVER DOLL YOU OWE SATCHEL.
KIT 'N' NIBBLES
WHOA, WHOA, WHOA! CHILL, SUCKY! YOU CAN'T BREAK UP THE SET!
I WANT YOU TO WEAR THE MISSING BEAVER'S SHIRT UNTIL THEN, TOO.
darb
3 BAND-AIDS LATER....
THIS IS ABUSE.
HA HA! *HELLOOO KITTY!*

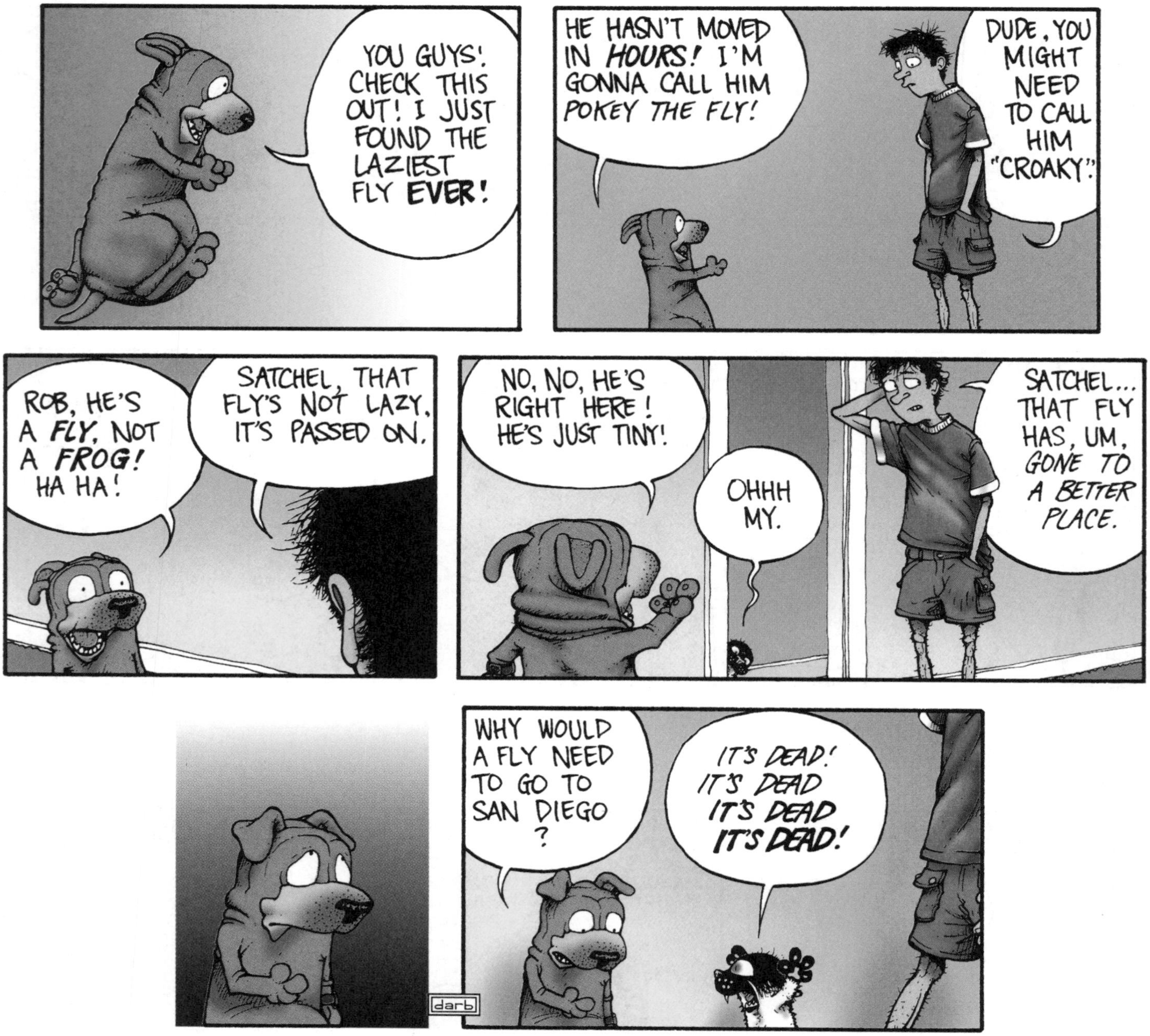
YOU GUYS! CHECK THIS OUT! I JUST FOUND THE LAZIEST FLY **EVER**!
HE HASN'T MOVED IN ***HOURS!*** I'M GONNA CALL HIM *POKEY THE FLY!*
DUDE, YOU MIGHT NEED TO CALL HIM "CROAKY."
ROB, HE'S A ***FLY***, NOT A ***FROG!*** HA HA!
SATCHEL, THAT FLY'S NOT LAZY. IT'S PASSED ON.
NO, NO, HE'S RIGHT HERE! HE'S JUST TINY!
OHHH MY.
SATCHEL... THAT FLY HAS, UM, *GONE TO A BETTER PLACE.*
WHY WOULD A FLY NEED TO GO TO SAN DIEGO?
IT'S DEAD! IT'S DEAD ***IT'S DEAD IT'S DEAD!***
darb

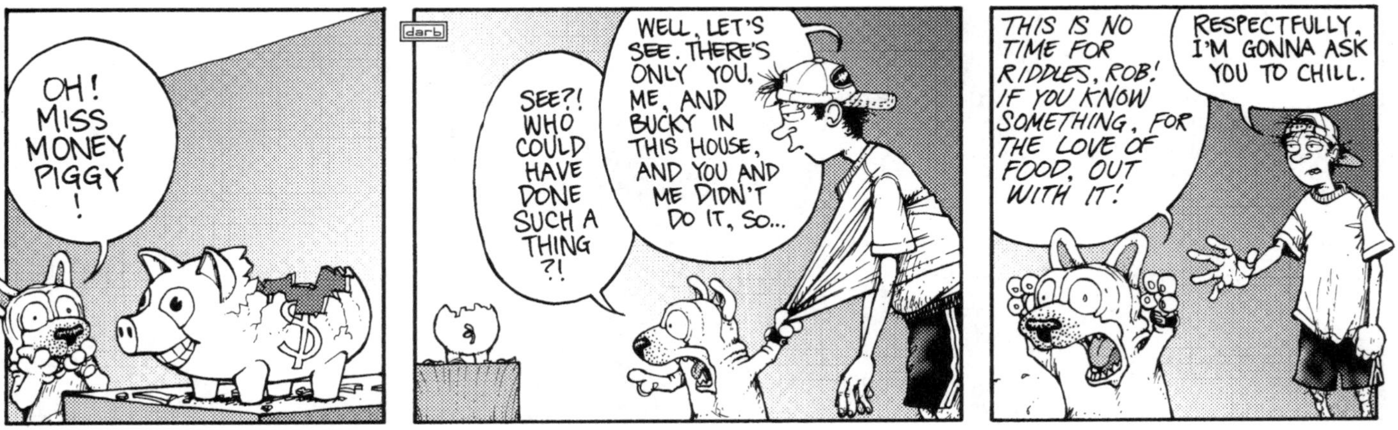
OH! MISS MONEY PIGGY!
darb
SEE?! WHO COULD HAVE DONE SUCH A THING?!
WELL, LET'S SEE. THERE'S ONLY YOU, ME, AND BUCKY IN THIS HOUSE, AND YOU AND ME DIDN'T DO IT, SO...
THIS IS NO TIME FOR RIDDLES, ROB! IF YOU KNOW SOMETHING, FOR THE LOVE OF FOOD, OUT WITH IT!
RESPECTFULLY, I'M GONNA ASK YOU TO CHILL.

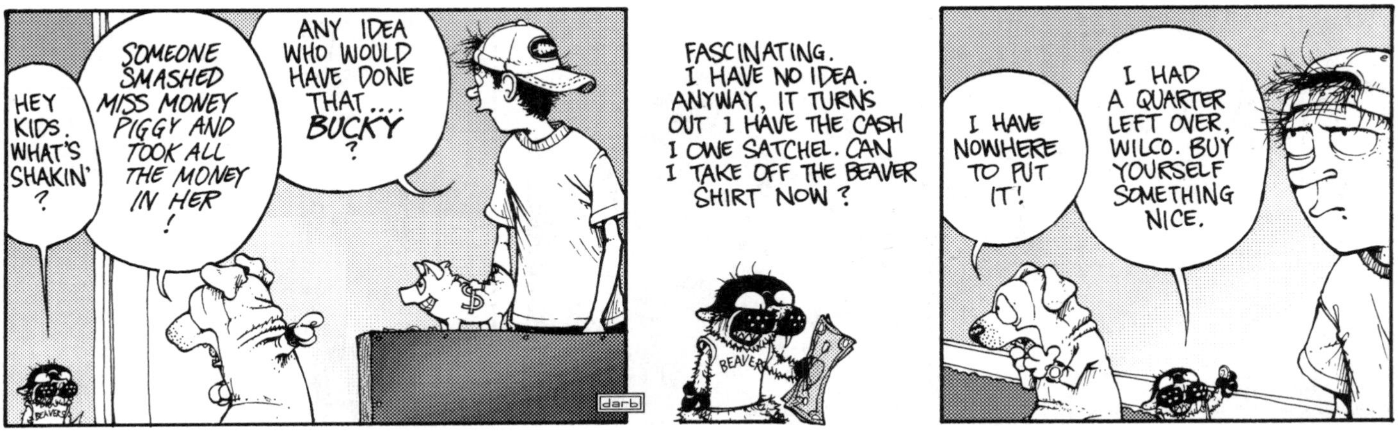
HEY KIDS. WHAT'S SHAKIN'?
SOMEONE SMASHED MISS MONEY PIGGY AND TOOK ALL THE MONEY IN HER!
ANY IDEA WHO WOULD HAVE DONE THAT.... BUCKY?
darb
FASCINATING. I HAVE NO IDEA. ANYWAY, IT TURNS OUT I HAVE THE CASH I OWE SATCHEL. CAN I TAKE OFF THE BEAVER SHIRT NOW?
BEAVER
I HAVE NOWHERE TO PUT IT!
I HAD A QUARTER LEFT OVER, WILCO. BUY YOURSELF SOMETHING NICE.

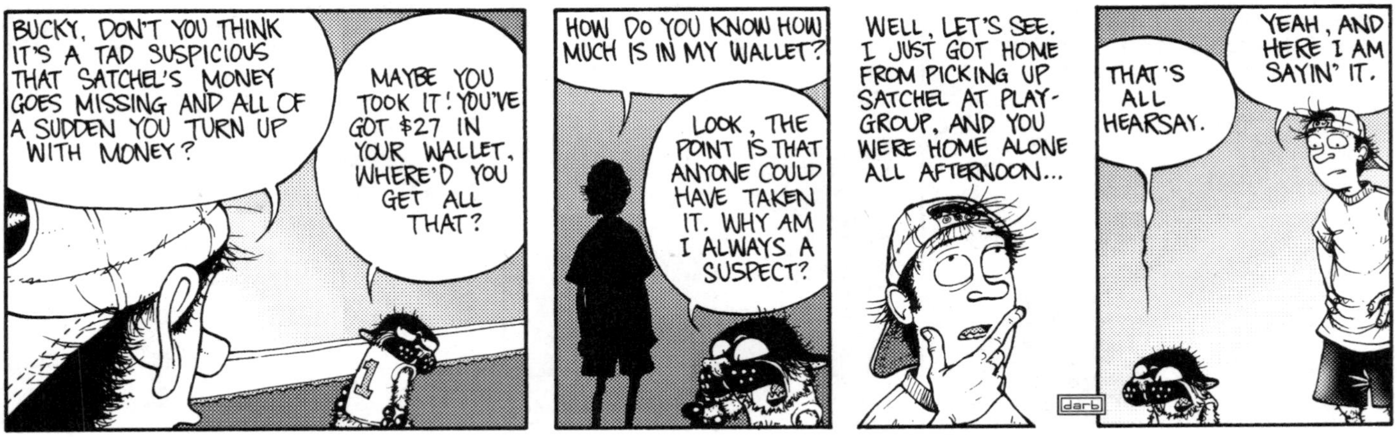
BUCKY, DON'T YOU THINK IT'S A TAD SUSPICIOUS THAT SATCHEL'S MONEY GOES MISSING AND ALL OF A SUDDEN YOU TURN UP WITH MONEY?
MAYBE YOU TOOK IT! YOU'VE GOT $27 IN YOUR WALLET. WHERE'D YOU GET ALL THAT?
HOW DO YOU KNOW HOW MUCH IS IN MY WALLET?
LOOK, THE POINT IS THAT ANYONE COULD HAVE TAKEN IT. WHY AM I ALWAYS A SUSPECT?
WELL, LET'S SEE. I JUST GOT HOME FROM PICKING UP SATCHEL AT PLAY-GROUP, AND YOU WERE HOME ALONE ALL AFTERNOON...
darb
THAT'S ALL HEARSAY.
YEAH, AND HERE I AM SAYIN' IT.

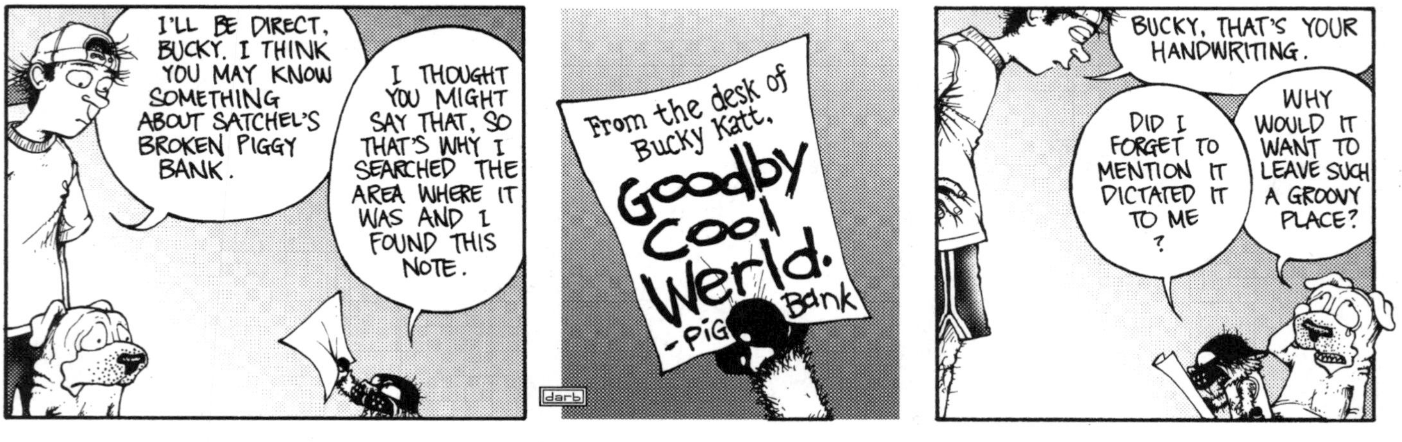
I'LL BE DIRECT, BUCKY. I THINK YOU MAY KNOW SOMETHING ABOUT SATCHEL'S BROKEN PIGGY BANK.
I THOUGHT YOU MIGHT SAY THAT, SO THAT'S WHY I SEARCHED THE AREA WHERE IT WAS AND I FOUND THIS NOTE.
From the desk of Bucky Katt,
Goodby Cool Werld.
-PIG Bank
darb
BUCKY, THAT'S YOUR HANDWRITING.
DID I FORGET TO MENTION IT DICTATED IT TO ME ?
WHY WOULD IT WANT TO LEAVE SUCH A GROOVY PLACE?

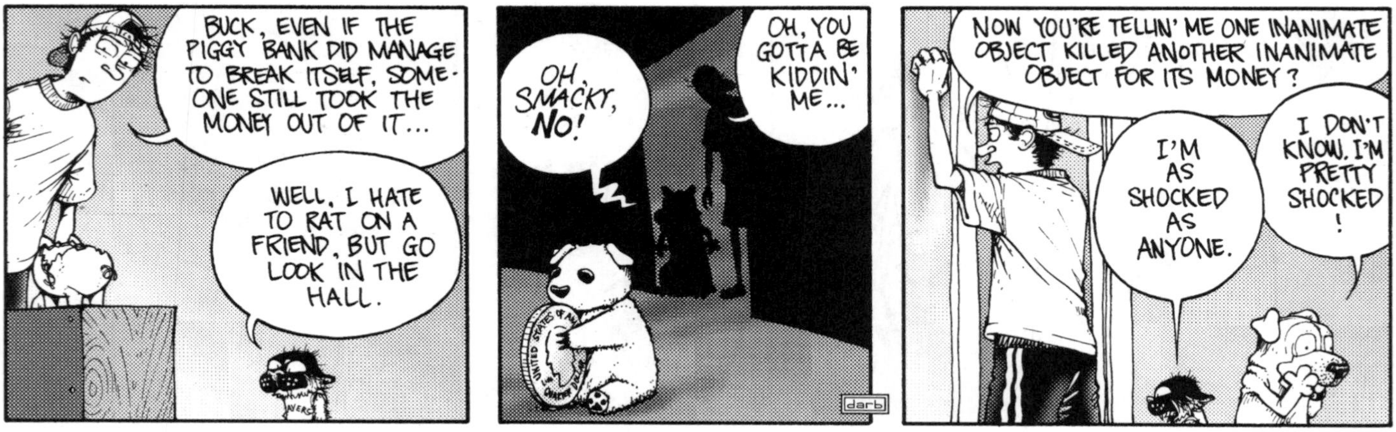
BUCK, EVEN IF THE PIGGY BANK DID MANAGE TO BREAK ITSELF, SOMEONE STILL TOOK THE MONEY OUT OF IT...
WELL, I HATE TO RAT ON A FRIEND, BUT GO LOOK IN THE HALL.
OH, SMACKY, NO!
OH, YOU GOTTA BE KIDDIN' ME...
darb
NOW YOU'RE TELLIN' ME ONE INANIMATE OBJECT KILLED ANOTHER INANIMATE OBJECT FOR ITS MONEY ?
I'M AS SHOCKED AS ANYONE.
I DON'T KNOW. I'M PRETTY SHOCKED !

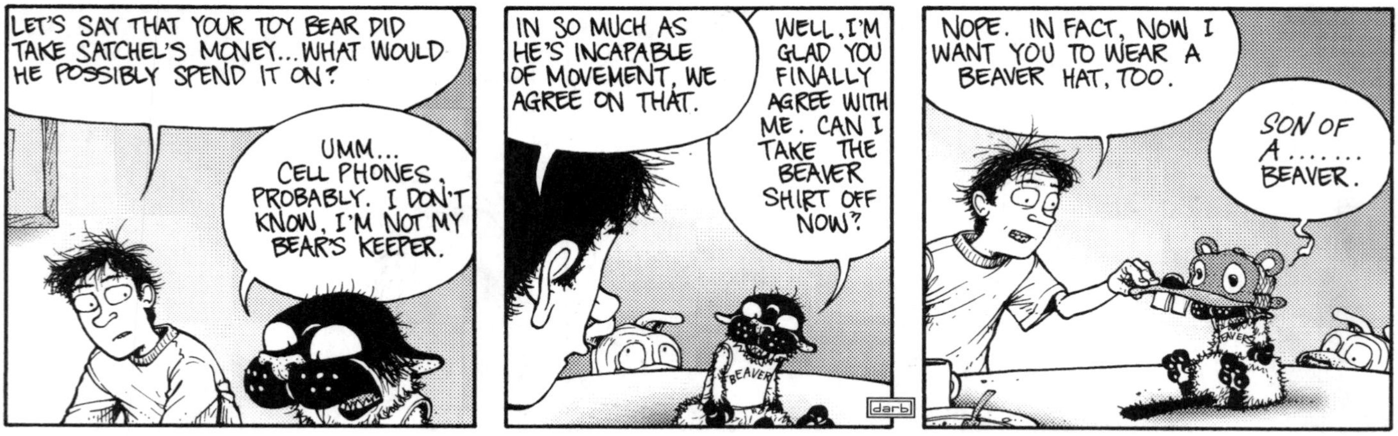
LET'S SAY THAT YOUR TOY BEAR DID TAKE SATCHEL'S MONEY... WHAT WOULD HE POSSIBLY SPEND IT ON?
UMM... CELL PHONES, PROBABLY. I DON'T KNOW, I'M NOT MY BEAR'S KEEPER.
IN SO MUCH AS HE'S INCAPABLE OF MOVEMENT, WE AGREE ON THAT.
WELL, I'M GLAD YOU FINALLY AGREE WITH ME. CAN I TAKE THE BEAVER SHIRT OFF NOW?
BEAVER
darb
NOPE. IN FACT, NOW I WANT YOU TO WEAR A BEAVER HAT, TOO.
SON OF A....... BEAVER.

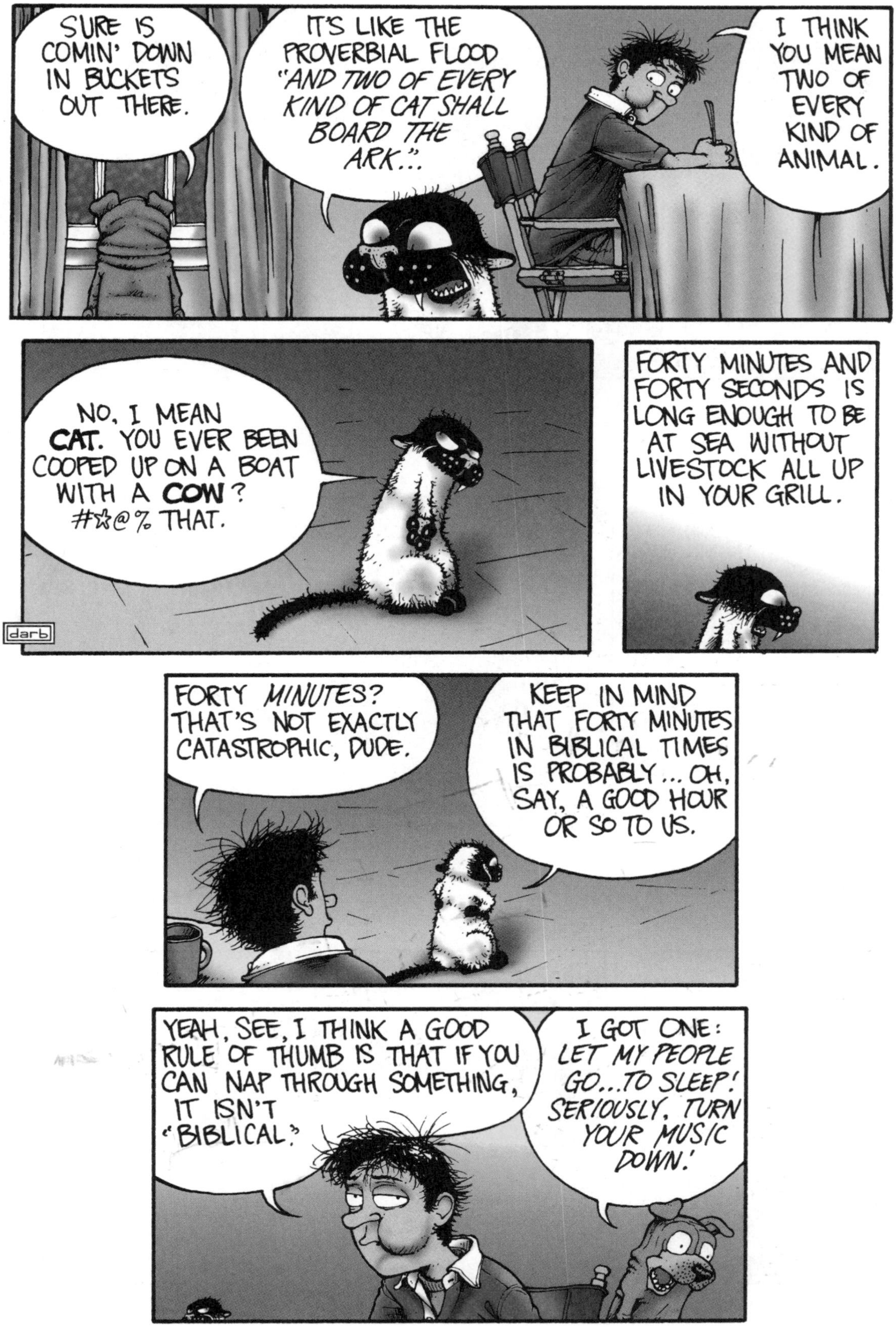
SURE IS COMIN' DOWN IN BUCKETS OUT THERE.
IT'S LIKE THE PROVERBIAL FLOOD "AND TWO OF EVERY KIND OF CAT SHALL BOARD THE ARK."
I THINK YOU MEAN TWO OF EVERY KIND OF ANIMAL.
NO, I MEAN **CAT**. YOU EVER BEEN COOPED UP ON A BOAT WITH A **COW**? #✫@% THAT.
darb
FORTY MINUTES AND FORTY SECONDS IS LONG ENOUGH TO BE AT SEA WITHOUT LIVESTOCK ALL UP IN YOUR GRILL.
FORTY *MINUTES*? THAT'S NOT EXACTLY CATASTROPHIC, DUDE.
KEEP IN MIND THAT FORTY MINUTES IN BIBLICAL TIMES IS PROBABLY... OH, SAY, A GOOD HOUR OR SO TO US.
YEAH, SEE, I THINK A GOOD RULE OF THUMB IS THAT IF YOU CAN NAP THROUGH SOMETHING, IT ISN'T "BIBLICAL."
I GOT ONE: *LET MY PEOPLE GO... TO SLEEP! SERIOUSLY, TURN YOUR MUSIC DOWN.'*

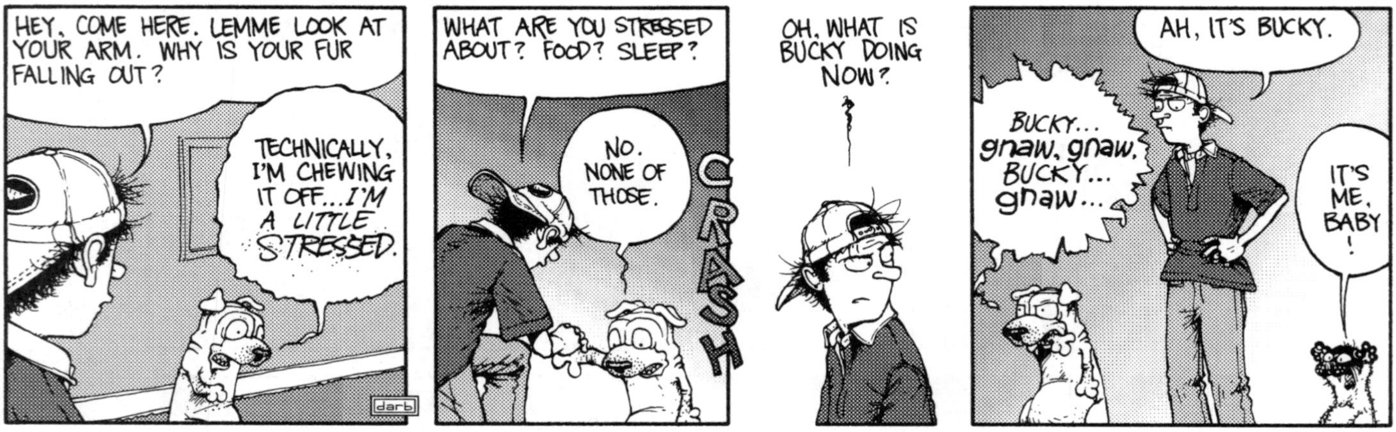
HEY, COME HERE. LEMME LOOK AT YOUR ARM. WHY IS YOUR FUR FALLING OUT?
TECHNICALLY, I'M CHEWING IT OFF... I'M A LITTLE STRESSED.
darb
WHAT ARE YOU STRESSED ABOUT? FOOD? SLEEP?
NO. NONE OF THOSE.
CRASH
OH, WHAT IS BUCKY DOING NOW?
AH, IT'S BUCKY.
BUCKY... gnaw, gnaw, BUCKY... gnaw...
IT'S ME, BABY!

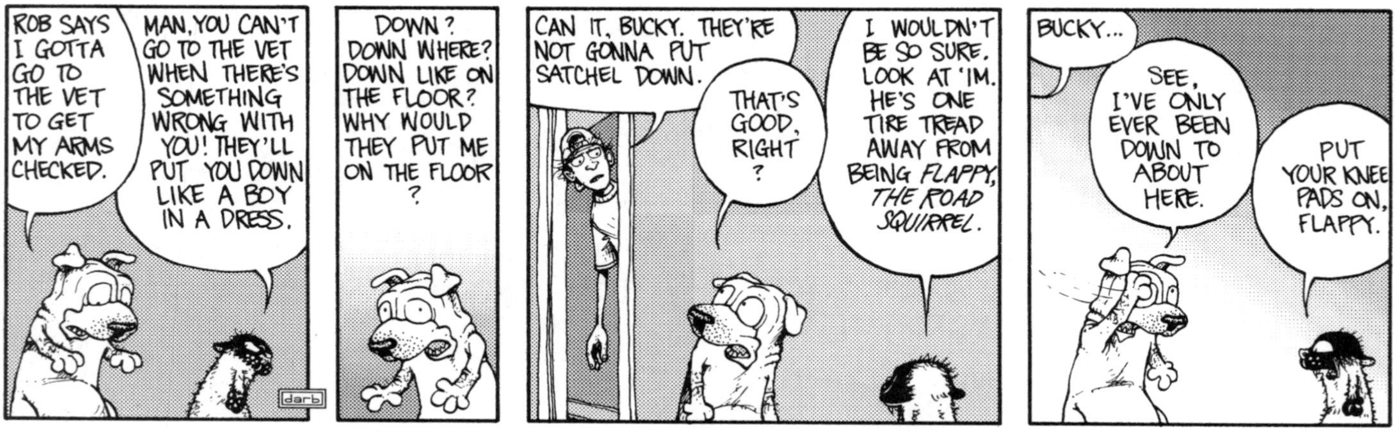
ROB SAYS I GOTTA GO TO THE VET TO GET MY ARMS CHECKED.
MAN, YOU CAN'T GO TO THE VET WHEN THERE'S SOMETHING WRONG WITH YOU! THEY'LL PUT YOU DOWN LIKE A BOY IN A DRESS.
darb
DOWN? DOWN WHERE? DOWN LIKE ON THE FLOOR? WHY WOULD THEY PUT ME ON THE FLOOR?
CAN IT, BUCKY. THEY'RE NOT GONNA PUT SATCHEL DOWN.
THAT'S GOOD, RIGHT?
I WOULDN'T BE SO SURE. LOOK AT 'IM. HE'S ONE TIRE TREAD AWAY FROM BEING FLAPPY, THE ROAD SQUIRREL.
BUCKY...
SEE, I'VE ONLY EVER BEEN DOWN TO ABOUT HERE.
PUT YOUR KNEE PADS ON, FLAPPY.

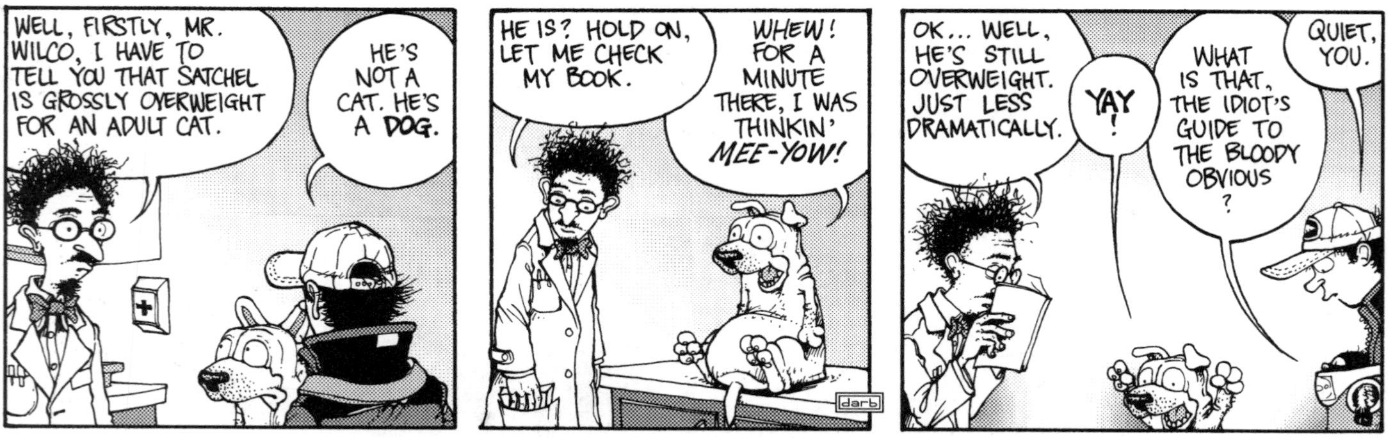
WELL, FIRSTLY, MR. WILCO, I HAVE TO TELL YOU THAT SATCHEL IS GROSSLY OVERWEIGHT FOR AN ADULT CAT.
HE'S NOT A CAT. HE'S A DOG.
HE IS? HOLD ON, LET ME CHECK MY BOOK.
WHEW! FOR A MINUTE THERE, I WAS THINKIN' MEE-YOW!
darb
OK... WELL, HE'S STILL OVERWEIGHT. JUST LESS DRAMATICALLY.
YAY!
WHAT IS THAT, THE IDIOT'S GUIDE TO THE BLOODY OBVIOUS?
QUIET, YOU.

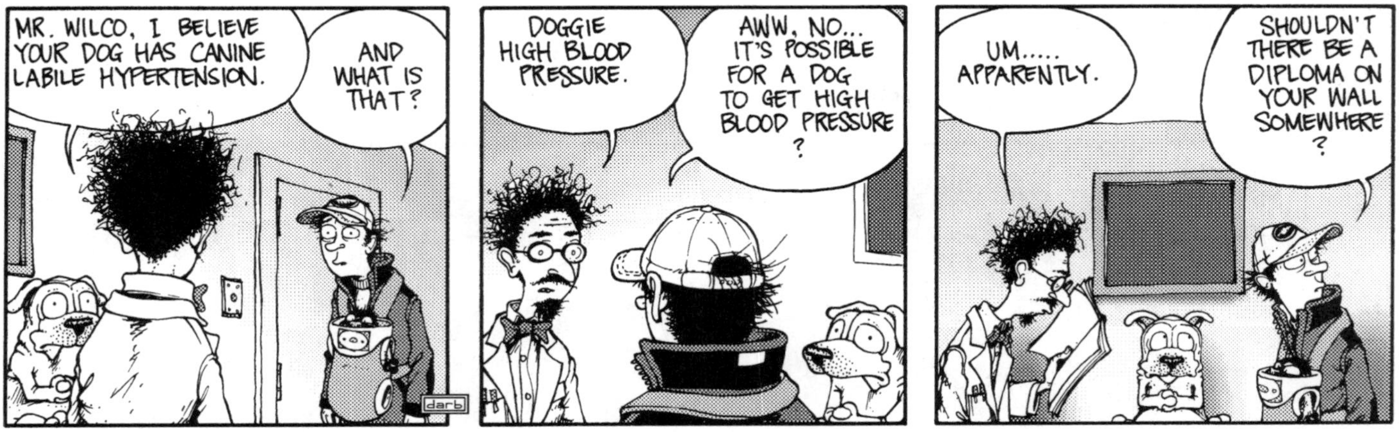
MR. WILCO, I BELIEVE YOUR DOG HAS CANINE LABILE HYPERTENSION.
AND WHAT IS THAT?
DOGGIE HIGH BLOOD PRESSURE.
AWW, NO... IT'S POSSIBLE FOR A DOG TO GET HIGH BLOOD PRESSURE?
UM..... APPARENTLY.
SHOULDN'T THERE BE A DIPLOMA ON YOUR WALL SOMEWHERE?

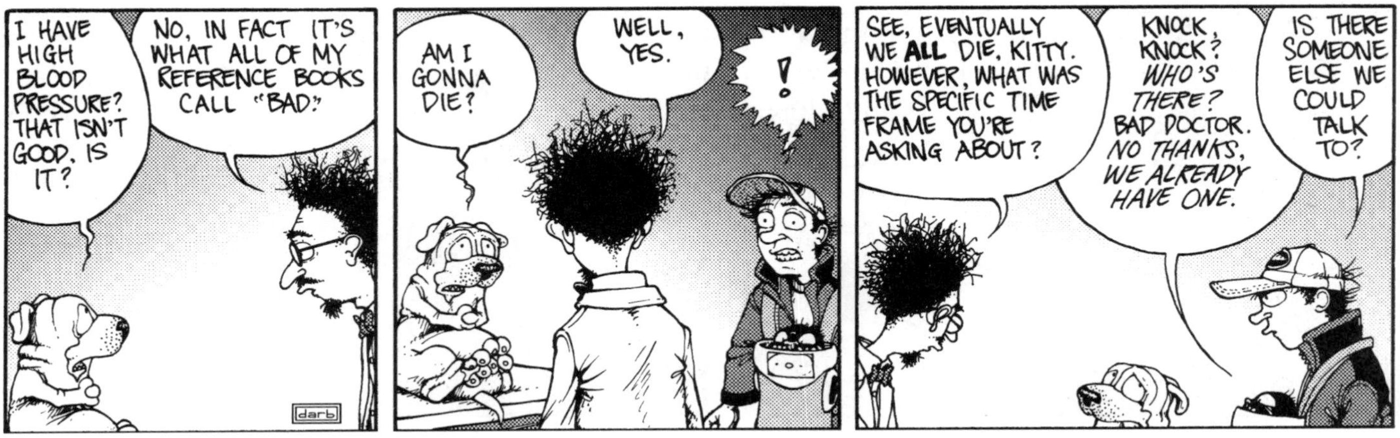
I HAVE HIGH BLOOD PRESSURE? THAT ISN'T GOOD, IS IT?
NO, IN FACT IT'S WHAT ALL OF MY REFERENCE BOOKS CALL "BAD."
AM I GONNA DIE?
WELL, YES.
!
SEE, EVENTUALLY WE **ALL** DIE, KITTY. HOWEVER, WHAT WAS THE SPECIFIC TIME FRAME YOU'RE ASKING ABOUT?
KNOCK, KNOCK? *WHO'S THERE?* BAD DOCTOR. *NO THANKS, WE ALREADY HAVE ONE.*
IS THERE SOMEONE ELSE WE COULD TALK TO?

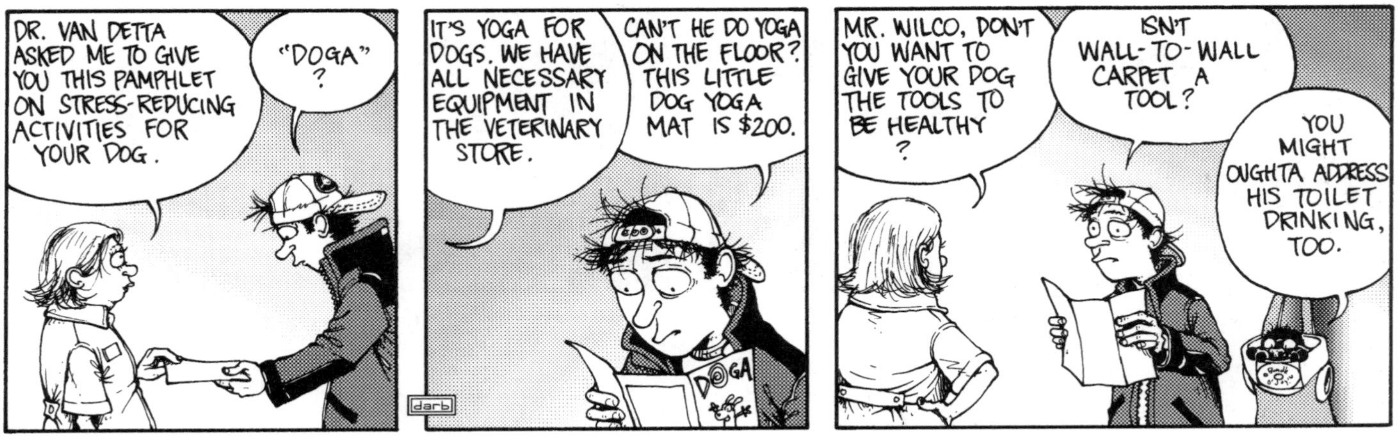
DR. VAN DETTA ASKED ME TO GIVE YOU THIS PAMPHLET ON STRESS-REDUCING ACTIVITIES FOR YOUR DOG.
"DOGA"?
IT'S YOGA FOR DOGS. WE HAVE ALL NECESSARY EQUIPMENT IN THE VETERINARY STORE.
CAN'T HE DO YOGA ON THE FLOOR? THIS LITTLE DOG YOGA MAT IS $200.
DOGA
MR. WILCO, DON'T YOU WANT TO GIVE YOUR DOG THE TOOLS TO BE HEALTHY?
ISN'T WALL-TO-WALL CARPET A TOOL?
YOU MIGHT OUGHTA ADDRESS HIS TOILET DRINKING, TOO.

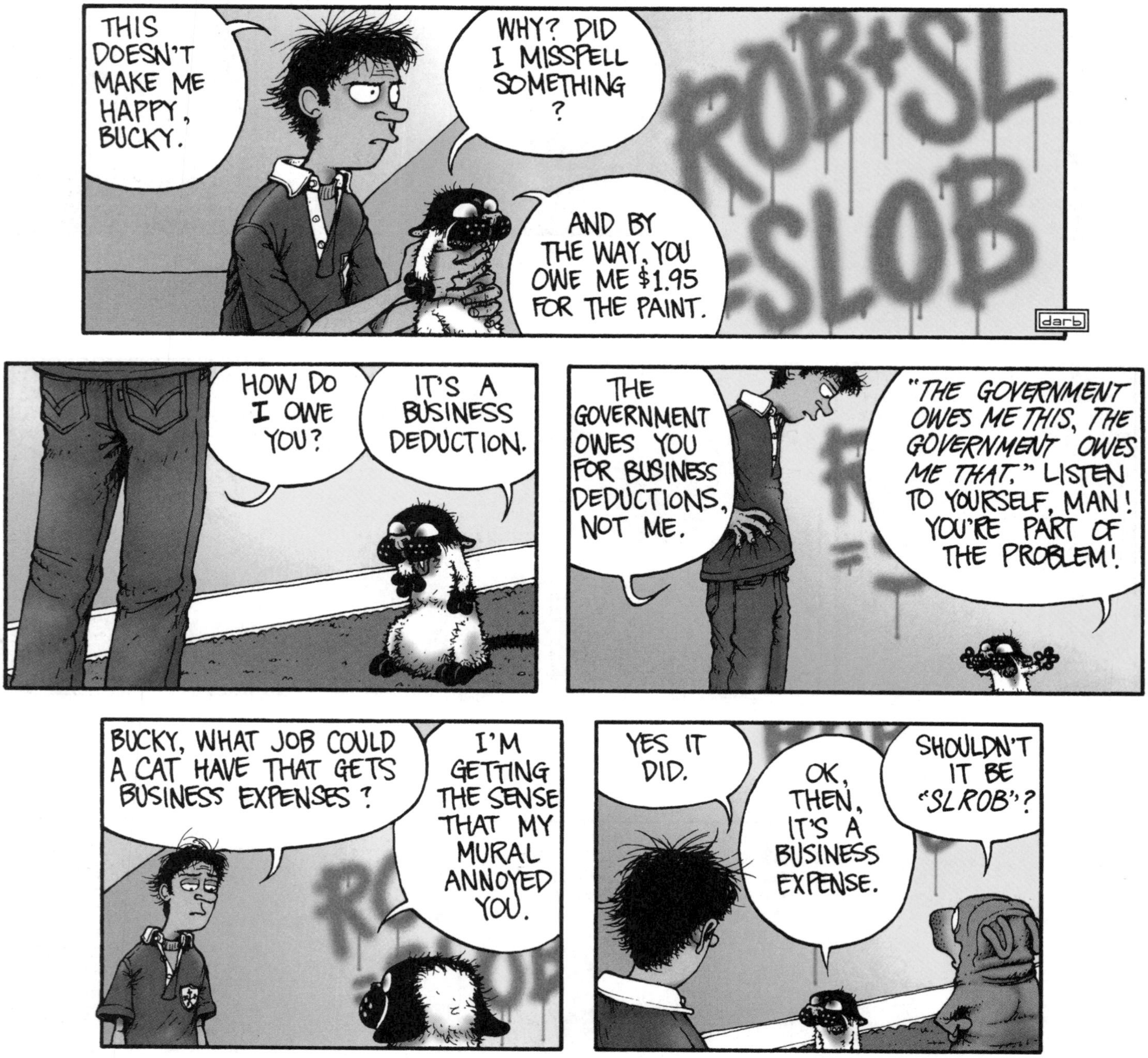
THIS DOESN'T MAKE ME HAPPY, BUCKY.
WHY? DID I MISSPELL SOMETHING?
ROB+SL =SLOB
AND BY THE WAY, YOU OWE ME $1.95 FOR THE PAINT.
darb
HOW DO I OWE YOU?
IT'S A BUSINESS DEDUCTION.
THE GOVERNMENT OWES YOU FOR BUSINESS DEDUCTIONS, NOT ME.
"THE GOVERNMENT OWES ME THIS, THE GOVERNMENT OWES ME THAT." LISTEN TO YOURSELF, MAN! YOU'RE PART OF THE PROBLEM!
BUCKY, WHAT JOB COULD A CAT HAVE THAT GETS BUSINESS EXPENSES?
I'M GETTING THE SENSE THAT MY MURAL ANNOYED YOU.
YES IT DID.
OK, THEN, IT'S A BUSINESS EXPENSE.
SHOULDN'T IT BE "SLROB"?

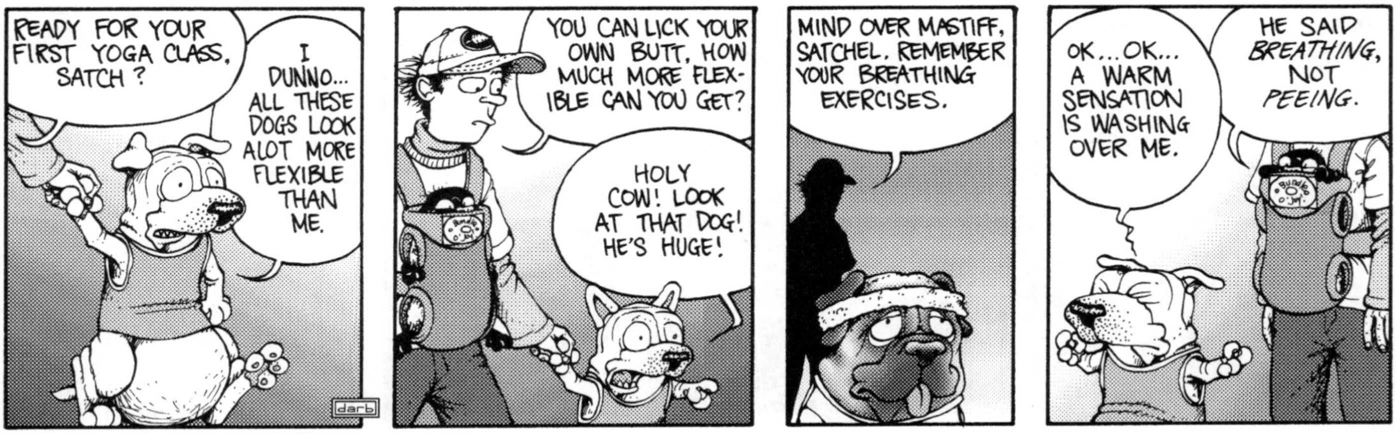
READY FOR YOUR FIRST YOGA CLASS, SATCH ?
I DUNNO... ALL THESE DOGS LOOK ALOT MORE FLEXIBLE THAN ME.
YOU CAN LICK YOUR OWN BUTT, HOW MUCH MORE FLEX-IBLE CAN YOU GET?
HOLY COW! LOOK AT THAT DOG! HE'S HUGE!
MIND OVER MASTIFF, SATCHEL. REMEMBER YOUR BREATHING EXERCISES.
OK...OK... A WARM SENSATION IS WASHING OVER ME.
HE SAID *BREATHING*, NOT *PEEING*.
darb

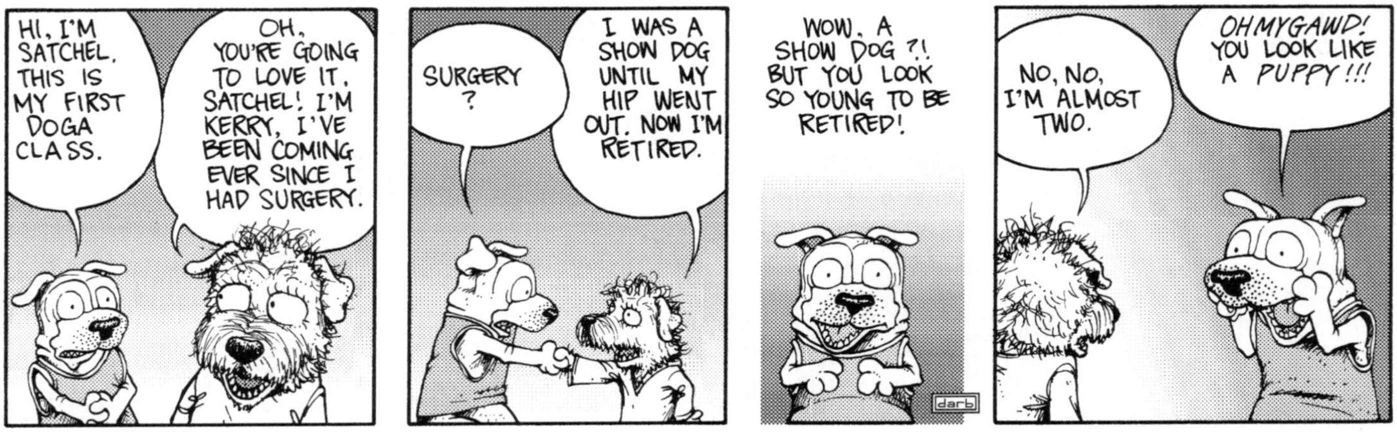
HI, I'M SATCHEL. THIS IS MY FIRST DOGA CLASS.
OH, YOU'RE GOING TO LOVE IT, SATCHEL! I'M KERRY, I'VE BEEN COMING EVER SINCE I HAD SURGERY.
SURGERY ?
I WAS A SHOW DOG UNTIL MY HIP WENT OUT. NOW I'M RETIRED.
WOW, A SHOW DOG ?! BUT YOU LOOK SO YOUNG TO BE RETIRED!
darb
NO, NO, I'M ALMOST TWO.
OHMYGAWD! YOU LOOK LIKE A *PUPPY!!!*

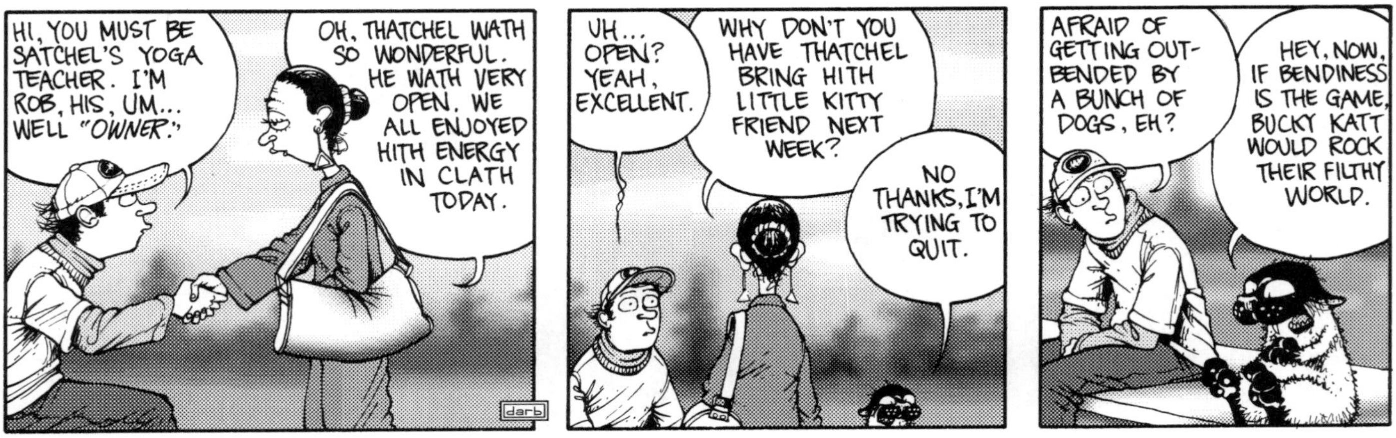
HI, YOU MUST BE SATCHEL'S YOGA TEACHER. I'M ROB, HIS, UM... WELL "*OWNER*."
OH, THATCHEL WATH SO WONDERFUL. HE WATH VERY OPEN. WE ALL ENJOYED HITH ENERGY IN CLATH TODAY.
darb
UH... OPEN? YEAH, EXCELLENT.
WHY DON'T YOU HAVE THATCHEL BRING HITH LITTLE KITTY FRIEND NEXT WEEK?
NO THANKS, I'M TRYING TO QUIT.
AFRAID OF GETTING OUT-BENDED BY A BUNCH OF DOGS, EH?
HEY, NOW, IF BENDINESS IS THE GAME, BUCKY KATT WOULD ROCK THEIR FILTHY WORLD.

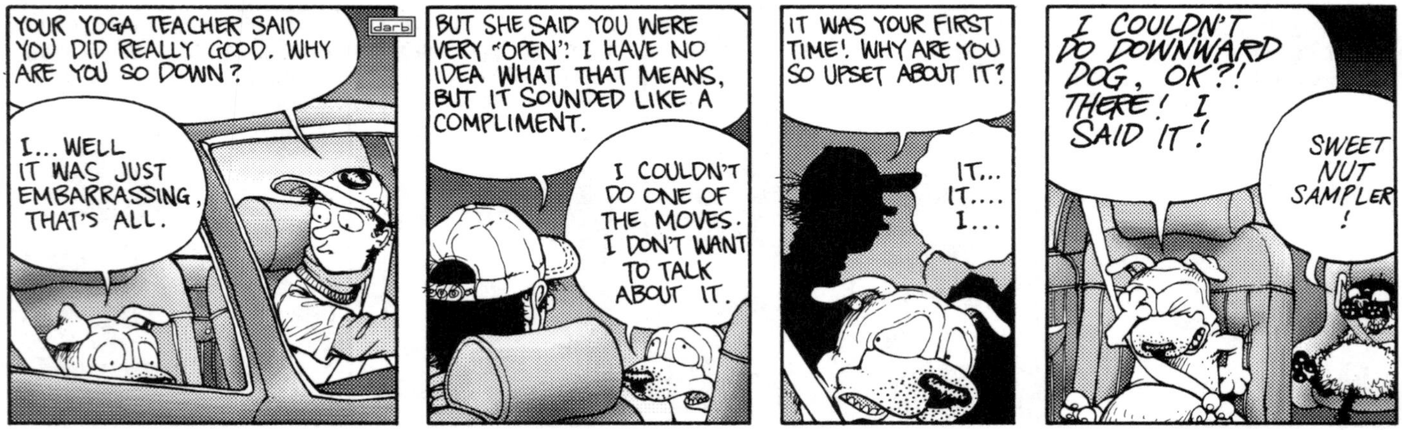
YOUR YOGA TEACHER SAID YOU DID REALLY GOOD. WHY ARE YOU SO DOWN?
I... WELL IT WAS JUST EMBARRASSING, THAT'S ALL.
BUT SHE SAID YOU WERE VERY "OPEN": I HAVE NO IDEA WHAT THAT MEANS, BUT IT SOUNDED LIKE A COMPLIMENT.
I COULDN'T DO ONE OF THE MOVES. I DON'T WANT TO TALK ABOUT IT.
IT WAS YOUR FIRST TIME! WHY ARE YOU SO UPSET ABOUT IT?
IT... IT.... I...
I COULDN'T DO DOWNWARD DOG, OK?! THERE! I SAID IT!
SWEET NUT SAMPLER!

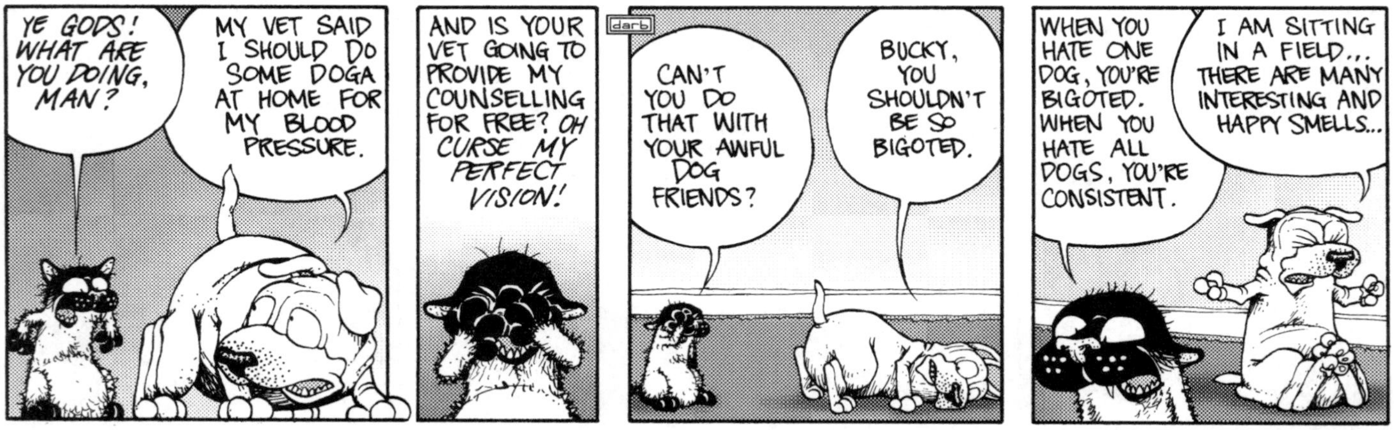
YE GODS! WHAT ARE YOU DOING, MAN?
MY VET SAID I SHOULD DO SOME DOGA AT HOME FOR MY BLOOD PRESSURE.
AND IS YOUR VET GOING TO PROVIDE MY COUNSELLING FOR FREE? OH CURSE MY PERFECT VISION!
CAN'T YOU DO THAT WITH YOUR AWFUL DOG FRIENDS?
BUCKY, YOU SHOULDN'T BE SO BIGOTED.
WHEN YOU HATE ONE DOG, YOU'RE BIGOTED. WHEN YOU HATE ALL DOGS, YOU'RE CONSISTENT.
I AM SITTING IN A FIELD... THERE ARE MANY INTERESTING AND HAPPY SMELLS...

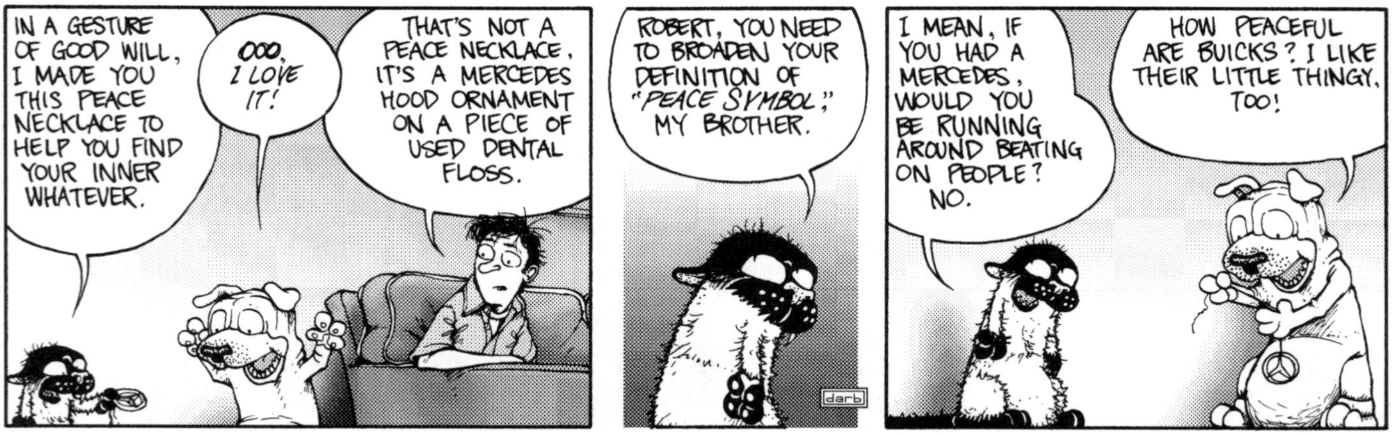
IN A GESTURE OF GOOD WILL, I MADE YOU THIS PEACE NECKLACE TO HELP YOU FIND YOUR INNER WHATEVER.
OOO, I LOVE IT!
THAT'S NOT A PEACE NECKLACE, IT'S A MERCEDES HOOD ORNAMENT ON A PIECE OF USED DENTAL FLOSS.
ROBERT, YOU NEED TO BROADEN YOUR DEFINITION OF "PEACE SYMBOL," MY BROTHER.
I MEAN, IF YOU HAD A MERCEDES, WOULD YOU BE RUNNING AROUND BEATING ON PEOPLE? NO.
HOW PEACEFUL ARE BUICKS? I LIKE THEIR LITTLE THINGY, TOO!

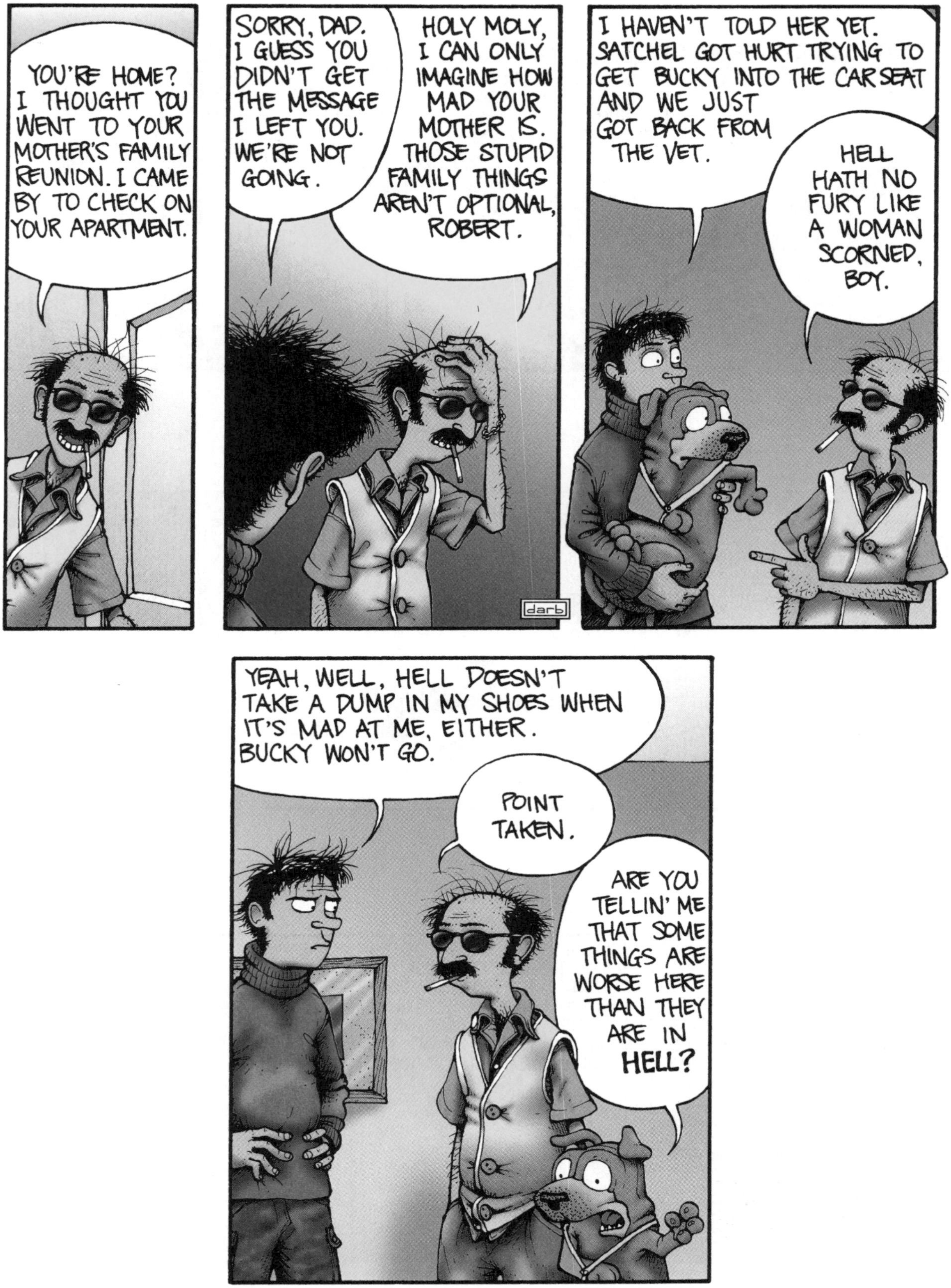
YOU'RE HOME? I THOUGHT YOU WENT TO YOUR MOTHER'S FAMILY REUNION. I CAME BY TO CHECK ON YOUR APARTMENT.
SORRY, DAD. I GUESS YOU DIDN'T GET THE MESSAGE I LEFT YOU. WE'RE NOT GOING.
HOLY MOLY, I CAN ONLY IMAGINE HOW MAD YOUR MOTHER IS. THOSE STUPID FAMILY THINGS AREN'T OPTIONAL, ROBERT.
darb
I HAVEN'T TOLD HER YET. SATCHEL GOT HURT TRYING TO GET BUCKY INTO THE CAR SEAT AND WE JUST GOT BACK FROM THE VET.
HELL HATH NO FURY LIKE A WOMAN SCORNED, BOY.
YEAH, WELL, HELL DOESN'T TAKE A DUMP IN MY SHOES WHEN IT'S MAD AT ME, EITHER. BUCKY WON'T GO.
POINT TAKEN.
ARE YOU TELLIN' ME THAT SOME THINGS ARE WORSE HERE THAN THEY ARE IN HELL?

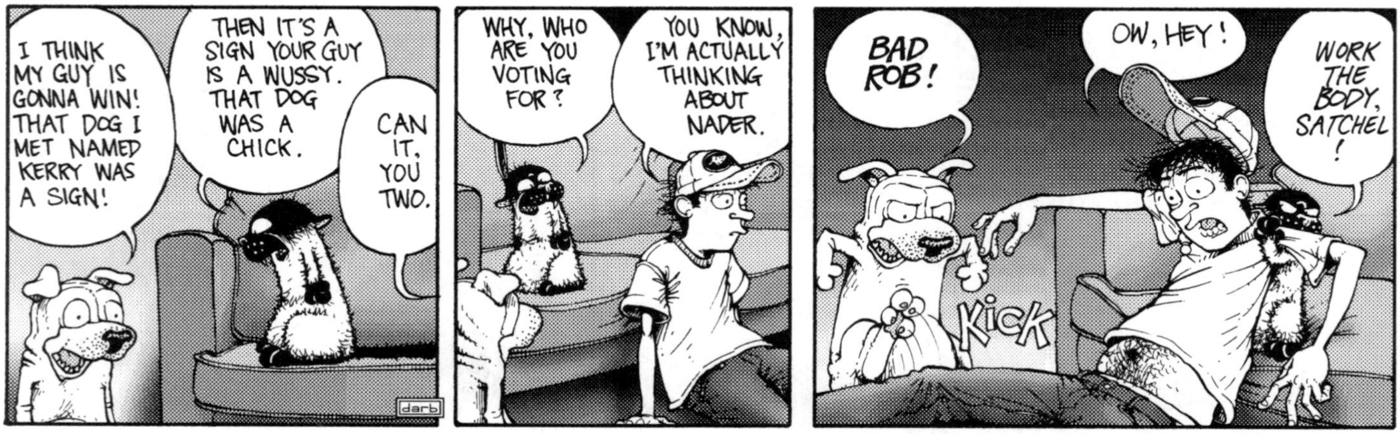
I THINK MY GUY IS GONNA WIN! THAT DOG I MET NAMED KERRY WAS A SIGN!
THEN IT'S A SIGN YOUR GUY IS A WUSSY. THAT DOG WAS A CHICK.
CAN IT, YOU TWO.
darb
WHY, WHO ARE YOU VOTING FOR?
YOU KNOW, I'M ACTUALLY THINKING ABOUT NADER.
BAD ROB!
OW, HEY!
WORK THE BODY, SATCHEL!
KICK

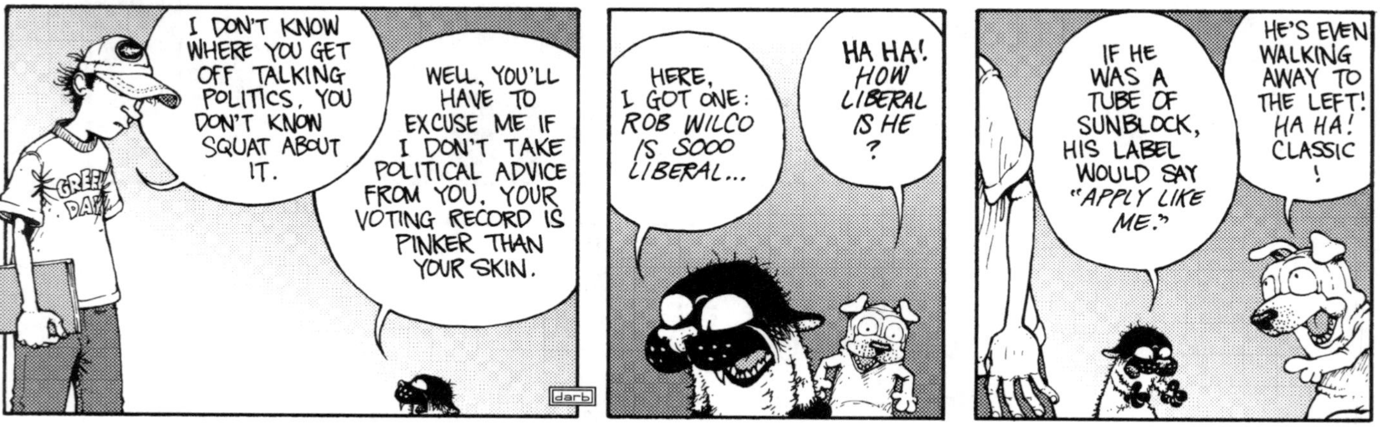
GREEN DAY
I DON'T KNOW WHERE YOU GET OFF TALKING POLITICS, YOU DON'T KNOW SQUAT ABOUT IT.
WELL, YOU'LL HAVE TO EXCUSE ME IF I DON'T TAKE POLITICAL ADVICE FROM YOU. YOUR VOTING RECORD IS PINKER THAN YOUR SKIN.
darb
HERE, I GOT ONE: ROB WILCO IS SOOO LIBERAL...
HA HA! HOW LIBERAL IS HE?
IF HE WAS A TUBE OF SUNBLOCK, HIS LABEL WOULD SAY "APPLY LIKE ME."
HE'S EVEN WALKING AWAY TO THE LEFT! HA HA! CLASSIC!

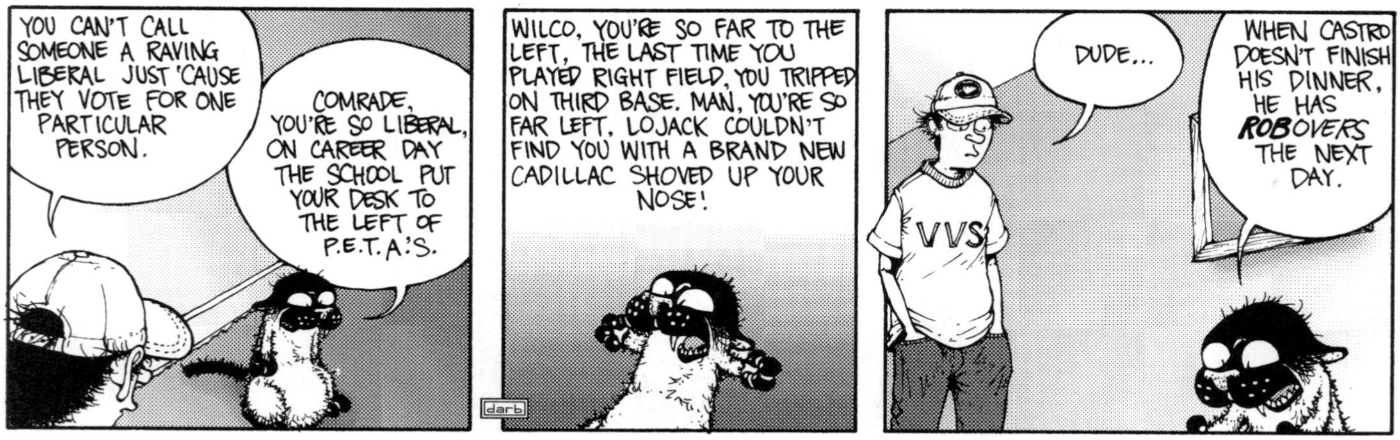
YOU CAN'T CALL SOMEONE A RAVING LIBERAL JUST 'CAUSE THEY VOTE FOR ONE PARTICULAR PERSON.
COMRADE, YOU'RE SO LIBERAL, ON CAREER DAY THE SCHOOL PUT YOUR DESK TO THE LEFT OF P.E.T.A.'S.
darb
WILCO, YOU'RE SO FAR TO THE LEFT, THE LAST TIME YOU PLAYED RIGHT FIELD, YOU TRIPPED ON THIRD BASE. MAN, YOU'RE SO FAR LEFT, LOJACK COULDN'T FIND YOU WITH A BRAND NEW CADILLAC SHOVED UP YOUR NOSE!
DUDE...
VVS
WHEN CASTRO DOESN'T FINISH HIS DINNER, HE HAS ROBOVERS THE NEXT DAY.

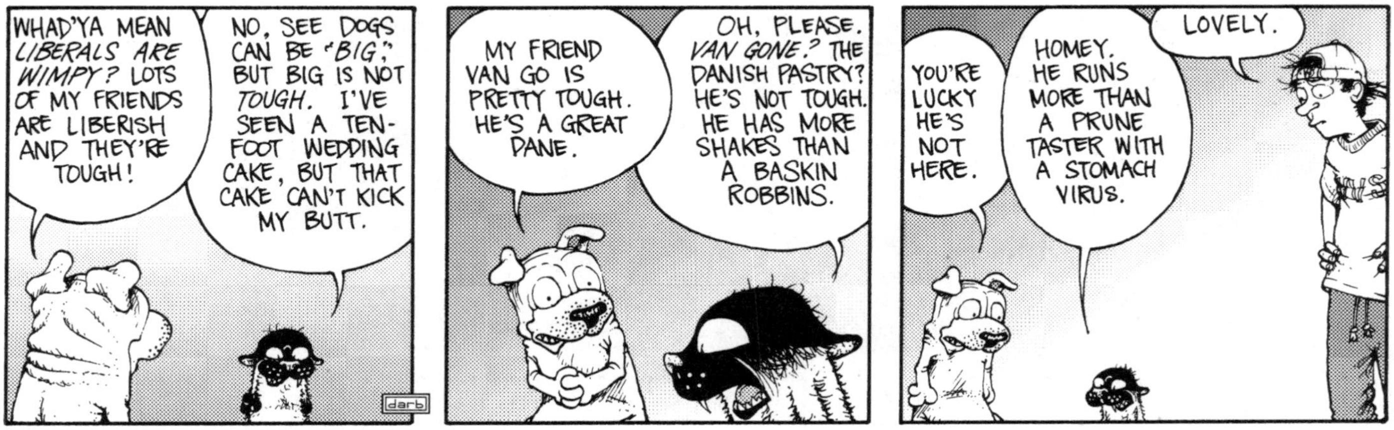
WHAD'YA MEAN *LIBERALS ARE WIMPY?* LOTS OF MY FRIENDS ARE LIBERISH AND THEY'RE TOUGH!
NO, SEE DOGS CAN BE "*BIG*," BUT BIG IS NOT *TOUGH.* I'VE SEEN A TEN-FOOT WEDDING CAKE, BUT THAT CAKE CAN'T KICK MY BUTT.
darb
MY FRIEND VAN GO IS PRETTY TOUGH. HE'S A GREAT DANE.
OH, PLEASE. *VAN GONE?* THE DANISH PASTRY? HE'S NOT TOUGH. HE HAS MORE SHAKES THAN A BASKIN ROBBINS.
YOU'RE LUCKY HE'S NOT HERE.
HOMEY. HE RUNS MORE THAN A PRUNE TASTER WITH A STOMACH VIRUS.
LOVELY.

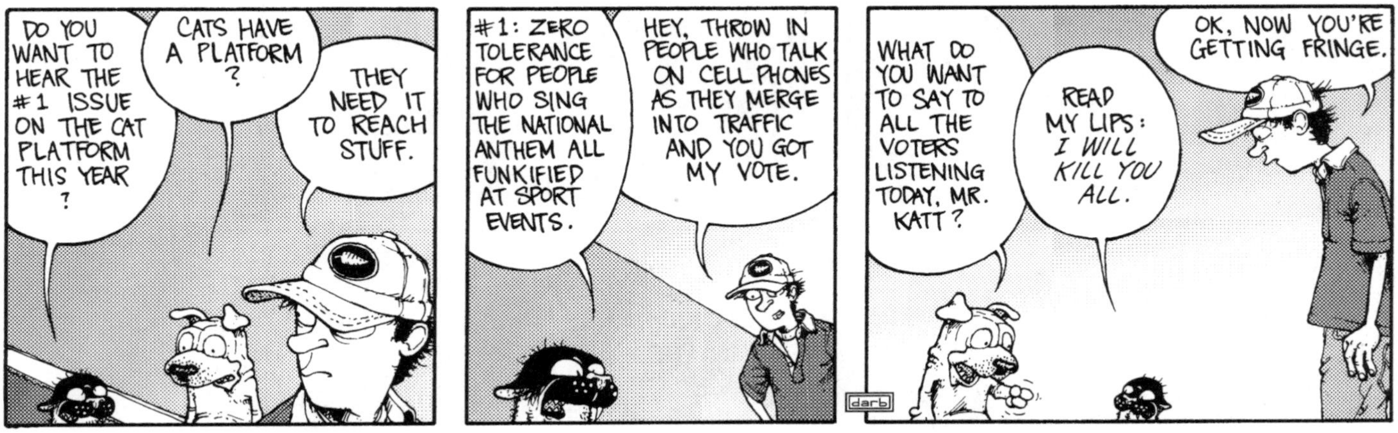
DO YOU WANT TO HEAR THE #1 ISSUE ON THE CAT PLATFORM THIS YEAR?
CATS HAVE A PLATFORM?
THEY NEED IT TO REACH STUFF.
#1: ZERO TOLERANCE FOR PEOPLE WHO SING THE NATIONAL ANTHEM ALL FUNKIFIED AT SPORT EVENTS.
HEY, THROW IN PEOPLE WHO TALK ON CELL PHONES AS THEY MERGE INTO TRAFFIC AND YOU GOT MY VOTE.
darb
WHAT DO YOU WANT TO SAY TO ALL THE VOTERS LISTENING TODAY, MR. KATT?
READ MY LIPS: *I WILL KILL YOU ALL.*
OK, NOW YOU'RE GETTING FRINGE.

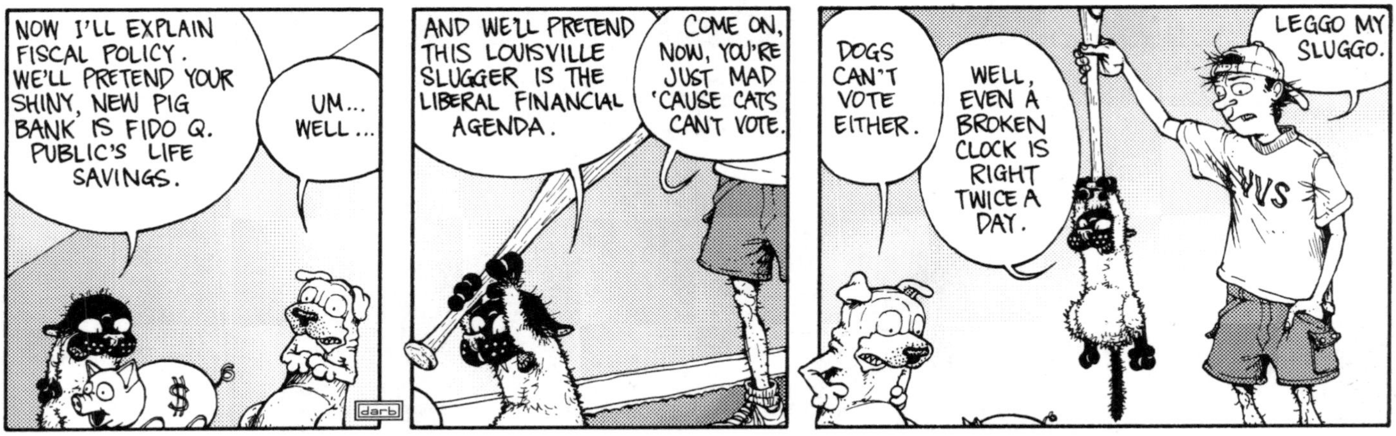
NOW I'LL EXPLAIN FISCAL POLICY. WE'LL PRETEND YOUR SHINY, NEW PIG BANK IS FIDO Q. PUBLIC'S LIFE SAVINGS.
UM... WELL...
darb
AND WE'LL PRETEND THIS LOUISVILLE SLUGGER IS THE LIBERAL FINANCIAL AGENDA.
COME ON, NOW, YOU'RE JUST MAD 'CAUSE CATS CAN'T VOTE.
DOGS CAN'T VOTE EITHER.
WELL, EVEN A BROKEN CLOCK IS RIGHT TWICE A DAY.
LEGGO MY SLUGGO.

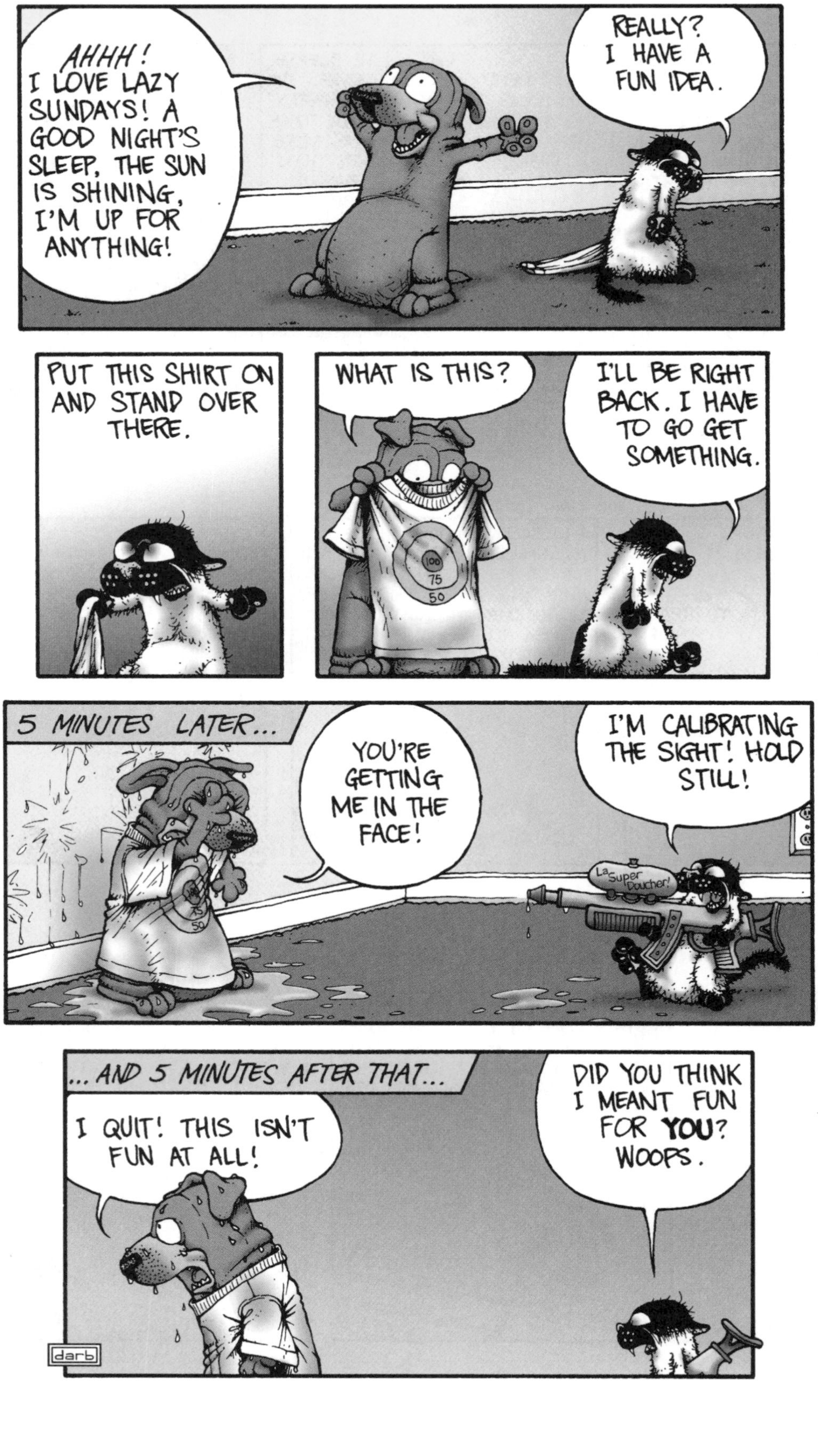
AHHH! I LOVE LAZY SUNDAYS! A GOOD NIGHT'S SLEEP, THE SUN IS SHINING, I'M UP FOR ANYTHING!
REALLY? I HAVE A FUN IDEA.
PUT THIS SHIRT ON AND STAND OVER THERE.
WHAT IS THIS?
I'LL BE RIGHT BACK. I HAVE TO GO GET SOMETHING.
100
75
50
5 MINUTES LATER...
YOU'RE GETTING ME IN THE FACE!
I'M CALIBRATING THE SIGHT! HOLD STILL!
La Super Doucher!
... AND 5 MINUTES AFTER THAT...
I QUIT! THIS ISN'T FUN AT ALL!
DID YOU THINK I MEANT FUN FOR **YOU**? WOOPS.
darb

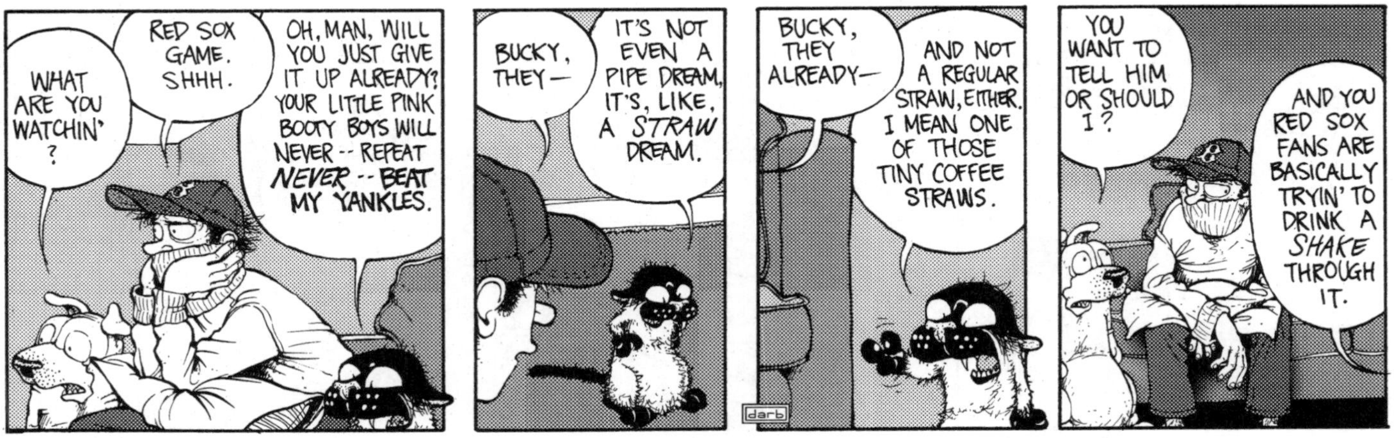
WHAT ARE YOU WATCHIN'?
RED SOX GAME. SHHH.
OH, MAN, WILL YOU JUST GIVE IT UP ALREADY? YOUR LITTLE PINK BOOTY BOYS WILL NEVER -- REPEAT *NEVER* -- BEAT MY YANKLES.
BUCKY, THEY—
IT'S NOT EVEN A PIPE DREAM, IT'S, LIKE, A *STRAW* DREAM.
BUCKY, THEY ALREADY—
AND NOT A REGULAR STRAW, EITHER. I MEAN ONE OF THOSE TINY COFFEE STRAWS.
darb
YOU WANT TO TELL HIM OR SHOULD I?
AND YOU RED SOX FANS ARE BASICALLY TRYIN' TO DRINK A *SHAKE* THROUGH IT.

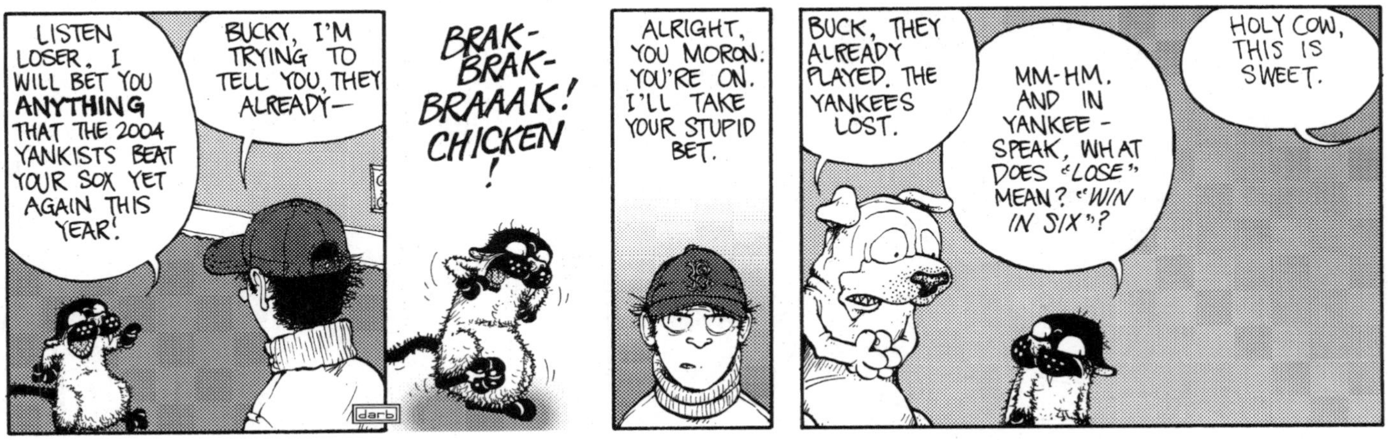
LISTEN LOSER. I WILL BET YOU **ANYTHING** THAT THE 2004 YANKISTS BEAT YOUR SOX YET AGAIN THIS YEAR!
BUCKY, I'M TRYING TO TELL YOU, THEY ALREADY—
darb
BRAK-BRAK-BRAAAK! CHICKEN!
ALRIGHT, YOU MORON. YOU'RE ON. I'LL TAKE YOUR STUPID BET.
BUCK, THEY ALREADY PLAYED. THE YANKEES LOST.
MM-HM. AND IN YANKEE-SPEAK, WHAT DOES "*LOSE*" MEAN? "*WIN IN SIX*"?
HOLY COW, THIS IS SWEET.

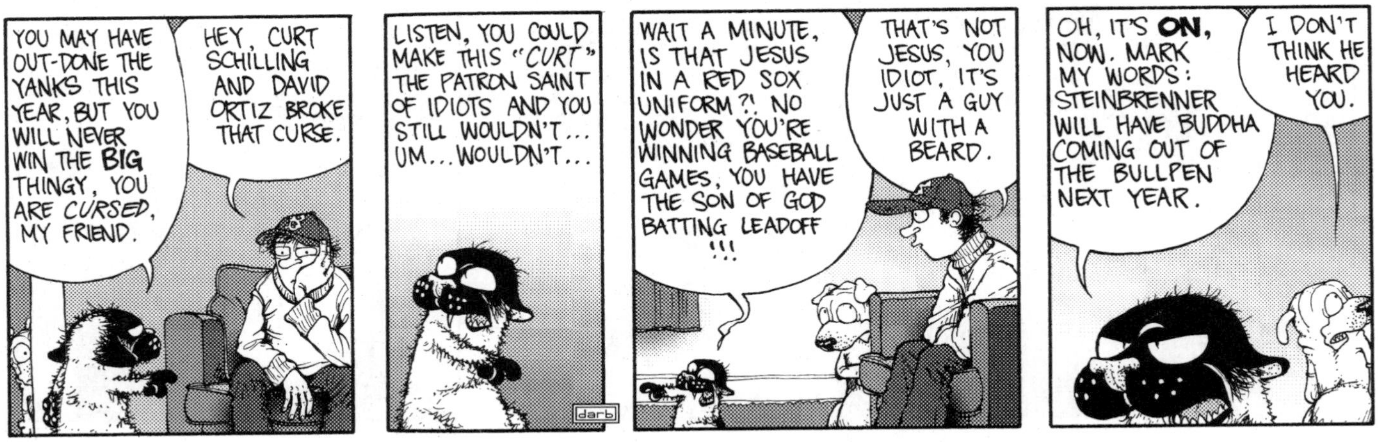
YOU MAY HAVE OUT-DONE THE YANKS THIS YEAR, BUT YOU WILL NEVER WIN THE **BIG** THINGY, YOU ARE *CURSED*, MY FRIEND.
HEY, CURT SCHILLING AND DAVID ORTIZ BROKE THAT CURSE.
LISTEN, YOU COULD MAKE THIS "*CURT*" THE PATRON SAINT OF IDIOTS AND YOU STILL WOULDN'T... UM... WOULDN'T...
darb
WAIT A MINUTE, IS THAT JESUS IN A RED SOX UNIFORM?! NO WONDER YOU'RE WINNING BASEBALL GAMES, YOU HAVE THE SON OF GOD BATTING LEADOFF!!!
THAT'S NOT JESUS, YOU IDIOT, IT'S JUST A GUY WITH A BEARD.
OH, IT'S **ON**, NOW. MARK MY WORDS: STEINBRENNER WILL HAVE BUDDHA COMING OUT OF THE BULLPEN NEXT YEAR.
I DON'T THINK HE HEARD YOU.

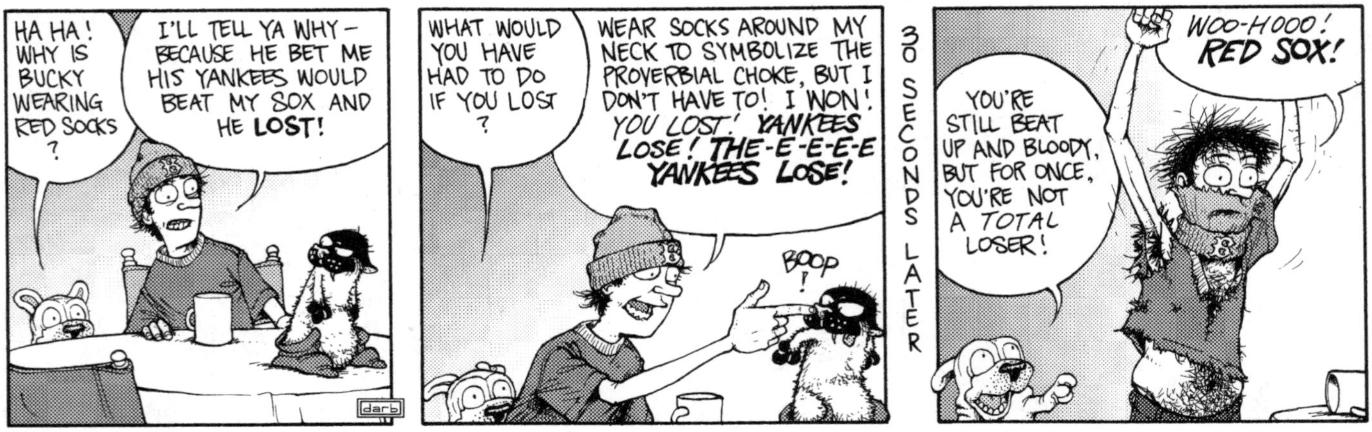
HA HA! WHY IS BUCKY WEARING RED SOCKS?
I'LL TELL YA WHY– BECAUSE HE BET ME HIS YANKEES WOULD BEAT MY SOX AND HE **LOST**!
WHAT WOULD YOU HAVE HAD TO DO IF YOU LOST?
WEAR SOCKS AROUND MY NECK TO SYMBOLIZE THE PROVERBIAL CHOKE, BUT I DON'T HAVE TO! I WON! *YOU LOST!* ***YANKEES LOSE! THE-E-E-E-E YANKEES LOSE!***
BOOP!
30 SECONDS LATER
WOO-HOOO! **RED SOX!**
YOU'RE STILL BEAT UP AND BLOODY, BUT FOR ONCE, YOU'RE NOT A *TOTAL* LOSER!
darb

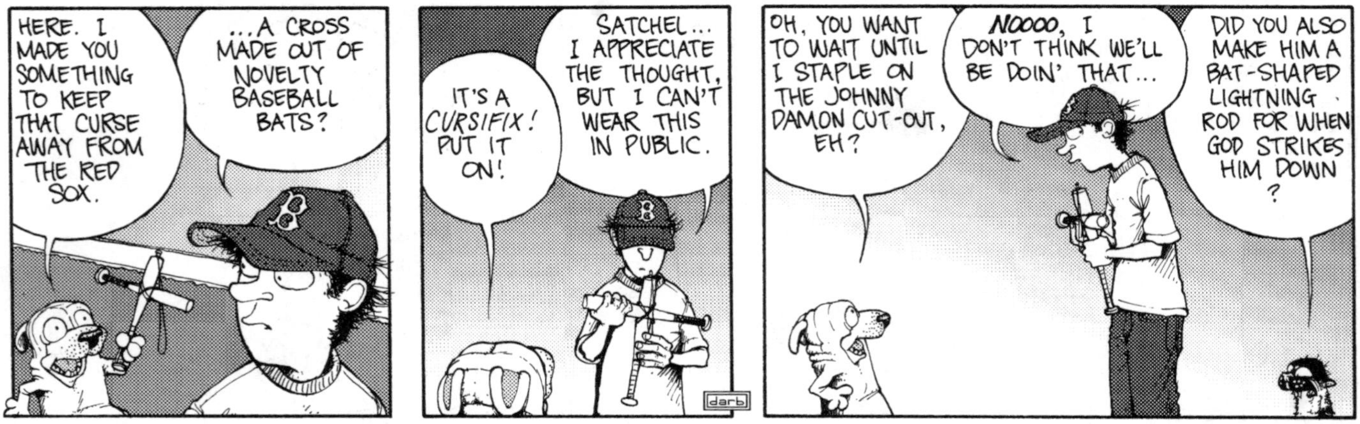
HERE. I MADE YOU SOMETHING TO KEEP THAT CURSE AWAY FROM THE RED SOX.
...A CROSS MADE OUT OF NOVELTY BASEBALL BATS?
IT'S A *CURSIFIX!* PUT IT ON!
SATCHEL... I APPRECIATE THE THOUGHT, BUT I CAN'T WEAR THIS IN PUBLIC.
darb
OH, YOU WANT TO WAIT UNTIL I STAPLE ON THE JOHNNY DAMON CUT-OUT, EH?
NOOOO, I DON'T THINK WE'LL BE DOIN' THAT...
DID YOU ALSO MAKE HIM A BAT-SHAPED LIGHTNING ROD FOR WHEN GOD STRIKES HIM DOWN?

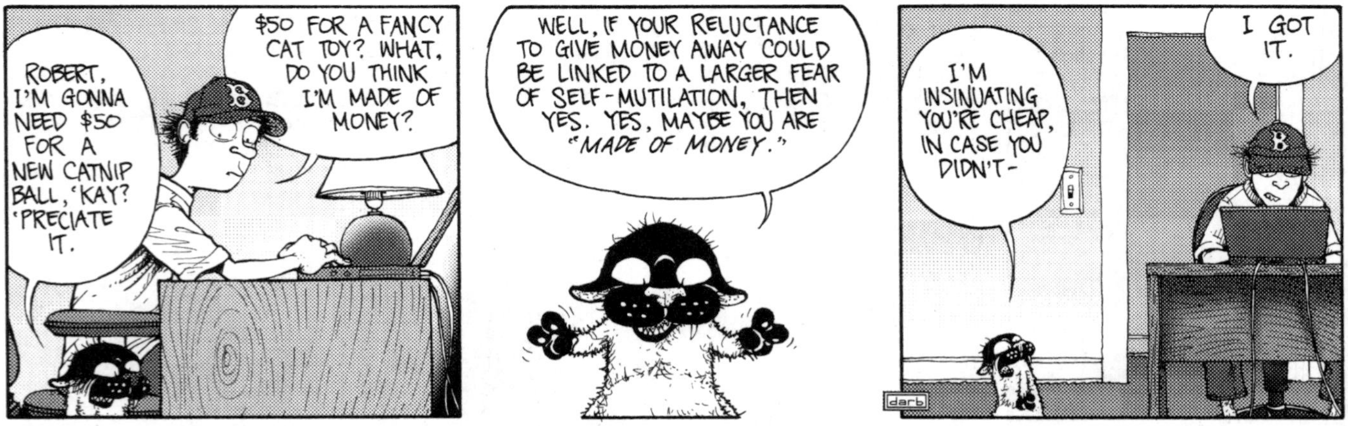
ROBERT, I'M GONNA NEED $50 FOR A NEW CATNIP BALL, 'KAY? 'PRECIATE IT.
$50 FOR A FANCY CAT TOY? WHAT, DO YOU THINK I'M MADE OF MONEY?
WELL, IF YOUR RELUCTANCE TO GIVE MONEY AWAY COULD BE LINKED TO A LARGER FEAR OF SELF-MUTILATION, THEN YES. YES, MAYBE YOU ARE *"MADE OF MONEY."*
I'M INSINUATING YOU'RE CHEAP, IN CASE YOU DIDN'T–
I GOT IT.
darb

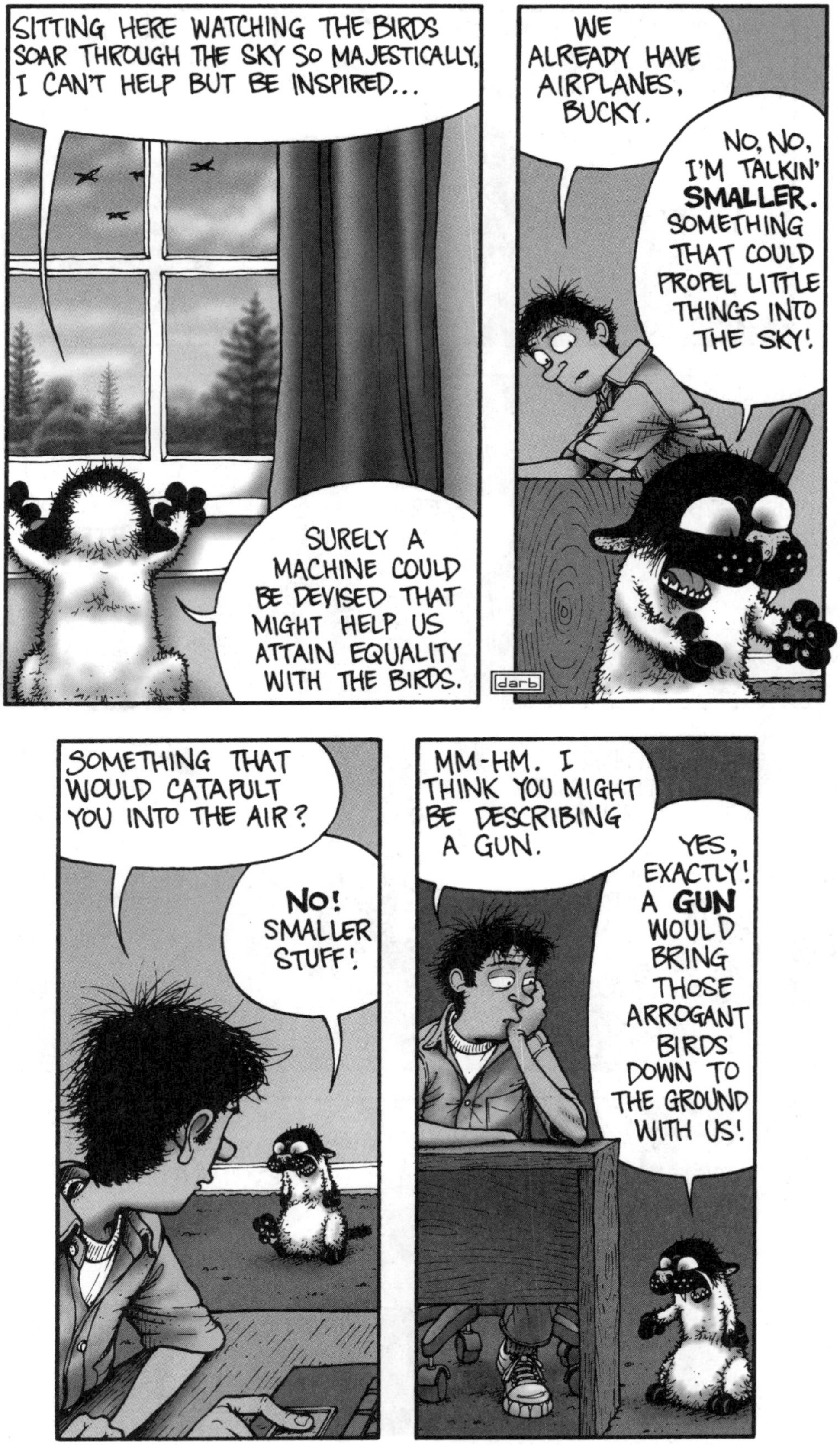
SITTING HERE WATCHING THE BIRDS SOAR THROUGH THE SKY SO MAJESTICALLY, I CAN'T HELP BUT BE INSPIRED...
SURELY A MACHINE COULD BE DEVISED THAT MIGHT HELP US ATTAIN EQUALITY WITH THE BIRDS.
WE ALREADY HAVE AIRPLANES, BUCKY.
NO, NO, I'M TALKIN' **SMALLER**. SOMETHING THAT COULD PROPEL LITTLE THINGS INTO THE SKY!
darb
SOMETHING THAT WOULD CATAPULT YOU INTO THE AIR?
NO! SMALLER STUFF!
MM-HM. I THINK YOU MIGHT BE DESCRIBING A GUN.
YES, EXACTLY! A **GUN** WOULD BRING THOSE ARROGANT BIRDS DOWN TO THE GROUND WITH US!

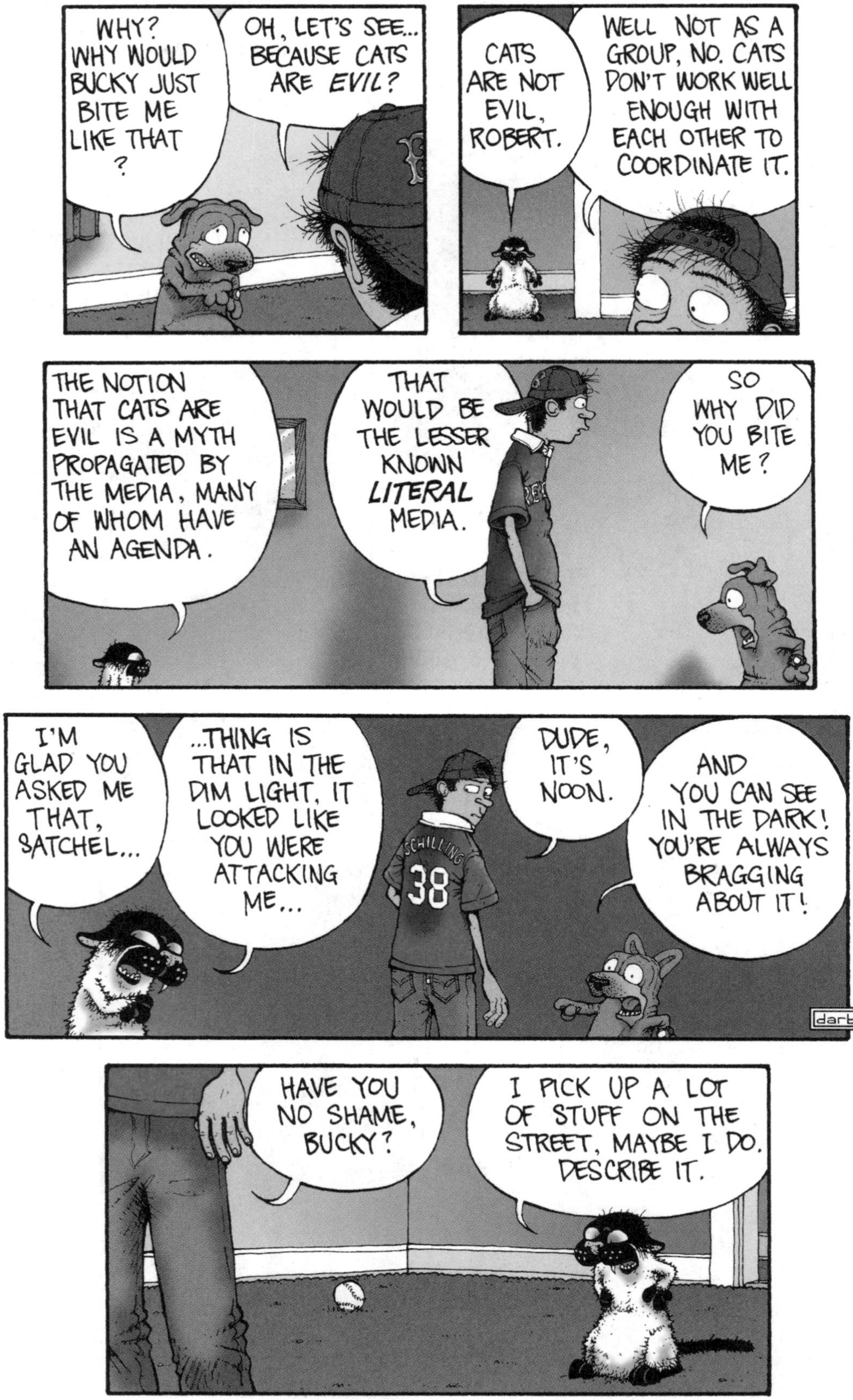
WHY? WHY WOULD BUCKY JUST BITE ME LIKE THAT ?
OH, LET'S SEE... BECAUSE CATS ARE *EVIL*?
CATS ARE NOT EVIL, ROBERT.
WELL NOT AS A GROUP, NO. CATS DON'T WORK WELL ENOUGH WITH EACH OTHER TO COORDINATE IT.
THE NOTION THAT CATS ARE EVIL IS A MYTH PROPAGATED BY THE MEDIA, MANY OF WHOM HAVE AN AGENDA.
THAT WOULD BE THE LESSER KNOWN ***LITERAL*** MEDIA.
SO WHY DID YOU BITE ME?
I'M GLAD YOU ASKED ME THAT, SATCHEL...
...THING IS THAT IN THE DIM LIGHT, IT LOOKED LIKE YOU WERE ATTACKING ME...
SCHILLING
38
DUDE, IT'S NOON.
AND YOU CAN SEE IN THE DARK! YOU'RE ALWAYS BRAGGING ABOUT IT!
darb
HAVE YOU NO SHAME, BUCKY?
I PICK UP A LOT OF STUFF ON THE STREET, MAYBE I DO. DESCRIBE IT.

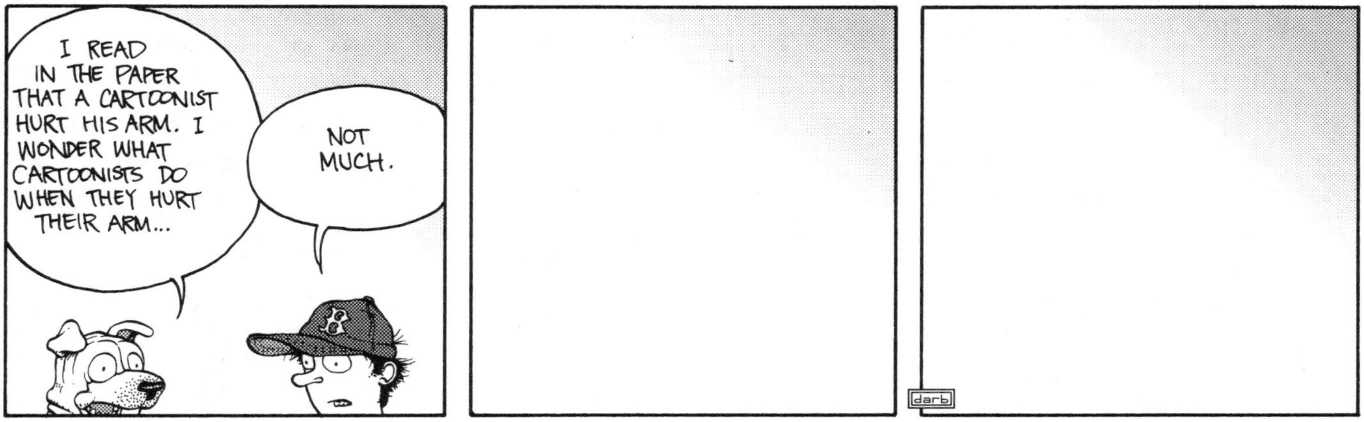
I READ IN THE PAPER THAT A CARTOONIST HURT HIS ARM. I WONDER WHAT CARTOONISTS DO WHEN THEY HURT THEIR ARM...
NOT MUCH.
darb

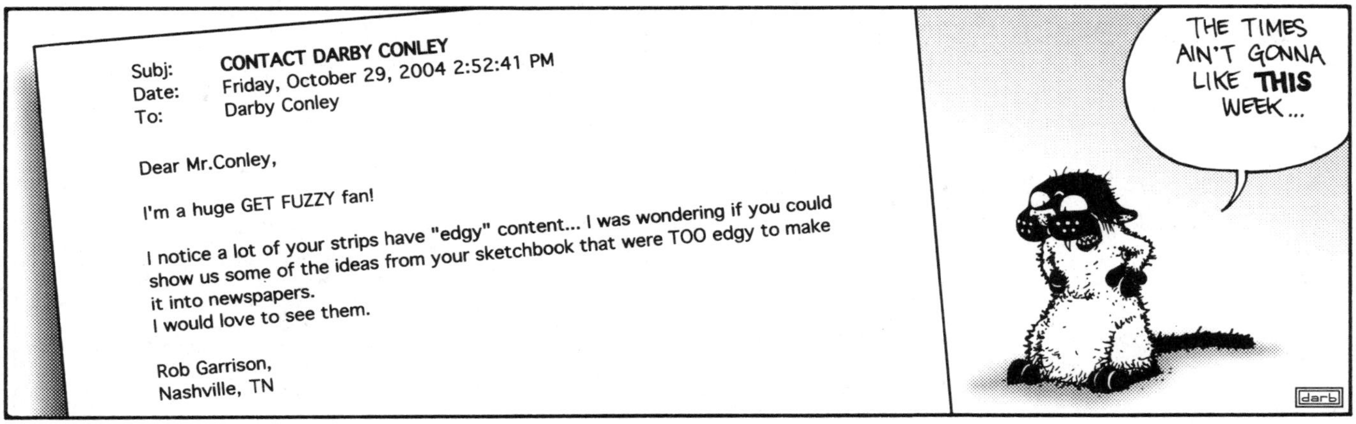
Subj: CONTACT DARBY CONLEY
Date: Friday, October 29, 2004 2:52:41 PM
To: Darby Conley
Dear Mr.Conley,
I'm a huge GET FUZZY fan!
I notice a lot of your strips have "edgy" content... I was wondering if you could show us some of the ideas from your sketchbook that were TOO edgy to make it into newspapers.
I would love to see them.
Rob Garrison,
Nashville, TN
THE TIMES AIN'T GONNA LIKE **THIS** WEEK...
darb

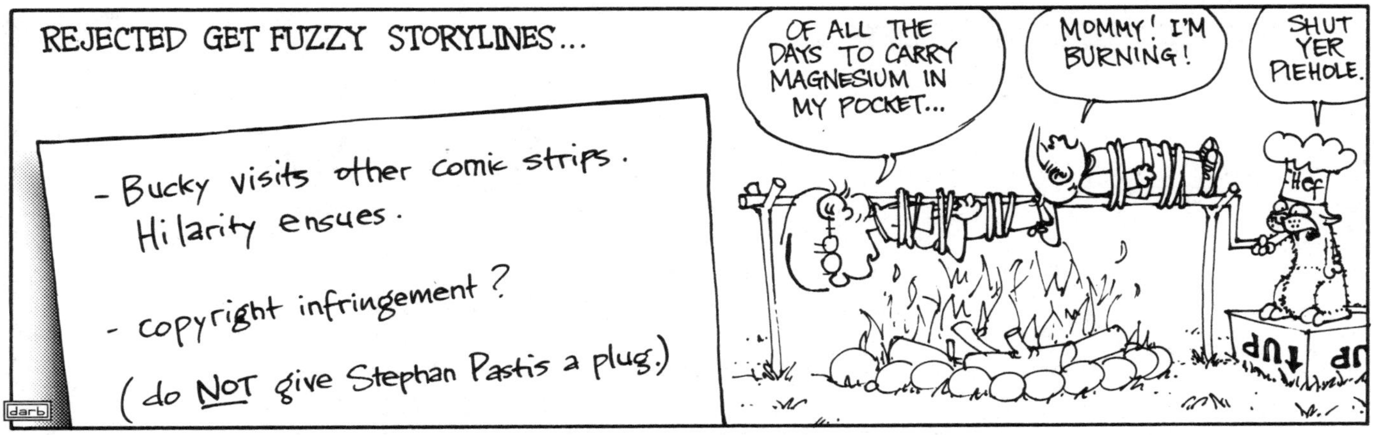
REJECTED GET FUZZY STORYLINES...
- Bucky visits other comic strips. Hilarity ensues.
- copyright infringement?
(do NOT give Stephan Pastis a plug.)
OF ALL THE DAYS TO CARRY MAGNESIUM IN MY POCKET...
MOMMY! I'M BURNING!
SHUT YER PIEHOLE.
Chef
UP
UP
darb

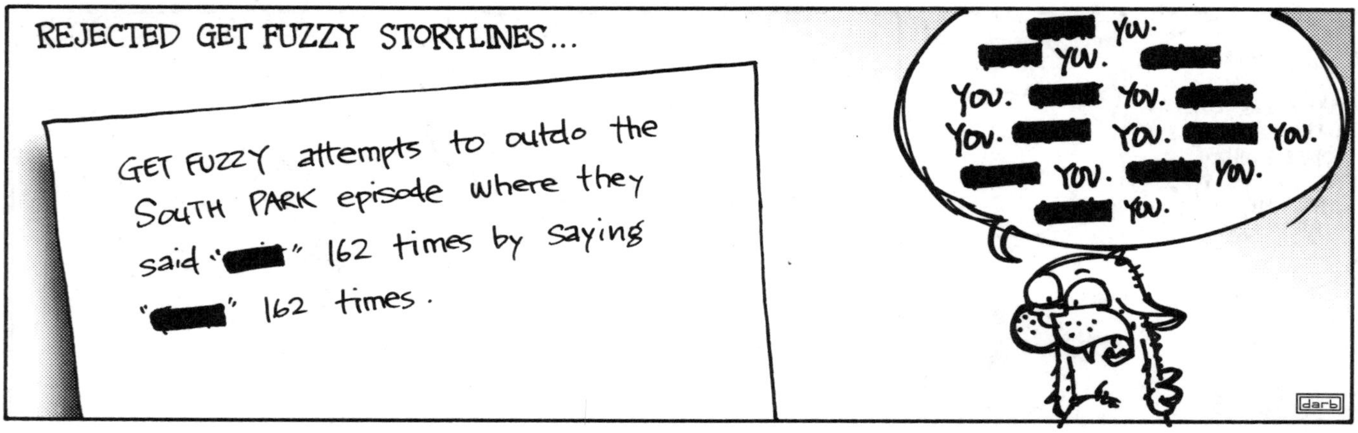
REJECTED GET FUZZY STORYLINES...
GET FUZZY attempts to outdo the SOUTH PARK episode where they said "[redacted]" 162 times by saying "[redacted]" 162 times.
[redacted] YOU. [redacted] YOU. [redacted] YOU. [redacted] YOU. [redacted] YOU. [redacted] YOU. [redacted] YOU. [redacted] YOU. [redacted] YOU. [redacted] YOU.
darb

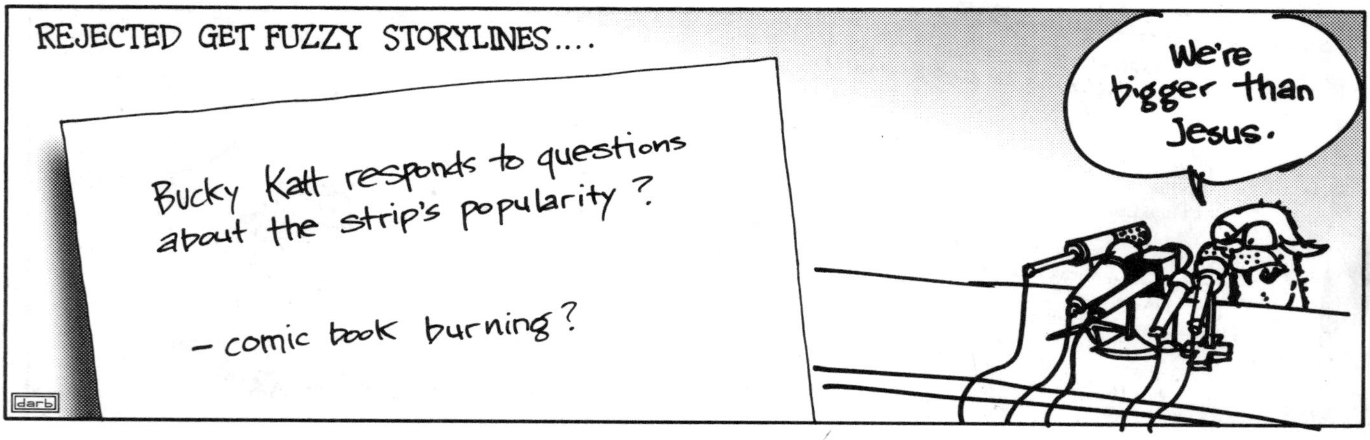
REJECTED GET FUZZY STORYLINES....
Bucky Katt responds to questions about the strip's popularity?
- comic book burning?
We're bigger than Jesus.
darb

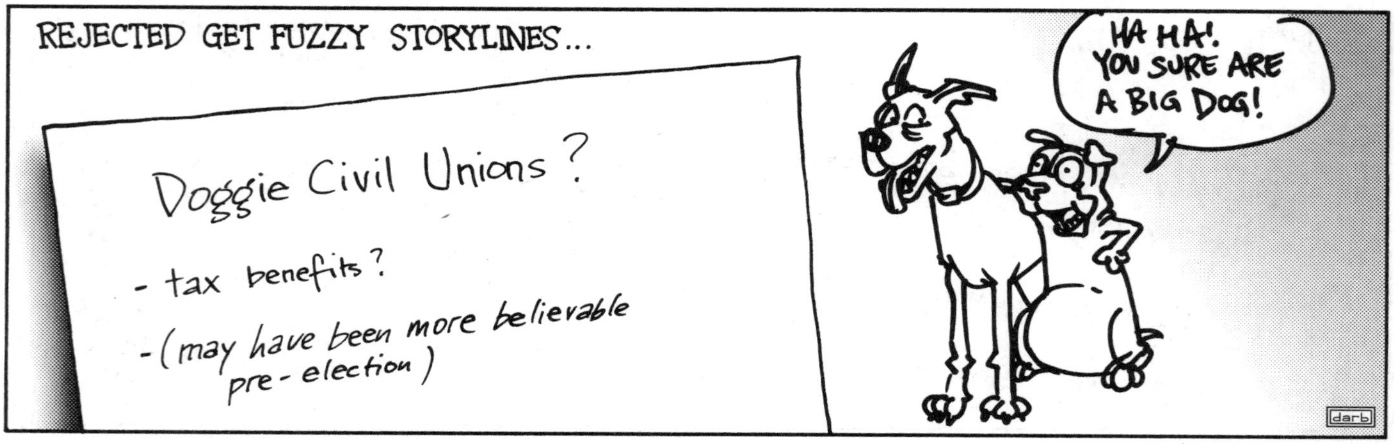
REJECTED GET FUZZY STORYLINES...
Doggie Civil Unions?
- tax benefits?
- (may have been more believable pre-election)
HA HA! YOU SURE ARE A BIG DOG!
darb

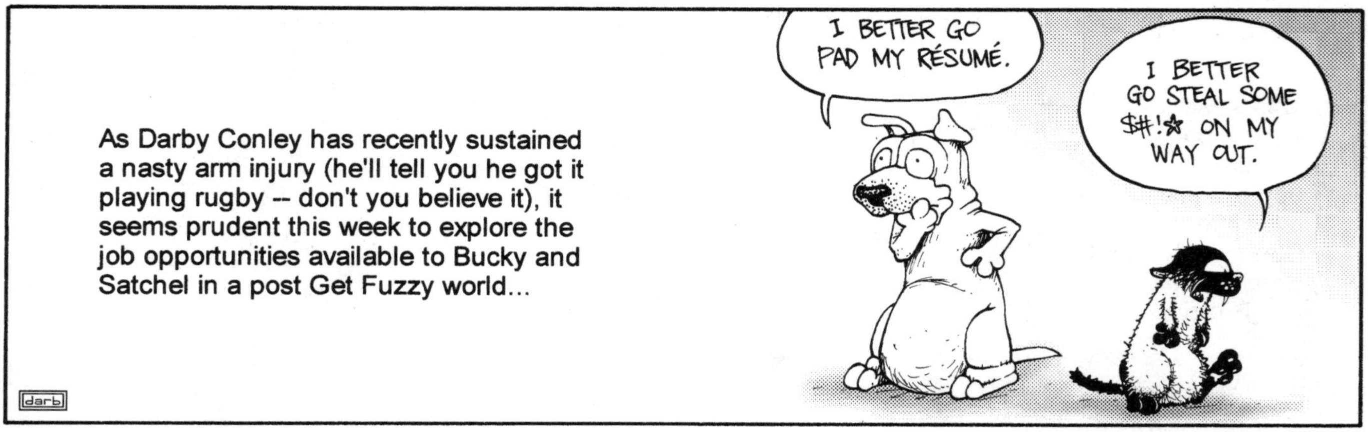
As Darby Conley has recently sustained a nasty arm injury (he'll tell you he got it playing rugby -- don't you believe it), it seems prudent this week to explore the job opportunities available to Bucky and Satchel in a post Get Fuzzy world...
I BETTER GO PAD MY RÉSUMÉ.
I BETTER GO STEAL SOME $#!☆ ON MY WAY OUT.
darb

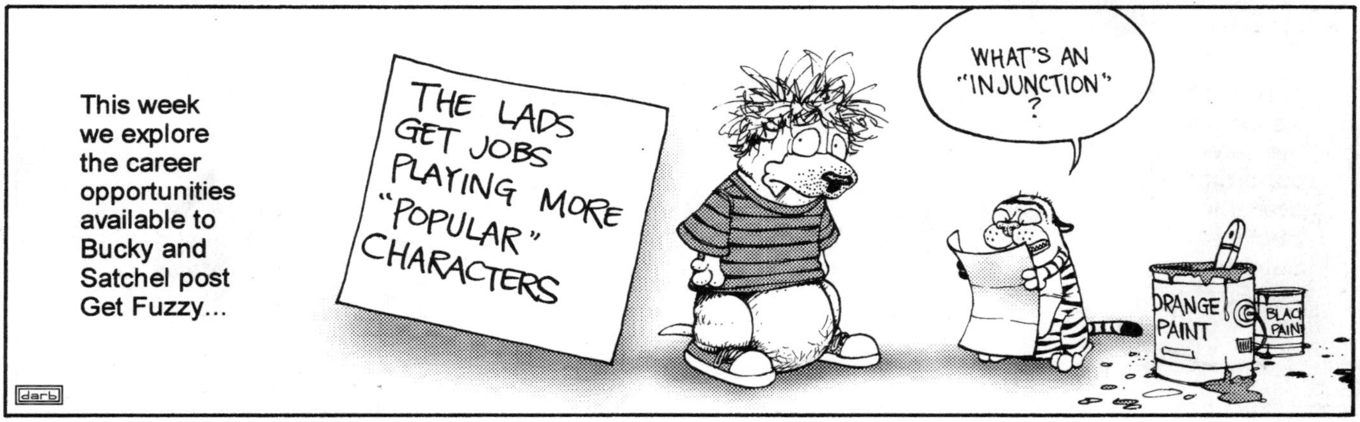
This week we explore the career opportunities available to Bucky and Satchel post Get Fuzzy...
THE LADS GET JOBS PLAYING MORE "POPULAR" CHARACTERS
WHAT'S AN "INJUNCTION"?
ORANGE PAINT
darb

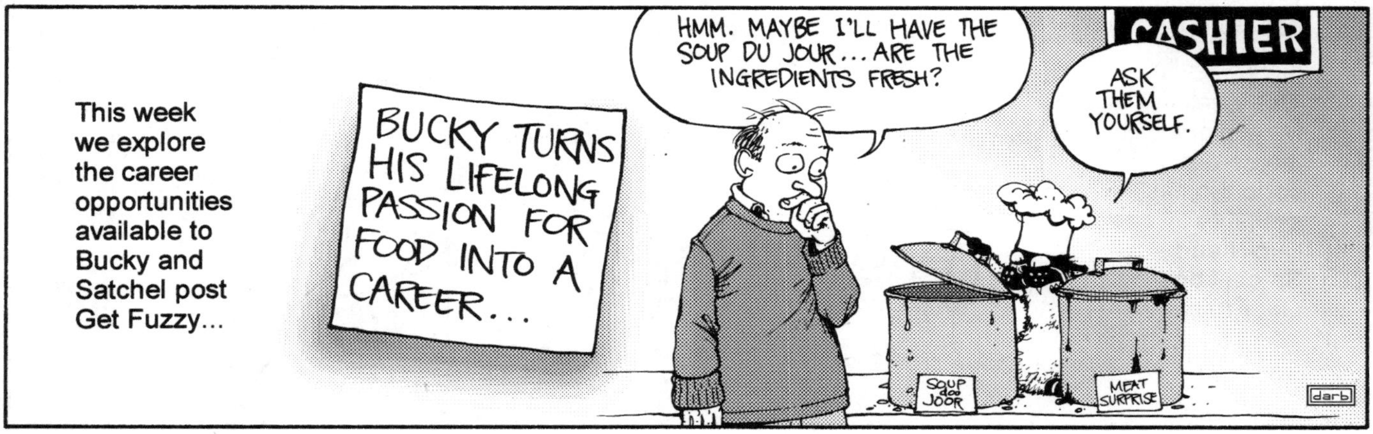
This week we explore the career opportunities available to Bucky and Satchel post Get Fuzzy...
BUCKY TURNS HIS LIFELONG PASSION FOR FOOD INTO A CAREER...
CASHIER
HMM. MAYBE I'LL HAVE THE SOUP DU JOUR... ARE THE INGREDIENTS FRESH?
ASK THEM YOURSELF.
SOUP doo JOOR
MEAT SURPRISE
darb

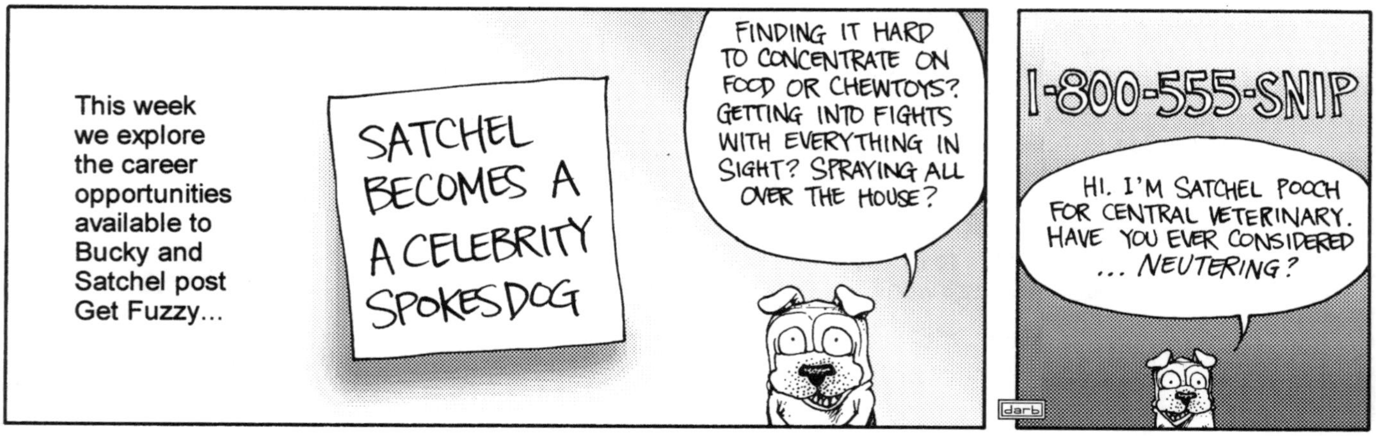
This week we explore the career opportunities available to Bucky and Satchel post Get Fuzzy...
SATCHEL BECOMES A A CELEBRITY SPOKESDOG
FINDING IT HARD TO CONCENTRATE ON FOOD OR CHEWTOYS? GETTING INTO FIGHTS WITH EVERYTHING IN SIGHT? SPRAYING ALL OVER THE HOUSE?
1-800-555-SNIP
HI. I'M SATCHEL POOCH FOR CENTRAL VETERINARY. HAVE YOU EVER CONSIDERED ... NEUTERING?
darb

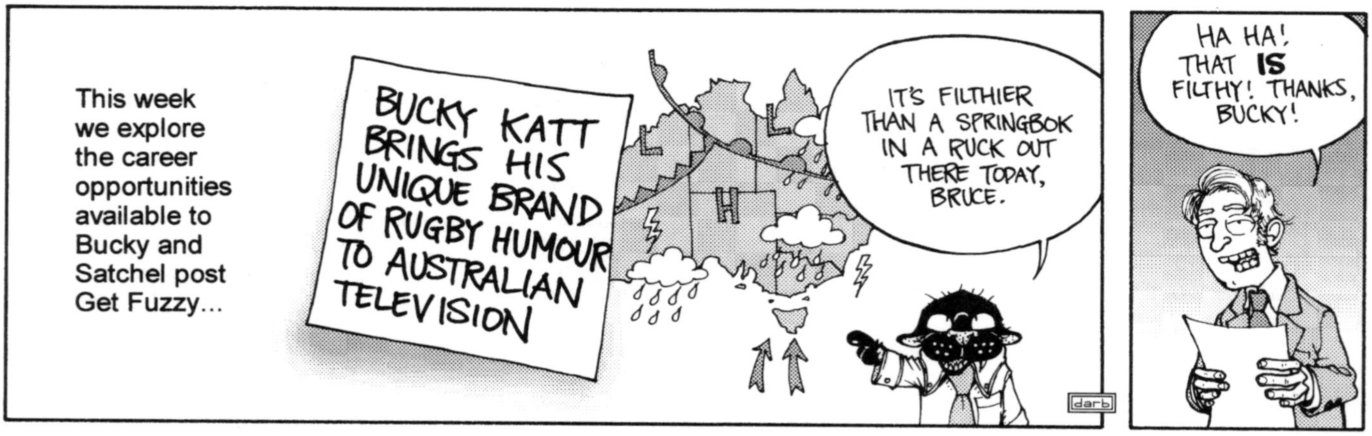
This week we explore the career opportunities available to Bucky and Satchel post Get Fuzzy...
BUCKY KATT BRINGS HIS UNIQUE BRAND OF RUGBY HUMOUR TO AUSTRALIAN TELEVISION
IT'S FILTHIER THAN A SPRINGBOK IN A RUCK OUT THERE TODAY, BRUCE.
HA HA! THAT **IS** FILTHY! THANKS, BUCKY!
darb

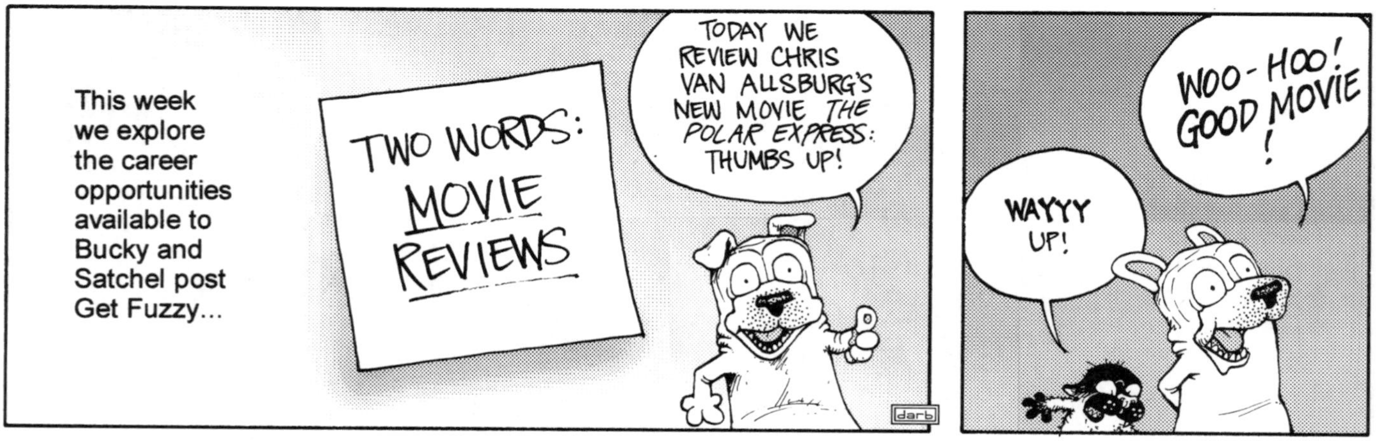
This week we explore the career opportunities available to Bucky and Satchel post Get Fuzzy...
TWO WORDS: MOVIE REVIEWS
TODAY WE REVIEW CHRIS VAN ALLSBURG'S NEW MOVIE *THE POLAR EXPRESS*: THUMBS UP!
WOO-HOO! GOOD MOVIE!
WAYYY UP!
darb

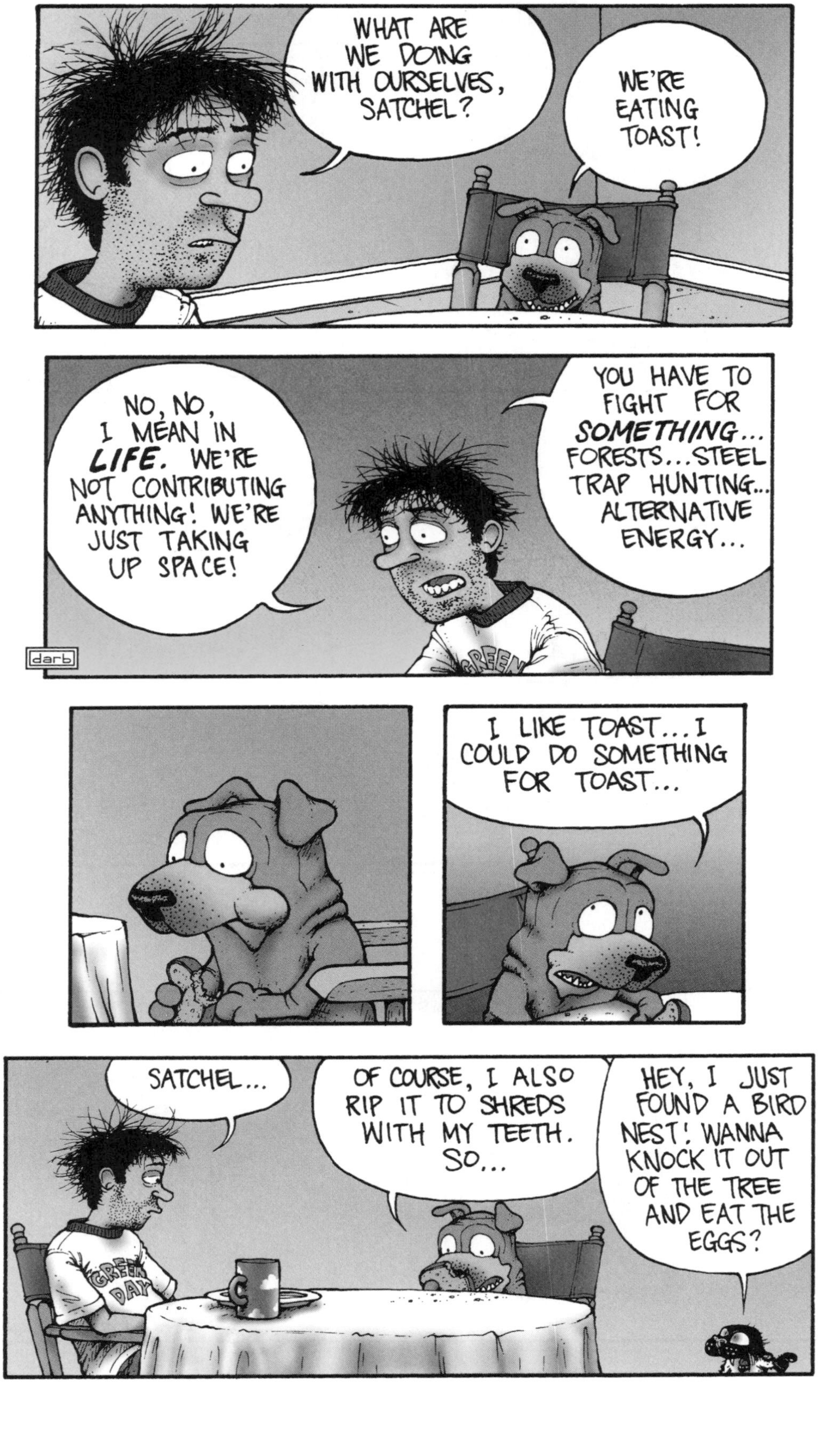
WHAT ARE WE DOING WITH OURSELVES, SATCHEL?
WE'RE EATING TOAST!
NO, NO, I MEAN IN LIFE. WE'RE NOT CONTRIBUTING ANYTHING! WE'RE JUST TAKING UP SPACE!
YOU HAVE TO FIGHT FOR SOMETHING... FORESTS...STEEL TRAP HUNTING... ALTERNATIVE ENERGY...
I LIKE TOAST... I COULD DO SOMETHING FOR TOAST...
SATCHEL...
OF COURSE, I ALSO RIP IT TO SHREDS WITH MY TEETH. SO...
HEY, I JUST FOUND A BIRD NEST! WANNA KNOCK IT OUT OF THE TREE AND EAT THE EGGS?

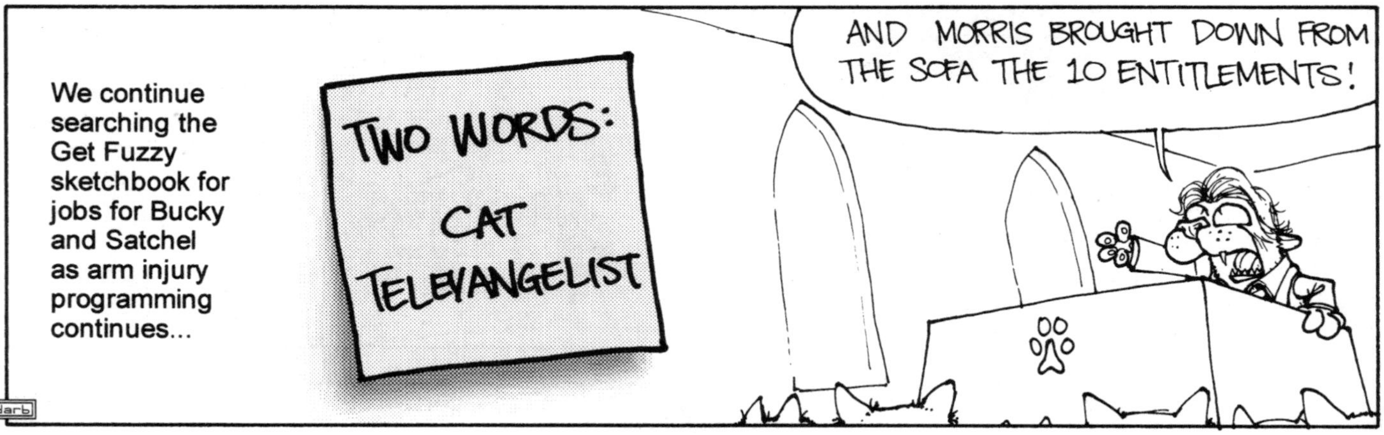
We continue searching the Get Fuzzy sketchbook for jobs for Bucky and Satchel as arm injury programming continues...
TWO WORDS: CAT TELEVANGELIST
AND MORRIS BROUGHT DOWN FROM THE SOFA THE 10 ENTITLEMENTS!
darb

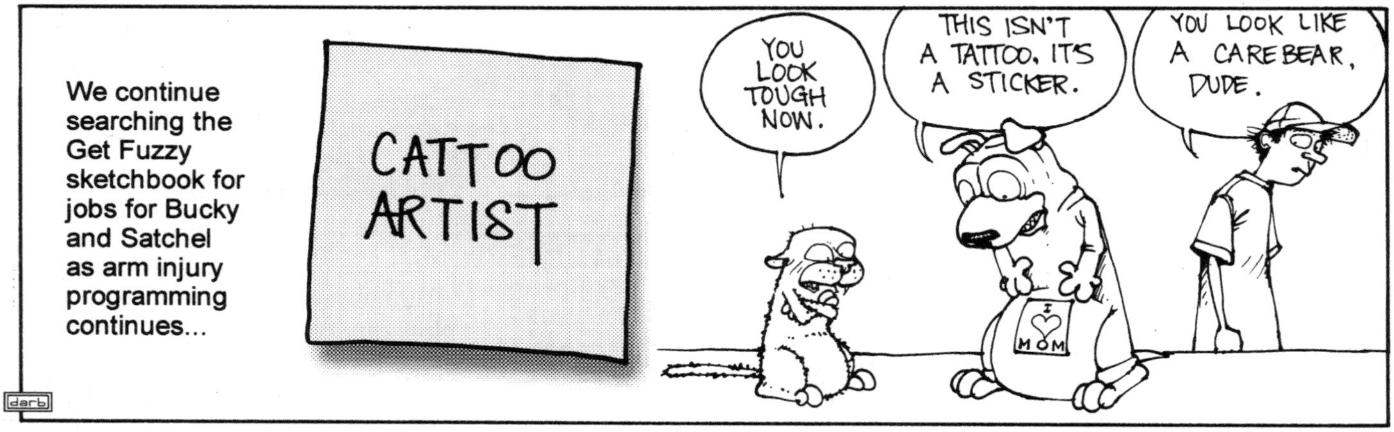
We continue searching the Get Fuzzy sketchbook for jobs for Bucky and Satchel as arm injury programming continues...
CATTOO ARTIST
YOU LOOK TOUGH NOW.
THIS ISN'T A TATTOO, IT'S A STICKER.
YOU LOOK LIKE A CAREBEAR, DUDE.
I ♥ MOM
darb

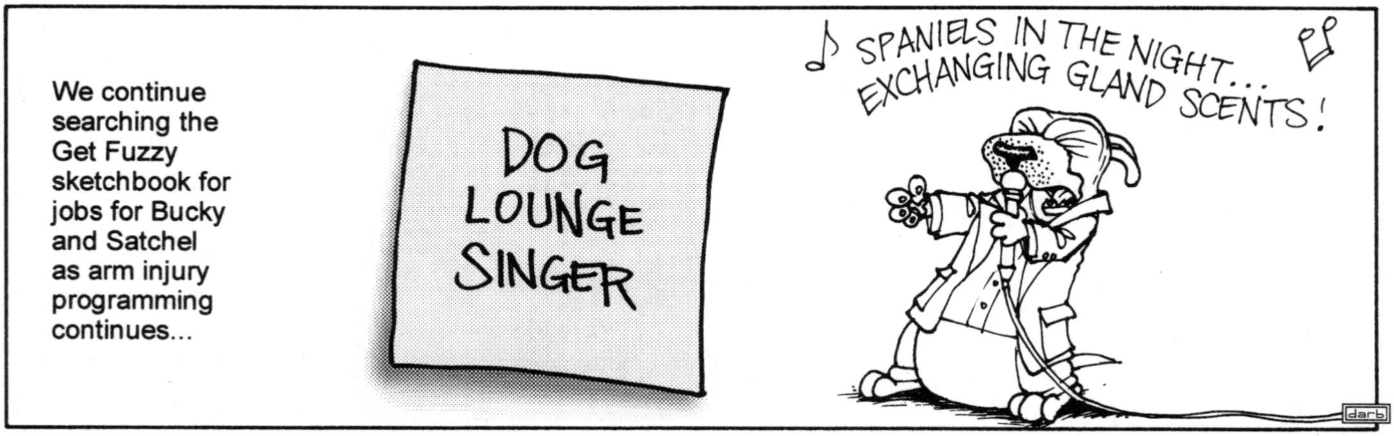
We continue searching the Get Fuzzy sketchbook for jobs for Bucky and Satchel as arm injury programming continues...
DOG LOUNGE SINGER
SPANIELS IN THE NIGHT... EXCHANGING GLAND SCENTS!
darb

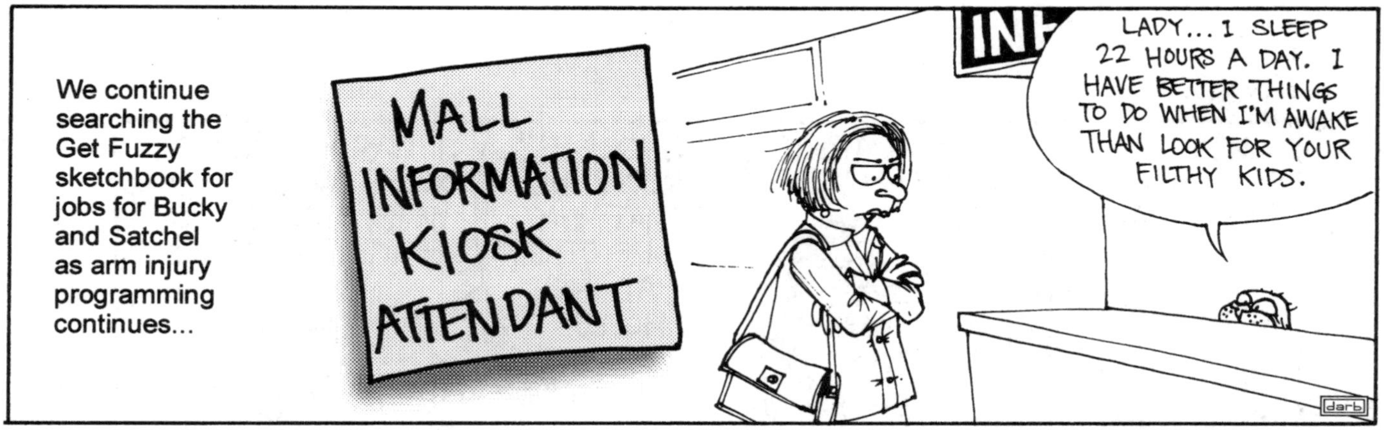
We continue searching the Get Fuzzy sketchbook for jobs for Bucky and Satchel as arm injury programming continues...
MALL INFORMATION KIOSK ATTENDANT
LADY... I SLEEP 22 HOURS A DAY. I HAVE BETTER THINGS TO DO WHEN I'M AWAKE THAN LOOK FOR YOUR FILTHY KIDS.
darb

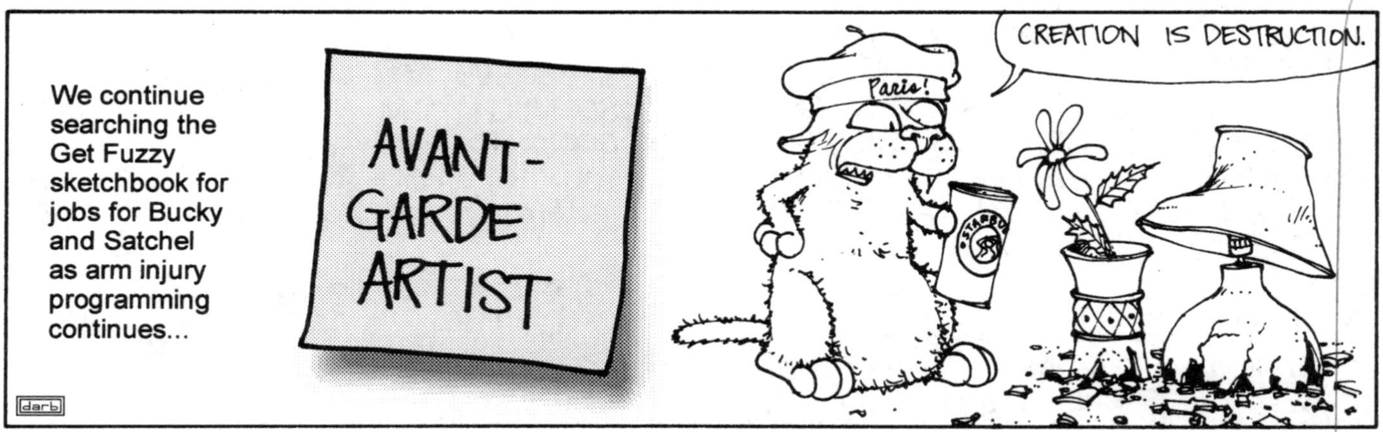
We continue searching the Get Fuzzy sketchbook for jobs for Bucky and Satchel as arm injury programming continues...
AVANT-GARDE ARTIST
Paris!
CREATION IS DESTRUCTION.
darb

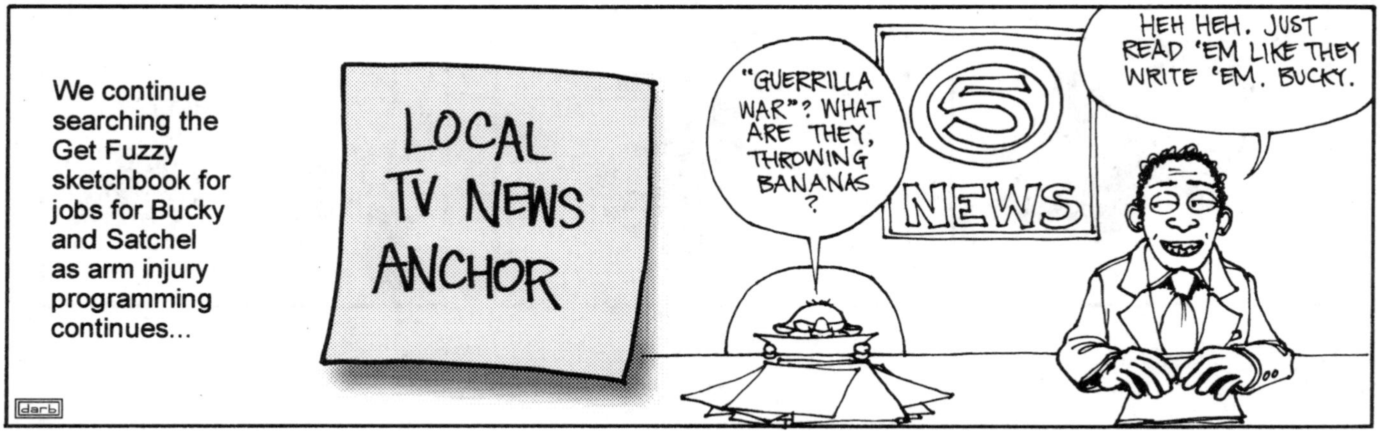
We continue searching the Get Fuzzy sketchbook for jobs for Bucky and Satchel as arm injury programming continues...
LOCAL TV NEWS ANCHOR
"GUERRILLA WAR"? WHAT ARE THEY, THROWING BANANAS?
5 NEWS
HEH HEH. JUST READ 'EM LIKE THEY WRITE 'EM, BUCKY.
darb

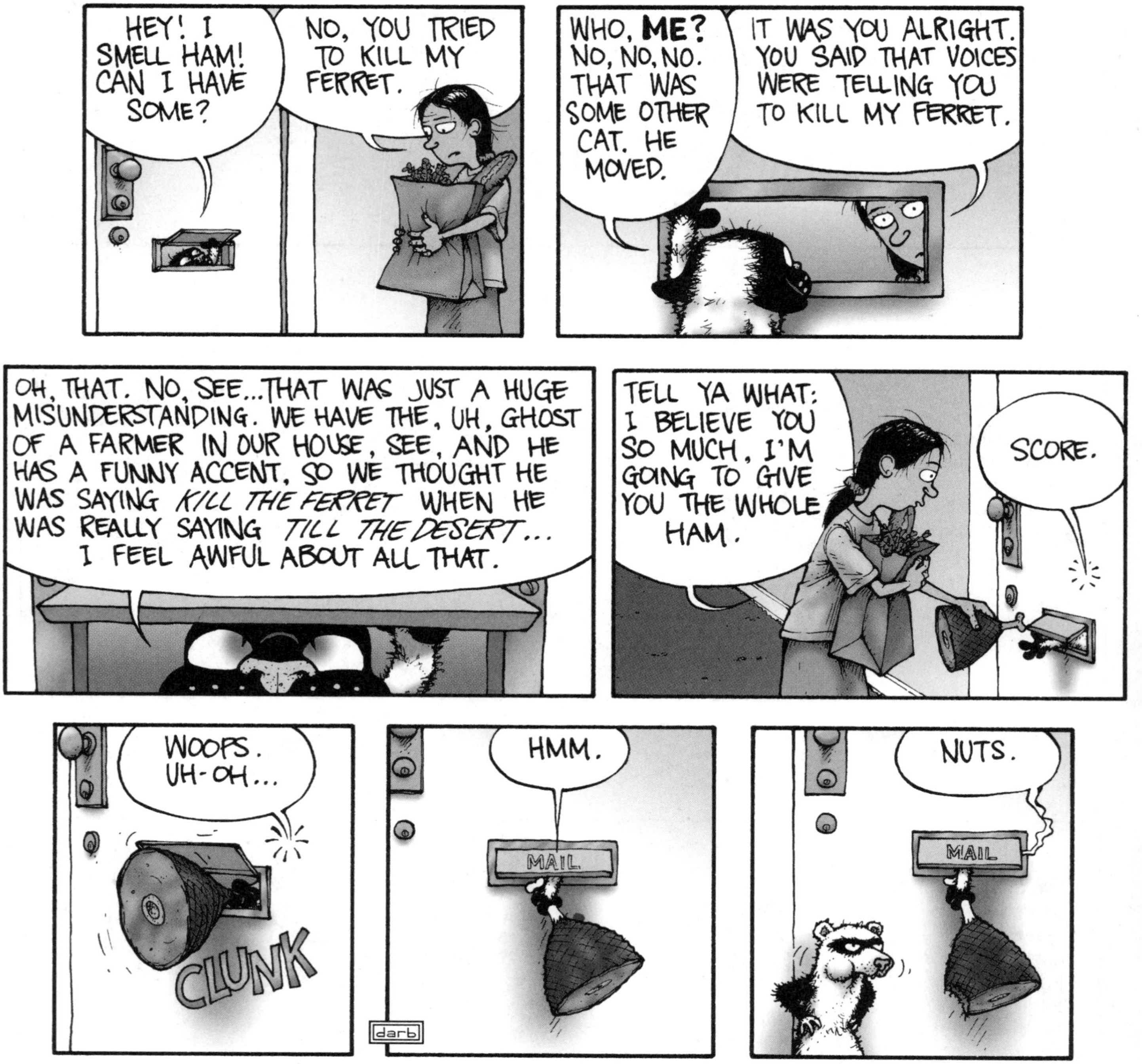
HEY! I SMELL HAM! CAN I HAVE SOME?
NO, YOU TRIED TO KILL MY FERRET.
WHO, **ME?** NO, NO, NO. THAT WAS SOME OTHER CAT. HE MOVED.
IT WAS YOU ALRIGHT. YOU SAID THAT VOICES WERE TELLING YOU TO KILL MY FERRET.
OH, THAT. NO, SEE...THAT WAS JUST A HUGE MISUNDERSTANDING. WE HAVE THE, UH, GHOST OF A FARMER IN OUR HOUSE, SEE, AND HE HAS A FUNNY ACCENT, SO WE THOUGHT HE WAS SAYING *KILL THE FERRET* WHEN HE WAS REALLY SAYING *TILL THE DESERT...* I FEEL AWFUL ABOUT ALL THAT.
TELL YA WHAT: I BELIEVE YOU SO MUCH, I'M GOING TO GIVE YOU THE WHOLE HAM.
SCORE.
WOOPS. UH-OH...
CLUNK
HMM.
MAIL
darb
NUTS.
MAIL

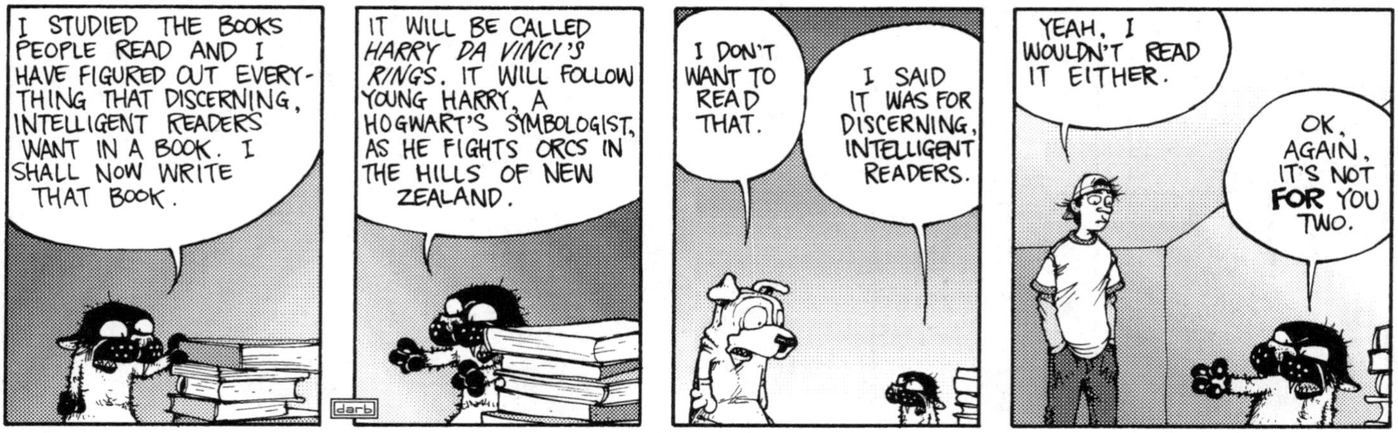
I STUDIED THE BOOKS PEOPLE READ AND I HAVE FIGURED OUT EVERYTHING THAT DISCERNING, INTELLIGENT READERS WANT IN A BOOK. I SHALL NOW WRITE THAT BOOK.
IT WILL BE CALLED *HARRY DA VINCI'S RINGS*. IT WILL FOLLOW YOUNG HARRY, A HOGWART'S SYMBOLOGIST, AS HE FIGHTS ORCS IN THE HILLS OF NEW ZEALAND.
darb
I DON'T WANT TO READ THAT.
I SAID IT WAS FOR DISCERNING, INTELLIGENT READERS.
YEAH, I WOULDN'T READ IT EITHER.
OK. AGAIN, IT'S NOT **FOR** YOU TWO.

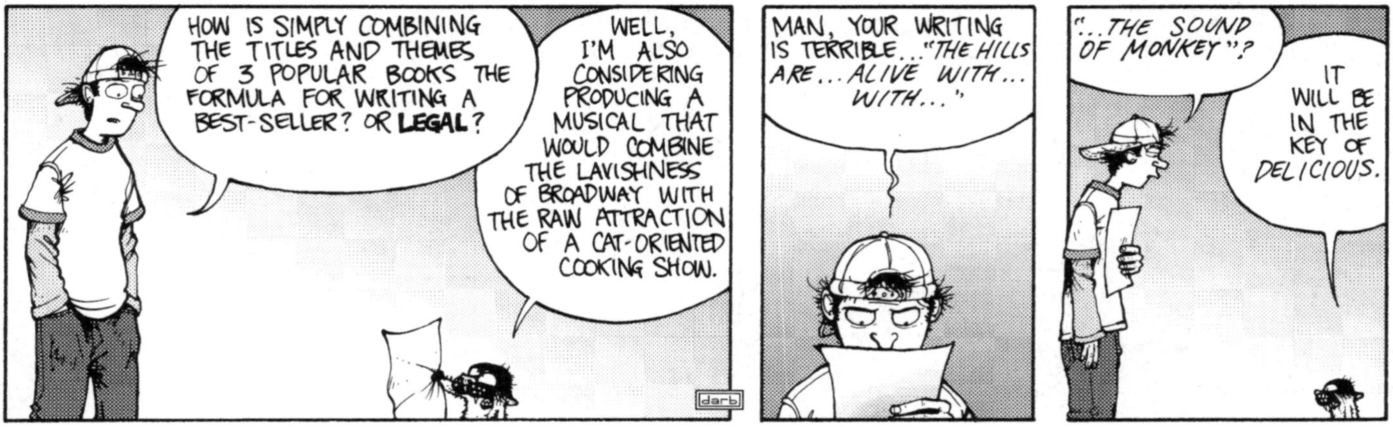
HOW IS SIMPLY COMBINING THE TITLES AND THEMES OF 3 POPULAR BOOKS THE FORMULA FOR WRITING A BEST-SELLER? OR **LEGAL**?
WELL, I'M ALSO CONSIDERING PRODUCING A MUSICAL THAT WOULD COMBINE THE LAVISHNESS OF BROADWAY WITH THE RAW ATTRACTION OF A CAT-ORIENTED COOKING SHOW.
darb
MAN, YOUR WRITING IS TERRIBLE... *"THE HILLS ARE... ALIVE WITH... WITH..."*
"...THE SOUND OF MONKEY"?
IT WILL BE IN THE KEY OF *DELICIOUS*.

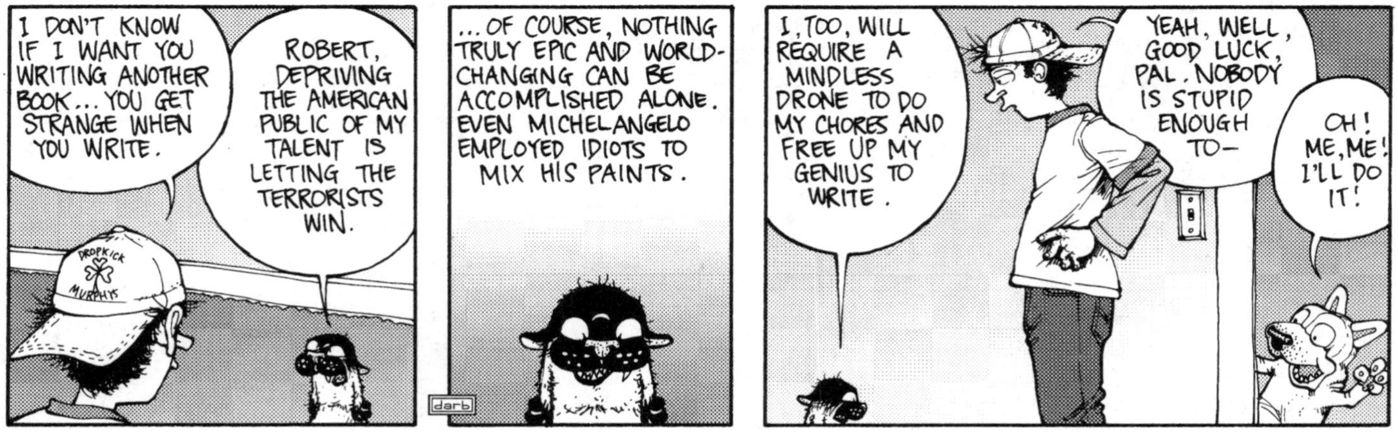
I DON'T KNOW IF I WANT YOU WRITING ANOTHER BOOK... YOU GET STRANGE WHEN YOU WRITE.
ROBERT, DEPRIVING THE AMERICAN PUBLIC OF MY TALENT IS LETTING THE TERRORISTS WIN.
DROPKICK MURPHYS
darb
...OF COURSE, NOTHING TRULY EPIC AND WORLD-CHANGING CAN BE ACCOMPLISHED ALONE. EVEN MICHELANGELO EMPLOYED IDIOTS TO MIX HIS PAINTS.
I, TOO, WILL REQUIRE A MINDLESS DRONE TO DO MY CHORES AND FREE UP MY GENIUS TO WRITE.
YEAH, WELL, GOOD LUCK, PAL. NOBODY IS STUPID ENOUGH TO—
OH! ME, ME! I'LL DO IT!

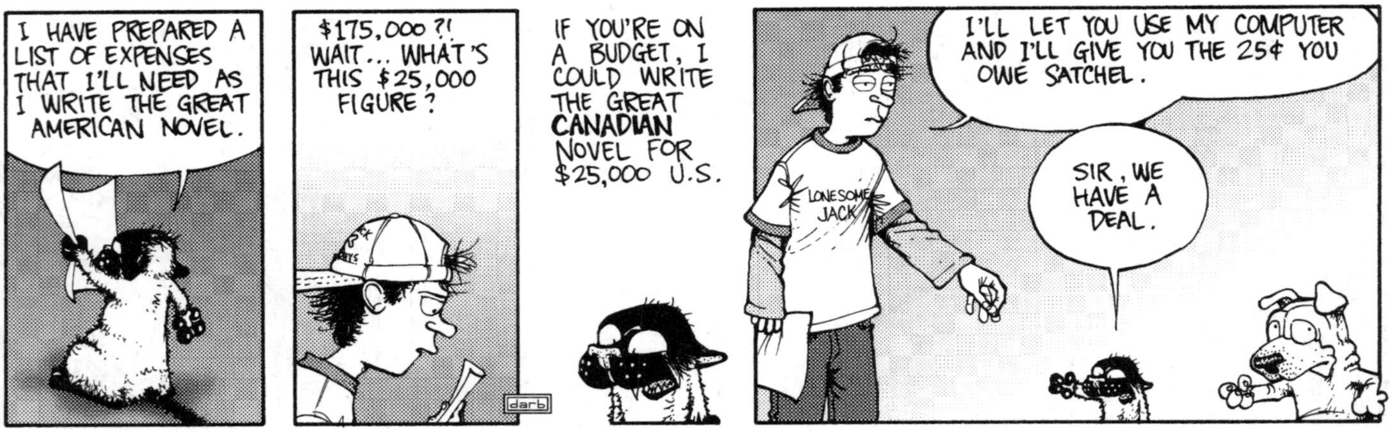
I HAVE PREPARED A LIST OF EXPENSES THAT I'LL NEED AS I WRITE THE GREAT AMERICAN NOVEL.
$175,000?! WAIT... WHAT'S THIS $25,000 FIGURE?
IF YOU'RE ON A BUDGET, I COULD WRITE THE GREAT **CANADIAN** NOVEL FOR $25,000 U.S.
I'LL LET YOU USE MY COMPUTER AND I'LL GIVE YOU THE 25¢ YOU OWE SATCHEL.
SIR, WE HAVE A DEAL.
LONESOME JACK
darb

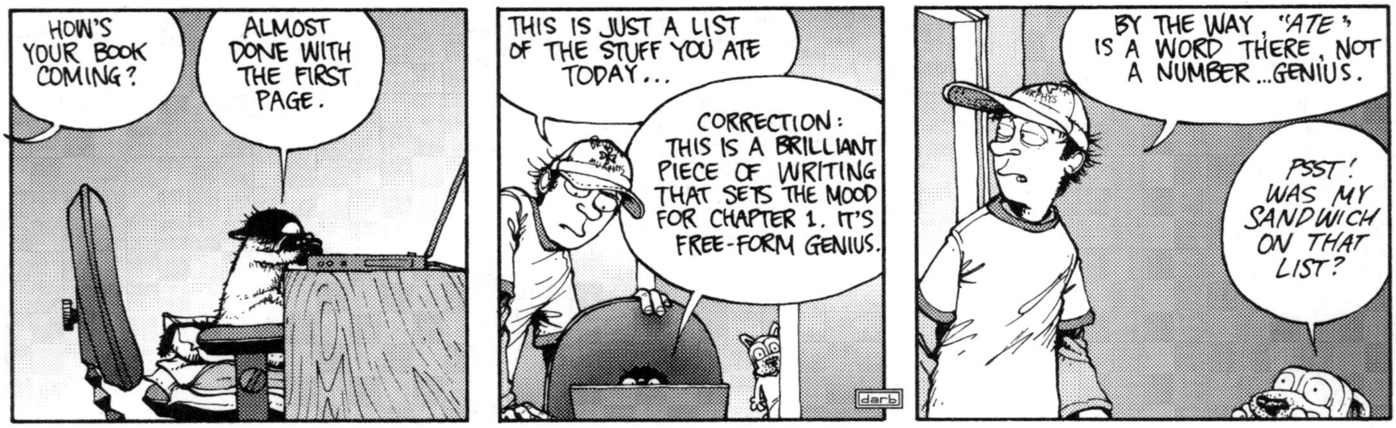
HOW'S YOUR BOOK COMING?
ALMOST DONE WITH THE FIRST PAGE.
THIS IS JUST A LIST OF THE STUFF YOU ATE TODAY...
CORRECTION: THIS IS A BRILLIANT PIECE OF WRITING THAT SETS THE MOOD FOR CHAPTER 1. IT'S FREE-FORM GENIUS.
darb
BY THE WAY, *"ATE"* IS A WORD THERE, NOT A NUMBER...GENIUS.
PSST! WAS MY SANDWICH ON THAT LIST?

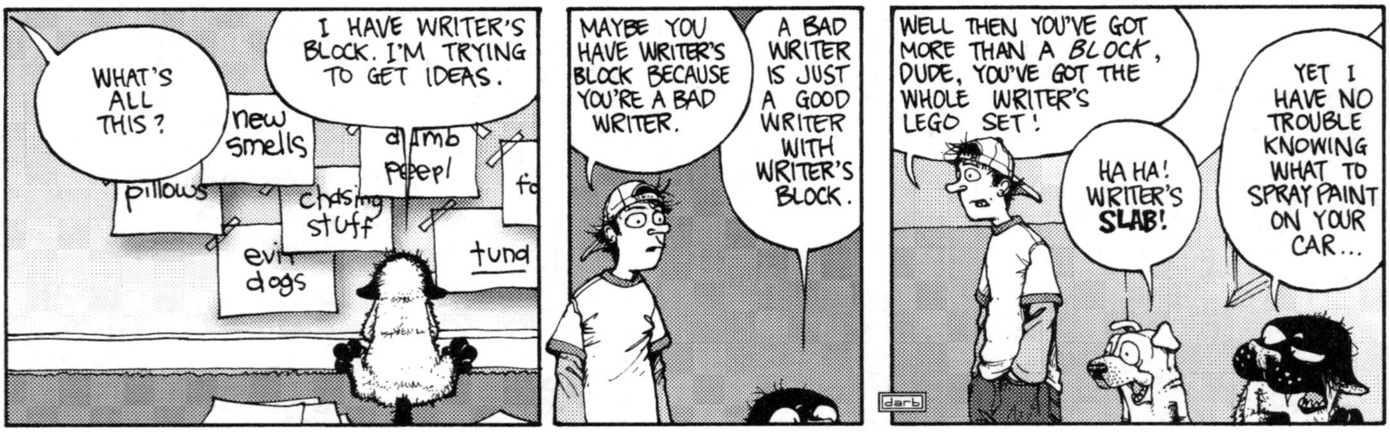
WHAT'S ALL THIS?
I HAVE WRITER'S BLOCK. I'M TRYING TO GET IDEAS.
new smells
pillows
tuna
MAYBE YOU HAVE WRITER'S BLOCK BECAUSE YOU'RE A BAD WRITER.
A BAD WRITER IS JUST A GOOD WRITER WITH WRITER'S BLOCK.
WELL THEN YOU'VE GOT MORE THAN A *BLOCK*, DUDE, YOU'VE GOT THE WHOLE WRITER'S LEGO SET!
HA HA! WRITER'S **SLAB**!
YET I HAVE NO TROUBLE KNOWING WHAT TO SPRAY PAINT ON YOUR CAR...
darb

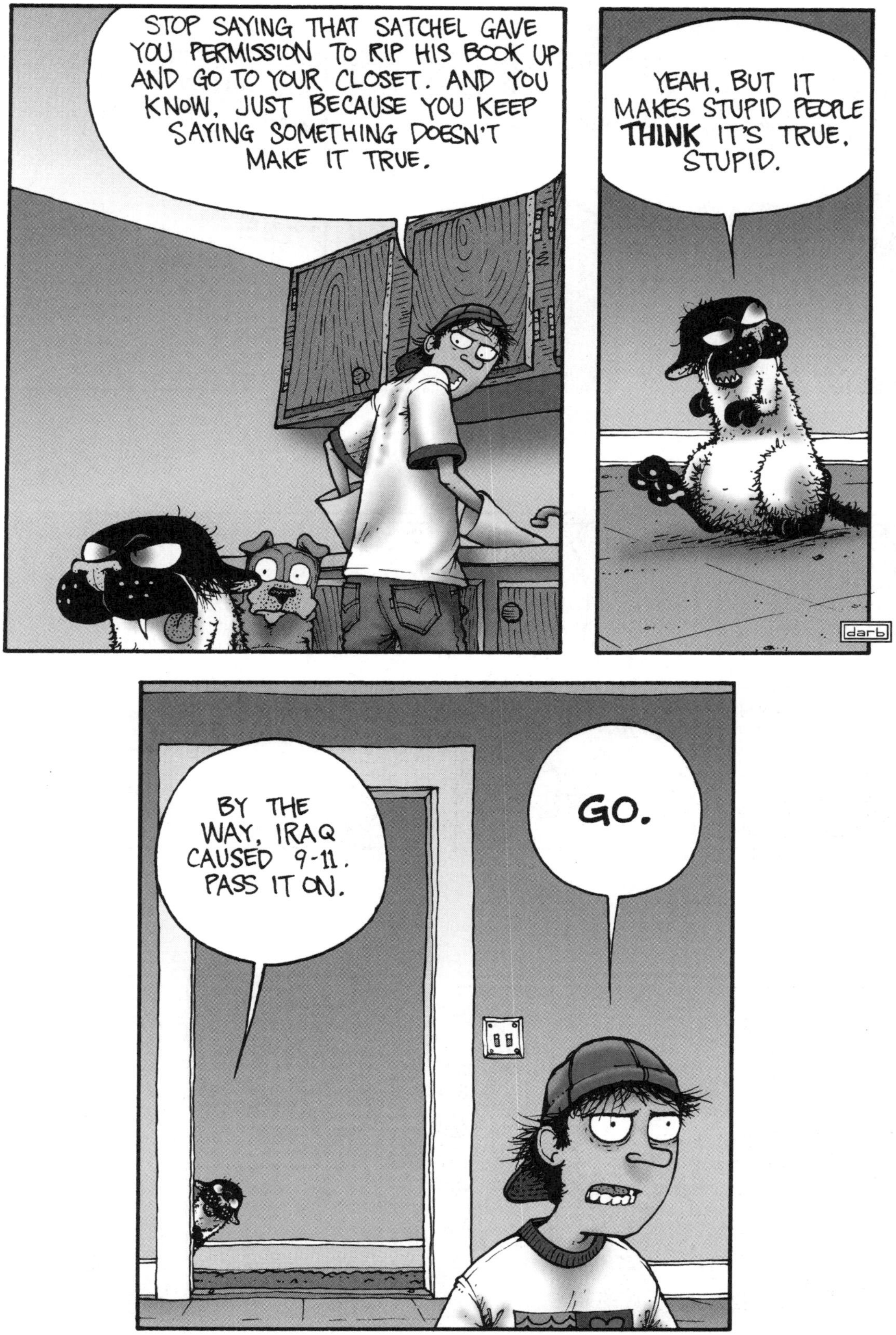
STOP SAYING THAT SATCHEL GAVE YOU PERMISSION TO RIP HIS BOOK UP AND GO TO YOUR CLOSET. AND YOU KNOW, JUST BECAUSE YOU KEEP SAYING SOMETHING DOESN'T MAKE IT TRUE.
YEAH, BUT IT MAKES STUPID PEOPLE **THINK** IT'S TRUE. STUPID.
darb
BY THE WAY, IRAQ CAUSED 9-11. PASS IT ON.
GO.

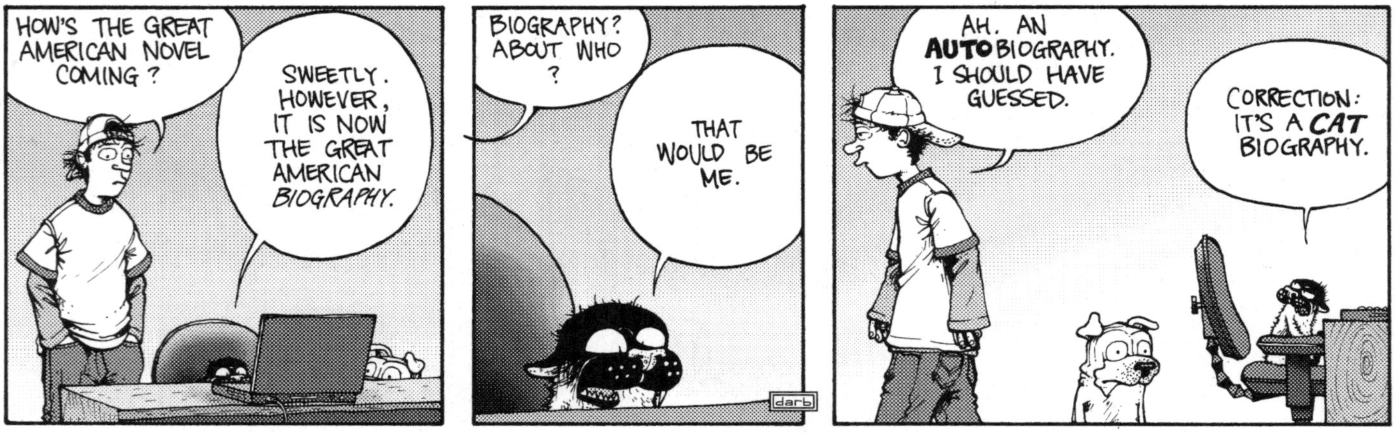
HOW'S THE GREAT AMERICAN NOVEL COMING ?
SWEETLY. HOWEVER, IT IS NOW THE GREAT AMERICAN *BIOGRAPHY.*
BIOGRAPHY? ABOUT WHO ?
THAT WOULD BE ME.
darb
AH. AN **AUTO**BIOGRAPHY. I SHOULD HAVE GUESSED.
CORRECTION: IT'S A ***CAT*** BIOGRAPHY.

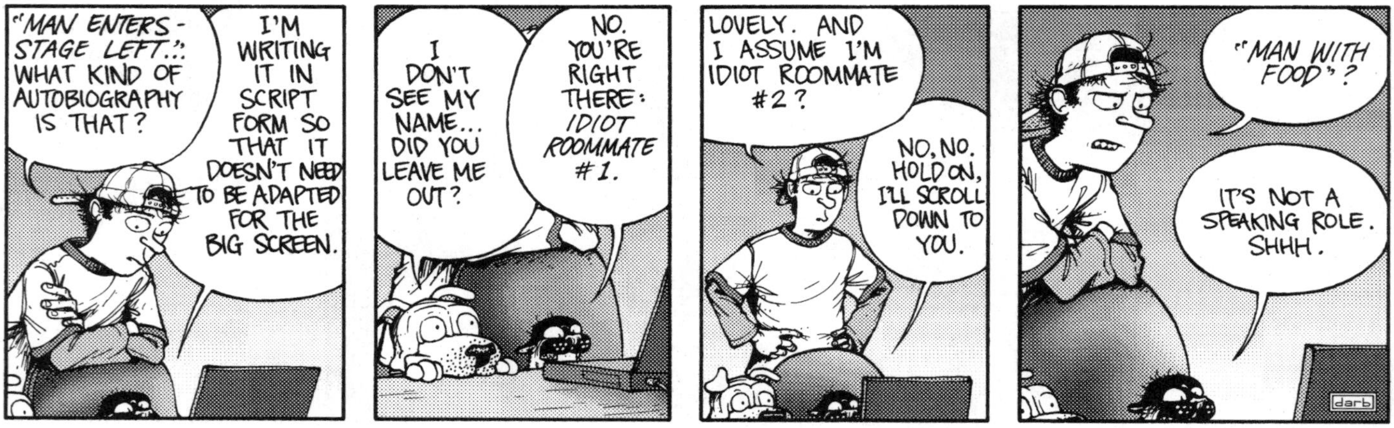
"*MAN ENTERS - STAGE LEFT.*": WHAT KIND OF AUTOBIOGRAPHY IS THAT?
I'M WRITING IT IN SCRIPT FORM SO THAT IT DOESN'T NEED TO BE ADAPTED FOR THE BIG SCREEN.
I DON'T SEE MY NAME... DID YOU LEAVE ME OUT?
NO. YOU'RE RIGHT THERE: *IDIOT ROOMMATE #1.*
LOVELY. AND I ASSUME I'M IDIOT ROOMMATE #2?
NO, NO. HOLD ON, I'LL SCROLL DOWN TO YOU.
"*MAN WITH FOOD*"?
IT'S NOT A SPEAKING ROLE. SHHH.
darb

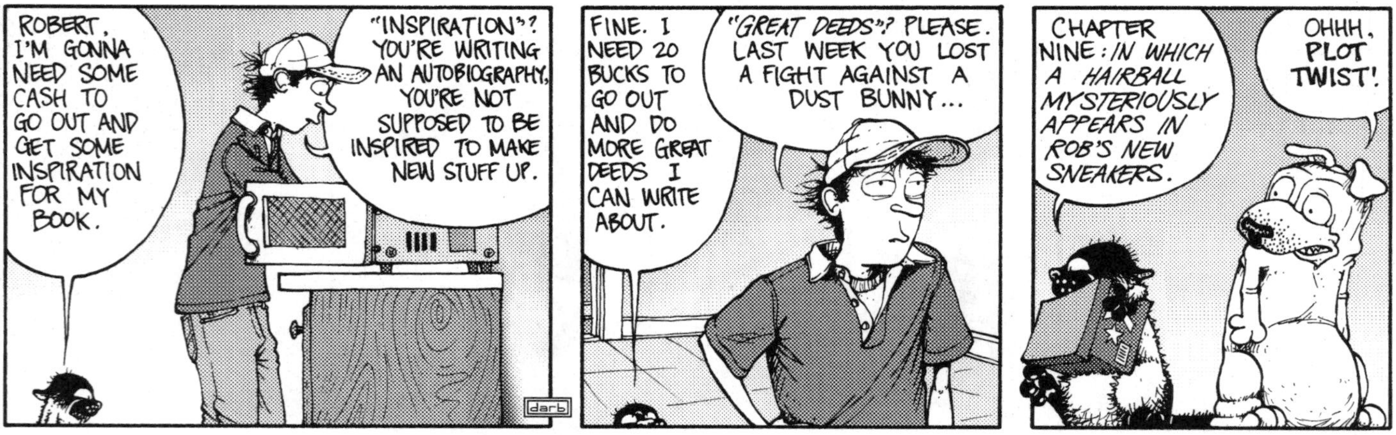
ROBERT, I'M GONNA NEED SOME CASH TO GO OUT AND GET SOME INSPIRATION FOR MY BOOK.
"INSPIRATION"? YOU'RE WRITING AN AUTOBIOGRAPHY, YOU'RE NOT SUPPOSED TO BE INSPIRED TO MAKE NEW STUFF UP.
darb
FINE. I NEED 20 BUCKS TO GO OUT AND DO MORE GREAT DEEDS I CAN WRITE ABOUT.
"*GREAT DEEDS*"? PLEASE. LAST WEEK YOU LOST A FIGHT AGAINST A DUST BUNNY...
CHAPTER NINE: *IN WHICH A HAIRBALL MYSTERIOUSLY APPEARS IN ROB'S NEW SNEAKERS.*
OHHH, **PLOT TWIST!**

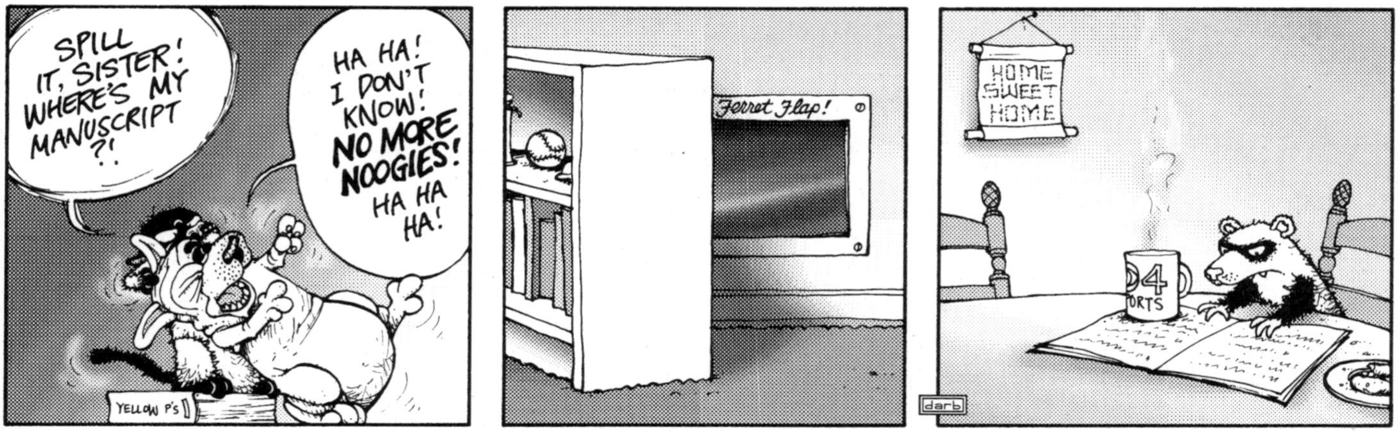
SPILL IT, SISTER! WHERE'S MY MANUSCRIPT ?!
HA HA! I DON'T KNOW! NO MORE NOOGIES! HA HA HA!
YELLOW P'S
Ferret Flap!
HOME SWEET HOME
darb

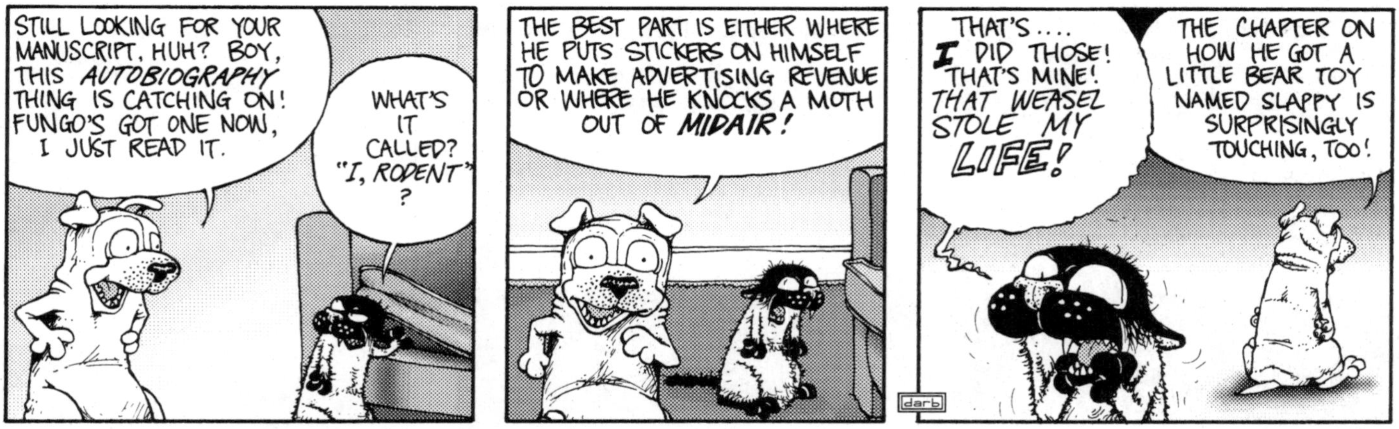
STILL LOOKING FOR YOUR MANUSCRIPT, HUH? BOY, THIS AUTOBIOGRAPHY THING IS CATCHING ON! FUNGO'S GOT ONE NOW, I JUST READ IT.
WHAT'S IT CALLED? "I, RODENT" ?
THE BEST PART IS EITHER WHERE HE PUTS STICKERS ON HIMSELF TO MAKE ADVERTISING REVENUE OR WHERE HE KNOCKS A MOTH OUT OF MIDAIR!
darb
THAT'S.... I DID THOSE! THAT'S MINE! THAT WEASEL STOLE MY LIFE!
THE CHAPTER ON HOW HE GOT A LITTLE BEAR TOY NAMED SLAPPY IS SURPRISINGLY TOUCHING, TOO!

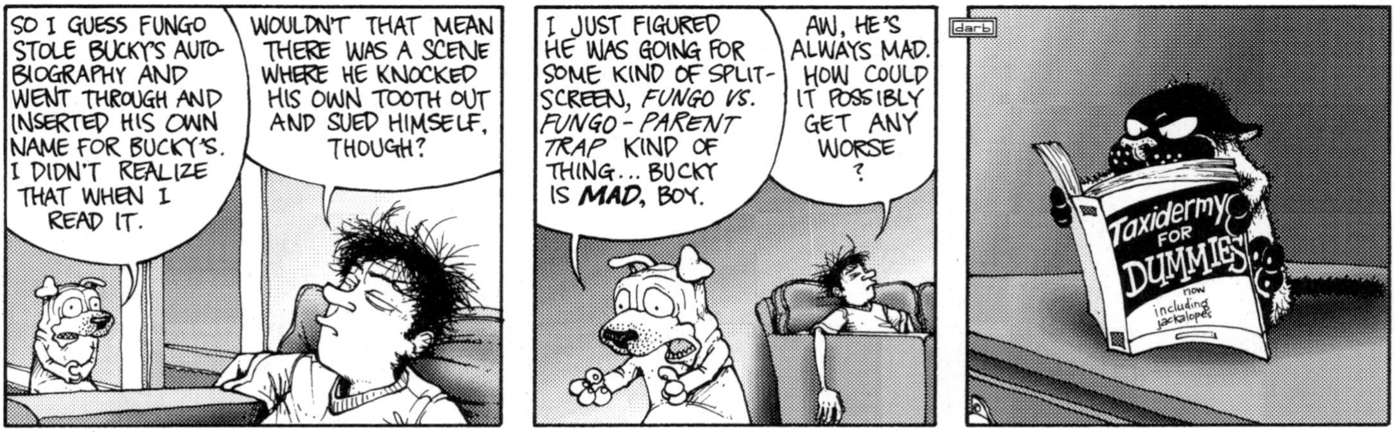
SO I GUESS FUNGO STOLE BUCKY'S AUTOBIOGRAPHY AND WENT THROUGH AND INSERTED HIS OWN NAME FOR BUCKY'S. I DIDN'T REALIZE THAT WHEN I READ IT.
WOULDN'T THAT MEAN THERE WAS A SCENE WHERE HE KNOCKED HIS OWN TOOTH OUT AND SUED HIMSELF, THOUGH?
I JUST FIGURED HE WAS GOING FOR SOME KIND OF SPLIT-SCREEN, FUNGO VS. FUNGO - PARENT TRAP KIND OF THING... BUCKY IS MAD, BOY.
AW, HE'S ALWAYS MAD. HOW COULD IT POSSIBLY GET ANY WORSE ?
darb
Taxidermy FOR DUMMIES
now including jackalopes

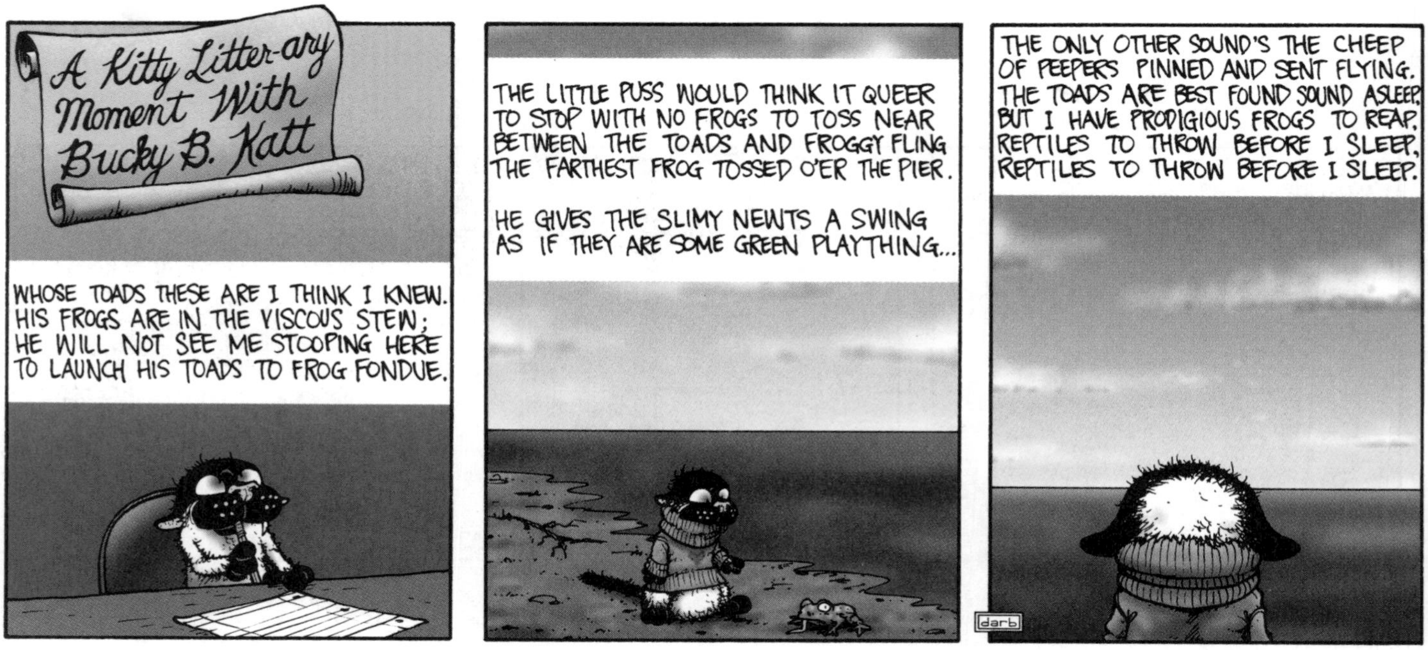
A Kitty Litter-ary Moment With Bucky B. Katt
WHOSE TOADS THESE ARE I THINK I KNEW. HIS FROGS ARE IN THE VISCOUS STEW; HE WILL NOT SEE ME STOOPING HERE TO LAUNCH HIS TOADS TO FROG FONDUE.
THE LITTLE PUSS WOULD THINK IT QUEER TO STOP WITH NO FROGS TO TOSS NEAR BETWEEN THE TOADS AND FROGGY FLING THE FARTHEST FROG TOSSED O'ER THE PIER.
HE GIVES THE SLIMY NEWTS A SWING AS IF THEY ARE SOME GREEN PLAYTHING...
THE ONLY OTHER SOUND'S THE CHEEP OF PEEPERS PINNED AND SENT FLYING. THE TOADS ARE BEST FOUND SOUND ASLEEP, BUT I HAVE PRODIGIOUS FROGS TO REAP, REPTILES TO THROW BEFORE I SLEEP, REPTILES TO THROW BEFORE I SLEEP.
darb

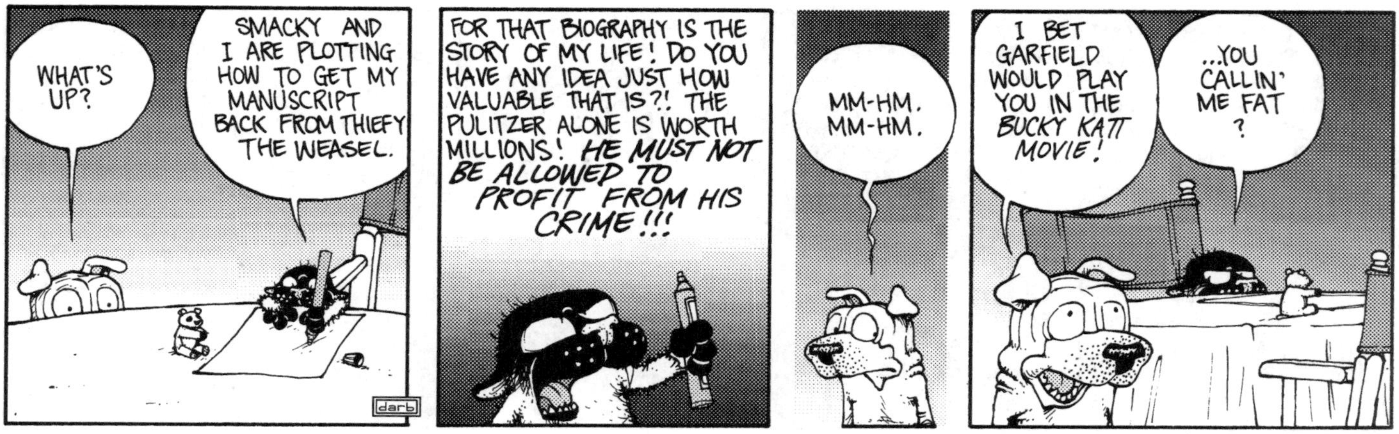
WHAT'S UP?
SMACKY AND I ARE PLOTTING HOW TO GET MY MANUSCRIPT BACK FROM THIEFY THE WEASEL.
FOR THAT BIOGRAPHY IS THE STORY OF MY LIFE! DO YOU HAVE ANY IDEA JUST HOW VALUABLE THAT IS?! THE PULITZER ALONE IS WORTH MILLIONS! HE MUST NOT BE ALLOWED TO PROFIT FROM HIS CRIME!!!
MM-HM. MM-HM.
I BET GARFIELD WOULD PLAY YOU IN THE BUCKY KATT MOVIE!
...YOU CALLIN' ME FAT?

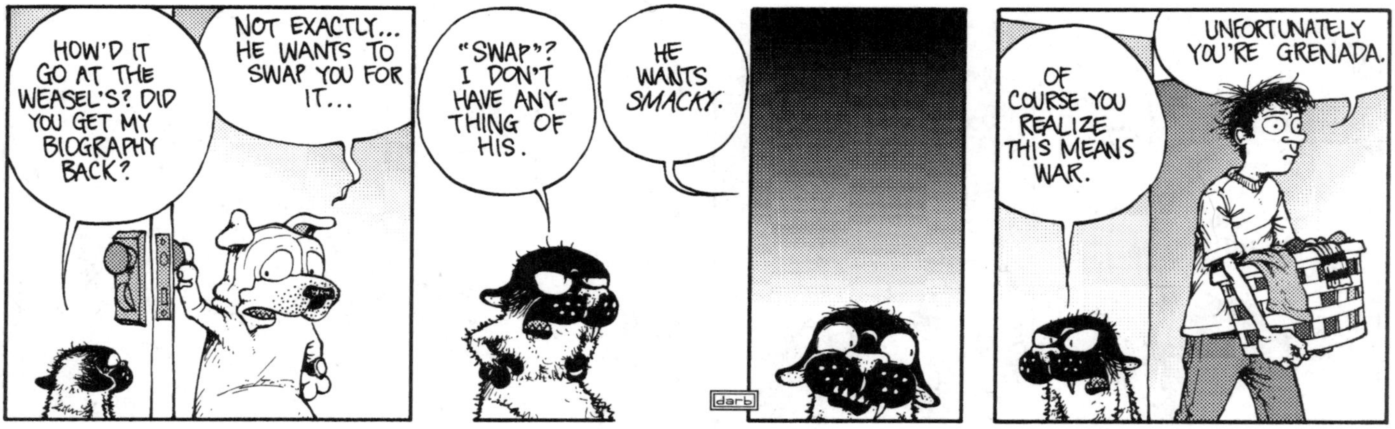
HOW'D IT GO AT THE WEASEL'S? DID YOU GET MY BIOGRAPHY BACK?
NOT EXACTLY... HE WANTS TO SWAP YOU FOR IT...
"SWAP"? I DON'T HAVE ANY-THING OF HIS.
HE WANTS SMACKY.
OF COURSE YOU REALIZE THIS MEANS WAR.
UNFORTUNATELY YOU'RE GRENADA.

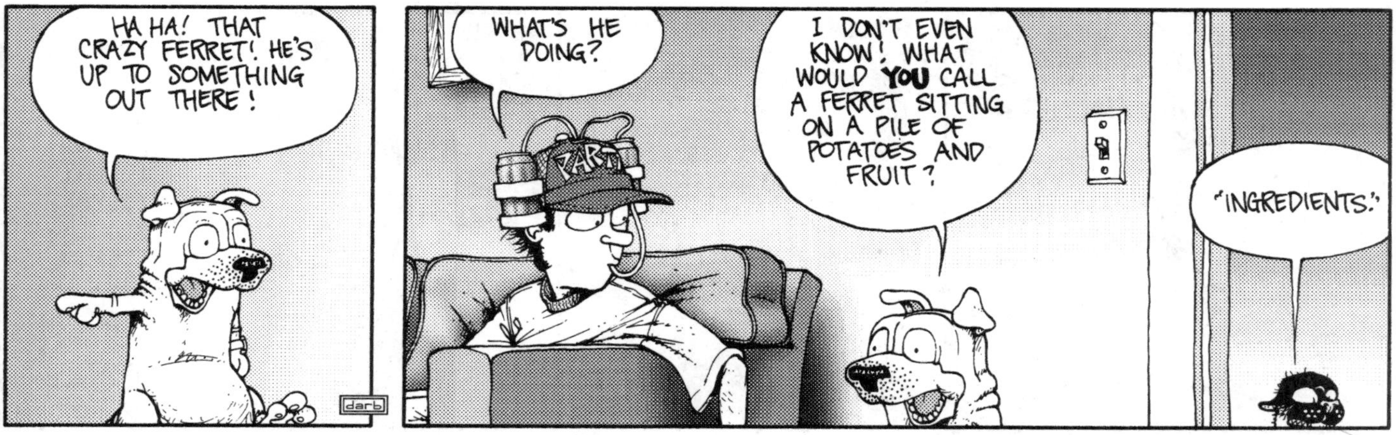
HA HA! THAT CRAZY FERRET! HE'S UP TO SOMETHING OUT THERE!
WHAT'S HE DOING?
I DON'T EVEN KNOW! WHAT WOULD YOU CALL A FERRET SITTING ON A PILE OF POTATOES AND FRUIT?
"INGREDIENTS."

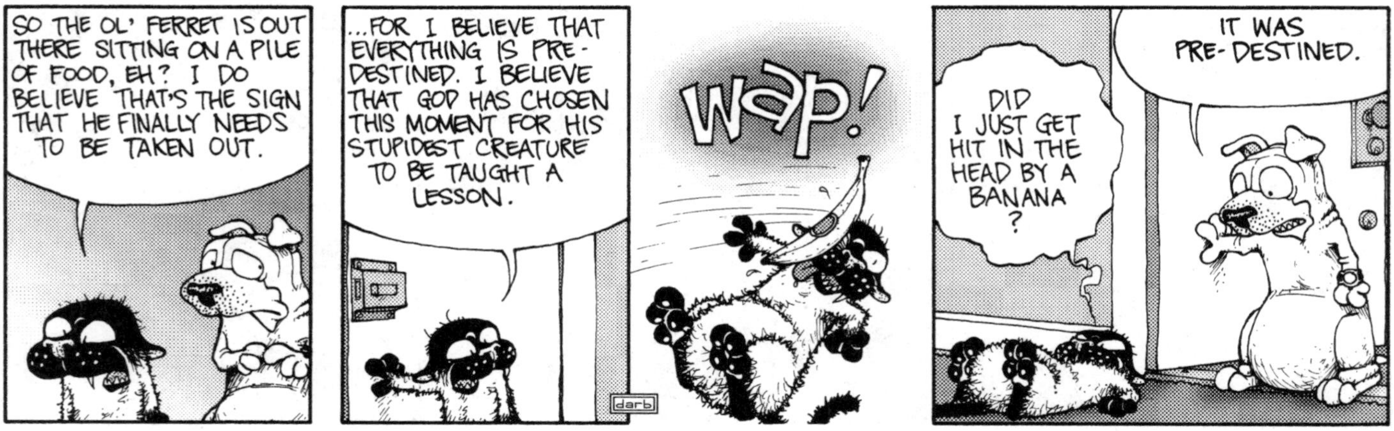
SO THE OL' FERRET IS OUT THERE SITTING ON A PILE OF FOOD, EH? I DO BELIEVE THAT'S THE SIGN THAT HE FINALLY NEEDS TO BE TAKEN OUT.
...FOR I BELIEVE THAT EVERYTHING IS PRE-DESTINED. I BELIEVE THAT GOD HAS CHOSEN THIS MOMENT FOR HIS STUPIDEST CREATURE TO BE TAUGHT A LESSON.
darb
WAP!
DID I JUST GET HIT IN THE HEAD BY A BANANA ?
IT WAS PRE-DESTINED.

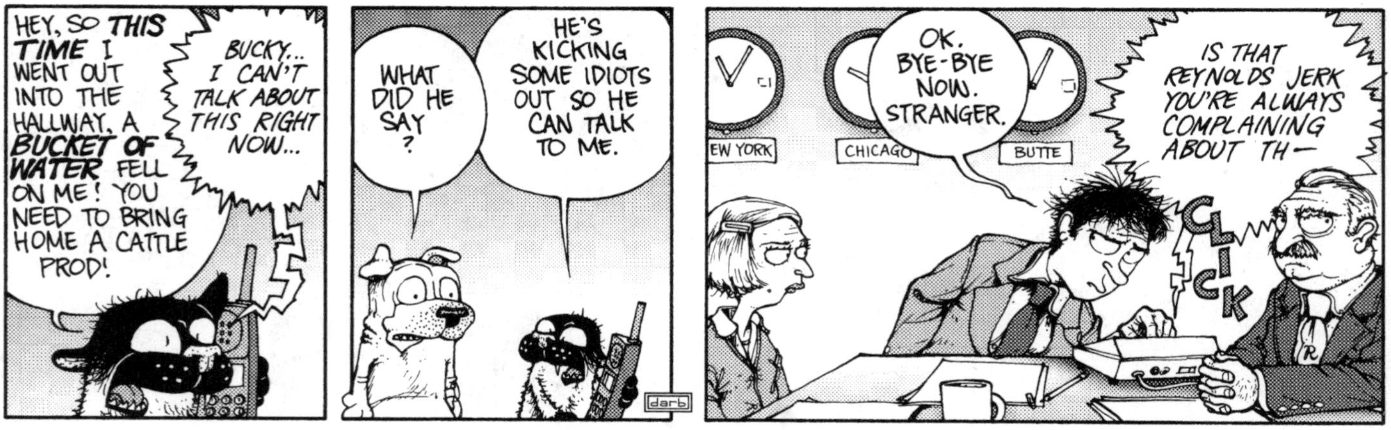
HEY, SO **THIS TIME** I WENT OUT INTO THE HALLWAY, A **BUCKET OF WATER** FELL ON ME! YOU NEED TO BRING HOME A CATTLE PROD!
BUCKY... I CAN'T TALK ABOUT THIS RIGHT NOW...
WHAT DID HE SAY ?
HE'S KICKING SOME IDIOTS OUT SO HE CAN TALK TO ME.
darb
EW YORK
CHICAGO
BUTTE
OK. BYE-BYE NOW. STRANGER.
IS THAT REYNOLDS JERK YOU'RE ALWAYS COMPLAINING ABOUT TH—
CLICK

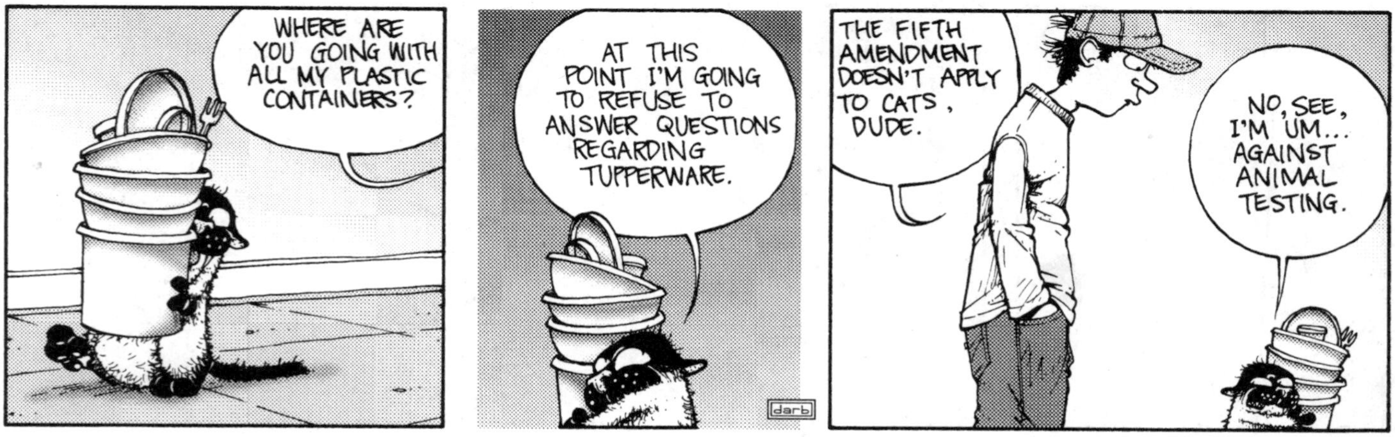
WHERE ARE YOU GOING WITH ALL MY PLASTIC CONTAINERS?
AT THIS POINT I'M GOING TO REFUSE TO ANSWER QUESTIONS REGARDING TUPPERWARE.
darb
THE FIFTH AMENDMENT DOESN'T APPLY TO CATS, DUDE.
NO, SEE, I'M UM... AGAINST ANIMAL TESTING.

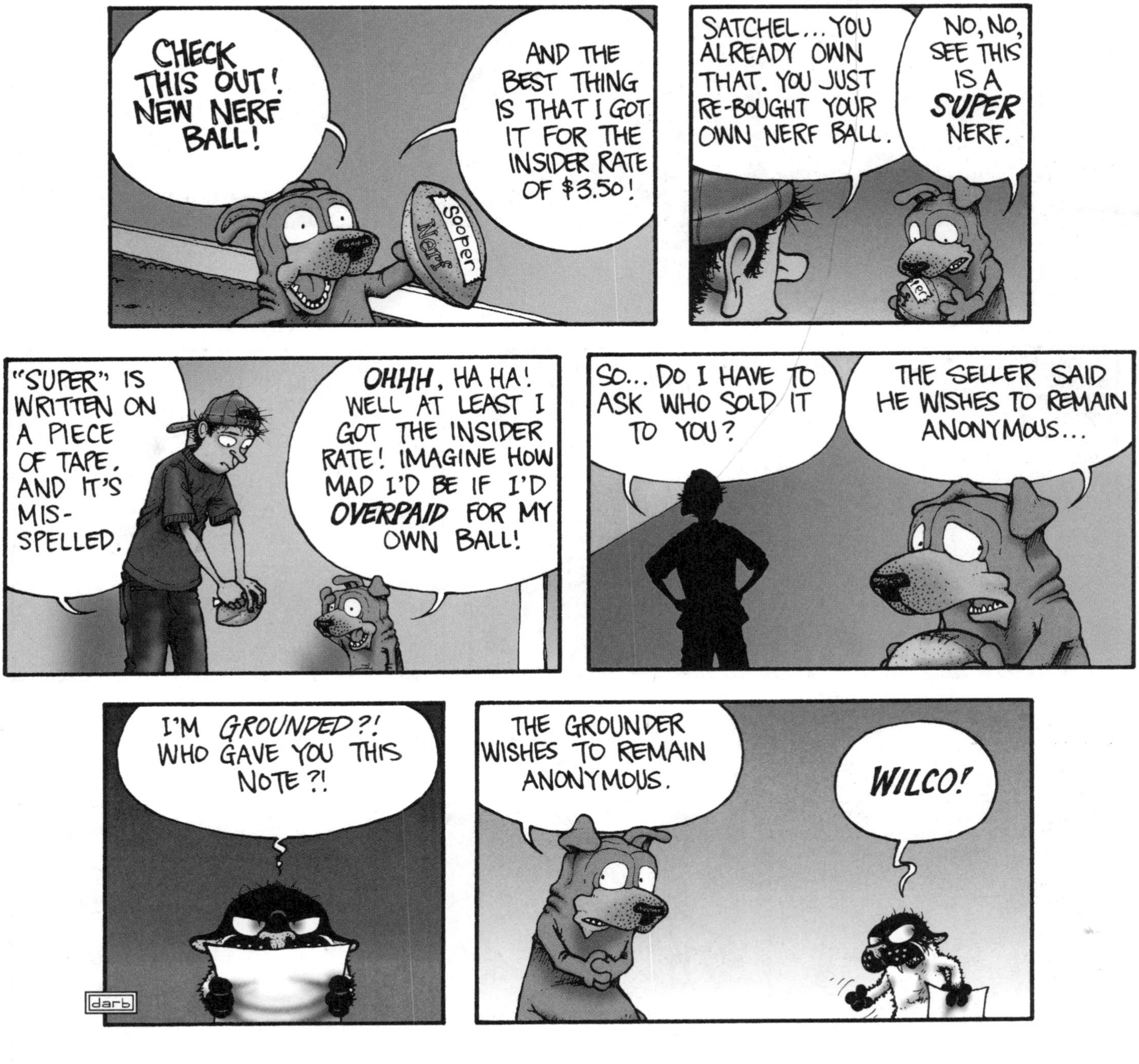
CHECK THIS OUT! NEW NERF BALL!
AND THE BEST THING IS THAT I GOT IT FOR THE INSIDER RATE OF $3.50!
Sooper Nerf
SATCHEL... YOU ALREADY OWN THAT. YOU JUST RE-BOUGHT YOUR OWN NERF BALL.
NO, NO, SEE THIS IS A SUPER NERF.
"SUPER" IS WRITTEN ON A PIECE OF TAPE. AND IT'S MIS-SPELLED.
OHHH, HA HA! WELL AT LEAST I GOT THE INSIDER RATE! IMAGINE HOW MAD I'D BE IF I'D OVERPAID FOR MY OWN BALL!
SO... DO I HAVE TO ASK WHO SOLD IT TO YOU?
THE SELLER SAID HE WISHES TO REMAIN ANONYMOUS...
I'M GROUNDED?! WHO GAVE YOU THIS NOTE?!
darb
THE GROUNDER WISHES TO REMAIN ANONYMOUS.
WILCO!

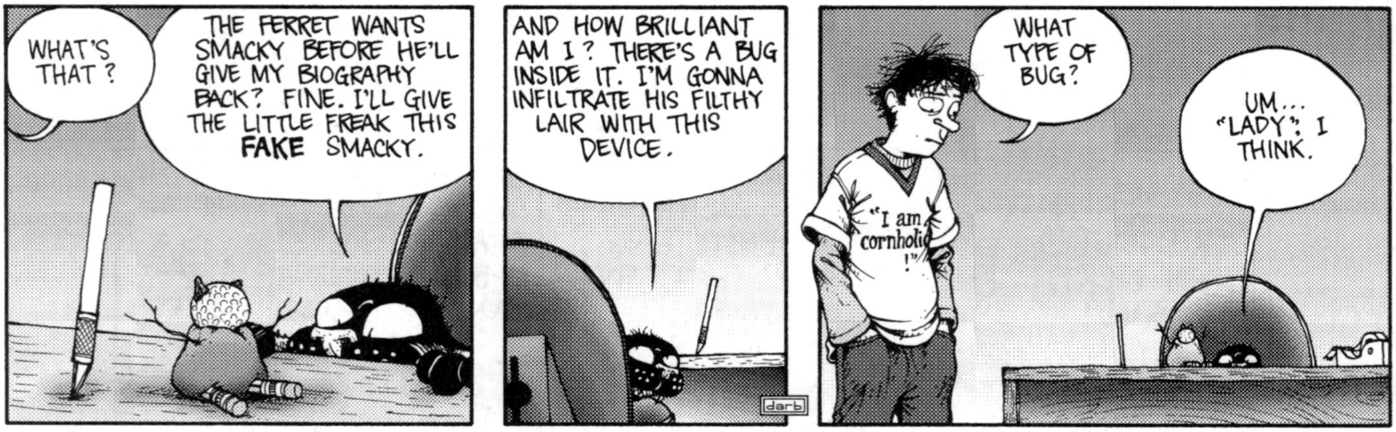
WHAT'S THAT?
THE FERRET WANTS SMACKY BEFORE HE'LL GIVE MY BIOGRAPHY BACK? FINE. I'LL GIVE THE LITTLE FREAK THIS FAKE SMACKY.
AND HOW BRILLIANT AM I? THERE'S A BUG INSIDE IT. I'M GONNA INFILTRATE HIS FILTHY LAIR WITH THIS DEVICE.
"I am cornholio!"
WHAT TYPE OF BUG?
UM... "LADY", I THINK.

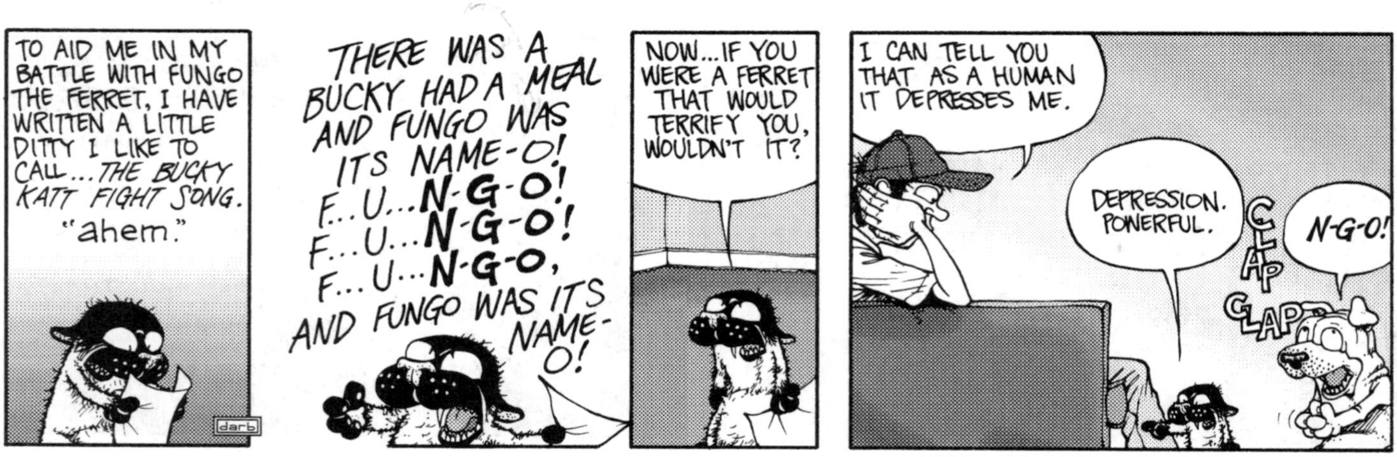
TO AID ME IN MY BATTLE WITH FUNGO THE FERRET, I HAVE WRITTEN A LITTLE DITTY I LIKE TO CALL... THE BUCKY KATT FIGHT SONG.
"ahem."
THERE WAS A BUCKY HAD A MEAL AND FUNGO WAS ITS NAME-O! F...U...N-G-O! F...U...N-G-O! F...U...N-G-O, AND FUNGO WAS ITS NAME-O!
NOW...IF YOU WERE A FERRET THAT WOULD TERRIFY YOU, WOULDN'T IT?
I CAN TELL YOU THAT AS A HUMAN IT DEPRESSES ME.
DEPRESSION. POWERFUL.
CLAP
CLAP
N-G-O!

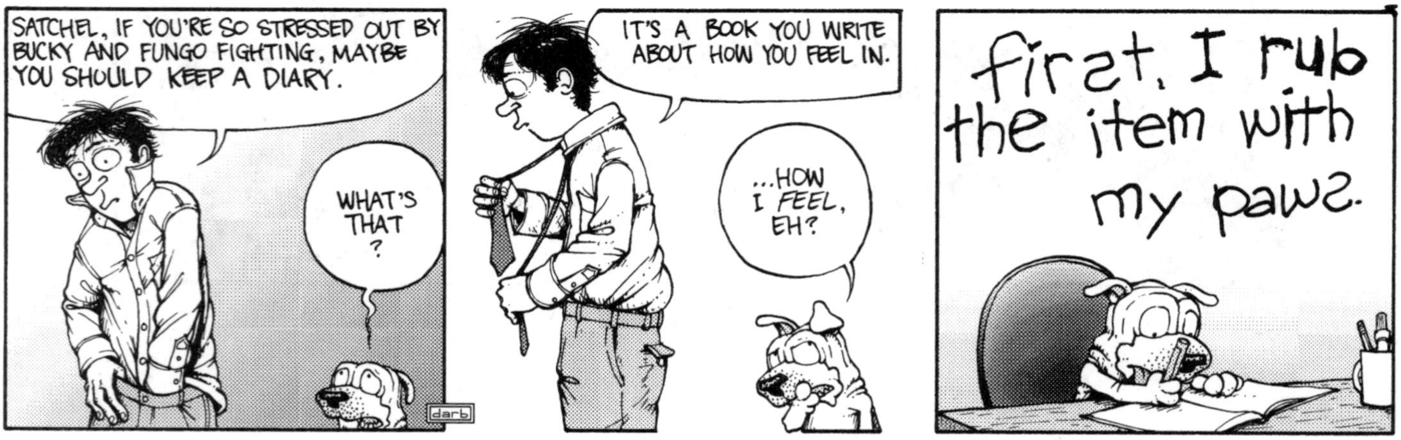
SATCHEL, IF YOU'RE SO STRESSED OUT BY BUCKY AND FUNGO FIGHTING, MAYBE YOU SHOULD KEEP A DIARY.
WHAT'S THAT?
IT'S A BOOK YOU WRITE ABOUT HOW YOU FEEL IN.
...HOW I FEEL, EH?
first, I rub the item with my paws.

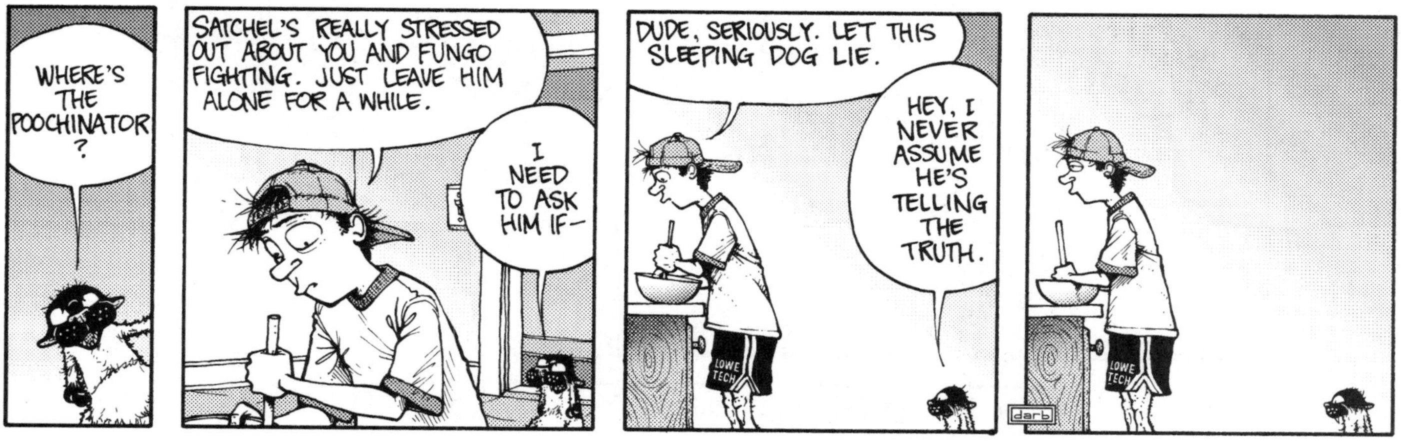
WHERE'S THE POOCHINATOR?
SATCHEL'S REALLY STRESSED OUT ABOUT YOU AND FUNGO FIGHTING. JUST LEAVE HIM ALONE FOR A WHILE.
I NEED TO ASK HIM IF—
DUDE, SERIOUSLY. LET THIS SLEEPING DOG LIE.
HEY, I NEVER ASSUME HE'S TELLING THE TRUTH.
LOWE TECH
LOWE TECH
darb

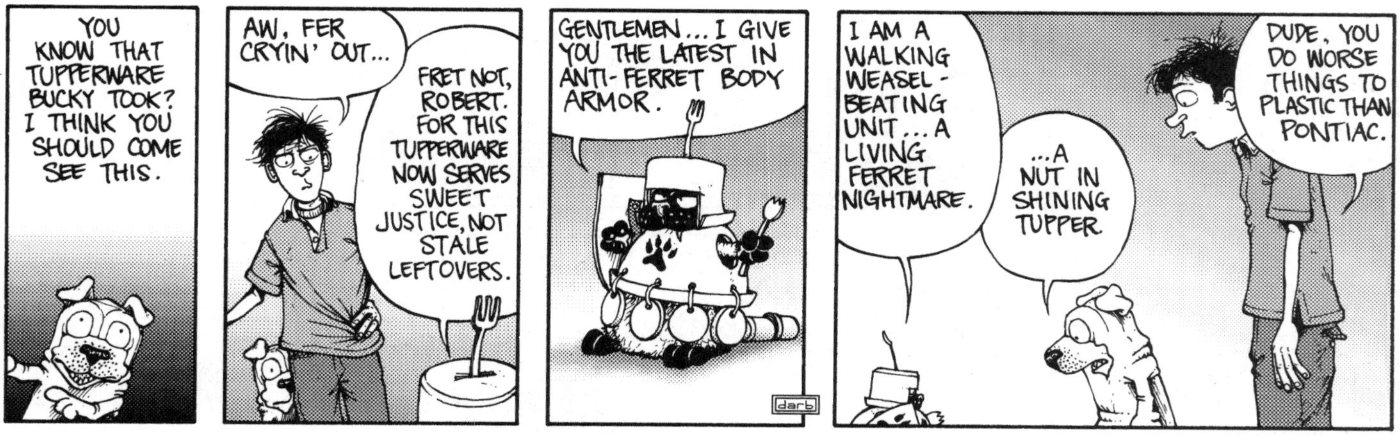
YOU KNOW THAT TUPPERWARE BUCKY TOOK? I THINK YOU SHOULD COME SEE THIS.
AW, FER CRYIN' OUT...
FRET NOT, ROBERT. FOR THIS TUPPERWARE NOW SERVES SWEET JUSTICE, NOT STALE LEFTOVERS.
GENTLEMEN... I GIVE YOU THE LATEST IN ANTI-FERRET BODY ARMOR.
darb
I AM A WALKING WEASEL-BEATING UNIT... A LIVING FERRET NIGHTMARE.
...A NUT IN SHINING TUPPER.
DUDE, YOU DO WORSE THINGS TO PLASTIC THAN PONTIAC.

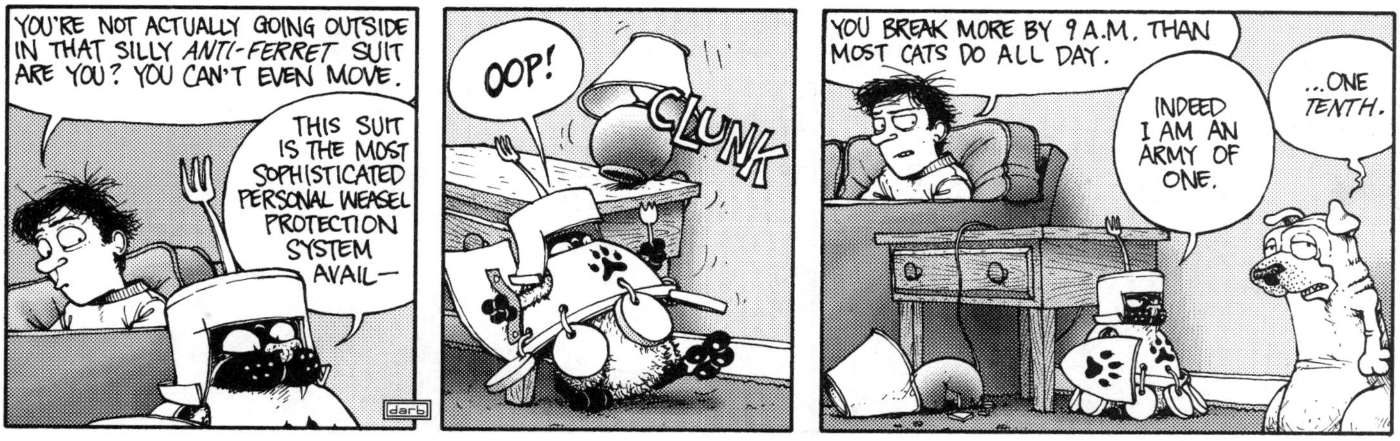
YOU'RE NOT ACTUALLY GOING OUTSIDE IN THAT SILLY *ANTI-FERRET* SUIT ARE YOU? YOU CAN'T EVEN MOVE.
THIS SUIT IS THE MOST SOPHISTICATED PERSONAL WEASEL PROTECTION SYSTEM AVAIL—
darb
OOP!
CLUNK
YOU BREAK MORE BY 9 A.M. THAN MOST CATS DO ALL DAY.
INDEED I AM AN ARMY OF ONE.
...ONE *TENTH*.

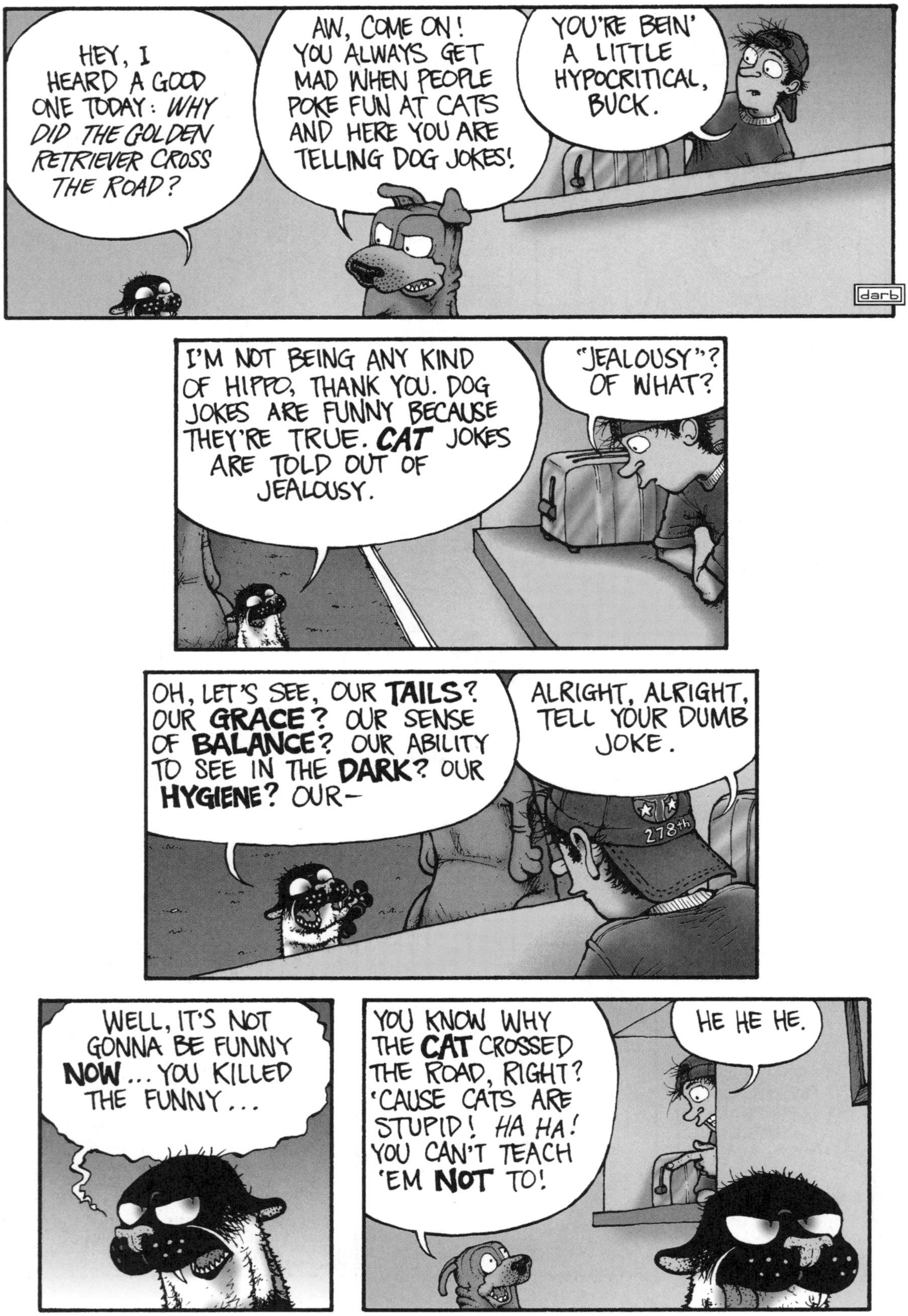
HEY, I HEARD A GOOD ONE TODAY: *WHY DID THE GOLDEN RETRIEVER CROSS THE ROAD?*
AW, COME ON! YOU ALWAYS GET MAD WHEN PEOPLE POKE FUN AT CATS AND HERE YOU ARE TELLING DOG JOKES!
YOU'RE BEIN' A LITTLE HYPOCRITICAL, BUCK.
darb
I'M NOT BEING ANY KIND OF HIPPO, THANK YOU. DOG JOKES ARE FUNNY BECAUSE THEY'RE TRUE. ***CAT*** JOKES ARE TOLD OUT OF JEALOUSY.
"JEALOUSY"? OF WHAT?
OH, LET'S SEE, OUR **TAILS**? OUR **GRACE**? OUR SENSE OF **BALANCE**? OUR ABILITY TO SEE IN THE **DARK**? OUR **HYGIENE**? OUR–
ALRIGHT, ALRIGHT, TELL YOUR DUMB JOKE.
278th
WELL, IT'S NOT GONNA BE FUNNY **NOW**... YOU KILLED THE FUNNY...
YOU KNOW WHY THE **CAT** CROSSED THE ROAD, RIGHT? 'CAUSE CATS ARE STUPID! *HA HA!* YOU CAN'T TEACH 'EM **NOT** TO!
HE HE HE.

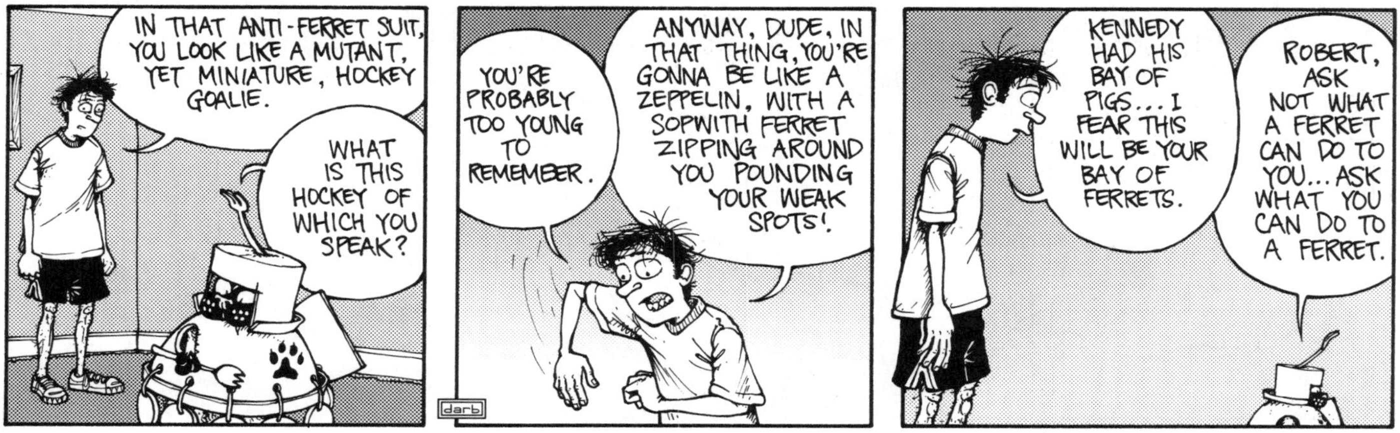
IN THAT ANTI-FERRET SUIT, YOU LOOK LIKE A MUTANT, YET MINIATURE, HOCKEY GOALIE.
WHAT IS THIS HOCKEY OF WHICH YOU SPEAK?
YOU'RE PROBABLY TOO YOUNG TO REMEMBER.
ANYWAY, DUDE, IN THAT THING, YOU'RE GONNA BE LIKE A ZEPPELIN, WITH A SOPWITH FERRET ZIPPING AROUND YOU POUNDING YOUR WEAK SPOTS!
darb
KENNEDY HAD HIS BAY OF PIGS... I FEAR THIS WILL BE YOUR BAY OF FERRETS.
ROBERT, ASK NOT WHAT A FERRET CAN DO TO YOU... ASK WHAT YOU CAN DO TO A FERRET.

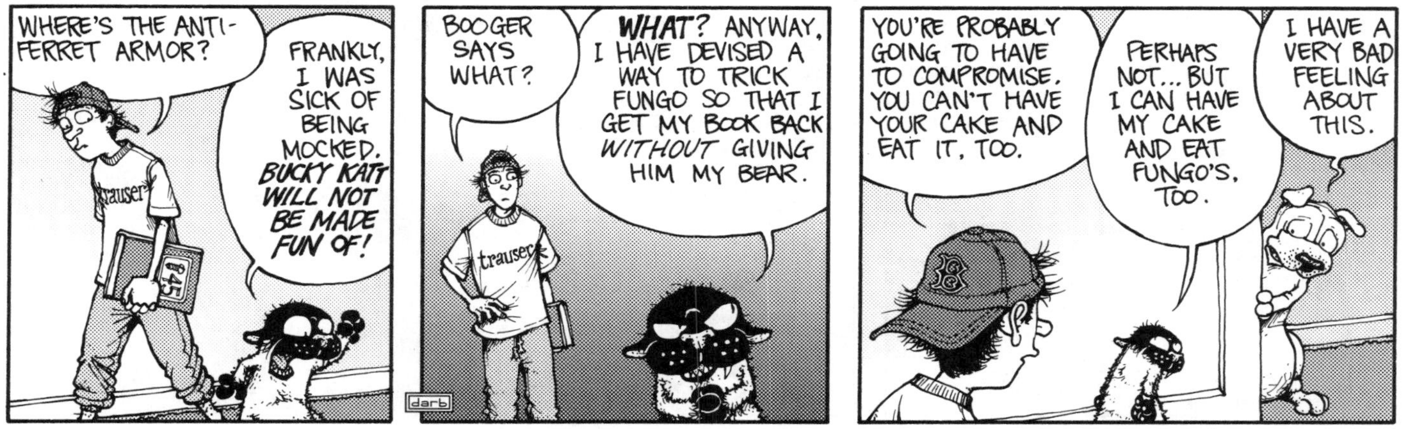
WHERE'S THE ANTI-FERRET ARMOR?
FRANKLY, I WAS SICK OF BEING MOCKED. BUCKY KATT WILL NOT BE MADE FUN OF!
trauser
BOOGER SAYS WHAT?
WHAT? ANYWAY, I HAVE DEVISED A WAY TO TRICK FUNGO SO THAT I GET MY BOOK BACK WITHOUT GIVING HIM MY BEAR.
darb
YOU'RE PROBABLY GOING TO HAVE TO COMPROMISE. YOU CAN'T HAVE YOUR CAKE AND EAT IT, TOO.
PERHAPS NOT... BUT I CAN HAVE MY CAKE AND EAT FUNGO'S, TOO.
I HAVE A VERY BAD FEELING ABOUT THIS.

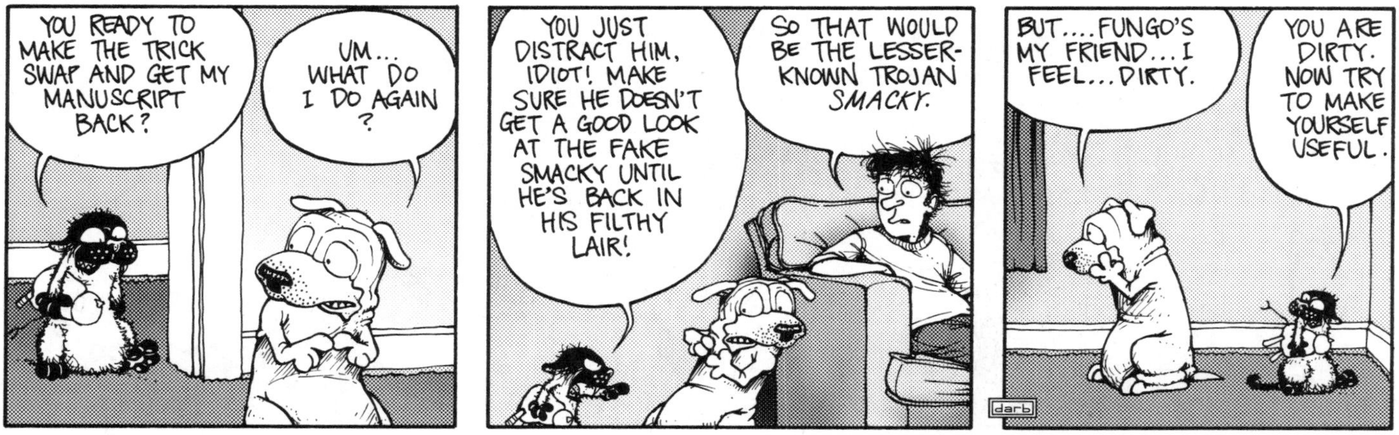
YOU READY TO MAKE THE TRICK SWAP AND GET MY MANUSCRIPT BACK?
UM... WHAT DO I DO AGAIN?
YOU JUST DISTRACT HIM, IDIOT! MAKE SURE HE DOESN'T GET A GOOD LOOK AT THE FAKE SMACKY UNTIL HE'S BACK IN HIS FILTHY LAIR!
SO THAT WOULD BE THE LESSER-KNOWN TROJAN SMACKY.
darb
BUT.... FUNGO'S MY FRIEND... I FEEL... DIRTY.
YOU ARE DIRTY. NOW TRY TO MAKE YOURSELF USEFUL.

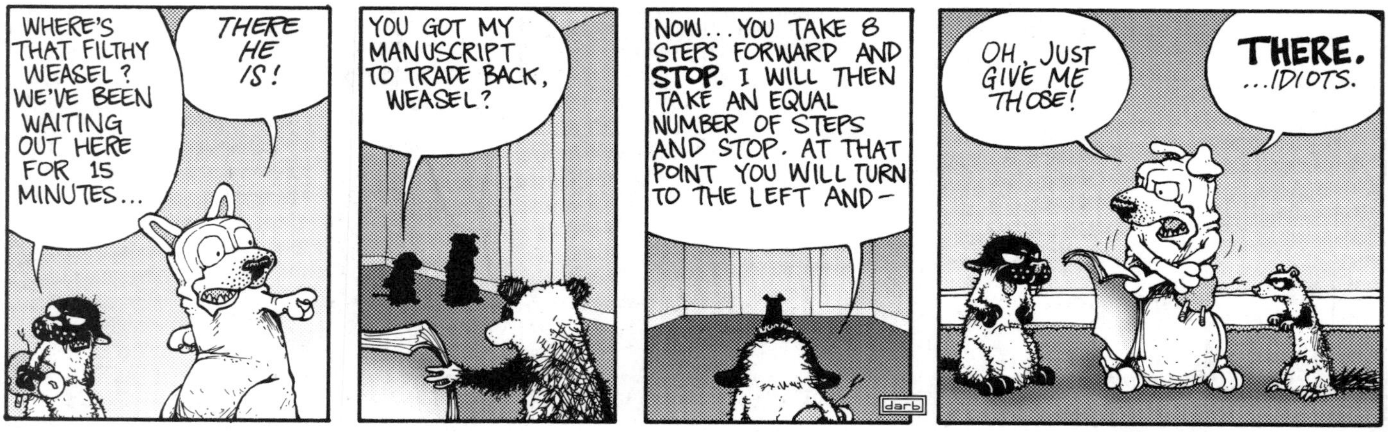
WHERE'S THAT FILTHY WEASEL? WE'VE BEEN WAITING OUT HERE FOR 15 MINUTES...
THERE HE IS!
YOU GOT MY MANUSCRIPT TO TRADE BACK, WEASEL?
NOW... YOU TAKE 8 STEPS FORWARD AND STOP. I WILL THEN TAKE AN EQUAL NUMBER OF STEPS AND STOP. AT THAT POINT YOU WILL TURN TO THE LEFT AND–
darb
OH, JUST GIVE ME THOSE!
THERE. ...IDIOTS.

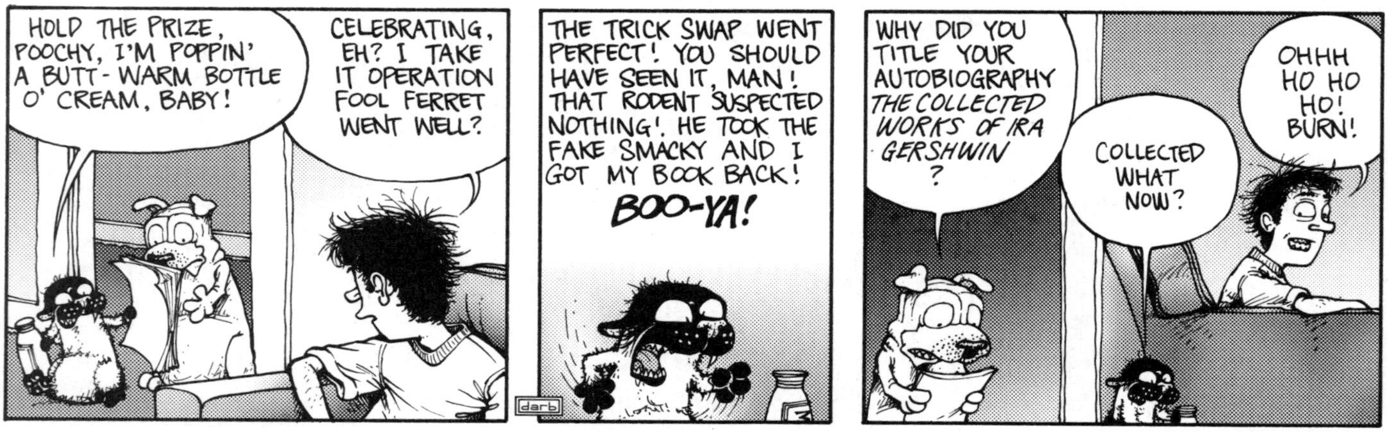
HOLD THE PRIZE, POOCHY, I'M POPPIN' A BUTT-WARM BOTTLE O' CREAM, BABY!
CELEBRATING, EH? I TAKE IT OPERATION FOOL FERRET WENT WELL?
darb
THE TRICK SWAP WENT PERFECT! YOU SHOULD HAVE SEEN IT, MAN! THAT RODENT SUSPECTED NOTHING! HE TOOK THE FAKE SMACKY AND I GOT MY BOOK BACK!
BOO-YA!
WHY DID YOU TITLE YOUR AUTOBIOGRAPHY THE COLLECTED WORKS OF IRA GERSHWIN?
COLLECTED WHAT NOW?
OHHH HO HO HO! BURN!

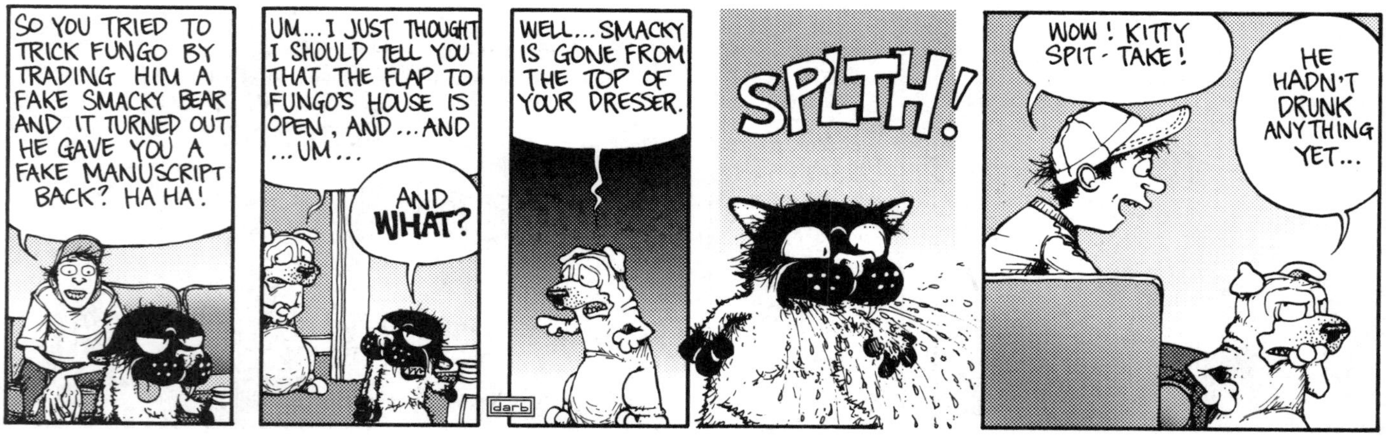
SO YOU TRIED TO TRICK FUNGO BY TRADING HIM A FAKE SMACKY BEAR AND IT TURNED OUT HE GAVE YOU A FAKE MANUSCRIPT BACK? HA HA!
UM... I JUST THOUGHT I SHOULD TELL YOU THAT THE FLAP TO FUNGO'S HOUSE IS OPEN, AND... AND ...UM...
AND WHAT?
darb
WELL... SMACKY IS GONE FROM THE TOP OF YOUR DRESSER.
SPLTH!
WOW! KITTY SPIT-TAKE!
HE HADN'T DRUNK ANYTHING YET...

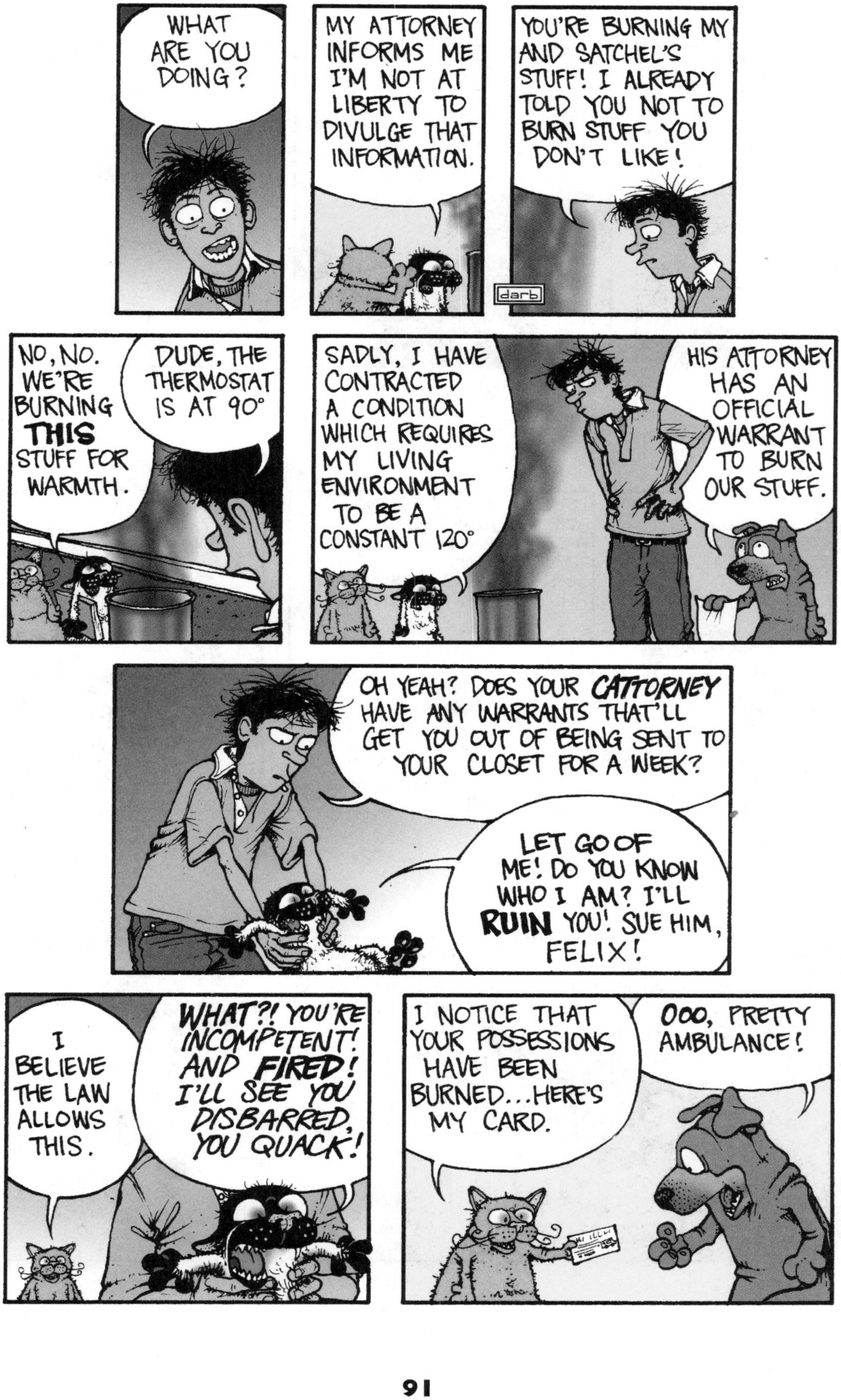
WHAT ARE YOU DOING?
MY ATTORNEY INFORMS ME I'M NOT AT LIBERTY TO DIVULGE THAT INFORMATION.
YOU'RE BURNING MY AND SATCHEL'S STUFF! I ALREADY TOLD YOU NOT TO BURN STUFF YOU DON'T LIKE!
NO, NO. WE'RE BURNING THIS STUFF FOR WARMTH.
DUDE, THE THERMOSTAT IS AT 90°
SADLY, I HAVE CONTRACTED A CONDITION WHICH REQUIRES MY LIVING ENVIRONMENT TO BE A CONSTANT 120°
HIS ATTORNEY HAS AN OFFICIAL WARRANT TO BURN OUR STUFF.
OH YEAH? DOES YOUR CATTORNEY HAVE ANY WARRANTS THAT'LL GET YOU OUT OF BEING SENT TO YOUR CLOSET FOR A WEEK?
LET GO OF ME! DO YOU KNOW WHO I AM? I'LL RUIN YOU! SUE HIM, FELIX!
I BELIEVE THE LAW ALLOWS THIS.
WHAT?! YOU'RE INCOMPETENT! AND FIRED! I'LL SEE YOU DISBARRED, YOU QUACK!
I NOTICE THAT YOUR POSSESSIONS HAVE BEEN BURNED... HERE'S MY CARD.
OOO, PRETTY AMBULANCE!

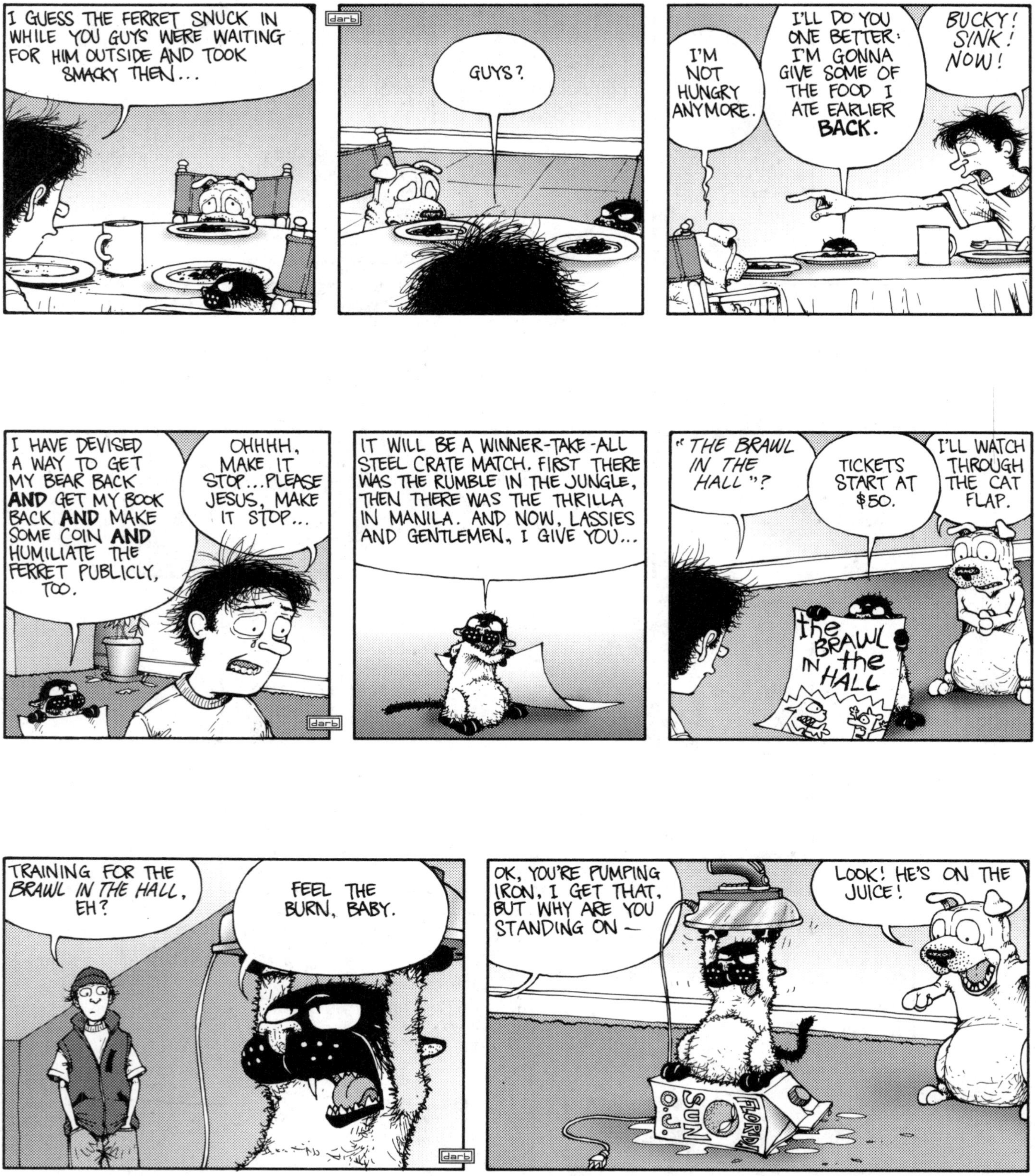

I GUESS THE FERRET SNUCK IN WHILE YOU GUYS WERE WAITING FOR HIM OUTSIDE AND TOOK SMACKY THEN...
GUYS?
I'M NOT HUNGRY ANYMORE.
I'LL DO YOU ONE BETTER: I'M GONNA GIVE SOME OF THE FOOD I ATE EARLIER **BACK**.
BUCKY! SINK! NOW!
I HAVE DEVISED A WAY TO GET MY BEAR BACK **AND** GET MY BOOK BACK **AND** MAKE SOME COIN **AND** HUMILIATE THE FERRET PUBLICLY, TOO.
OHHHH, MAKE IT STOP...PLEASE JESUS, MAKE IT STOP...
IT WILL BE A WINNER-TAKE-ALL STEEL CRATE MATCH. FIRST THERE WAS THE RUMBLE IN THE JUNGLE, THEN THERE WAS THE THRILLA IN MANILA. AND NOW, LASSIES AND GENTLEMEN, I GIVE YOU...
"*THE BRAWL IN THE HALL*"?
TICKETS START AT $50.
I'LL WATCH THROUGH THE CAT FLAP.
the BRAWL IN the HALL
TRAINING FOR THE *BRAWL IN THE HALL*, EH?
FEEL THE BURN, BABY.
OK, YOU'RE PUMPING IRON, I GET THAT, BUT WHY ARE YOU STANDING ON –
LOOK! HE'S ON THE JUICE!
SUN O.J. FLORIDA

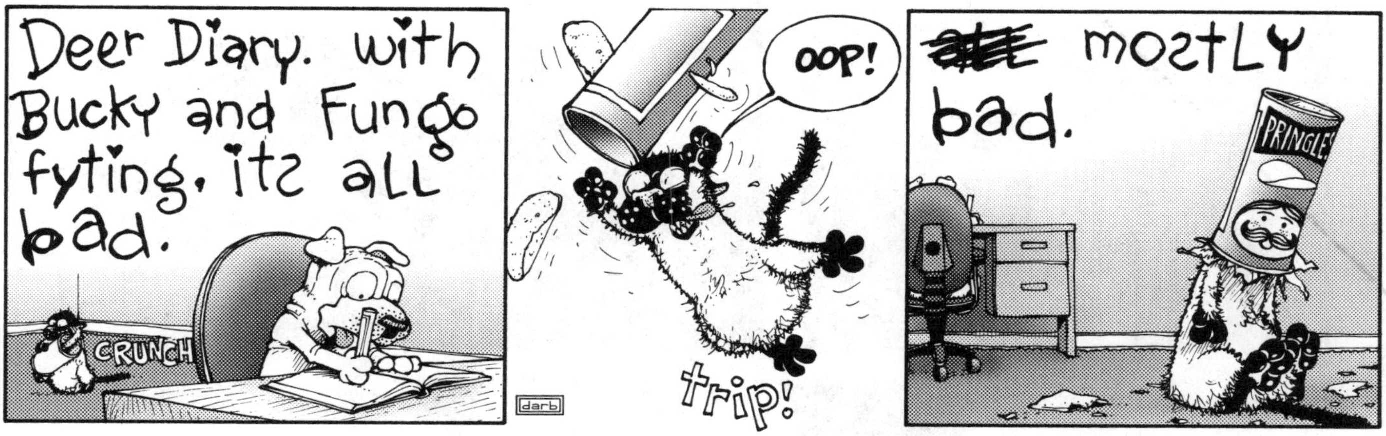
Deer Diary. with Bucky and Fungo fyting. itz aLL bad.
CRUNCH
darb
OOP!
trip!
mostLY bad.
PRINGLES

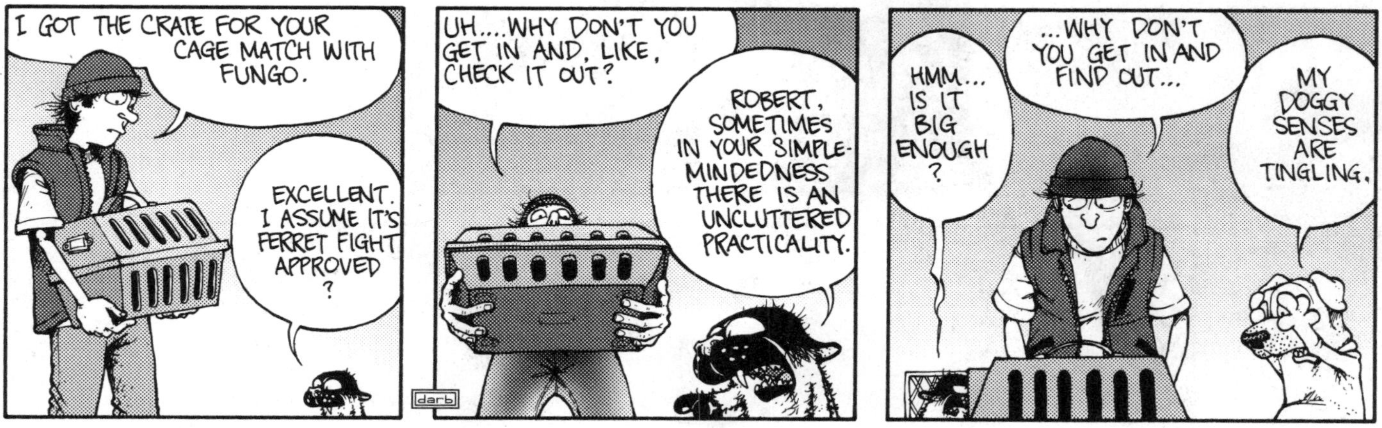
I GOT THE CRATE FOR YOUR CAGE MATCH WITH FUNGO.
EXCELLENT. I ASSUME IT'S FERRET FIGHT APPROVED ?
darb
UH....WHY DON'T YOU GET IN AND, LIKE, CHECK IT OUT?
ROBERT, SOMETIMES IN YOUR SIMPLE-MINDEDNESS THERE IS AN UNCLUTTERED PRACTICALITY.
HMM... IS IT BIG ENOUGH ?
...WHY DON'T YOU GET IN AND FIND OUT...
MY DOGGY SENSES ARE TINGLING.

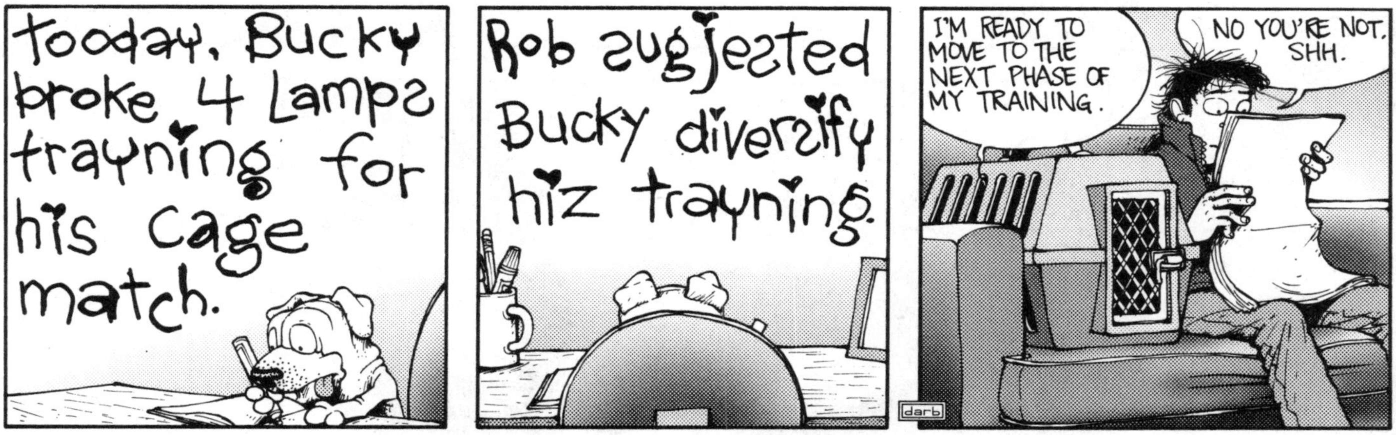
toodaY. Bucky broke 4 Lampz trayning for his cage match.
Rob sugjested Bucky diverzify hiz trayning.
darb
I'M READY TO MOVE TO THE NEXT PHASE OF MY TRAINING.
NO YOU'RE NOT. SHH.

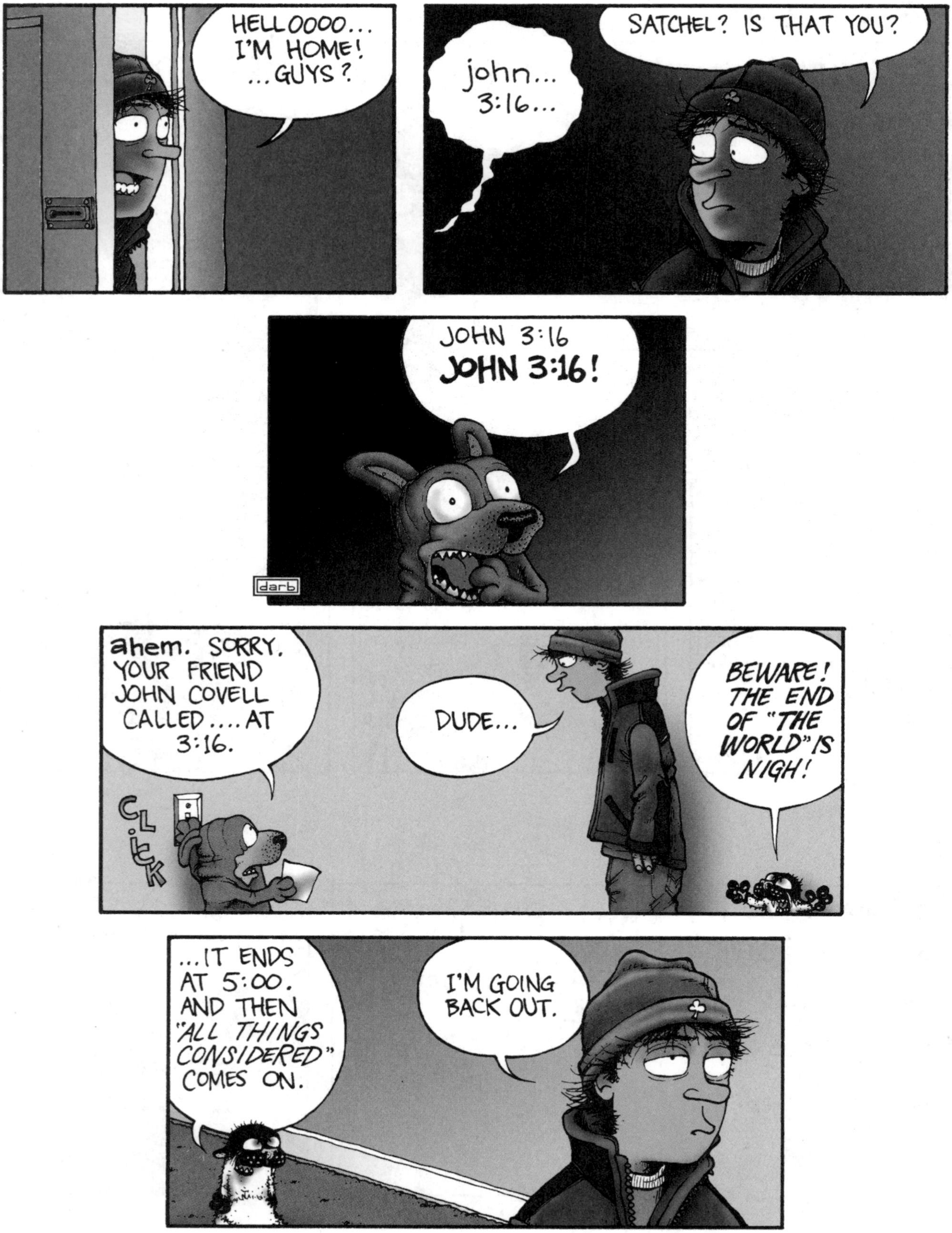
HELLOOOO... I'M HOME! ...GUYS?
SATCHEL? IS THAT YOU?
john... 3:16...
JOHN 3:16 JOHN 3:16!
darb
ahem. SORRY. YOUR FRIEND JOHN COVELL CALLED.... AT 3:16.
CLICK
DUDE...
BEWARE! THE END OF "THE WORLD" IS NIGH!
...IT ENDS AT 5:00. AND THEN "ALL THINGS CONSIDERED" COMES ON.
I'M GOING BACK OUT.

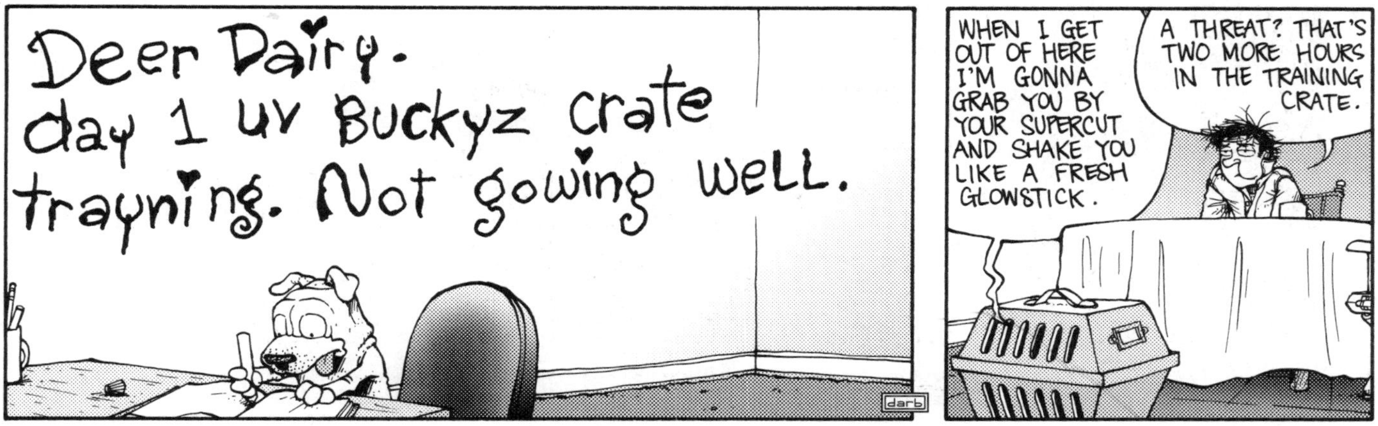
Deer Dairy. day 1 uv Buckyz crate trayning. Not gowing well.
darb
WHEN I GET OUT OF HERE I'M GONNA GRAB YOU BY YOUR SUPERCUT AND SHAKE YOU LIKE A FRESH GLOWSTICK.
A THREAT? THAT'S TWO MORE HOURS IN THE TRAINING CRATE.

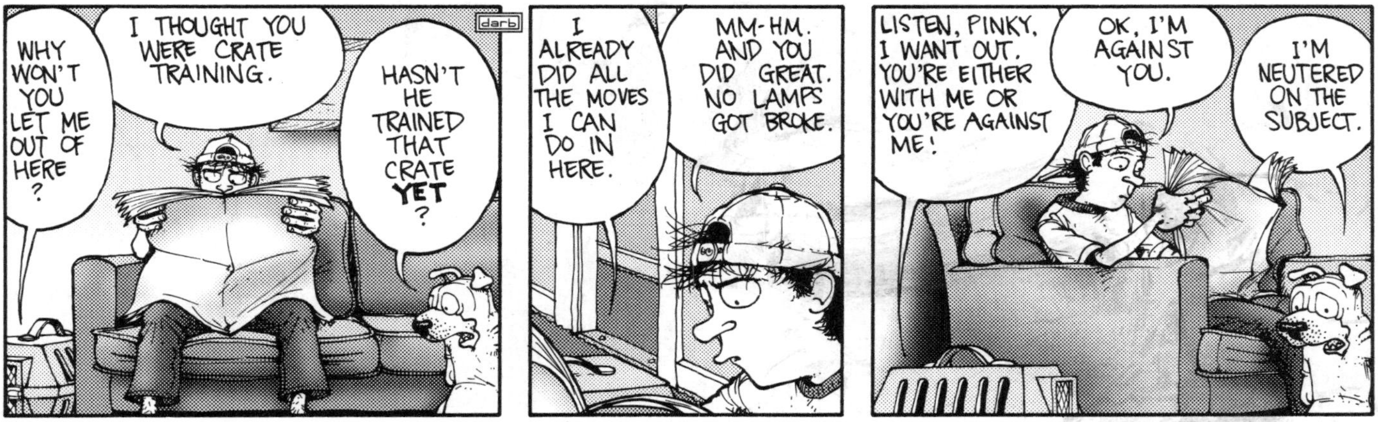
darb
WHY WON'T YOU LET ME OUT OF HERE?
I THOUGHT YOU WERE CRATE TRAINING.
HASN'T HE TRAINED THAT CRATE YET?
I ALREADY DID ALL THE MOVES I CAN DO IN HERE.
MM-HM. AND YOU DID GREAT. NO LAMPS GOT BROKE.
LISTEN, PINKY. I WANT OUT. YOU'RE EITHER WITH ME OR YOU'RE AGAINST ME!
OK, I'M AGAINST YOU.
I'M NEUTERED ON THE SUBJECT.

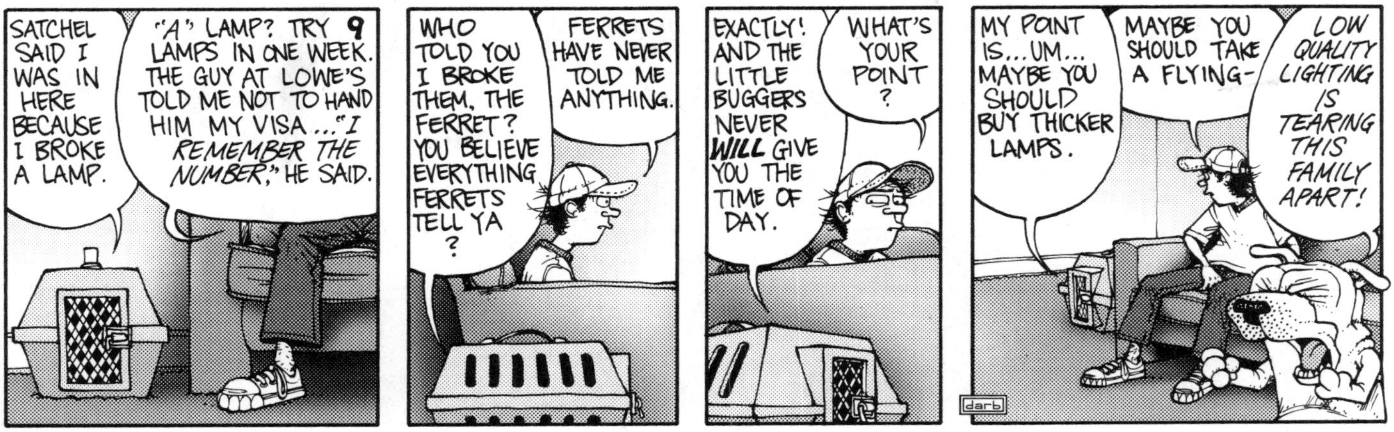
SATCHEL SAID I WAS IN HERE BECAUSE I BROKE A LAMP.
"A" LAMP? TRY 9 LAMPS IN ONE WEEK. THE GUY AT LOWE'S TOLD ME NOT TO HAND HIM MY VISA... "I REMEMBER THE NUMBER," HE SAID.
WHO TOLD YOU I BROKE THEM, THE FERRET? YOU BELIEVE EVERYTHING FERRETS TELL YA?
FERRETS HAVE NEVER TOLD ME ANYTHING.
EXACTLY! AND THE LITTLE BUGGERS NEVER WILL GIVE YOU THE TIME OF DAY.
WHAT'S YOUR POINT?
MY POINT IS... UM... MAYBE YOU SHOULD BUY THICKER LAMPS.
MAYBE YOU SHOULD TAKE A FLYING-
LOW QUALITY LIGHTING IS TEARING THIS FAMILY APART!
darb

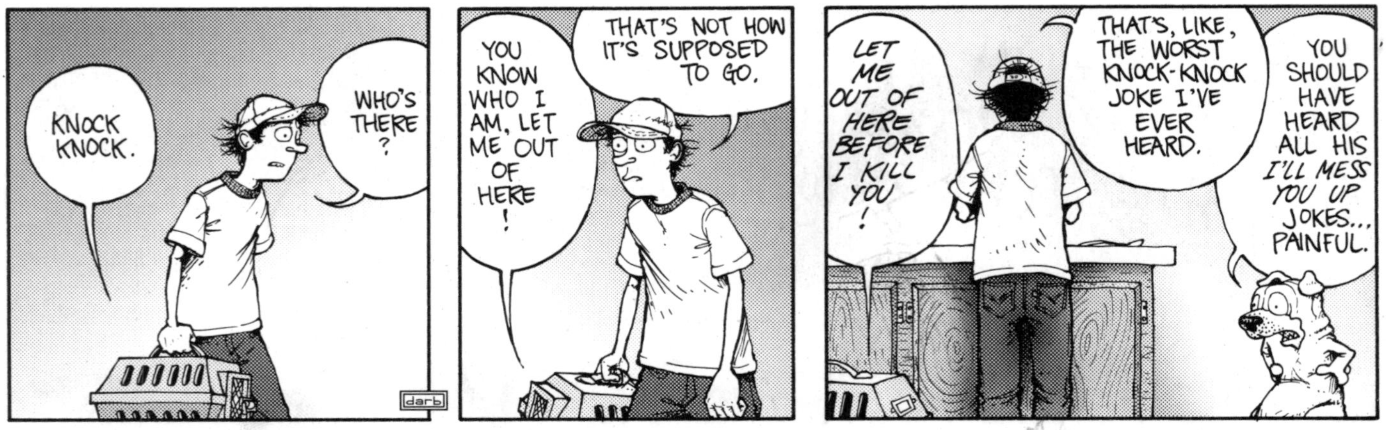
KNOCK KNOCK.
WHO'S THERE?
YOU KNOW WHO I AM, LET ME OUT OF HERE!
THAT'S NOT HOW IT'S SUPPOSED TO GO.
LET ME OUT OF HERE BEFORE I KILL YOU!
THAT'S, LIKE, THE WORST KNOCK-KNOCK JOKE I'VE EVER HEARD.
YOU SHOULD HAVE HEARD ALL HIS *I'LL MESS YOU UP* JOKES... PAINFUL.
darb

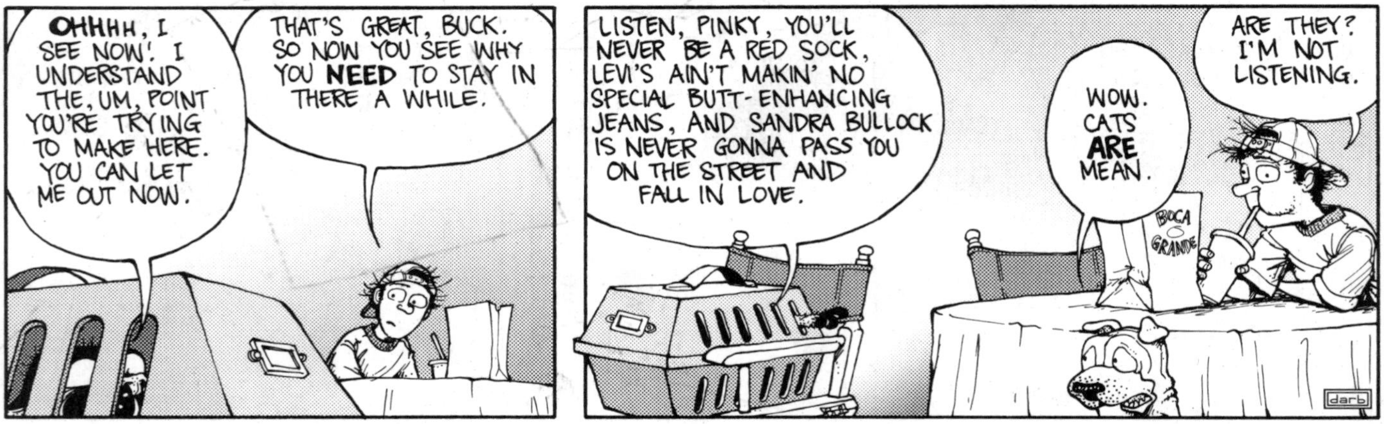
OHHHHH, I SEE NOW! I UNDERSTAND THE, UM, POINT YOU'RE TRYING TO MAKE HERE. YOU CAN LET ME OUT NOW.
THAT'S GREAT, BUCK. SO NOW YOU SEE WHY YOU **NEED** TO STAY IN THERE A WHILE.
LISTEN, PINKY, YOU'LL NEVER BE A RED SOCK, LEVI'S AIN'T MAKIN' NO SPECIAL BUTT-ENHANCING JEANS, AND SANDRA BULLOCK IS NEVER GONNA PASS YOU ON THE STREET AND FALL IN LOVE.
WOW. CATS **ARE** MEAN.
ARE THEY? I'M NOT LISTENING.
BOCA GRANDE
darb

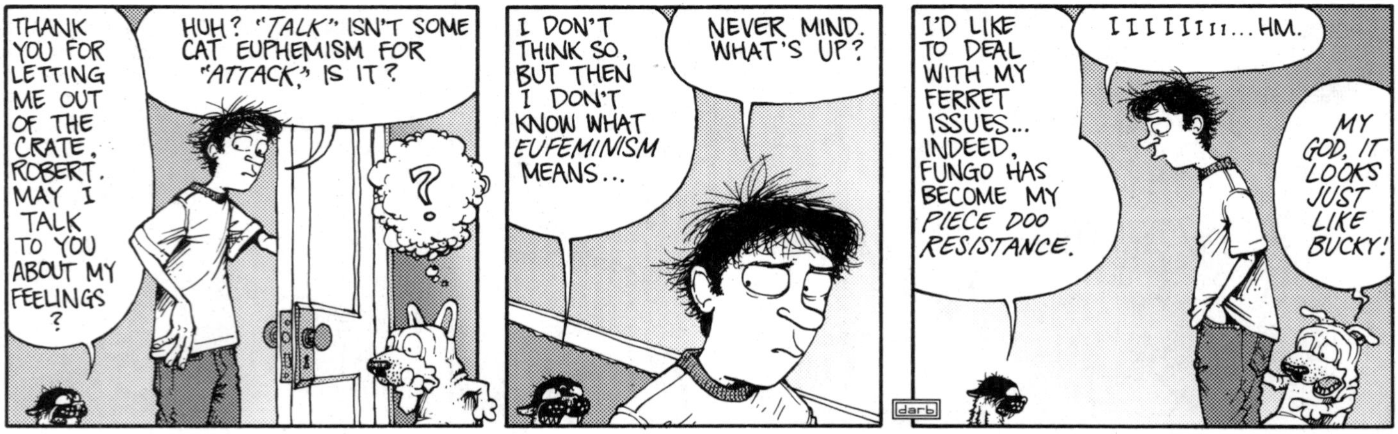
THANK YOU FOR LETTING ME OUT OF THE CRATE, ROBERT. MAY I TALK TO YOU ABOUT MY FEELINGS?
HUH? "*TALK*" ISN'T SOME CAT EUPHEMISM FOR "*ATTACK*," IS IT?
?
I DON'T THINK SO, BUT THEN I DON'T KNOW WHAT *EUFEMINISM* MEANS...
NEVER MIND. WHAT'S UP?
I'D LIKE TO DEAL WITH MY FERRET ISSUES... INDEED, FUNGO HAS BECOME MY *PIECE DOO RESISTANCE*.
IIIIIIII... HM.
MY GOD, IT LOOKS JUST LIKE BUCKY!
darb

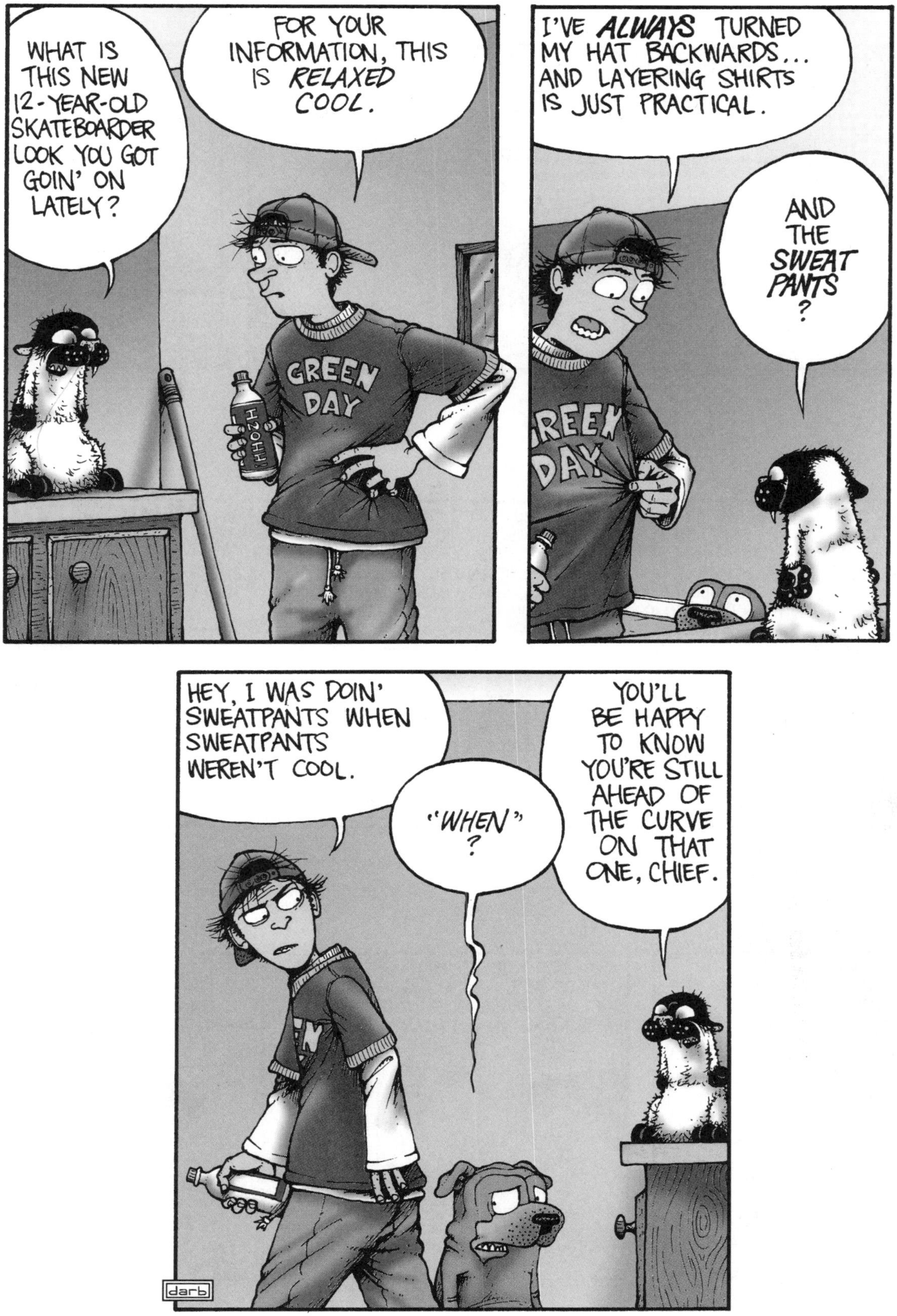
WHAT IS THIS NEW 12-YEAR-OLD SKATEBOARDER LOOK YOU GOT GOIN' ON LATELY?
FOR YOUR INFORMATION, THIS IS RELAXED COOL.
GREEN DAY
H2OHH
I'VE ALWAYS TURNED MY HAT BACKWARDS... AND LAYERING SHIRTS IS JUST PRACTICAL.
AND THE SWEAT PANTS?
HEY, I WAS DOIN' SWEATPANTS WHEN SWEATPANTS WEREN'T COOL.
"WHEN"?
YOU'LL BE HAPPY TO KNOW YOU'RE STILL AHEAD OF THE CURVE ON THAT ONE, CHIEF.
darb

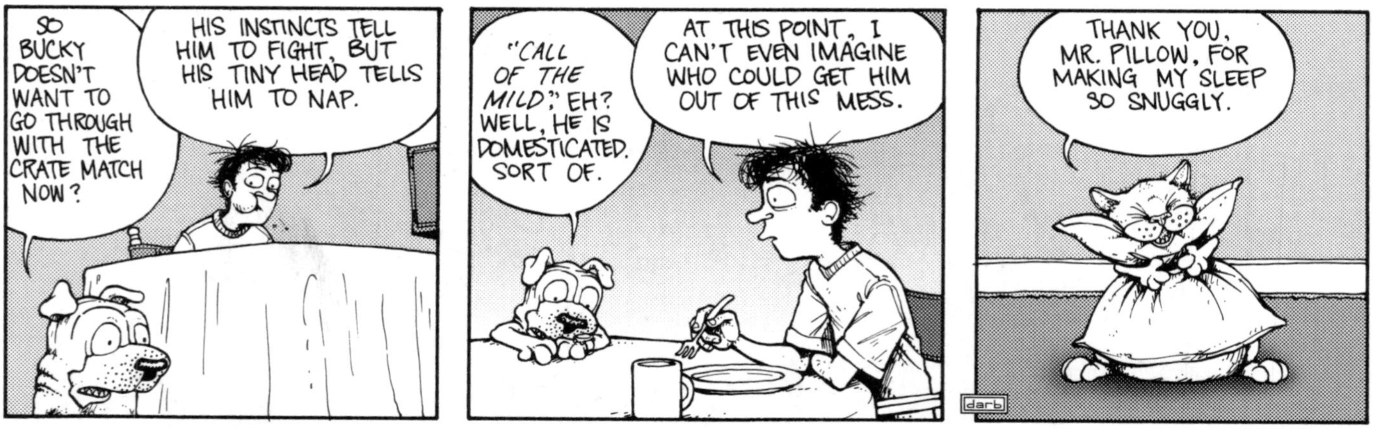
SO BUCKY DOESN'T WANT TO GO THROUGH WITH THE CRATE MATCH NOW?
HIS INSTINCTS TELL HIM TO FIGHT, BUT HIS TINY HEAD TELLS HIM TO NAP.
"CALL OF THE MILD," EH? WELL, HE IS DOMESTICATED. SORT OF.
AT THIS POINT, I CAN'T EVEN IMAGINE WHO COULD GET HIM OUT OF THIS MESS.
THANK YOU, MR. PILLOW, FOR MAKING MY SLEEP SO SNUGGLY.
darb

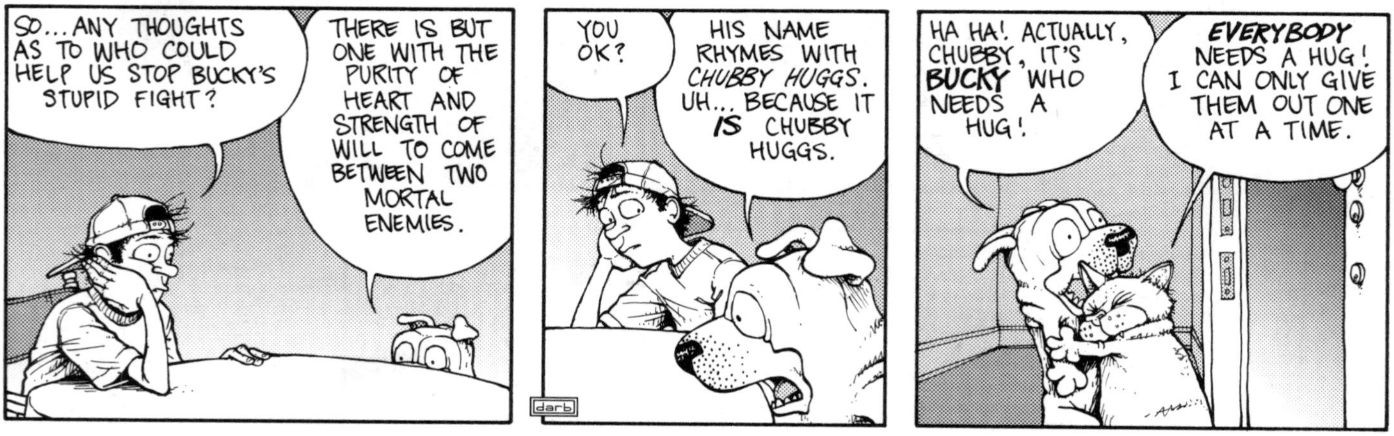
SO... ANY THOUGHTS AS TO WHO COULD HELP US STOP BUCKY'S STUPID FIGHT?
THERE IS BUT ONE WITH THE PURITY OF HEART AND STRENGTH OF WILL TO COME BETWEEN TWO MORTAL ENEMIES.
darb
YOU OK?
HIS NAME RHYMES WITH CHUBBY HUGGS. UH... BECAUSE IT IS CHUBBY HUGGS.
HA HA! ACTUALLY, CHUBBY, IT'S BUCKY WHO NEEDS A HUG!
EVERYBODY NEEDS A HUG! I CAN ONLY GIVE THEM OUT ONE AT A TIME.

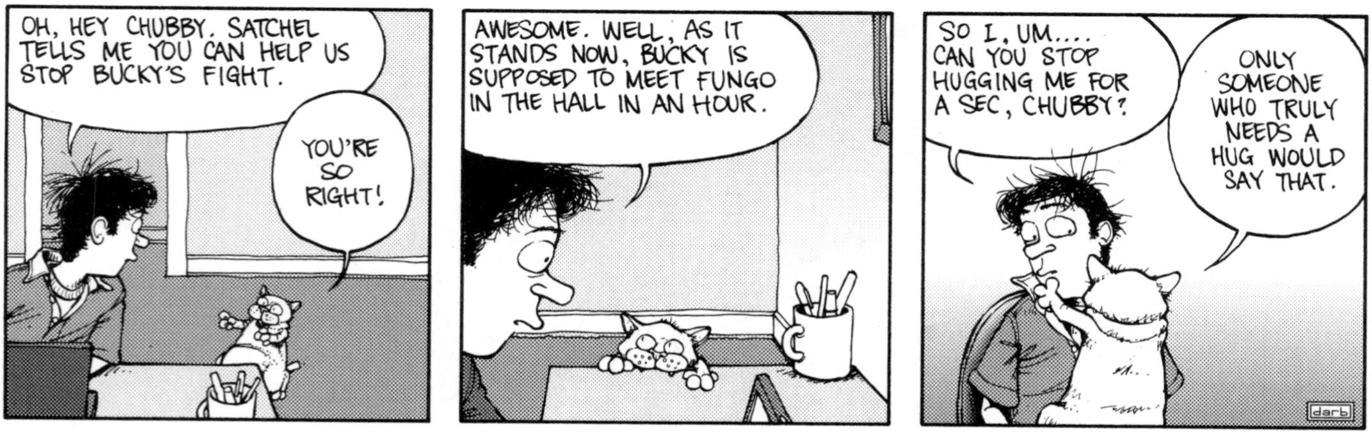
OH, HEY CHUBBY. SATCHEL TELLS ME YOU CAN HELP US STOP BUCKY'S FIGHT.
YOU'RE SO RIGHT!
AWESOME. WELL, AS IT STANDS NOW, BUCKY IS SUPPOSED TO MEET FUNGO IN THE HALL IN AN HOUR.
SO I, UM.... CAN YOU STOP HUGGING ME FOR A SEC, CHUBBY?
ONLY SOMEONE WHO TRULY NEEDS A HUG WOULD SAY THAT.
darb

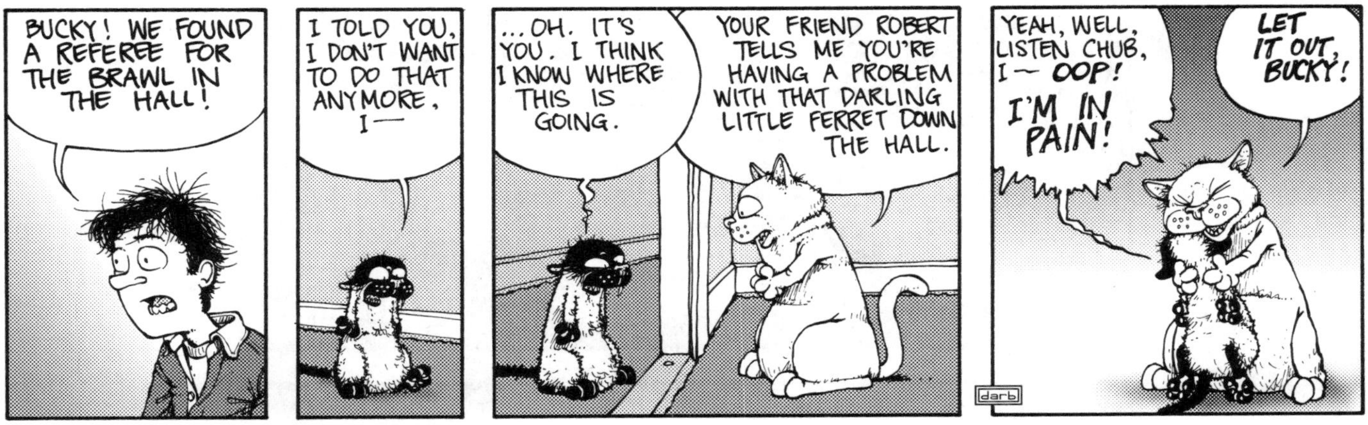
BUCKY! WE FOUND A REFEREE FOR THE BRAWL IN THE HALL!
I TOLD YOU, I DON'T WANT TO DO THAT ANYMORE, I—
...OH. IT'S YOU. I THINK I KNOW WHERE THIS IS GOING.
YOUR FRIEND ROBERT TELLS ME YOU'RE HAVING A PROBLEM WITH THAT DARLING LITTLE FERRET DOWN THE HALL.
YEAH, WELL, LISTEN CHUB, I— OOP!
I'M IN PAIN!
LET IT OUT, BUCKY!
darb

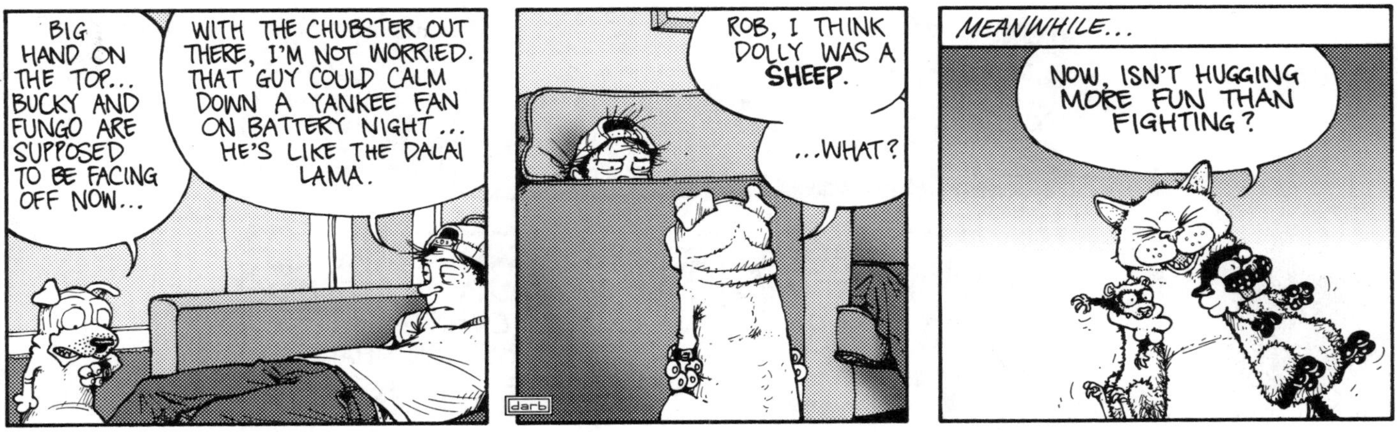
BIG HAND ON THE TOP... BUCKY AND FUNGO ARE SUPPOSED TO BE FACING OFF NOW...
WITH THE CHUBSTER OUT THERE, I'M NOT WORRIED. THAT GUY COULD CALM DOWN A YANKEE FAN ON BATTERY NIGHT... HE'S LIKE THE DALAI LAMA.
darb
ROB, I THINK DOLLY WAS A SHEEP.
...WHAT?
MEANWHILE...
NOW, ISN'T HUGGING MORE FUN THAN FIGHTING?

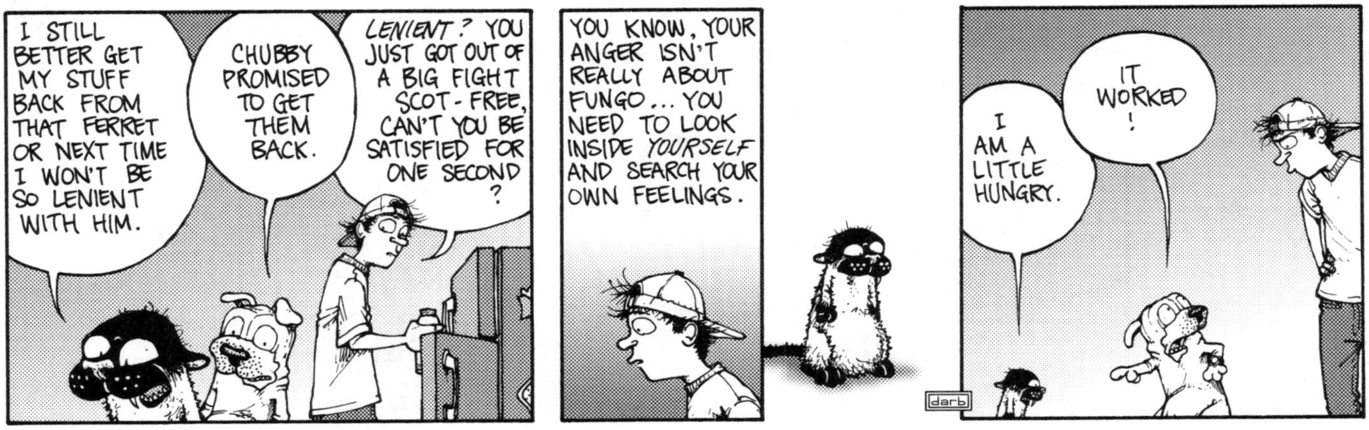
I STILL BETTER GET MY STUFF BACK FROM THAT FERRET OR NEXT TIME I WON'T BE SO LENIENT WITH HIM.
CHUBBY PROMISED TO GET THEM BACK.
LENIENT? YOU JUST GOT OUT OF A BIG FIGHT SCOT-FREE, CAN'T YOU BE SATISFIED FOR ONE SECOND?
YOU KNOW, YOUR ANGER ISN'T REALLY ABOUT FUNGO... YOU NEED TO LOOK INSIDE YOURSELF AND SEARCH YOUR OWN FEELINGS.
I AM A LITTLE HUNGRY.
IT WORKED!
darb

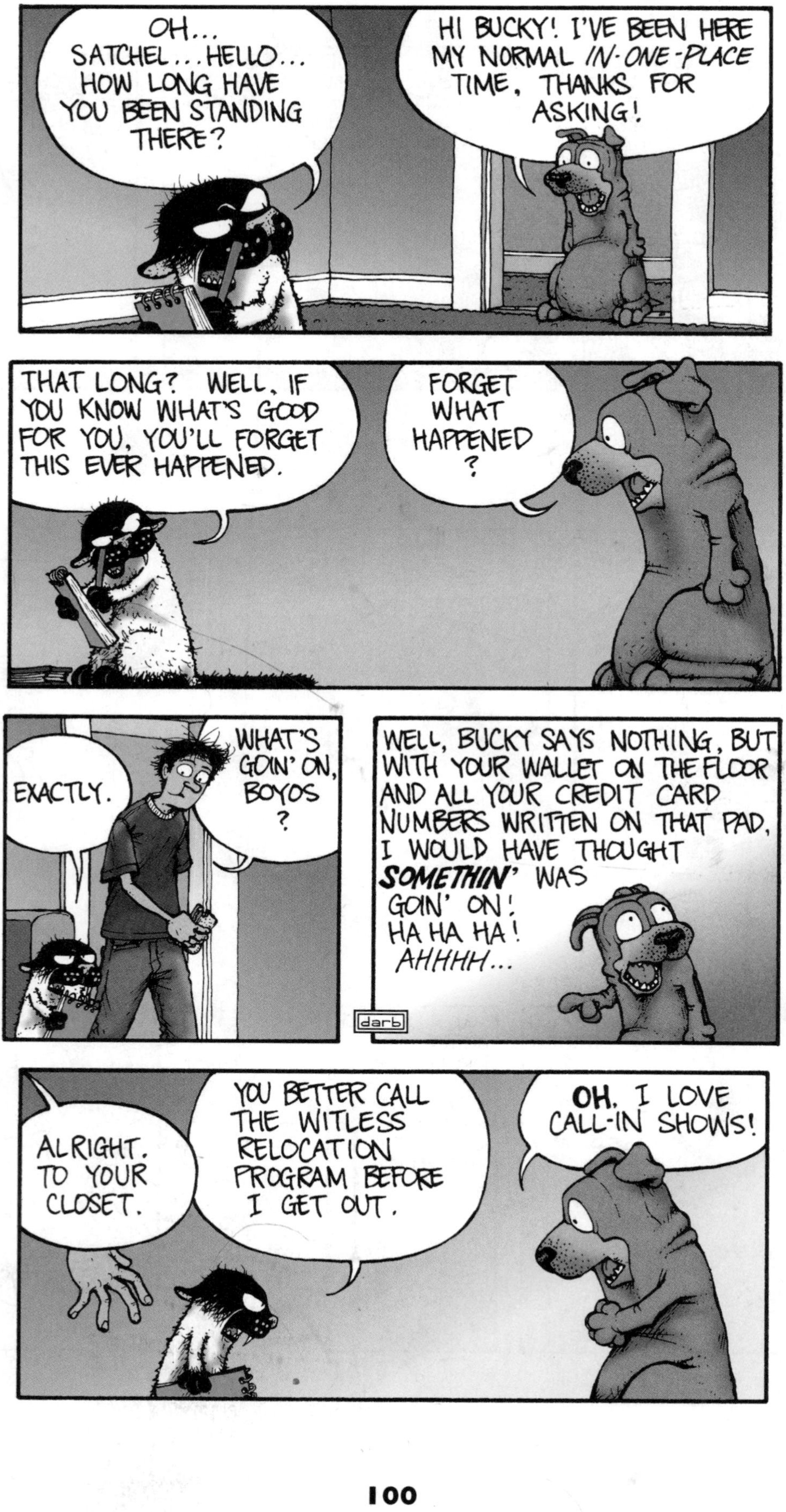
OH... SATCHEL... HELLO... HOW LONG HAVE YOU BEEN STANDING THERE?
HI BUCKY! I'VE BEEN HERE MY NORMAL *IN-ONE-PLACE* TIME, THANKS FOR ASKING!
THAT LONG? WELL, IF YOU KNOW WHAT'S GOOD FOR YOU, YOU'LL FORGET THIS EVER HAPPENED.
FORGET WHAT HAPPENED ?
EXACTLY.
WHAT'S GOIN' ON, BOYOS ?
WELL, BUCKY SAYS NOTHING, BUT WITH YOUR WALLET ON THE FLOOR AND ALL YOUR CREDIT CARD NUMBERS WRITTEN ON THAT PAD, I WOULD HAVE THOUGHT ***SOMETHIN'*** WAS GOIN' ON! HA HA HA! *AHHHH...*
darb
ALRIGHT. TO YOUR CLOSET.
YOU BETTER CALL THE WITLESS RELOCATION PROGRAM BEFORE I GET OUT.
OH, I LOVE CALL-IN SHOWS!

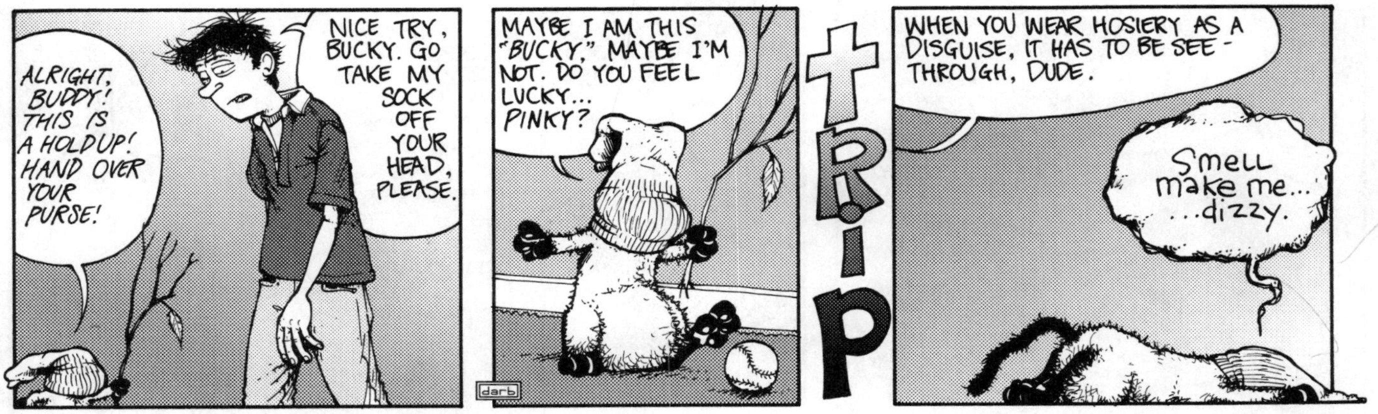
ALRIGHT, BUDDY! THIS IS A HOLDUP! HAND OVER YOUR PURSE!
NICE TRY, BUCKY. GO TAKE MY SOCK OFF YOUR HEAD, PLEASE.
MAYBE I AM THIS "BUCKY," MAYBE I'M NOT. DO YOU FEEL LUCKY... PINKY?
TRIP
WHEN YOU WEAR HOSIERY AS A DISGUISE, IT HAS TO BE SEE-THROUGH, DUDE.
Smell make me... ...dizzy.
darb

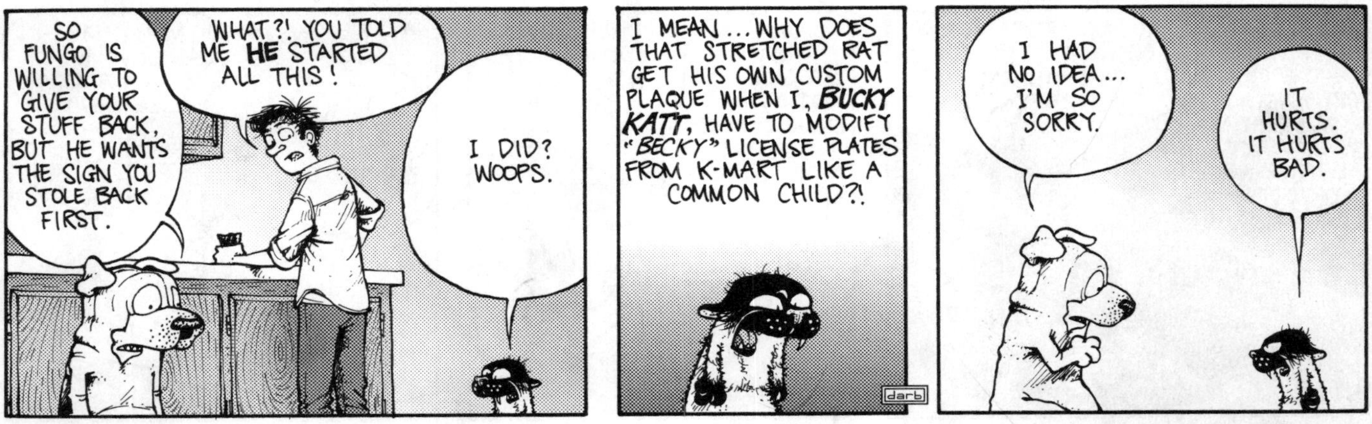
SO FUNGO IS WILLING TO GIVE YOUR STUFF BACK, BUT HE WANTS THE SIGN YOU STOLE BACK FIRST.
WHAT?! YOU TOLD ME **HE** STARTED ALL THIS!
I DID? WOOPS.
I MEAN... WHY DOES THAT STRETCHED RAT GET HIS OWN CUSTOM PLAQUE WHEN I, *BUCKY KATT*, HAVE TO MODIFY "*BECKY*" LICENSE PLATES FROM K-MART LIKE A COMMON CHILD?!
darb
I HAD NO IDEA... I'M SO SORRY.
IT HURTS. IT HURTS BAD.

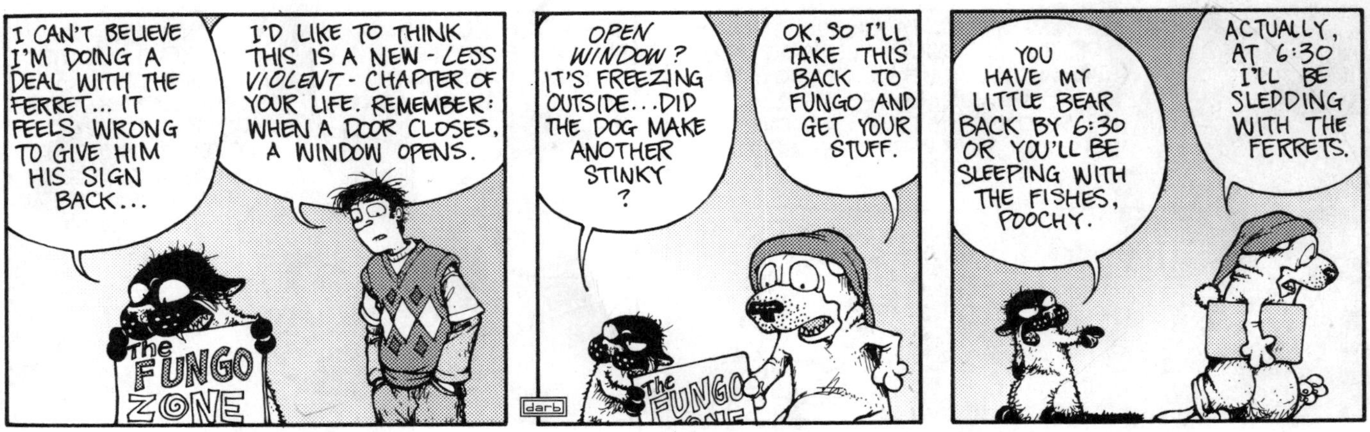
I CAN'T BELIEVE I'M DOING A DEAL WITH THE FERRET... IT FEELS WRONG TO GIVE HIM HIS SIGN BACK...
I'D LIKE TO THINK THIS IS A NEW - *LESS VIOLENT* - CHAPTER OF YOUR LIFE. REMEMBER: WHEN A DOOR CLOSES, A WINDOW OPENS.
The FUNGO ZONE
darb
OPEN WINDOW? IT'S FREEZING OUTSIDE... DID THE DOG MAKE ANOTHER STINKY?
OK, SO I'LL TAKE THIS BACK TO FUNGO AND GET YOUR STUFF.
YOU HAVE MY LITTLE BEAR BACK BY 6:30 OR YOU'LL BE SLEEPING WITH THE FISHES, POOCHY.
ACTUALLY, AT 6:30 I'LL BE SLEDDING WITH THE FERRETS.

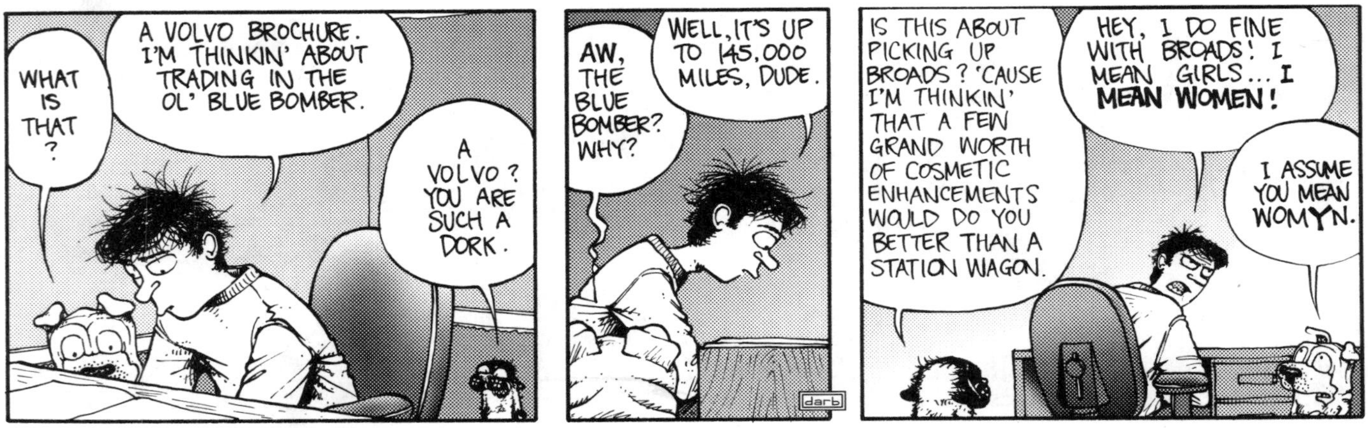
WHAT IS THAT?
A VOLVO BROCHURE. I'M THINKIN' ABOUT TRADING IN THE OL' BLUE BOMBER.
A VOLVO? YOU ARE SUCH A DORK.
AW, THE BLUE BOMBER? WHY?
WELL, IT'S UP TO 145,000 MILES, DUDE.
IS THIS ABOUT PICKING UP BROADS? 'CAUSE I'M THINKIN' THAT A FEW GRAND WORTH OF COSMETIC ENHANCEMENTS WOULD DO YOU BETTER THAN A STATION WAGON.
HEY, I DO FINE WITH BROADS! I MEAN GIRLS... I MEAN WOMEN!
I ASSUME YOU MEAN WOMYN.
darb

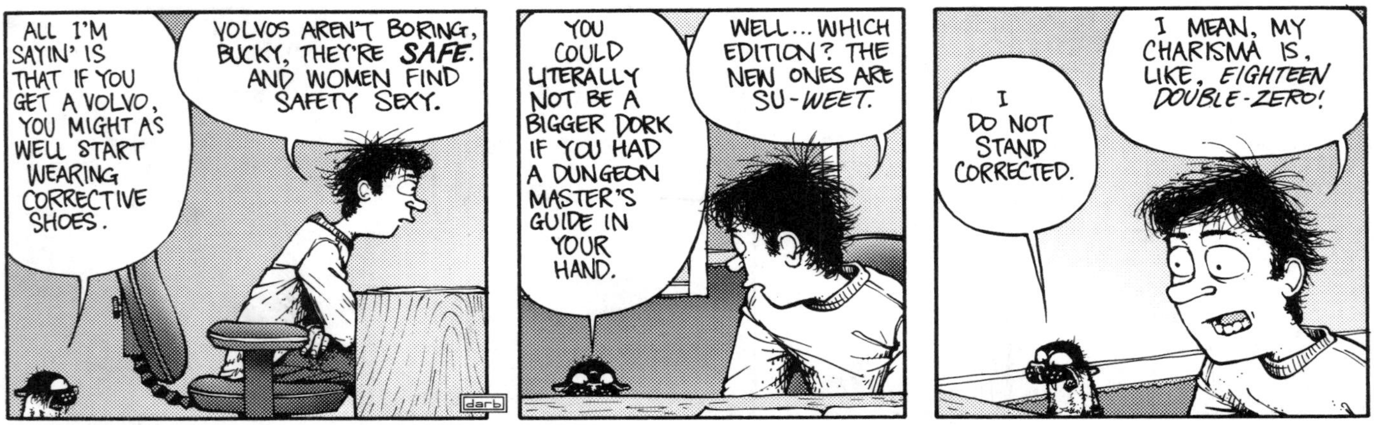
ALL I'M SAYIN' IS THAT IF YOU GET A VOLVO, YOU MIGHT AS WELL START WEARING CORRECTIVE SHOES.
VOLVOS AREN'T BORING, BUCKY, THEY'RE SAFE. AND WOMEN FIND SAFETY SEXY.
YOU COULD LITERALLY NOT BE A BIGGER DORK IF YOU HAD A DUNGEON MASTER'S GUIDE IN YOUR HAND.
WELL... WHICH EDITION? THE NEW ONES ARE SU-WEET.
I DO NOT STAND CORRECTED.
I MEAN, MY CHARISMA IS, LIKE, EIGHTEEN DOUBLE-ZERO!
darb

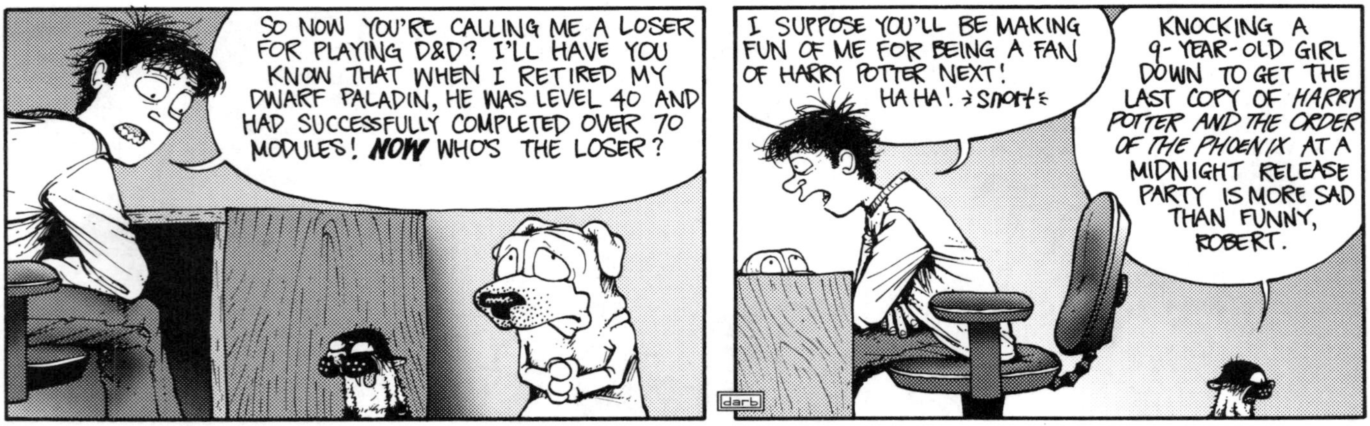
SO NOW YOU'RE CALLING ME A LOSER FOR PLAYING D&D? I'LL HAVE YOU KNOW THAT WHEN I RETIRED MY DWARF PALADIN, HE WAS LEVEL 40 AND HAD SUCCESSFULLY COMPLETED OVER 70 MODULES! NOW WHO'S THE LOSER?
I SUPPOSE YOU'LL BE MAKING FUN OF ME FOR BEING A FAN OF HARRY POTTER NEXT! HA HA! snort
KNOCKING A 9-YEAR-OLD GIRL DOWN TO GET THE LAST COPY OF HARRY POTTER AND THE ORDER OF THE PHOENIX AT A MIDNIGHT RELEASE PARTY IS MORE SAD THAN FUNNY, ROBERT.
darb

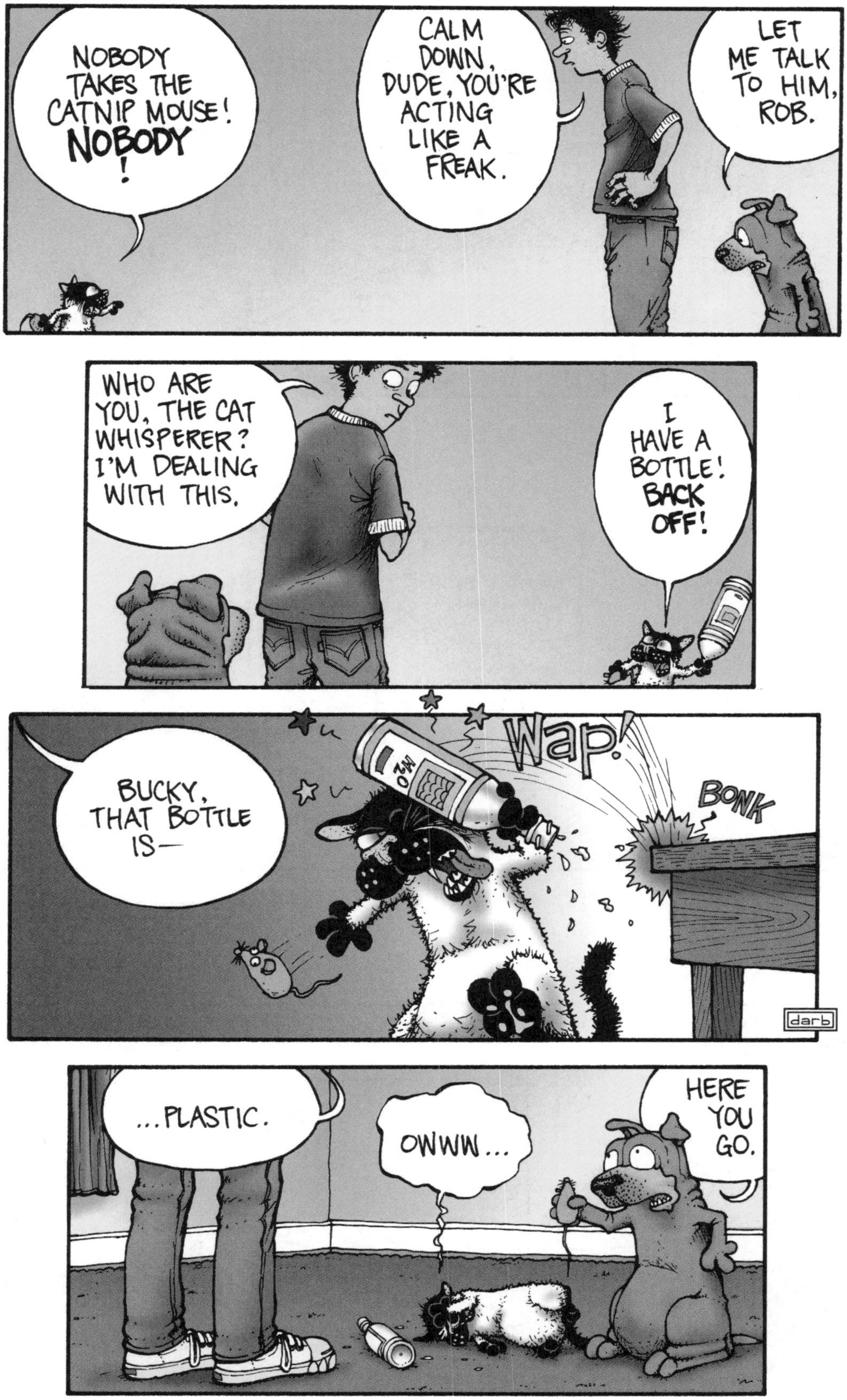
NOBODY TAKES THE CATNIP MOUSE! NOBODY!
CALM DOWN, DUDE, YOU'RE ACTING LIKE A FREAK.
LET ME TALK TO HIM, ROB.
WHO ARE YOU, THE CAT WHISPERER? I'M DEALING WITH THIS.
I HAVE A BOTTLE! BACK OFF!
BUCKY, THAT BOTTLE IS—
WAP!
BONK
darb
...PLASTIC.
OWWW...
HERE YOU GO.

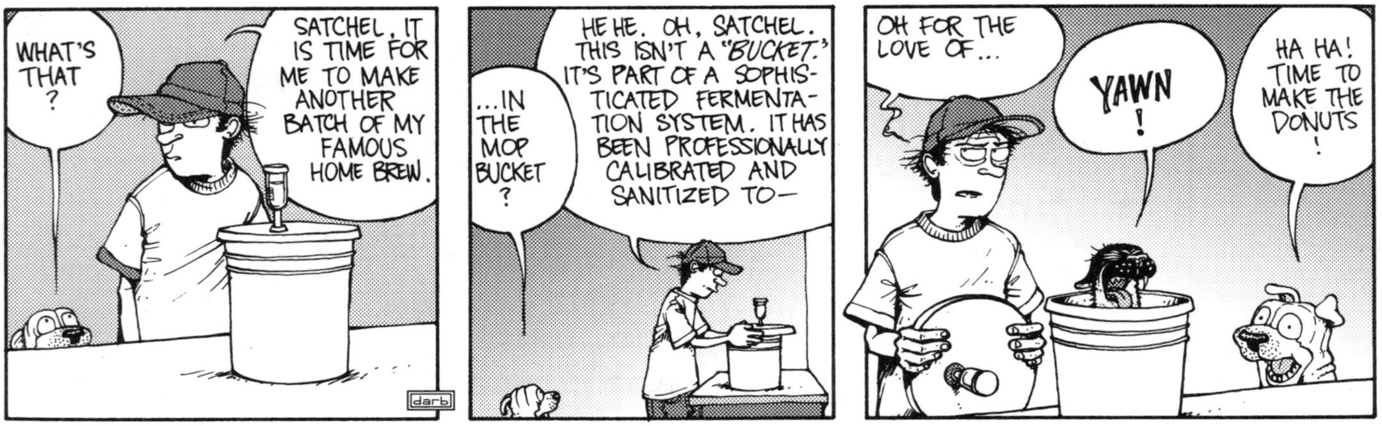
WHAT'S THAT?
SATCHEL, IT IS TIME FOR ME TO MAKE ANOTHER BATCH OF MY FAMOUS HOME BREW.
...IN THE MOP BUCKET?
HE HE. OH, SATCHEL. THIS ISN'T A "*BUCKET*." IT'S PART OF A SOPHISTICATED FERMENTATION SYSTEM. IT HAS BEEN PROFESSIONALLY CALIBRATED AND SANITIZED TO—
OH FOR THE LOVE OF...
YAWN!
HA HA! TIME TO MAKE THE DONUTS!
darb

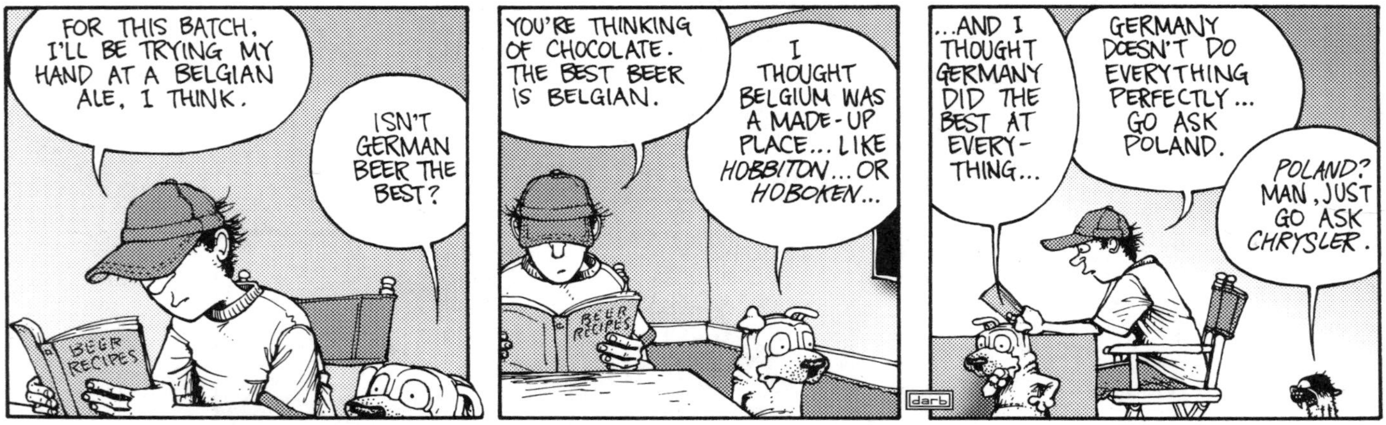
FOR THIS BATCH, I'LL BE TRYING MY HAND AT A BELGIAN ALE, I THINK.
ISN'T GERMAN BEER THE BEST?
BEER RECIPES
YOU'RE THINKING OF CHOCOLATE. THE BEST BEER IS BELGIAN.
I THOUGHT BELGIUM WAS A MADE-UP PLACE... LIKE *HOBBITON*... OR *HOBOKEN*...
...AND I THOUGHT GERMANY DID THE BEST AT EVERYTHING...
GERMANY DOESN'T DO EVERYTHING PERFECTLY... GO ASK POLAND.
POLAND? MAN, JUST GO ASK *CHRYSLER*.
darb

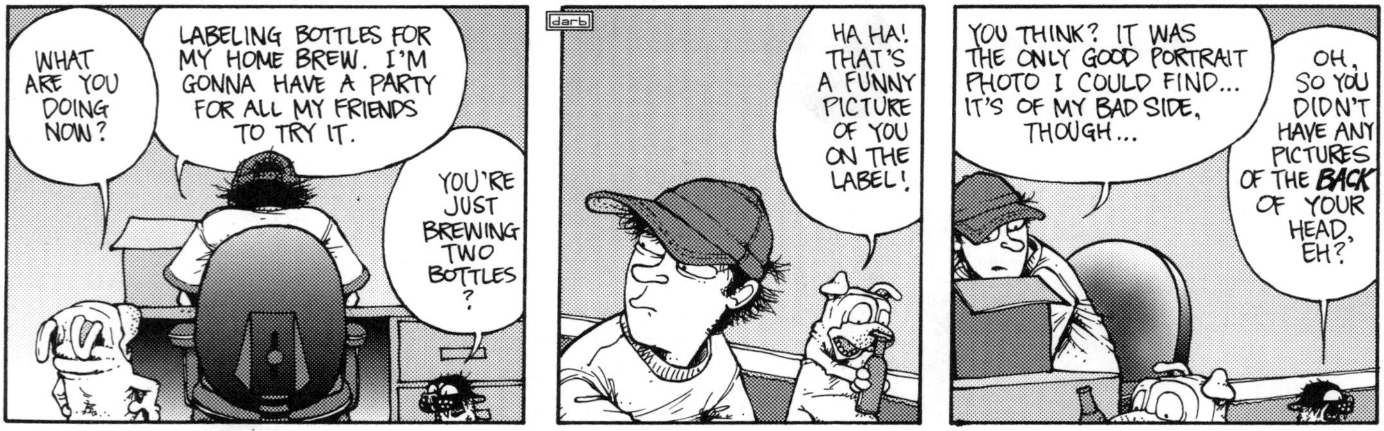
WHAT ARE YOU DOING NOW?
LABELING BOTTLES FOR MY HOME BREW. I'M GONNA HAVE A PARTY FOR ALL MY FRIENDS TO TRY IT.
YOU'RE JUST BREWING TWO BOTTLES?
darb
HA HA! THAT'S A FUNNY PICTURE OF YOU ON THE LABEL!
YOU THINK? IT WAS THE ONLY GOOD PORTRAIT PHOTO I COULD FIND... IT'S OF MY BAD SIDE, THOUGH...
OH, SO YOU DIDN'T HAVE ANY PICTURES OF THE *BACK* OF YOUR HEAD, EH?

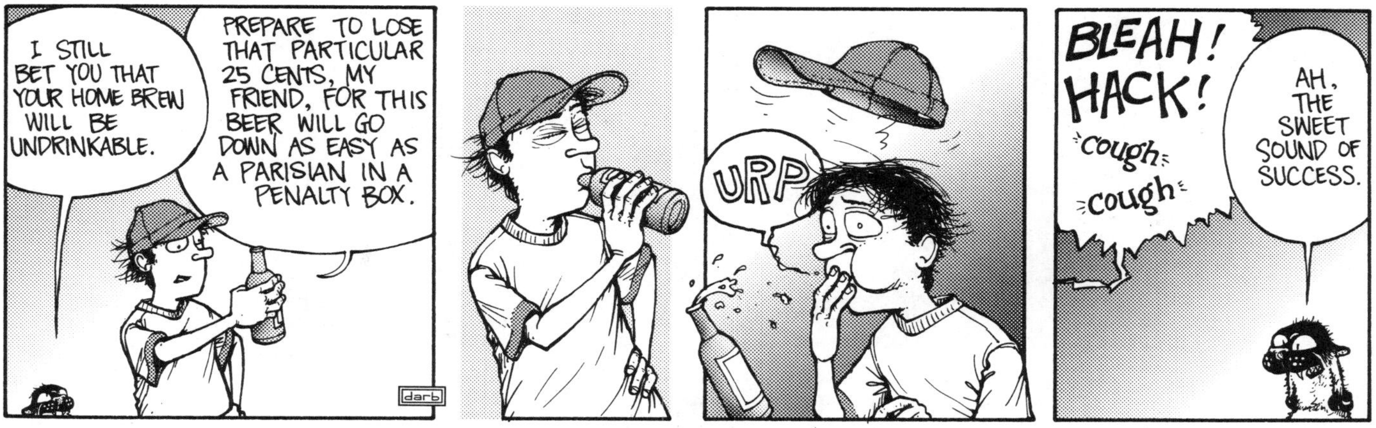
I STILL BET YOU THAT YOUR HOME BREW WILL BE UNDRINKABLE.
PREPARE TO LOSE THAT PARTICULAR 25 CENTS, MY FRIEND, FOR THIS BEER WILL GO DOWN AS EASY AS A PARISIAN IN A PENALTY BOX.
darb
URP
BLEAH! HACK! cough cough
AH, THE SWEET SOUND OF SUCCESS.

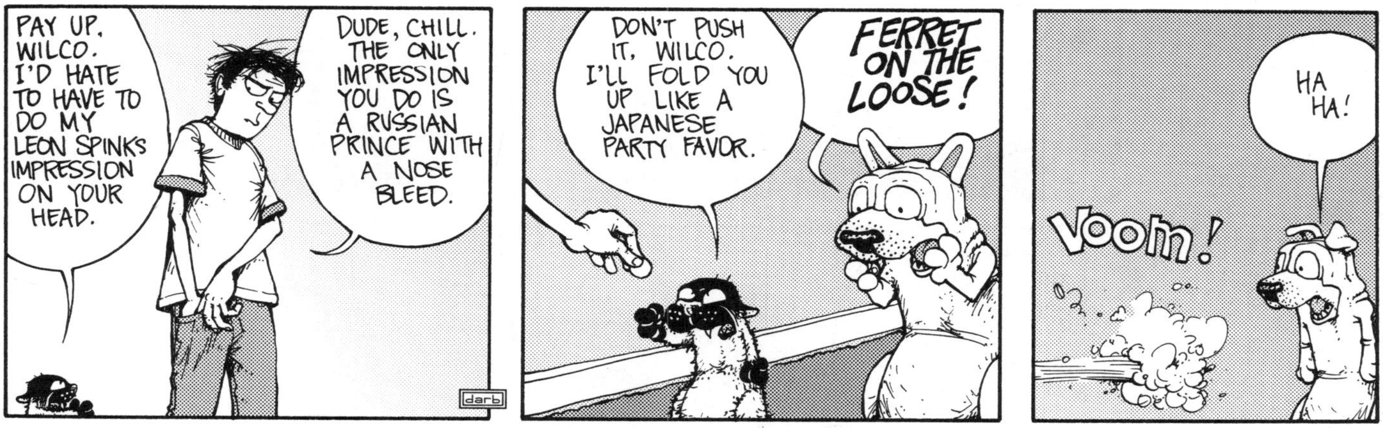
PAY UP, WILCO. I'D HATE TO HAVE TO DO MY LEON SPINKS IMPRESSION ON YOUR HEAD.
DUDE, CHILL. THE ONLY IMPRESSION YOU DO IS A RUSSIAN PRINCE WITH A NOSE BLEED.
darb
DON'T PUSH IT, WILCO. I'LL FOLD YOU UP LIKE A JAPANESE PARTY FAVOR.
FERRET ON THE LOOSE!
Voom!
HA HA!

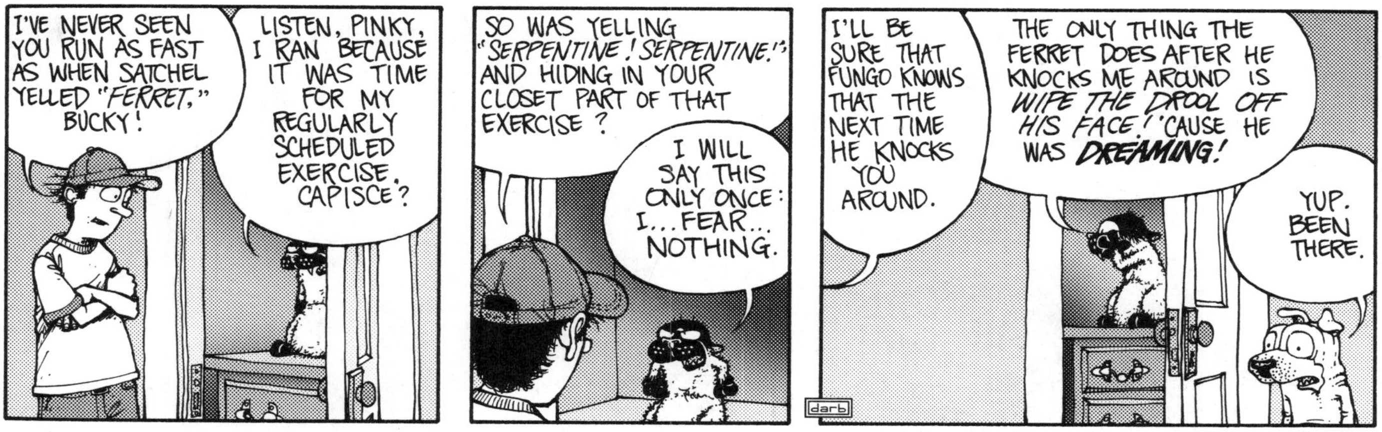
I'VE NEVER SEEN YOU RUN AS FAST AS WHEN SATCHEL YELLED "FERRET," BUCKY!
LISTEN, PINKY, I RAN BECAUSE IT WAS TIME FOR MY REGULARLY SCHEDULED EXERCISE. CAPISCE?
SO WAS YELLING "SERPENTINE! SERPENTINE!" AND HIDING IN YOUR CLOSET PART OF THAT EXERCISE?
I WILL SAY THIS ONLY ONCE: I... FEAR... NOTHING.
darb
I'LL BE SURE THAT FUNGO KNOWS THAT THE NEXT TIME HE KNOCKS YOU AROUND.
THE ONLY THING THE FERRET DOES AFTER HE KNOCKS ME AROUND IS WIPE THE DROOL OFF HIS FACE! 'CAUSE HE WAS DREAMING!
YUP. BEEN THERE.

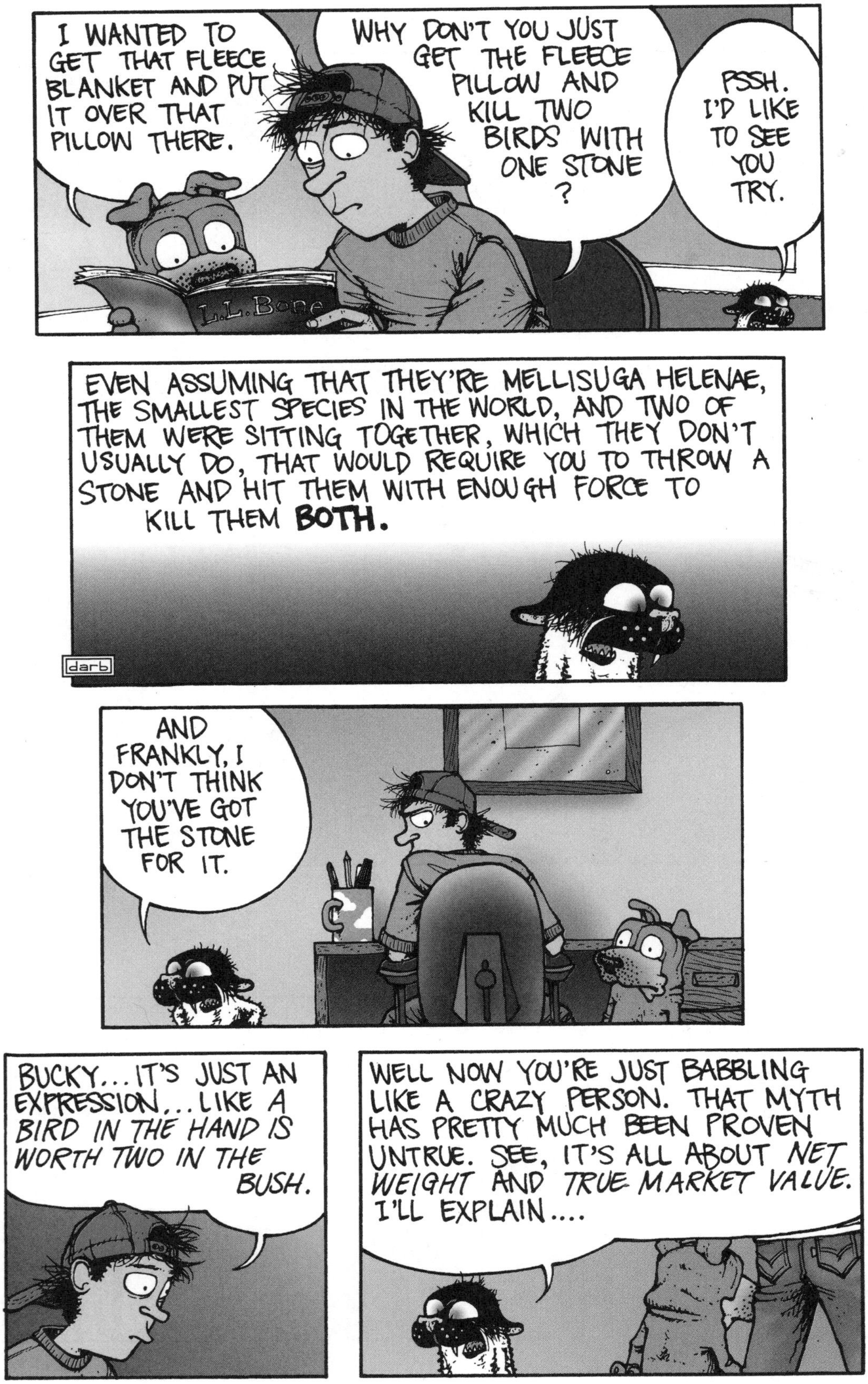
I WANTED TO GET THAT FLEECE BLANKET AND PUT IT OVER THAT PILLOW THERE.
WHY DON'T YOU JUST GET THE FLEECE PILLOW AND KILL TWO BIRDS WITH ONE STONE ?
PSSH. I'D LIKE TO SEE YOU TRY.
L.L.Bone
EVEN ASSUMING THAT THEY'RE MELLISUGA HELENAE, THE SMALLEST SPECIES IN THE WORLD, AND TWO OF THEM WERE SITTING TOGETHER, WHICH THEY DON'T USUALLY DO, THAT WOULD REQUIRE YOU TO THROW A STONE AND HIT THEM WITH ENOUGH FORCE TO KILL THEM **BOTH.**
darb
AND FRANKLY, I DON'T THINK YOU'VE GOT THE STONE FOR IT.
BUCKY... IT'S JUST AN EXPRESSION... LIKE *A BIRD IN THE HAND IS WORTH TWO IN THE BUSH.*
WELL NOW YOU'RE JUST BABBLING LIKE A CRAZY PERSON. THAT MYTH HAS PRETTY MUCH BEEN PROVEN UNTRUE. SEE, IT'S ALL ABOUT *NET WEIGHT* AND *TRUE MARKET VALUE.* I'LL EXPLAIN....

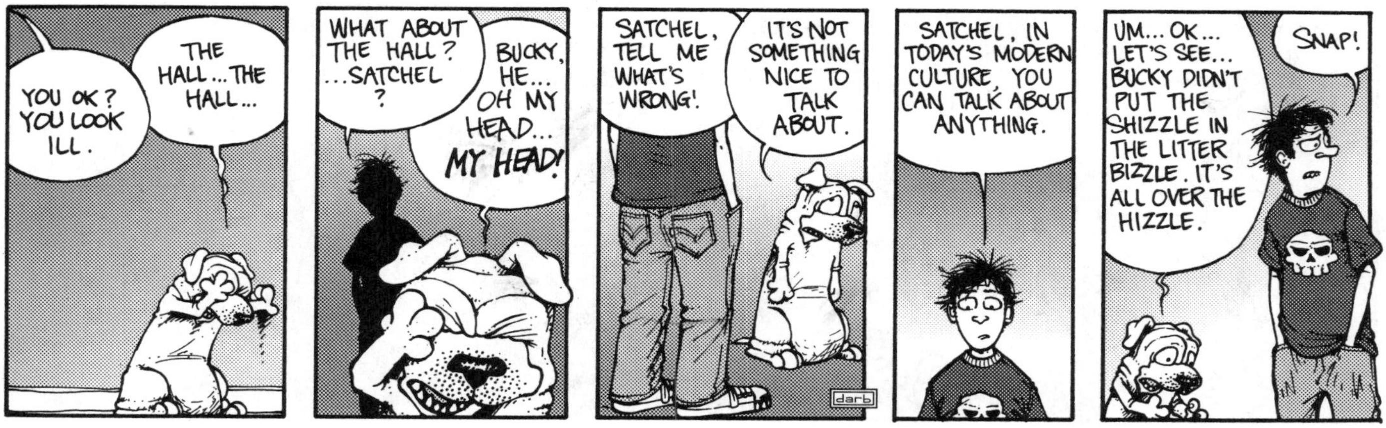
YOU OK? YOU LOOK ILL.
THE HALL... THE HALL...
WHAT ABOUT THE HALL? ...SATCHEL?
BUCKY, HE... OH MY HEAD... MY HEAD!
SATCHEL, TELL ME WHAT'S WRONG!
IT'S NOT SOMETHING NICE TO TALK ABOUT.
SATCHEL, IN TODAY'S MODERN CULTURE, YOU CAN TALK ABOUT ANYTHING.
UM... OK... LET'S SEE... BUCKY DIDN'T PUT THE SHIZZLE IN THE LITTER BIZZLE. IT'S ALL OVER THE HIZZLE.
SNAP!

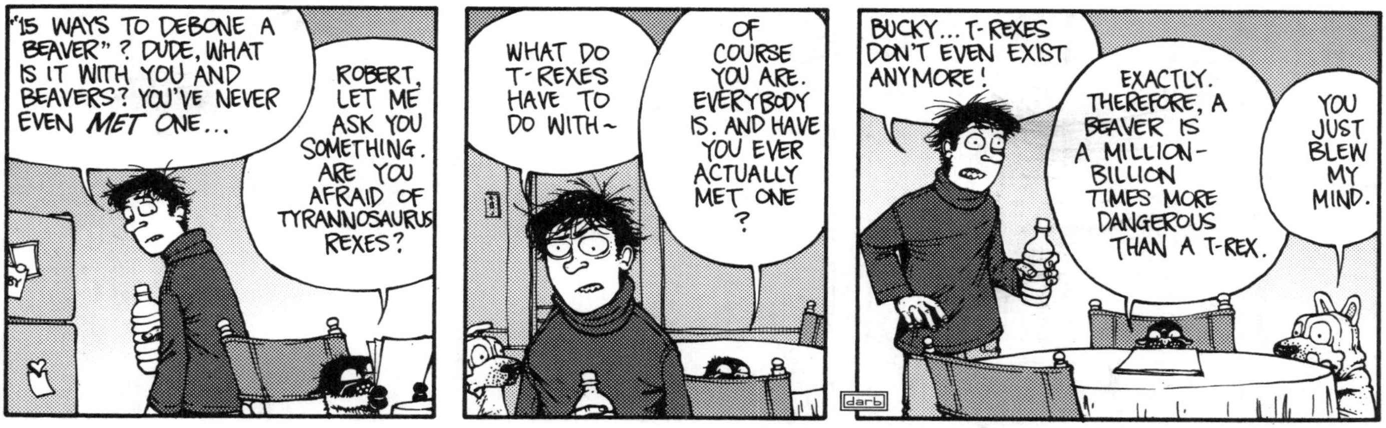
"15 WAYS TO DEBONE A BEAVER"? DUDE, WHAT IS IT WITH YOU AND BEAVERS? YOU'VE NEVER EVEN MET ONE...
ROBERT, LET ME ASK YOU SOMETHING. ARE YOU AFRAID OF TYRANNOSAURUS REXES?
WHAT DO T-REXES HAVE TO DO WITH~
OF COURSE YOU ARE. EVERYBODY IS. AND HAVE YOU EVER ACTUALLY MET ONE?
BUCKY... T-REXES DON'T EVEN EXIST ANYMORE!
EXACTLY. THEREFORE, A BEAVER IS A MILLION-BILLION TIMES MORE DANGEROUS THAN A T-REX.
YOU JUST BLEW MY MIND.

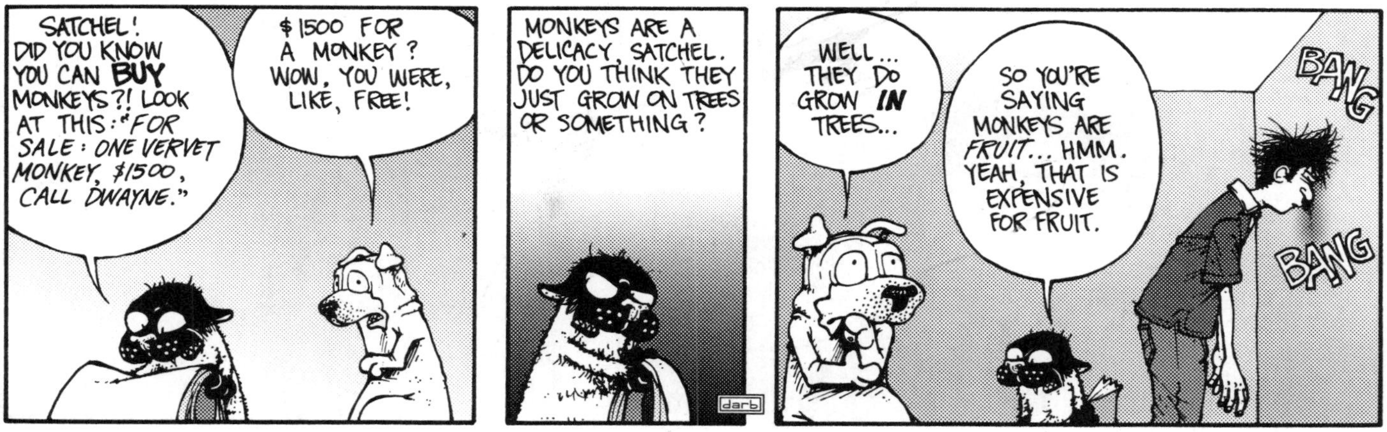
SATCHEL! DID YOU KNOW YOU CAN BUY MONKEYS?! LOOK AT THIS: "FOR SALE: ONE VERVET MONKEY, $1500, CALL DWAYNE."
$1500 FOR A MONKEY? WOW, YOU WERE, LIKE, FREE!
MONKEYS ARE A DELICACY, SATCHEL. DO YOU THINK THEY JUST GROW ON TREES OR SOMETHING?
WELL... THEY DO GROW IN TREES...
SO YOU'RE SAYING MONKEYS ARE FRUIT... HMM. YEAH, THAT IS EXPENSIVE FOR FRUIT.
BANG
BANG

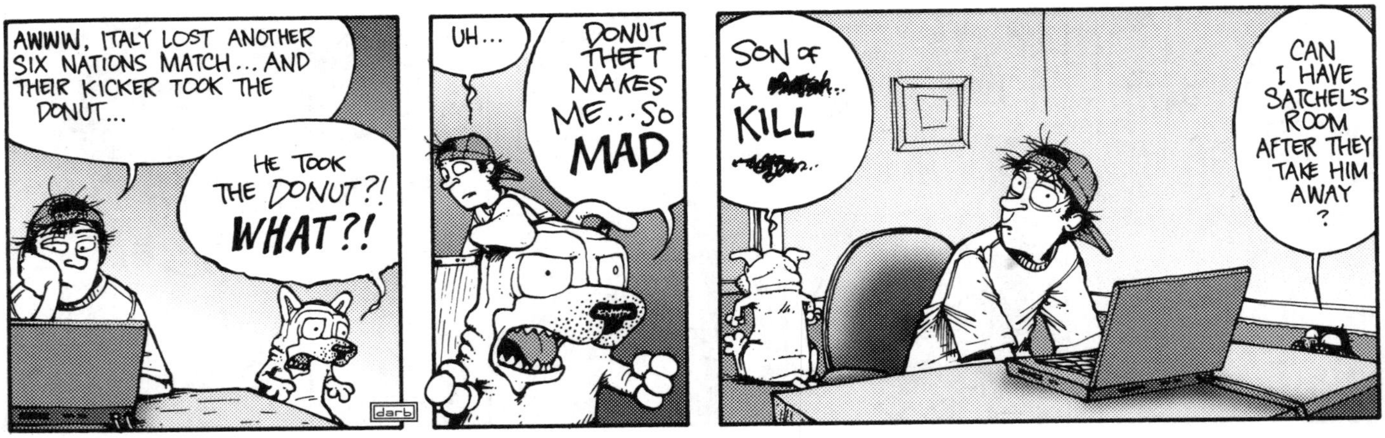
AWWW, ITALY LOST ANOTHER SIX NATIONS MATCH... AND THEIR KICKER TOOK THE DONUT...
HE TOOK THE DONUT?! WHAT?!
UH...
DONUT THEFT MAKES ME... SO MAD
SON OF A [redacted]... KILL [redacted]...
CAN I HAVE SATCHEL'S ROOM AFTER THEY TAKE HIM AWAY?
darb

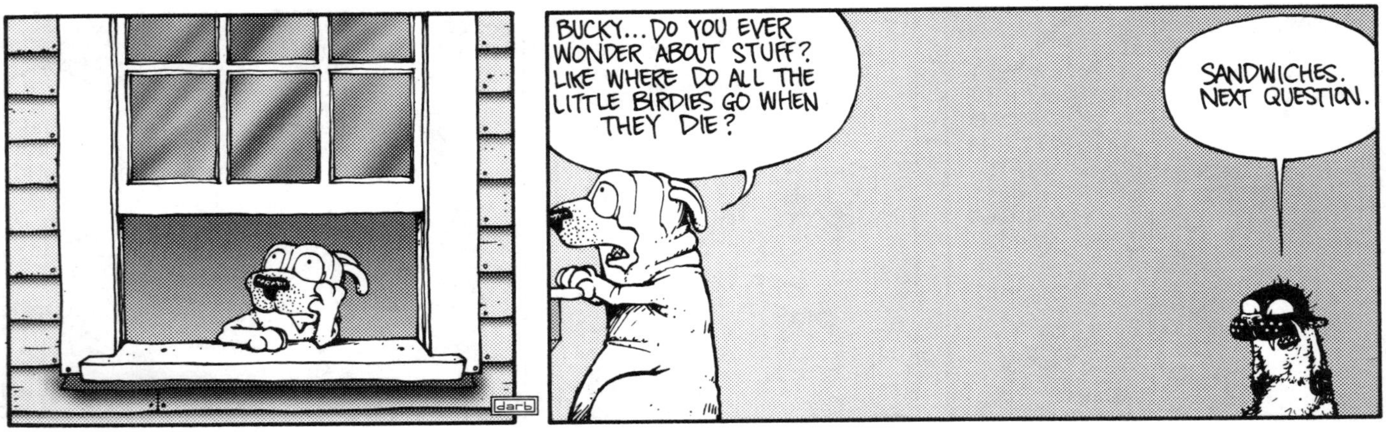
darb
BUCKY... DO YOU EVER WONDER ABOUT STUFF? LIKE WHERE DO ALL THE LITTLE BIRDIES GO WHEN THEY DIE?
SANDWICHES. NEXT QUESTION.

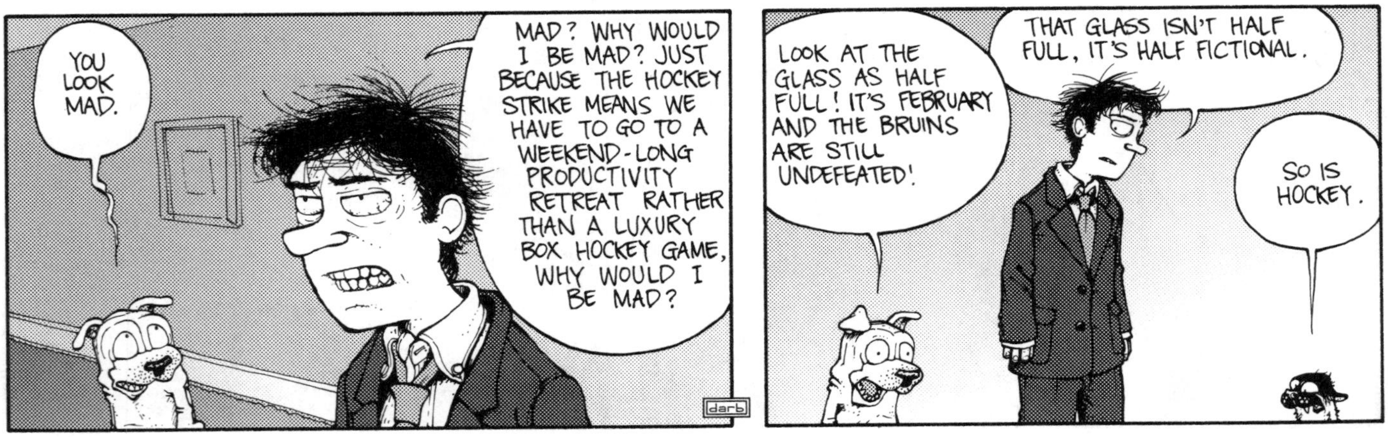
YOU LOOK MAD.
MAD? WHY WOULD I BE MAD? JUST BECAUSE THE HOCKEY STRIKE MEANS WE HAVE TO GO TO A WEEKEND-LONG PRODUCTIVITY RETREAT RATHER THAN A LUXURY BOX HOCKEY GAME, WHY WOULD I BE MAD?
darb
LOOK AT THE GLASS AS HALF FULL! IT'S FEBRUARY AND THE BRUINS ARE STILL UNDEFEATED!
THAT GLASS ISN'T HALF FULL, IT'S HALF FICTIONAL.
SO IS HOCKEY.

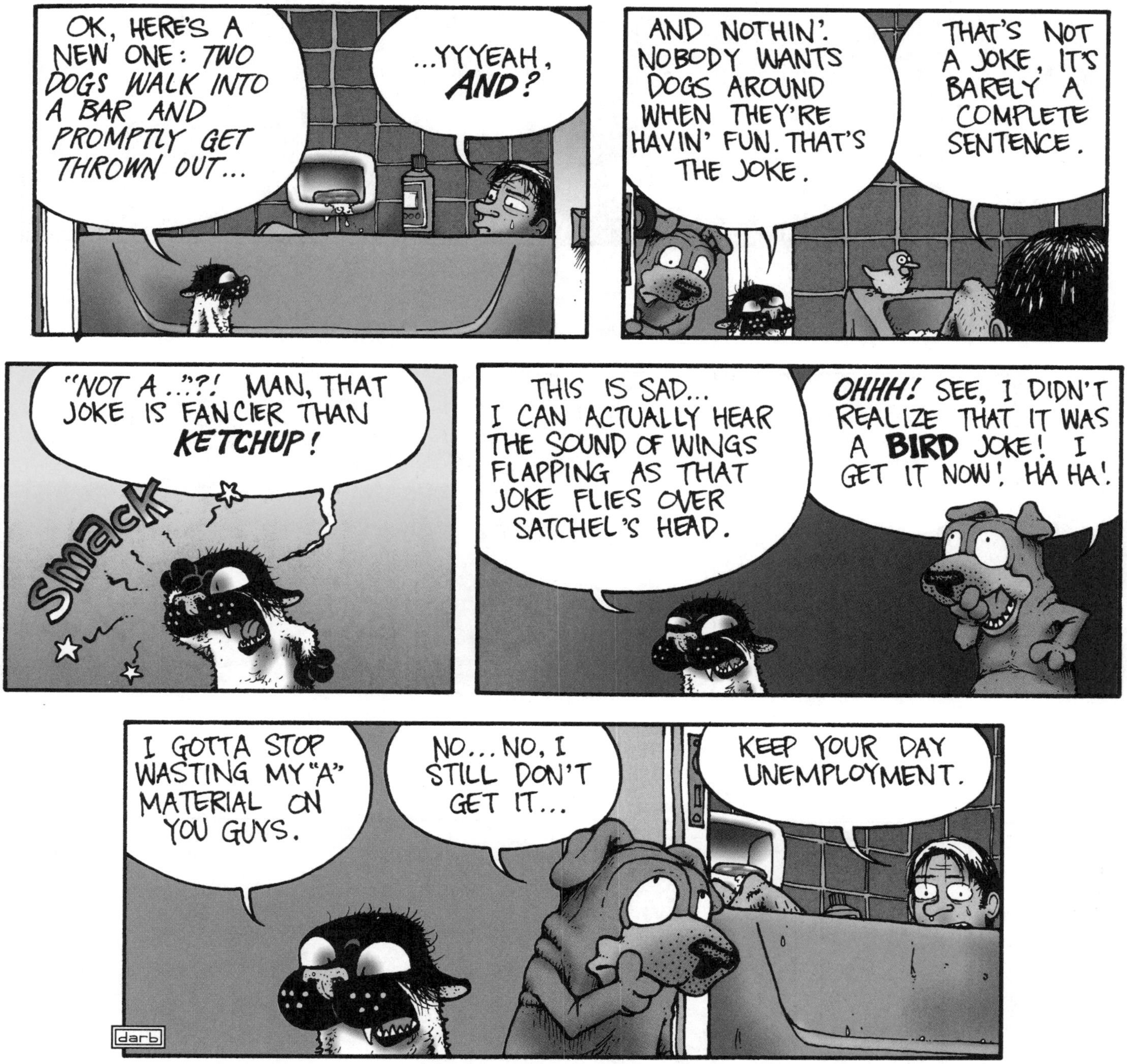
OK, HERE'S A NEW ONE: TWO DOGS WALK INTO A BAR AND PROMPTLY GET THROWN OUT...
...YYYEAH, AND?
AND NOTHIN'. NOBODY WANTS DOGS AROUND WHEN THEY'RE HAVIN' FUN. THAT'S THE JOKE.
THAT'S NOT A JOKE, IT'S BARELY A COMPLETE SENTENCE.
"NOT A..."?! MAN, THAT JOKE IS FANCIER THAN KETCHUP!
SMACK
THIS IS SAD... I CAN ACTUALLY HEAR THE SOUND OF WINGS FLAPPING AS THAT JOKE FLIES OVER SATCHEL'S HEAD.
OHHH! SEE, I DIDN'T REALIZE THAT IT WAS A BIRD JOKE! I GET IT NOW! HA HA!
I GOTTA STOP WASTING MY "A" MATERIAL ON YOU GUYS.
NO...NO, I STILL DON'T GET IT...
KEEP YOUR DAY UNEMPLOYMENT.
darb

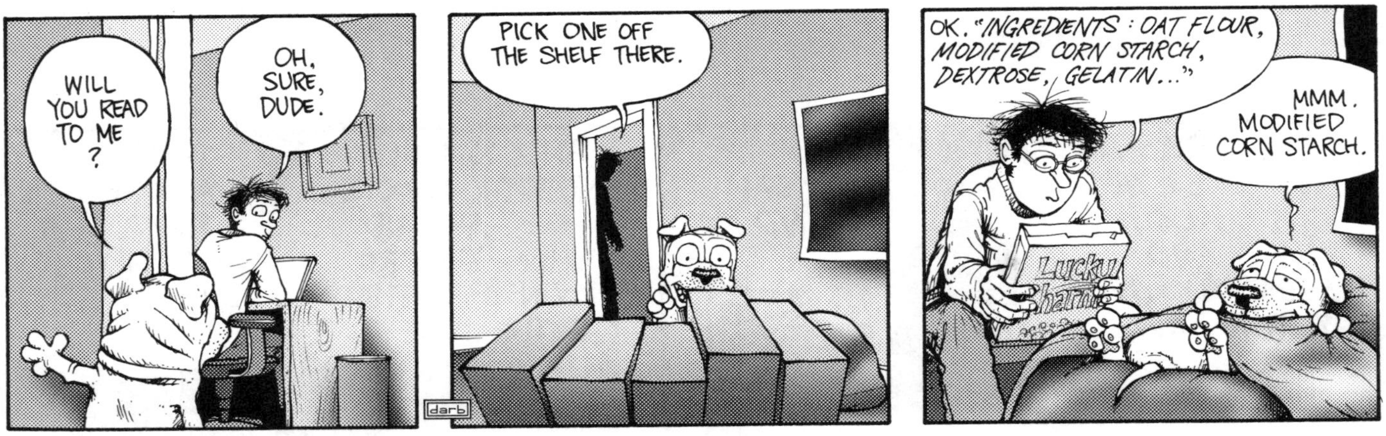
WILL YOU READ TO ME ?
OH, SURE, DUDE.
PICK ONE OFF THE SHELF THERE.
OK. "INGREDIENTS: OAT FLOUR, MODIFIED CORN STARCH, DEXTROSE, GELATIN..."
MMM. MODIFIED CORN STARCH.

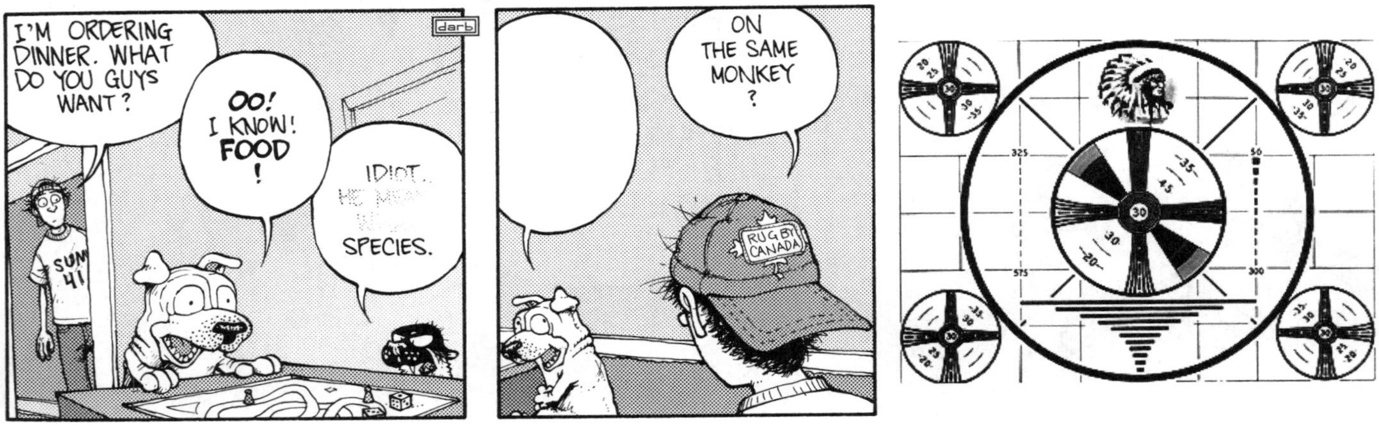
I'M ORDERING DINNER. WHAT DO YOU GUYS WANT?
SUM 41
OO! I KNOW! FOOD !
IDIOT.
SPECIES.
ON THE SAME MONKEY ?
RUGBY CANADA

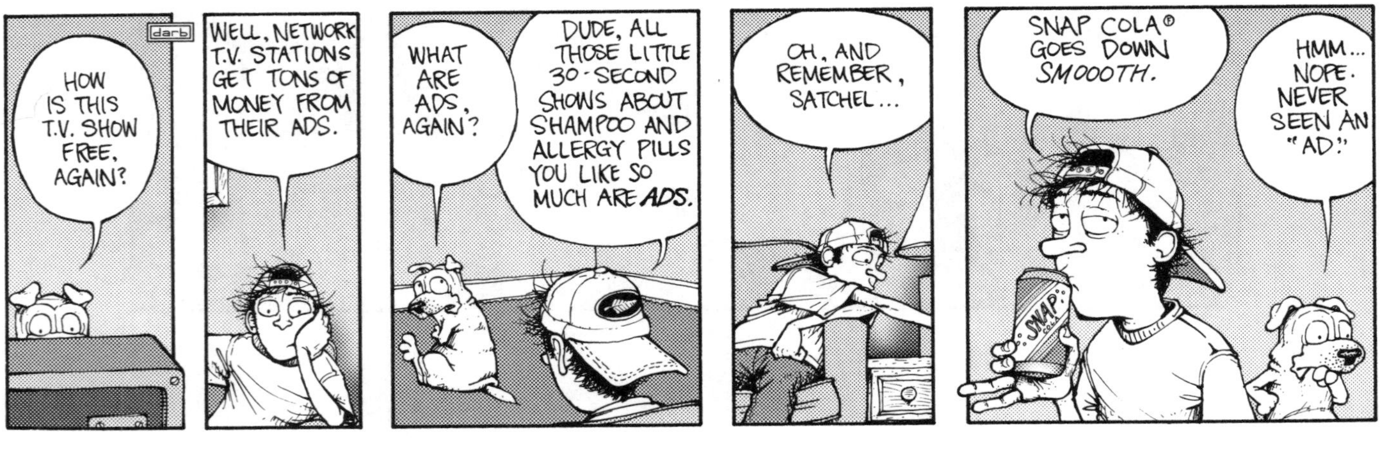
HOW IS THIS T.V. SHOW FREE, AGAIN?
WELL, NETWORK T.V. STATIONS GET TONS OF MONEY FROM THEIR ADS.
WHAT ARE ADS, AGAIN?
DUDE, ALL THOSE LITTLE 30-SECOND SHOWS ABOUT SHAMPOO AND ALLERGY PILLS YOU LIKE SO MUCH ARE ADS.
OH, AND REMEMBER, SATCHEL...
SNAP COLA® GOES DOWN SMOOOTH.
HMM... NOPE. NEVER SEEN AN "AD."

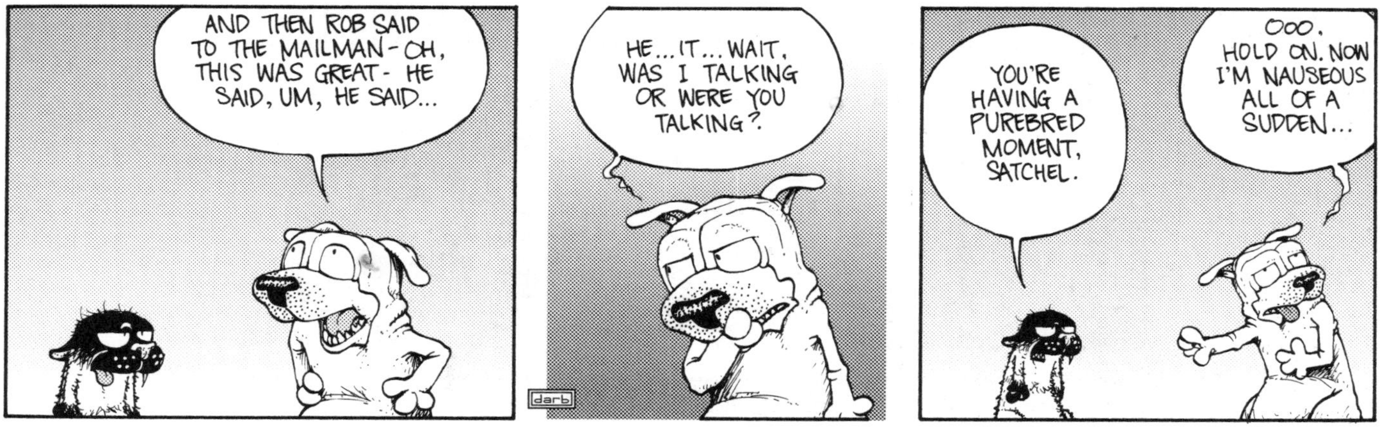
AND THEN ROB SAID TO THE MAILMAN- OH, THIS WAS GREAT- HE SAID, UM, HE SAID...
HE... IT... WAIT, WAS I TALKING OR WERE YOU TALKING?
YOU'RE HAVING A PUREBRED MOMENT, SATCHEL.
OOO. HOLD ON. NOW I'M NAUSEOUS ALL OF A SUDDEN...

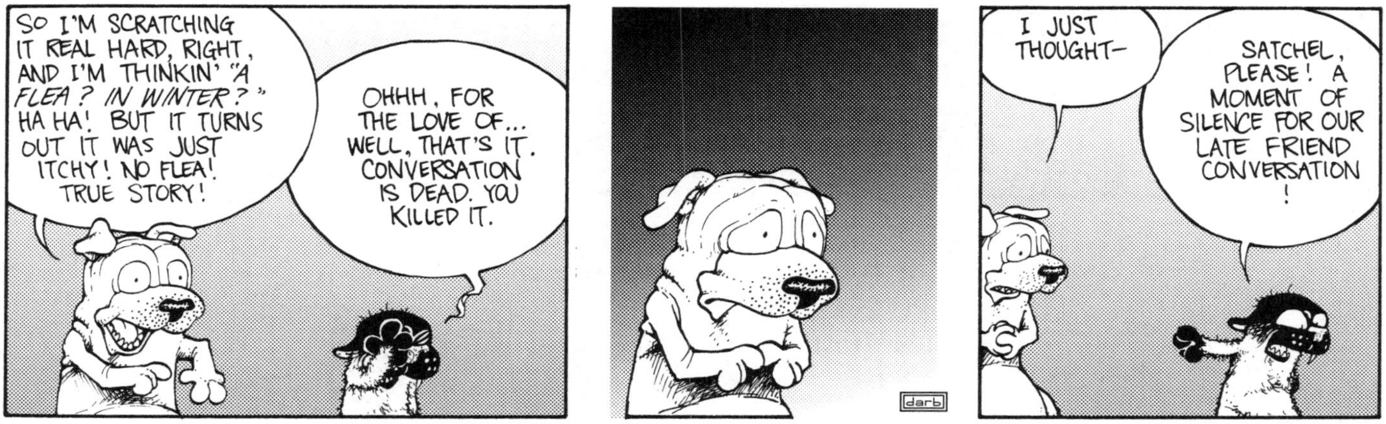
SO I'M SCRATCHING IT REAL HARD, RIGHT, AND I'M THINKIN' "*A FLEA? IN WINTER?*" HA HA! BUT IT TURNS OUT IT WAS JUST ITCHY! NO FLEA! TRUE STORY!
OHHH, FOR THE LOVE OF... WELL, THAT'S IT. CONVERSATION IS DEAD. YOU KILLED IT.
I JUST THOUGHT-
SATCHEL, PLEASE! A MOMENT OF SILENCE FOR OUR LATE FRIEND CONVERSATION!

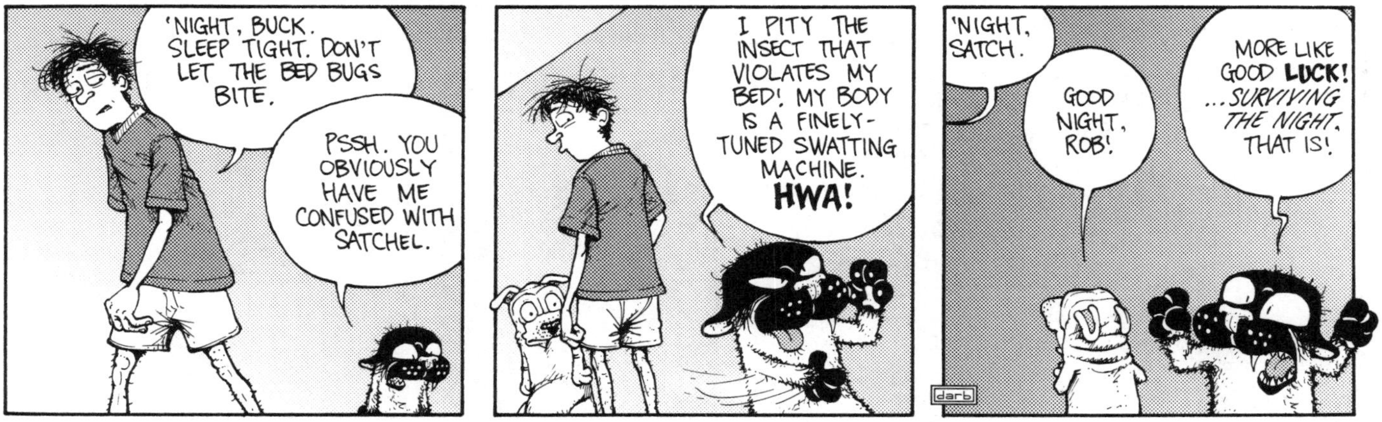
'NIGHT, BUCK. SLEEP TIGHT. DON'T LET THE BED BUGS BITE.
PSSH. YOU OBVIOUSLY HAVE ME CONFUSED WITH SATCHEL.
I PITY THE INSECT THAT VIOLATES MY BED! MY BODY IS A FINELY-TUNED SWATTING MACHINE. **HWA!**
'NIGHT, SATCH.
GOOD NIGHT, ROB!
MORE LIKE GOOD **LUCK!** ...*SURVIVING THE NIGHT*, THAT IS!

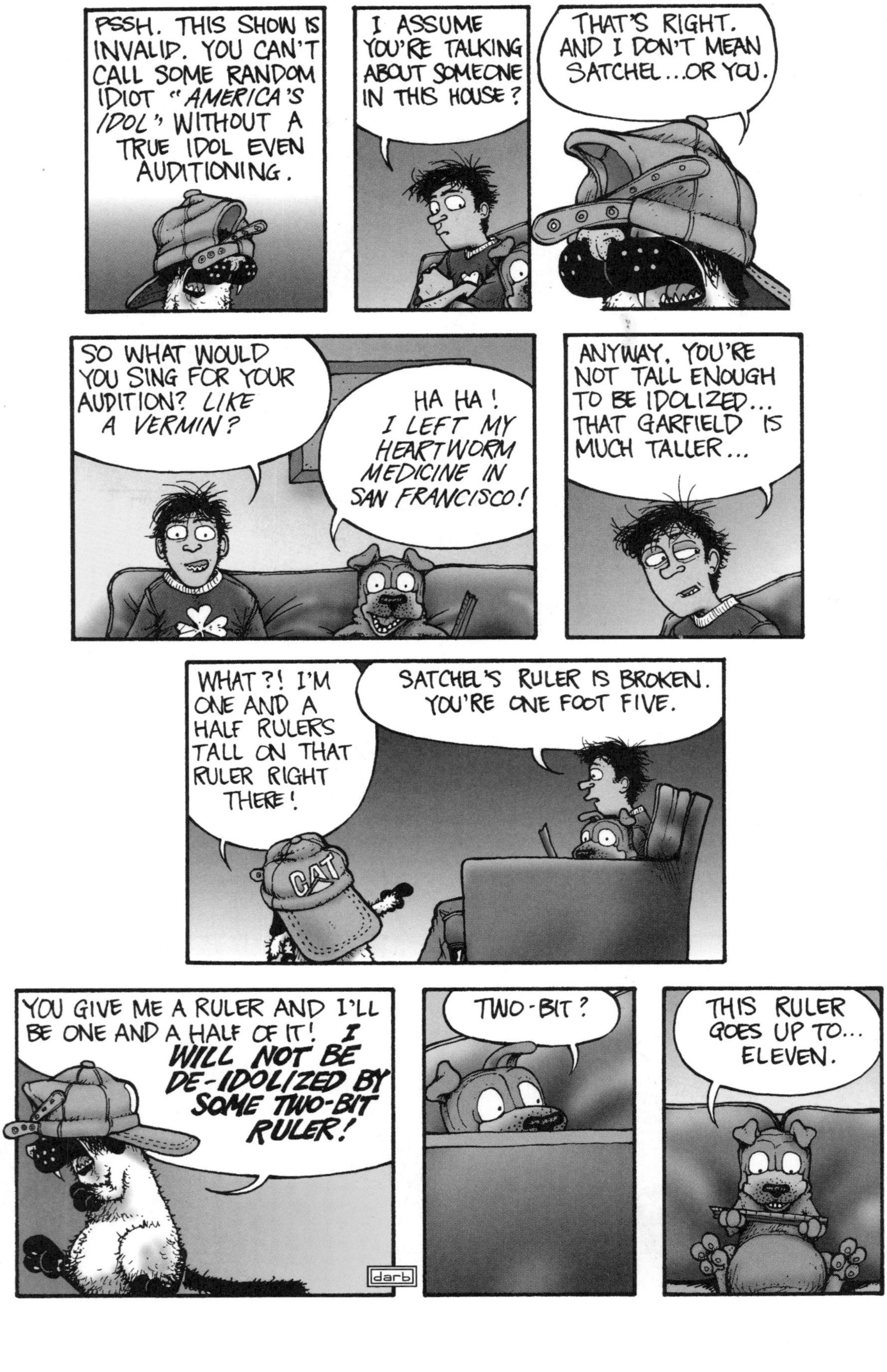
PSSH. THIS SHOW IS INVALID. YOU CAN'T CALL SOME RANDOM IDIOT "AMERICA'S IDOL" WITHOUT A TRUE IDOL EVEN AUDITIONING.
I ASSUME YOU'RE TALKING ABOUT SOMEONE IN THIS HOUSE?
THAT'S RIGHT. AND I DON'T MEAN SATCHEL...OR YOU.
SO WHAT WOULD YOU SING FOR YOUR AUDITION? LIKE A VERMIN?
HA HA! I LEFT MY HEARTWORM MEDICINE IN SAN FRANCISCO!
ANYWAY, YOU'RE NOT TALL ENOUGH TO BE IDOLIZED... THAT GARFIELD IS MUCH TALLER...
WHAT?! I'M ONE AND A HALF RULERS TALL ON THAT RULER RIGHT THERE!
SATCHEL'S RULER IS BROKEN. YOU'RE ONE FOOT FIVE.
CAT
YOU GIVE ME A RULER AND I'LL BE ONE AND A HALF OF IT! I WILL NOT BE DE-IDOLIZED BY SOME TWO-BIT RULER!
darb
TWO-BIT?
THIS RULER GOES UP TO... ELEVEN.

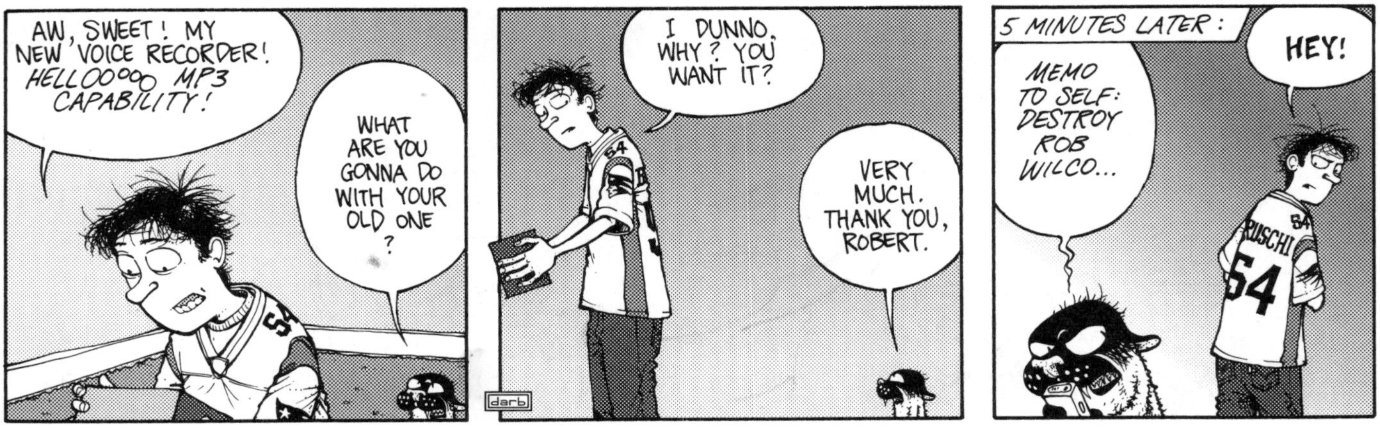
AW, SWEET! MY NEW VOICE RECORDER! HELLOOOOO MP3 CAPABILITY!
WHAT ARE YOU GONNA DO WITH YOUR OLD ONE?
I DUNNO. WHY? YOU WANT IT?
VERY MUCH. THANK YOU, ROBERT.
darb
5 MINUTES LATER:
MEMO TO SELF: DESTROY ROB WILCO...
HEY!

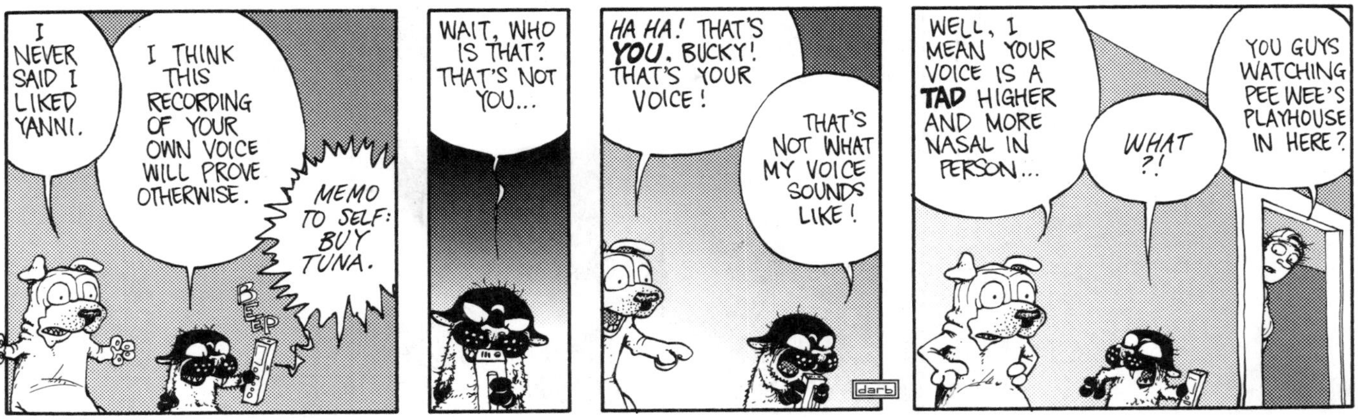
I NEVER SAID I LIKED YANNI.
I THINK THIS RECORDING OF YOUR OWN VOICE WILL PROVE OTHERWISE.
BEEP
MEMO TO SELF: BUY TUNA.
WAIT, WHO IS THAT? THAT'S NOT YOU...
HA HA! THAT'S **YOU**, BUCKY! THAT'S YOUR VOICE!
THAT'S NOT WHAT MY VOICE SOUNDS LIKE!
darb
WELL, I MEAN YOUR VOICE IS A **TAD** HIGHER AND MORE NASAL IN PERSON...
WHAT?!
YOU GUYS WATCHING PEE WEE'S PLAYHOUSE IN HERE?

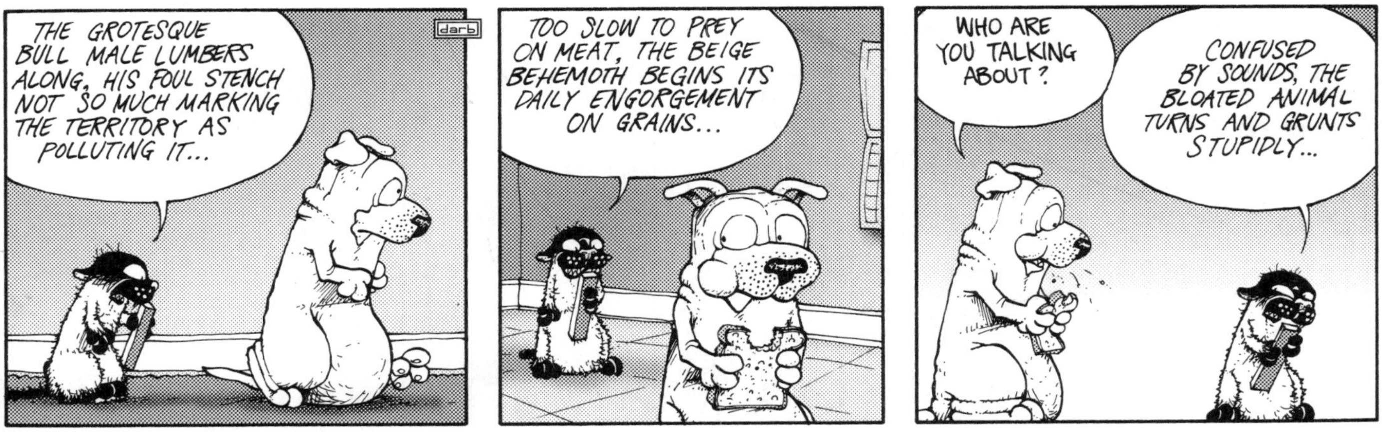
THE GROTESQUE BULL MALE LUMBERS ALONG, HIS FOUL STENCH NOT SO MUCH MARKING THE TERRITORY AS POLLUTING IT...
darb
TOO SLOW TO PREY ON MEAT, THE BEIGE BEHEMOTH BEGINS ITS DAILY ENGORGEMENT ON GRAINS...
WHO ARE YOU TALKING ABOUT?
CONFUSED BY SOUNDS, THE BLOATED ANIMAL TURNS AND GRUNTS STUPIDLY...

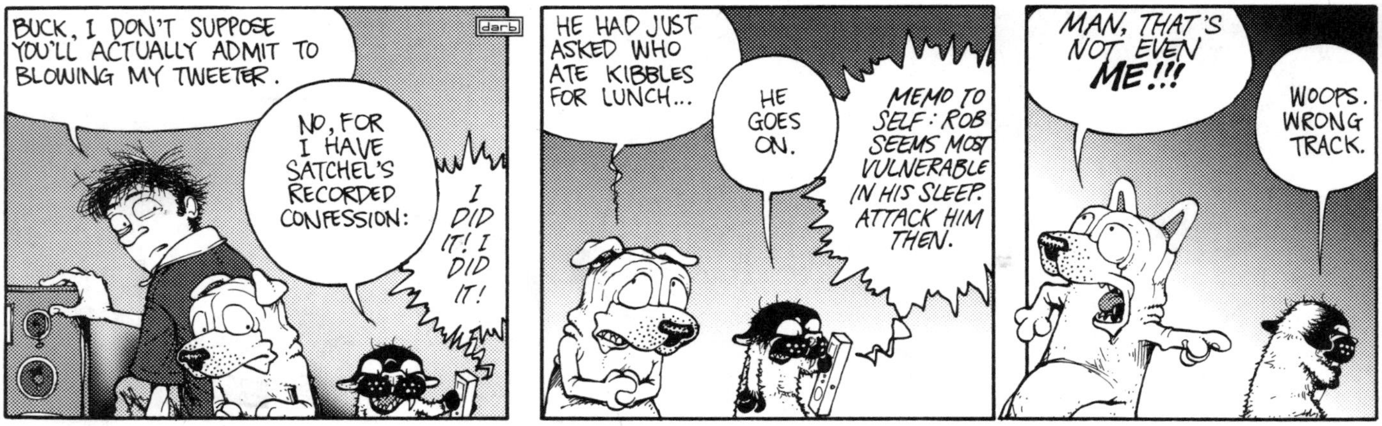
darb
BUCK, I DON'T SUPPOSE YOU'LL ACTUALLY ADMIT TO BLOWING MY TWEETER.
NO, FOR I HAVE SATCHEL'S RECORDED CONFESSION:
I DID IT! I DID IT!
HE HAD JUST ASKED WHO ATE KIBBLES FOR LUNCH...
HE GOES ON.
MEMO TO SELF: ROB SEEMS MOST VULNERABLE IN HIS SLEEP. ATTACK HIM THEN.
MAN, THAT'S NOT EVEN ME!!!
WOOPS. WRONG TRACK.

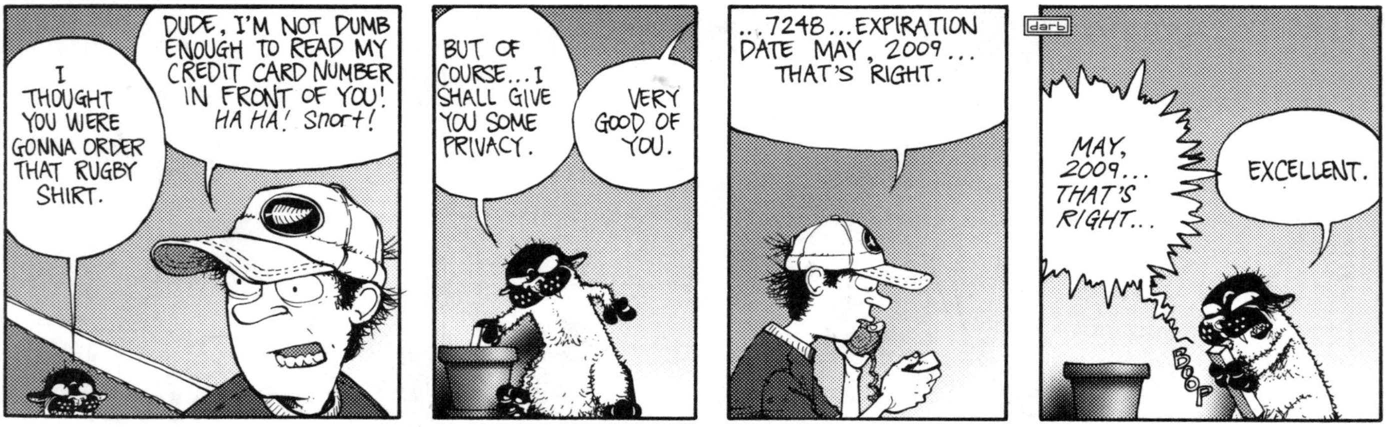
I THOUGHT YOU WERE GONNA ORDER THAT RUGBY SHIRT.
DUDE, I'M NOT DUMB ENOUGH TO READ MY CREDIT CARD NUMBER IN FRONT OF YOU! HA HA! Snort!
BUT OF COURSE... I SHALL GIVE YOU SOME PRIVACY.
VERY GOOD OF YOU.
...7248... EXPIRATION DATE MAY, 2009... THAT'S RIGHT.
darb
MAY, 2009... THAT'S RIGHT...
EXCELLENT.
BOOP

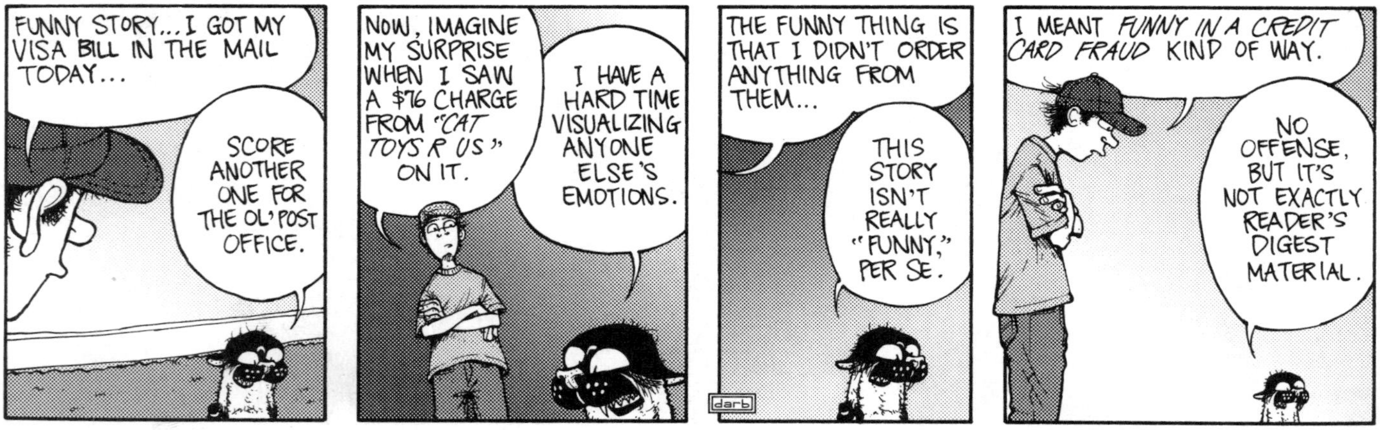
FUNNY STORY... I GOT MY VISA BILL IN THE MAIL TODAY...
SCORE ANOTHER ONE FOR THE OL' POST OFFICE.
NOW, IMAGINE MY SURPRISE WHEN I SAW A $76 CHARGE FROM "CAT TOYS R US" ON IT.
I HAVE A HARD TIME VISUALIZING ANYONE ELSE'S EMOTIONS.
THE FUNNY THING IS THAT I DIDN'T ORDER ANYTHING FROM THEM...
THIS STORY ISN'T REALLY "FUNNY," PER SE.
darb
I MEANT FUNNY IN A CREDIT CARD FRAUD KIND OF WAY.
NO OFFENSE, BUT IT'S NOT EXACTLY READER'S DIGEST MATERIAL.

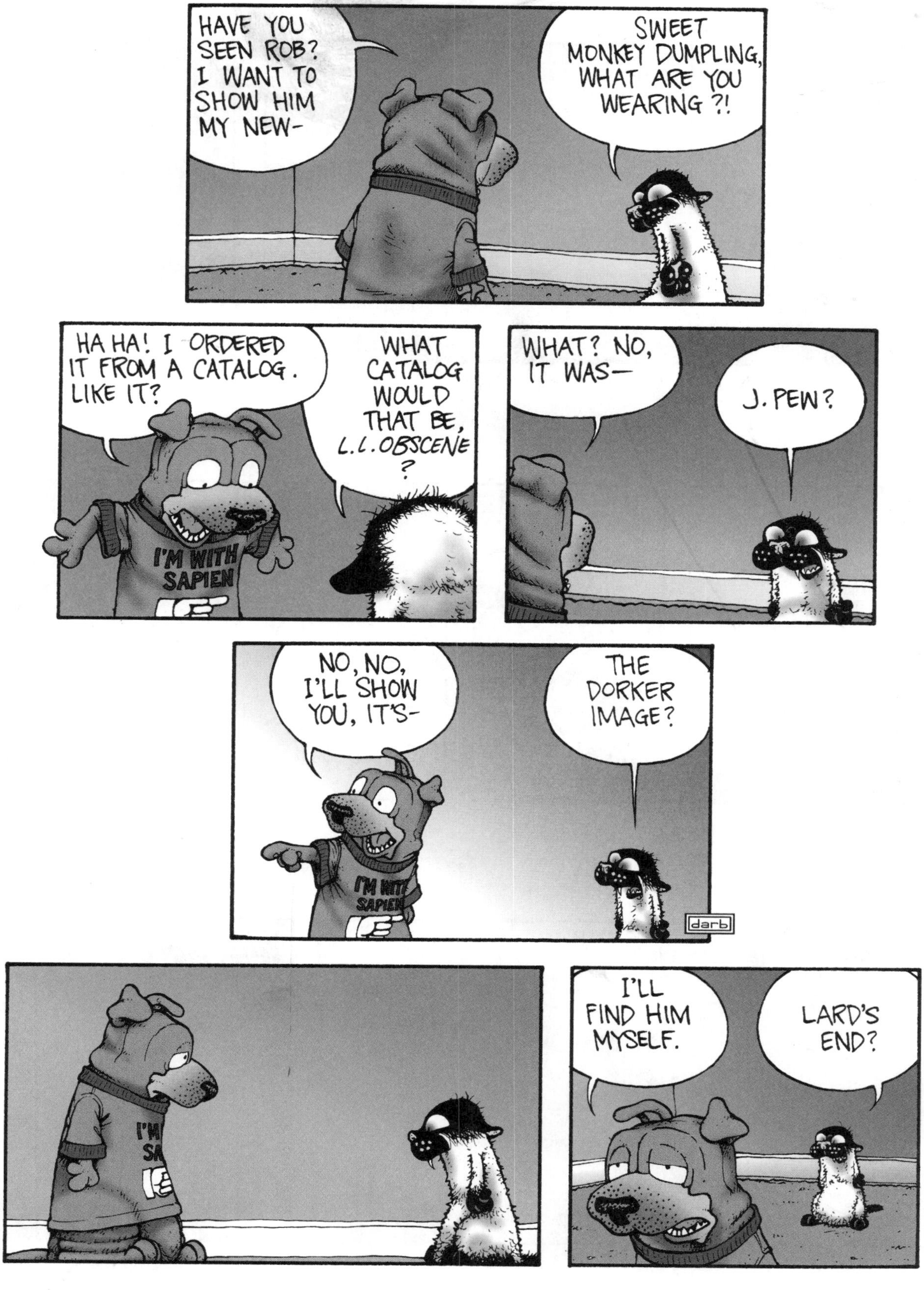
HAVE YOU SEEN ROB? I WANT TO SHOW HIM MY NEW-
SWEET MONKEY DUMPLING, WHAT ARE YOU WEARING ?!
HA HA! I ORDERED IT FROM A CATALOG. LIKE IT?
I'M WITH SAPIEN
WHAT CATALOG WOULD THAT BE, L.L. OBSCENE ?
WHAT? NO, IT WAS—
J. PEW?
NO, NO, I'LL SHOW YOU, IT'S-
THE DORKER IMAGE?
darb
I'LL FIND HIM MYSELF.
LARD'S END?

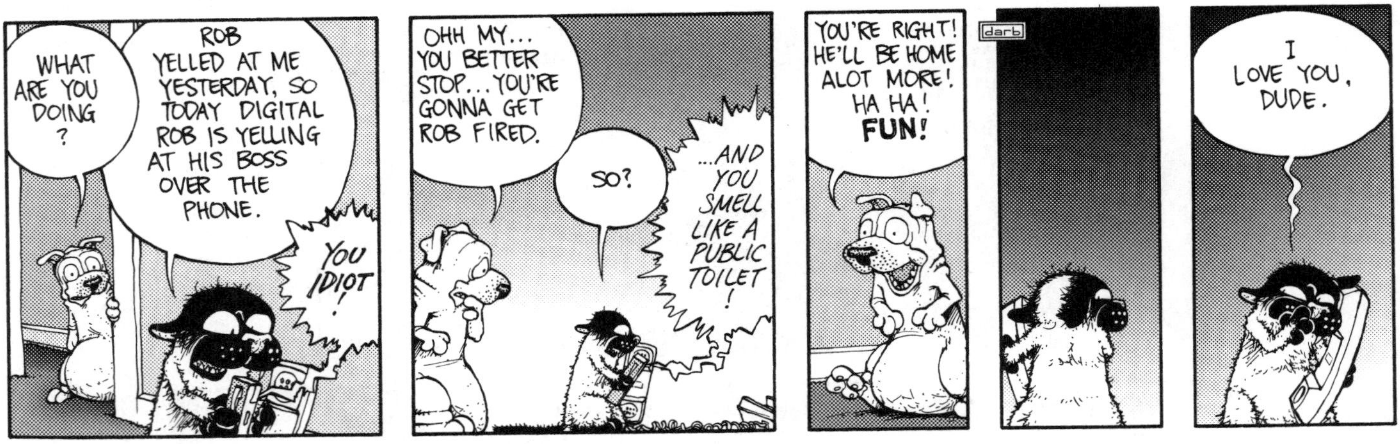
WHAT ARE YOU DOING ?
ROB YELLED AT ME YESTERDAY, SO TODAY DIGITAL ROB IS YELLING AT HIS BOSS OVER THE PHONE.
YOU IDIOT!
OHH MY... YOU BETTER STOP... YOU'RE GONNA GET ROB FIRED.
SO?
...AND YOU SMELL LIKE A PUBLIC TOILET!
YOU'RE RIGHT! HE'LL BE HOME ALOT MORE! HA HA! FUN!
I LOVE YOU, DUDE.

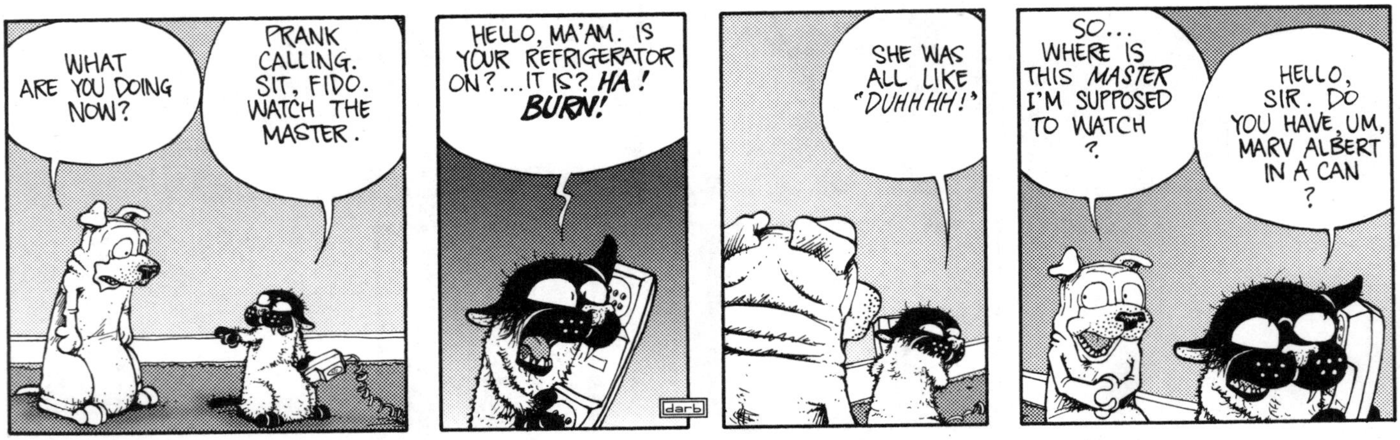
WHAT ARE YOU DOING NOW?
PRANK CALLING. SIT, FIDO. WATCH THE MASTER.
HELLO, MA'AM. IS YOUR REFRIGERATOR ON?... IT IS? HA! BURN!
SHE WAS ALL LIKE "DUHHHH!"
SO... WHERE IS THIS MASTER I'M SUPPOSED TO WATCH ?
HELLO, SIR. DO YOU HAVE, UM, MARV ALBERT IN A CAN ?

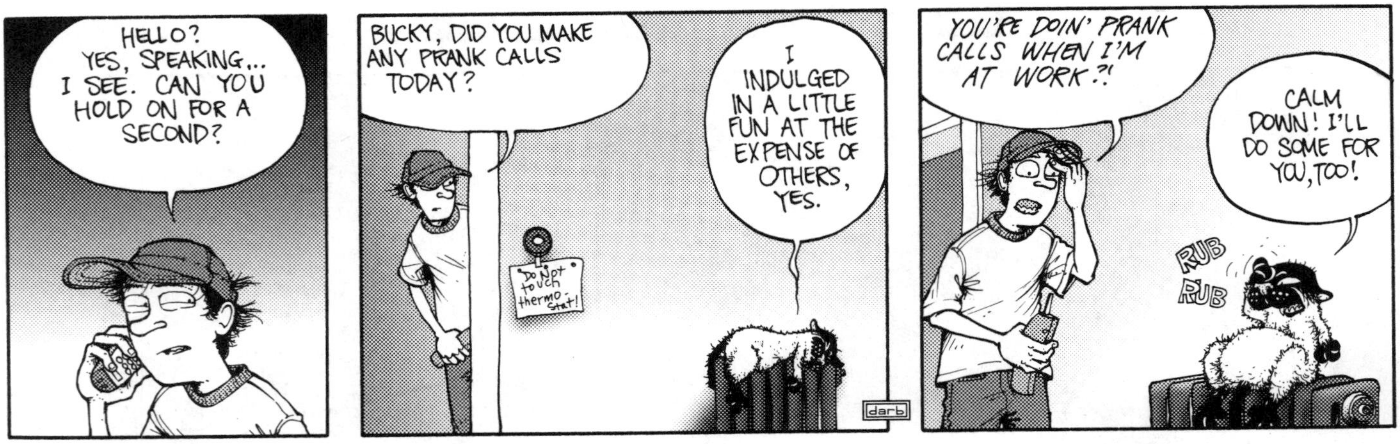
HELLO? YES, SPEAKING... I SEE. CAN YOU HOLD ON FOR A SECOND?
BUCKY, DID YOU MAKE ANY PRANK CALLS TODAY?
Do Not touch thermo-stat!
I INDULGED IN A LITTLE FUN AT THE EXPENSE OF OTHERS, YES.
YOU'RE DOIN' PRANK CALLS WHEN I'M AT WORK?!
CALM DOWN! I'LL DO SOME FOR YOU, TOO!
RUB RUB

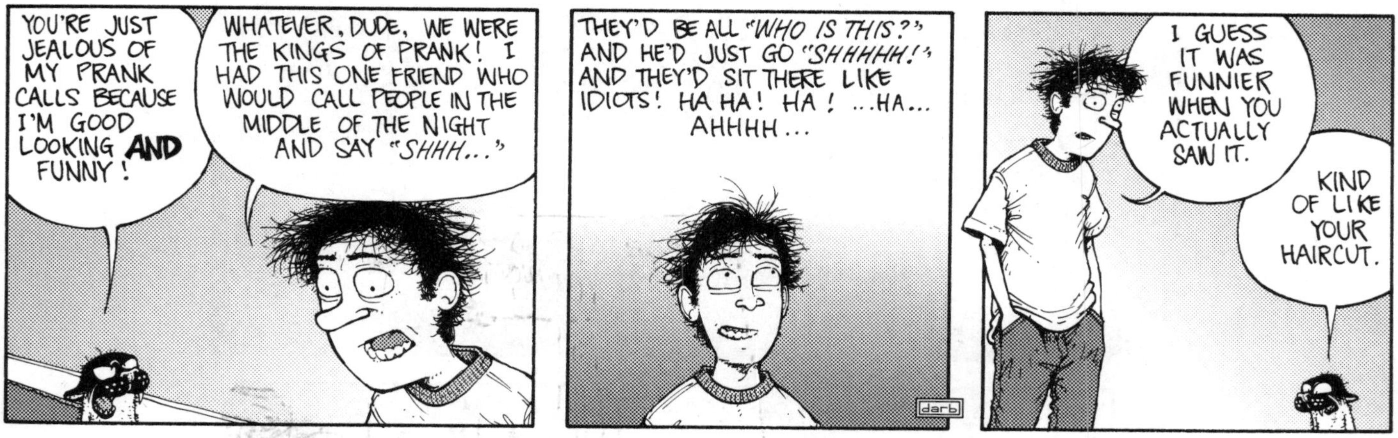
YOU'RE JUST JEALOUS OF MY PRANK CALLS BECAUSE I'M GOOD LOOKING AND FUNNY!
WHATEVER, DUDE, WE WERE THE KINGS OF PRANK! I HAD THIS ONE FRIEND WHO WOULD CALL PEOPLE IN THE MIDDLE OF THE NIGHT AND SAY "SHHH..."
THEY'D BE ALL "WHO IS THIS?" AND HE'D JUST GO "SHHHHH!" AND THEY'D SIT THERE LIKE IDIOTS! HA HA! HA! ...HA... AHHHH...
darb
I GUESS IT WAS FUNNIER WHEN YOU ACTUALLY SAW IT.
KIND OF LIKE YOUR HAIRCUT.

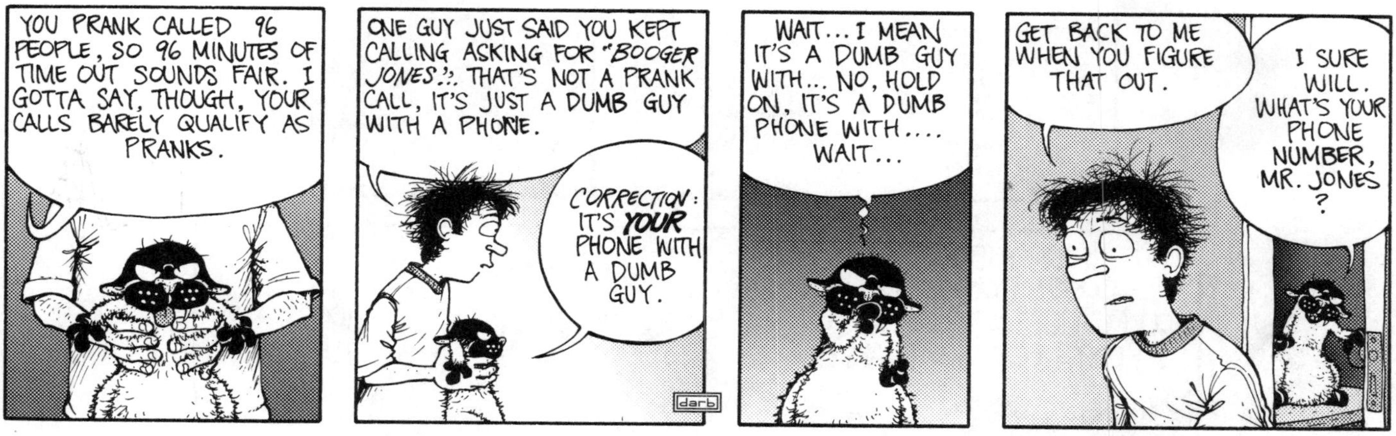
YOU PRANK CALLED 96 PEOPLE, SO 96 MINUTES OF TIME OUT SOUNDS FAIR. I GOTTA SAY, THOUGH, YOUR CALLS BARELY QUALIFY AS PRANKS.
ONE GUY JUST SAID YOU KEPT CALLING ASKING FOR "BOOGER JONES". THAT'S NOT A PRANK CALL, IT'S JUST A DUMB GUY WITH A PHONE.
CORRECTION: IT'S YOUR PHONE WITH A DUMB GUY.
darb
WAIT... I MEAN IT'S A DUMB GUY WITH... NO, HOLD ON, IT'S A DUMB PHONE WITH.... WAIT...
GET BACK TO ME WHEN YOU FIGURE THAT OUT.
I SURE WILL. WHAT'S YOUR PHONE NUMBER, MR. JONES?

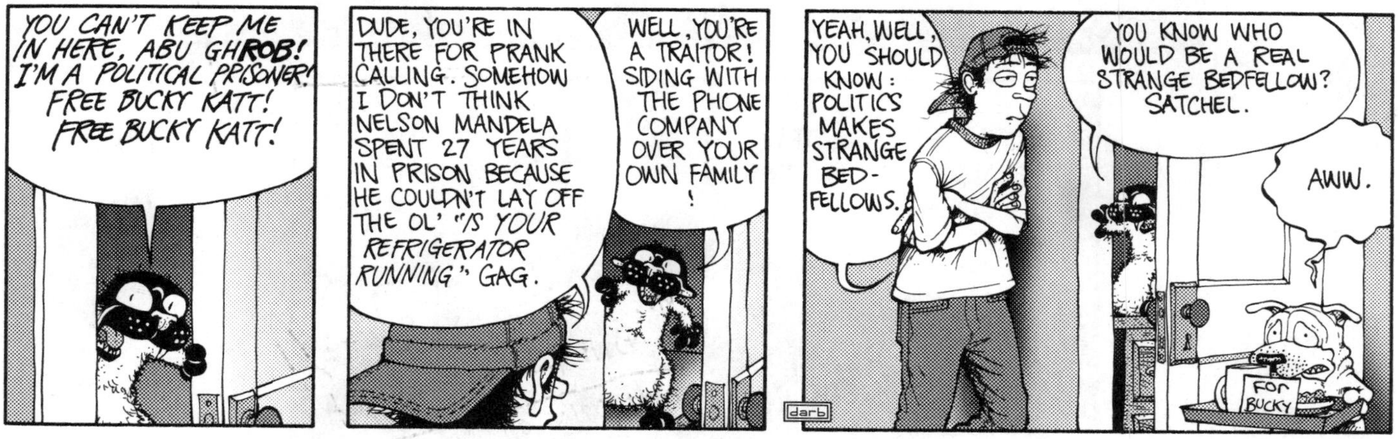
YOU CAN'T KEEP ME IN HERE, ABU GHROB! I'M A POLITICAL PRISONER! FREE BUCKY KATT! FREE BUCKY KATT!
DUDE, YOU'RE IN THERE FOR PRANK CALLING. SOMEHOW I DON'T THINK NELSON MANDELA SPENT 27 YEARS IN PRISON BECAUSE HE COULDN'T LAY OFF THE OL' "IS YOUR REFRIGERATOR RUNNING" GAG.
WELL, YOU'RE A TRAITOR! SIDING WITH THE PHONE COMPANY OVER YOUR OWN FAMILY!
darb
YEAH, WELL, YOU SHOULD KNOW: POLITICS MAKES STRANGE BED-FELLOWS.
YOU KNOW WHO WOULD BE A REAL STRANGE BEDFELLOW? SATCHEL.
AWW.
FOR BUCKY

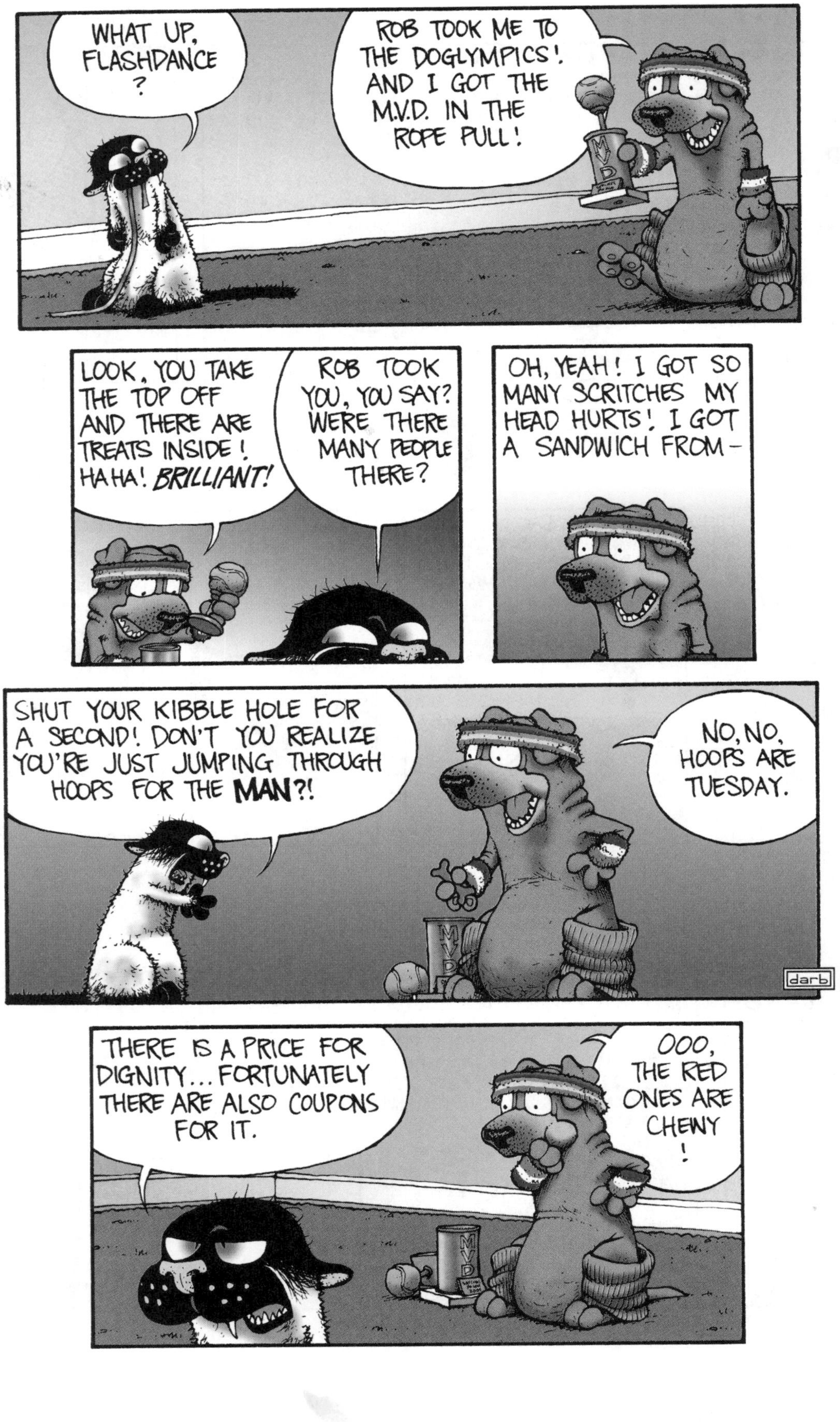
WHAT UP, FLASHDANCE ?
ROB TOOK ME TO THE DOGLYMPICS! AND I GOT THE M.V.D. IN THE ROPE PULL!
LOOK, YOU TAKE THE TOP OFF AND THERE ARE TREATS INSIDE! HAHA! BRILLIANT!
ROB TOOK YOU, YOU SAY? WERE THERE MANY PEOPLE THERE?
OH, YEAH! I GOT SO MANY SCRITCHES MY HEAD HURTS! I GOT A SANDWICH FROM-
SHUT YOUR KIBBLE HOLE FOR A SECOND! DON'T YOU REALIZE YOU'RE JUST JUMPING THROUGH HOOPS FOR THE MAN?!
NO, NO, HOOPS ARE TUESDAY.
darb
THERE IS A PRICE FOR DIGNITY... FORTUNATELY THERE ARE ALSO COUPONS FOR IT.
OOO, THE RED ONES ARE CHEWY !

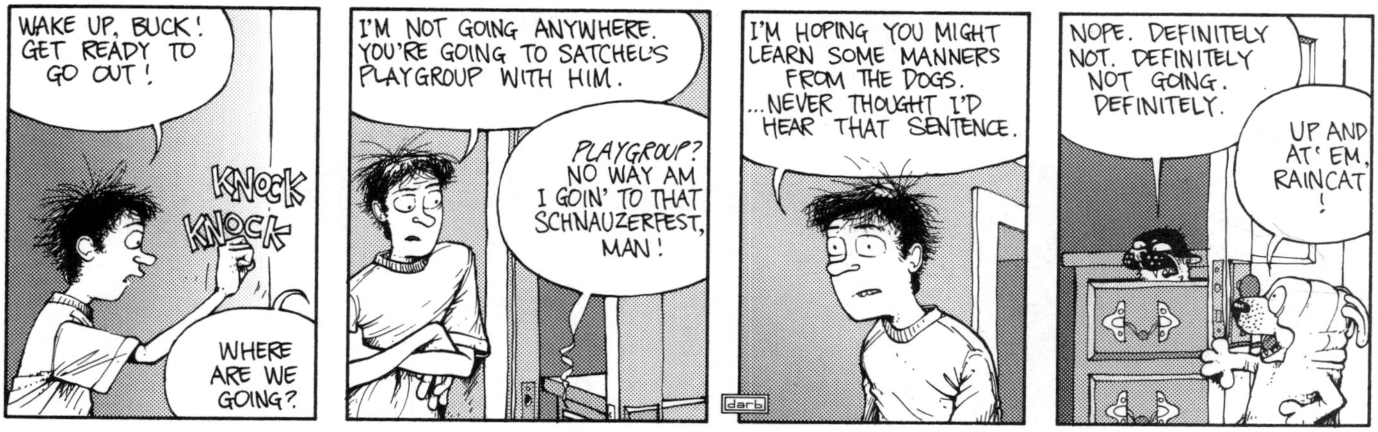
WAKE UP, BUCK! GET READY TO GO OUT!
KNOCK
KNOCK
WHERE ARE WE GOING?
I'M NOT GOING ANYWHERE. YOU'RE GOING TO SATCHEL'S PLAYGROUP WITH HIM.
PLAYGROUP? NO WAY AM I GOIN' TO THAT SCHNAUZERFEST, MAN!
I'M HOPING YOU MIGHT LEARN SOME MANNERS FROM THE DOGS. ...NEVER THOUGHT I'D HEAR THAT SENTENCE.
darb
NOPE. DEFINITELY NOT. DEFINITELY NOT GOING. DEFINITELY.
UP AND AT' EM, RAINCAT!

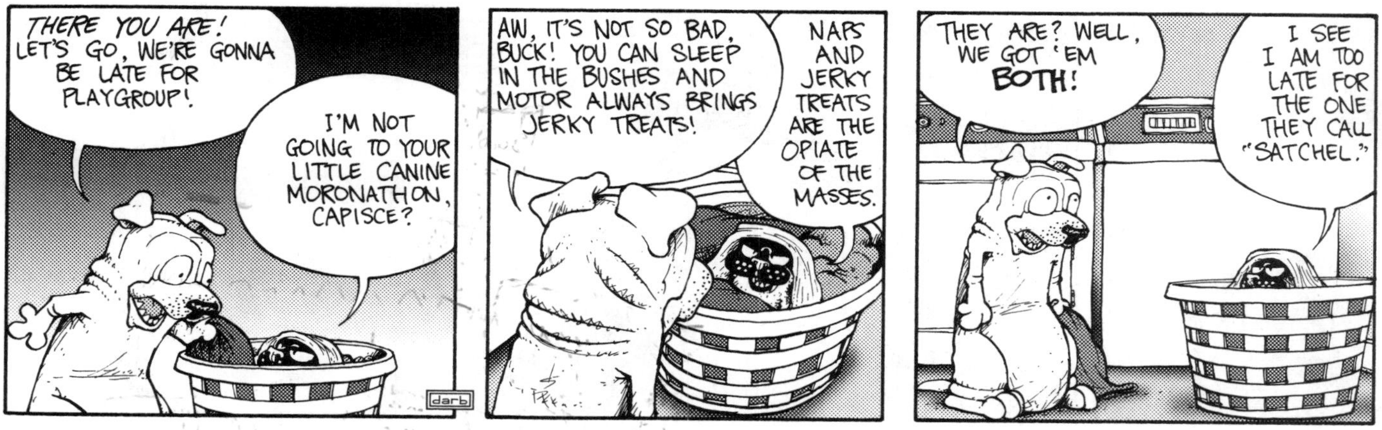
THERE YOU ARE! LET'S GO, WE'RE GONNA BE LATE FOR PLAYGROUP!
I'M NOT GOING TO YOUR LITTLE CANINE MORONATHON, CAPISCE?
darb
AW, IT'S NOT SO BAD, BUCK! YOU CAN SLEEP IN THE BUSHES AND MOTOR ALWAYS BRINGS JERKY TREATS!
NAPS AND JERKY TREATS ARE THE OPIATE OF THE MASSES.
THEY ARE? WELL, WE GOT 'EM **BOTH**!
I SEE I AM TOO LATE FOR THE ONE THEY CALL "SATCHEL."

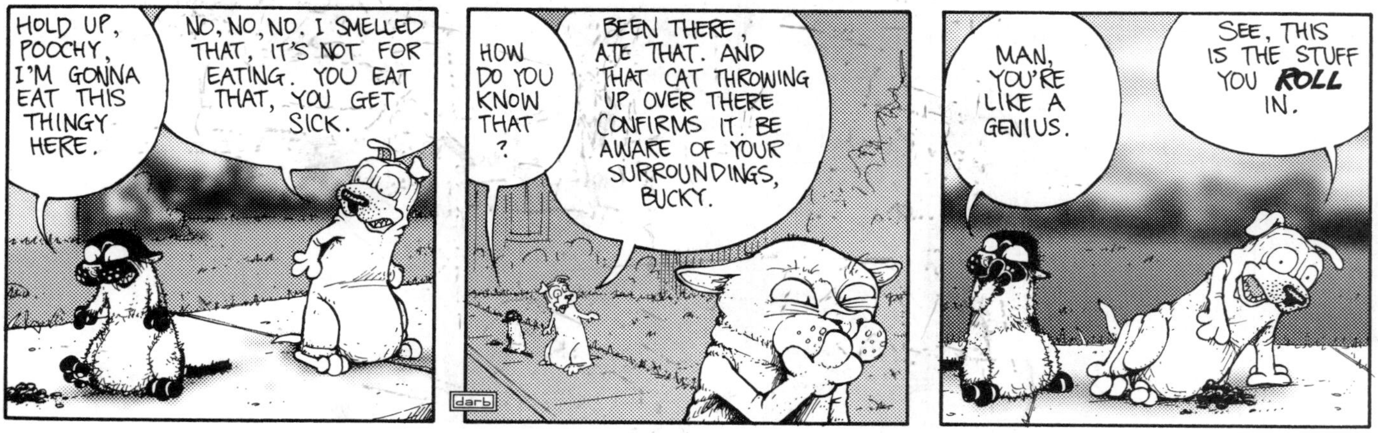
HOLD UP, POOCHY, I'M GONNA EAT THIS THINGY HERE.
NO, NO, NO. I SMELLED THAT, IT'S NOT FOR EATING. YOU EAT THAT, YOU GET SICK.
HOW DO YOU KNOW THAT?
BEEN THERE, ATE THAT. AND THAT CAT THROWING UP OVER THERE CONFIRMS IT. BE AWARE OF YOUR SURROUNDINGS, BUCKY.
darb
MAN, YOU'RE LIKE A GENIUS.
SEE, THIS IS THE STUFF YOU ***ROLL*** IN.

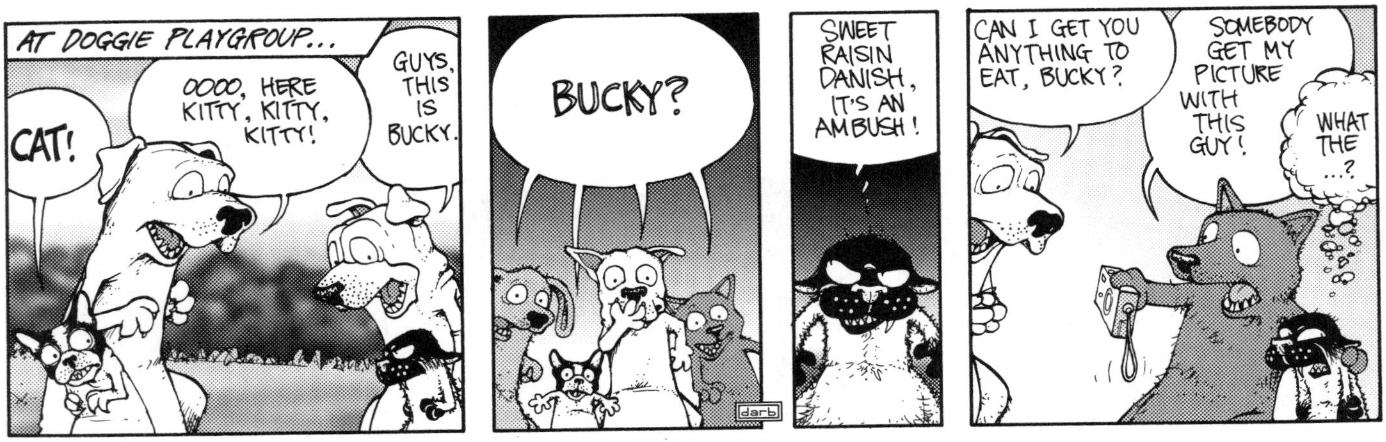
AT DOGGIE PLAYGROUP...
CAT!
OOOO, HERE KITTY, KITTY, KITTY!
GUYS, THIS IS BUCKY.
BUCKY?
SWEET RAISIN DANISH, IT'S AN AMBUSH!
CAN I GET YOU ANYTHING TO EAT, BUCKY?
SOMEBODY GET MY PICTURE WITH THIS GUY!
WHAT THE ...?
darb

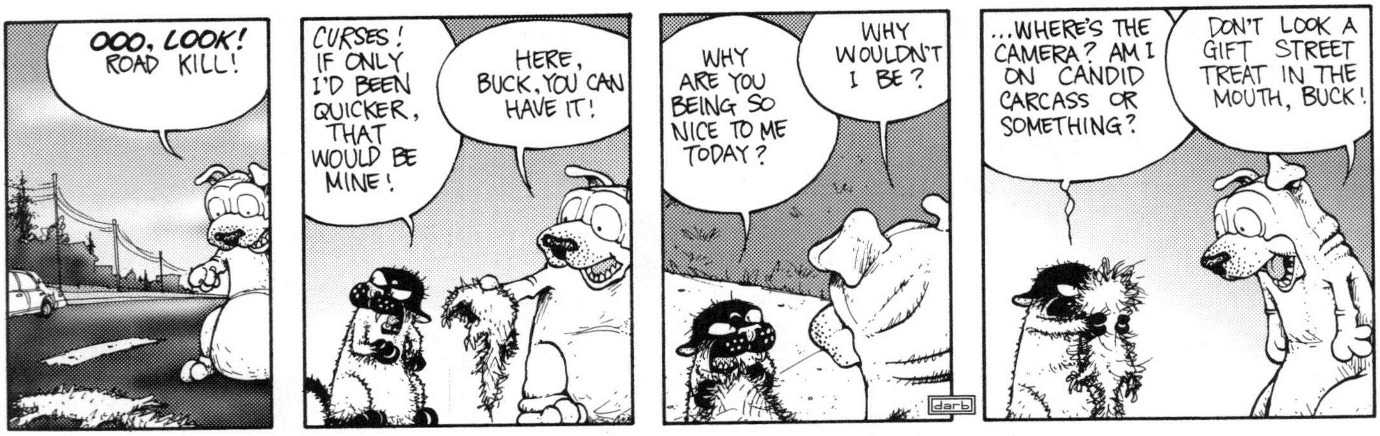
OOO, LOOK! ROAD KILL!
CURSES! IF ONLY I'D BEEN QUICKER, THAT WOULD BE MINE!
HERE, BUCK, YOU CAN HAVE IT!
WHY ARE YOU BEING SO NICE TO ME TODAY?
WHY WOULDN'T I BE?
...WHERE'S THE CAMERA? AM I ON CANDID CARCASS OR SOMETHING?
DON'T LOOK A GIFT STREET TREAT IN THE MOUTH, BUCK!
darb

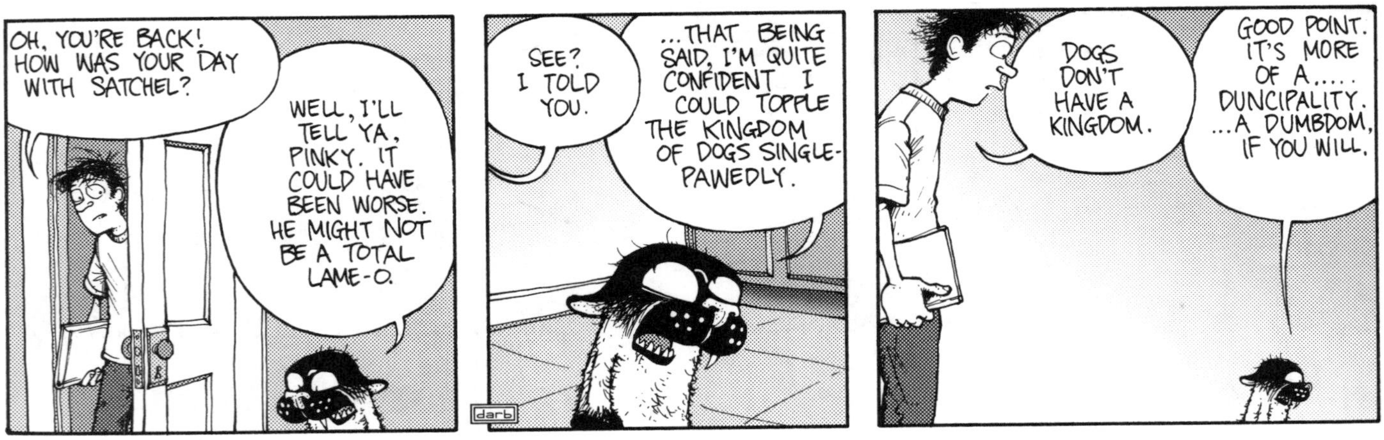
OH, YOU'RE BACK! HOW WAS YOUR DAY WITH SATCHEL?
WELL, I'LL TELL YA, PINKY. IT COULD HAVE BEEN WORSE. HE MIGHT NOT BE A TOTAL LAME-O.
SEE? I TOLD YOU.
...THAT BEING SAID, I'M QUITE CONFIDENT I COULD TOPPLE THE KINGDOM OF DOGS SINGLE-PAWEDLY.
DOGS DON'T HAVE A KINGDOM.
GOOD POINT. IT'S MORE OF A..... DUNCIPALITY. ...A DUMBDOM, IF YOU WILL.
darb

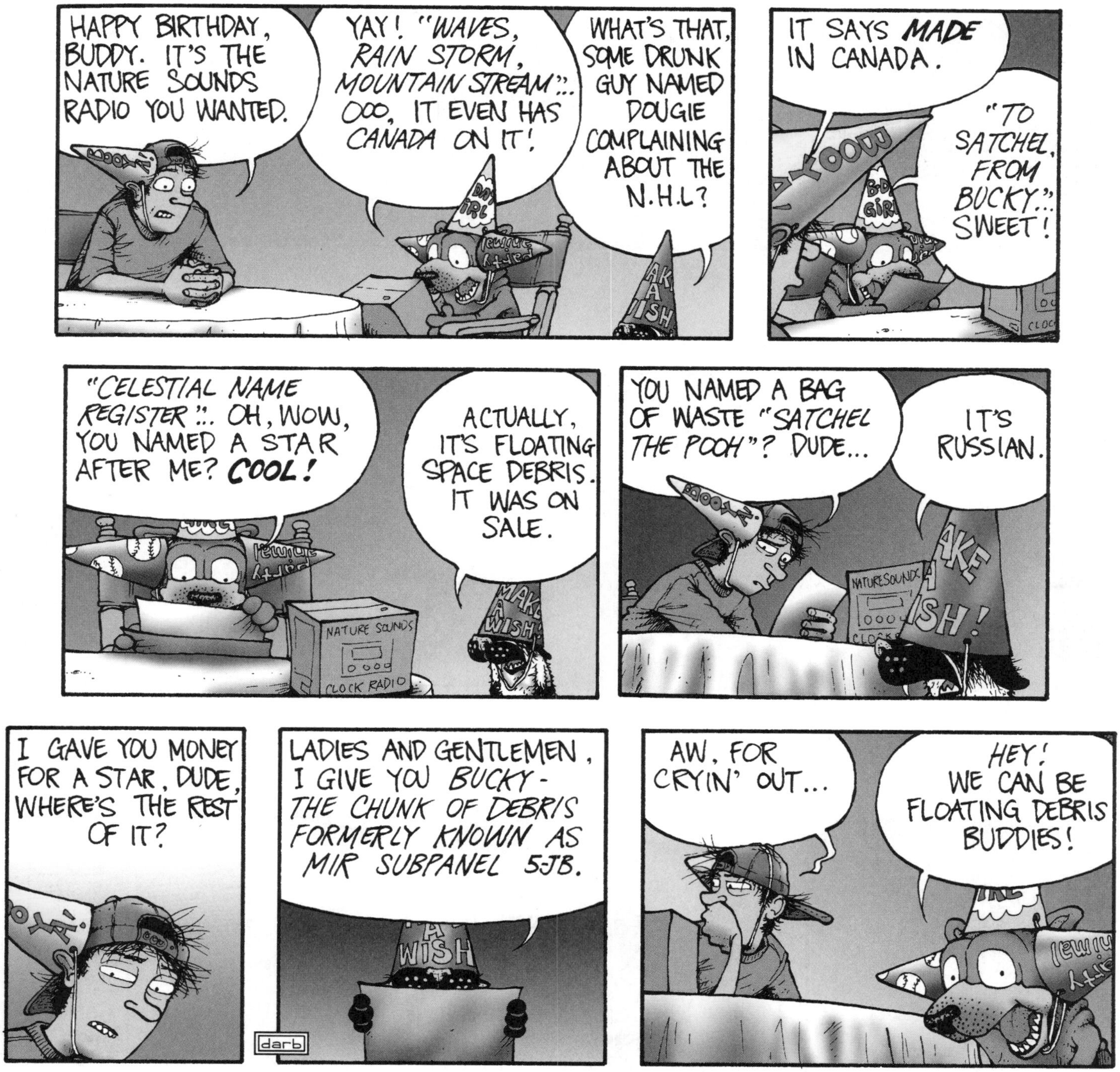
HAPPY BIRTHDAY, BUDDY. IT'S THE NATURE SOUNDS RADIO YOU WANTED.
YAY! "WAVES, RAIN STORM, MOUNTAIN STREAM"... OOO, IT EVEN HAS CANADA ON IT!
WHAT'S THAT, SOME DRUNK GUY NAMED DOUGIE COMPLAINING ABOUT THE N.H.L?
IT SAYS MADE IN CANADA.
"TO SATCHEL, FROM BUCKY."... SWEET!
"CELESTIAL NAME REGISTER"... OH, WOW, YOU NAMED A STAR AFTER ME? COOL!
ACTUALLY, IT'S FLOATING SPACE DEBRIS. IT WAS ON SALE.
NATURE SOUNDS
CLOCK RADIO
YOU NAMED A BAG OF WASTE "SATCHEL THE POOH"? DUDE...
IT'S RUSSIAN.
I GAVE YOU MONEY FOR A STAR, DUDE, WHERE'S THE REST OF IT?
LADIES AND GENTLEMEN, I GIVE YOU BUCKY - THE CHUNK OF DEBRIS FORMERLY KNOWN AS MIR SUBPANEL 5-JB.
AW, FOR CRYIN' OUT...
HEY! WE CAN BE FLOATING DEBRIS BUDDIES!

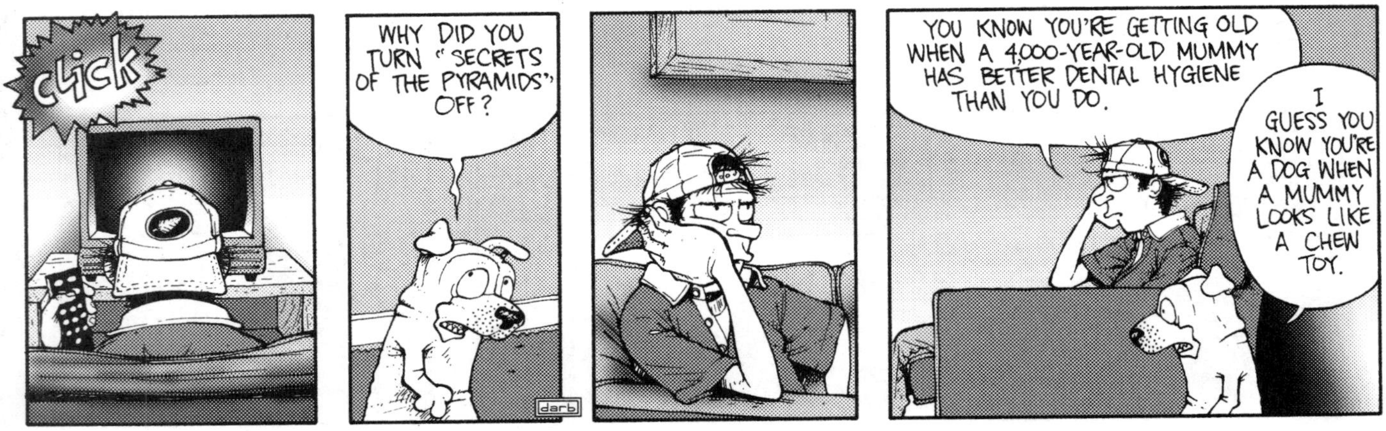
CLICK
WHY DID YOU TURN "SECRETS OF THE PYRAMIDS" OFF?
YOU KNOW YOU'RE GETTING OLD WHEN A 4,000-YEAR-OLD MUMMY HAS BETTER DENTAL HYGIENE THAN YOU DO.
I GUESS YOU KNOW YOU'RE A DOG WHEN A MUMMY LOOKS LIKE A CHEW TOY.
darb

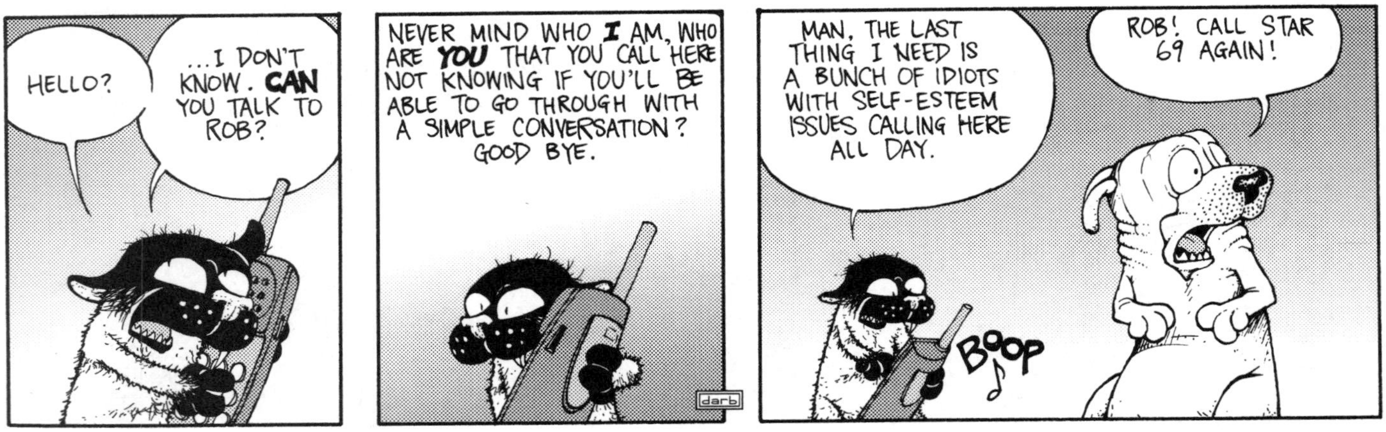
HELLO?
...I DON'T KNOW. CAN YOU TALK TO ROB?
NEVER MIND WHO I AM, WHO ARE YOU THAT YOU CALL HERE NOT KNOWING IF YOU'LL BE ABLE TO GO THROUGH WITH A SIMPLE CONVERSATION? GOOD BYE.
MAN, THE LAST THING I NEED IS A BUNCH OF IDIOTS WITH SELF-ESTEEM ISSUES CALLING HERE ALL DAY.
BOOP
ROB! CALL STAR 69 AGAIN!
darb

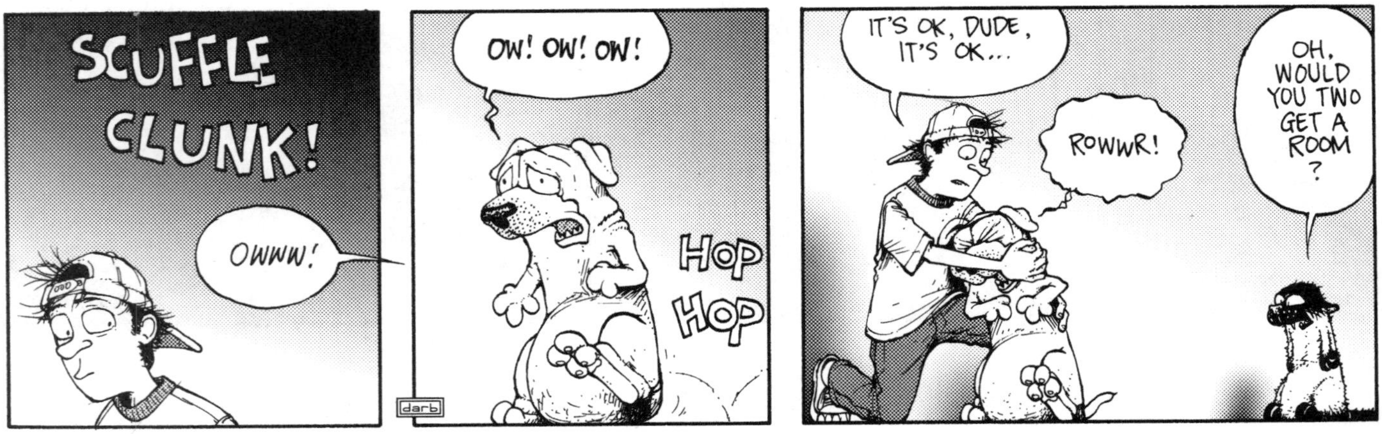
SCUFFLE
CLUNK!
OWWW!
OW! OW! OW!
HOP
HOP
IT'S OK, DUDE, IT'S OK...
ROWWR!
OH, WOULD YOU TWO GET A ROOM?
darb

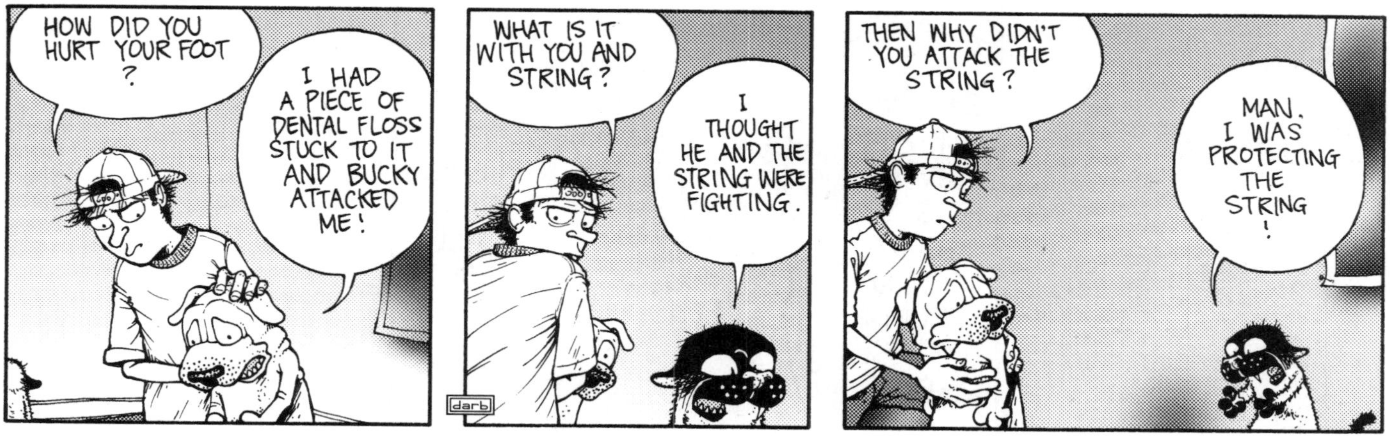
HOW DID YOU HURT YOUR FOOT ?
I HAD A PIECE OF DENTAL FLOSS STUCK TO IT AND BUCKY ATTACKED ME!
WHAT IS IT WITH YOU AND STRING ?
I THOUGHT HE AND THE STRING WERE FIGHTING.
THEN WHY DIDN'T YOU ATTACK THE STRING ?
MAN. I WAS PROTECTING THE STRING !

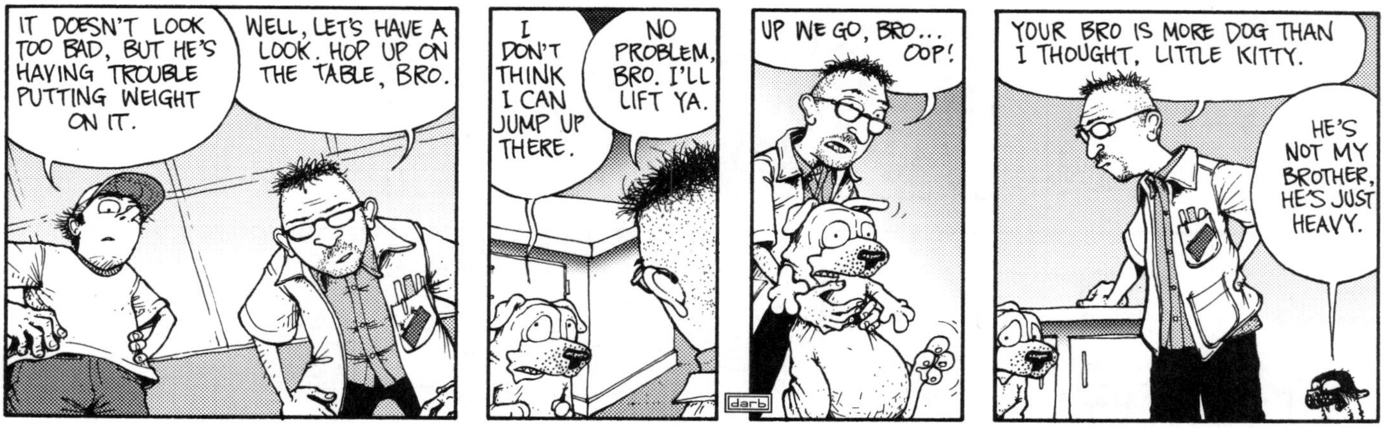
IT DOESN'T LOOK TOO BAD, BUT HE'S HAVING TROUBLE PUTTING WEIGHT ON IT.
WELL, LET'S HAVE A LOOK. HOP UP ON THE TABLE, BRO.
I DON'T THINK I CAN JUMP UP THERE.
NO PROBLEM, BRO. I'LL LIFT YA.
UP WE GO, BRO... OOP!
YOUR BRO IS MORE DOG THAN I THOUGHT, LITTLE KITTY.
HE'S NOT MY BROTHER, HE'S JUST HEAVY.

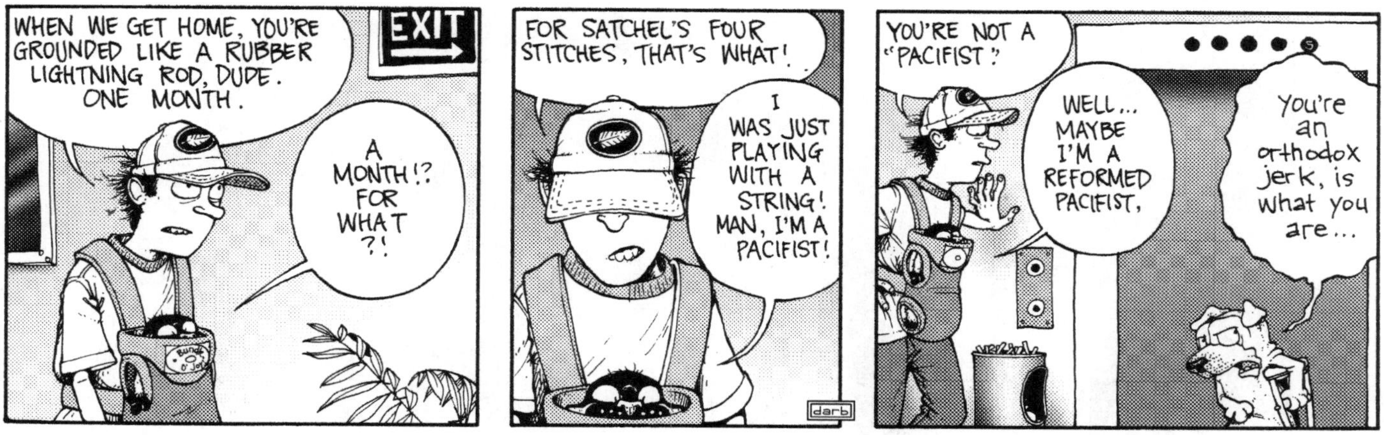
WHEN WE GET HOME, YOU'RE GROUNDED LIKE A RUBBER LIGHTNING ROD, DUDE. ONE MONTH.
EXIT
A MONTH!? FOR WHAT ?!
FOR SATCHEL'S FOUR STITCHES, THAT'S WHAT!
I WAS JUST PLAYING WITH A STRING! MAN, I'M A PACIFIST!
YOU'RE NOT A "PACIFIST."
WELL... MAYBE I'M A REFORMED PACIFIST,
You're an orthodox jerk, is what you are...

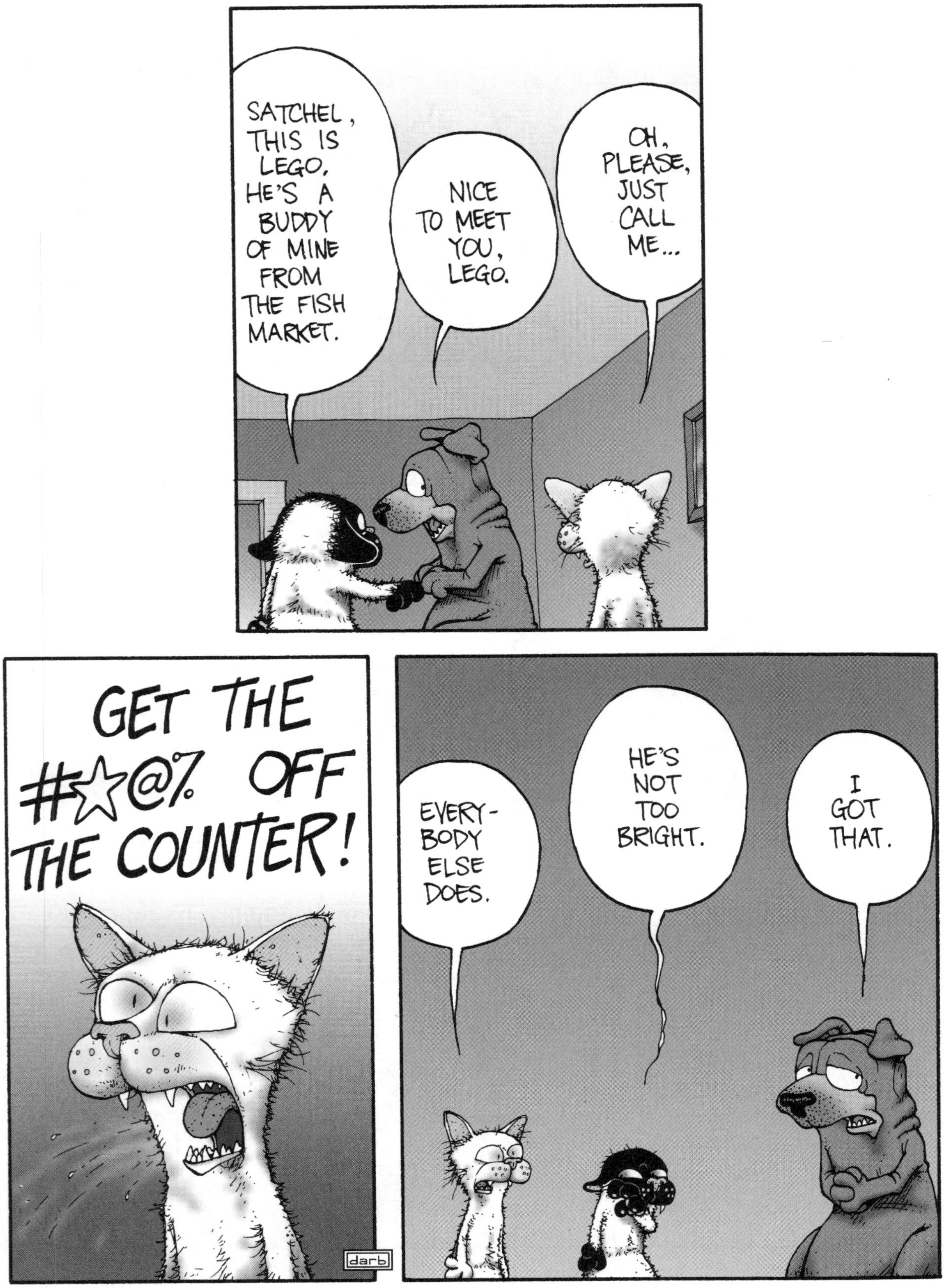
SATCHEL, THIS IS LEGO. HE'S A BUDDY OF MINE FROM THE FISH MARKET.
NICE TO MEET YOU, LEGO.
OH, PLEASE, JUST CALL ME...
GET THE #☆@% OFF THE COUNTER!
darb
EVERY-BODY ELSE DOES.
HE'S NOT TOO BRIGHT.
I GOT THAT.

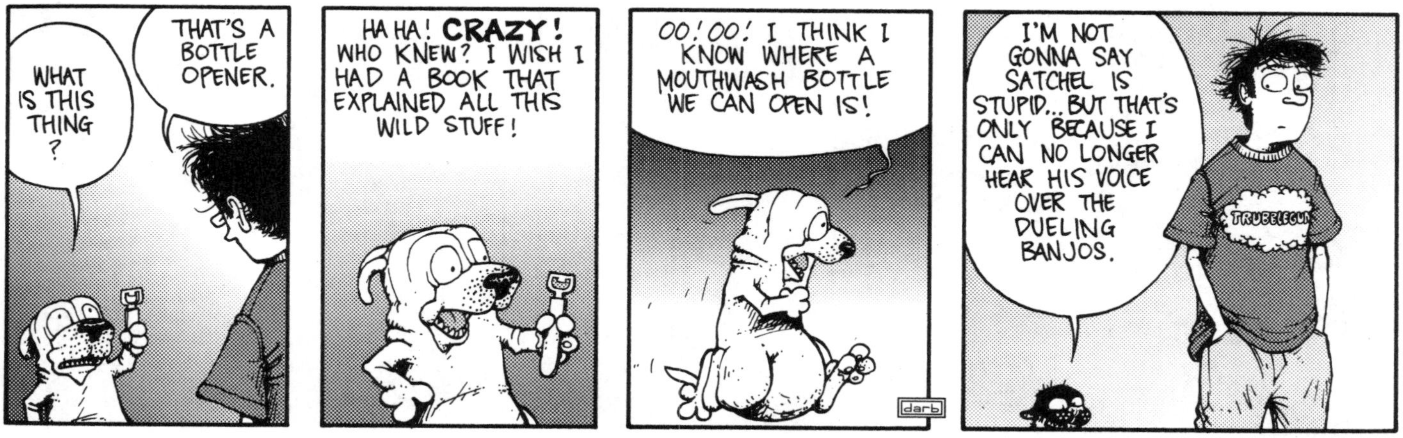
WHAT IS THIS THING ?
THAT'S A BOTTLE OPENER.
HA HA! **CRAZY!** WHO KNEW? I WISH I HAD A BOOK THAT EXPLAINED ALL THIS WILD STUFF!
OO! OO! I THINK I KNOW WHERE A MOUTHWASH BOTTLE WE CAN OPEN IS!
darb
I'M NOT GONNA SAY SATCHEL IS STUPID... BUT THAT'S ONLY BECAUSE I CAN NO LONGER HEAR HIS VOICE OVER THE DUELING BANJOS.
TRUBBLEGUM

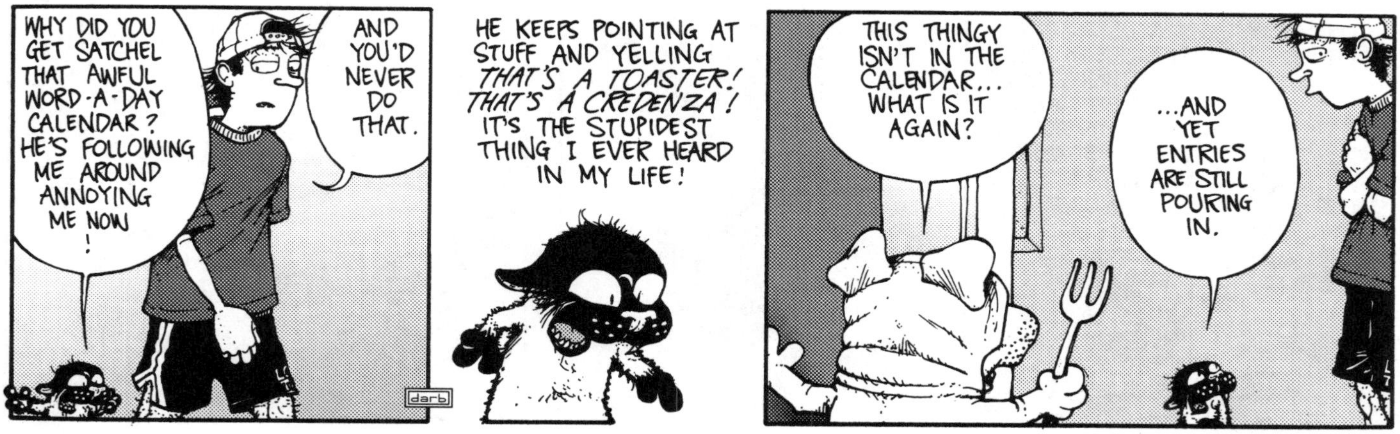
WHY DID YOU GET SATCHEL THAT AWFUL WORD-A-DAY CALENDAR? HE'S FOLLOWING ME AROUND ANNOYING ME NOW !
AND YOU'D NEVER DO THAT.
darb
HE KEEPS POINTING AT STUFF AND YELLING *THAT'S A TOASTER! THAT'S A CREDENZA!* IT'S THE STUPIDEST THING I EVER HEARD IN MY LIFE!
THIS THINGY ISN'T IN THE CALENDAR... WHAT IS IT AGAIN?
...AND YET ENTRIES ARE STILL POURING IN.

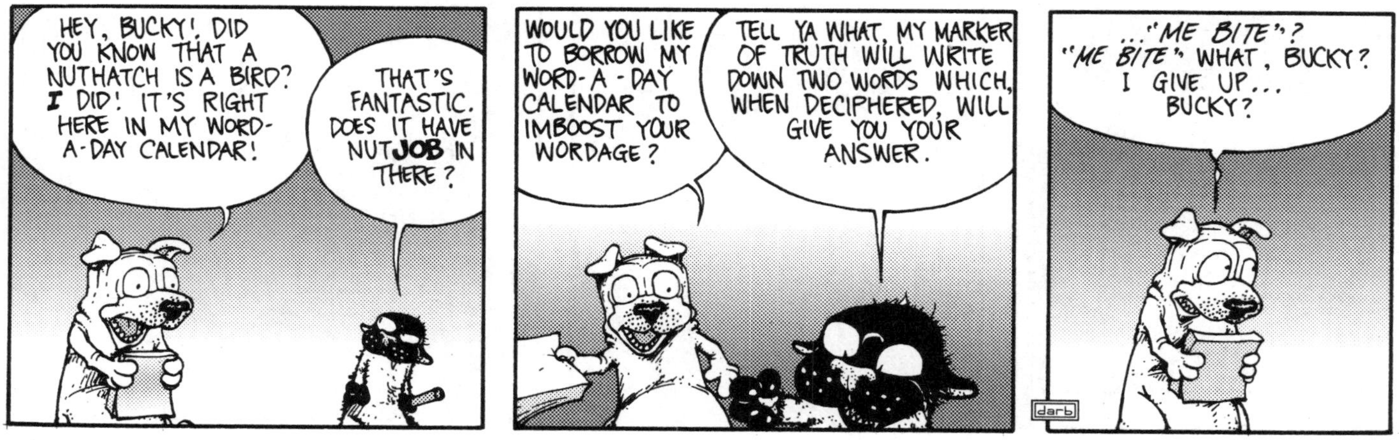
HEY, BUCKY! DID YOU KNOW THAT A NUTHATCH IS A BIRD? **I** DID! IT'S RIGHT HERE IN MY WORD-A-DAY CALENDAR!
THAT'S FANTASTIC. DOES IT HAVE NUT**JOB** IN THERE?
WOULD YOU LIKE TO BORROW MY WORD-A-DAY CALENDAR TO IMBOOST YOUR WORDAGE?
TELL YA WHAT, MY MARKER OF TRUTH WILL WRITE DOWN TWO WORDS WHICH, WHEN DECIPHERED, WILL GIVE YOU YOUR ANSWER.
darb
..."*ME BITE*"? "*ME BITE*" WHAT, BUCKY? I GIVE UP... BUCKY?

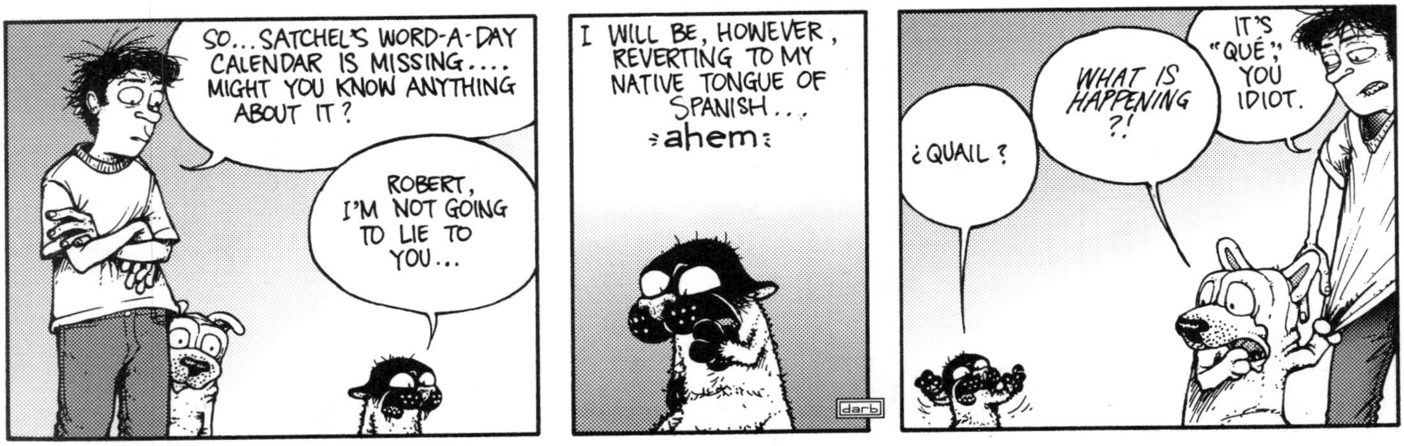
SO... SATCHEL'S WORD-A-DAY CALENDAR IS MISSING.... MIGHT YOU KNOW ANYTHING ABOUT IT?
ROBERT, I'M NOT GOING TO LIE TO YOU...
I WILL BE, HOWEVER, REVERTING TO MY NATIVE TONGUE OF SPANISH...
ahem
¿QUAIL?
WHAT IS HAPPENING ?!
IT'S "QUÉ," YOU IDIOT.

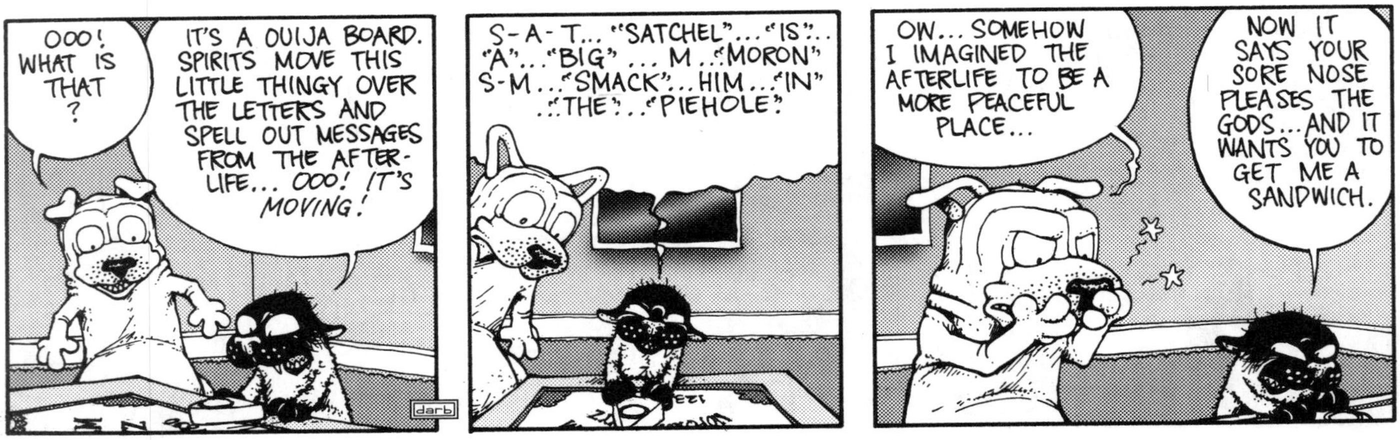
OOO! WHAT IS THAT ?
IT'S A OUIJA BOARD. SPIRITS MOVE THIS LITTLE THINGY OVER THE LETTERS AND SPELL OUT MESSAGES FROM THE AFTER-LIFE... OOO! IT'S MOVING!
S-A-T... "SATCHEL"... "IS"... "A"... "BIG"... M... "MORON" S-M... "SMACK"... HIM... "IN" ... "THE"... "PIEHOLE"
OW... SOMEHOW I IMAGINED THE AFTERLIFE TO BE A MORE PEACEFUL PLACE...
NOW IT SAYS YOUR SORE NOSE PLEASES THE GODS... AND IT WANTS YOU TO GET ME A SANDWICH.

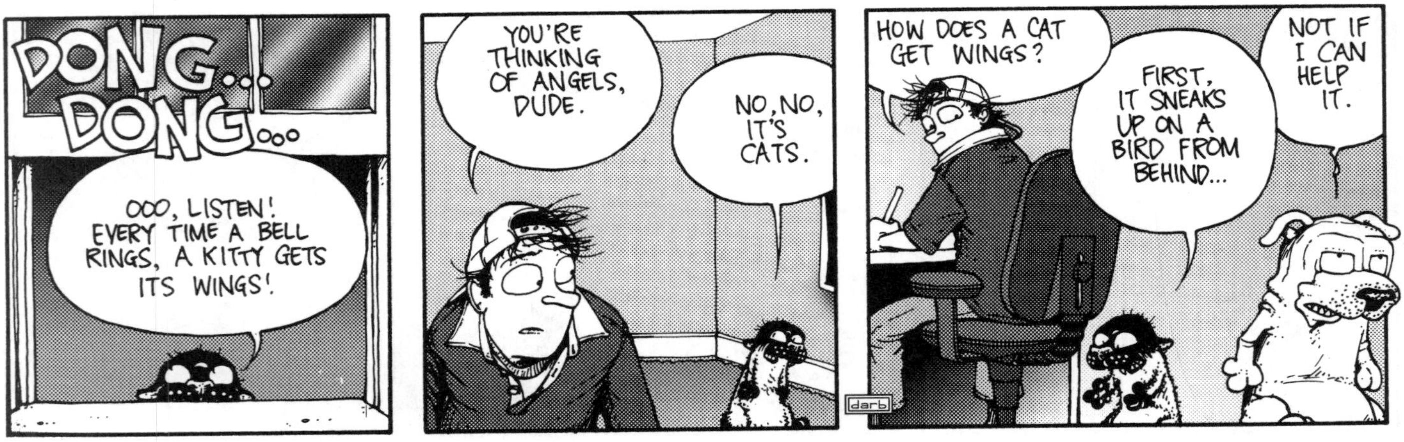
DONG... DONG...
OOO, LISTEN! EVERY TIME A BELL RINGS, A KITTY GETS ITS WINGS!
YOU'RE THINKING OF ANGELS, DUDE.
NO, NO, IT'S CATS.
HOW DOES A CAT GET WINGS?
FIRST, IT SNEAKS UP ON A BIRD FROM BEHIND...
NOT IF I CAN HELP IT.

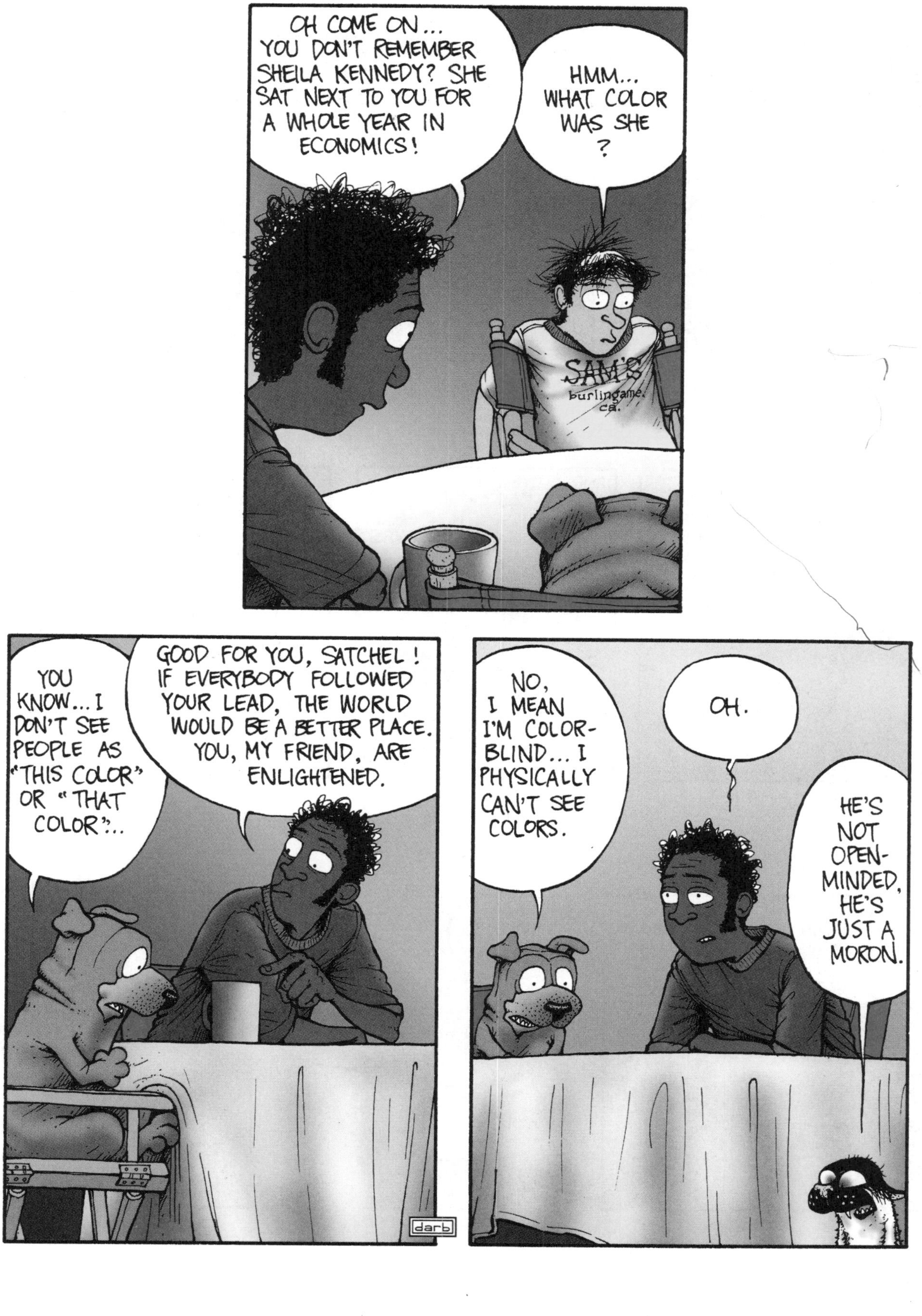
OH COME ON... YOU DON'T REMEMBER SHEILA KENNEDY? SHE SAT NEXT TO YOU FOR A WHOLE YEAR IN ECONOMICS!
HMM... WHAT COLOR WAS SHE ?
SAM'S burlingame. ca.
YOU KNOW... I DON'T SEE PEOPLE AS "THIS COLOR" OR "THAT COLOR"...
GOOD FOR YOU, SATCHEL! IF EVERYBODY FOLLOWED YOUR LEAD, THE WORLD WOULD BE A BETTER PLACE. YOU, MY FRIEND, ARE ENLIGHTENED.
darb
NO, I MEAN I'M COLOR-BLIND... I PHYSICALLY CAN'T SEE COLORS.
OH.
HE'S NOT OPEN-MINDED, HE'S JUST A MORON.

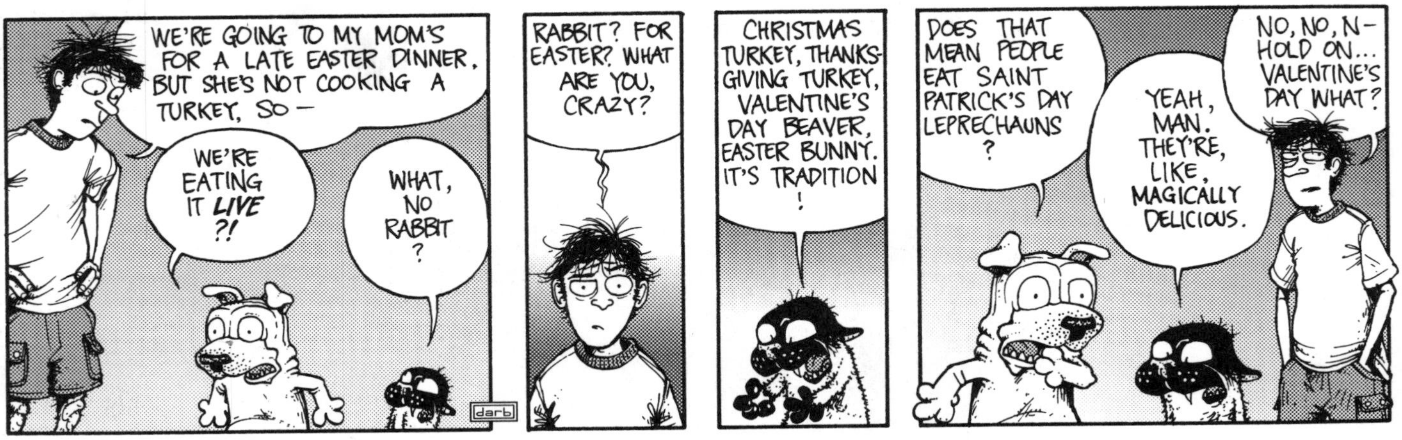
WE'RE GOING TO MY MOM'S FOR A LATE EASTER DINNER, BUT SHE'S NOT COOKING A TURKEY, SO—
WE'RE EATING IT **LIVE** ?!
WHAT, NO RABBIT ?
RABBIT? FOR EASTER? WHAT ARE YOU, CRAZY?
CHRISTMAS TURKEY, THANKSGIVING TURKEY, VALENTINE'S DAY BEAVER, EASTER BUNNY. IT'S TRADITION !
DOES THAT MEAN PEOPLE EAT SAINT PATRICK'S DAY LEPRECHAUNS ?
YEAH, MAN. THEY'RE, LIKE, MAGICALLY DELICIOUS.
NO, NO, N— HOLD ON... VALENTINE'S DAY WHAT?
darb

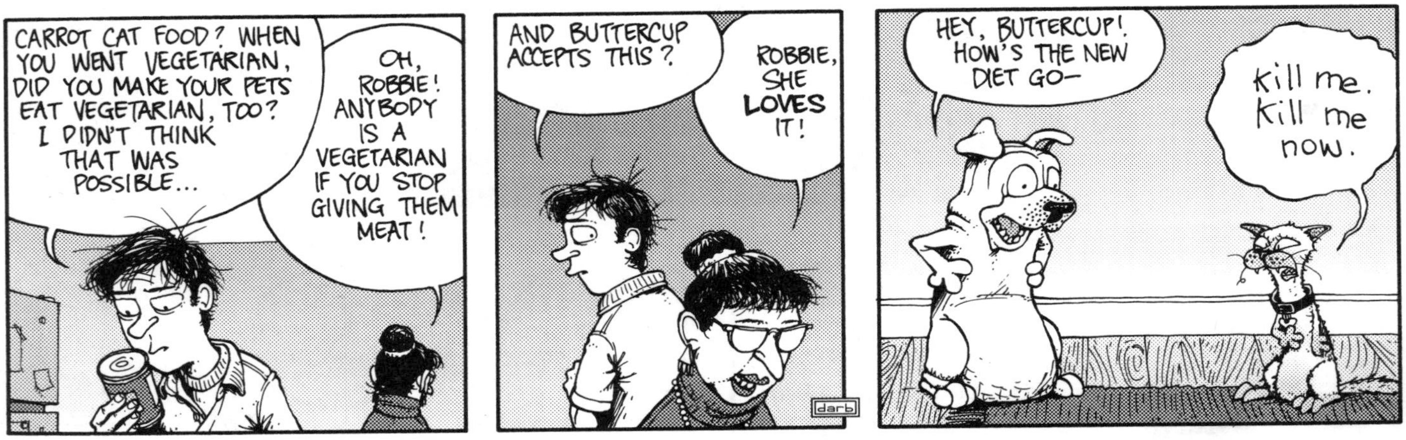
CARROT CAT FOOD? WHEN YOU WENT VEGETARIAN, DID YOU MAKE YOUR PETS EAT VEGETARIAN, TOO? I DIDN'T THINK THAT WAS POSSIBLE...
OH, ROBBIE! ANYBODY IS A VEGETARIAN IF YOU STOP GIVING THEM MEAT!
AND BUTTERCUP ACCEPTS THIS?
ROBBIE, SHE **LOVES** IT!
darb
HEY, BUTTERCUP! HOW'S THE NEW DIET GO—
Kill me. Kill me now.

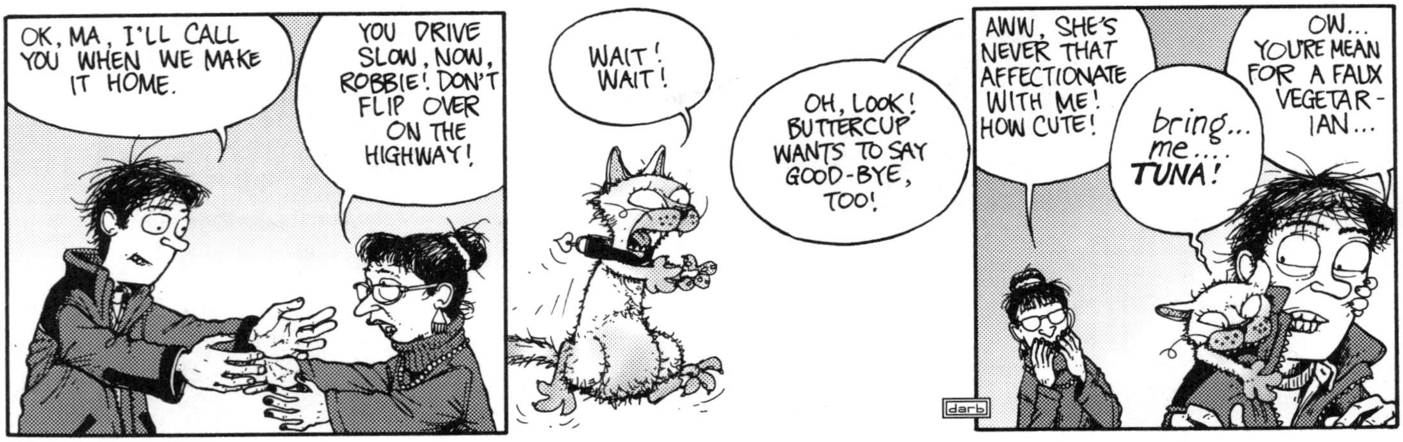
OK, MA, I'LL CALL YOU WHEN WE MAKE IT HOME.
YOU DRIVE SLOW, NOW, ROBBIE! DON'T FLIP OVER ON THE HIGHWAY!
WAIT! WAIT!
OH, LOOK! BUTTERCUP WANTS TO SAY GOOD-BYE, TOO!
AWW, SHE'S NEVER THAT AFFECTIONATE WITH ME! HOW CUTE!
bring... me.... **TUNA!**
OW... YOU'RE MEAN FOR A FAUX VEGETAR-IAN...
darb

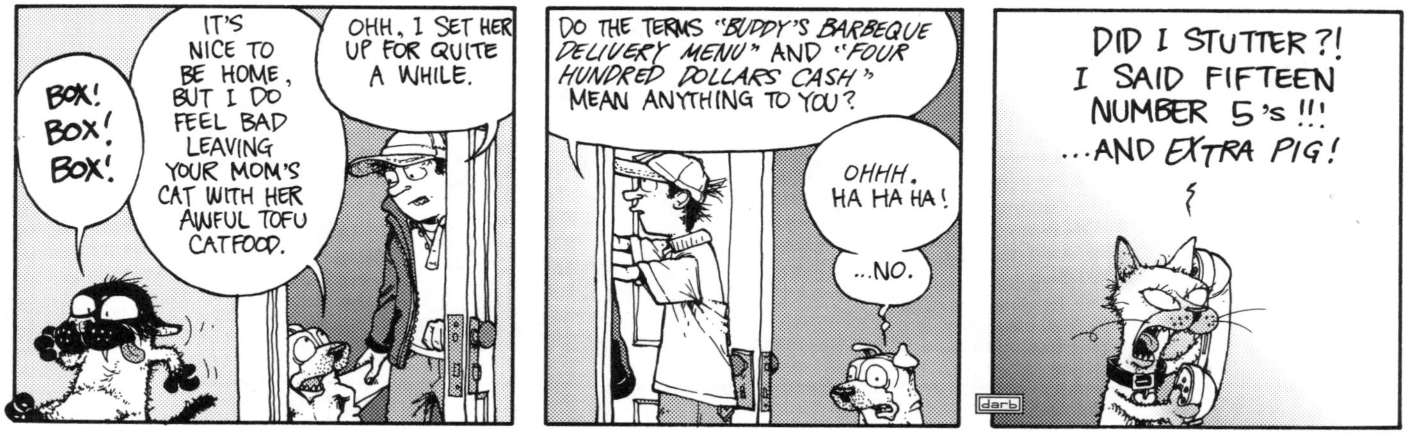
BOX! BOX! BOX!
IT'S NICE TO BE HOME, BUT I DO FEEL BAD LEAVING YOUR MOM'S CAT WITH HER AWFUL TOFU CATFOOD.
OHH, I SET HER UP FOR QUITE A WHILE.
DO THE TERMS "BUDDY'S BARBEQUE DELIVERY MENU" AND "FOUR HUNDRED DOLLARS CASH" MEAN ANYTHING TO YOU?
OHHH. HA HA HA!
...NO.
DID I STUTTER?! I SAID FIFTEEN NUMBER 5's!!! ...AND EXTRA PIG!
darb

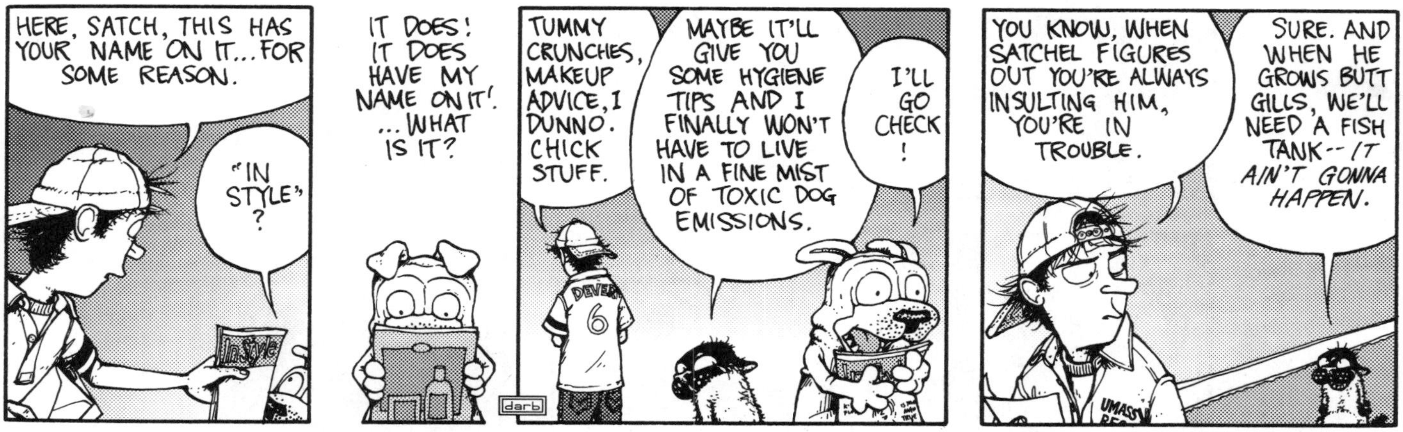
HERE, SATCH, THIS HAS YOUR NAME ON IT... FOR SOME REASON.
"IN STYLE"?
IT DOES! IT DOES HAVE MY NAME ON IT! ...WHAT IS IT?
darb
TUMMY CRUNCHES, MAKEUP ADVICE, I DUNNO. CHICK STUFF.
MAYBE IT'LL GIVE YOU SOME HYGIENE TIPS AND I FINALLY WON'T HAVE TO LIVE IN A FINE MIST OF TOXIC DOG EMISSIONS.
I'LL GO CHECK!
YOU KNOW, WHEN SATCHEL FIGURES OUT YOU'RE ALWAYS INSULTING HIM, YOU'RE IN TROUBLE.
SURE. AND WHEN HE GROWS BUTT GILLS, WE'LL NEED A FISH TANK-- IT AIN'T GONNA HAPPEN.

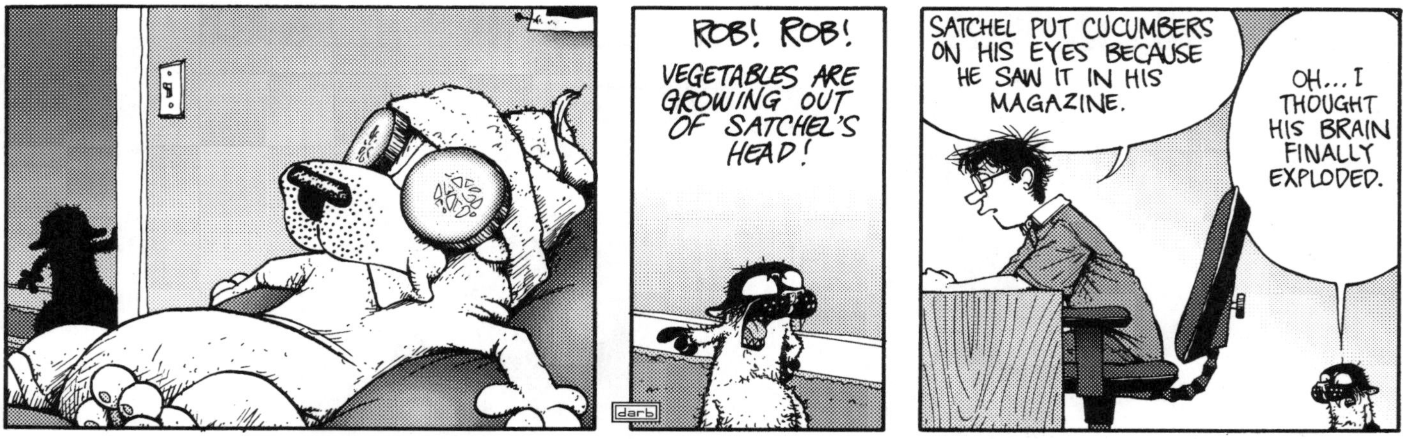
darb
ROB! ROB!
VEGETABLES ARE GROWING OUT OF SATCHEL'S HEAD!
SATCHEL PUT CUCUMBERS ON HIS EYES BECAUSE HE SAW IT IN HIS MAGAZINE.
OH... I THOUGHT HIS BRAIN FINALLY EXPLODED.

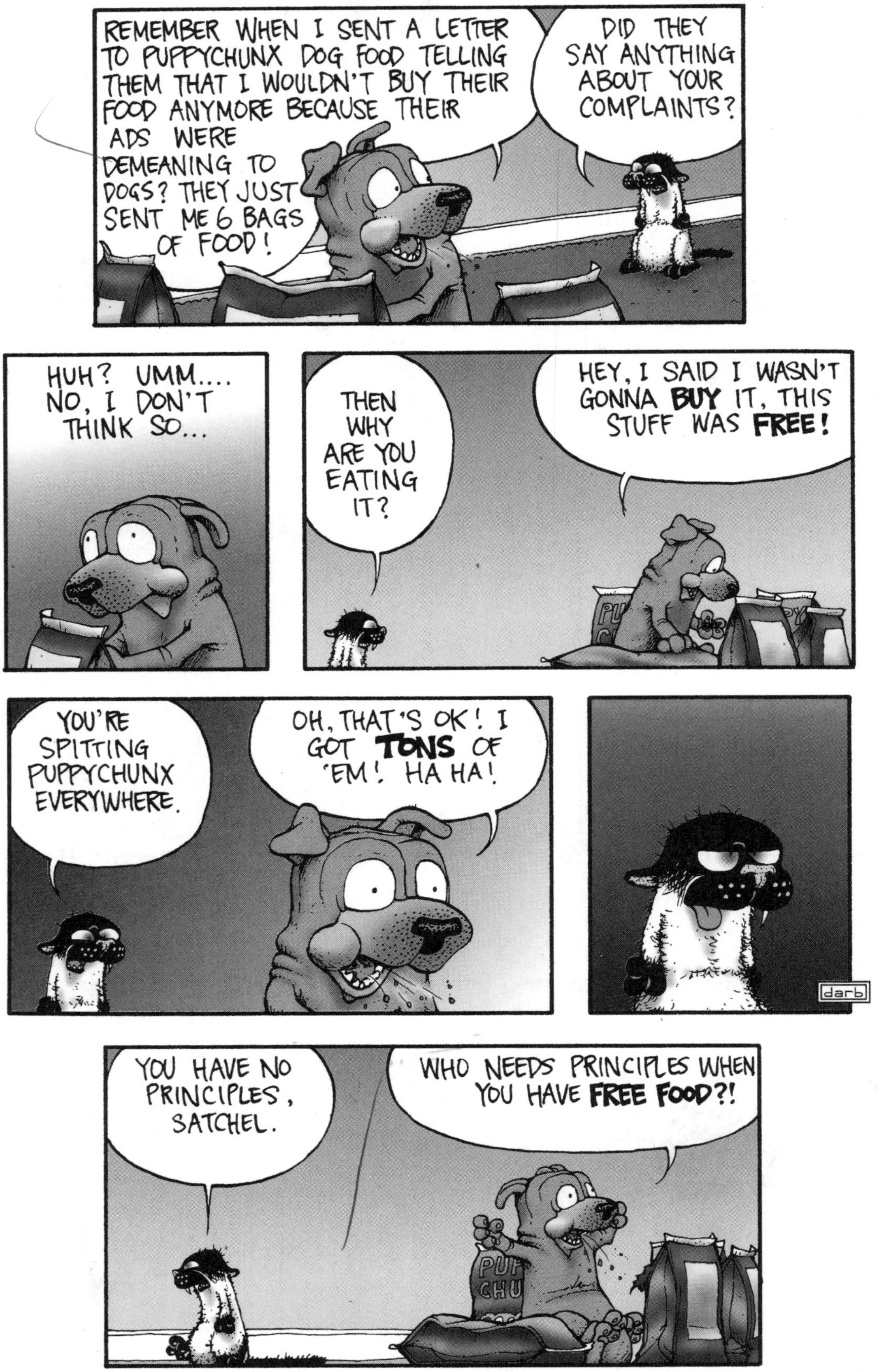
REMEMBER WHEN I SENT A LETTER TO PUPPYCHUNX DOG FOOD TELLING THEM THAT I WOULDN'T BUY THEIR FOOD ANYMORE BECAUSE THEIR ADS WERE DEMEANING TO DOGS? THEY JUST SENT ME 6 BAGS OF FOOD!
DID THEY SAY ANYTHING ABOUT YOUR COMPLAINTS?
HUH? UMM.... NO, I DON'T THINK SO...
THEN WHY ARE YOU EATING IT?
HEY, I SAID I WASN'T GONNA **BUY** IT, THIS STUFF WAS **FREE!**
YOU'RE SPITTING PUPPYCHUNX EVERYWHERE.
OH, THAT'S OK! I GOT **TONS** OF 'EM! HA HA!
darb
YOU HAVE NO PRINCIPLES, SATCHEL.
WHO NEEDS PRINCIPLES WHEN YOU HAVE **FREE FOOD**?!

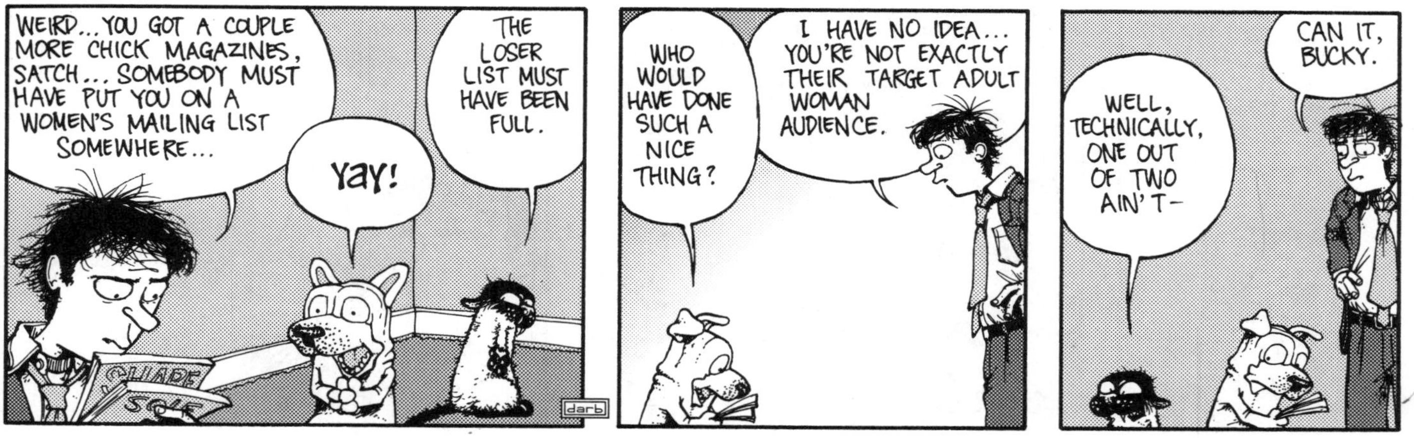
WEIRD... YOU GOT A COUPLE MORE CHICK MAGAZINES, SATCH... SOMEBODY MUST HAVE PUT YOU ON A WOMEN'S MAILING LIST SOMEWHERE...
YAY!
THE LOSER LIST MUST HAVE BEEN FULL.
darb
WHO WOULD HAVE DONE SUCH A NICE THING?
I HAVE NO IDEA... YOU'RE NOT EXACTLY THEIR TARGET ADULT WOMAN AUDIENCE.
WELL, TECHNICALLY, ONE OUT OF TWO AIN'T-
CAN IT, BUCKY.

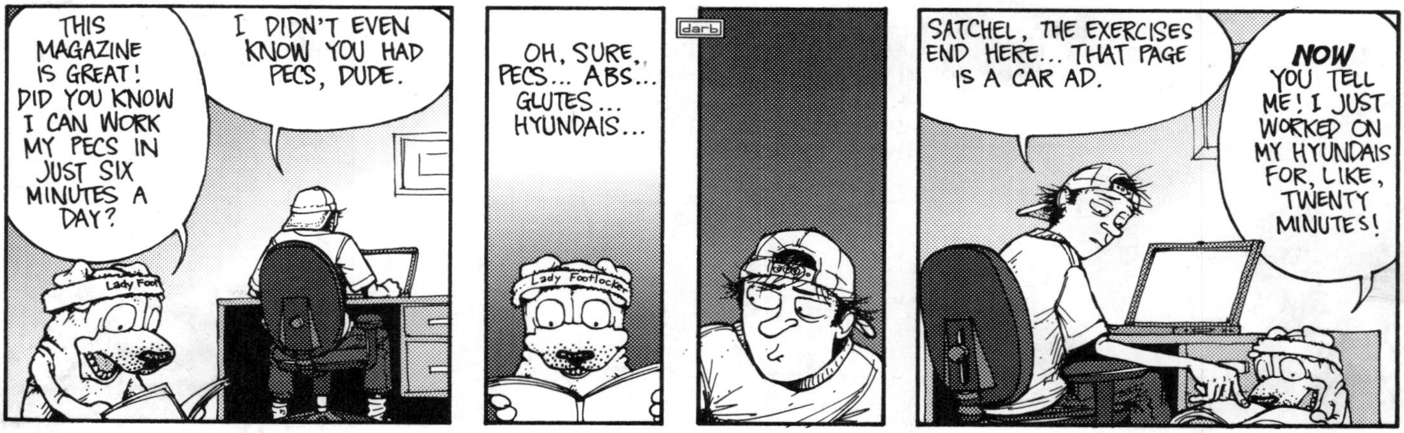
THIS MAGAZINE IS GREAT! DID YOU KNOW I CAN WORK MY PECS IN JUST SIX MINUTES A DAY?
I DIDN'T EVEN KNOW YOU HAD PECS, DUDE.
OH, SURE. PECS... ABS... GLUTES... HYUNDAIS...
Lady Footlocker
darb
SATCHEL, THE EXERCISES END HERE... THAT PAGE IS A CAR AD.
NOW YOU TELL ME! I JUST WORKED ON MY HYUNDAIS FOR, LIKE, TWENTY MINUTES!

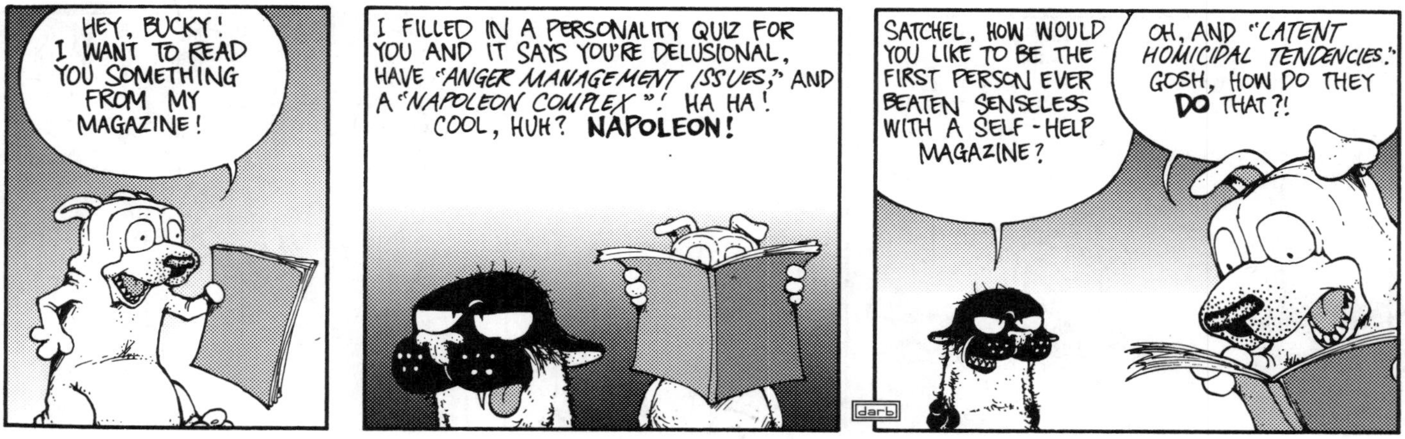
HEY, BUCKY! I WANT TO READ YOU SOMETHING FROM MY MAGAZINE!
I FILLED IN A PERSONALITY QUIZ FOR YOU AND IT SAYS YOU'RE DELUSIONAL, HAVE "ANGER MANAGEMENT ISSUES," AND A "NAPOLEON COMPLEX"! HA HA! COOL, HUH? NAPOLEON!
darb
SATCHEL, HOW WOULD YOU LIKE TO BE THE FIRST PERSON EVER BEATEN SENSELESS WITH A SELF-HELP MAGAZINE?
OH, AND "LATENT HOMICIDAL TENDENCIES." GOSH, HOW DO THEY DO THAT?!

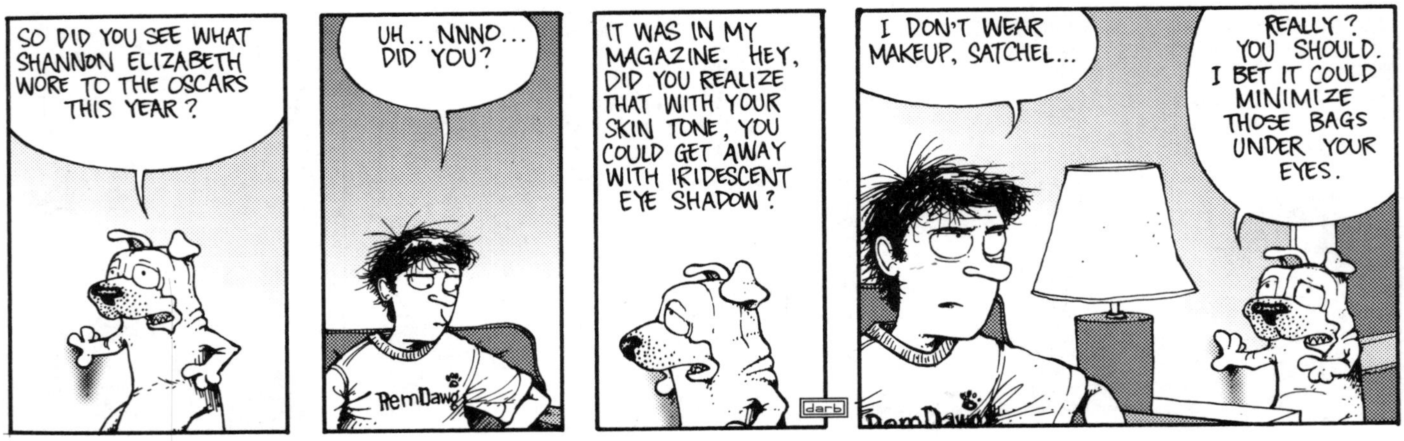
SO DID YOU SEE WHAT SHANNON ELIZABETH WORE TO THE OSCARS THIS YEAR?
UH...NNNO... DID YOU?
RemDawg
IT WAS IN MY MAGAZINE. HEY, DID YOU REALIZE THAT WITH YOUR SKIN TONE, YOU COULD GET AWAY WITH IRIDESCENT EYE SHADOW?
darb
I DON'T WEAR MAKEUP, SATCHEL...
REALLY? YOU SHOULD. I BET IT COULD MINIMIZE THOSE BAGS UNDER YOUR EYES.

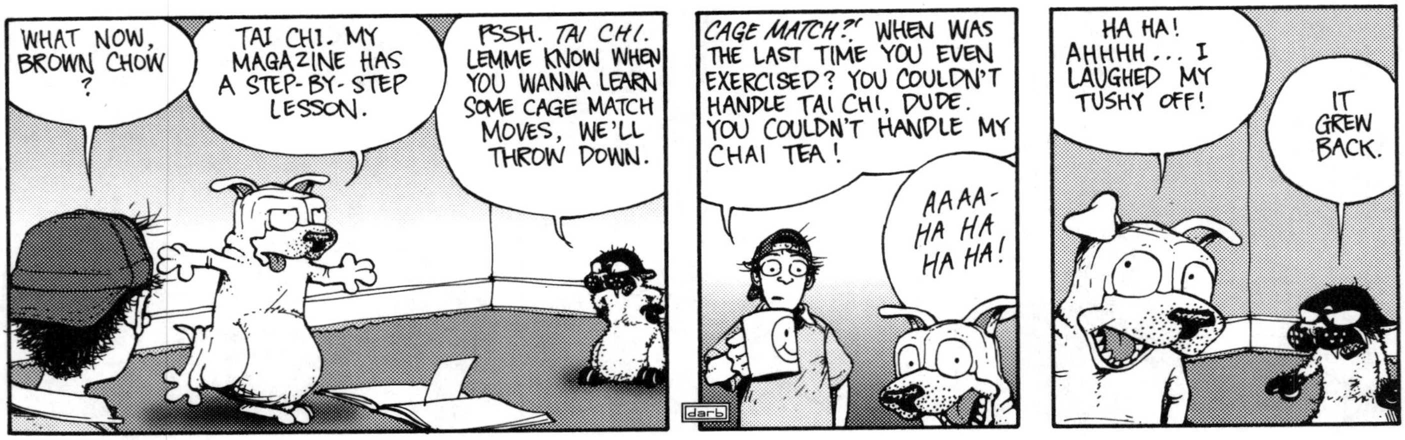
WHAT NOW, BROWN CHOW?
TAI CHI. MY MAGAZINE HAS A STEP-BY-STEP LESSON.
PSSH. TAI CHI. LEMME KNOW WHEN YOU WANNA LEARN SOME CAGE MATCH MOVES, WE'LL THROW DOWN.
CAGE MATCH?! WHEN WAS THE LAST TIME YOU EVEN EXERCISED? YOU COULDN'T HANDLE TAI CHI, DUDE. YOU COULDN'T HANDLE MY CHAI TEA!
AAAA-HA HA HA HA!
darb
HA HA! AHHHH... I LAUGHED MY TUSHY OFF!
IT GREW BACK.

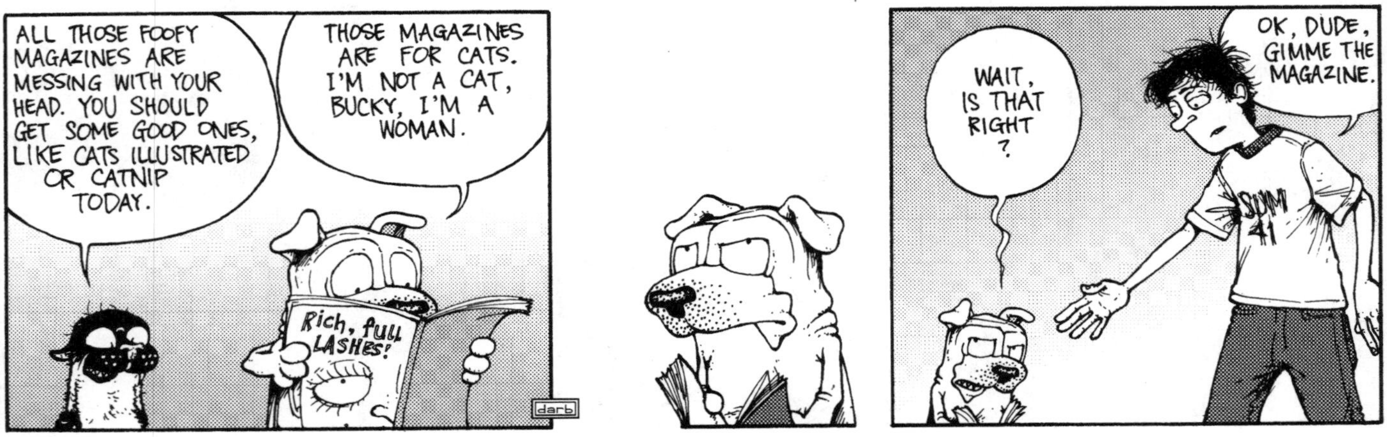
ALL THOSE FOOFY MAGAZINES ARE MESSING WITH YOUR HEAD. YOU SHOULD GET SOME GOOD ONES, LIKE CATS ILLUSTRATED OR CATNIP TODAY.
THOSE MAGAZINES ARE FOR CATS. I'M NOT A CAT, BUCKY, I'M A WOMAN.
Rich, full LASHES!
darb
WAIT, IS THAT RIGHT?
OK, DUDE, GIMME THE MAGAZINE.
SUM 41

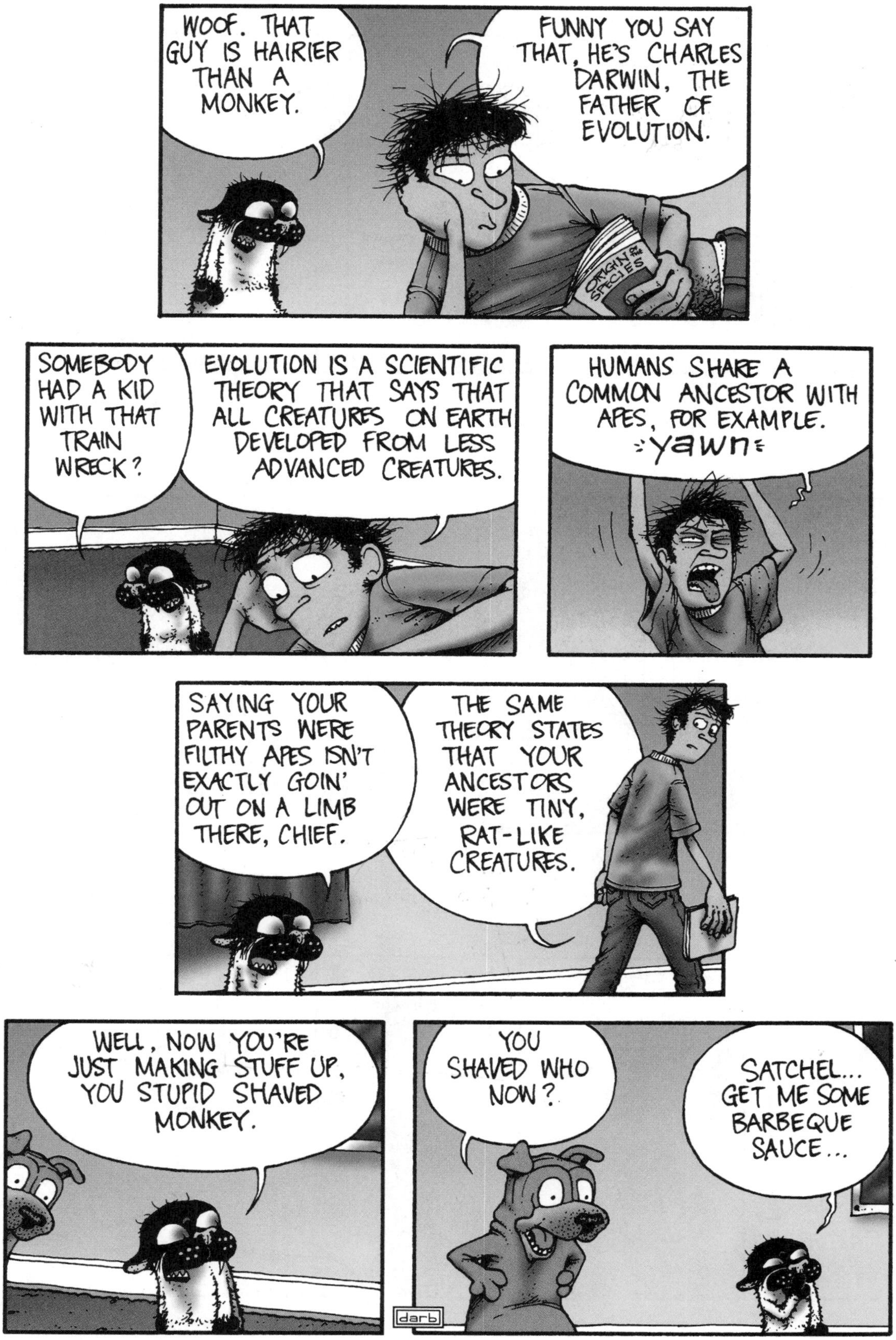
WOOF. THAT GUY IS HAIRIER THAN A MONKEY.
FUNNY YOU SAY THAT, HE'S CHARLES DARWIN, THE FATHER OF EVOLUTION.
ORIGIN OF THE SPECIES
SOMEBODY HAD A KID WITH THAT TRAIN WRECK?
EVOLUTION IS A SCIENTIFIC THEORY THAT SAYS THAT ALL CREATURES ON EARTH DEVELOPED FROM LESS ADVANCED CREATURES.
HUMANS SHARE A COMMON ANCESTOR WITH APES, FOR EXAMPLE.
yawn
SAYING YOUR PARENTS WERE FILTHY APES ISN'T EXACTLY GOIN' OUT ON A LIMB THERE, CHIEF.
THE SAME THEORY STATES THAT YOUR ANCESTORS WERE TINY, RAT-LIKE CREATURES.
WELL, NOW YOU'RE JUST MAKING STUFF UP, YOU STUPID SHAVED MONKEY.
darb
YOU SHAVED WHO NOW?
SATCHEL... GET ME SOME BARBEQUE SAUCE...

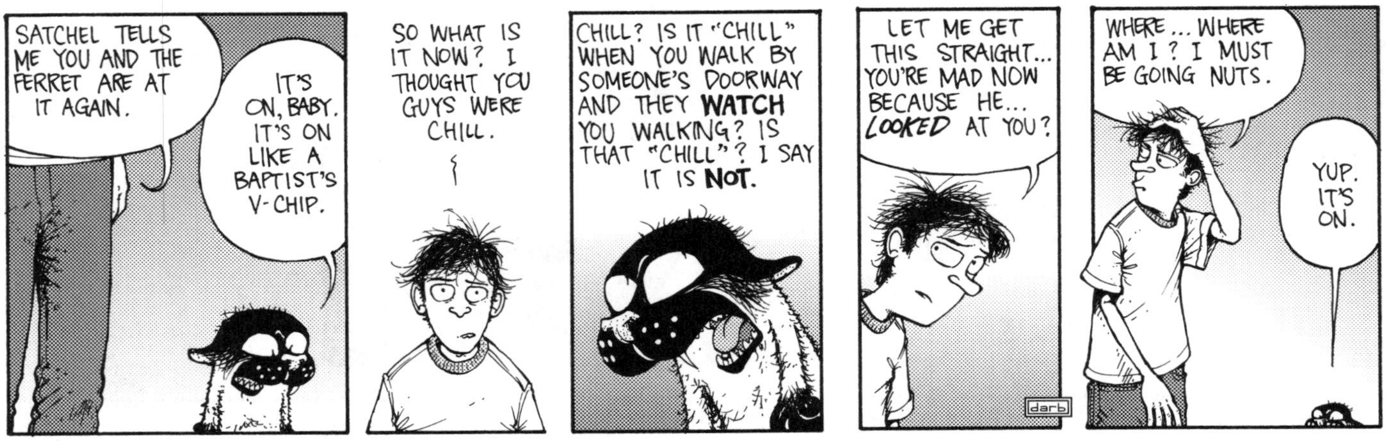
SATCHEL TELLS ME YOU AND THE FERRET ARE AT IT AGAIN.
IT'S ON, BABY. IT'S ON LIKE A BAPTIST'S V-CHIP.
SO WHAT IS IT NOW? I THOUGHT YOU GUYS WERE CHILL.
CHILL? IS IT "CHILL" WHEN YOU WALK BY SOMEONE'S DOORWAY AND THEY **WATCH** YOU WALKING? IS THAT "CHILL"? I SAY IT IS **NOT**.
LET ME GET THIS STRAIGHT... YOU'RE MAD NOW BECAUSE HE... *LOOKED* AT YOU?
darb
WHERE... WHERE AM I? I MUST BE GOING NUTS.
YUP. IT'S ON.

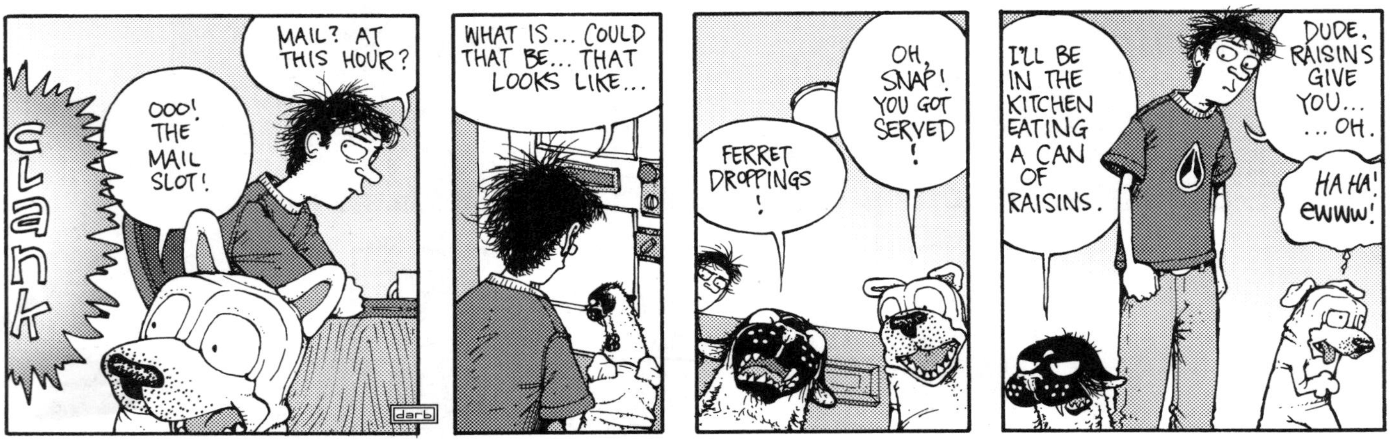
CLANK
MAIL? AT THIS HOUR?
OOO! THE MAIL SLOT!
darb
WHAT IS... COULD THAT BE... THAT LOOKS LIKE...
FERRET DROPPINGS!
OH, SNAP! YOU GOT SERVED!
I'LL BE IN THE KITCHEN EATING A CAN OF RAISINS.
DUDE. RAISINS GIVE YOU... ...OH.
HA HA! EWWW!

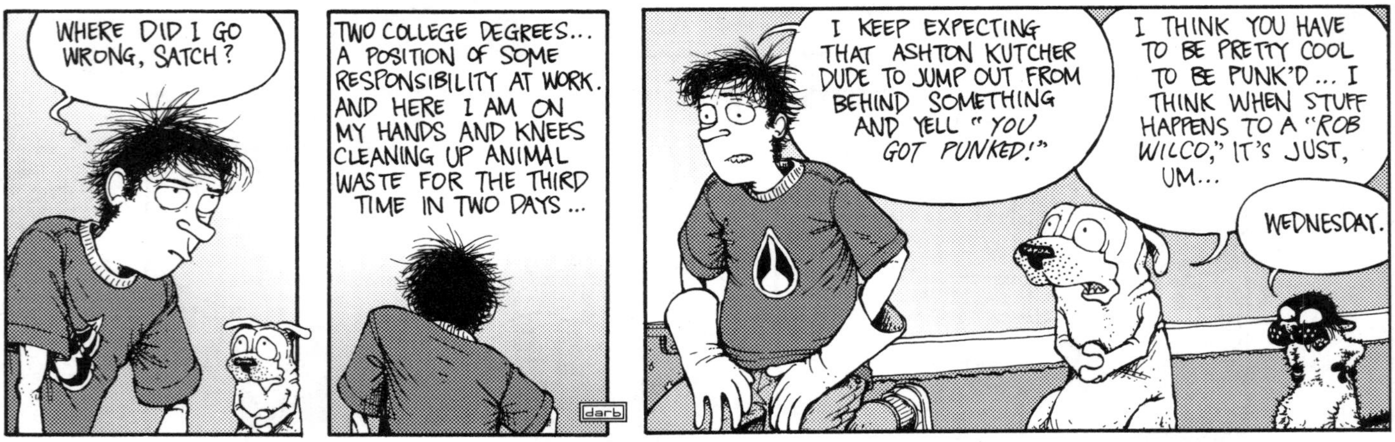
WHERE DID I GO WRONG, SATCH?
TWO COLLEGE DEGREES... A POSITION OF SOME RESPONSIBILITY AT WORK. AND HERE I AM ON MY HANDS AND KNEES CLEANING UP ANIMAL WASTE FOR THE THIRD TIME IN TWO DAYS...
darb
I KEEP EXPECTING THAT ASHTON KUTCHER DUDE TO JUMP OUT FROM BEHIND SOMETHING AND YELL "*YOU GOT PUNKED!*"
I THINK YOU HAVE TO BE PRETTY COOL TO BE PUNK'D... I THINK WHEN STUFF HAPPENS TO A "*ROB WILCO*," IT'S JUST, UM...
WEDNESDAY.

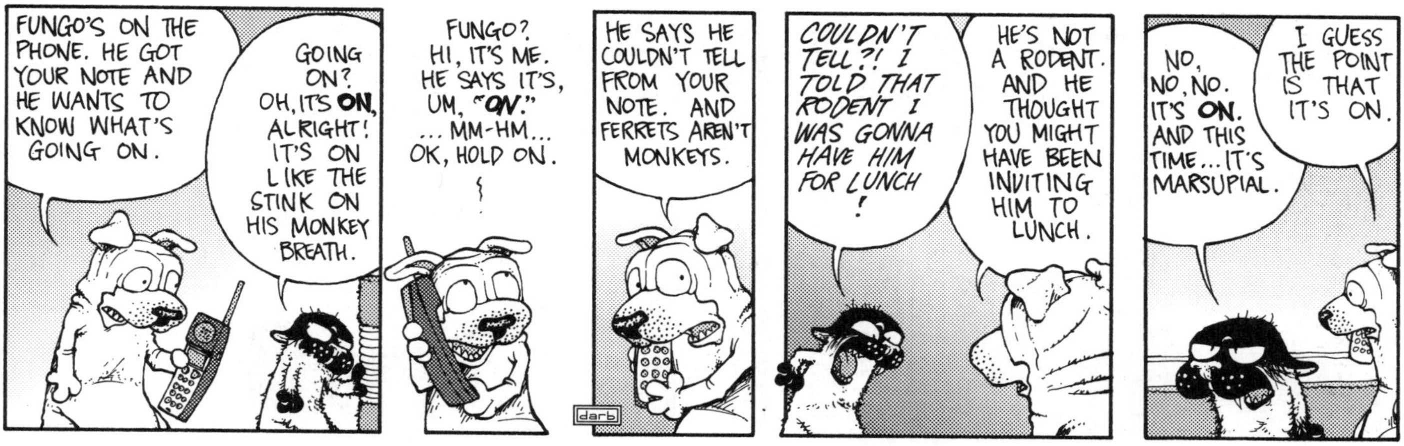
FUNGO'S ON THE PHONE. HE GOT YOUR NOTE AND HE WANTS TO KNOW WHAT'S GOING ON.
GOING ON? OH, IT'S **ON**, ALRIGHT! IT'S ON LIKE THE STINK ON HIS MONKEY BREATH.
FUNGO? HI, IT'S ME. HE SAYS IT'S, UM, "**ON**." ... MM-HM... OK, HOLD ON.
HE SAYS HE COULDN'T TELL FROM YOUR NOTE. AND FERRETS AREN'T MONKEYS.
COULDN'T TELL?! I TOLD THAT RODENT I WAS GONNA HAVE HIM FOR LUNCH!
HE'S NOT A RODENT. AND HE THOUGHT YOU MIGHT HAVE BEEN INVITING HIM TO LUNCH.
NO, NO, NO. IT'S **ON**. AND THIS TIME... IT'S MARSUPIAL.
I GUESS THE POINT IS THAT IT'S ON.
darb

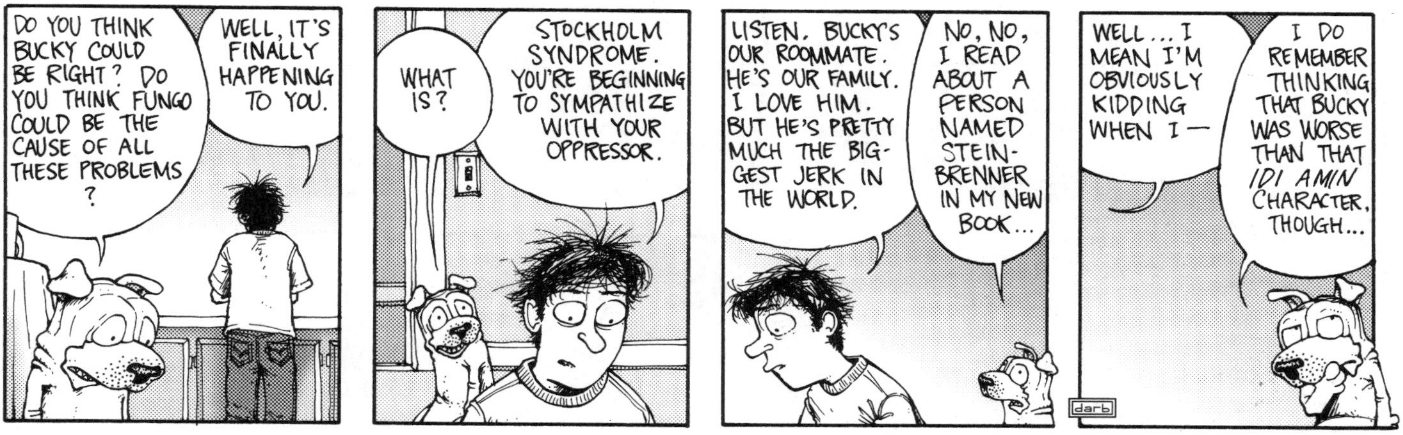
DO YOU THINK BUCKY COULD BE RIGHT? DO YOU THINK FUNGO COULD BE THE CAUSE OF ALL THESE PROBLEMS?
WELL, IT'S FINALLY HAPPENING TO YOU.
WHAT IS?
STOCKHOLM SYNDROME. YOU'RE BEGINNING TO SYMPATHIZE WITH YOUR OPPRESSOR.
LISTEN. BUCKY'S OUR ROOMMATE. HE'S OUR FAMILY. I LOVE HIM. BUT HE'S PRETTY MUCH THE BIGGEST JERK IN THE WORLD.
NO, NO, I READ ABOUT A PERSON NAMED STEINBRENNER IN MY NEW BOOK...
darb
WELL... I MEAN I'M OBVIOUSLY KIDDING WHEN I—
I DO REMEMBER THINKING THAT BUCKY WAS WORSE THAN THAT *IDI AMIN* CHARACTER, THOUGH...

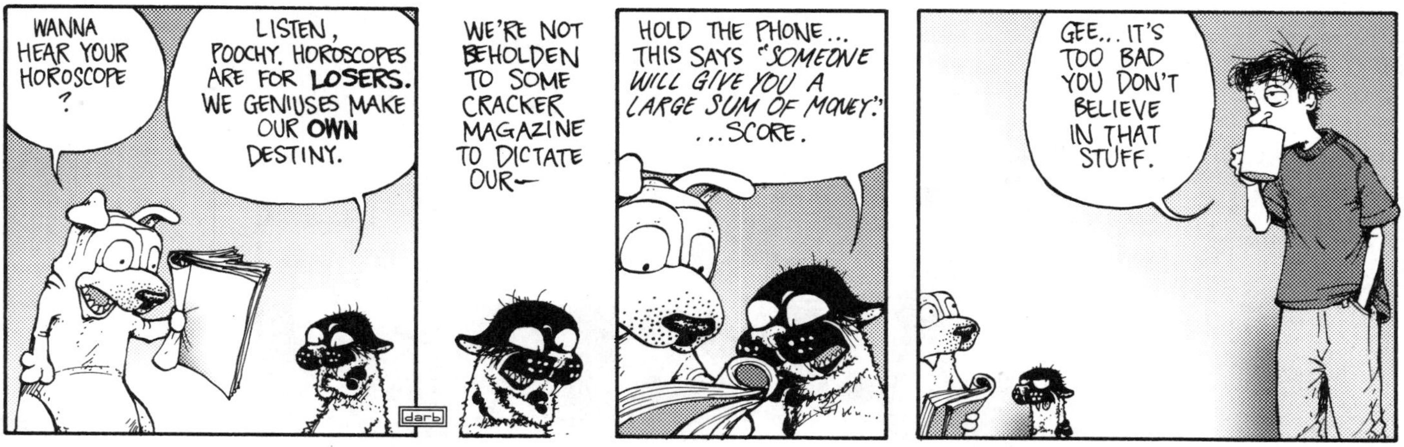
WANNA HEAR YOUR HOROSCOPE?
LISTEN, POOCHY. HOROSCOPES ARE FOR **LOSERS.** WE GENIUSES MAKE OUR **OWN** DESTINY.
darb
WE'RE NOT BEHOLDEN TO SOME CRACKER MAGAZINE TO DICTATE OUR—
HOLD THE PHONE... THIS SAYS "*SOMEONE WILL GIVE YOU A LARGE SUM OF MONEY*." ...SCORE.
GEE... IT'S TOO BAD YOU DON'T BELIEVE IN THAT STUFF.

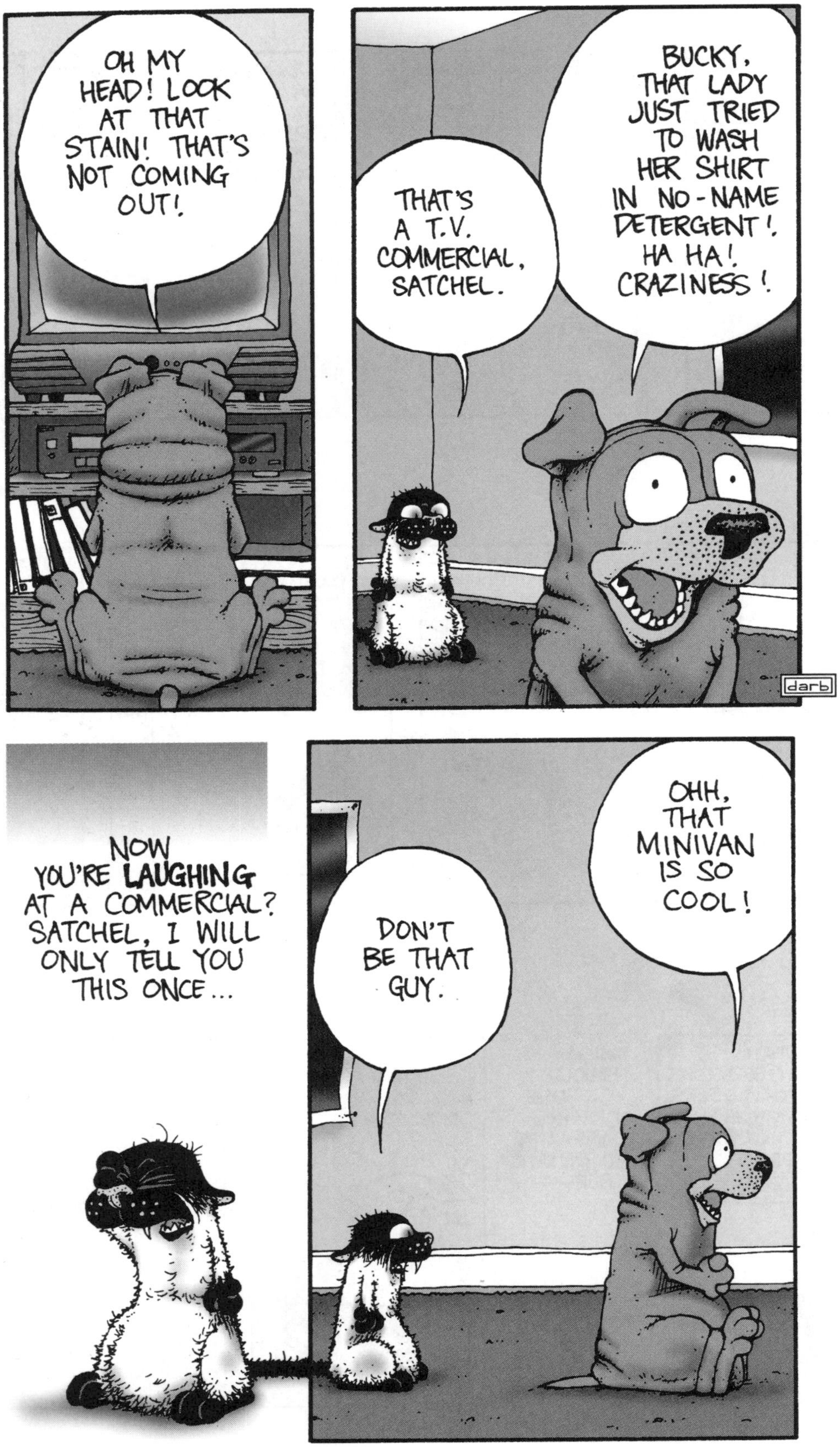
OH MY HEAD! LOOK AT THAT STAIN! THAT'S NOT COMING OUT!
BUCKY, THAT LADY JUST TRIED TO WASH HER SHIRT IN NO-NAME DETERGENT! HA HA! CRAZINESS!
THAT'S A T.V. COMMERCIAL, SATCHEL.
darb
NOW YOU'RE **LAUGHING** AT A COMMERCIAL? SATCHEL, I WILL ONLY TELL YOU THIS ONCE...
OHH, THAT MINIVAN IS SO COOL!
DON'T BE THAT GUY.

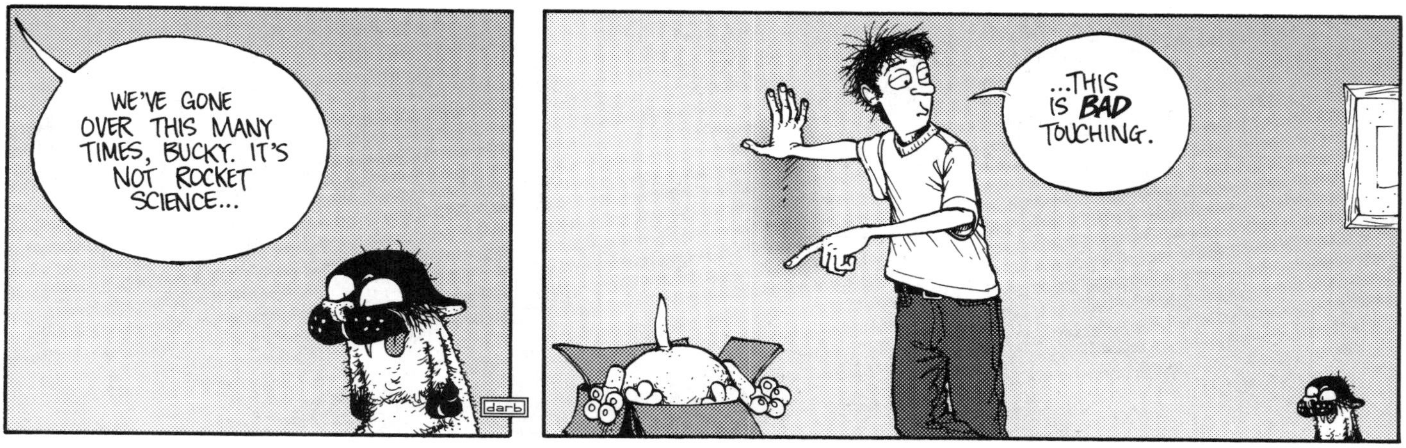
WE'VE GONE OVER THIS MANY TIMES, BUCKY. IT'S NOT ROCKET SCIENCE...
...THIS IS **BAD** TOUCHING.
darb

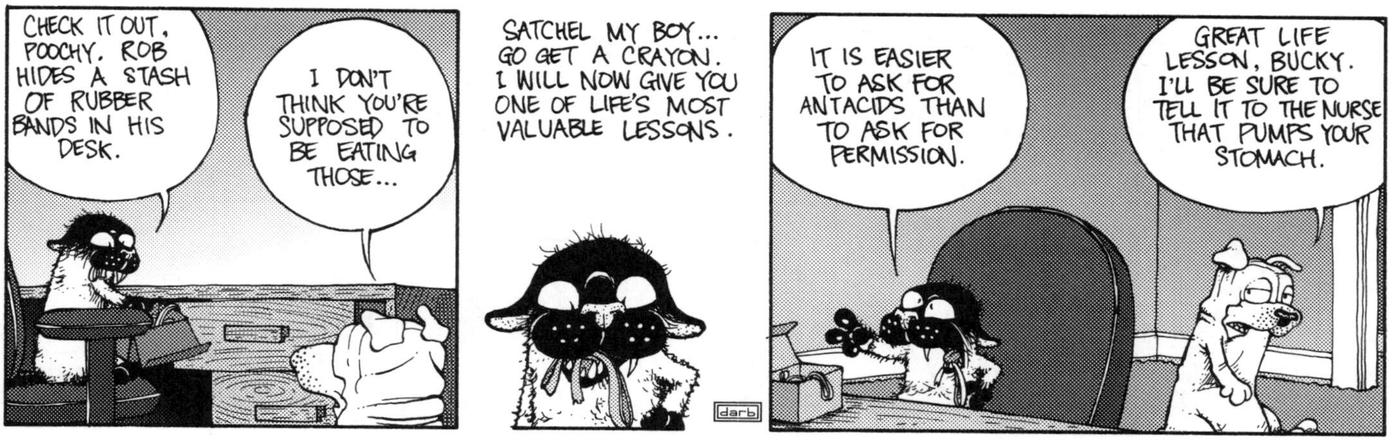
CHECK IT OUT, POOCHY. ROB HIDES A STASH OF RUBBER BANDS IN HIS DESK.
I DON'T THINK YOU'RE SUPPOSED TO BE EATING THOSE...
SATCHEL MY BOY... GO GET A CRAYON. I WILL NOW GIVE YOU ONE OF LIFE'S MOST VALUABLE LESSONS.
IT IS EASIER TO ASK FOR ANTACIDS THAN TO ASK FOR PERMISSION.
GREAT LIFE LESSON, BUCKY. I'LL BE SURE TO TELL IT TO THE NURSE THAT PUMPS YOUR STOMACH.
darb

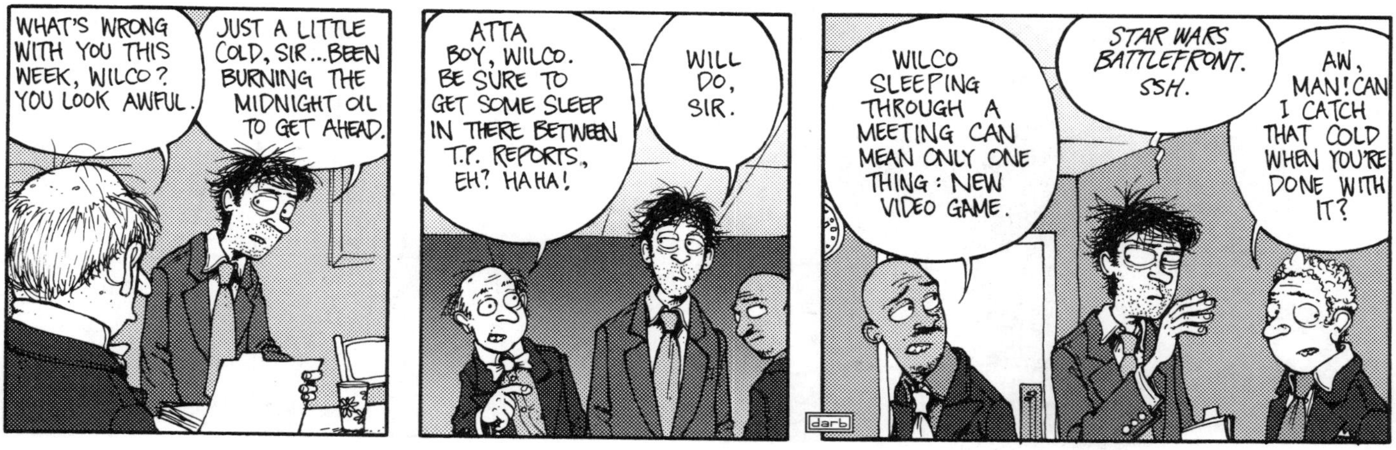
WHAT'S WRONG WITH YOU THIS WEEK, WILCO? YOU LOOK AWFUL.
JUST A LITTLE COLD, SIR...BEEN BURNING THE MIDNIGHT OIL TO GET AHEAD.
ATTA BOY, WILCO. BE SURE TO GET SOME SLEEP IN THERE BETWEEN T.P. REPORTS, EH? HAHA!
WILL DO, SIR.
WILCO SLEEPING THROUGH A MEETING CAN MEAN ONLY ONE THING: NEW VIDEO GAME.
STAR WARS BATTLEFRONT. SSH.
AW, MAN! CAN I CATCH THAT COLD WHEN YOU'RE DONE WITH IT?
darb

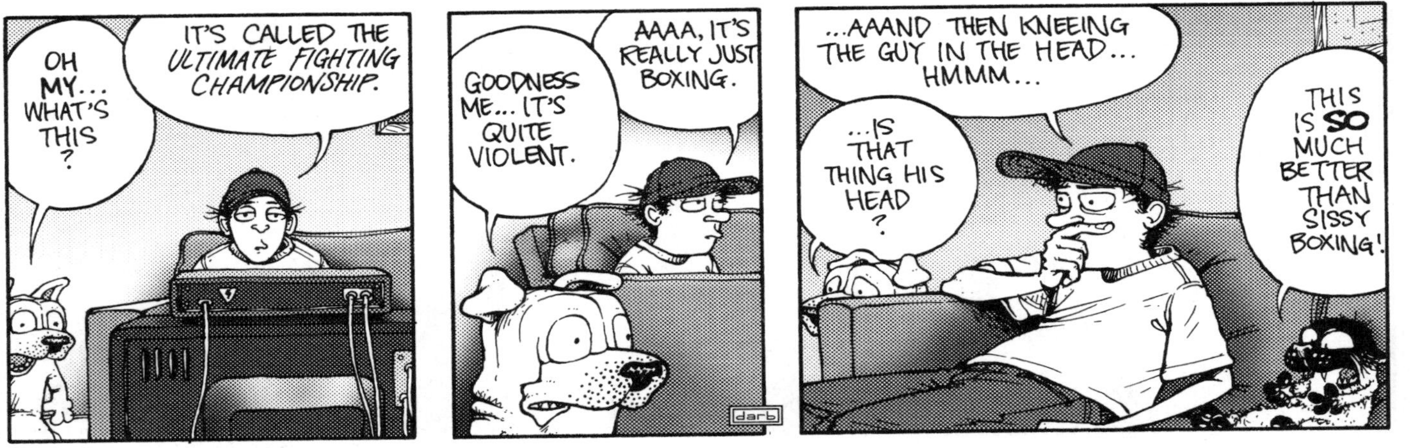
OH MY... WHAT'S THIS ?
IT'S CALLED THE ULTIMATE FIGHTING CHAMPIONSHIP.
GOODNESS ME... IT'S QUITE VIOLENT.
AAAA, IT'S REALLY JUST BOXING.
...AAAND THEN KNEEING THE GUY IN THE HEAD... HMMM...
...IS THAT THING HIS HEAD ?
THIS IS SO MUCH BETTER THAN SISSY BOXING!
darb

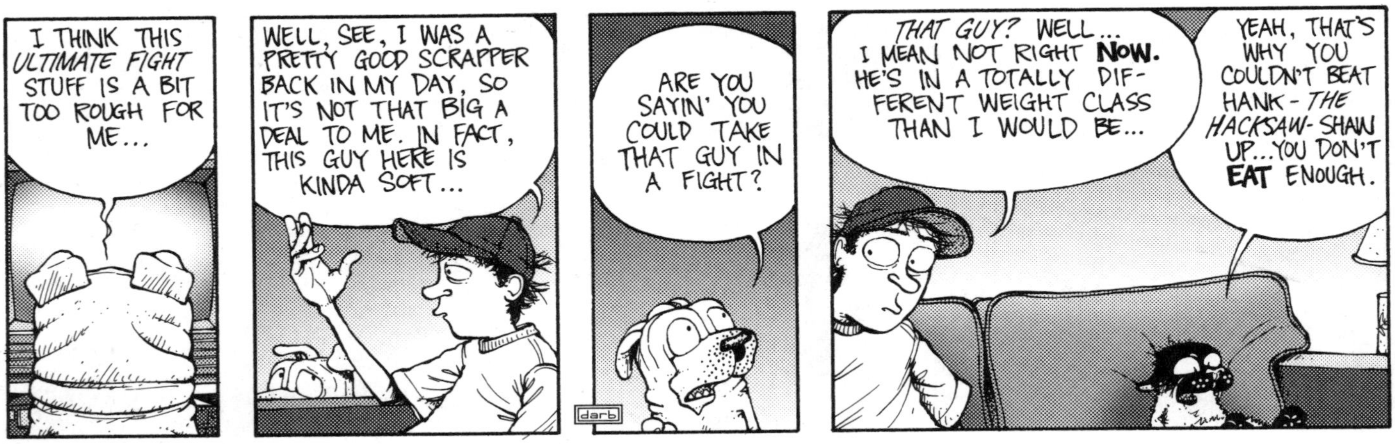
I THINK THIS ULTIMATE FIGHT STUFF IS A BIT TOO ROUGH FOR ME...
WELL, SEE, I WAS A PRETTY GOOD SCRAPPER BACK IN MY DAY, SO IT'S NOT THAT BIG A DEAL TO ME. IN FACT, THIS GUY HERE IS KINDA SOFT...
ARE YOU SAYIN' YOU COULD TAKE THAT GUY IN A FIGHT?
THAT GUY? WELL... I MEAN NOT RIGHT NOW. HE'S IN A TOTALLY DIFFERENT WEIGHT CLASS THAN I WOULD BE...
YEAH, THAT'S WHY YOU COULDN'T BEAT HANK-THE HACKSAW-SHAW UP...YOU DON'T EAT ENOUGH.
darb

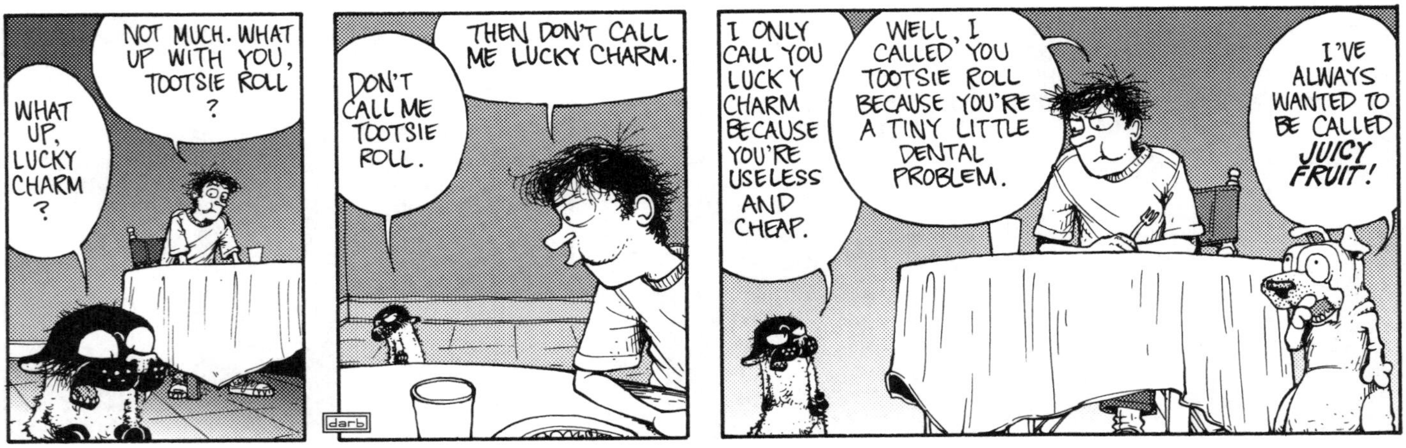
WHAT UP, LUCKY CHARM ?
NOT MUCH. WHAT UP WITH YOU, TOOTSIE ROLL ?
DON'T CALL ME TOOTSIE ROLL.
THEN DON'T CALL ME LUCKY CHARM.
I ONLY CALL YOU LUCKY CHARM BECAUSE YOU'RE USELESS AND CHEAP.
WELL, I CALLED YOU TOOTSIE ROLL BECAUSE YOU'RE A TINY LITTLE DENTAL PROBLEM.
I'VE ALWAYS WANTED TO BE CALLED JUICY FRUIT!
darb

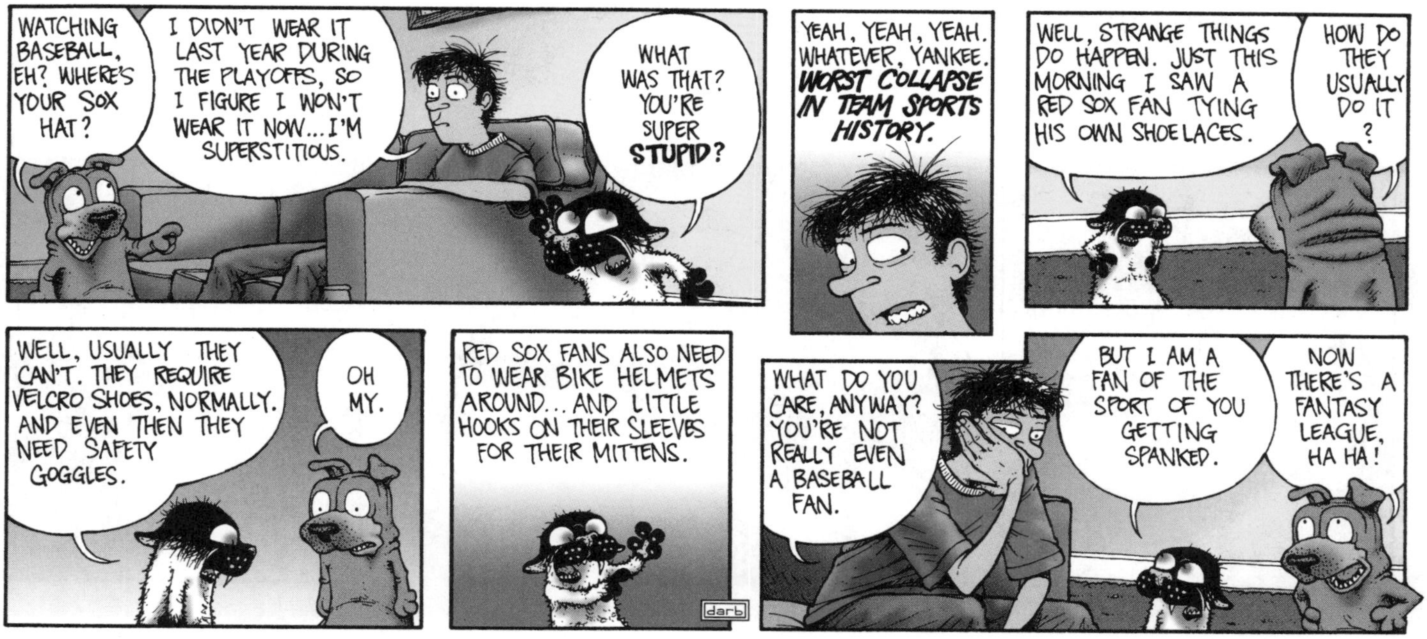
WATCHING BASEBALL, EH? WHERE'S YOUR SOX HAT?
I DIDN'T WEAR IT LAST YEAR DURING THE PLAYOFFS, SO I FIGURE I WON'T WEAR IT NOW... I'M SUPERSTITIOUS.
WHAT WAS THAT? YOU'RE SUPER **STUPID**?
YEAH, YEAH, YEAH. WHATEVER, YANKEE. ***WORST COLLAPSE IN TEAM SPORTS HISTORY.***
WELL, STRANGE THINGS DO HAPPEN. JUST THIS MORNING I SAW A RED SOX FAN TYING HIS OWN SHOELACES.
HOW DO THEY USUALLY DO IT ?
WELL, USUALLY THEY CAN'T. THEY REQUIRE VELCRO SHOES, NORMALLY. AND EVEN THEN THEY NEED SAFETY GOGGLES.
OH MY.
RED SOX FANS ALSO NEED TO WEAR BIKE HELMETS AROUND... AND LITTLE HOOKS ON THEIR SLEEVES FOR THEIR MITTENS.
darb
WHAT DO YOU CARE, ANYWAY? YOU'RE NOT REALLY EVEN A BASEBALL FAN.
BUT I AM A FAN OF THE SPORT OF YOU GETTING SPANKED.
NOW THERE'S A FANTASY LEAGUE, HA HA!

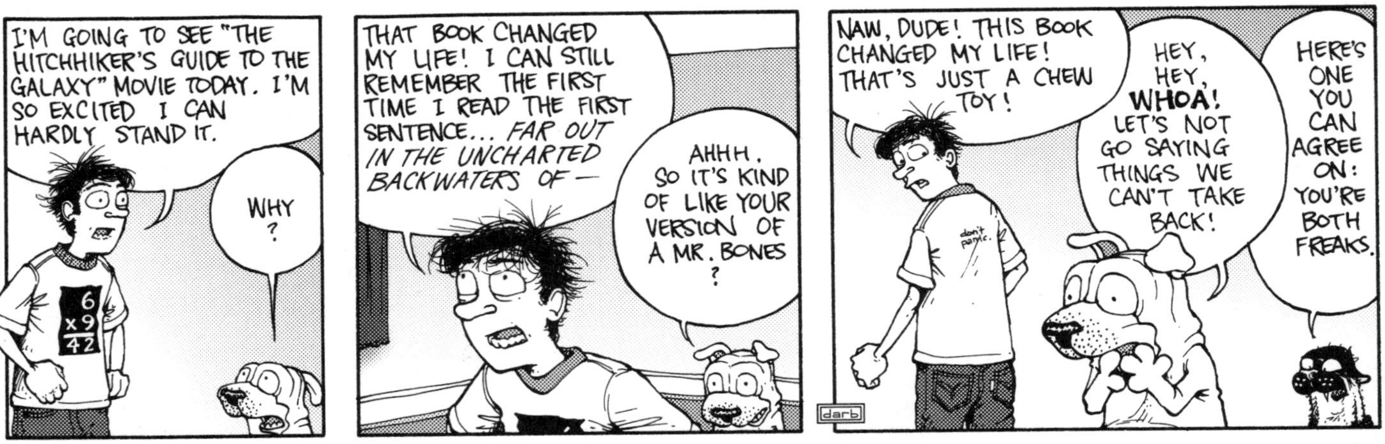
I'M GOING TO SEE "THE HITCHHIKER'S GUIDE TO THE GALAXY" MOVIE TODAY. I'M SO EXCITED I CAN HARDLY STAND IT.
WHY?
6 x9 42
THAT BOOK CHANGED MY LIFE! I CAN STILL REMEMBER THE FIRST TIME I READ THE FIRST SENTENCE... *FAR OUT IN THE UNCHARTED BACKWATERS OF—*
AHHH. SO IT'S KIND OF LIKE YOUR VERSION OF A MR. BONES?
NAW, DUDE! THIS BOOK CHANGED MY LIFE! THAT'S JUST A CHEW TOY!
HEY, HEY, **WHOA!** LET'S NOT GO SAYING THINGS WE CAN'T TAKE BACK!
HERE'S ONE YOU CAN AGREE ON: YOU'RE BOTH FREAKS.
darb

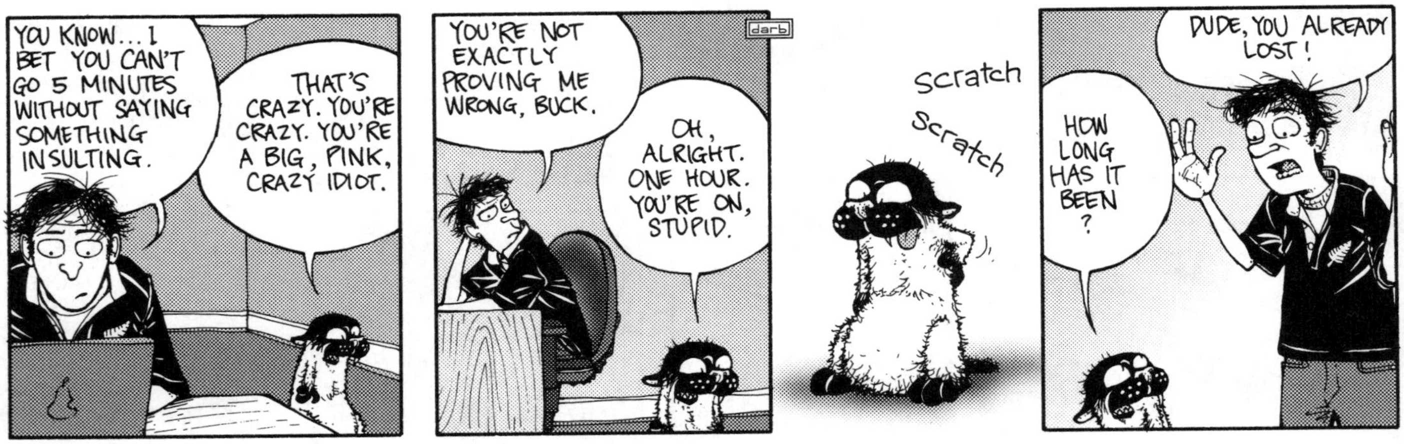
YOU KNOW... I BET YOU CAN'T GO 5 MINUTES WITHOUT SAYING SOMETHING INSULTING.
THAT'S CRAZY. YOU'RE CRAZY. YOU'RE A BIG, PINK, CRAZY IDIOT.
YOU'RE NOT EXACTLY PROVING ME WRONG, BUCK.
OH, ALRIGHT. ONE HOUR. YOU'RE ON, STUPID.
darb
Scratch
Scratch
HOW LONG HAS IT BEEN?
DUDE, YOU ALREADY LOST!

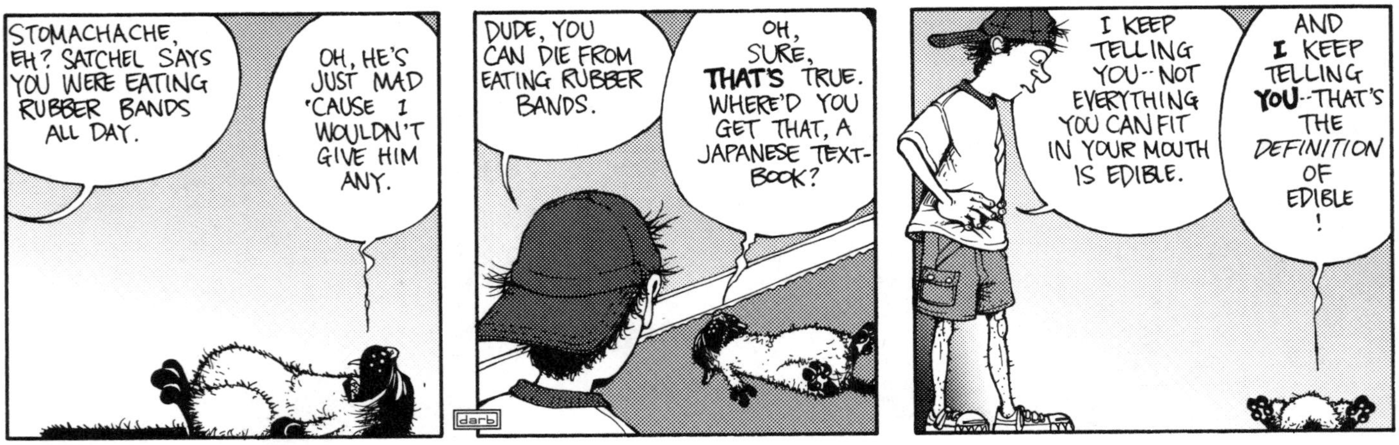
STOMACHACHE, EH? SATCHEL SAYS YOU WERE EATING RUBBER BANDS ALL DAY.
OH, HE'S JUST MAD 'CAUSE I WOULDN'T GIVE HIM ANY.
DUDE, YOU CAN DIE FROM EATING RUBBER BANDS.
OH, SURE, **THAT'S** TRUE. WHERE'D YOU GET THAT, A JAPANESE TEXT-BOOK?
darb
I KEEP TELLING YOU--NOT EVERYTHING YOU CAN FIT IN YOUR MOUTH IS EDIBLE.
AND **I** KEEP TELLING **YOU**--THAT'S THE *DEFINITION* OF EDIBLE!

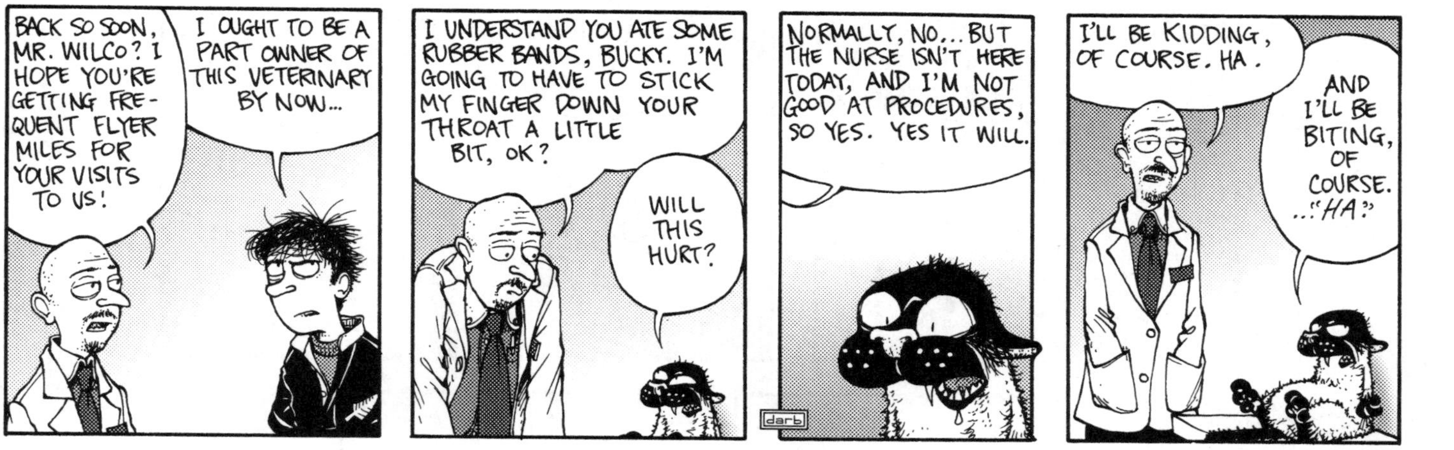
BACK SO SOON, MR. WILCO? I HOPE YOU'RE GETTING FRE-QUENT FLYER MILES FOR YOUR VISITS TO US!
I OUGHT TO BE A PART OWNER OF THIS VETERINARY BY NOW...
I UNDERSTAND YOU ATE SOME RUBBER BANDS, BUCKY. I'M GOING TO HAVE TO STICK MY FINGER DOWN YOUR THROAT A LITTLE BIT, OK?
WILL THIS HURT?
NORMALLY, NO... BUT THE NURSE ISN'T HERE TODAY, AND I'M NOT GOOD AT PROCEDURES, SO YES. YES IT WILL.
I'LL BE KIDDING, OF COURSE. HA.
AND I'LL BE BITING, OF COURSE. ..."HA."
darb

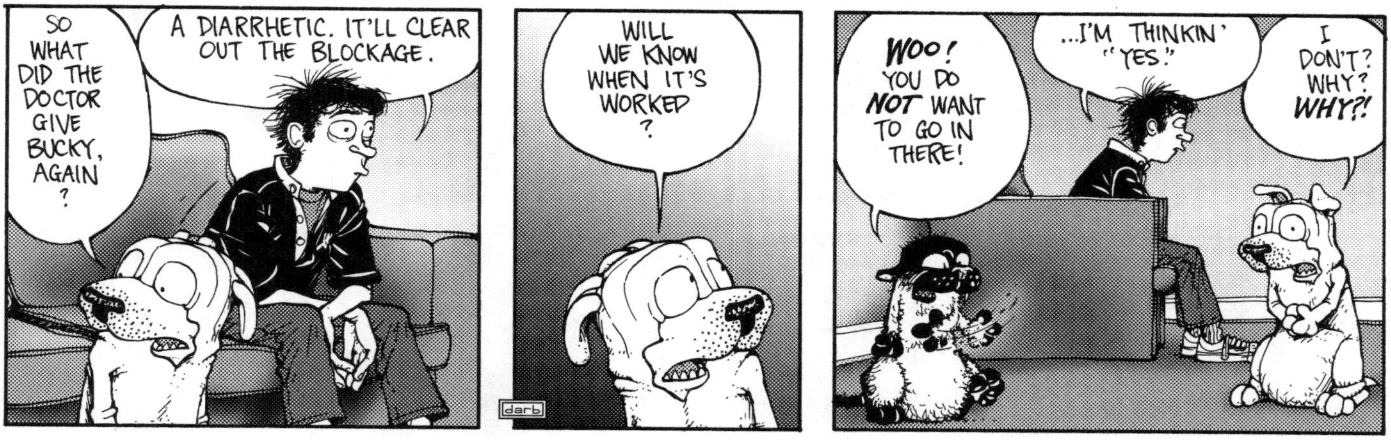
SO WHAT DID THE DOCTOR GIVE BUCKY, AGAIN?
A DIARRHETIC. IT'LL CLEAR OUT THE BLOCKAGE.
WILL WE KNOW WHEN IT'S WORKED?
WOO! YOU DO *NOT* WANT TO GO IN THERE!
...I'M THINKIN' "YES."
I DON'T? WHY? *WHY?!*
darb

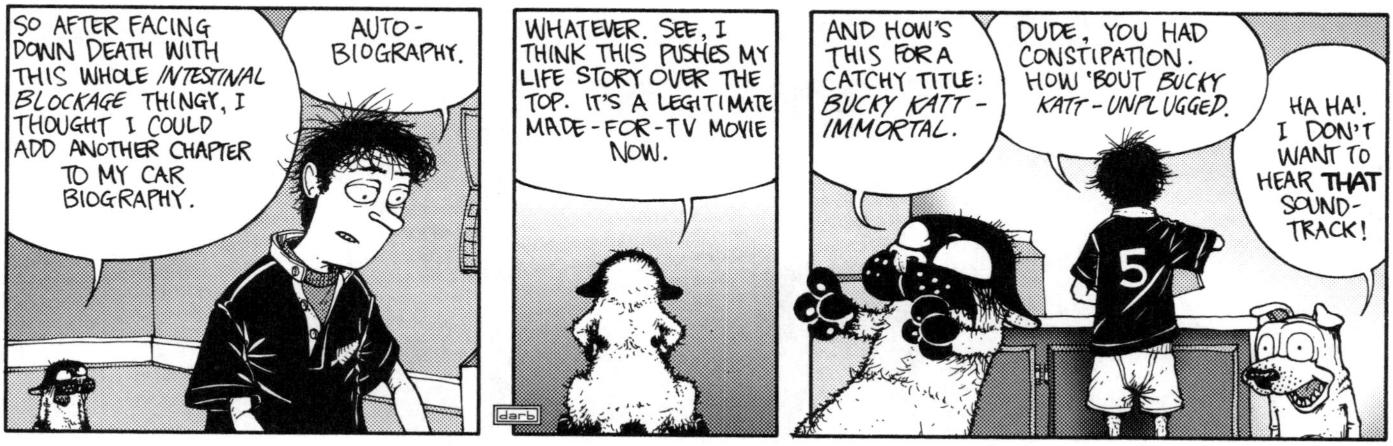
SO AFTER FACING DOWN DEATH WITH THIS WHOLE *INTESTINAL BLOCKAGE* THINGY, I THOUGHT I COULD ADD ANOTHER CHAPTER TO MY CAR BIOGRAPHY.
AUTO-BIOGRAPHY.
WHATEVER. SEE, I THINK THIS PUSHES MY LIFE STORY OVER THE TOP. IT'S A LEGITIMATE MADE-FOR-TV MOVIE NOW.
AND HOW'S THIS FOR A CATCHY TITLE: *BUCKY KATT - IMMORTAL.*
DUDE, YOU HAD CONSTIPATION. HOW 'BOUT *BUCKY KATT - UNPLUGGED.*
HA HA! I DON'T WANT TO HEAR **THAT** SOUND-TRACK!
darb

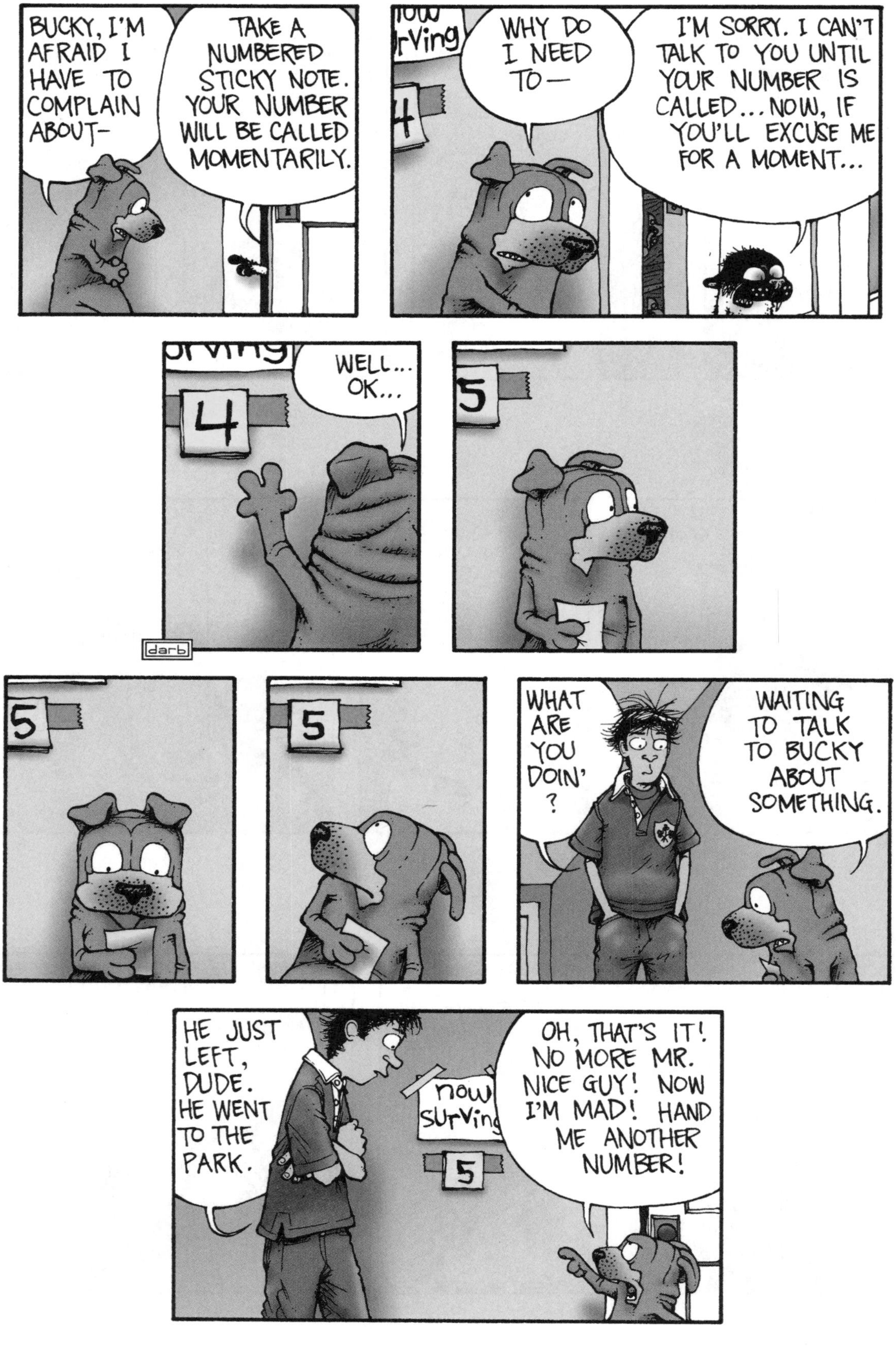
BUCKY, I'M AFRAID I HAVE TO COMPLAIN ABOUT-
TAKE A NUMBERED STICKY NOTE. YOUR NUMBER WILL BE CALLED MOMENTARILY.
WHY DO I NEED TO—
I'M SORRY. I CAN'T TALK TO YOU UNTIL YOUR NUMBER IS CALLED... NOW, IF YOU'LL EXCUSE ME FOR A MOMENT...
4
WELL... OK...
darb
5
5
5
WHAT ARE YOU DOIN' ?
WAITING TO TALK TO BUCKY ABOUT SOMETHING.
HE JUST LEFT, DUDE. HE WENT TO THE PARK.
now surving
5
OH, THAT'S IT! NO MORE MR. NICE GUY! NOW I'M MAD! HAND ME ANOTHER NUMBER!

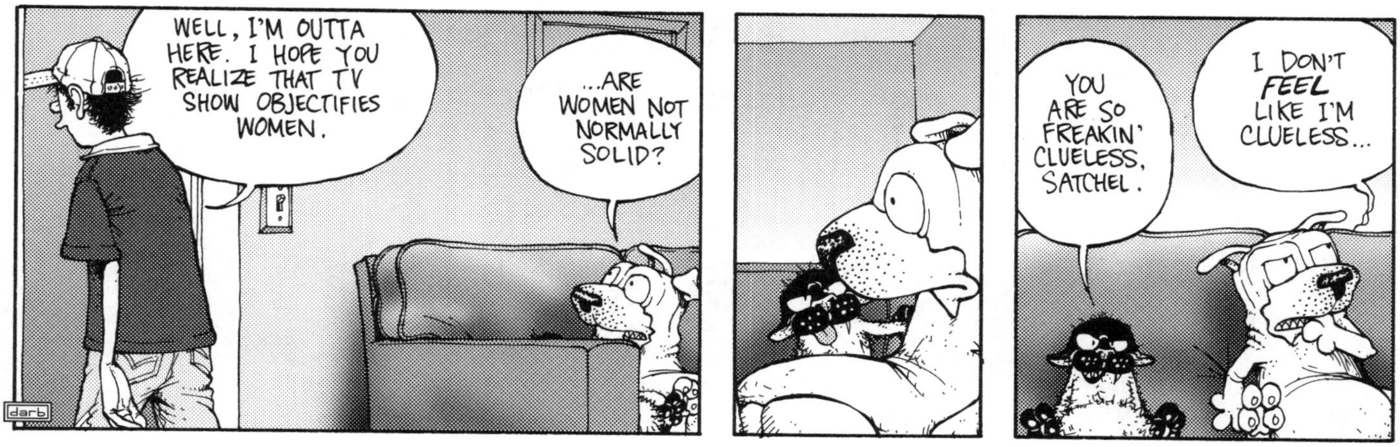
WELL, I'M OUTTA HERE. I HOPE YOU REALIZE THAT TV SHOW OBJECTIFIES WOMEN.
...ARE WOMEN NOT NORMALLY SOLID?
YOU ARE SO FREAKIN' CLUELESS, SATCHEL.
I DON'T FEEL LIKE I'M CLUELESS...
darb

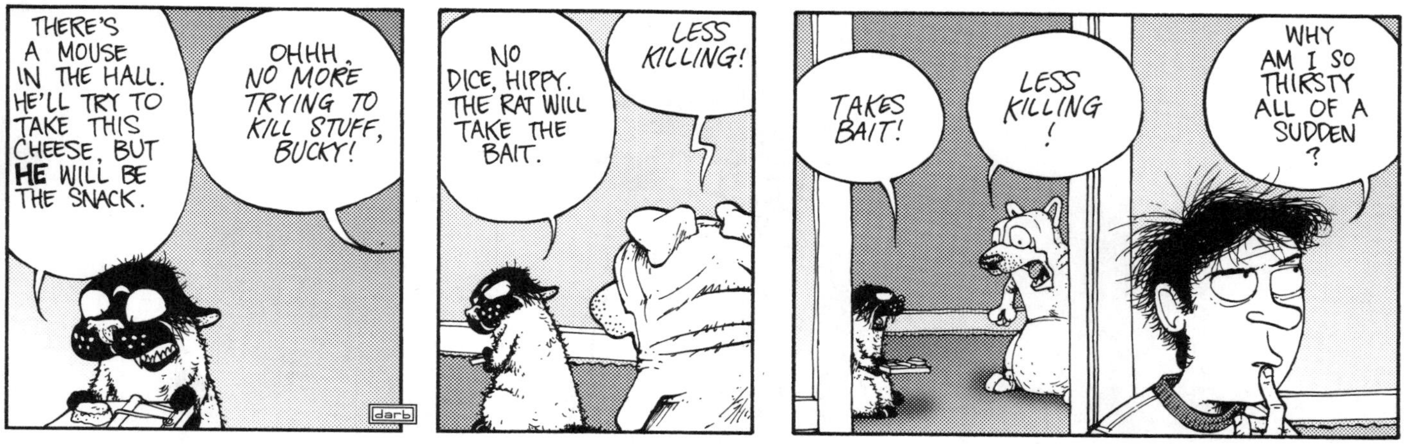
THERE'S A MOUSE IN THE HALL. HE'LL TRY TO TAKE THIS CHEESE, BUT HE WILL BE THE SNACK.
OHHH, NO MORE TRYING TO KILL STUFF, BUCKY!
darb
NO DICE, HIPPY. THE RAT WILL TAKE THE BAIT.
LESS KILLING!
TAKES BAIT!
LESS KILLING!
WHY AM I SO THIRSTY ALL OF A SUDDEN?

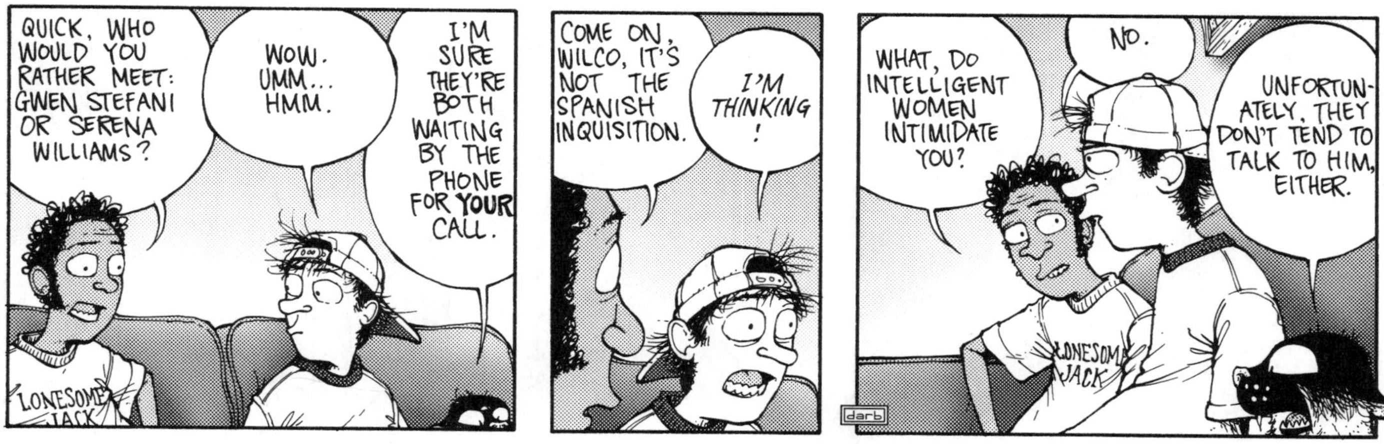
QUICK, WHO WOULD YOU RATHER MEET: GWEN STEFANI OR SERENA WILLIAMS?
WOW. UMM... HMM.
I'M SURE THEY'RE BOTH WAITING BY THE PHONE FOR YOUR CALL.
LONESOME JACK
COME ON, WILCO, IT'S NOT THE SPANISH INQUISITION.
I'M THINKING!
WHAT, DO INTELLIGENT WOMEN INTIMIDATE YOU?
NO.
UNFORTUNATELY, THEY DON'T TEND TO TALK TO HIM, EITHER.
LONESOME JACK
darb

SATCH, DO YOUR KEANU REEVES IMPRESSION FOR JOE.
DO YOU WANT ANGRY KEANU OR CONFUSED KEANU?
LET'S GO WITH CONFUSED KEANU.
LONESOME JACK
darb
UUUH?
NOW DO ANGRY KEANU.
UHHHH...
HE HE.
LONESOME JACK

WOW... IT SAYS HERE THERE ARE 140 SPECIES OF BIRDS IN HAWAII. YOU'D LIKE THAT, BUCK!
SATCHEL, I'M GOING TO START CALLING YOU SEA GULL... AS IN "OH, LOOK! SEE GULL-IBLE COMING DOWN THE STREET!"
BIRDS of the World
darb
I.... DON'T FOLLOW.
BIRDS, FLOWERS, SUN... HAWAII DOES NOT EXIST. IT'S A MYTH... LIKE TOUGH LIBERALS, OR THE CANADIAN ARMY.
HAWAII IS THE 50th STATE, YOU IDIOT, IT TOTALLY EXISTS.
IT DOES? BLOODY #$☆£! WHY DON'T WE LIVE THERE, THEN?
HA HA! 50th WHAT?!

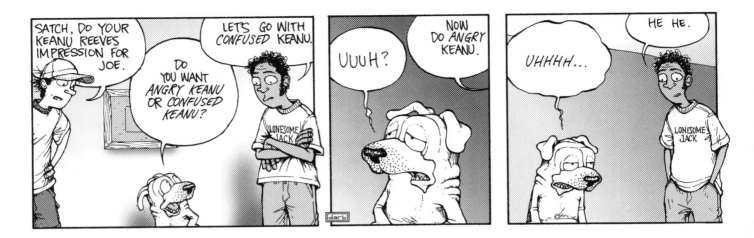

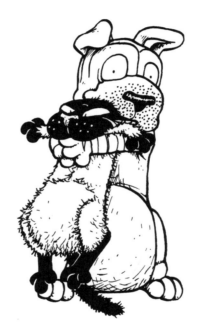

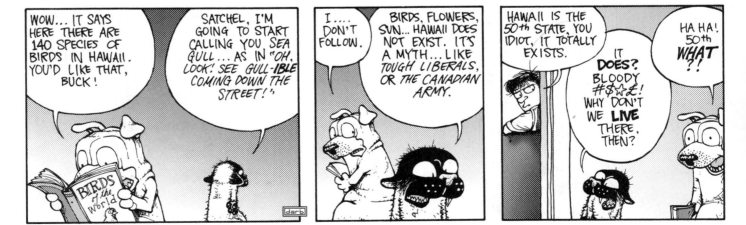

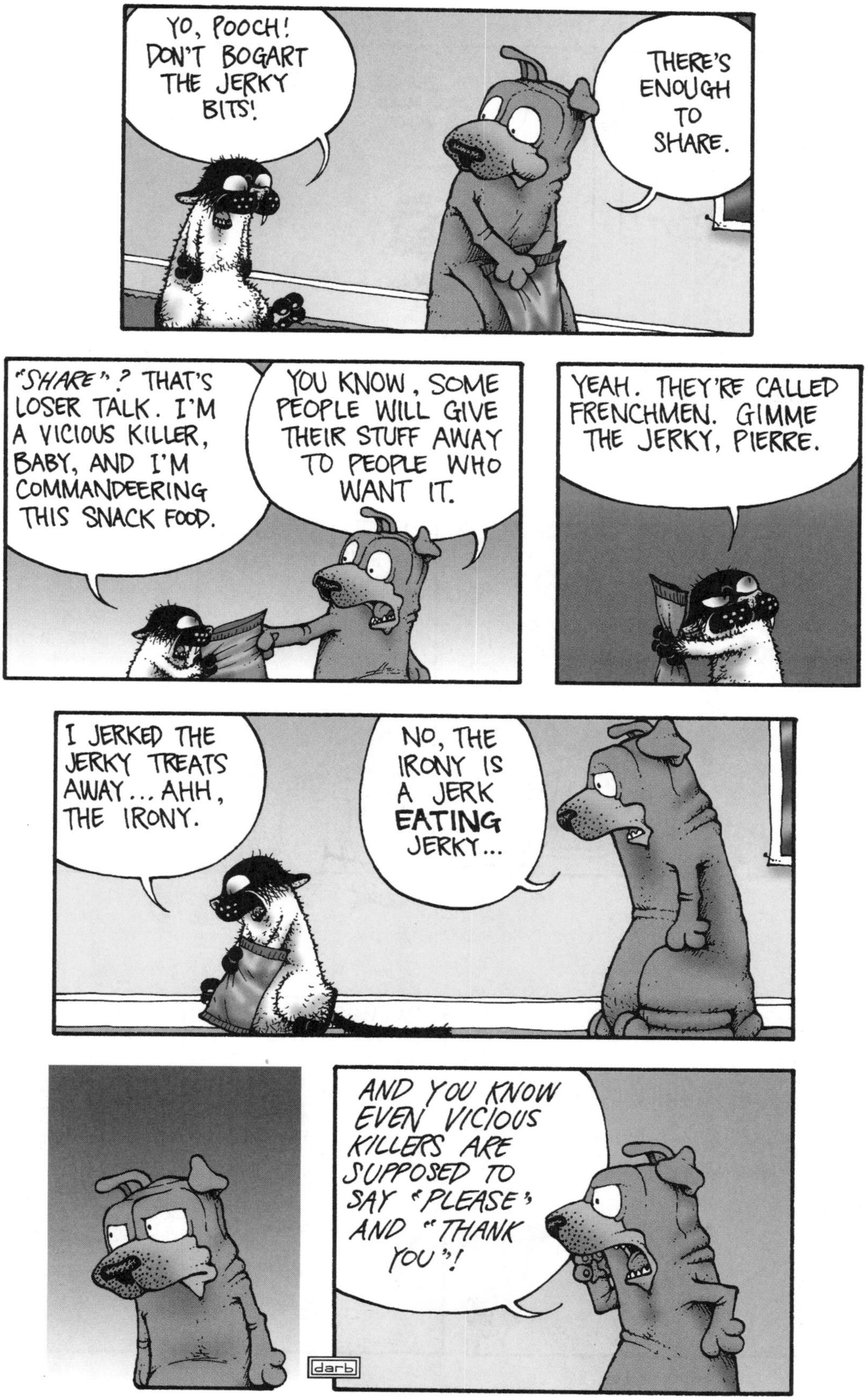
YO, POOCH! DON'T BOGART THE JERKY BITS!
THERE'S ENOUGH TO SHARE.
"SHARE"? THAT'S LOSER TALK. I'M A VICIOUS KILLER, BABY, AND I'M COMMANDEERING THIS SNACK FOOD.
YOU KNOW, SOME PEOPLE WILL GIVE THEIR STUFF AWAY TO PEOPLE WHO WANT IT.
YEAH. THEY'RE CALLED FRENCHMEN. GIMME THE JERKY, PIERRE.
I JERKED THE JERKY TREATS AWAY... AHH, THE IRONY.
NO, THE IRONY IS A JERK EATING JERKY...
AND YOU KNOW EVEN VICIOUS KILLERS ARE SUPPOSED TO SAY "PLEASE" AND "THANK YOU"!
darb

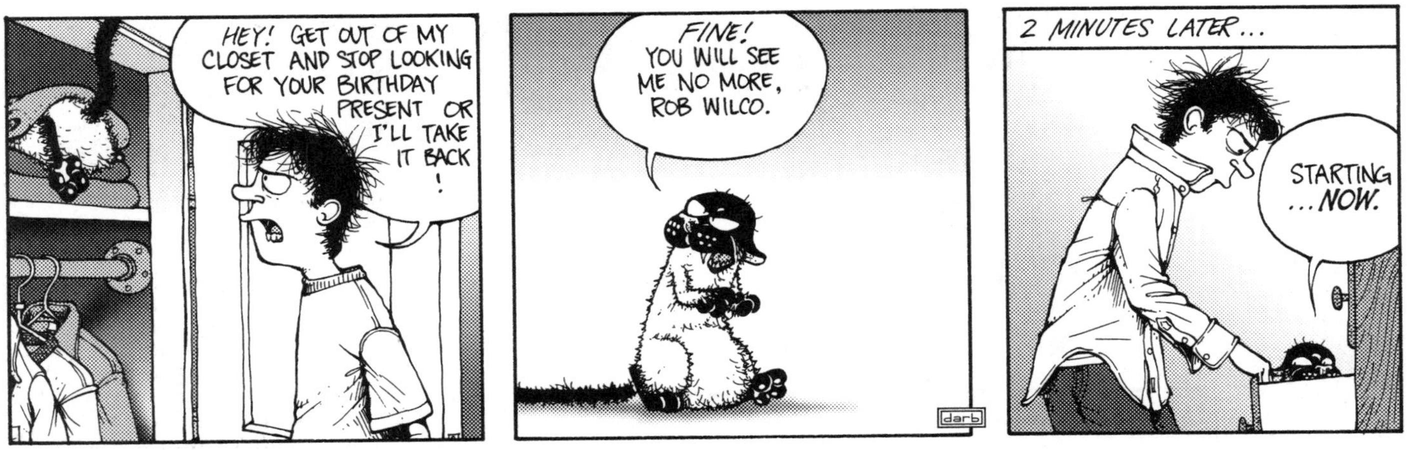
HEY! GET OUT OF MY CLOSET AND STOP LOOKING FOR YOUR BIRTHDAY PRESENT OR I'LL TAKE IT BACK!
FINE! YOU WILL SEE ME NO MORE, ROB WILCO.
darb
2 MINUTES LATER...
STARTING ...NOW.

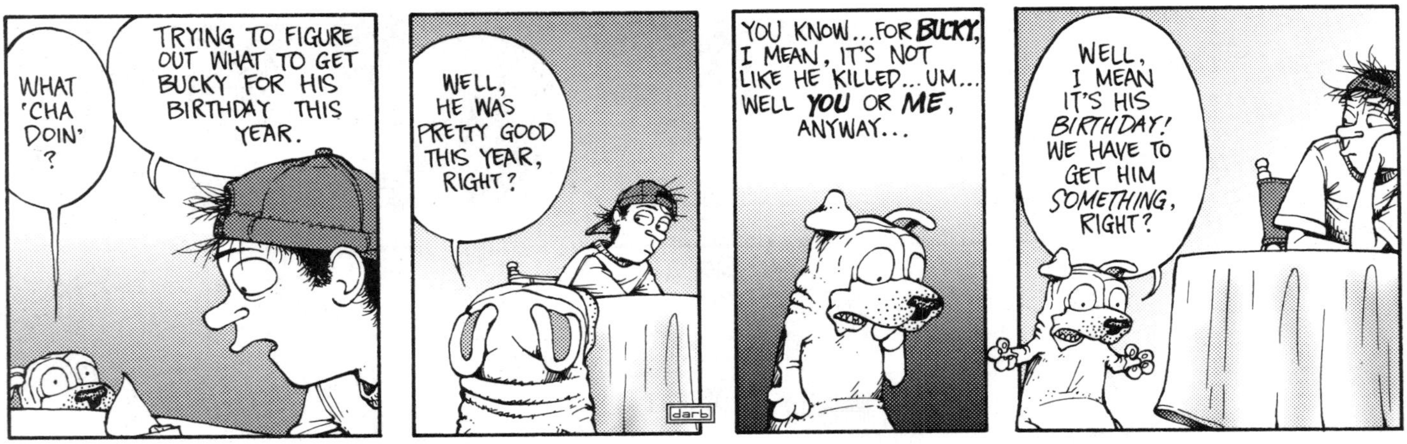
WHAT 'CHA DOIN'?
TRYING TO FIGURE OUT WHAT TO GET BUCKY FOR HIS BIRTHDAY THIS YEAR.
WELL, HE WAS PRETTY GOOD THIS YEAR, RIGHT?
darb
YOU KNOW...FOR BUCKY, I MEAN, IT'S NOT LIKE HE KILLED...UM... WELL YOU OR ME, ANYWAY...
WELL, I MEAN IT'S HIS BIRTHDAY! WE HAVE TO GET HIM SOMETHING, RIGHT?

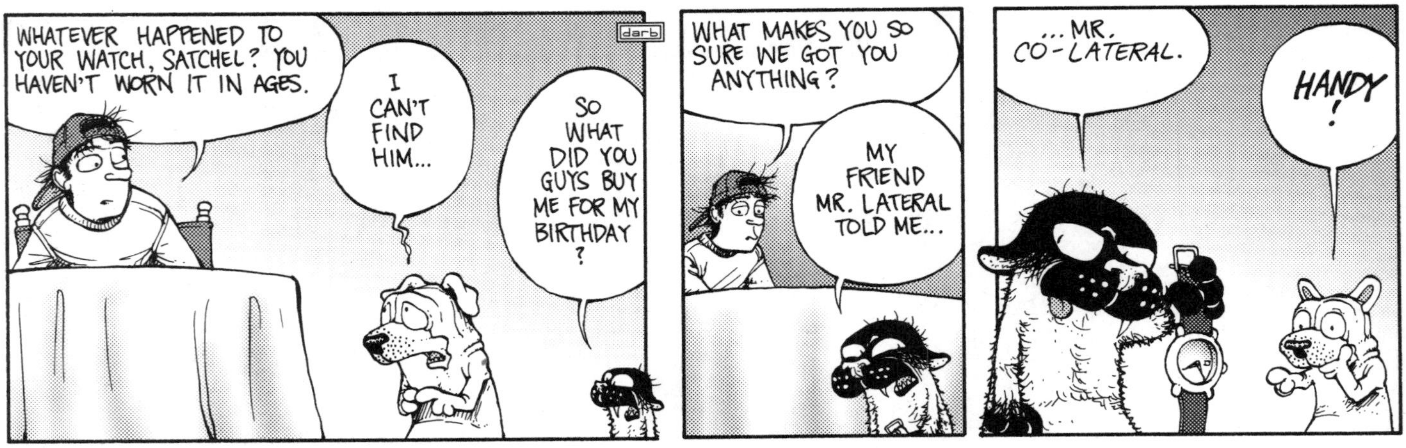
WHATEVER HAPPENED TO YOUR WATCH, SATCHEL? YOU HAVEN'T WORN IT IN AGES.
I CAN'T FIND HIM...
SO WHAT DID YOU GUYS BUY ME FOR MY BIRTHDAY?
darb
WHAT MAKES YOU SO SURE WE GOT YOU ANYTHING?
MY FRIEND MR. LATERAL TOLD ME...
...MR. CO-LATERAL.
HANDY!

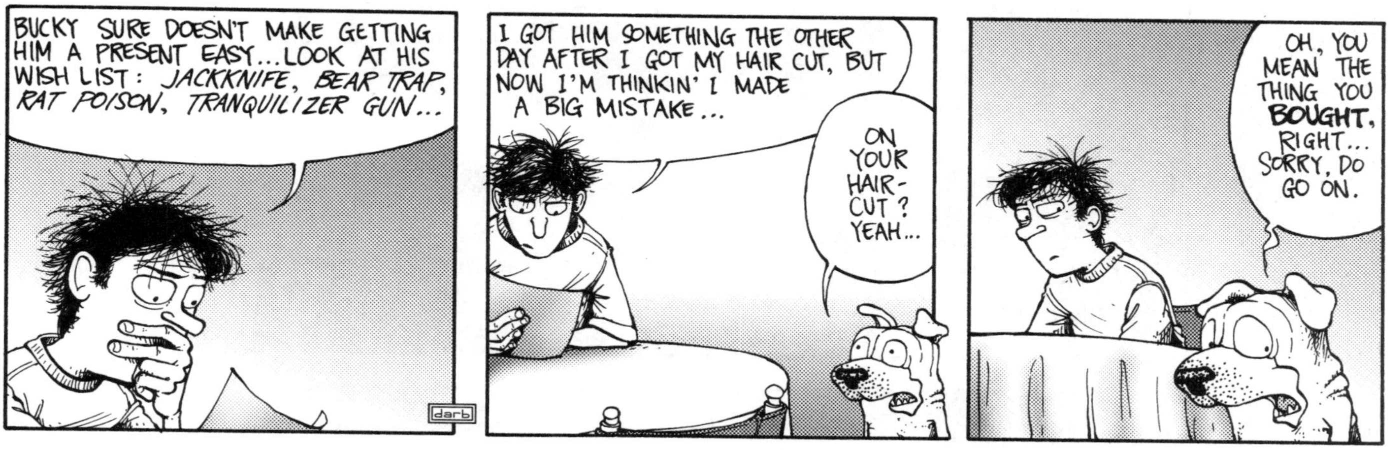
BUCKY SURE DOESN'T MAKE GETTING HIM A PRESENT EASY... LOOK AT HIS WISH LIST: *JACKKNIFE, BEAR TRAP, RAT POISON, TRANQUILIZER GUN...*
I GOT HIM SOMETHING THE OTHER DAY AFTER I GOT MY HAIR CUT, BUT NOW I'M THINKIN' I MADE A BIG MISTAKE...
ON YOUR HAIR-CUT? YEAH...
OH, YOU MEAN THE THING YOU **BOUGHT**, RIGHT... SORRY, DO GO ON.
darb

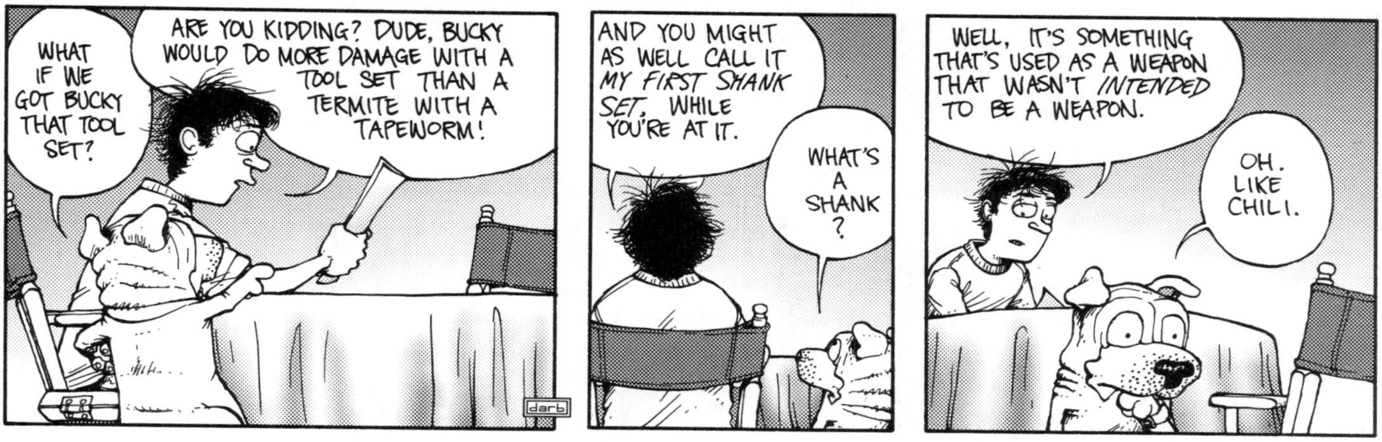
WHAT IF WE GOT BUCKY THAT TOOL SET?
ARE YOU KIDDING? DUDE, BUCKY WOULD DO MORE DAMAGE WITH A TOOL SET THAN A TERMITE WITH A TAPEWORM!
AND YOU MIGHT AS WELL CALL IT *MY FIRST SHANK SET*, WHILE YOU'RE AT IT.
WHAT'S A SHANK?
WELL, IT'S SOMETHING THAT'S USED AS A WEAPON THAT WASN'T *INTENDED* TO BE A WEAPON.
OH. LIKE CHILI.
darb

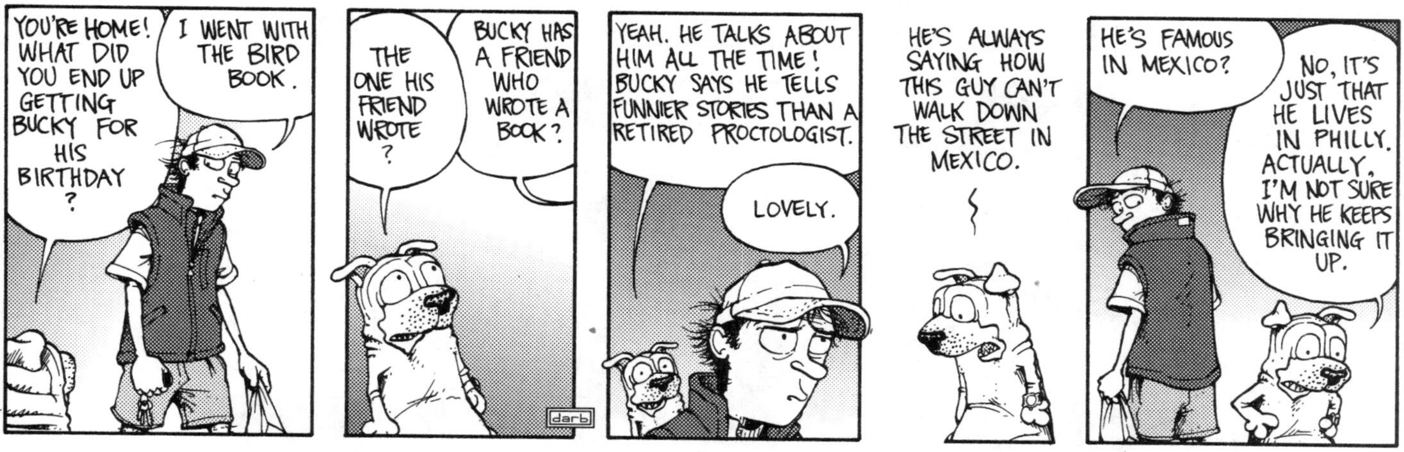
YOU'RE HOME! WHAT DID YOU END UP GETTING BUCKY FOR HIS BIRTHDAY?
I WENT WITH THE BIRD BOOK.
THE ONE HIS FRIEND WROTE?
BUCKY HAS A FRIEND WHO WROTE A BOOK?
YEAH. HE TALKS ABOUT HIM ALL THE TIME! BUCKY SAYS HE TELLS FUNNIER STORIES THAN A RETIRED PROCTOLOGIST.
LOVELY.
HE'S ALWAYS SAYING HOW THIS GUY CAN'T WALK DOWN THE STREET IN MEXICO.
HE'S FAMOUS IN MEXICO?
NO, IT'S JUST THAT HE LIVES IN PHILLY. ACTUALLY, I'M NOT SURE WHY HE KEEPS BRINGING IT UP.
darb

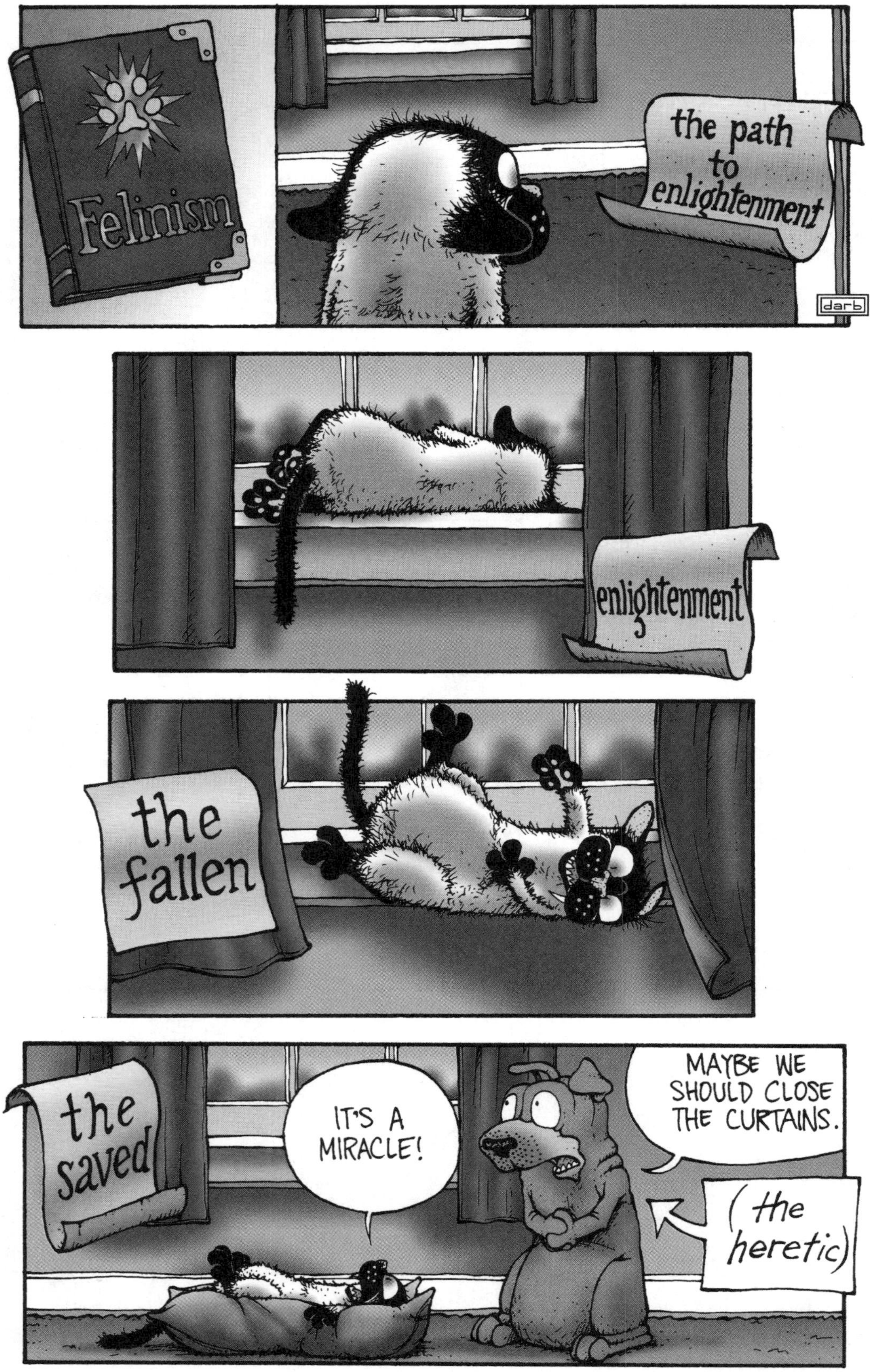
Felinism
the path to enlightenment
darb
enlightenment
the fallen
the saved
IT'S A MIRACLE!
MAYBE WE SHOULD CLOSE THE CURTAINS.
(the heretic)

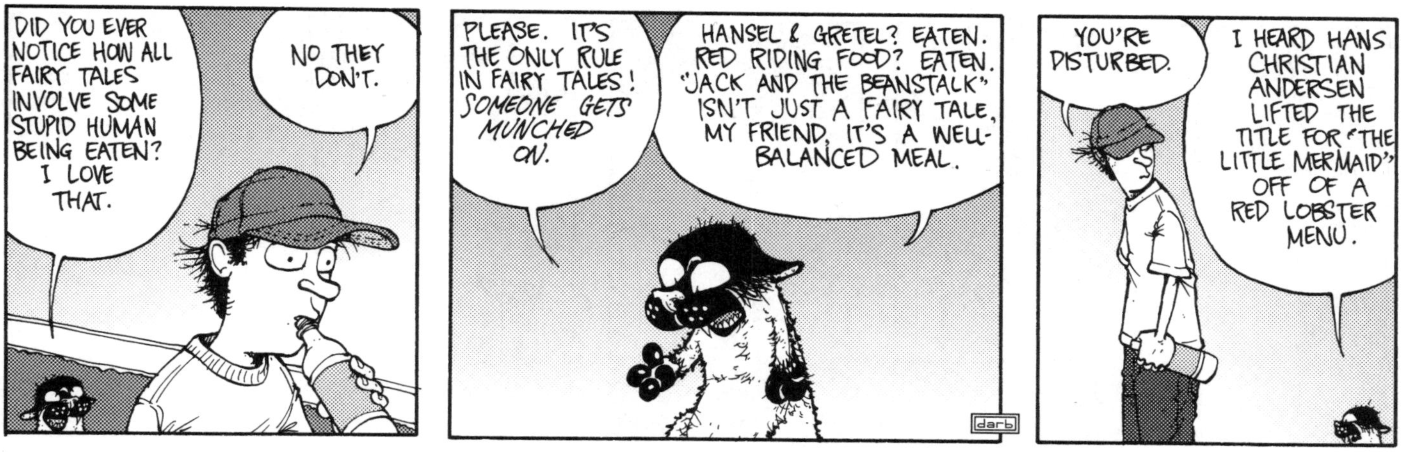
DID YOU EVER NOTICE HOW ALL FAIRY TALES INVOLVE SOME STUPID HUMAN BEING EATEN? I LOVE THAT.
NO THEY DON'T.
PLEASE. IT'S THE ONLY RULE IN FAIRY TALES! *SOMEONE GETS MUNCHED ON.*
HANSEL & GRETEL? EATEN. RED RIDING FOOD? EATEN. "JACK AND THE BEANSTALK" ISN'T JUST A FAIRY TALE, MY FRIEND, IT'S A WELL-BALANCED MEAL.
YOU'RE DISTURBED.
I HEARD HANS CHRISTIAN ANDERSEN LIFTED THE TITLE FOR "THE LITTLE MERMAID" OFF OF A RED LOBSTER MENU.
darb

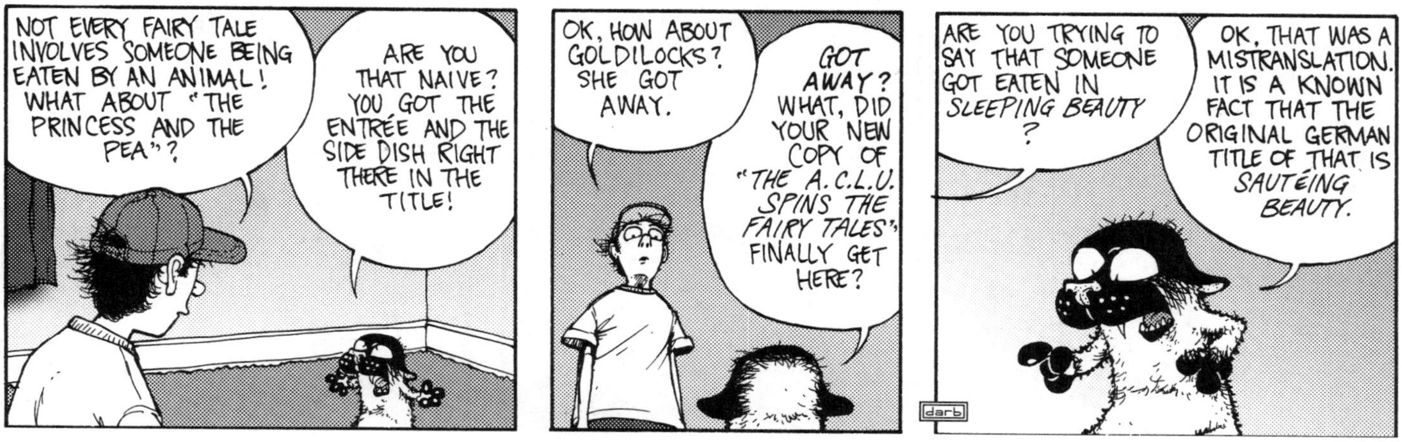
NOT EVERY FAIRY TALE INVOLVES SOMEONE BEING EATEN BY AN ANIMAL! WHAT ABOUT "THE PRINCESS AND THE PEA"?
ARE YOU THAT NAIVE? YOU GOT THE ENTRÉE AND THE SIDE DISH RIGHT THERE IN THE TITLE!
OK, HOW ABOUT GOLDILOCKS? SHE GOT AWAY.
GOT AWAY? WHAT, DID YOUR NEW COPY OF "*THE A.C.L.U. SPINS THE FAIRY TALES*" FINALLY GET HERE?
ARE YOU TRYING TO SAY THAT SOMEONE GOT EATEN IN *SLEEPING BEAUTY*?
OK, THAT WAS A MISTRANSLATION. IT IS A KNOWN FACT THAT THE ORIGINAL GERMAN TITLE OF THAT IS *SAUTÉING BEAUTY.*
darb

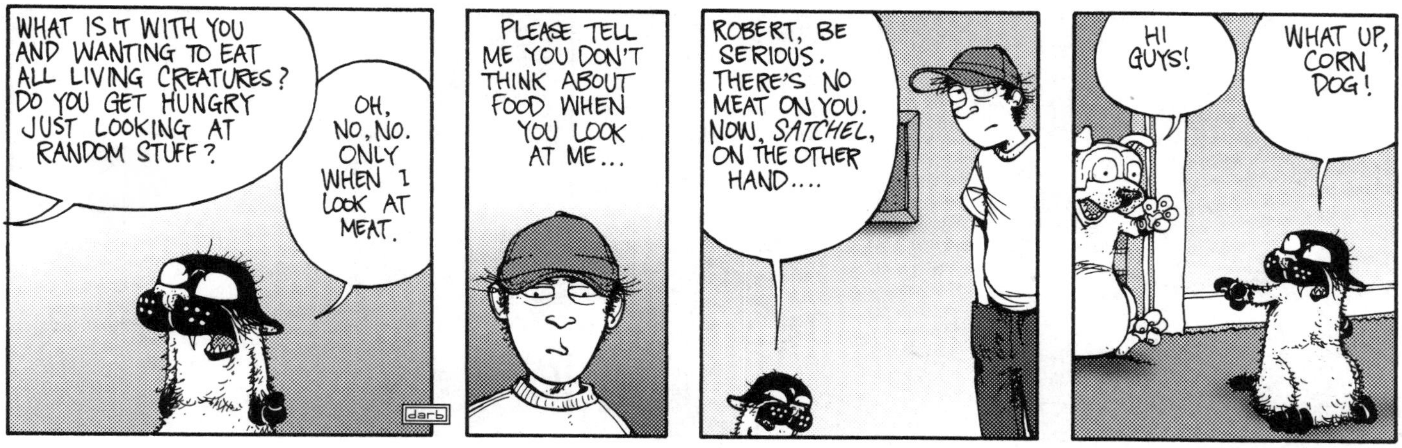
WHAT IS IT WITH YOU AND WANTING TO EAT ALL LIVING CREATURES? DO YOU GET HUNGRY JUST LOOKING AT RANDOM STUFF?
OH, NO, NO. ONLY WHEN I LOOK AT MEAT.
darb
PLEASE TELL ME YOU DON'T THINK ABOUT FOOD WHEN YOU LOOK AT ME...
ROBERT, BE SERIOUS. THERE'S NO MEAT ON YOU. NOW, *SATCHEL,* ON THE OTHER HAND....
HI GUYS!
WHAT UP, CORN DOG!

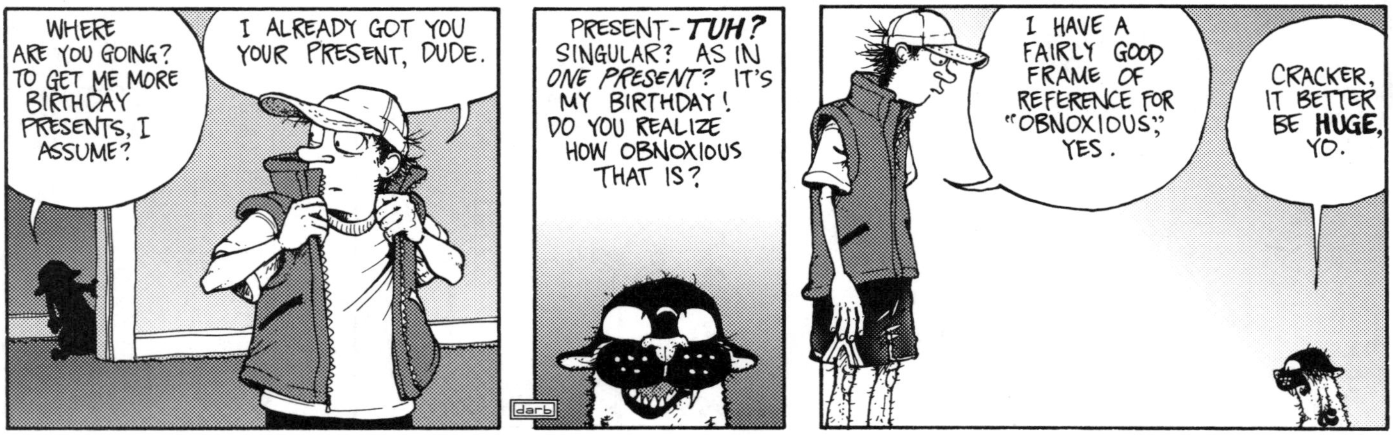
WHERE ARE YOU GOING? TO GET ME MORE BIRTHDAY PRESENTS, I ASSUME?
I ALREADY GOT YOU YOUR PRESENT, DUDE.
PRESENT-*TUH?* SINGULAR? AS IN *ONE PRESENT?* IT'S MY BIRTHDAY! DO YOU REALIZE HOW OBNOXIOUS THAT IS?
I HAVE A FAIRLY GOOD FRAME OF REFERENCE FOR "OBNOXIOUS," YES.
CRACKER, IT BETTER BE **HUGE**, YO.
darb

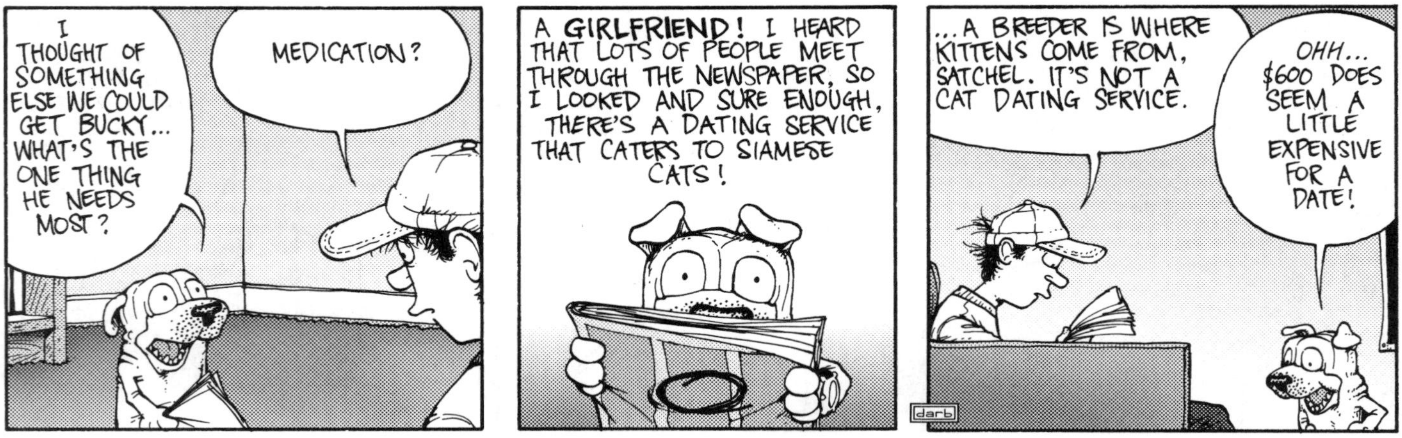
I THOUGHT OF SOMETHING ELSE WE COULD GET BUCKY... WHAT'S THE ONE THING HE NEEDS MOST?
MEDICATION?
A **GIRLFRIEND!** I HEARD THAT LOTS OF PEOPLE MEET THROUGH THE NEWSPAPER, SO I LOOKED AND SURE ENOUGH, THERE'S A DATING SERVICE THAT CATERS TO SIAMESE CATS!
darb
...A BREEDER IS WHERE KITTENS COME FROM, SATCHEL. IT'S NOT A CAT DATING SERVICE.
OHH... $600 DOES SEEM A LITTLE EXPENSIVE FOR A DATE!

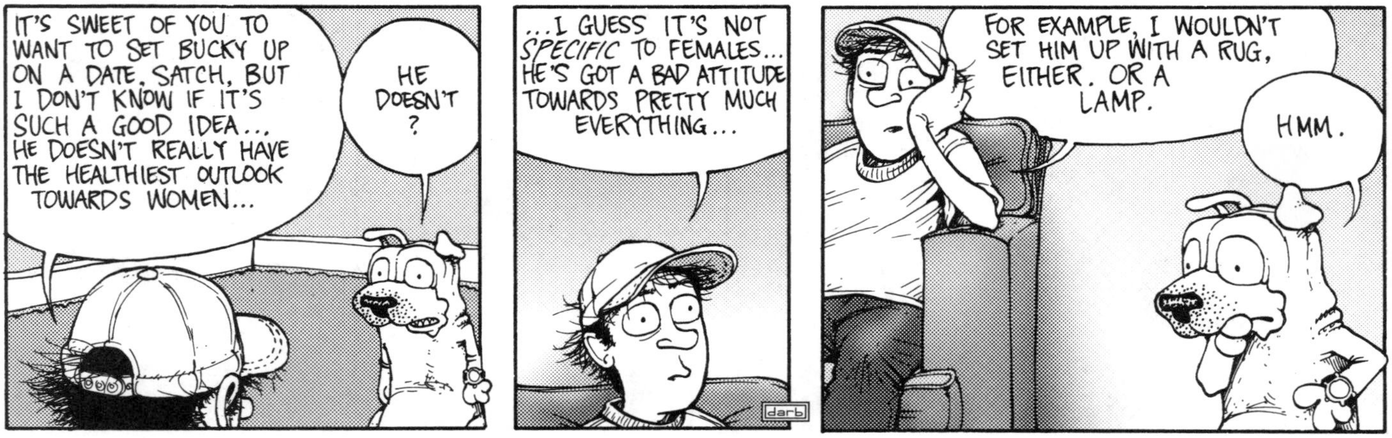
IT'S SWEET OF YOU TO WANT TO SET BUCKY UP ON A DATE, SATCH, BUT I DON'T KNOW IF IT'S SUCH A GOOD IDEA... HE DOESN'T REALLY HAVE THE HEALTHIEST OUTLOOK TOWARDS WOMEN...
HE DOESN'T?
...I GUESS IT'S NOT *SPECIFIC* TO FEMALES... HE'S GOT A BAD ATTITUDE TOWARDS PRETTY MUCH EVERYTHING...
darb
FOR EXAMPLE, I WOULDN'T SET HIM UP WITH A RUG, EITHER. OR A LAMP.
HMM.

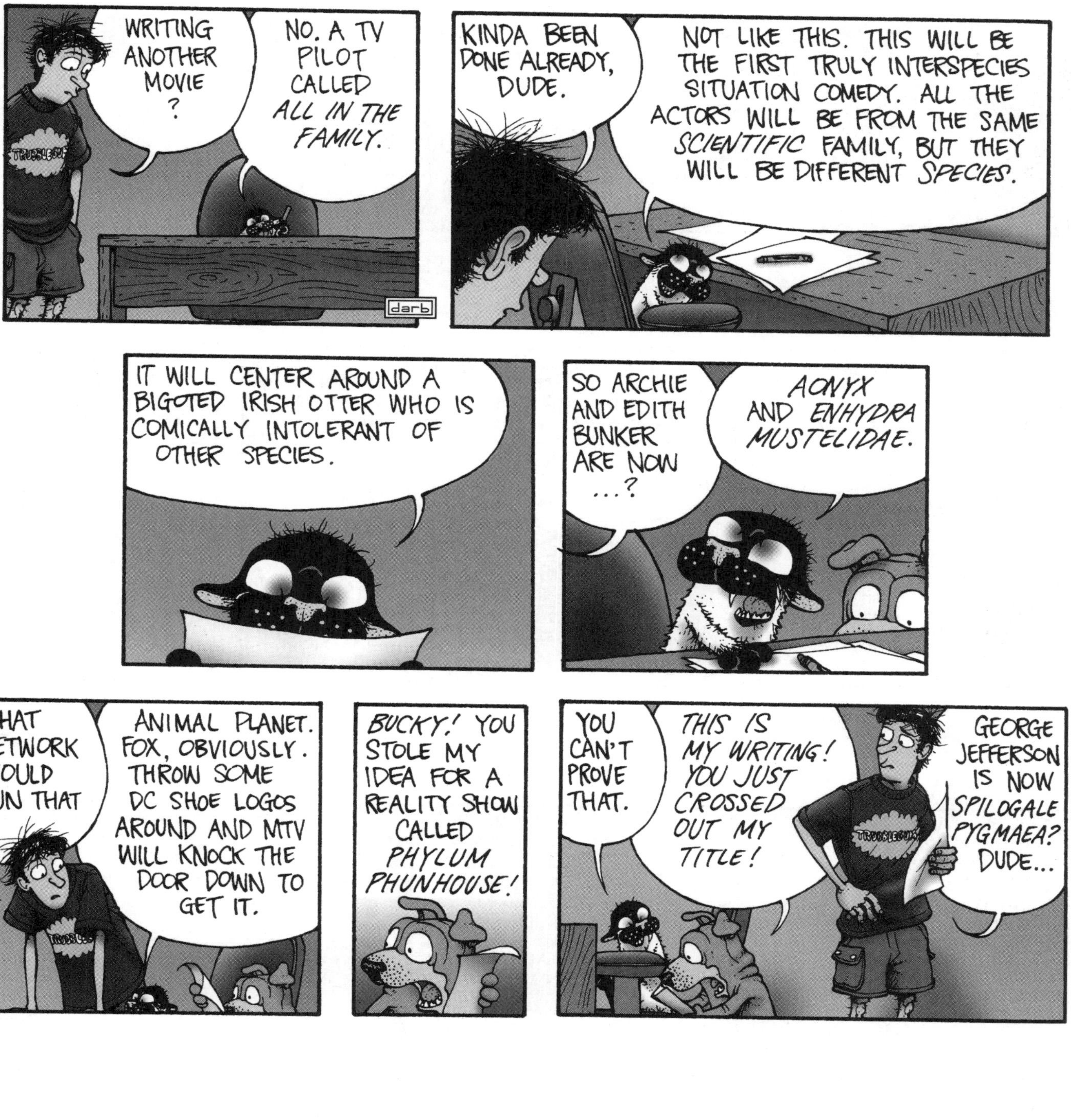
WRITING ANOTHER MOVIE ?
NO. A TV PILOT CALLED *ALL IN THE FAMILY.*
KINDA BEEN DONE ALREADY, DUDE.
NOT LIKE THIS. THIS WILL BE THE FIRST TRULY INTERSPECIES SITUATION COMEDY. ALL THE ACTORS WILL BE FROM THE SAME *SCIENTIFIC* FAMILY, BUT THEY WILL BE DIFFERENT *SPECIES*.
IT WILL CENTER AROUND A BIGOTED IRISH OTTER WHO IS COMICALLY INTOLERANT OF OTHER SPECIES.
SO ARCHIE AND EDITH BUNKER ARE NOW ...?
AONYX AND *ENHYDRA MUSTELIDAE.*
WHAT NETWORK WOULD RUN THAT ?
ANIMAL PLANET. FOX, OBVIOUSLY. THROW SOME DC SHOE LOGOS AROUND AND MTV WILL KNOCK THE DOOR DOWN TO GET IT.
BUCKY! YOU STOLE MY IDEA FOR A REALITY SHOW CALLED *PHYLUM PHUNHOUSE!*
YOU CAN'T PROVE THAT.
THIS IS MY WRITING! YOU JUST CROSSED OUT MY TITLE!
GEORGE JEFFERSON IS NOW *SPILOGALE PYGMAEA?* DUDE...

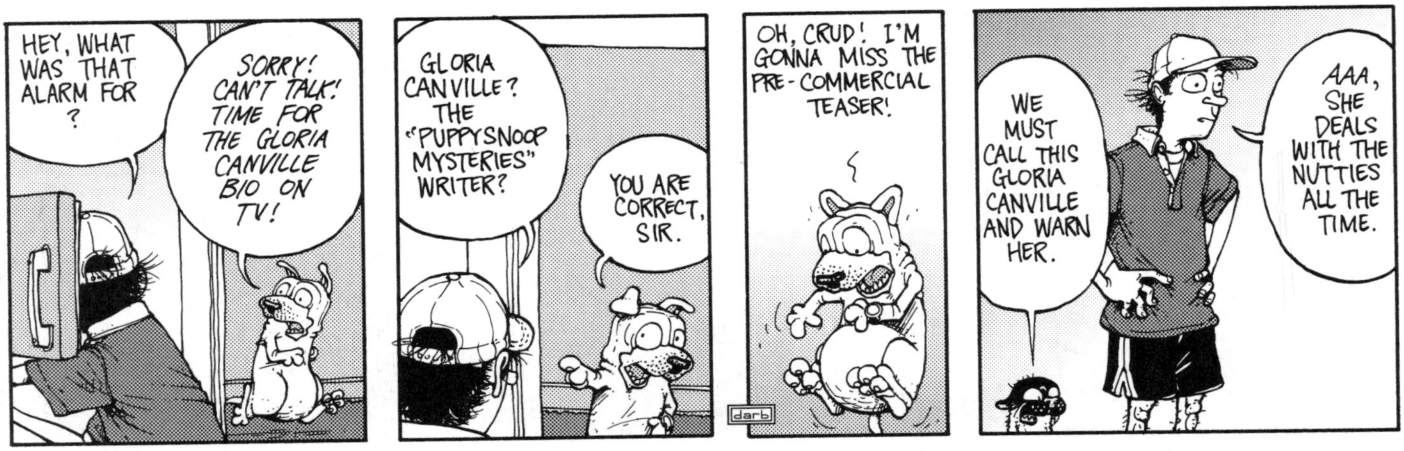
HEY, WHAT WAS THAT ALARM FOR?
SORRY! CAN'T TALK! TIME FOR THE GLORIA CANVILLE BIO ON TV!
GLORIA CANVILLE? THE "PUPPYSNOOP MYSTERIES" WRITER?
YOU ARE CORRECT, SIR.
OH, CRUD! I'M GONNA MISS THE PRE-COMMERCIAL TEASER!
WE MUST CALL THIS GLORIA CANVILLE AND WARN HER.
AAA, SHE DEALS WITH THE NUTTIES ALL THE TIME.

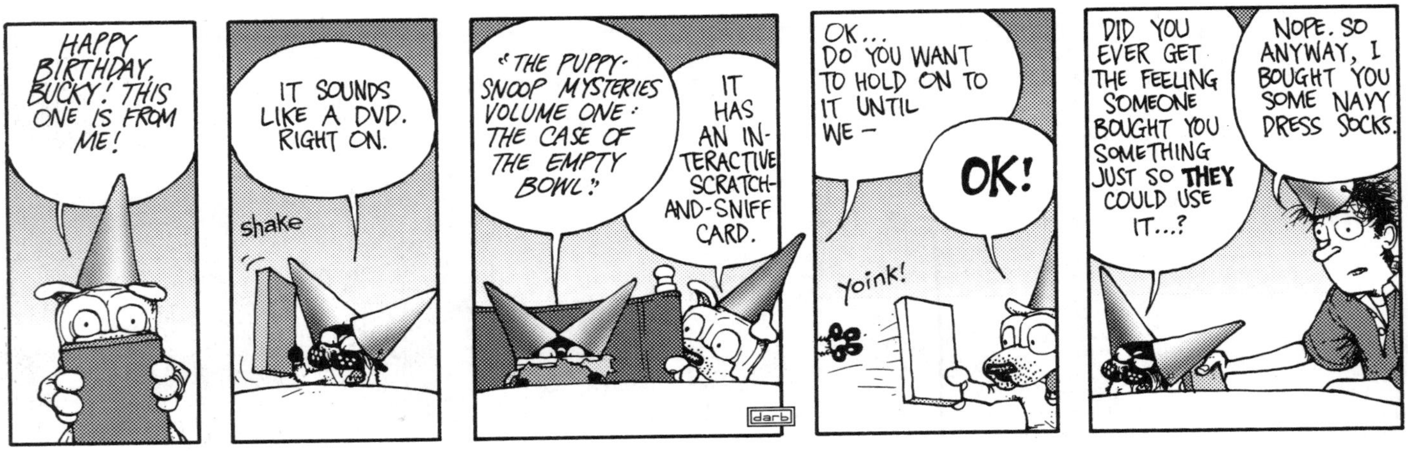
HAPPY BIRTHDAY, BUCKY! THIS ONE IS FROM ME!
shake
IT SOUNDS LIKE A DVD. RIGHT ON.
"THE PUPPY-SNOOP MYSTERIES VOLUME ONE: THE CASE OF THE EMPTY BOWL."
IT HAS AN INTERACTIVE SCRATCH-AND-SNIFF CARD.
OK... DO YOU WANT TO HOLD ON TO IT UNTIL WE –
OK!
yoink!
DID YOU EVER GET THE FEELING SOMEONE BOUGHT YOU SOMETHING JUST SO **THEY** COULD USE IT...?
NOPE. SO ANYWAY, I BOUGHT YOU SOME NAVY DRESS SOCKS.

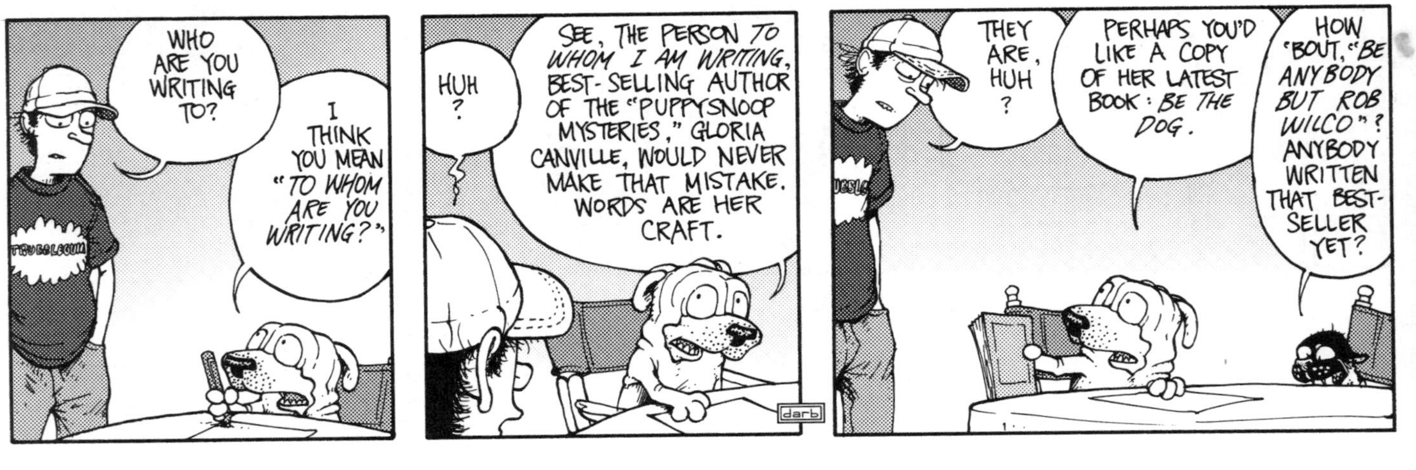
WHO ARE YOU WRITING TO?
I THINK YOU MEAN "TO WHOM ARE YOU WRITING?"
HUH?
SEE, THE PERSON TO WHOM I AM WRITING, BEST-SELLING AUTHOR OF THE "PUPPYSNOOP MYSTERIES," GLORIA CANVILLE, WOULD NEVER MAKE THAT MISTAKE. WORDS ARE HER CRAFT.
THEY ARE, HUH?
PERHAPS YOU'D LIKE A COPY OF HER LATEST BOOK: BE THE DOG.
HOW 'BOUT, "BE ANYBODY BUT ROB WILCO"? ANYBODY WRITTEN THAT BEST-SELLER YET?

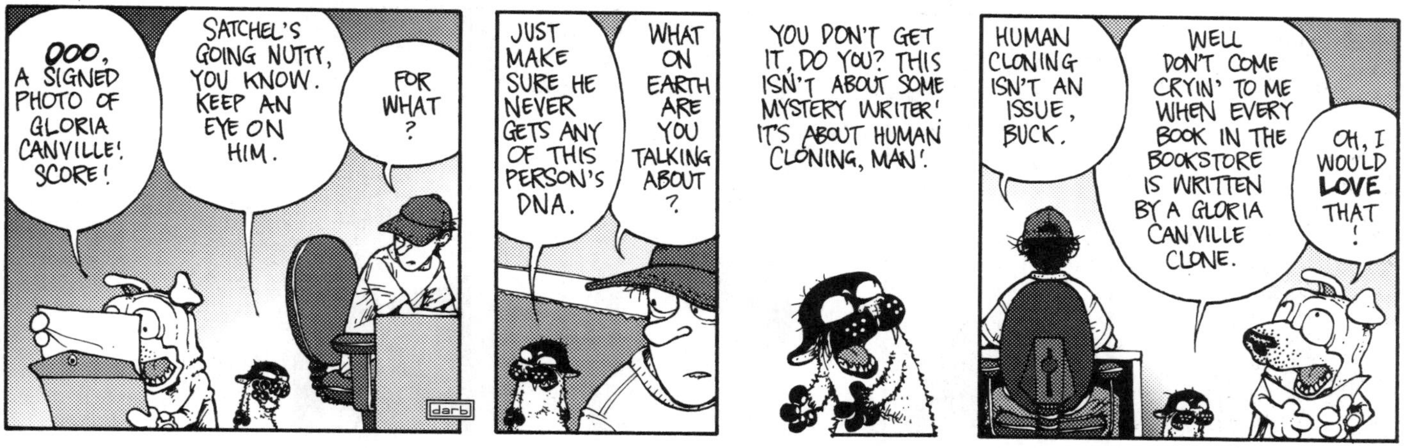
OOO, A SIGNED PHOTO OF GLORIA CANVILLE! SCORE!
SATCHEL'S GOING NUTTY, YOU KNOW. KEEP AN EYE ON HIM.
FOR WHAT?
darb
JUST MAKE SURE HE NEVER GETS ANY OF THIS PERSON'S DNA.
WHAT ON EARTH ARE YOU TALKING ABOUT?
YOU DON'T GET IT, DO YOU? THIS ISN'T ABOUT SOME MYSTERY WRITER! IT'S ABOUT HUMAN CLONING, MAN!
HUMAN CLONING ISN'T AN ISSUE, BUCK.
WELL DON'T COME CRYIN' TO ME WHEN EVERY BOOK IN THE BOOKSTORE IS WRITTEN BY A GLORIA CANVILLE CLONE.
OH, I WOULD LOVE THAT!

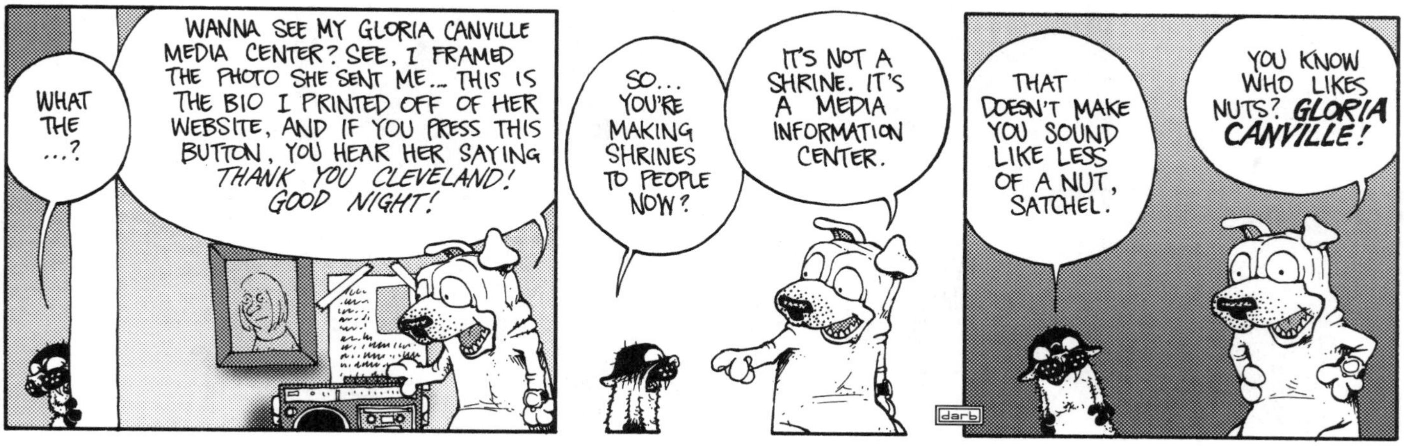
WHAT THE ...?
WANNA SEE MY GLORIA CANVILLE MEDIA CENTER? SEE, I FRAMED THE PHOTO SHE SENT ME... THIS IS THE BIO I PRINTED OFF OF HER WEBSITE, AND IF YOU PRESS THIS BUTTON, YOU HEAR HER SAYING *THANK YOU CLEVELAND! GOOD NIGHT!*
SO... YOU'RE MAKING SHRINES TO PEOPLE NOW?
IT'S NOT A SHRINE. IT'S A MEDIA INFORMATION CENTER.
darb
THAT DOESN'T MAKE YOU SOUND LIKE LESS OF A NUT, SATCHEL.
YOU KNOW WHO LIKES NUTS? **GLORIA CANVILLE!**

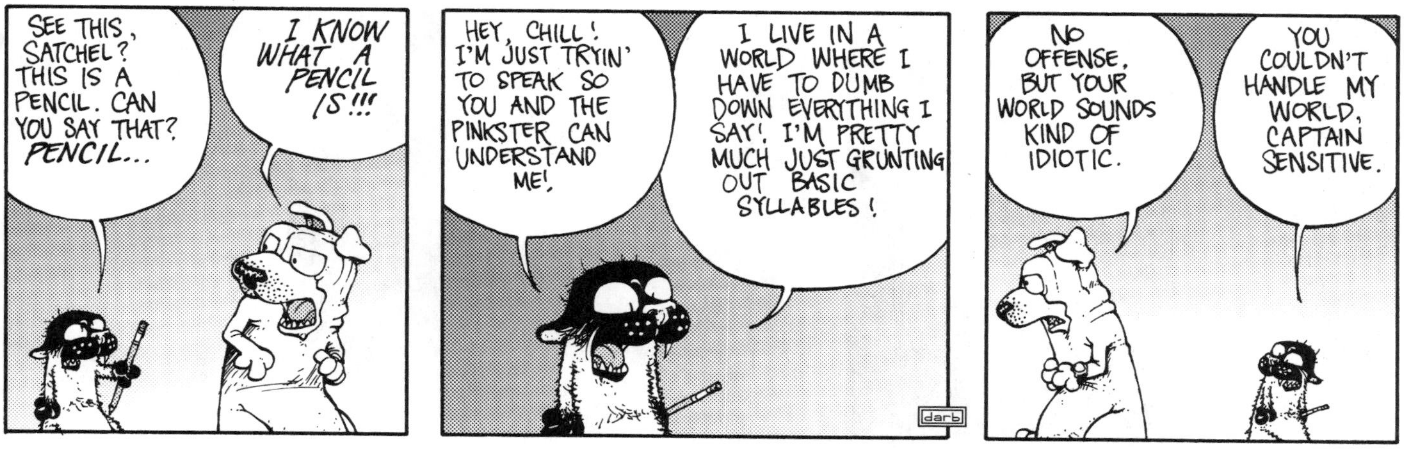
SEE THIS, SATCHEL? THIS IS A PENCIL. CAN YOU SAY THAT? *PENCIL...*
I KNOW WHAT A PENCIL IS!!!
HEY, CHILL! I'M JUST TRYIN' TO SPEAK SO YOU AND THE PINKSTER CAN UNDERSTAND ME!
I LIVE IN A WORLD WHERE I HAVE TO DUMB DOWN EVERYTHING I SAY! I'M PRETTY MUCH JUST GRUNTING OUT BASIC SYLLABLES!
darb
NO OFFENSE, BUT YOUR WORLD SOUNDS KIND OF IDIOTIC.
YOU COULDN'T HANDLE MY WORLD, CAPTAIN SENSITIVE.

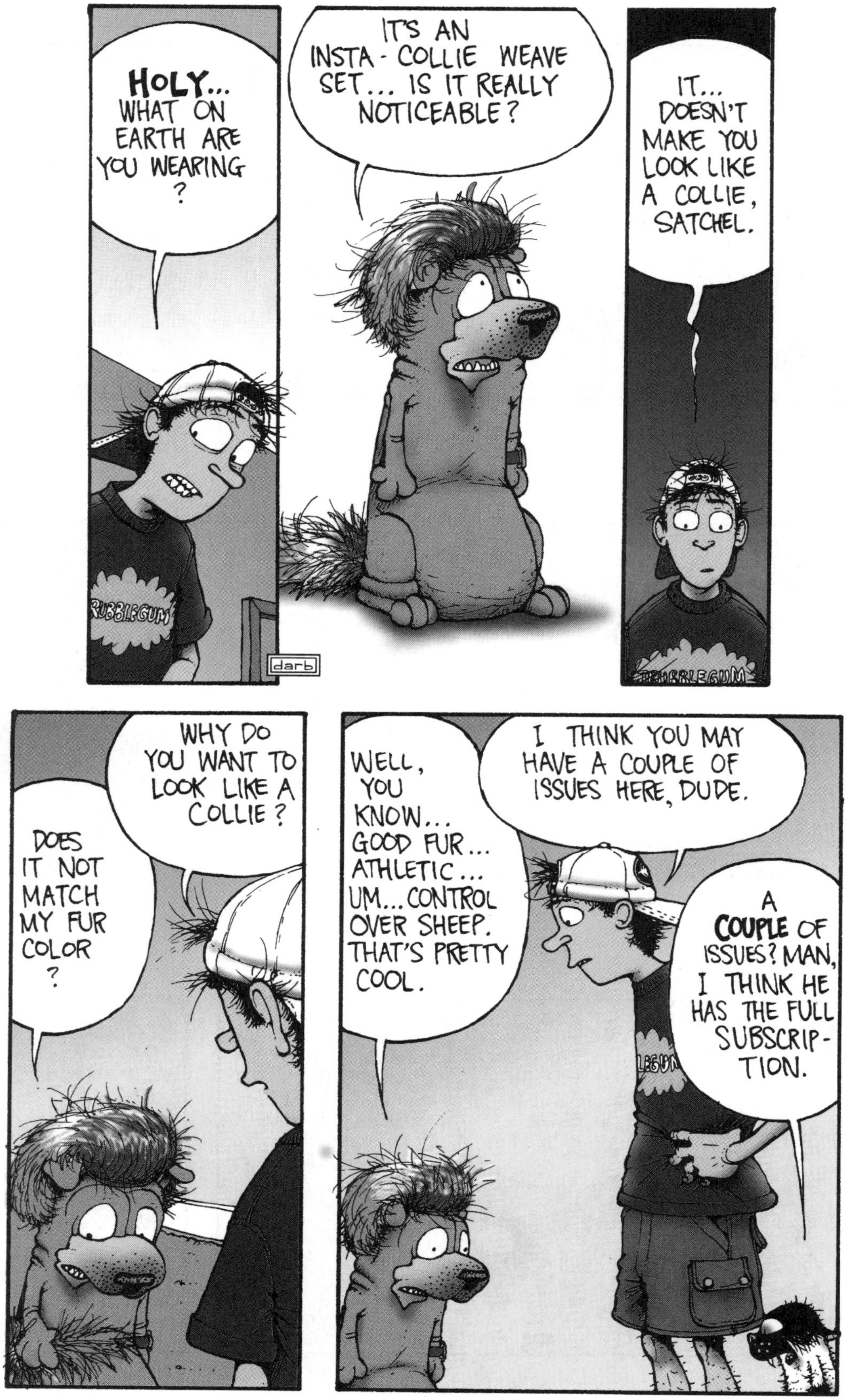
HOLY... WHAT ON EARTH ARE YOU WEARING ?
IT'S AN INSTA-COLLIE WEAVE SET... IS IT REALLY NOTICEABLE?
IT... DOESN'T MAKE YOU LOOK LIKE A COLLIE, SATCHEL.
darb
RUBBLEGUM
WHY DO YOU WANT TO LOOK LIKE A COLLIE?
DOES IT NOT MATCH MY FUR COLOR ?
WELL, YOU KNOW... GOOD FUR... ATHLETIC... UM... CONTROL OVER SHEEP. THAT'S PRETTY COOL.
I THINK YOU MAY HAVE A COUPLE OF ISSUES HERE, DUDE.
A **COUPLE** OF ISSUES? MAN, I THINK HE HAS THE FULL SUBSCRIP-TION.

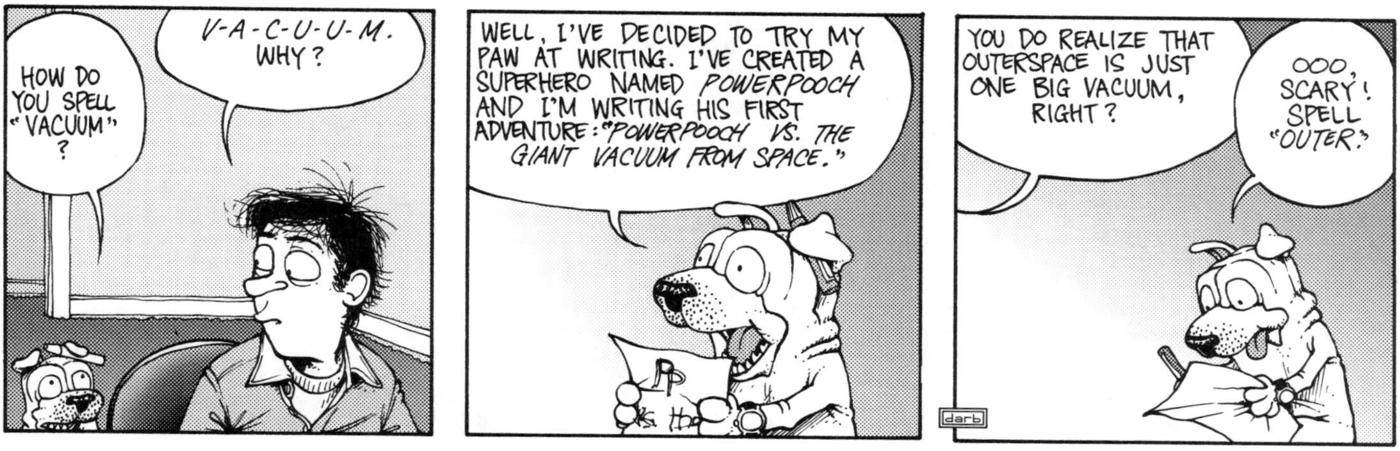
HOW DO YOU SPELL "VACUUM"?
V-A-C-U-U-M. WHY?
WELL, I'VE DECIDED TO TRY MY PAW AT WRITING. I'VE CREATED A SUPERHERO NAMED *POWERPOOCH* AND I'M WRITING HIS FIRST ADVENTURE: *"POWERPOOCH VS. THE GIANT VACUUM FROM SPACE."*
YOU DO REALIZE THAT OUTERSPACE IS JUST ONE BIG VACUUM, RIGHT?
OOO, SCARY! SPELL "OUTER."
darb

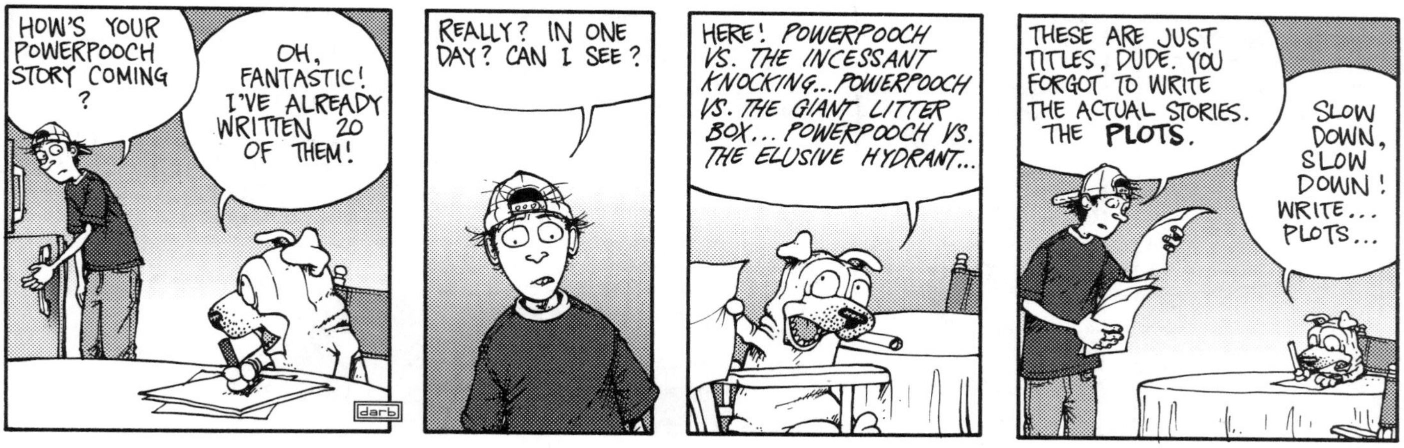
HOW'S YOUR POWERPOOCH STORY COMING?
OH, FANTASTIC! I'VE ALREADY WRITTEN 20 OF THEM!
darb
REALLY? IN ONE DAY? CAN I SEE?
HERE! *POWERPOOCH VS. THE INCESSANT KNOCKING... POWERPOOCH VS. THE GIANT LITTER BOX... POWERPOOCH VS. THE ELUSIVE HYDRANT...*
THESE ARE JUST TITLES, DUDE. YOU FORGOT TO WRITE THE ACTUAL STORIES. THE **PLOTS**.
SLOW DOWN, SLOW DOWN! WRITE... PLOTS...

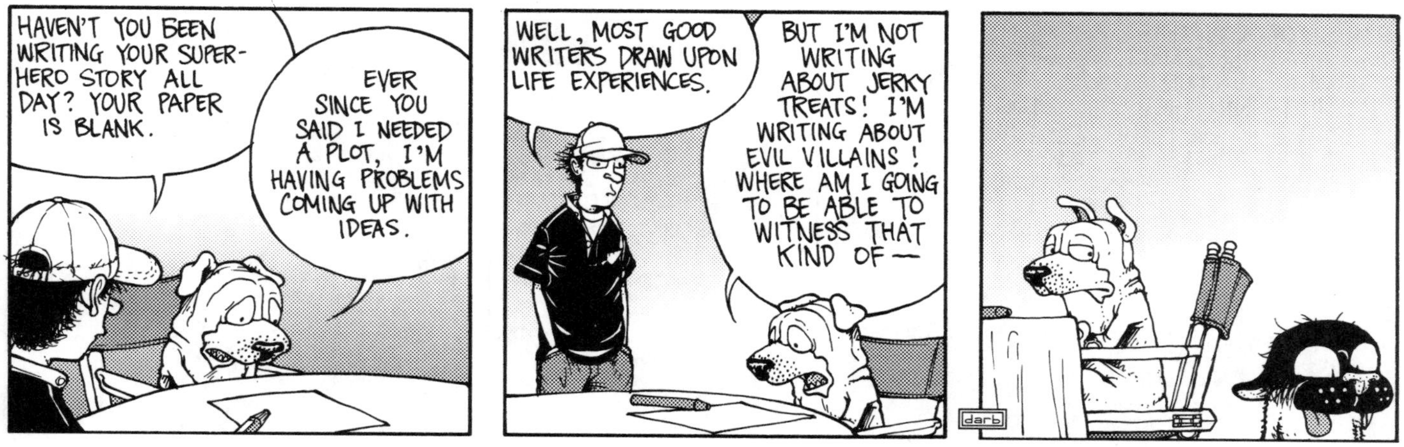
HAVEN'T YOU BEEN WRITING YOUR SUPER-HERO STORY ALL DAY? YOUR PAPER IS BLANK.
EVER SINCE YOU SAID I NEEDED A PLOT, I'M HAVING PROBLEMS COMING UP WITH IDEAS.
WELL, MOST GOOD WRITERS DRAW UPON LIFE EXPERIENCES.
BUT I'M NOT WRITING ABOUT JERKY TREATS! I'M WRITING ABOUT EVIL VILLAINS! WHERE AM I GOING TO BE ABLE TO WITNESS THAT KIND OF—
darb

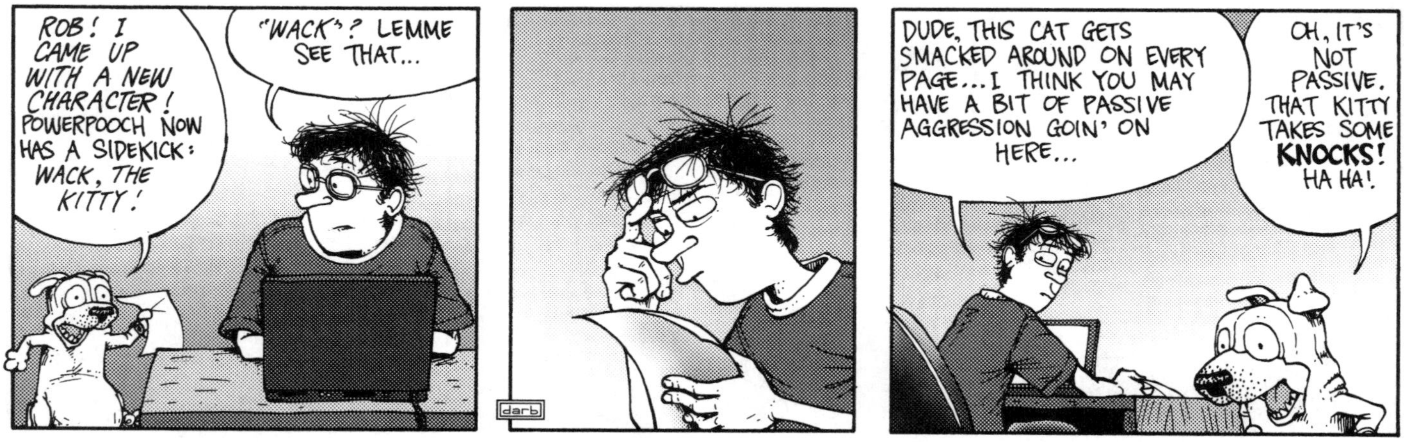
ROB! I CAME UP WITH A NEW CHARACTER! POWERPOOCH NOW HAS A SIDEKICK: WACK, THE KITTY!
"WACK"? LEMME SEE THAT...
DUDE, THIS CAT GETS SMACKED AROUND ON EVERY PAGE... I THINK YOU MAY HAVE A BIT OF PASSIVE AGGRESSION GOIN' ON HERE...
OH, IT'S NOT PASSIVE. THAT KITTY TAKES SOME **KNOCKS!** HA HA!

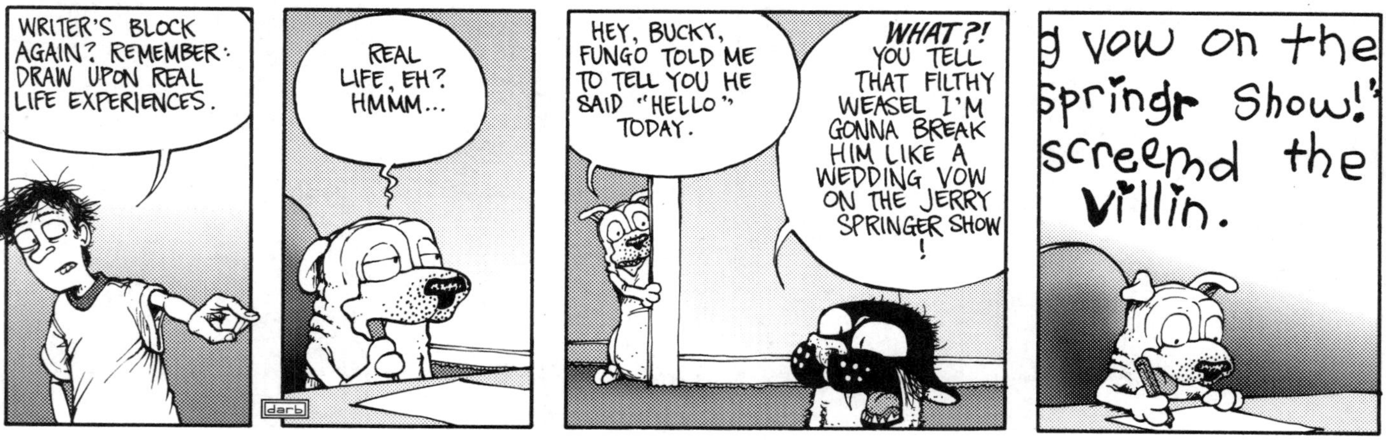
WRITER'S BLOCK AGAIN? REMEMBER: DRAW UPON REAL LIFE EXPERIENCES.
REAL LIFE, EH? HMMM...
HEY, BUCKY, FUNGO TOLD ME TO TELL YOU HE SAID "HELLO" TODAY.
WHAT?! YOU TELL THAT FILTHY WEASEL I'M GONNA BREAK HIM LIKE A WEDDING VOW ON THE JERRY SPRINGER SHOW!
g vow on the springr Show!" screemd the villin.

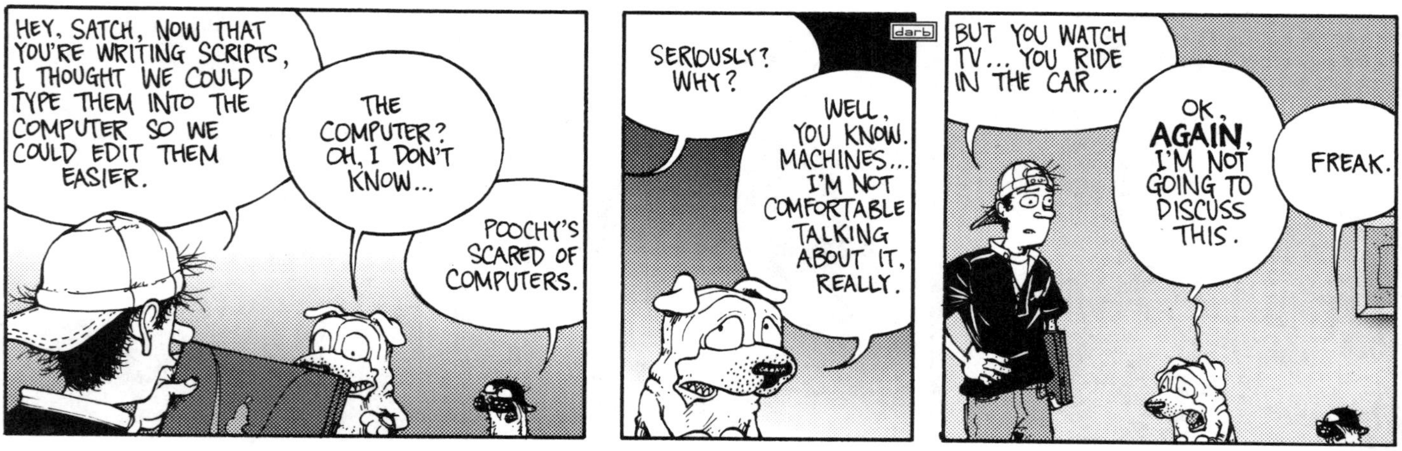
HEY, SATCH, NOW THAT YOU'RE WRITING SCRIPTS, I THOUGHT WE COULD TYPE THEM INTO THE COMPUTER SO WE COULD EDIT THEM EASIER.
THE COMPUTER? OH, I DON'T KNOW...
POOCHY'S SCARED OF COMPUTERS.
SERIOUSLY? WHY?
WELL, YOU KNOW. MACHINES... I'M NOT COMFORTABLE TALKING ABOUT IT, REALLY.
BUT YOU WATCH TV... YOU RIDE IN THE CAR...
OK, **AGAIN**, I'M NOT GOING TO DISCUSS THIS.
FREAK.

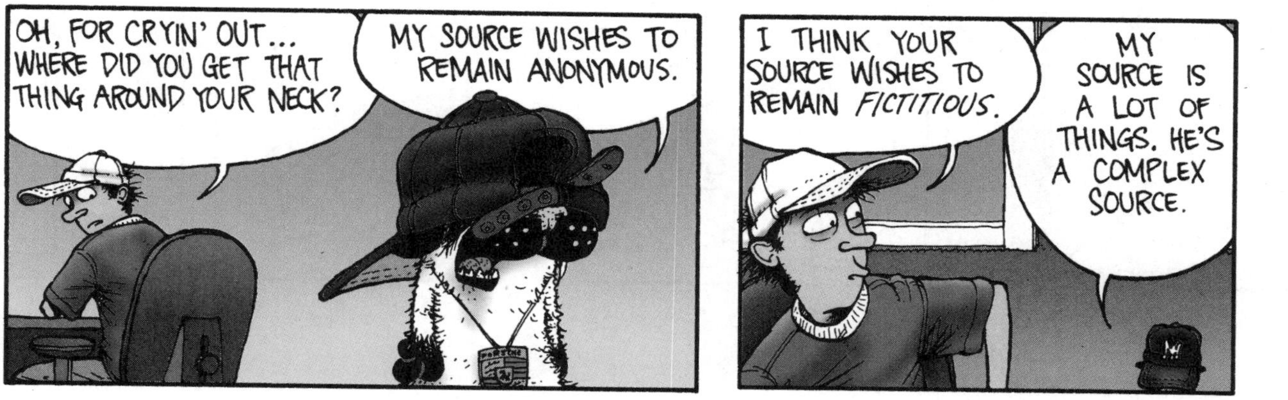
OH, FOR CRYIN' OUT... WHERE DID YOU GET THAT THING AROUND YOUR NECK?
MY SOURCE WISHES TO REMAIN ANONYMOUS.
I THINK YOUR SOURCE WISHES TO REMAIN *FICTITIOUS*.
MY SOURCE IS A LOT OF THINGS. HE'S A COMPLEX SOURCE.

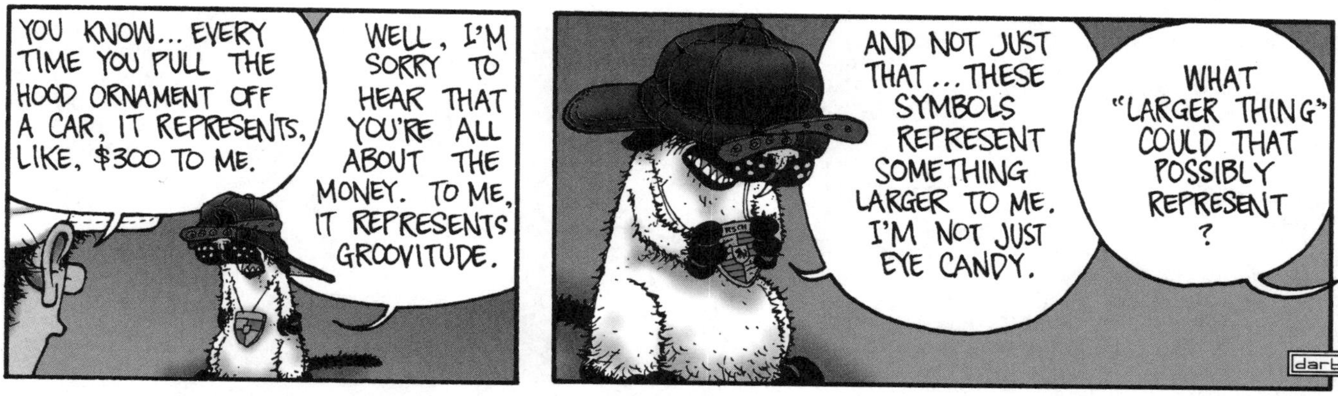
YOU KNOW... EVERY TIME YOU PULL THE HOOD ORNAMENT OFF A CAR, IT REPRESENTS, LIKE, $300 TO ME.
WELL, I'M SORRY TO HEAR THAT YOU'RE ALL ABOUT THE MONEY. TO ME, IT REPRESENTS GROOVITUDE.
AND NOT JUST THAT... THESE SYMBOLS REPRESENT SOMETHING LARGER TO ME. I'M NOT JUST EYE CANDY.
WHAT "LARGER THING" COULD THAT POSSIBLY REPRESENT?
darb

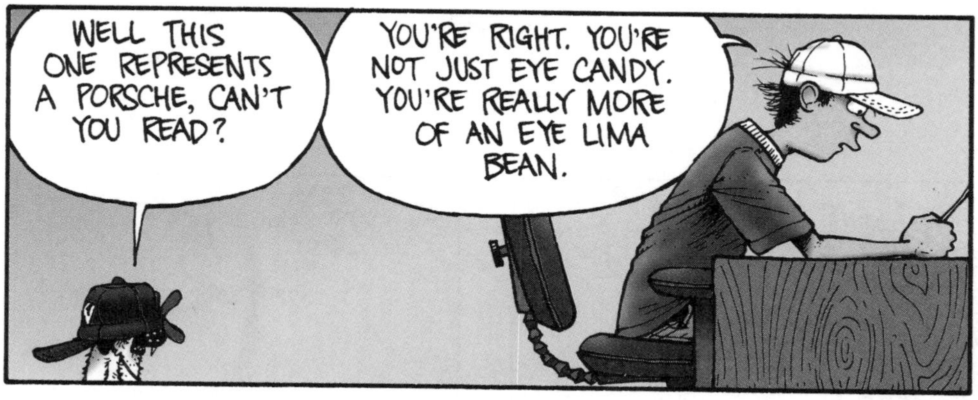
WELL THIS ONE REPRESENTS A PORSCHE, CAN'T YOU READ?
YOU'RE RIGHT. YOU'RE NOT JUST EYE CANDY. YOU'RE REALLY MORE OF AN EYE LIMA BEAN.

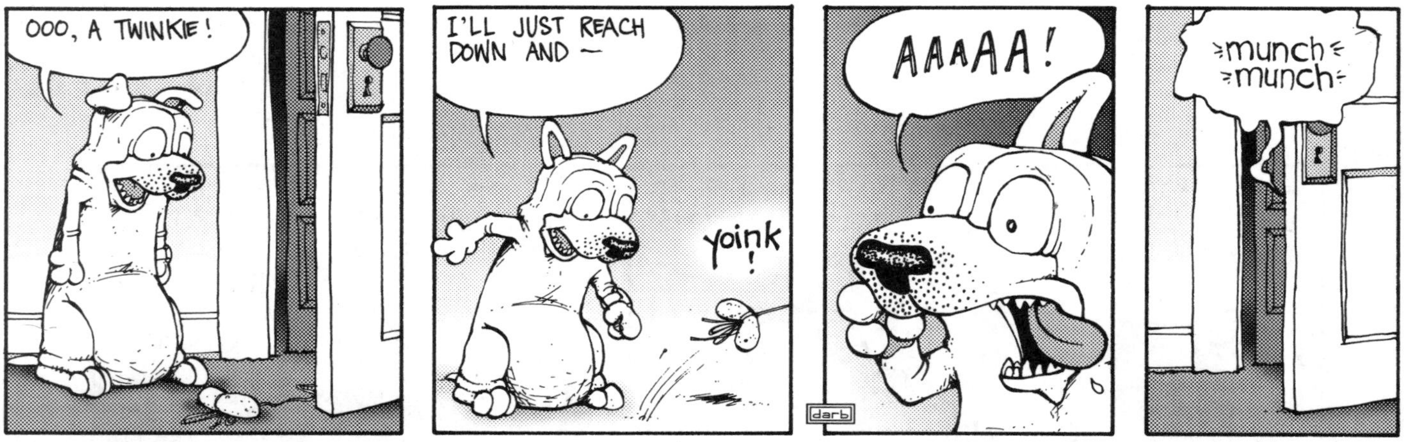
OOO, A TWINKIE!
I'LL JUST REACH DOWN AND ~
yoink!
AAAAA!
munch munch
darb

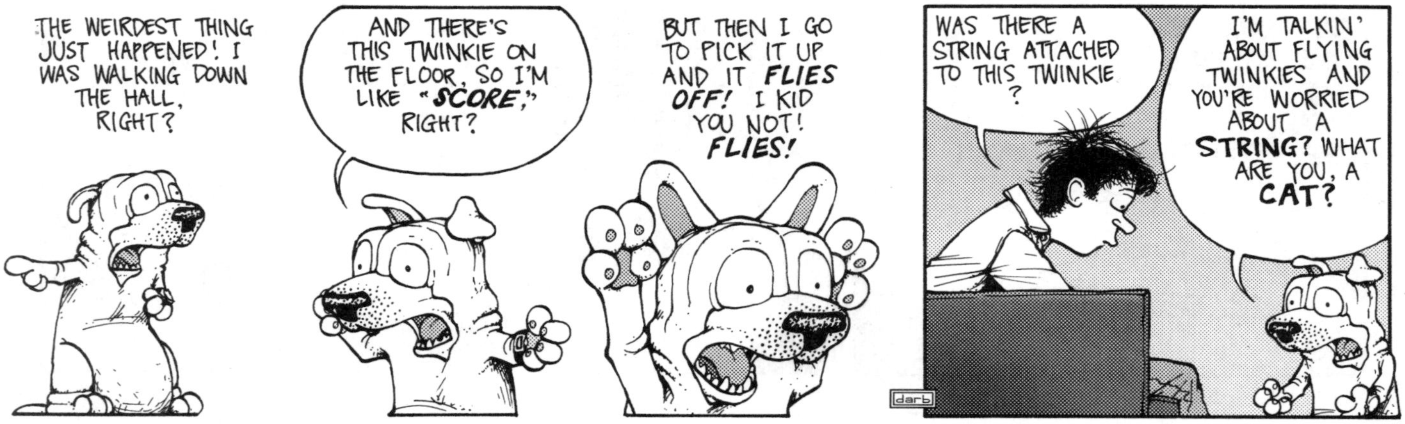
THE WEIRDEST THING JUST HAPPENED! I WAS WALKING DOWN THE HALL, RIGHT?
AND THERE'S THIS TWINKIE ON THE FLOOR, SO I'M LIKE "SCORE," RIGHT?
BUT THEN I GO TO PICK IT UP AND IT FLIES OFF! I KID YOU NOT! FLIES!
WAS THERE A STRING ATTACHED TO THIS TWINKIE?
I'M TALKIN' ABOUT FLYING TWINKIES AND YOU'RE WORRIED ABOUT A STRING? WHAT ARE YOU, A CAT?
darb

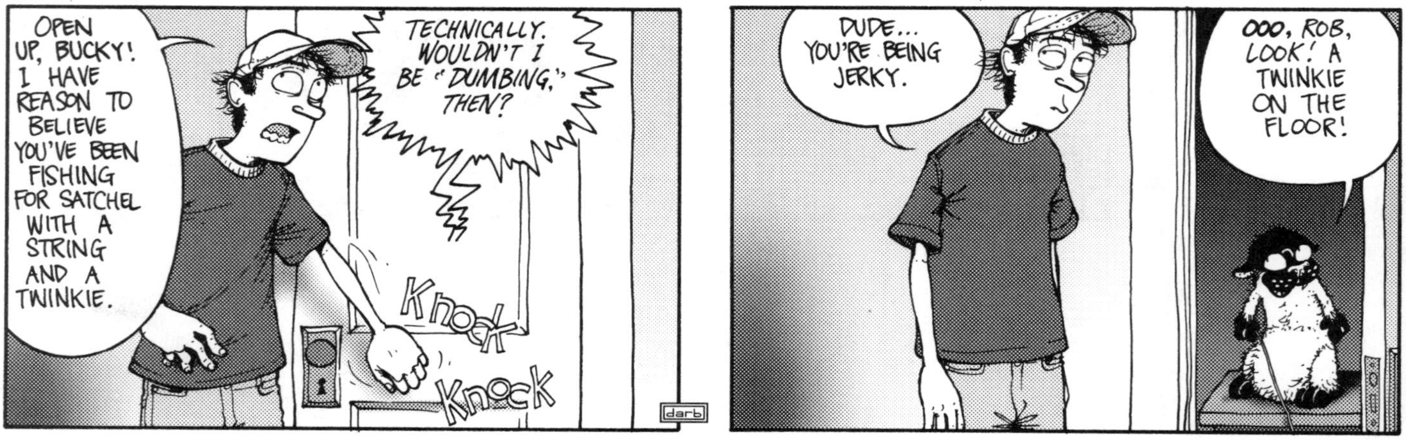
OPEN UP, BUCKY! I HAVE REASON TO BELIEVE YOU'VE BEEN FISHING FOR SATCHEL WITH A STRING AND A TWINKIE.
TECHNICALLY, WOULDN'T I BE "DUMBING," THEN?
Knock Knock
darb
DUDE... YOU'RE BEING JERKY.
OOO, ROB, LOOK! A TWINKIE ON THE FLOOR!

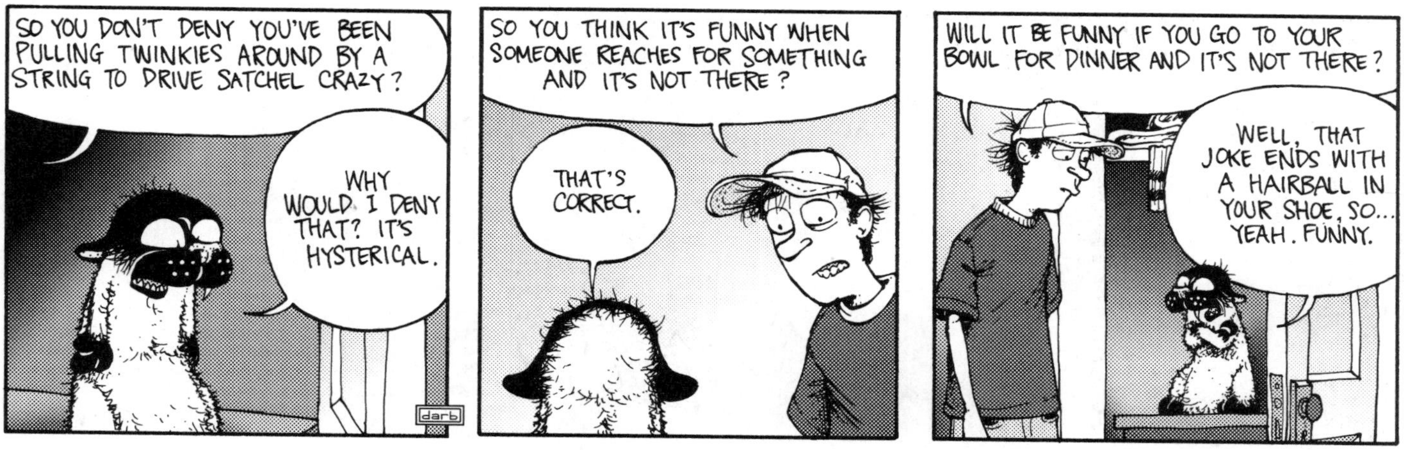
SO YOU DON'T DENY YOU'VE BEEN PULLING TWINKIES AROUND BY A STRING TO DRIVE SATCHEL CRAZY?
WHY WOULD I DENY THAT? IT'S HYSTERICAL.
darb
SO YOU THINK IT'S FUNNY WHEN SOMEONE REACHES FOR SOMETHING AND IT'S NOT THERE?
THAT'S CORRECT.
WILL IT BE FUNNY IF YOU GO TO YOUR BOWL FOR DINNER AND IT'S NOT THERE?
WELL, THAT JOKE ENDS WITH A HAIRBALL IN YOUR SHOE, SO... YEAH. FUNNY.

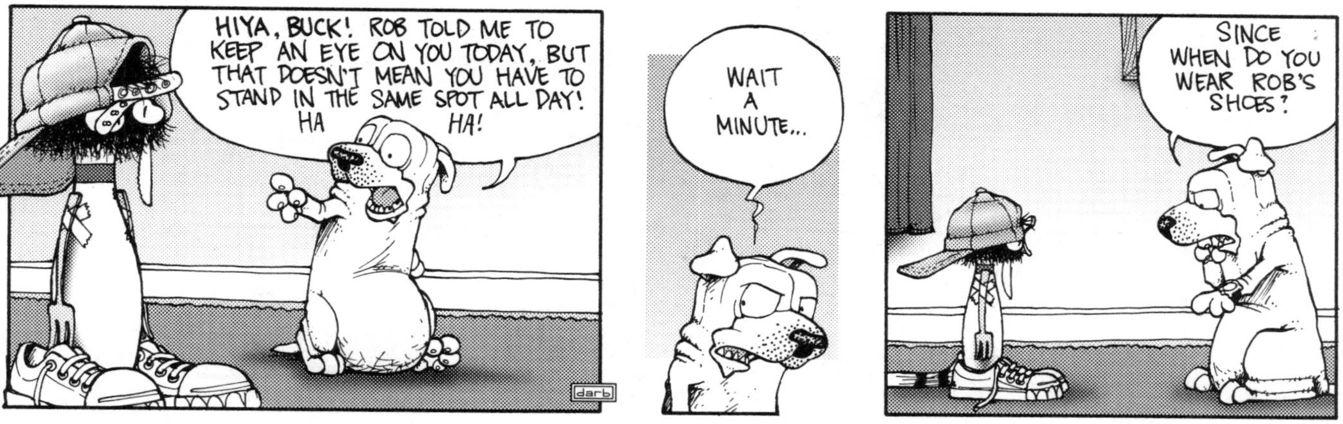
HIYA, BUCK! ROB TOLD ME TO KEEP AN EYE ON YOU TODAY, BUT THAT DOESN'T MEAN YOU HAVE TO STAND IN THE SAME SPOT ALL DAY! HA HA!
darb
WAIT A MINUTE...
SINCE WHEN DO YOU WEAR ROB'S SHOES?

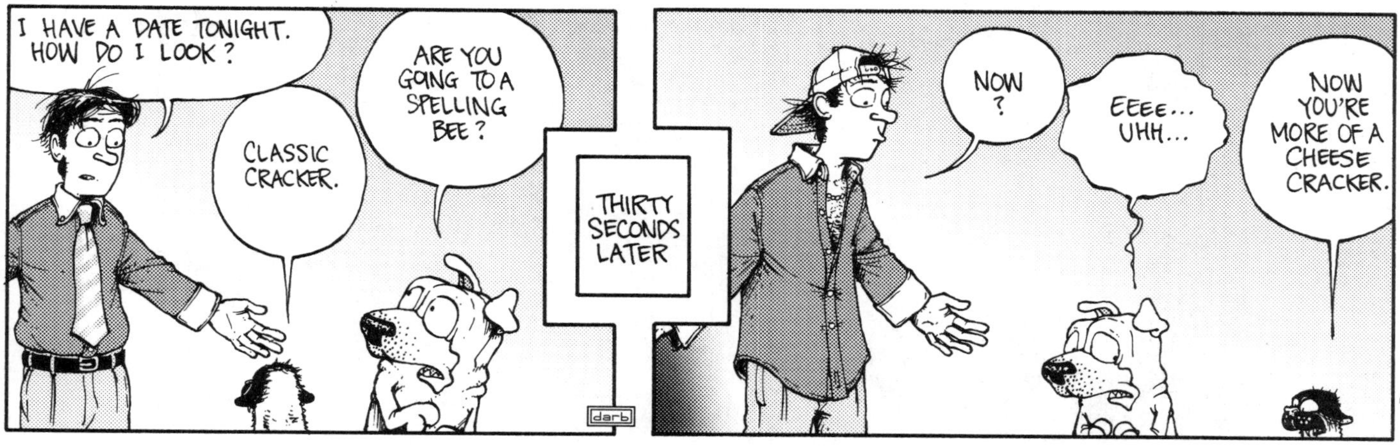
I HAVE A DATE TONIGHT. HOW DO I LOOK?
CLASSIC CRACKER.
ARE YOU GOING TO A SPELLING BEE?
darb
THIRTY SECONDS LATER
NOW?
EEEE... UHH...
NOW YOU'RE MORE OF A CHEESE CRACKER.

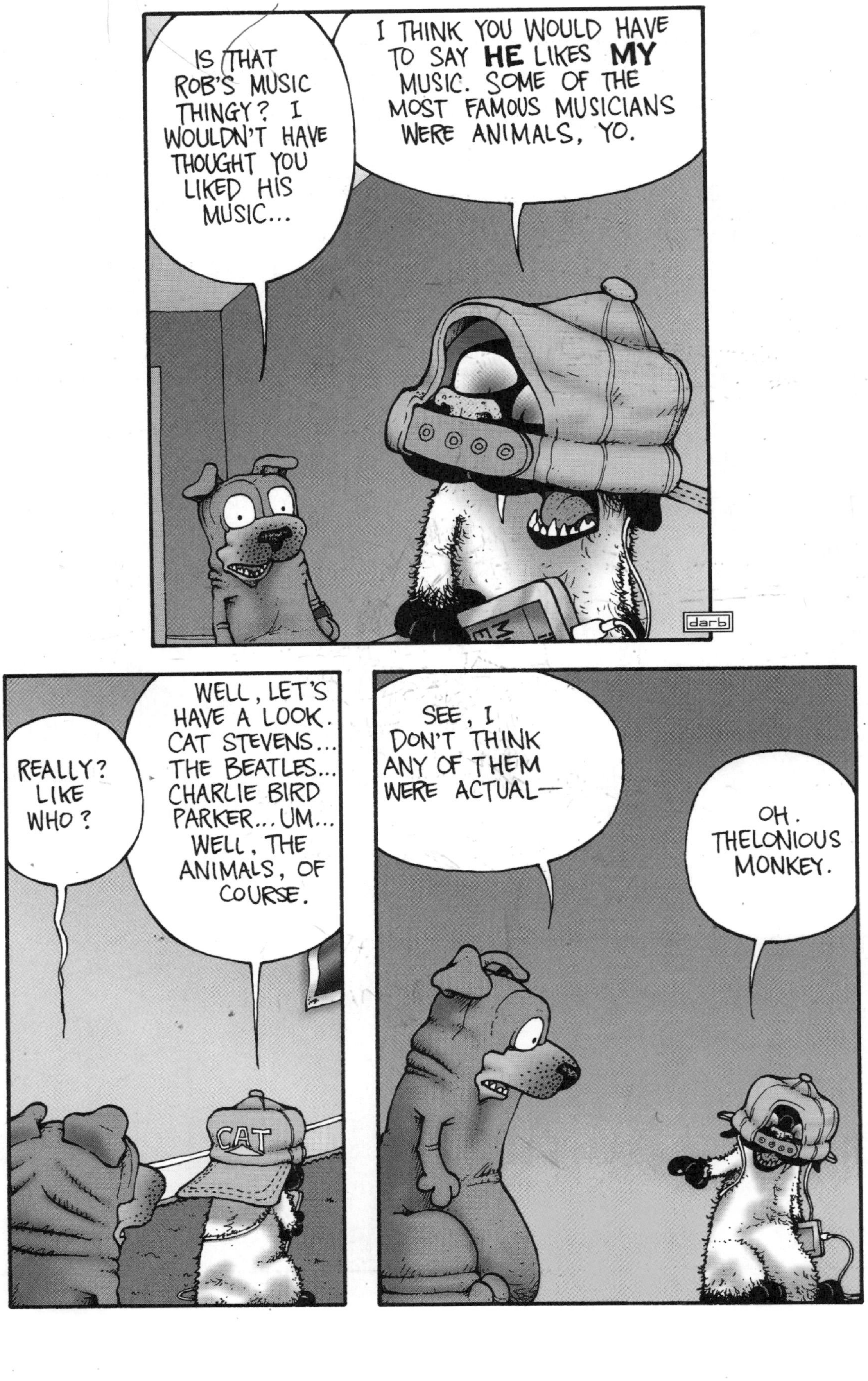
IS THAT ROB'S MUSIC THINGY? I WOULDN'T HAVE THOUGHT YOU LIKED HIS MUSIC...
I THINK YOU WOULD HAVE TO SAY HE LIKES MY MUSIC. SOME OF THE MOST FAMOUS MUSICIANS WERE ANIMALS, YO.
darb
REALLY? LIKE WHO?
WELL, LET'S HAVE A LOOK. CAT STEVENS... THE BEATLES... CHARLIE BIRD PARKER... UM... WELL, THE ANIMALS, OF COURSE.
CAT
SEE, I DON'T THINK ANY OF THEM WERE ACTUAL—
OH. THELONIOUS MONKEY.

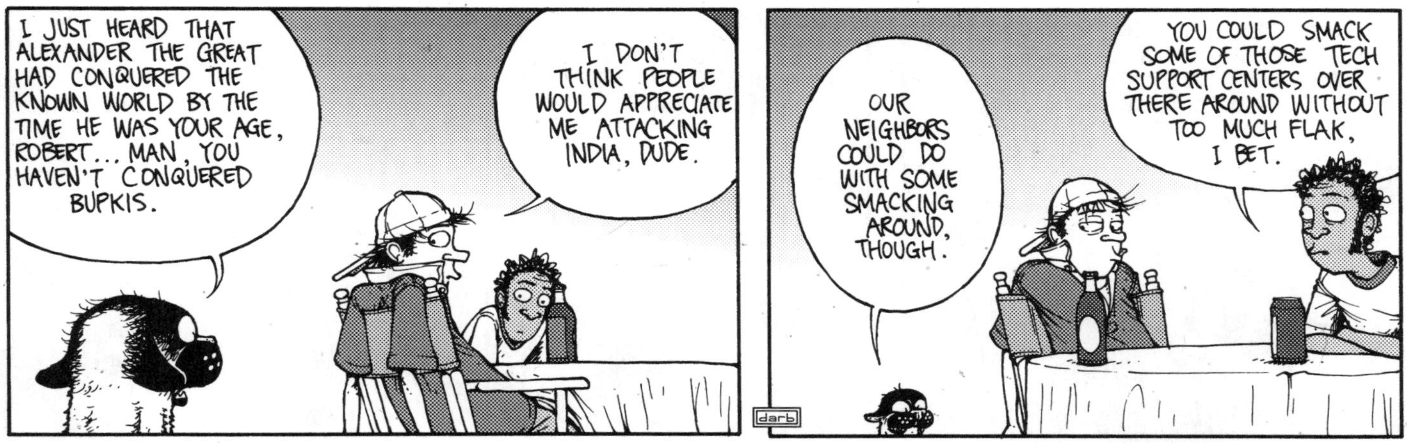
I JUST HEARD THAT ALEXANDER THE GREAT HAD CONQUERED THE KNOWN WORLD BY THE TIME HE WAS YOUR AGE, ROBERT... MAN, YOU HAVEN'T CONQUERED BUPKIS.
I DON'T THINK PEOPLE WOULD APPRECIATE ME ATTACKING INDIA, DUDE.
OUR NEIGHBORS COULD DO WITH SOME SMACKING AROUND, THOUGH.
YOU COULD SMACK SOME OF THOSE TECH SUPPORT CENTERS OVER THERE AROUND WITHOUT TOO MUCH FLAK, I BET.
darb

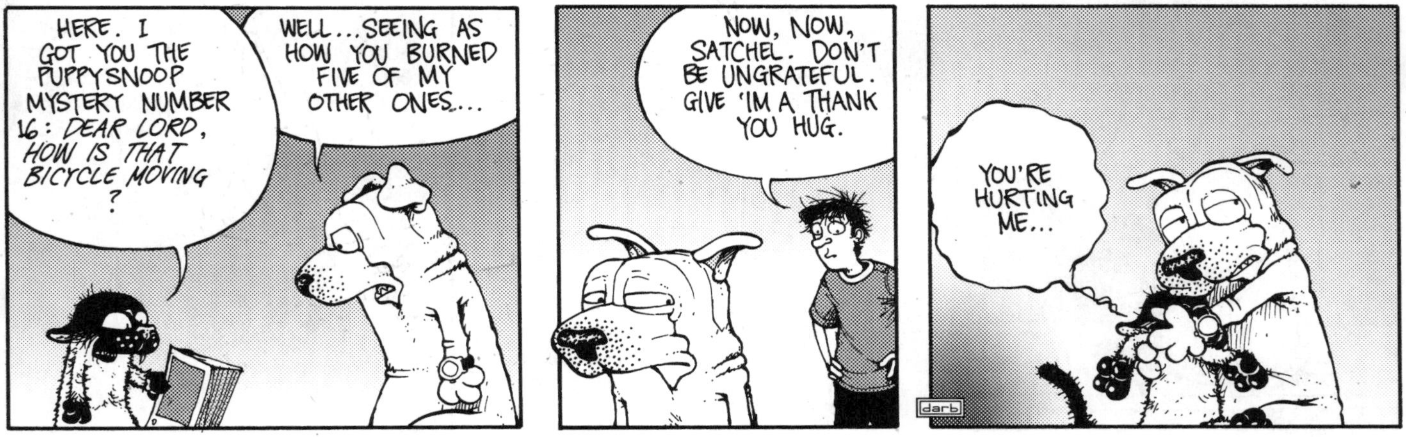
HERE. I GOT YOU THE PUPPYSNOOP MYSTERY NUMBER 16: *DEAR LORD, HOW IS THAT BICYCLE MOVING?*
WELL... SEEING AS HOW YOU BURNED FIVE OF MY OTHER ONES...
NOW, NOW, SATCHEL. DON'T BE UNGRATEFUL. GIVE 'IM A THANK YOU HUG.
YOU'RE HURTING ME...
darb

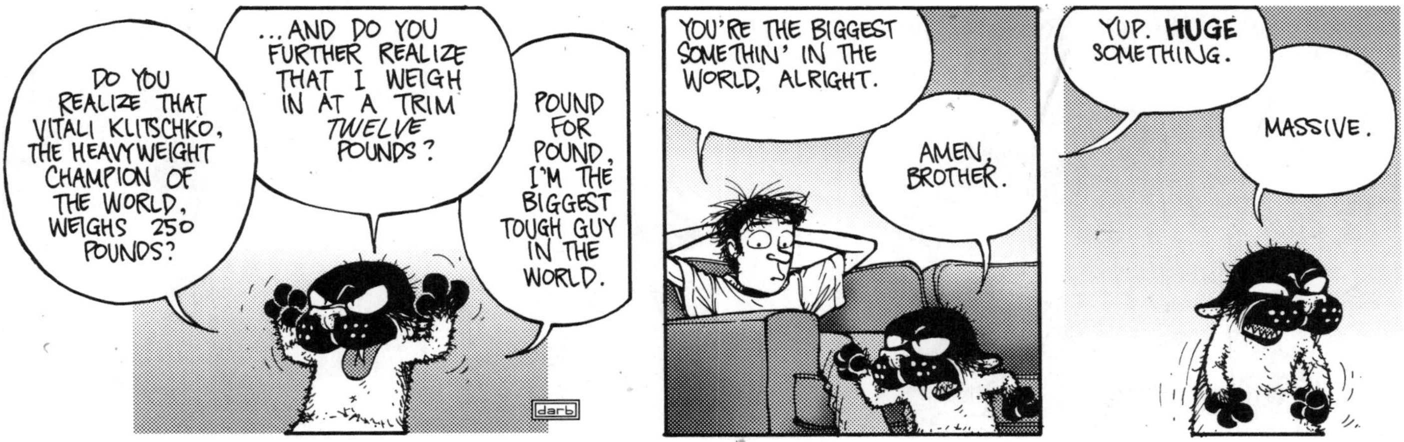
DO YOU REALIZE THAT VITALI KLITSCHKO, THE HEAVYWEIGHT CHAMPION OF THE WORLD, WEIGHS 250 POUNDS?
...AND DO YOU FURTHER REALIZE THAT I WEIGH IN AT A TRIM *TWELVE* POUNDS?
POUND FOR POUND, I'M THE BIGGEST TOUGH GUY IN THE WORLD.
darb
YOU'RE THE BIGGEST SOMETHIN' IN THE WORLD, ALRIGHT.
AMEN, BROTHER.
YUP. **HUGE** SOMETHING.
MASSIVE.

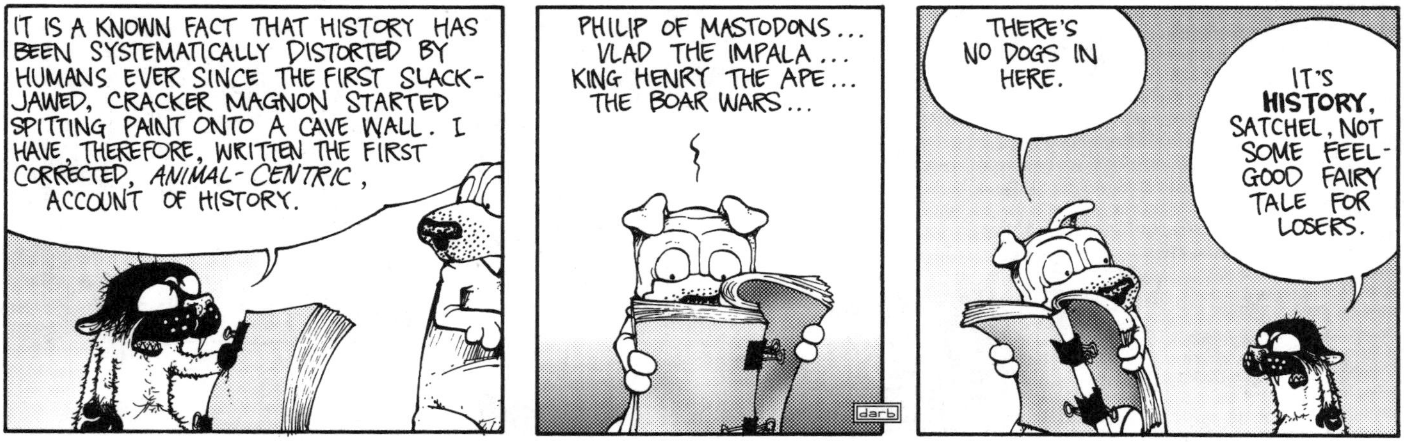
IT IS A KNOWN FACT THAT HISTORY HAS BEEN SYSTEMATICALLY DISTORTED BY HUMANS EVER SINCE THE FIRST SLACK-JAWED, CRACKER MAGNON STARTED SPITTING PAINT ONTO A CAVE WALL. I HAVE, THEREFORE, WRITTEN THE FIRST CORRECTED, *ANIMAL-CENTRIC*, ACCOUNT OF HISTORY.
PHILIP OF MASTODONS... VLAD THE IMPALA... KING HENRY THE APE... THE BOAR WARS...
darb
THERE'S NO DOGS IN HERE.
IT'S **HISTORY**, SATCHEL, NOT SOME FEEL-GOOD FAIRY TALE FOR LOSERS.

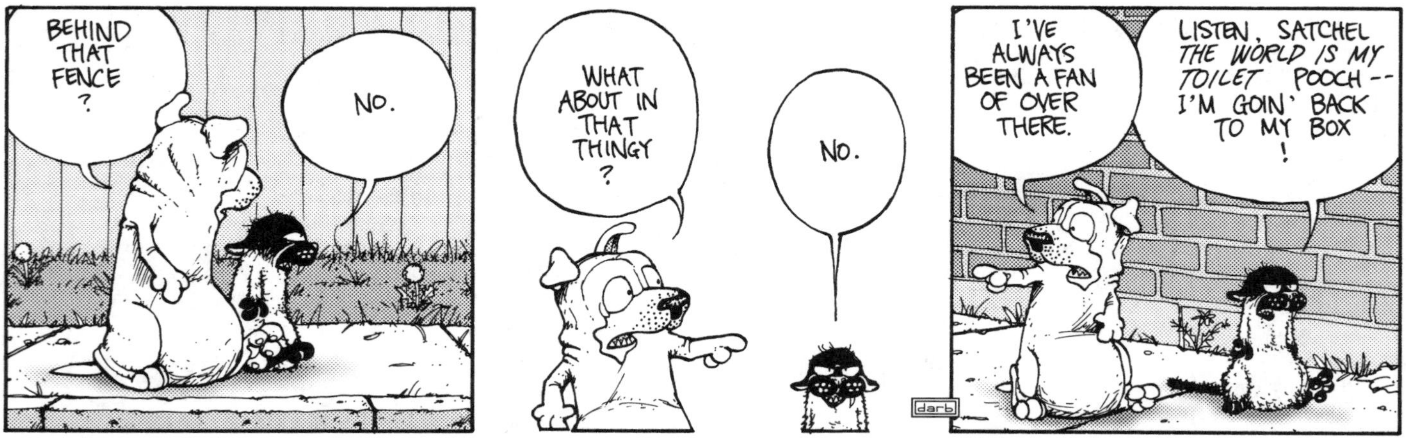
BEHIND THAT FENCE?
NO.
WHAT ABOUT IN THAT THINGY?
NO.
darb
I'VE ALWAYS BEEN A FAN OF OVER THERE.
LISTEN, SATCHEL *THE WORLD IS MY TOILET* POOCH -- I'M GOIN' BACK TO MY BOX!

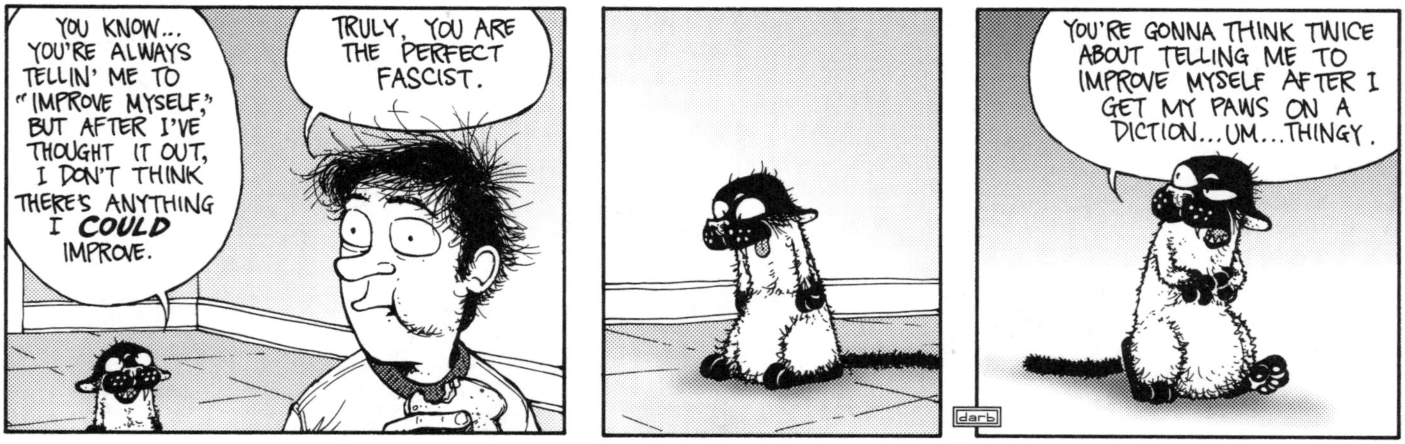
YOU KNOW... YOU'RE ALWAYS TELLIN' ME TO "IMPROVE MYSELF," BUT AFTER I'VE THOUGHT IT OUT, I DON'T THINK THERE'S ANYTHING I **COULD** IMPROVE.
TRULY, YOU ARE THE PERFECT FASCIST.
darb
YOU'RE GONNA THINK TWICE ABOUT TELLING ME TO IMPROVE MYSELF AFTER I GET MY PAWS ON A DICTION...UM...THINGY.

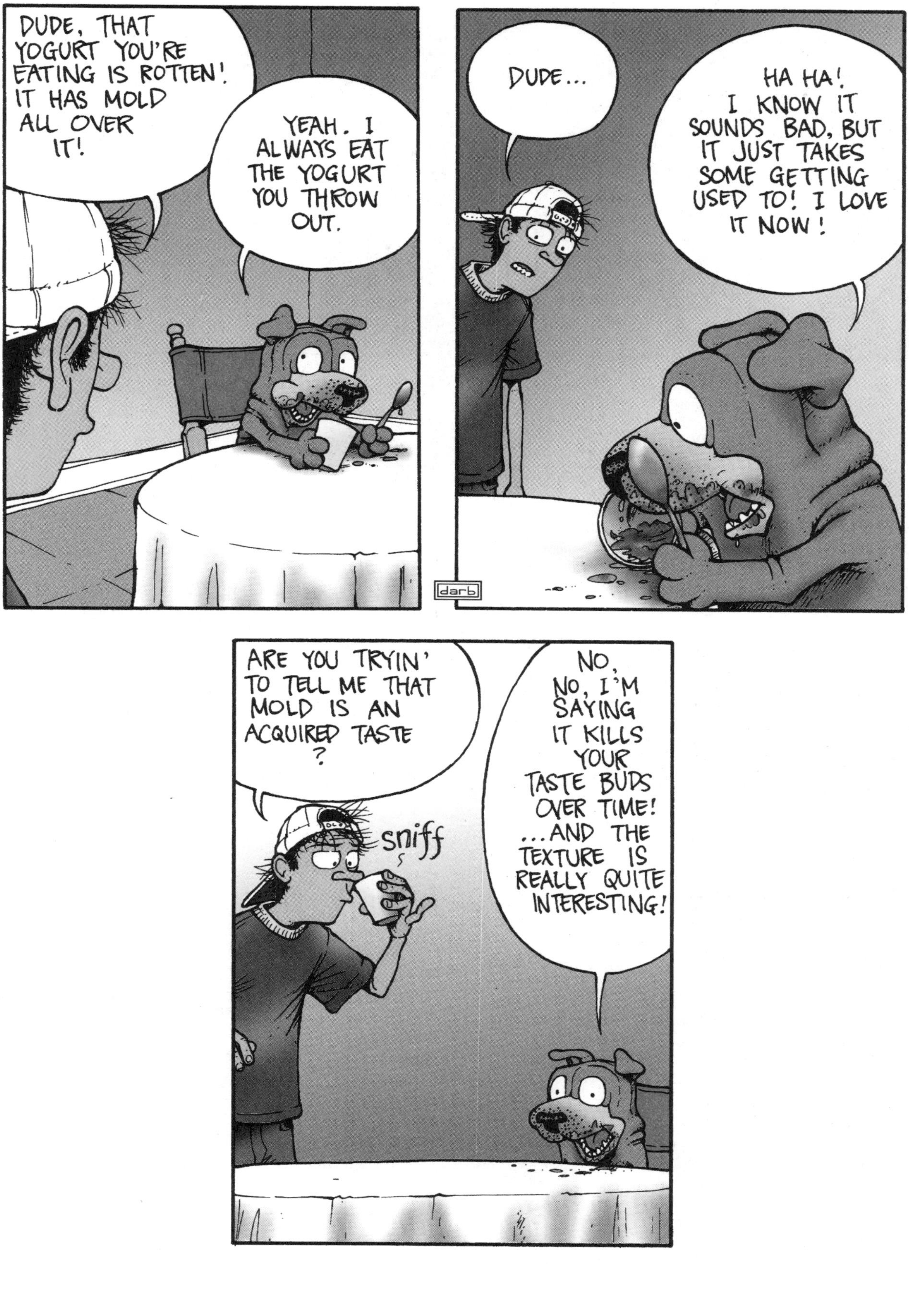
DUDE, THAT YOGURT YOU'RE EATING IS ROTTEN! IT HAS MOLD ALL OVER IT!
YEAH. I ALWAYS EAT THE YOGURT YOU THROW OUT.
DUDE...
HA HA! I KNOW IT SOUNDS BAD, BUT IT JUST TAKES SOME GETTING USED TO! I LOVE IT NOW!
darb
ARE YOU TRYIN' TO TELL ME THAT MOLD IS AN ACQUIRED TASTE?
sniff
NO, NO, I'M SAYING IT KILLS YOUR TASTE BUDS OVER TIME! ...AND THE TEXTURE IS REALLY QUITE INTERESTING!

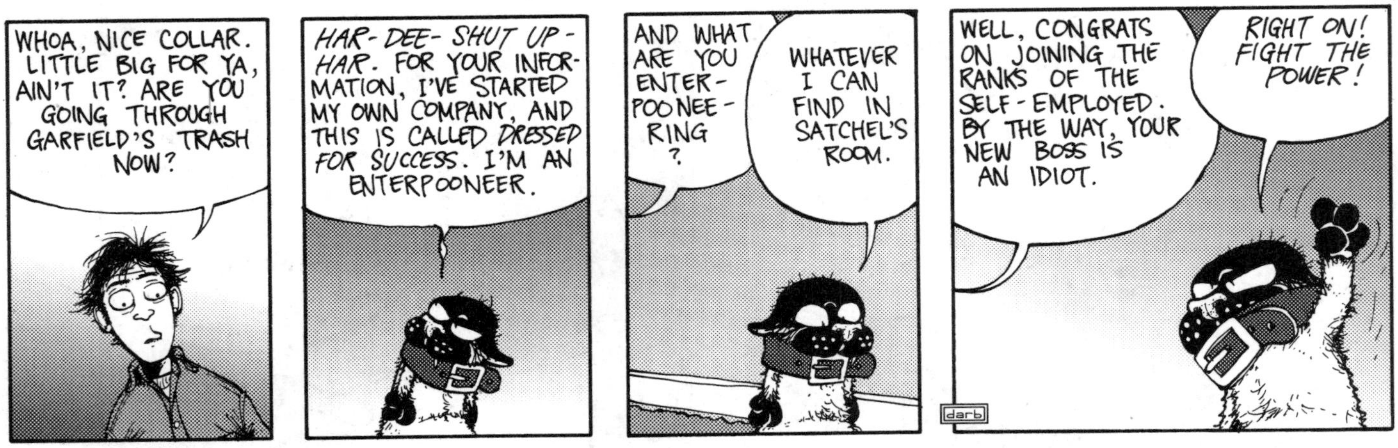
WHOA, NICE COLLAR. LITTLE BIG FOR YA, AIN'T IT? ARE YOU GOING THROUGH GARFIELD'S TRASH NOW?
HAR-DEE-SHUT UP-HAR. FOR YOUR INFORMATION, I'VE STARTED MY OWN COMPANY, AND THIS IS CALLED DRESSED FOR SUCCESS. I'M AN ENTERPOONEER.
AND WHAT ARE YOU ENTER-POONEE-RING?
WHATEVER I CAN FIND IN SATCHEL'S ROOM.
WELL, CONGRATS ON JOINING THE RANKS OF THE SELF-EMPLOYED. BY THE WAY, YOUR NEW BOSS IS AN IDIOT.
RIGHT ON! FIGHT THE POWER!
darb

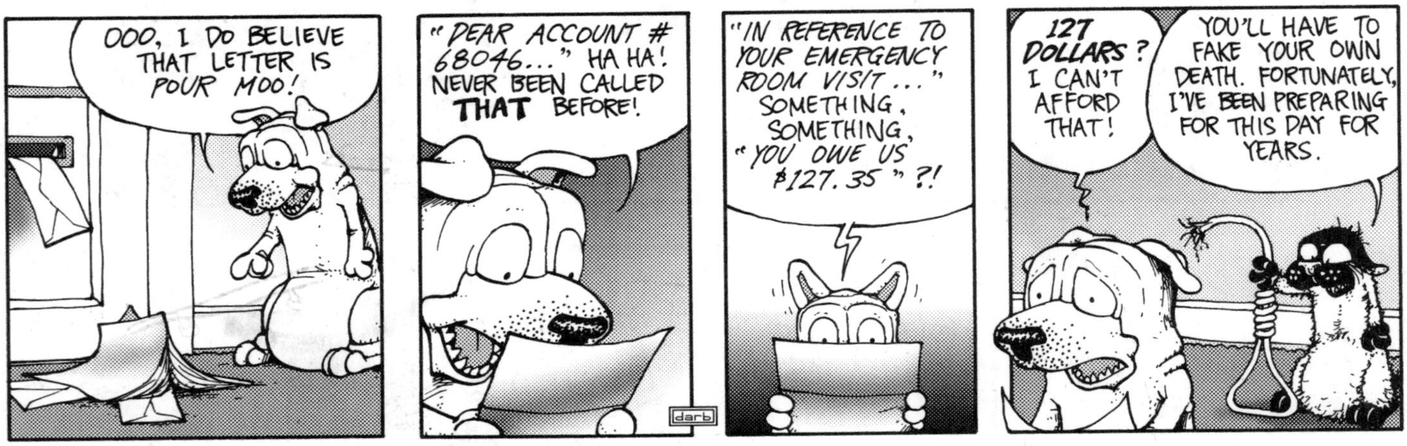
OOO, I DO BELIEVE THAT LETTER IS POUR MOO!
"DEAR ACCOUNT # 68046..." HA HA! NEVER BEEN CALLED **THAT** BEFORE!
darb
"IN REFERENCE TO YOUR EMERGENCY ROOM VISIT..." SOMETHING, SOMETHING, "YOU OWE US $127.35"?!
127 DOLLARS? I CAN'T AFFORD THAT!
YOU'LL HAVE TO FAKE YOUR OWN DEATH. FORTUNATELY, I'VE BEEN PREPARING FOR THIS DAY FOR YEARS.

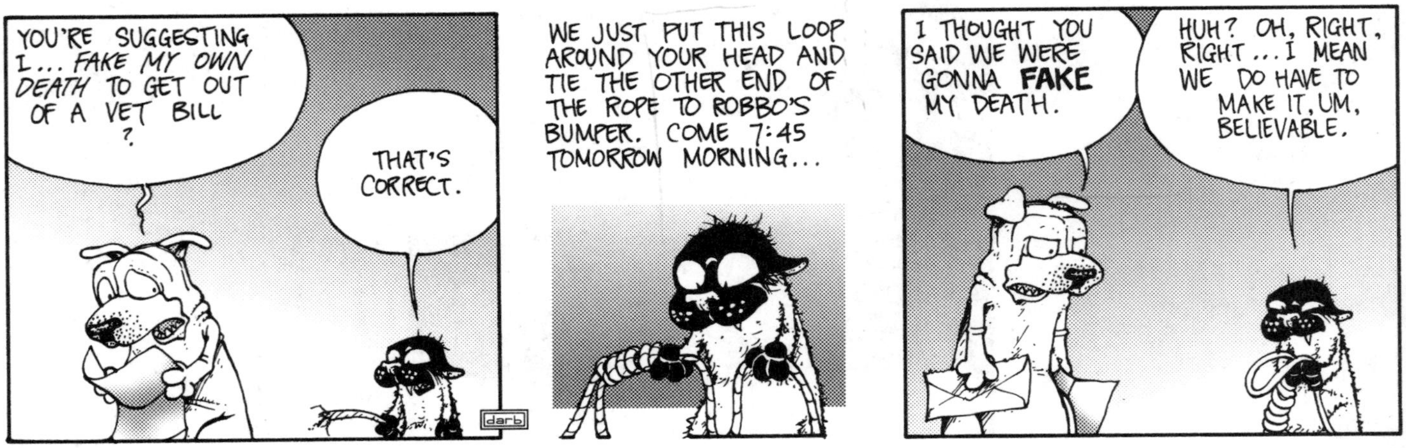
YOU'RE SUGGESTING I... FAKE MY OWN DEATH TO GET OUT OF A VET BILL?
THAT'S CORRECT.
darb
WE JUST PUT THIS LOOP AROUND YOUR HEAD AND TIE THE OTHER END OF THE ROPE TO ROBBO'S BUMPER. COME 7:45 TOMORROW MORNING...
I THOUGHT YOU SAID WE WERE GONNA **FAKE** MY DEATH.
HUH? OH, RIGHT, RIGHT... I MEAN WE DO HAVE TO MAKE IT, UM, BELIEVABLE.

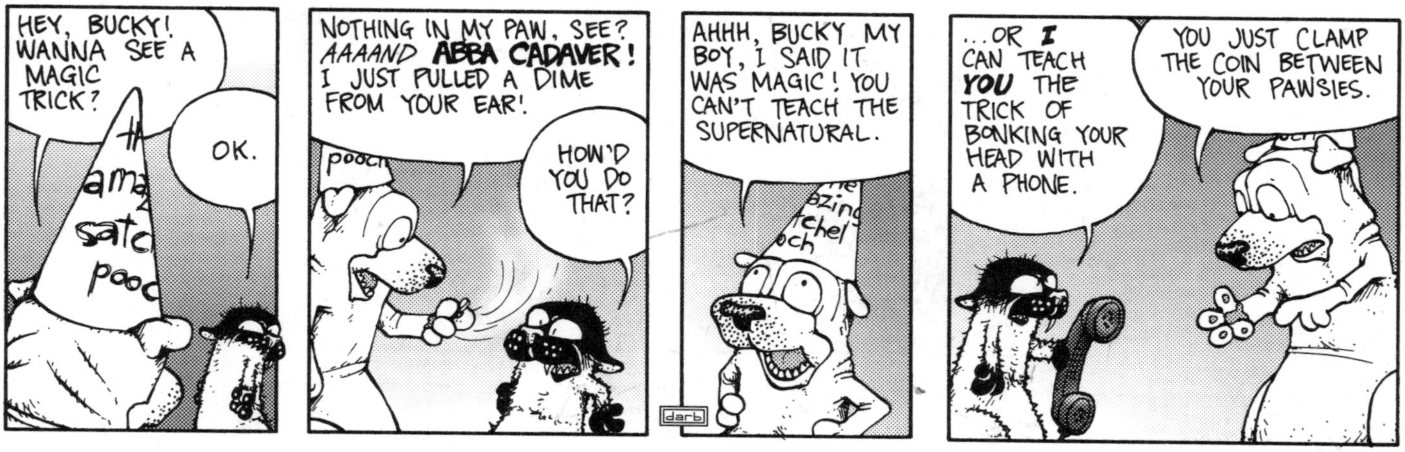
HEY, BUCKY! WANNA SEE A MAGIC TRICK?
OK.
NOTHING IN MY PAW, SEE? AAAAND ABBA CADAVER! I JUST PULLED A DIME FROM YOUR EAR!
HOW'D YOU DO THAT?
AHHH, BUCKY MY BOY, I SAID IT WAS MAGIC! YOU CAN'T TEACH THE SUPERNATURAL.
...OR I CAN TEACH YOU THE TRICK OF BONKING YOUR HEAD WITH A PHONE.
YOU JUST CLAMP THE COIN BETWEEN YOUR PAWSIES.

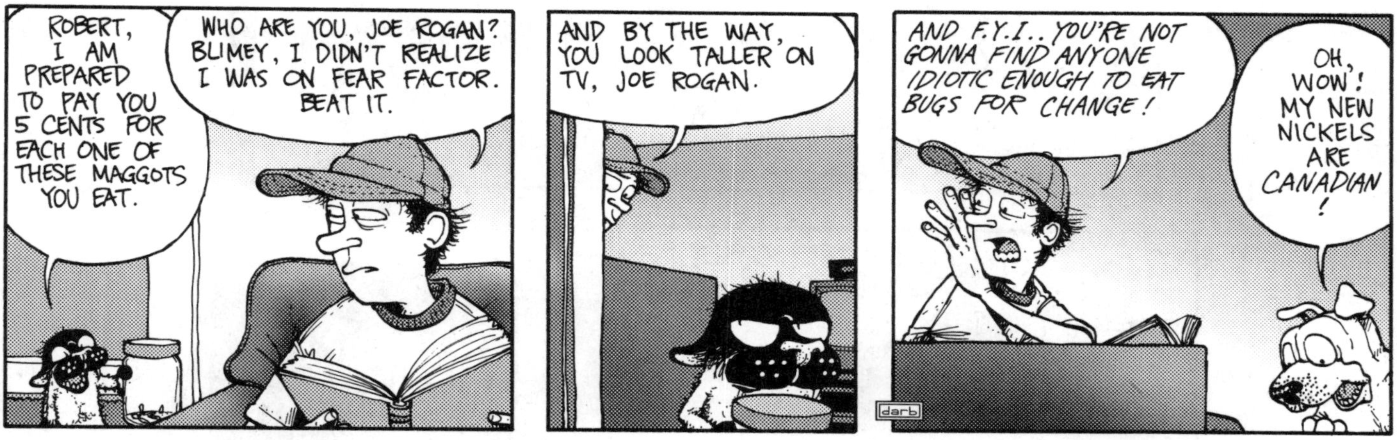
ROBERT, I AM PREPARED TO PAY YOU 5 CENTS FOR EACH ONE OF THESE MAGGOTS YOU EAT.
WHO ARE YOU, JOE ROGAN? BLIMEY, I DIDN'T REALIZE I WAS ON FEAR FACTOR. BEAT IT.
AND BY THE WAY, YOU LOOK TALLER ON TV, JOE ROGAN.
AND F.Y.I.. YOU'RE NOT GONNA FIND ANYONE IDIOTIC ENOUGH TO EAT BUGS FOR CHANGE!
OH, WOW! MY NEW NICKELS ARE CANADIAN!

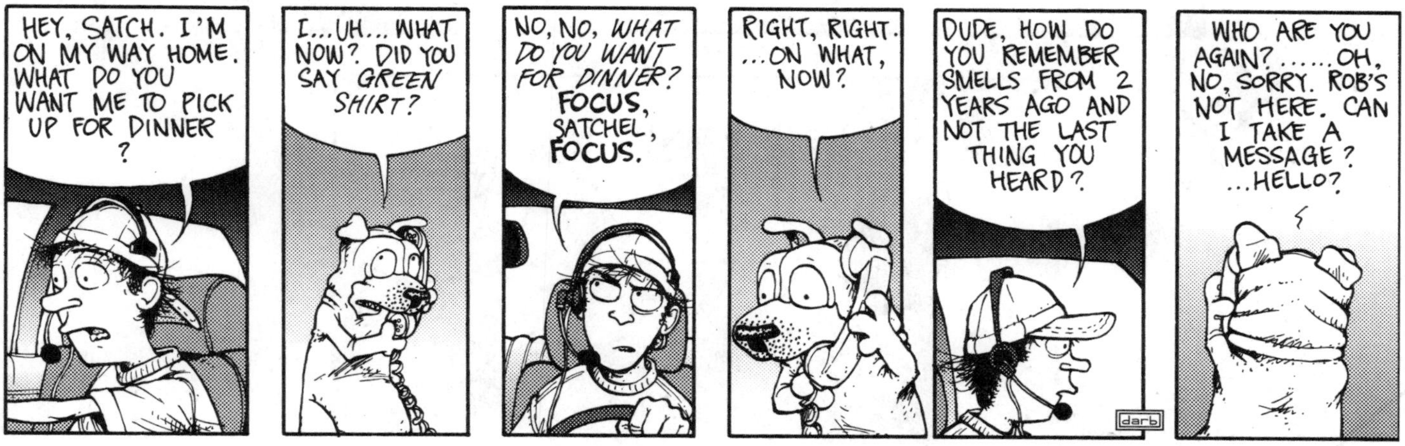
HEY, SATCH. I'M ON MY WAY HOME. WHAT DO YOU WANT ME TO PICK UP FOR DINNER?
I...UH...WHAT NOW? DID YOU SAY GREEN SHIRT?
NO, NO, WHAT DO YOU WANT FOR DINNER? FOCUS, SATCHEL, FOCUS.
RIGHT, RIGHT. ...ON WHAT, NOW?
DUDE, HOW DO YOU REMEMBER SMELLS FROM 2 YEARS AGO AND NOT THE LAST THING YOU HEARD?
WHO ARE YOU AGAIN? ......OH, NO, SORRY. ROB'S NOT HERE. CAN I TAKE A MESSAGE? ...HELLO?

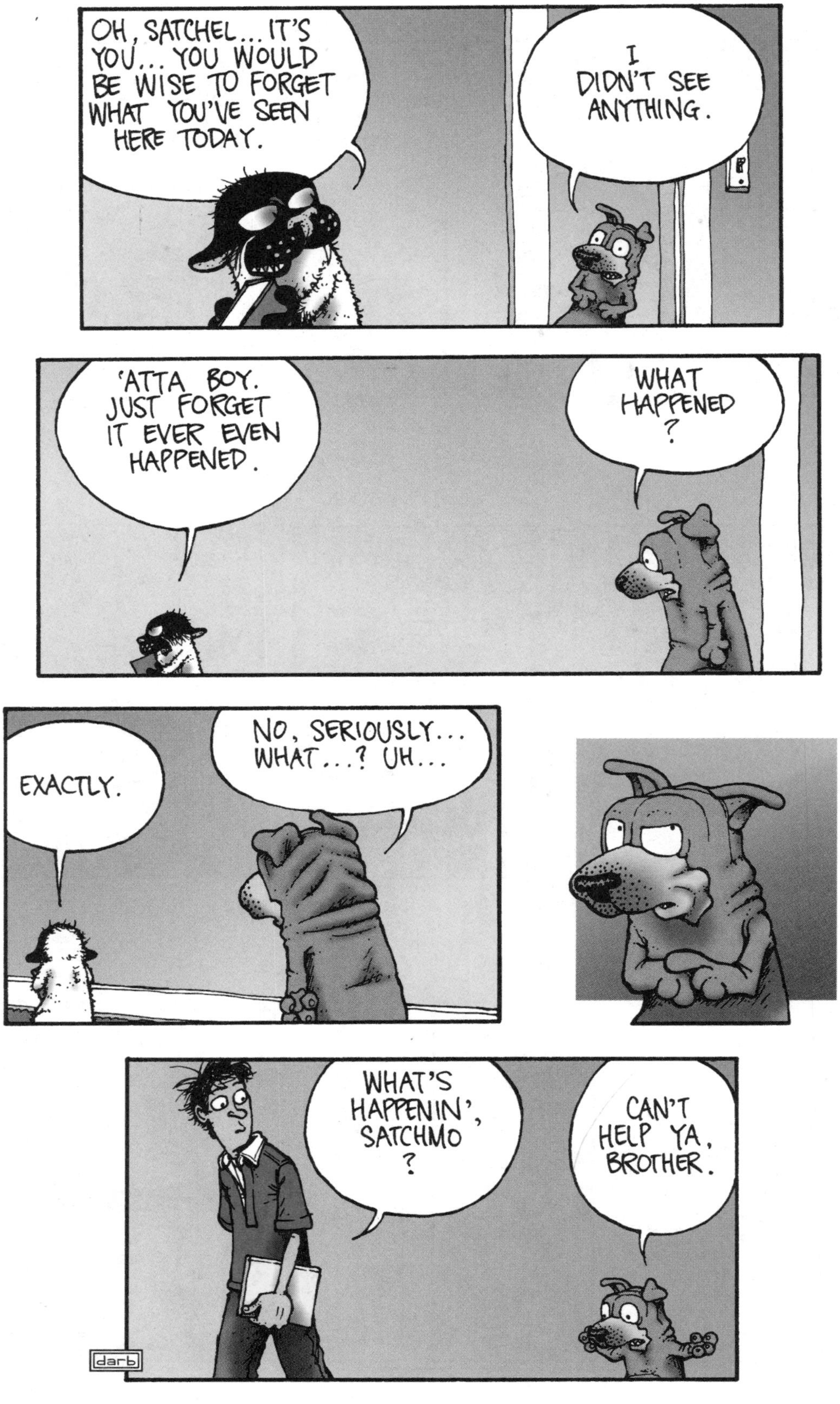
OH, SATCHEL... IT'S YOU... YOU WOULD BE WISE TO FORGET WHAT YOU'VE SEEN HERE TODAY.
I DIDN'T SEE ANYTHING.
'ATTA BOY. JUST FORGET IT EVER EVEN HAPPENED.
WHAT HAPPENED ?
EXACTLY.
NO, SERIOUSLY... WHAT...? UH...
WHAT'S HAPPENIN', SATCHMO ?
CAN'T HELP YA, BROTHER.
darb

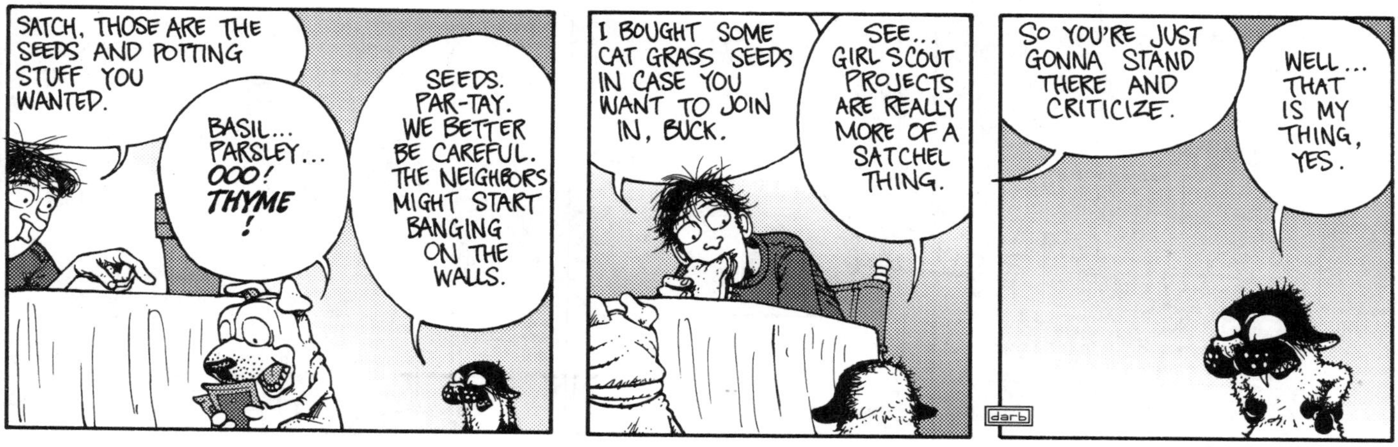
SATCH, THOSE ARE THE SEEDS AND POTTING STUFF YOU WANTED.
BASIL... PARSLEY... OOO! THYME!
SEEDS. PAR-TAY. WE BETTER BE CAREFUL. THE NEIGHBORS MIGHT START BANGING ON THE WALLS.
I BOUGHT SOME CAT GRASS SEEDS IN CASE YOU WANT TO JOIN IN, BUCK.
SEE... GIRL SCOUT PROJECTS ARE REALLY MORE OF A SATCHEL THING.
SO YOU'RE JUST GONNA STAND THERE AND CRITICIZE.
WELL... THAT IS MY THING, YES.
darb

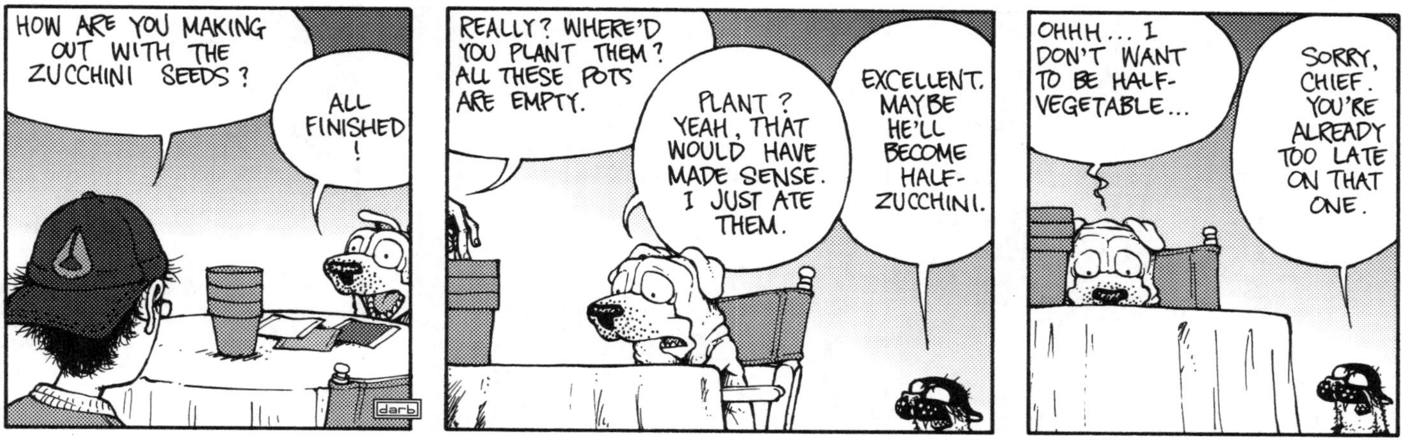
HOW ARE YOU MAKING OUT WITH THE ZUCCHINI SEEDS?
ALL FINISHED!
darb
REALLY? WHERE'D YOU PLANT THEM? ALL THESE POTS ARE EMPTY.
PLANT? YEAH, THAT WOULD HAVE MADE SENSE. I JUST ATE THEM.
EXCELLENT. MAYBE HE'LL BECOME HALF-ZUCCHINI.
OHHH... I DON'T WANT TO BE HALF-VEGETABLE...
SORRY, CHIEF. YOU'RE ALREADY TOO LATE ON THAT ONE.

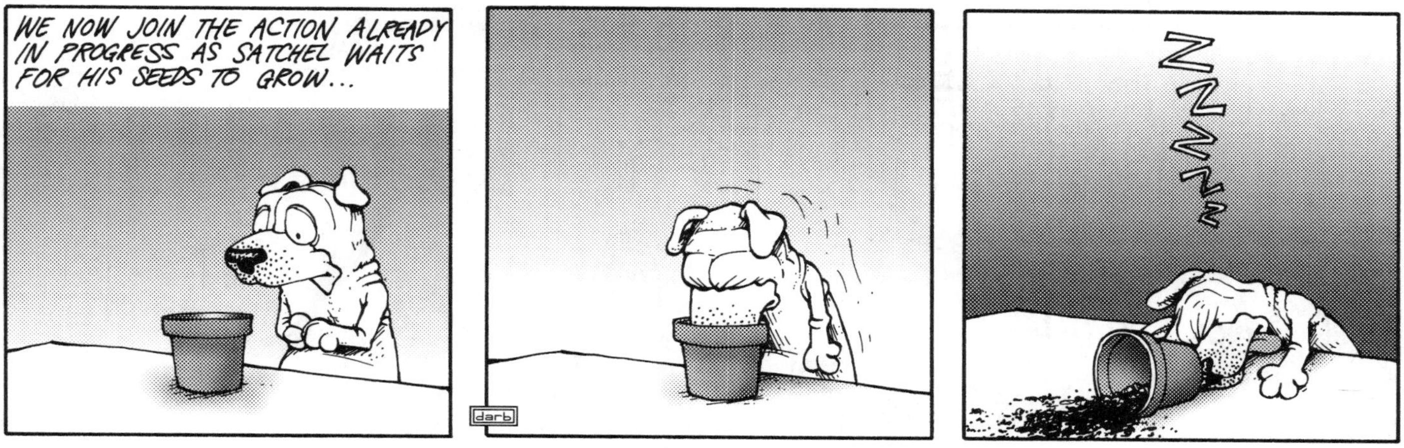
WE NOW JOIN THE ACTION ALREADY IN PROGRESS AS SATCHEL WAITS FOR HIS SEEDS TO GROW...
darb
ZZZZZ

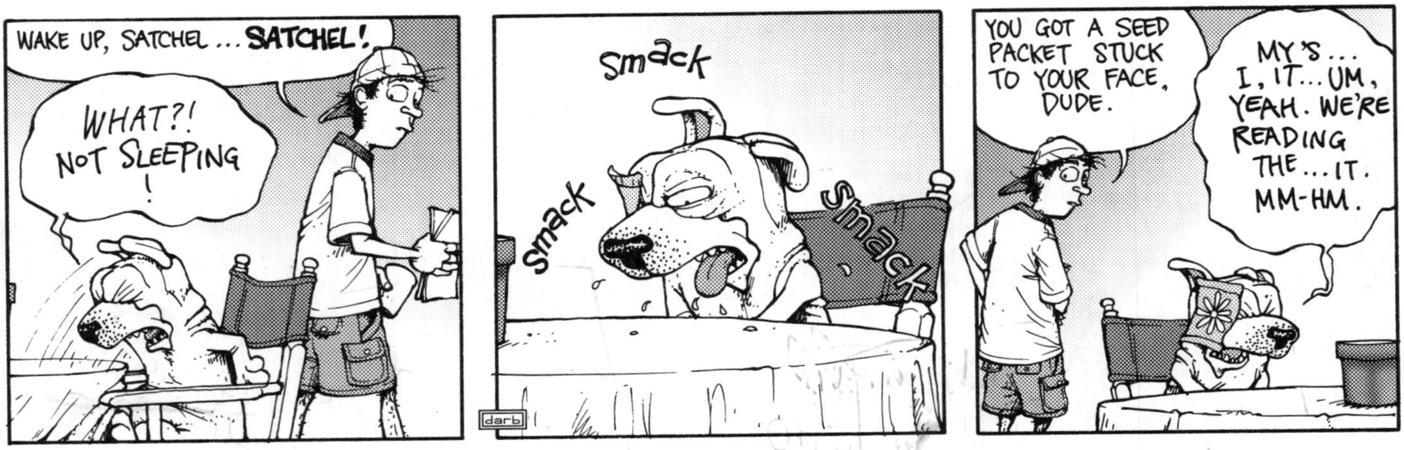
WAKE UP, SATCHEL ... **SATCHEL!**
WHAT?! NOT SLEEPING !
smack
smack
smack
YOU GOT A SEED PACKET STUCK TO YOUR FACE, DUDE.
MY'S ... I, IT... UM, YEAH. WE'RE READING THE... IT. MM-HM.

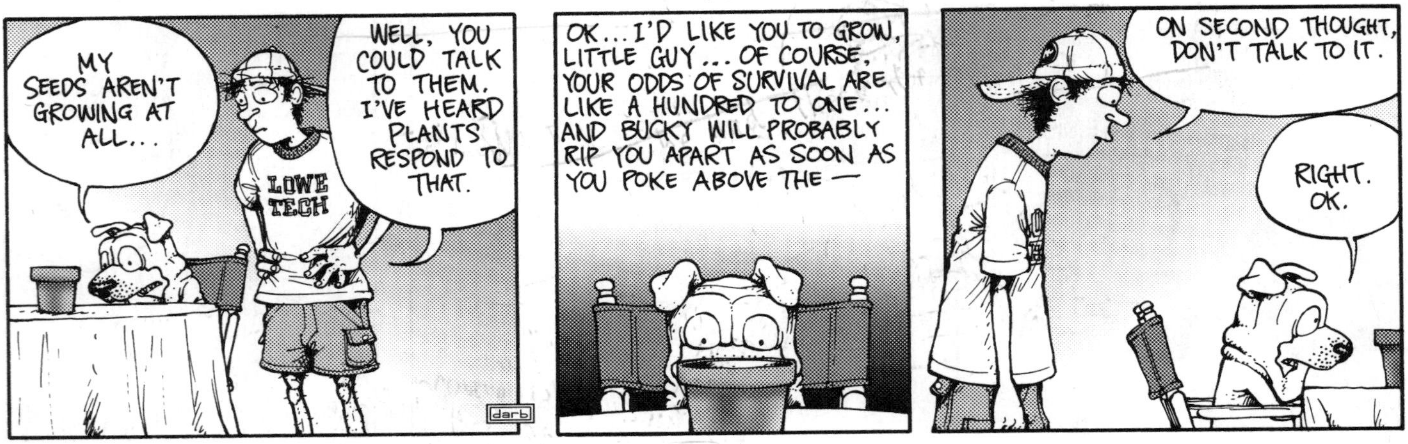
MY SEEDS AREN'T GROWING AT ALL...
LOWE TECH
WELL, YOU COULD TALK TO THEM. I'VE HEARD PLANTS RESPOND TO THAT.
OK... I'D LIKE YOU TO GROW, LITTLE GUY... OF COURSE, YOUR ODDS OF SURVIVAL ARE LIKE A HUNDRED TO ONE... AND BUCKY WILL PROBABLY RIP YOU APART AS SOON AS YOU POKE ABOVE THE —
ON SECOND THOUGHT, DON'T TALK TO IT.
RIGHT. OK.

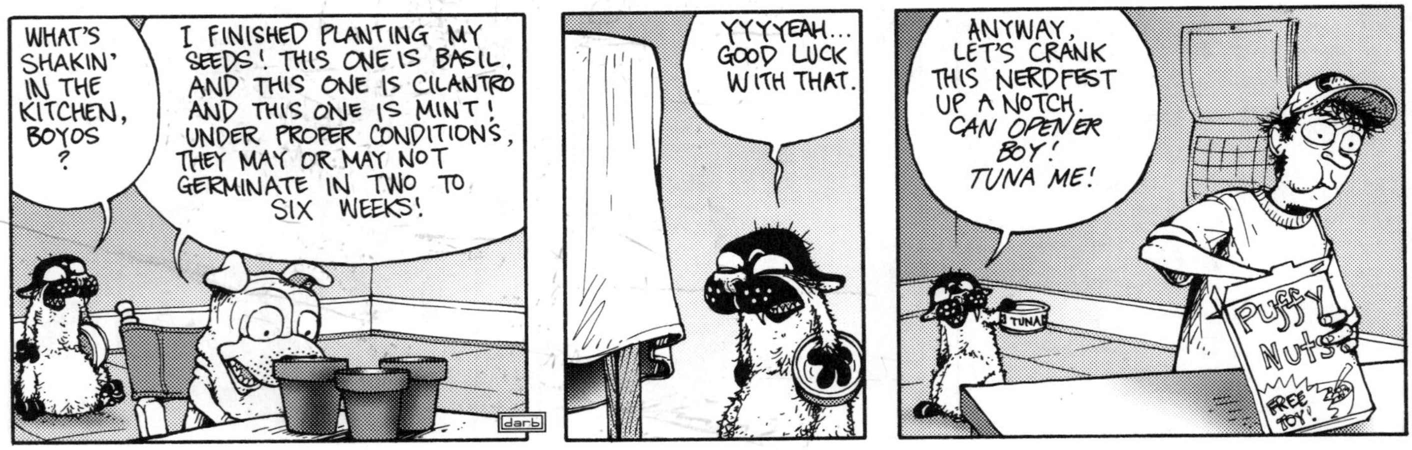
WHAT'S SHAKIN' IN THE KITCHEN, BOYOS ?
I FINISHED PLANTING MY SEEDS! THIS ONE IS BASIL, AND THIS ONE IS CILANTRO AND THIS ONE IS MINT! UNDER PROPER CONDITIONS, THEY MAY OR MAY NOT GERMINATE IN TWO TO SIX WEEKS!
YYYYEAH... GOOD LUCK WITH THAT.
ANYWAY, LET'S CRANK THIS NERDFEST UP A NOTCH. CAN OPENER BOY! TUNA ME!
TUNA
Puffy Nuts
FREE TOY!

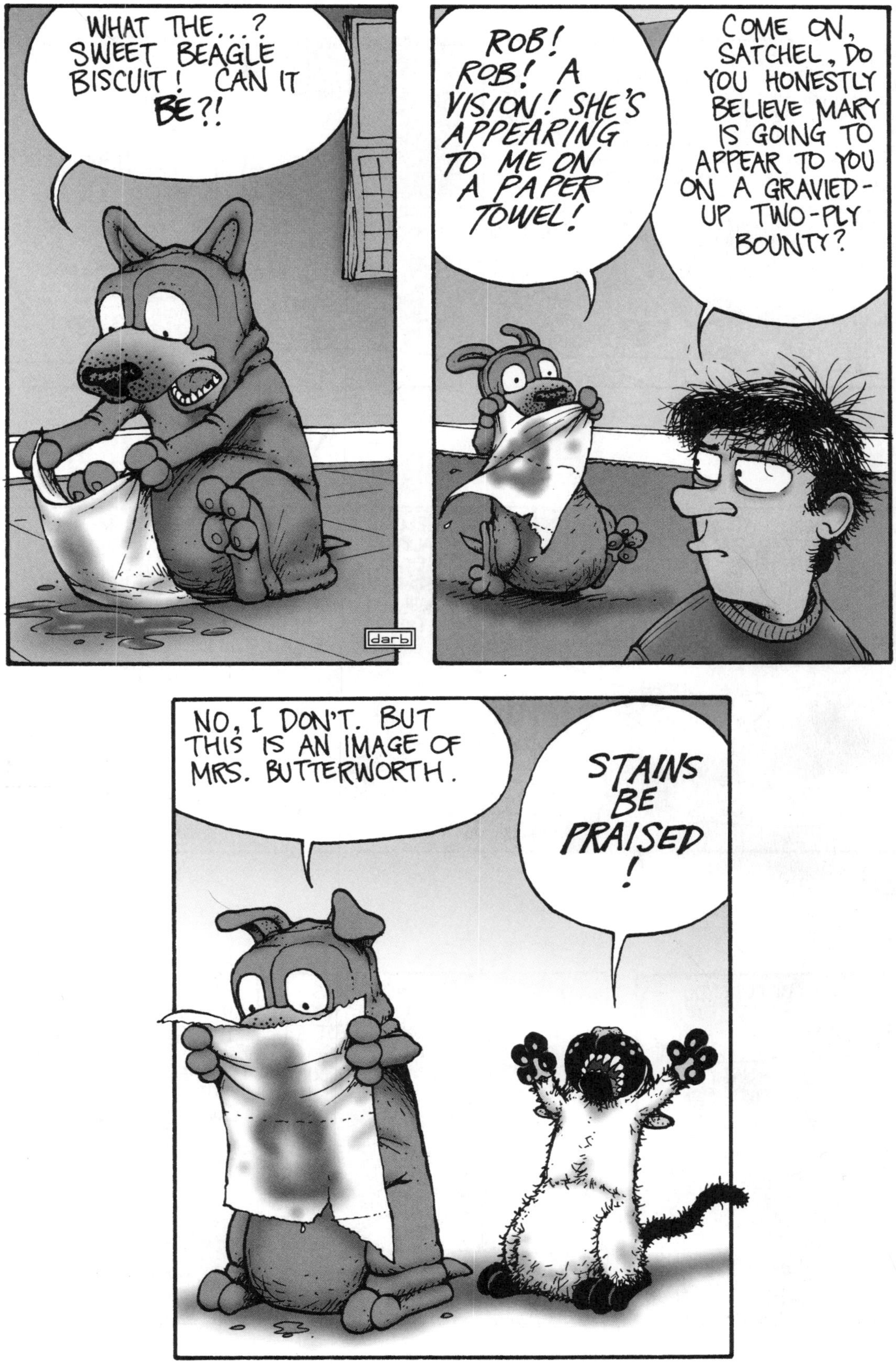
WHAT THE...? SWEET BEAGLE BISCUIT! CAN IT BE?!
darb
ROB! ROB! A VISION! SHE'S APPEARING TO ME ON A PAPER TOWEL!
COME ON, SATCHEL, DO YOU HONESTLY BELIEVE MARY IS GOING TO APPEAR TO YOU ON A GRAVIED-UP TWO-PLY BOUNTY?
NO, I DON'T. BUT THIS IS AN IMAGE OF MRS. BUTTERWORTH.
STAINS BE PRAISED!

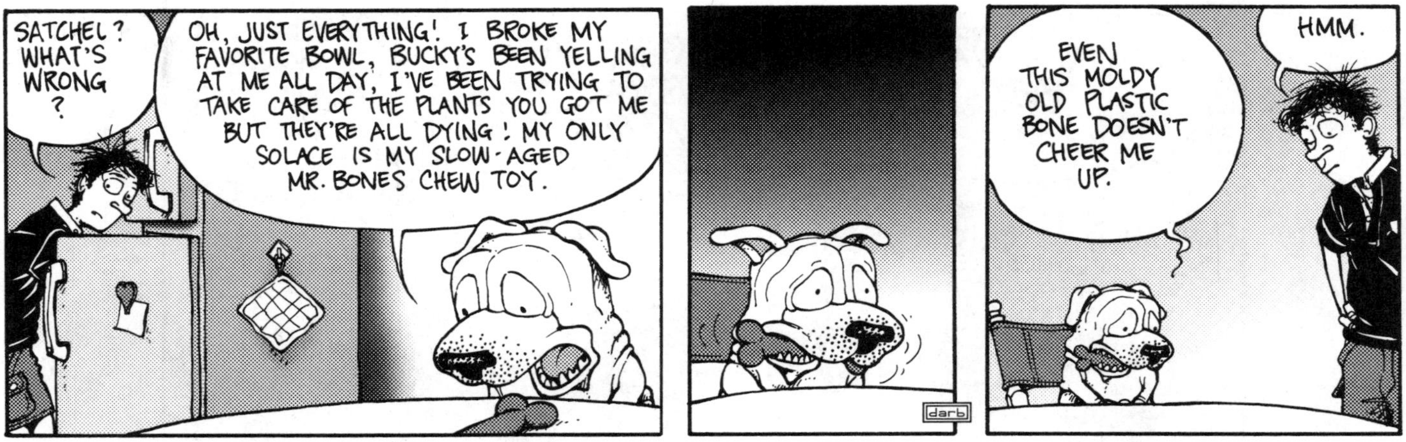
SATCHEL? WHAT'S WRONG?
OH, JUST EVERYTHING! I BROKE MY FAVORITE BOWL, BUCKY'S BEEN YELLING AT ME ALL DAY, I'VE BEEN TRYING TO TAKE CARE OF THE PLANTS YOU GOT ME BUT THEY'RE ALL DYING! MY ONLY SOLACE IS MY SLOW-AGED MR. BONES CHEW TOY.
EVEN THIS MOLDY OLD PLASTIC BONE DOESN'T CHEER ME UP.
HMM.
darb

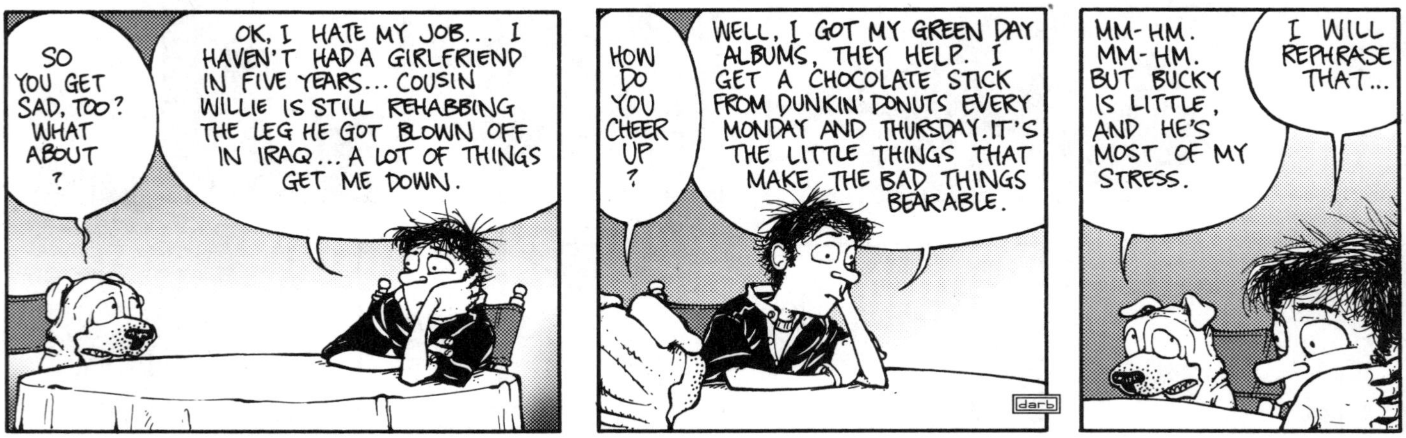
SO YOU GET SAD, TOO? WHAT ABOUT?
OK, I HATE MY JOB... I HAVEN'T HAD A GIRLFRIEND IN FIVE YEARS... COUSIN WILLIE IS STILL REHABBING THE LEG HE GOT BLOWN OFF IN IRAQ... A LOT OF THINGS GET ME DOWN.
HOW DO YOU CHEER UP?
WELL, I GOT MY GREEN DAY ALBUMS, THEY HELP. I GET A CHOCOLATE STICK FROM DUNKIN' DONUTS EVERY MONDAY AND THURSDAY. IT'S THE LITTLE THINGS THAT MAKE THE BAD THINGS BEARABLE.
darb
MM-HM. MM-HM. BUT BUCKY IS LITTLE, AND HE'S MOST OF MY STRESS.
I WILL REPHRASE THAT...

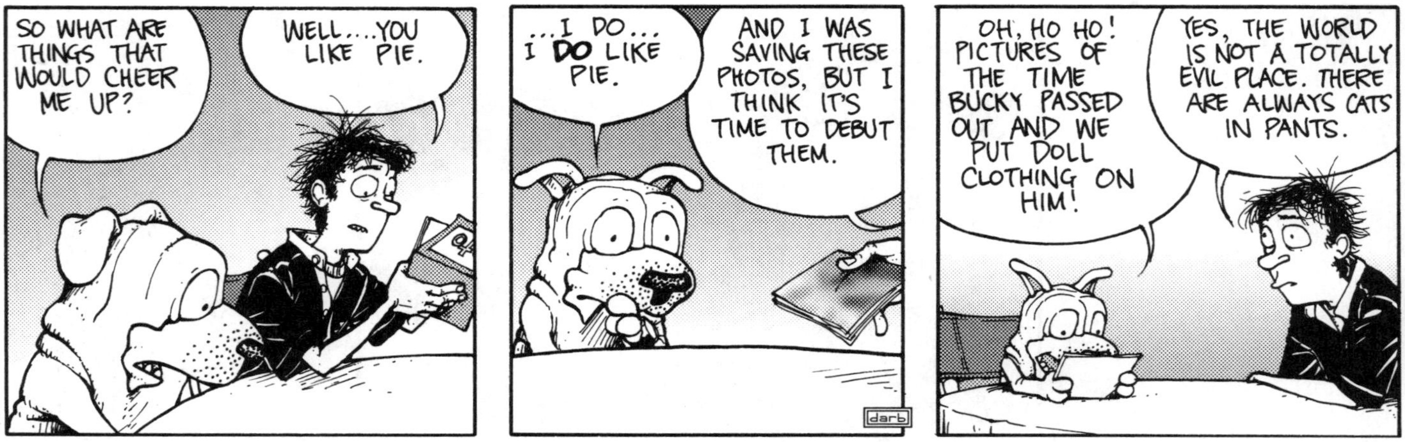
SO WHAT ARE THINGS THAT WOULD CHEER ME UP?
WELL....YOU LIKE PIE.
...I DO... I **DO** LIKE PIE.
AND I WAS SAVING THESE PHOTOS, BUT I THINK IT'S TIME TO DEBUT THEM.
darb
OH, HO HO! PICTURES OF THE TIME BUCKY PASSED OUT AND WE PUT DOLL CLOTHING ON HIM!
YES, THE WORLD IS NOT A TOTALLY EVIL PLACE. THERE ARE ALWAYS CATS IN PANTS.

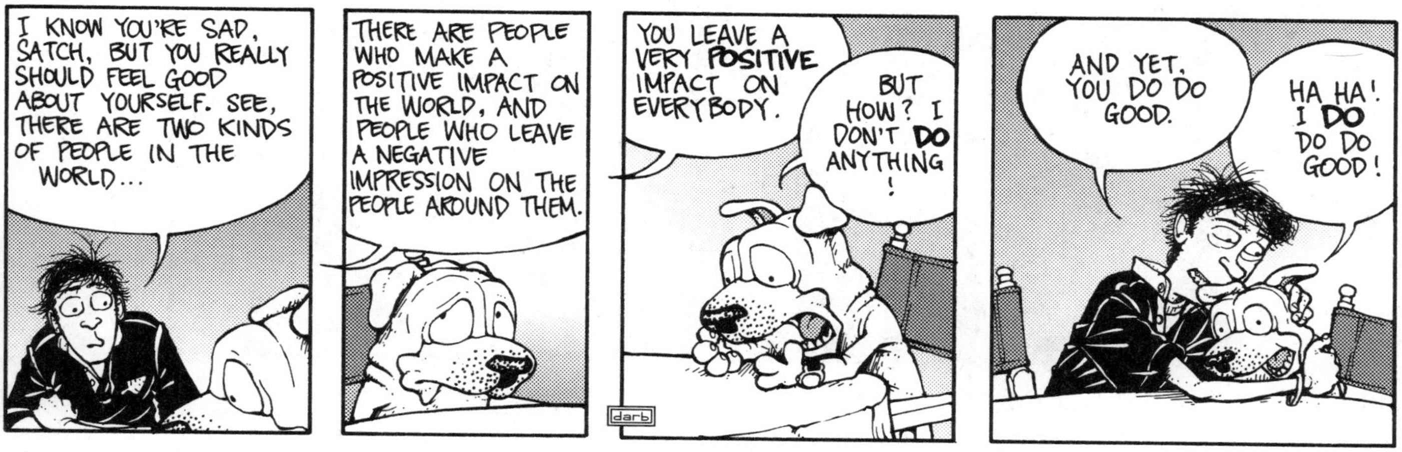
I KNOW YOU'RE SAD, SATCH, BUT YOU REALLY SHOULD FEEL GOOD ABOUT YOURSELF. SEE, THERE ARE TWO KINDS OF PEOPLE IN THE WORLD...
THERE ARE PEOPLE WHO MAKE A POSITIVE IMPACT ON THE WORLD, AND PEOPLE WHO LEAVE A NEGATIVE IMPRESSION ON THE PEOPLE AROUND THEM.
YOU LEAVE A VERY **POSITIVE** IMPACT ON EVERYBODY.
BUT HOW? I DON'T **DO** ANYTHING!
AND YET, YOU DO DO GOOD.
HA HA! I **DO** DO DO GOOD!
darb

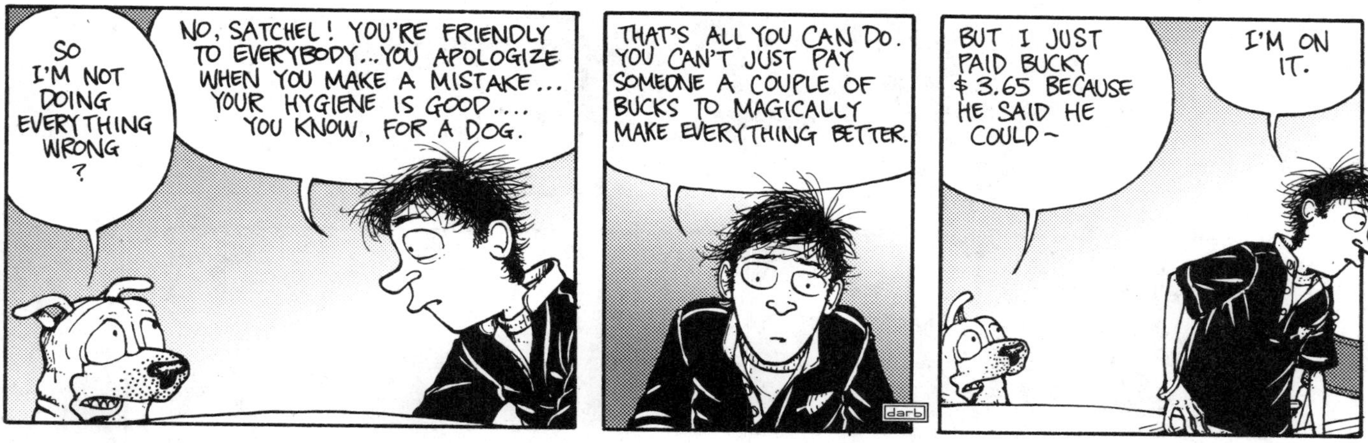
SO I'M NOT DOING EVERYTHING WRONG?
NO, SATCHEL! YOU'RE FRIENDLY TO EVERYBODY...YOU APOLOGIZE WHEN YOU MAKE A MISTAKE... YOUR HYGIENE IS GOOD.... YOU KNOW, FOR A DOG.
THAT'S ALL YOU CAN DO. YOU CAN'T JUST PAY SOMEONE A COUPLE OF BUCKS TO MAGICALLY MAKE EVERYTHING BETTER.
darb
BUT I JUST PAID BUCKY $3.65 BECAUSE HE SAID HE COULD~
I'M ON IT.

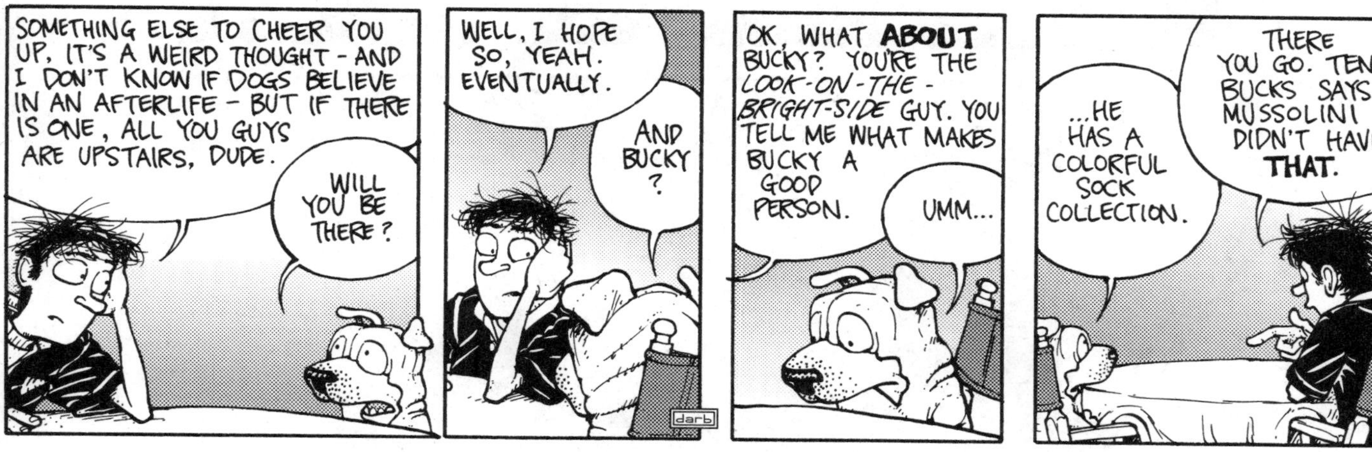
SOMETHING ELSE TO CHEER YOU UP, IT'S A WEIRD THOUGHT - AND I DON'T KNOW IF DOGS BELIEVE IN AN AFTERLIFE - BUT IF THERE IS ONE, ALL YOU GUYS ARE UPSTAIRS, DUDE.
WILL YOU BE THERE?
WELL, I HOPE SO, YEAH. EVENTUALLY.
AND BUCKY?
darb
OK, WHAT **ABOUT** BUCKY? YOU'RE THE *LOOK-ON-THE-BRIGHT-SIDE* GUY. YOU TELL ME WHAT MAKES BUCKY A GOOD PERSON.
UMM...
...HE HAS A COLORFUL SOCK COLLECTION.
THERE YOU GO. TEN BUCKS SAYS MUSSOLINI DIDN'T HAVE **THAT**.

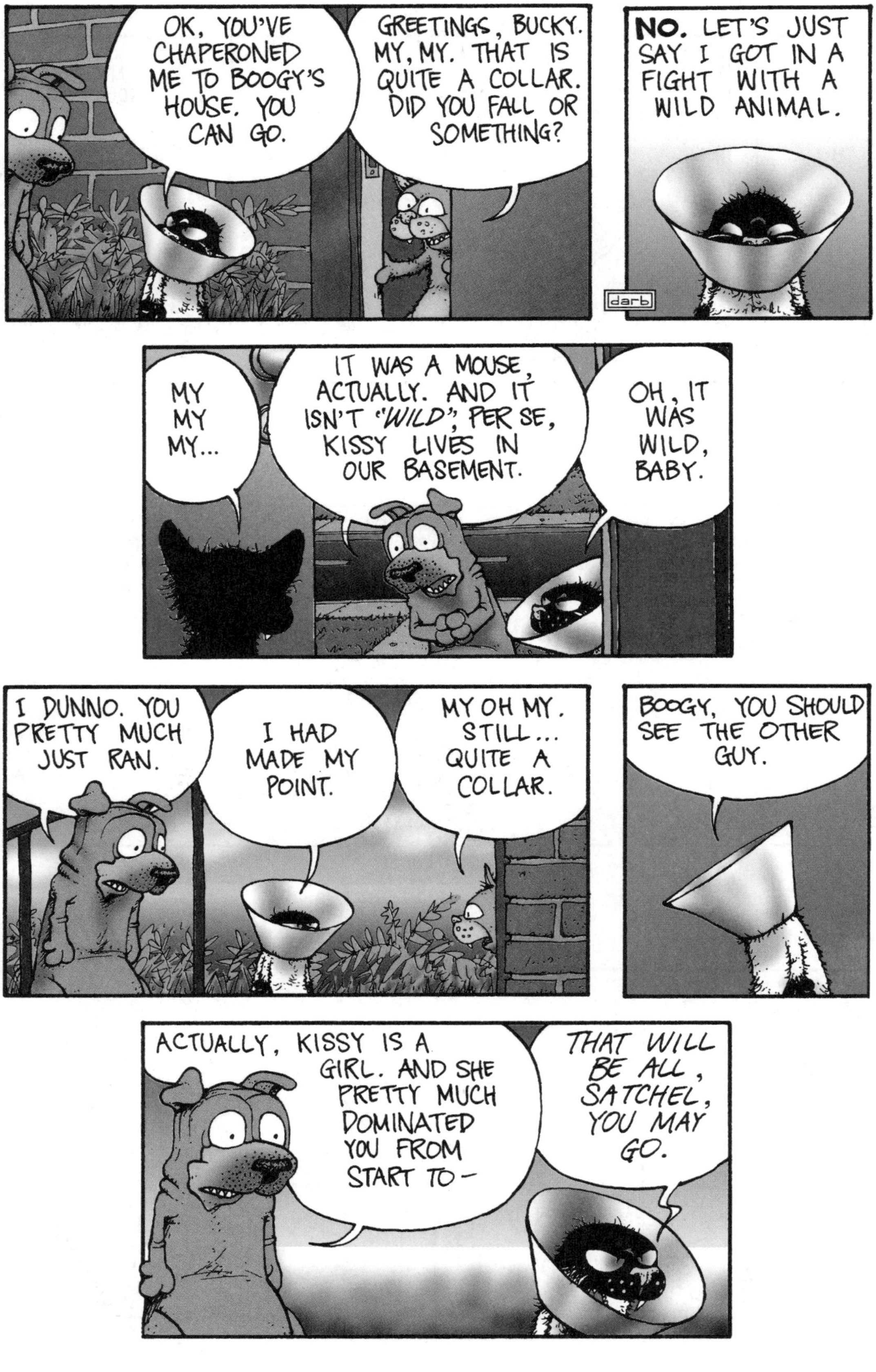
OK, YOU'VE CHAPERONED ME TO BOOGY'S HOUSE. YOU CAN GO.
GREETINGS, BUCKY. MY, MY. THAT IS QUITE A COLLAR. DID YOU FALL OR SOMETHING?
NO. LET'S JUST SAY I GOT IN A FIGHT WITH A WILD ANIMAL.
darb
MY MY MY...
IT WAS A MOUSE, ACTUALLY. AND IT ISN'T "WILD", PER SE, KISSY LIVES IN OUR BASEMENT.
OH, IT WAS WILD, BABY.
I DUNNO. YOU PRETTY MUCH JUST RAN.
I HAD MADE MY POINT.
MY OH MY. STILL... QUITE A COLLAR.
BOOGY, YOU SHOULD SEE THE OTHER GUY.
ACTUALLY, KISSY IS A GIRL. AND SHE PRETTY MUCH DOMINATED YOU FROM START TO-
THAT WILL BE ALL, SATCHEL, YOU MAY GO.

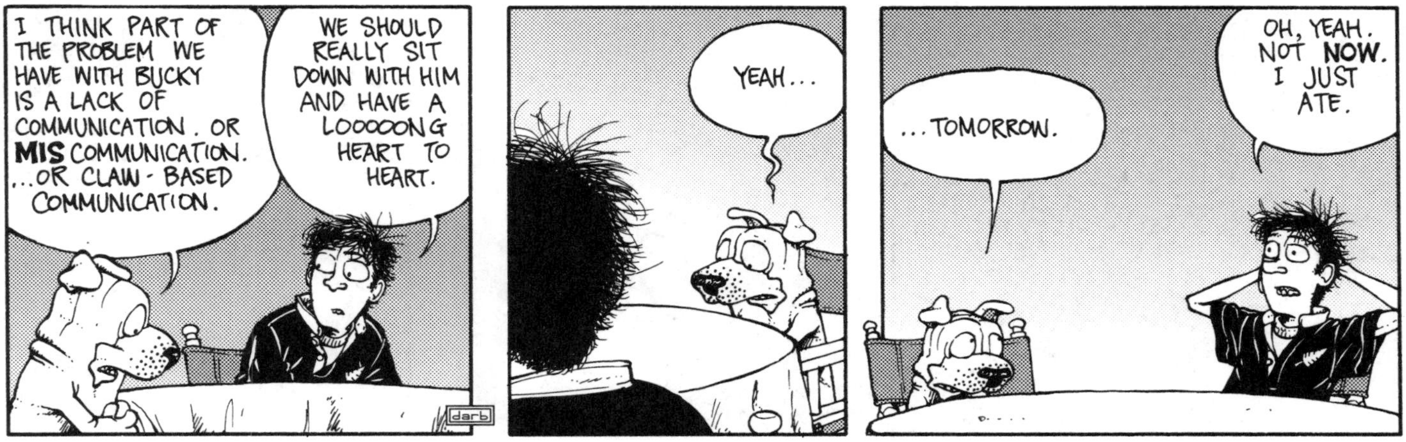
I THINK PART OF THE PROBLEM WE HAVE WITH BUCKY IS A LACK OF COMMUNICATION. OR **MIS**COMMUNICATION. ...OR CLAW-BASED COMMUNICATION.
WE SHOULD REALLY SIT DOWN WITH HIM AND HAVE A LOOOOONG HEART TO HEART.
YEAH...
...TOMORROW.
OH, YEAH. NOT **NOW**. I JUST ATE.
darb

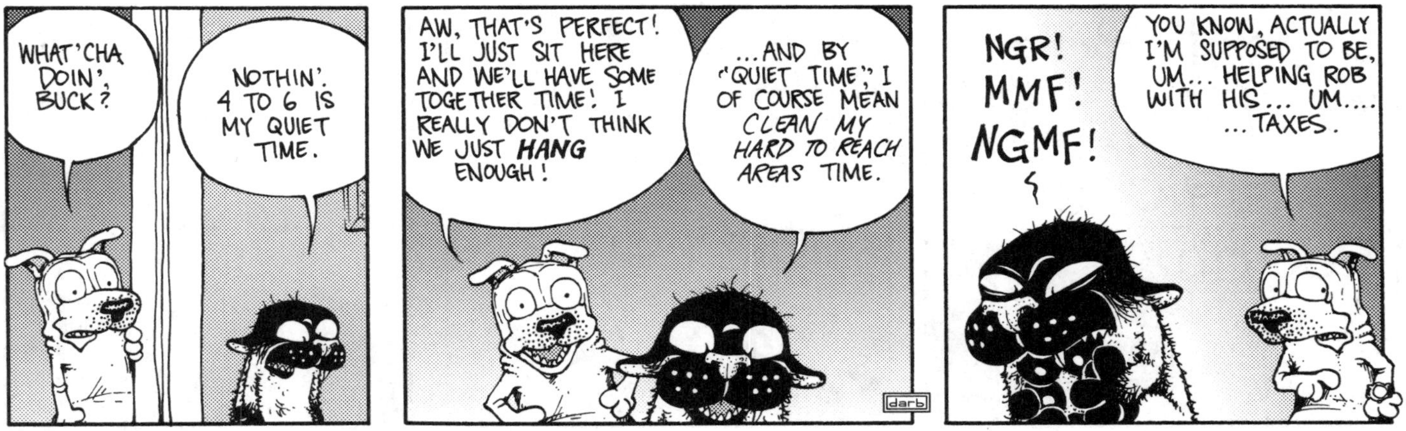
WHAT'CHA DOIN', BUCK?
NOTHIN'. 4 TO 6 IS MY QUIET TIME.
AW, THAT'S PERFECT! I'LL JUST SIT HERE AND WE'LL HAVE SOME TOGETHER TIME! I REALLY DON'T THINK WE JUST **HANG** ENOUGH!
...AND BY "QUIET TIME," I OF COURSE MEAN *CLEAN MY HARD TO REACH AREAS* TIME.
darb
NGR! MMF! NGMF!
YOU KNOW, ACTUALLY I'M SUPPOSED TO BE, UM... HELPING ROB WITH HIS... UM.... ...TAXES.

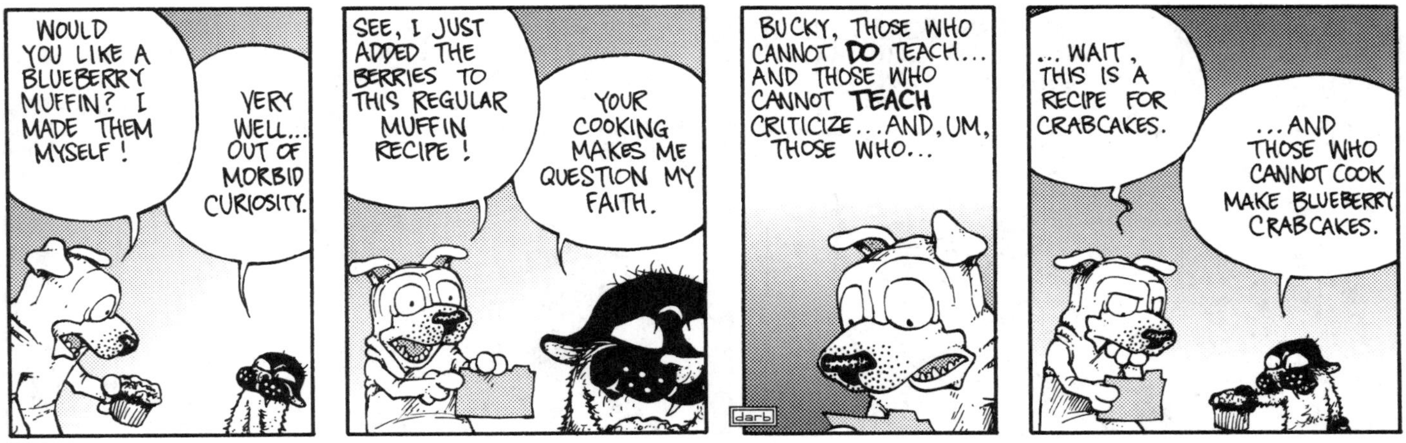
WOULD YOU LIKE A BLUEBERRY MUFFIN? I MADE THEM MYSELF!
VERY WELL... OUT OF MORBID CURIOSITY.
SEE, I JUST ADDED THE BERRIES TO THIS REGULAR MUFFIN RECIPE!
YOUR COOKING MAKES ME QUESTION MY FAITH.
BUCKY, THOSE WHO CANNOT **DO** TEACH... AND THOSE WHO CANNOT **TEACH** CRITICIZE... AND, UM, THOSE WHO...
darb
...WAIT, THIS IS A RECIPE FOR CRABCAKES.
...AND THOSE WHO CANNOT COOK MAKE BLUEBERRY CRABCAKES.

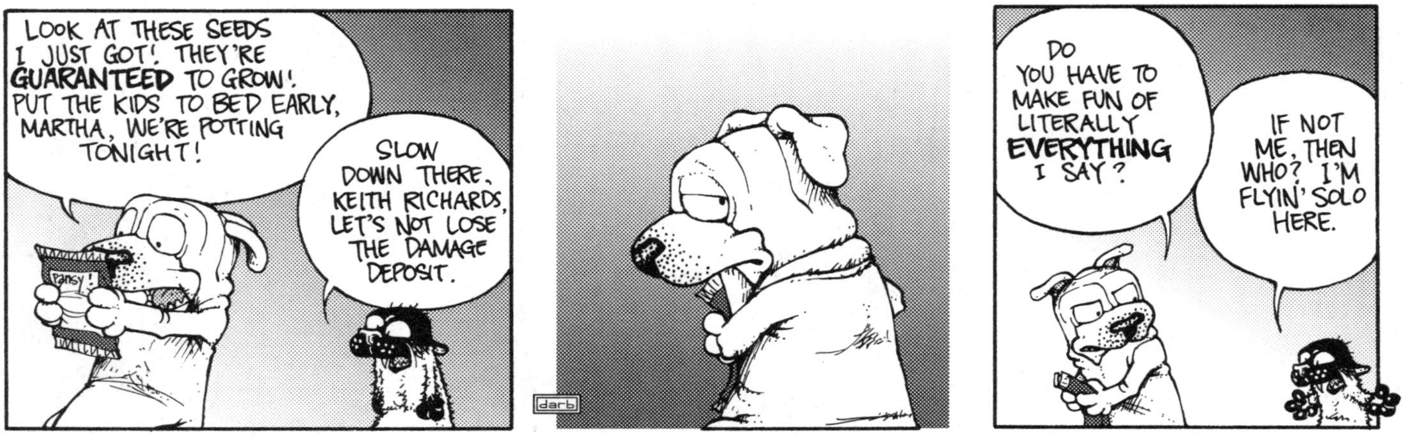
LOOK AT THESE SEEDS I JUST GOT! THEY'RE **GUARANTEED** TO GROW! PUT THE KIDS TO BED EARLY, MARTHA, WE'RE POTTING TONIGHT!
SLOW DOWN THERE, KEITH RICHARDS, LET'S NOT LOSE THE DAMAGE DEPOSIT.
darb
DO YOU HAVE TO MAKE FUN OF LITERALLY **EVERYTHING** I SAY?
IF NOT ME, THEN WHO? I'M FLYIN' SOLO HERE.

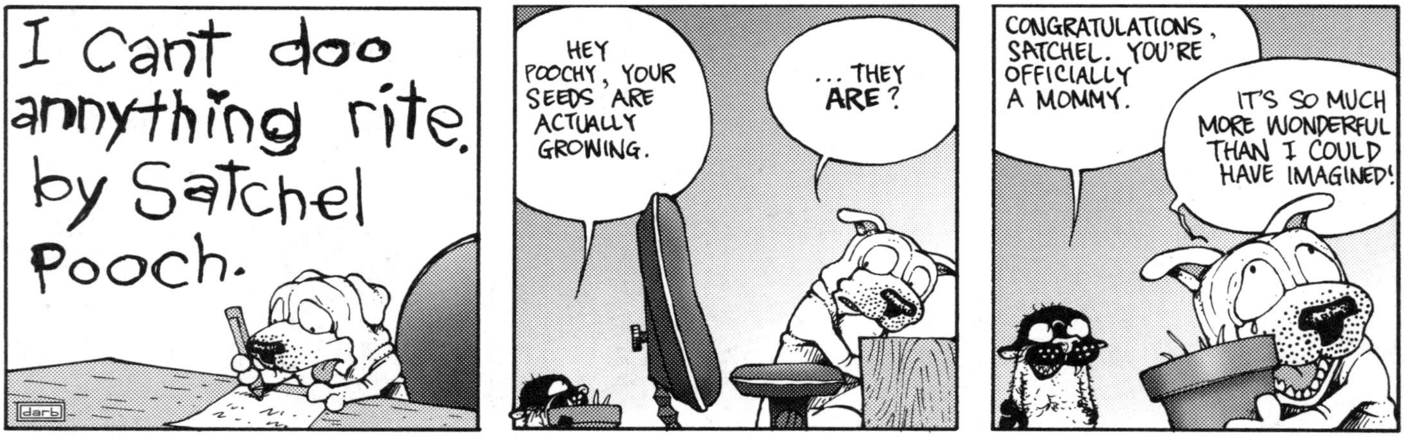
I cant doo annything rite. by Satchel Pooch.
darb
HEY POOCHY, YOUR SEEDS ARE ACTUALLY GROWING.
... THEY **ARE**?
CONGRATULATIONS, SATCHEL. YOU'RE OFFICIALLY A MOMMY.
IT'S SO MUCH MORE WONDERFUL THAN I COULD HAVE IMAGINED!

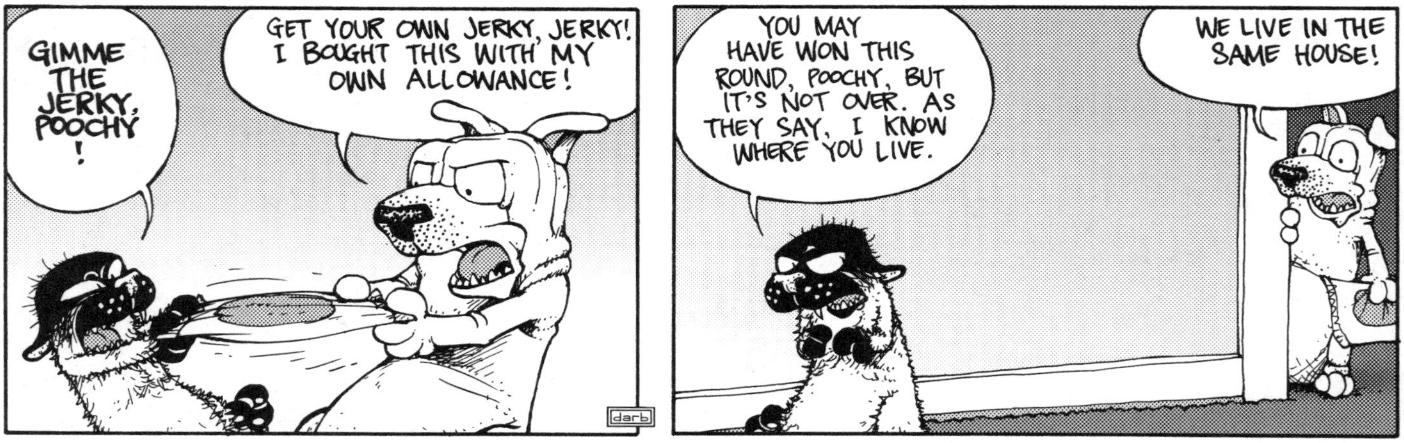
GIMME THE JERKY, POOCHY!
GET YOUR OWN JERKY, JERKY! I BOUGHT THIS WITH MY OWN ALLOWANCE!
darb
YOU MAY HAVE WON THIS ROUND, POOCHY, BUT IT'S NOT OVER. AS THEY SAY, I KNOW WHERE YOU LIVE.
WE LIVE IN THE SAME HOUSE!

I SUPPOSE YOU THINK THOSE SUNGLASSES MAKE YOU LOOK COOL, DO YA? NOT.
AND HEY! YOU'RE COPYING MY TRADEMARK RELAXED GUY SLUMP! CUT IT OUT!
OH, I GET IT. BLOWING ME OFF, EH? WELL LET'S JUST SEE WHO'S COOLEST! STARE OFF!
AWW, FORGET IT! BE THAT WAY!
zzzZZZ
darb

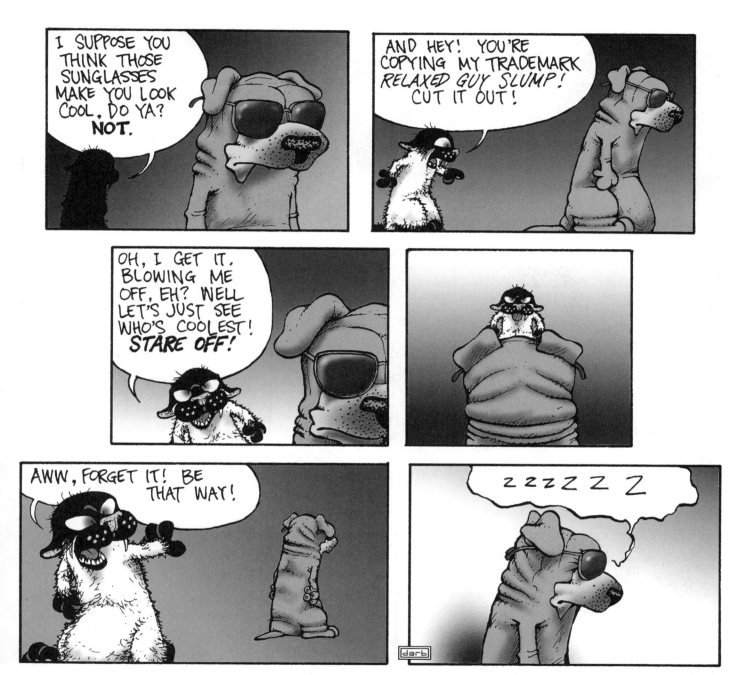

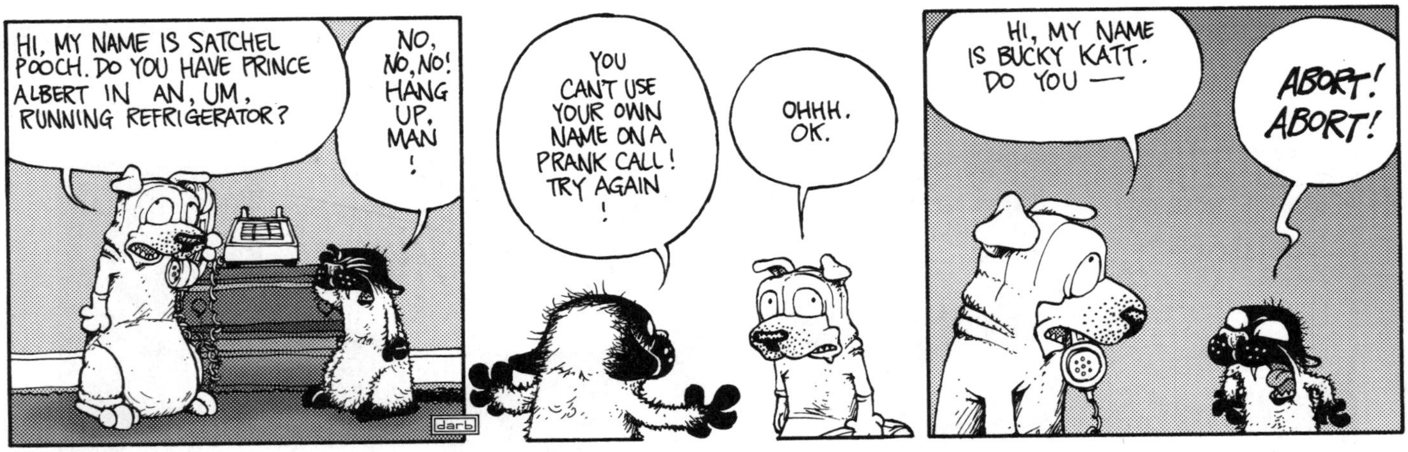
HI, MY NAME IS SATCHEL POOCH. DO YOU HAVE PRINCE ALBERT IN AN, UM, RUNNING REFRIGERATOR?
NO, NO, NO! HANG UP, MAN!
YOU CAN'T USE YOUR OWN NAME ON A PRANK CALL! TRY AGAIN!
OHHH. OK.
HI, MY NAME IS BUCKY KATT. DO YOU —
ABORT! ABORT!
darb

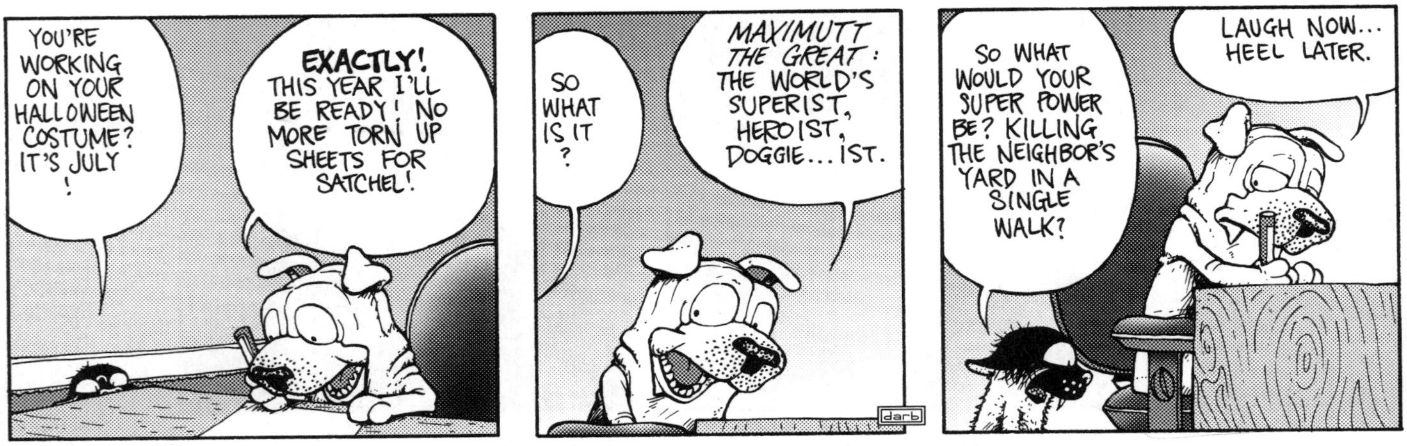
YOU'RE WORKING ON YOUR HALLOWEEN COSTUME? IT'S JULY!
EXACTLY! THIS YEAR I'LL BE READY! NO MORE TORN UP SHEETS FOR SATCHEL!
SO WHAT IS IT?
MAXIMUTT THE GREAT: THE WORLD'S SUPERIST, HEROIST, DOGGIE... IST.
SO WHAT WOULD YOUR SUPER POWER BE? KILLING THE NEIGHBOR'S YARD IN A SINGLE WALK?
LAUGH NOW... HEEL LATER.
darb

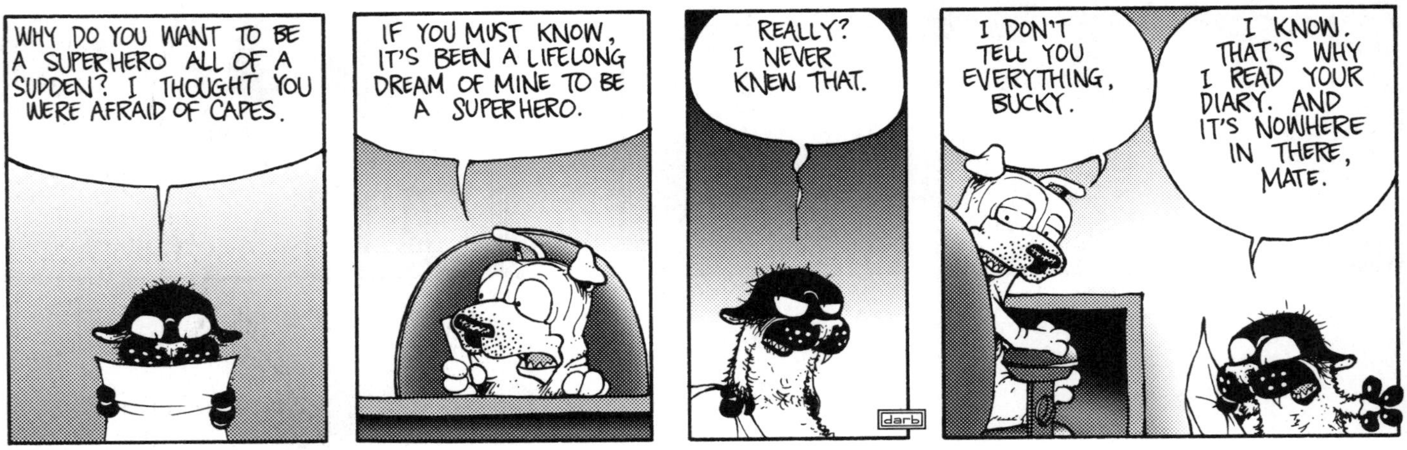
WHY DO YOU WANT TO BE A SUPERHERO ALL OF A SUDDEN? I THOUGHT YOU WERE AFRAID OF CAPES.
IF YOU MUST KNOW, IT'S BEEN A LIFELONG DREAM OF MINE TO BE A SUPERHERO.
REALLY? I NEVER KNEW THAT.
I DON'T TELL YOU EVERYTHING, BUCKY.
I KNOW. THAT'S WHY I READ YOUR DIARY. AND IT'S NOWHERE IN THERE, MATE.
darb

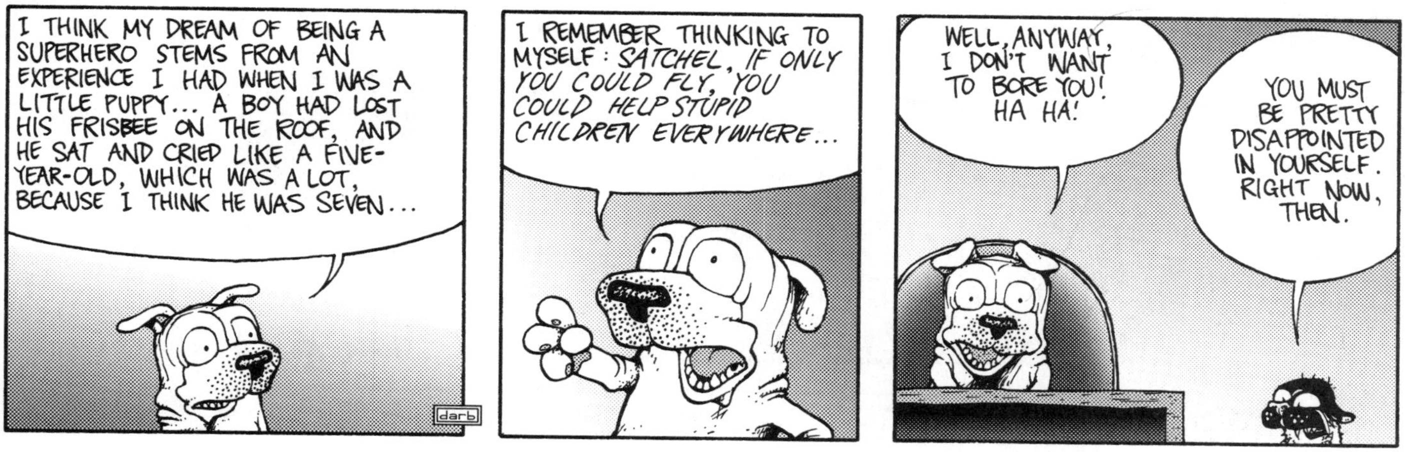
I THINK MY DREAM OF BEING A SUPERHERO STEMS FROM AN EXPERIENCE I HAD WHEN I WAS A LITTLE PUPPY... A BOY HAD LOST HIS FRISBEE ON THE ROOF, AND HE SAT AND CRIED LIKE A FIVE-YEAR-OLD, WHICH WAS A LOT, BECAUSE I THINK HE WAS SEVEN...
darb
I REMEMBER THINKING TO MYSELF: *SATCHEL, IF ONLY YOU COULD FLY, YOU COULD HELP STUPID CHILDREN EVERYWHERE...*
WELL, ANYWAY, I DON'T WANT TO BORE YOU! HA HA!
YOU MUST BE PRETTY DISAPPOINTED IN YOURSELF. RIGHT NOW, THEN.

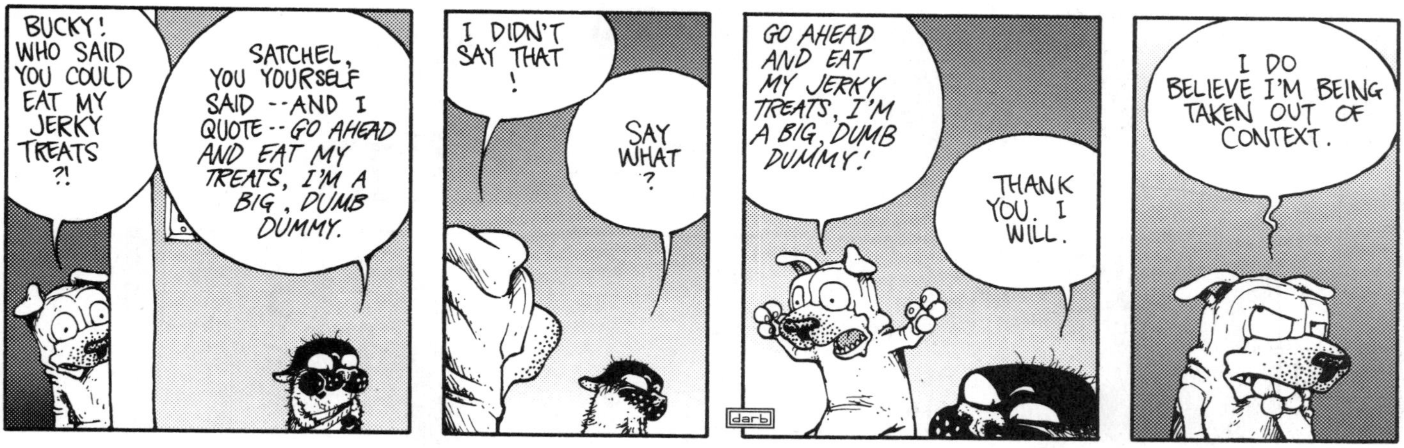
BUCKY! WHO SAID YOU COULD EAT MY JERKY TREATS ?!
SATCHEL, YOU YOURSELF SAID --AND I QUOTE-- *GO AHEAD AND EAT MY TREATS, I'M A BIG, DUMB DUMMY.*
I DIDN'T SAY THAT !
SAY WHAT ?
GO AHEAD AND EAT MY JERKY TREATS, I'M A BIG, DUMB DUMMY!
THANK YOU. I WILL.
darb
I DO BELIEVE I'M BEING TAKEN OUT OF CONTEXT.

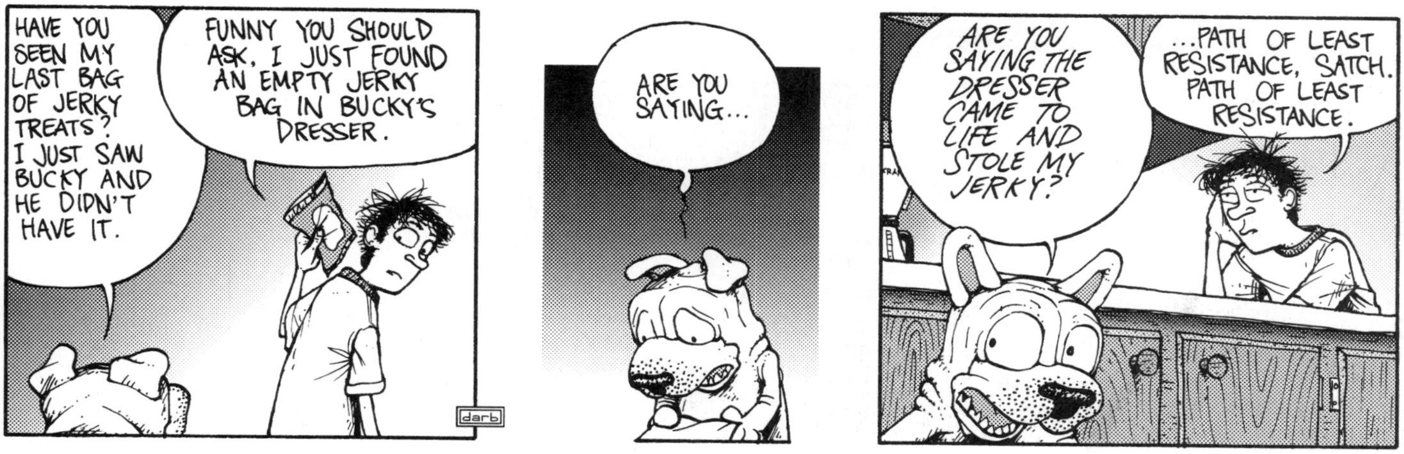
HAVE YOU SEEN MY LAST BAG OF JERKY TREATS? I JUST SAW BUCKY AND HE DIDN'T HAVE IT.
FUNNY YOU SHOULD ASK. I JUST FOUND AN EMPTY JERKY BAG IN BUCKY'S DRESSER.
darb
ARE YOU SAYING...
ARE YOU SAYING THE DRESSER CAME TO LIFE AND STOLE MY JERKY?
...PATH OF LEAST RESISTANCE, SATCH. PATH OF LEAST RESISTANCE.

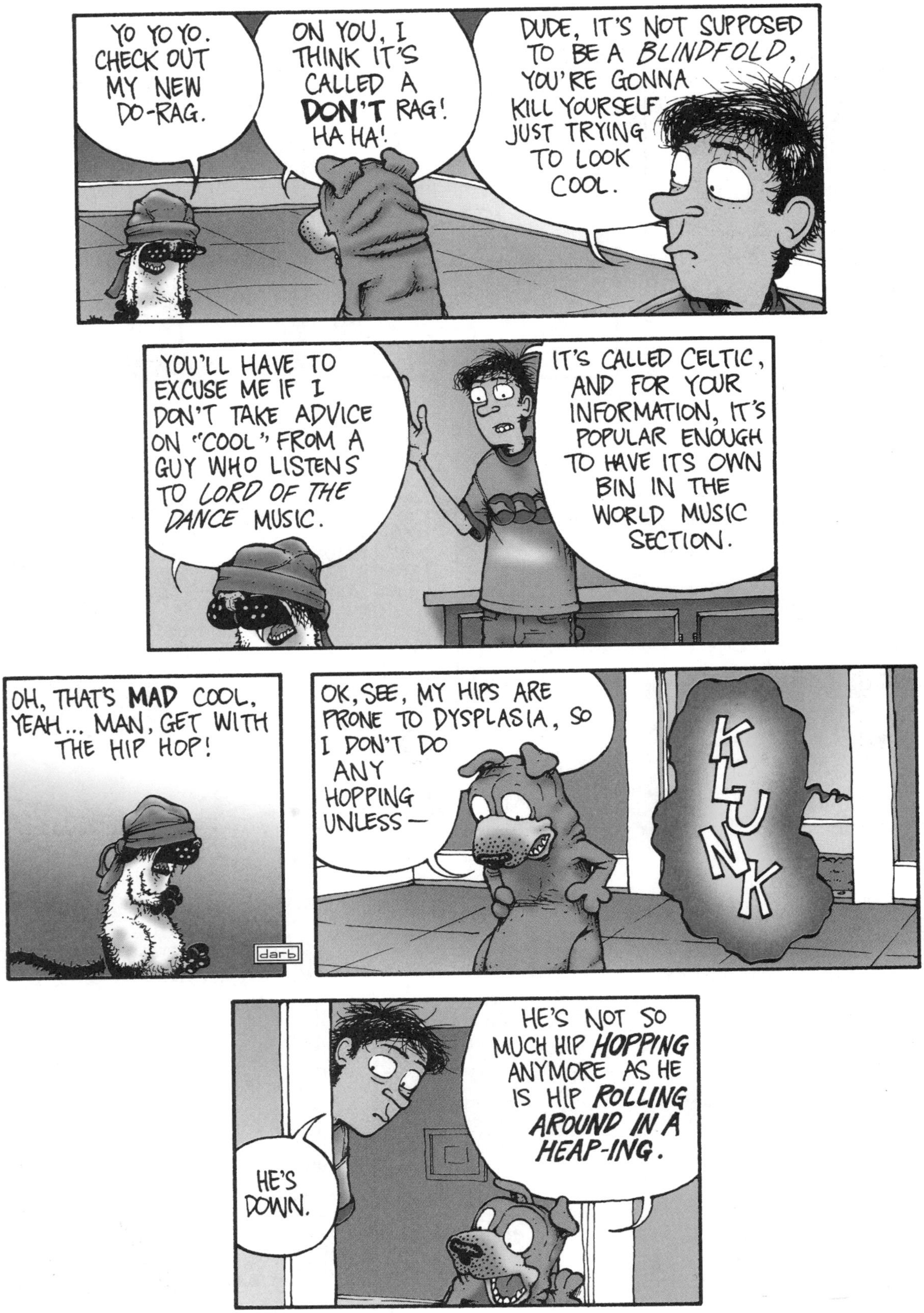
YO YO YO. CHECK OUT MY NEW DO-RAG.
ON YOU, I THINK IT'S CALLED A **DON'T** RAG! HA HA!
DUDE, IT'S NOT SUPPOSED TO BE A *BLINDFOLD*, YOU'RE GONNA KILL YOURSELF JUST TRYING TO LOOK COOL.
YOU'LL HAVE TO EXCUSE ME IF I DON'T TAKE ADVICE ON "COOL" FROM A GUY WHO LISTENS TO *LORD OF THE DANCE* MUSIC.
IT'S CALLED CELTIC, AND FOR YOUR INFORMATION, IT'S POPULAR ENOUGH TO HAVE ITS OWN BIN IN THE WORLD MUSIC SECTION.
OH, THAT'S **MAD** COOL, YEAH... MAN, GET WITH THE HIP HOP!
darb
OK, SEE, MY HIPS ARE PRONE TO DYSPLASIA, SO I DON'T DO ANY HOPPING UNLESS—
KLUNK
HE'S DOWN.
HE'S NOT SO MUCH HIP ***HOPPING*** ANYMORE AS HE IS HIP ***ROLLING AROUND IN A HEAP-ING***.

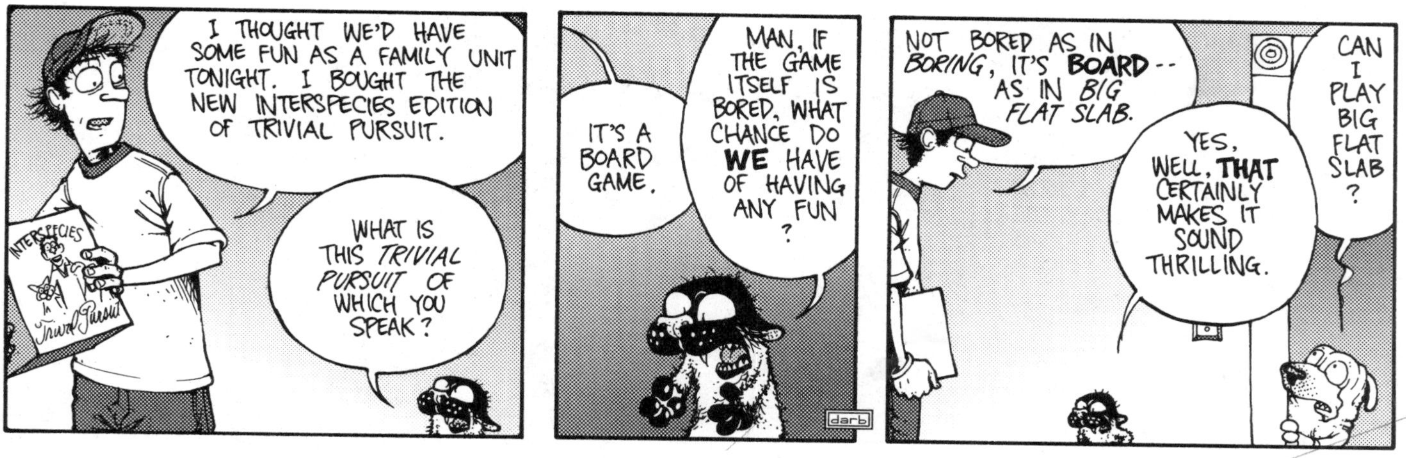
I THOUGHT WE'D HAVE SOME FUN AS A FAMILY UNIT TONIGHT. I BOUGHT THE NEW INTERSPECIES EDITION OF TRIVIAL PURSUIT.
WHAT IS THIS *TRIVIAL PURSUIT* OF WHICH YOU SPEAK?
INTERSPECIES
Trivial Pursuit
IT'S A BOARD GAME.
MAN, IF THE GAME ITSELF IS BORED, WHAT CHANCE DO **WE** HAVE OF HAVING ANY FUN?
NOT BORED AS IN *BORING*, IT'S **BOARD** -- AS IN *BIG FLAT SLAB.*
YES, WELL, **THAT** CERTAINLY MAKES IT SOUND THRILLING.
CAN I PLAY BIG FLAT SLAB?
darb

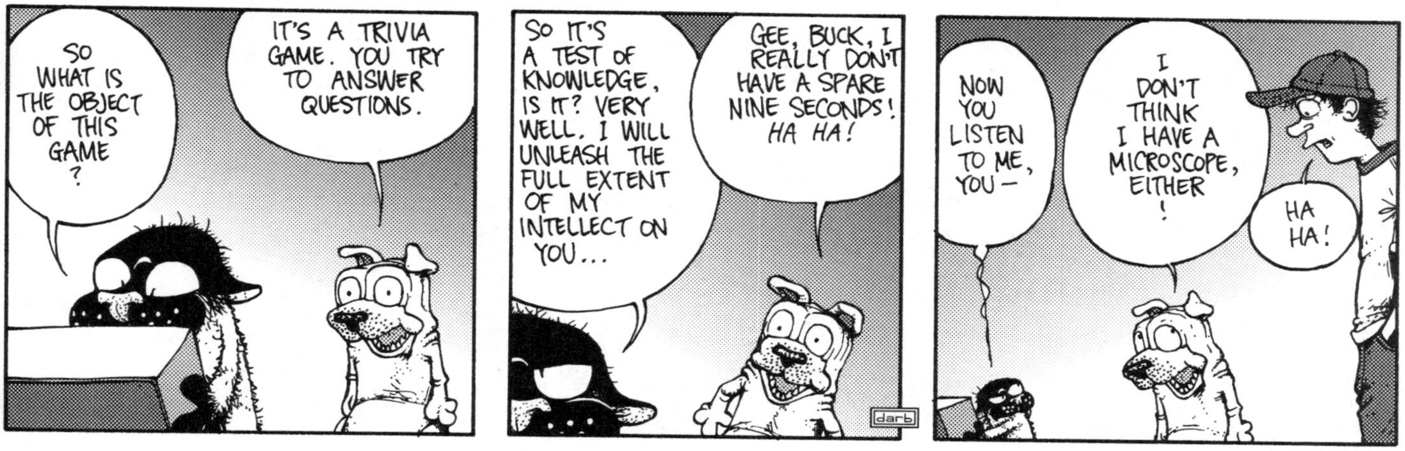
SO WHAT IS THE OBJECT OF THIS GAME?
IT'S A TRIVIA GAME. YOU TRY TO ANSWER QUESTIONS.
SO IT'S A TEST OF KNOWLEDGE, IS IT? VERY WELL. I WILL UNLEASH THE FULL EXTENT OF MY INTELLECT ON YOU...
GEE, BUCK, I REALLY DON'T HAVE A SPARE NINE SECONDS! *HA HA!*
NOW YOU LISTEN TO ME, YOU—
I DON'T THINK I HAVE A MICROSCOPE, EITHER!
HA HA!
darb

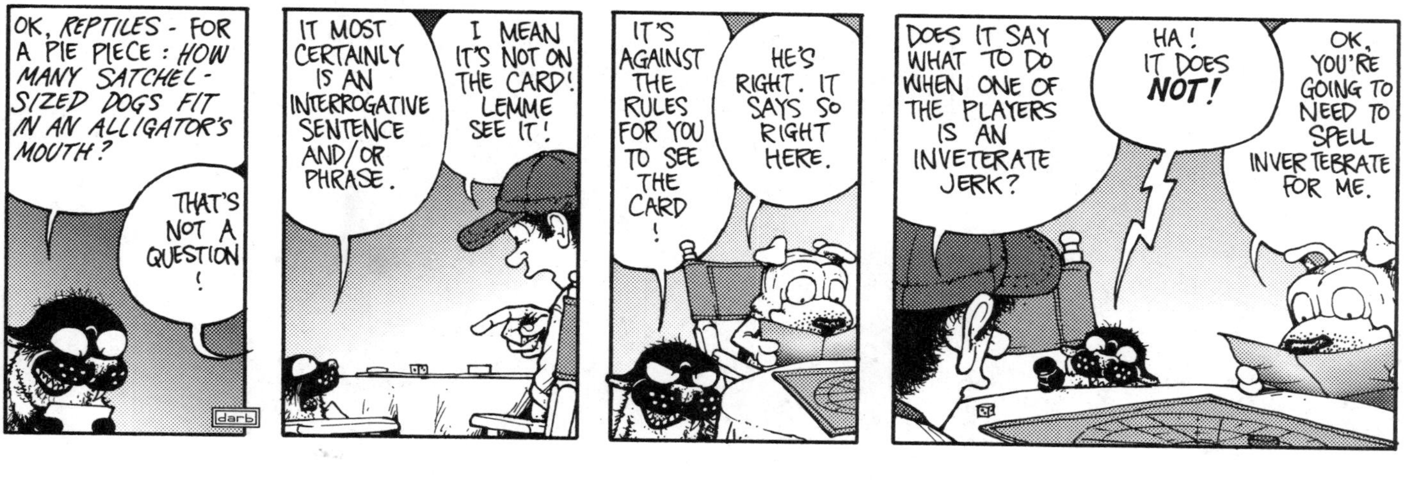
OK, *REPTILES* - FOR A PIE PIECE: *HOW MANY SATCHEL-SIZED DOGS FIT IN AN ALLIGATOR'S MOUTH?*
THAT'S NOT A QUESTION!
IT MOST CERTAINLY IS AN INTERROGATIVE SENTENCE AND/OR PHRASE.
I MEAN IT'S NOT ON THE CARD! LEMME SEE IT!
IT'S AGAINST THE RULES FOR YOU TO SEE THE CARD!
HE'S RIGHT. IT SAYS SO RIGHT HERE.
DOES IT SAY WHAT TO DO WHEN ONE OF THE PLAYERS IS AN INVETERATE JERK?
HA! IT DOES ***NOT!***
OK, YOU'RE GOING TO NEED TO SPELL INVERTEBRATE FOR ME.
darb

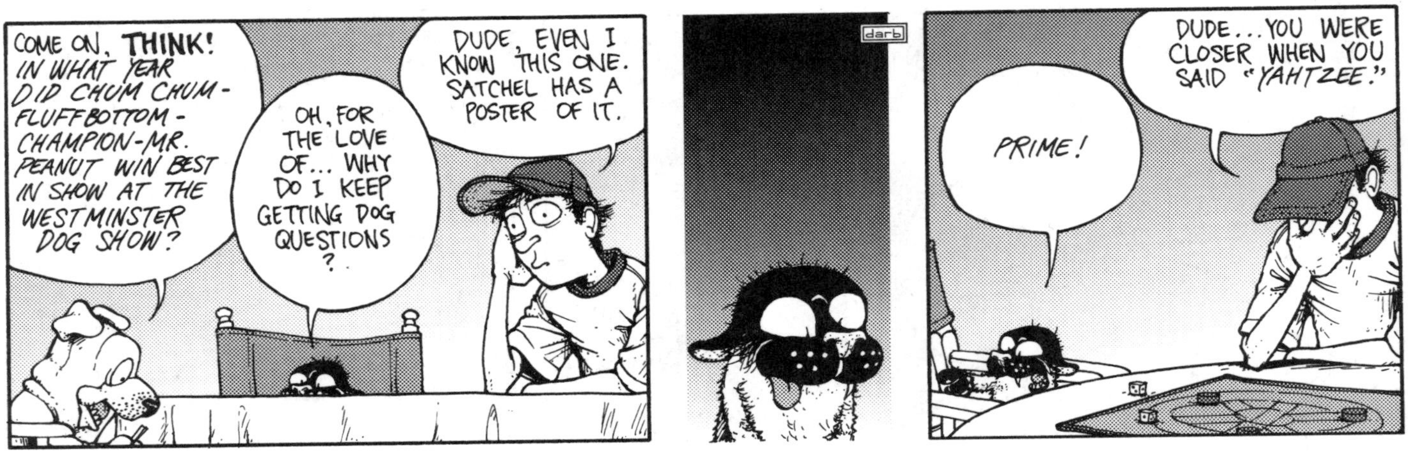
COME ON, THINK! IN WHAT YEAR DID CHUM CHUM-FLUFFBOTTOM-CHAMPION-MR. PEANUT WIN BEST IN SHOW AT THE WESTMINSTER DOG SHOW?
OH, FOR THE LOVE OF... WHY DO I KEEP GETTING DOG QUESTIONS?
DUDE, EVEN I KNOW THIS ONE. SATCHEL HAS A POSTER OF IT.
darb
darb
PRIME!
DUDE... YOU WERE CLOSER WHEN YOU SAID "YAHTZEE."

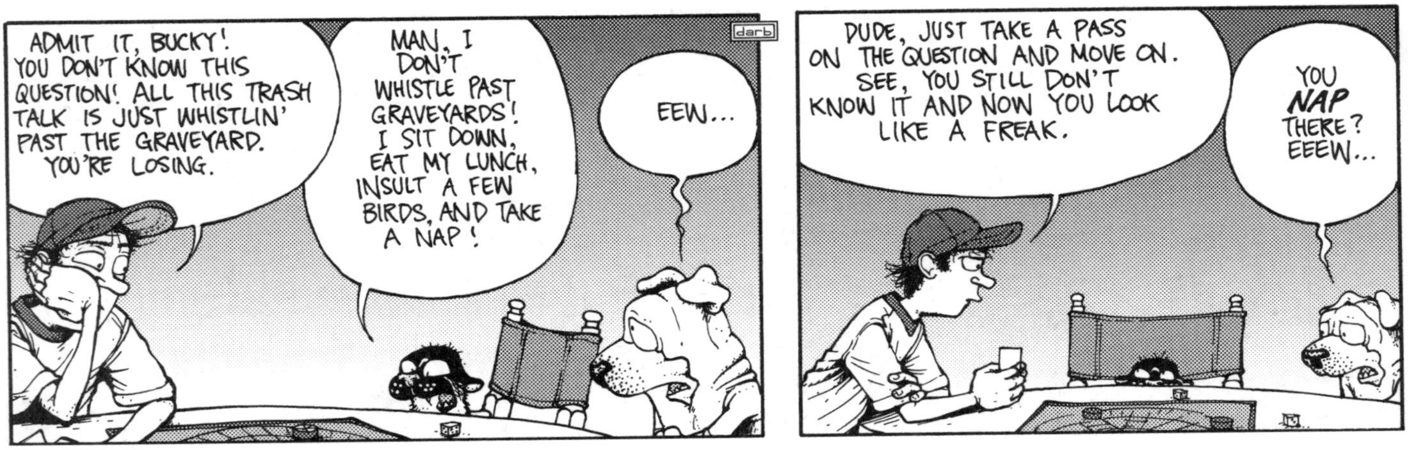
ADMIT IT, BUCKY! YOU DON'T KNOW THIS QUESTION! ALL THIS TRASH TALK IS JUST WHISTLIN' PAST THE GRAVEYARD. YOU'RE LOSING.
MAN, I DON'T WHISTLE PAST GRAVEYARDS! I SIT DOWN, EAT MY LUNCH, INSULT A FEW BIRDS, AND TAKE A NAP!
EEW...
darb
DUDE, JUST TAKE A PASS ON THE QUESTION AND MOVE ON. SEE, YOU STILL DON'T KNOW IT AND NOW YOU LOOK LIKE A FREAK.
YOU NAP THERE? EEEW...

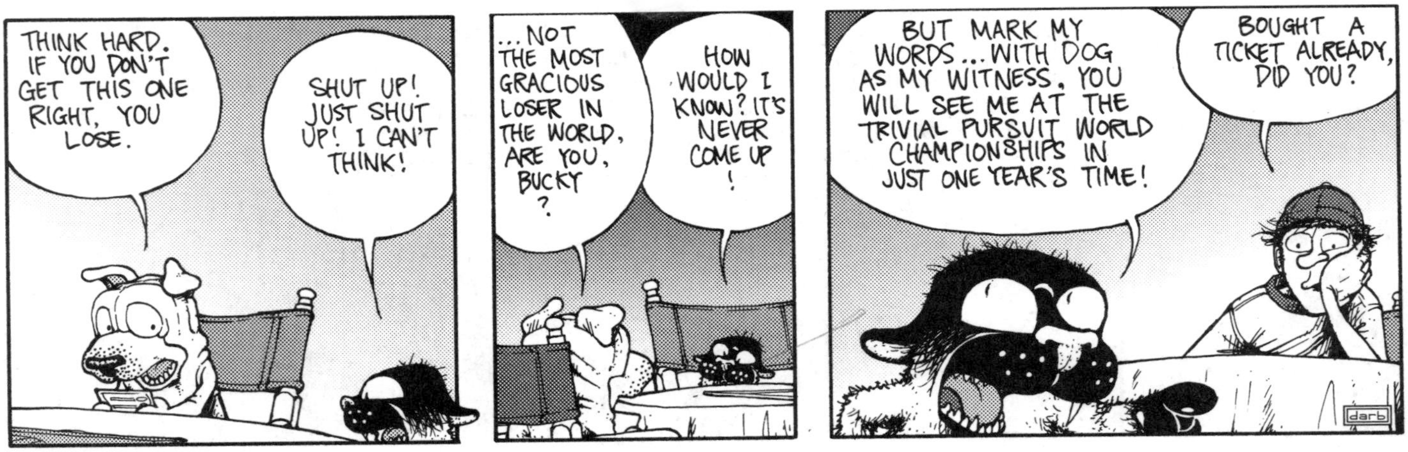
THINK HARD. IF YOU DON'T GET THIS ONE RIGHT, YOU LOSE.
SHUT UP! JUST SHUT UP! I CAN'T THINK!
...NOT THE MOST GRACIOUS LOSER IN THE WORLD, ARE YOU, BUCKY?
HOW WOULD I KNOW? IT'S NEVER COME UP!
BUT MARK MY WORDS... WITH DOG AS MY WITNESS, YOU WILL SEE ME AT THE TRIVIAL PURSUIT WORLD CHAMPIONSHIPS IN JUST ONE YEAR'S TIME!
BOUGHT A TICKET ALREADY, DID YOU?
darb

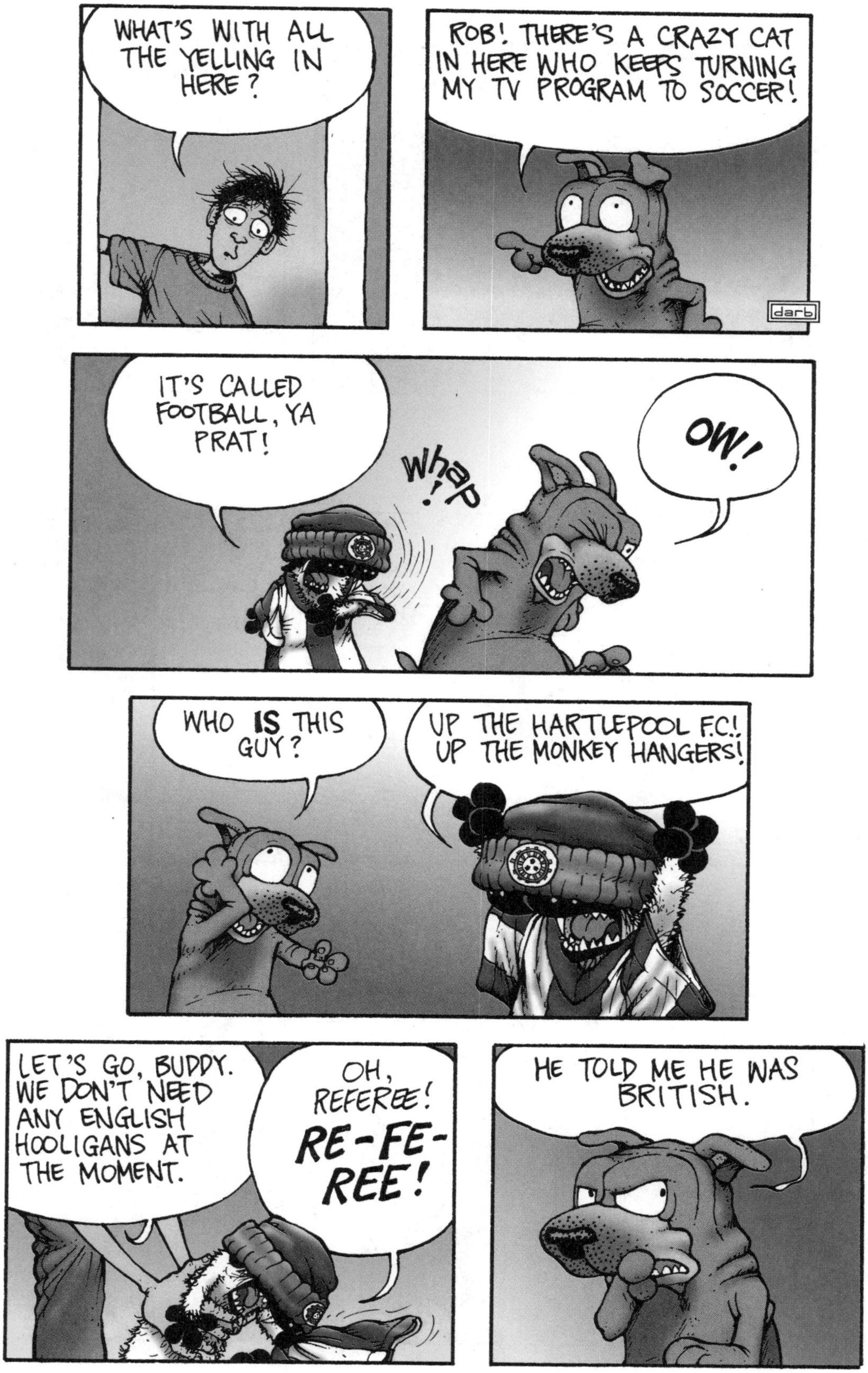
WHAT'S WITH ALL THE YELLING IN HERE?
ROB! THERE'S A CRAZY CAT IN HERE WHO KEEPS TURNING MY TV PROGRAM TO SOCCER!
darb
IT'S CALLED FOOTBALL, YA PRAT!
WHAP!
OW!
WHO IS THIS GUY?
UP THE HARTLEPOOL F.C.! UP THE MONKEY HANGERS!
LET'S GO, BUDDY. WE DON'T NEED ANY ENGLISH HOOLIGANS AT THE MOMENT.
OH, REFEREE! RE-FE-REE!
HE TOLD ME HE WAS BRITISH.

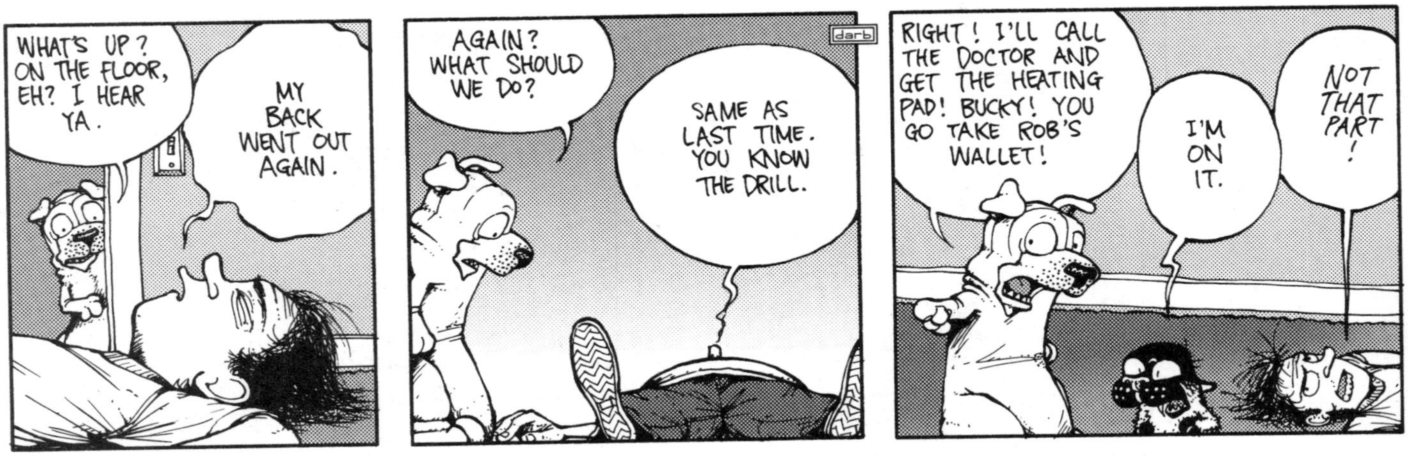
WHAT'S UP? ON THE FLOOR, EH? I HEAR YA.
MY BACK WENT OUT AGAIN.
AGAIN? WHAT SHOULD WE DO?
SAME AS LAST TIME. YOU KNOW THE DRILL.
RIGHT! I'LL CALL THE DOCTOR AND GET THE HEATING PAD! BUCKY! YOU GO TAKE ROB'S WALLET!
I'M ON IT.
NOT THAT PART!
darb

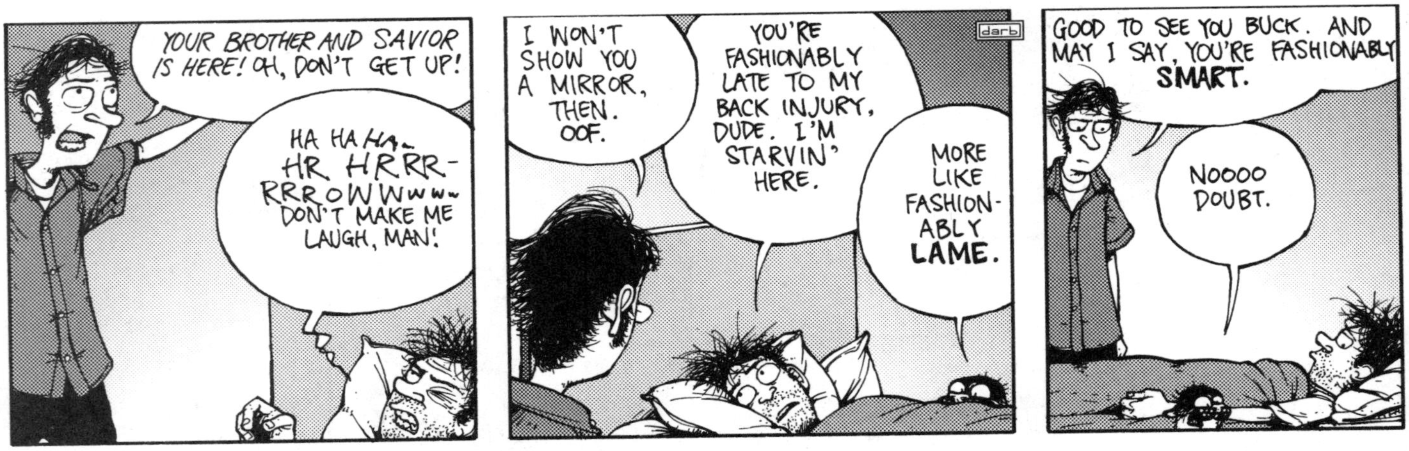
YOUR BROTHER AND SAVIOR IS HERE! OH, DON'T GET UP!
HA HA HA.. HR HRRR-RRROWWwww.. DON'T MAKE ME LAUGH, MAN!
I WON'T SHOW YOU A MIRROR, THEN. OOF.
YOU'RE FASHIONABLY LATE TO MY BACK INJURY, DUDE. I'M STARVIN' HERE.
MORE LIKE FASHION-ABLY **LAME**.
GOOD TO SEE YOU BUCK. AND MAY I SAY, YOU'RE FASHIONABLY **SMART**.
NOOOO DOUBT.
darb

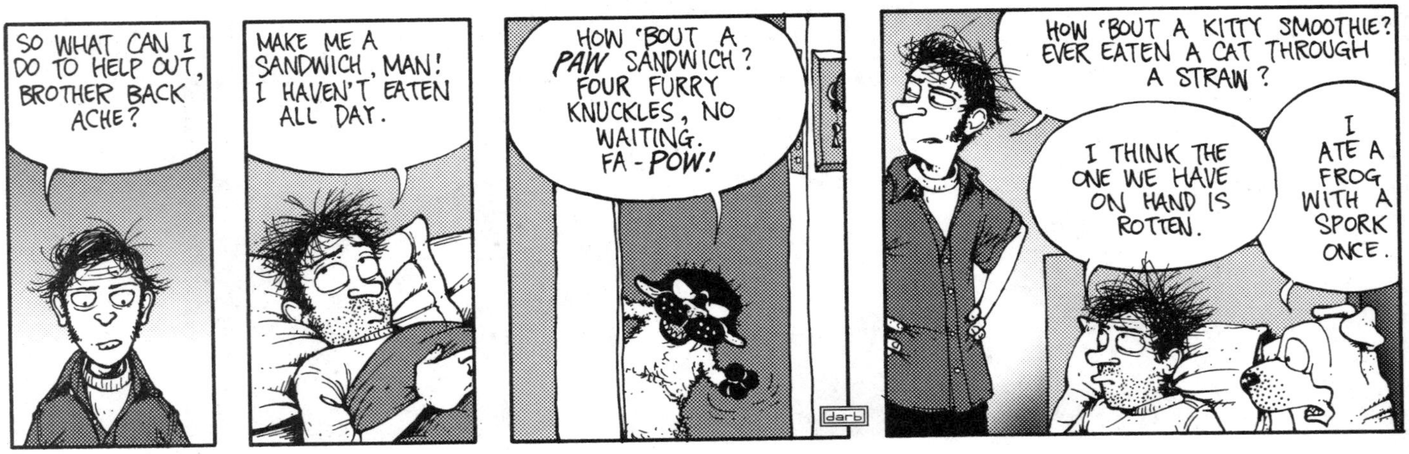
SO WHAT CAN I DO TO HELP OUT, BROTHER BACK ACHE?
MAKE ME A SANDWICH, MAN! I HAVEN'T EATEN ALL DAY.
HOW 'BOUT A *PAW* SANDWICH? FOUR FURRY KNUCKLES, NO WAITING. FA-*POW!*
HOW 'BOUT A KITTY SMOOTHIE? EVER EATEN A CAT THROUGH A STRAW?
I THINK THE ONE WE HAVE ON HAND IS ROTTEN.
I ATE A FROG WITH A SPORK ONCE.
darb

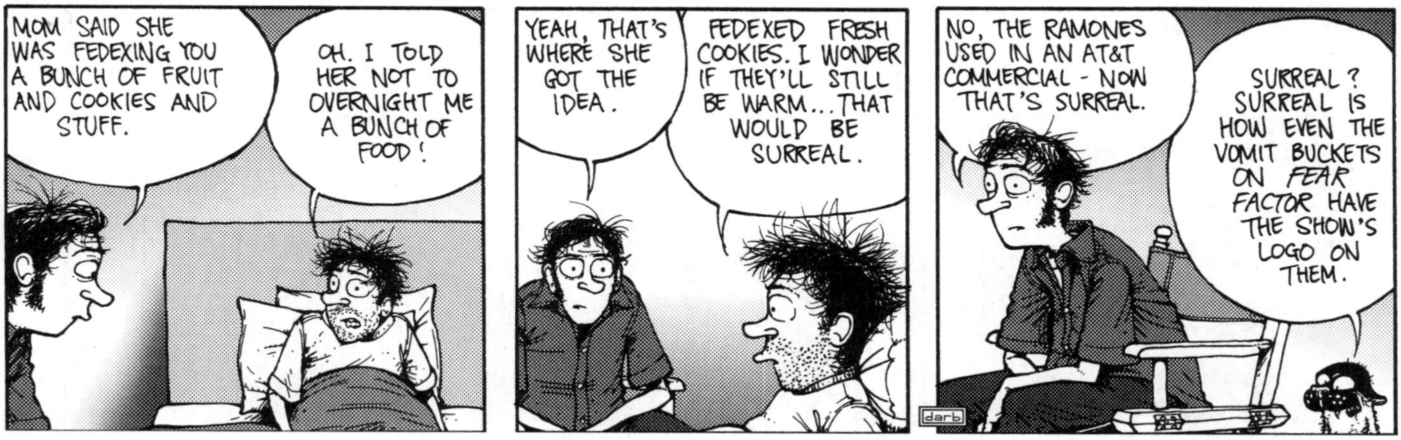
MOM SAID SHE WAS FEDEXING YOU A BUNCH OF FRUIT AND COOKIES AND STUFF.
OH. I TOLD HER NOT TO OVERNIGHT ME A BUNCH OF FOOD!
YEAH, THAT'S WHERE SHE GOT THE IDEA.
FEDEXED FRESH COOKIES. I WONDER IF THEY'LL STILL BE WARM... THAT WOULD BE SURREAL.
NO, THE RAMONES USED IN AN AT&T COMMERCIAL - NOW THAT'S SURREAL.
SURREAL? SURREAL IS HOW EVEN THE VOMIT BUCKETS ON *FEAR FACTOR* HAVE THE SHOW'S LOGO ON THEM.
darb

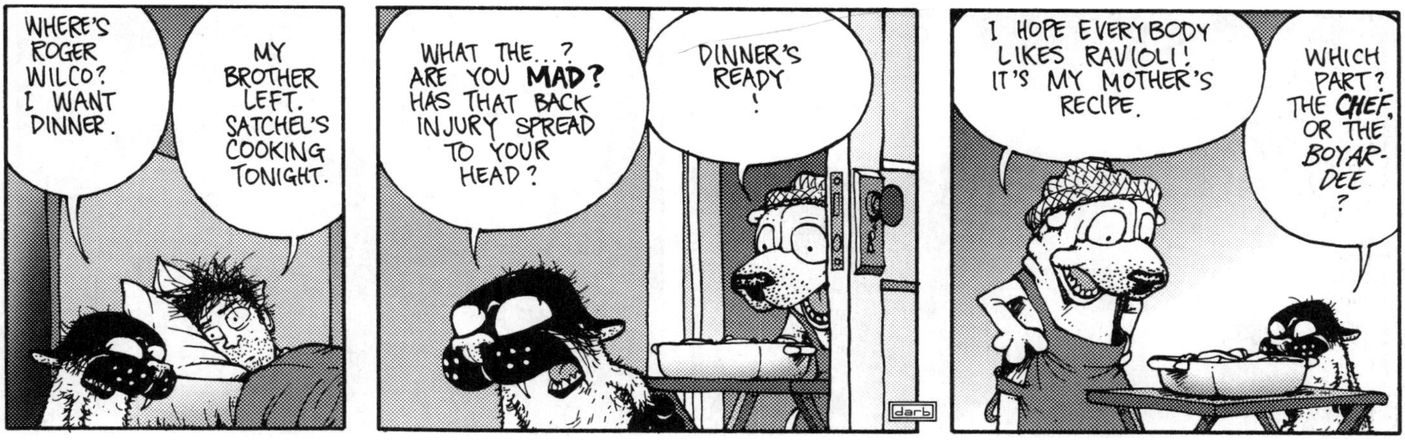
WHERE'S ROGER WILCO? I WANT DINNER.
MY BROTHER LEFT. SATCHEL'S COOKING TONIGHT.
WHAT THE...? ARE YOU **MAD?** HAS THAT BACK INJURY SPREAD TO YOUR HEAD?
DINNER'S READY!
darb
I HOPE EVERYBODY LIKES RAVIOLI! IT'S MY MOTHER'S RECIPE.
WHICH PART? THE **CHEF**, OR THE *BOYARDEE*?

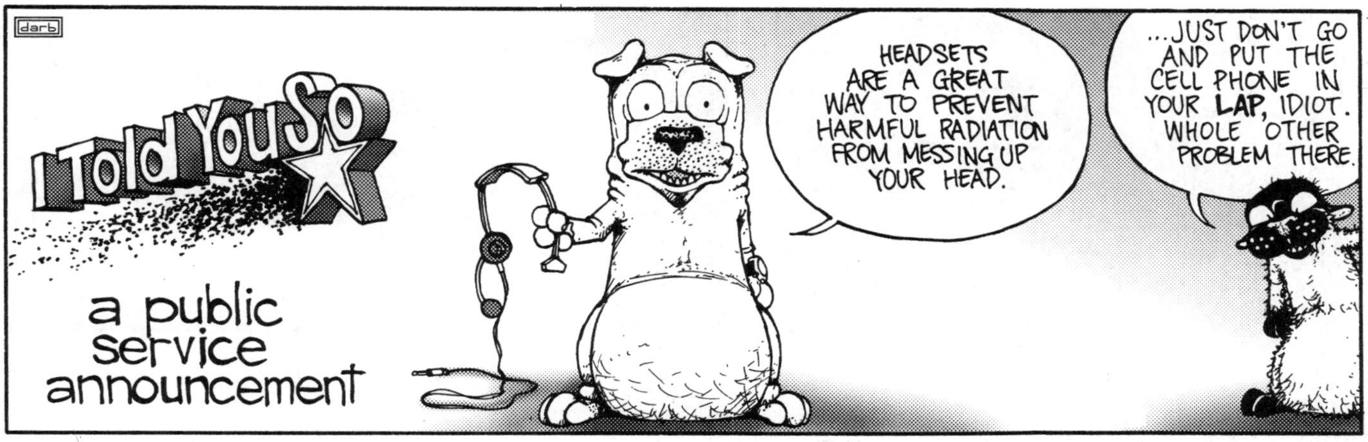
darb
I Told You So
a public service announcement
HEADSETS ARE A GREAT WAY TO PREVENT HARMFUL RADIATION FROM MESSING UP YOUR HEAD.
...JUST DON'T GO AND PUT THE CELL PHONE IN YOUR **LAP**, IDIOT. WHOLE OTHER PROBLEM THERE.

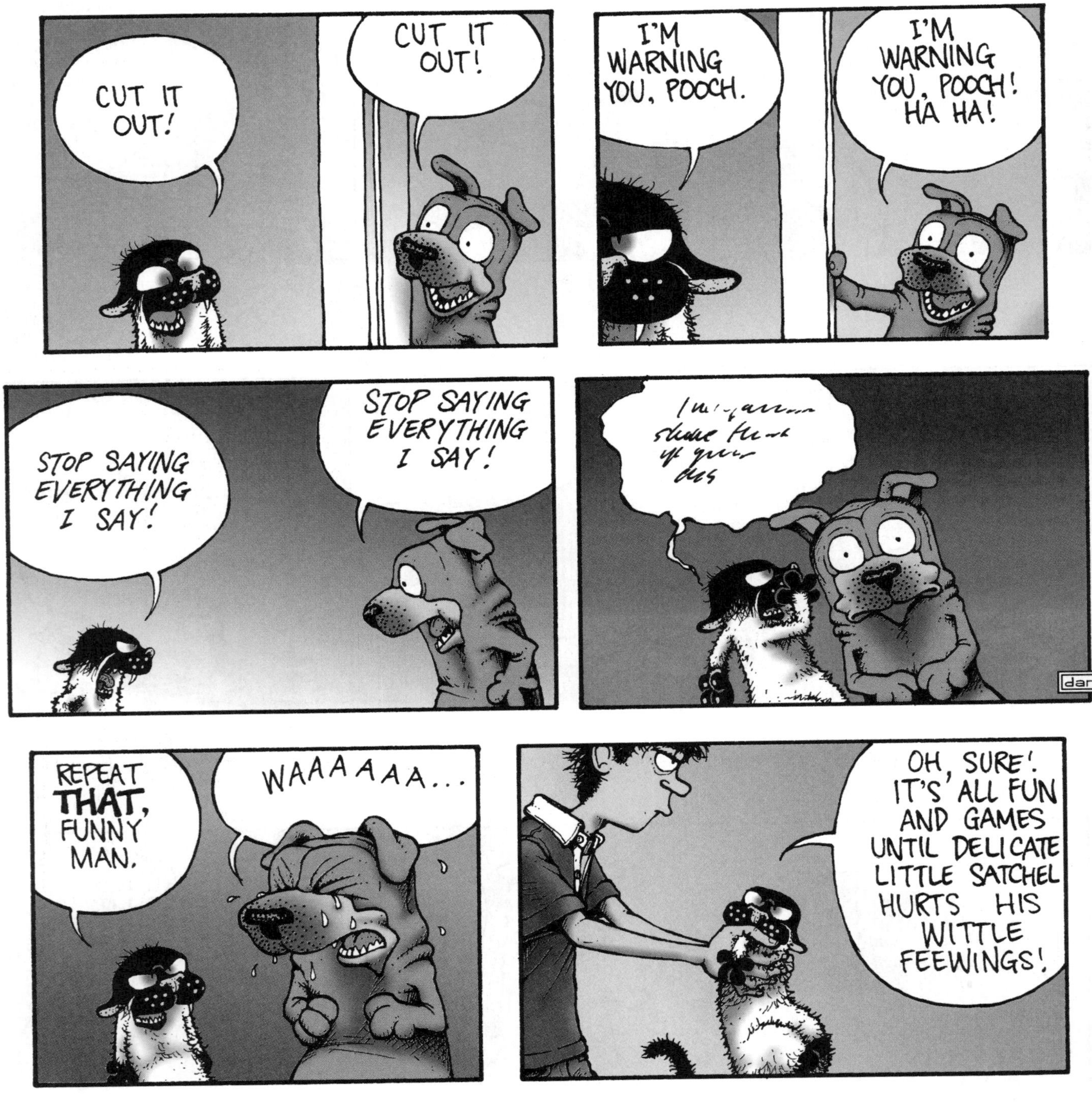
CUT IT OUT!
CUT IT OUT!
I'M WARNING YOU, POOCH.
I'M WARNING YOU, POOCH! HA HA!
STOP SAYING EVERYTHING I SAY!
STOP SAYING EVERYTHING I SAY!
darb
REPEAT **THAT**, FUNNY MAN.
WAAAAAA...
OH, SURE! IT'S ALL FUN AND GAMES UNTIL DELICATE LITTLE SATCHEL HURTS HIS WITTLE FEEWINGS!

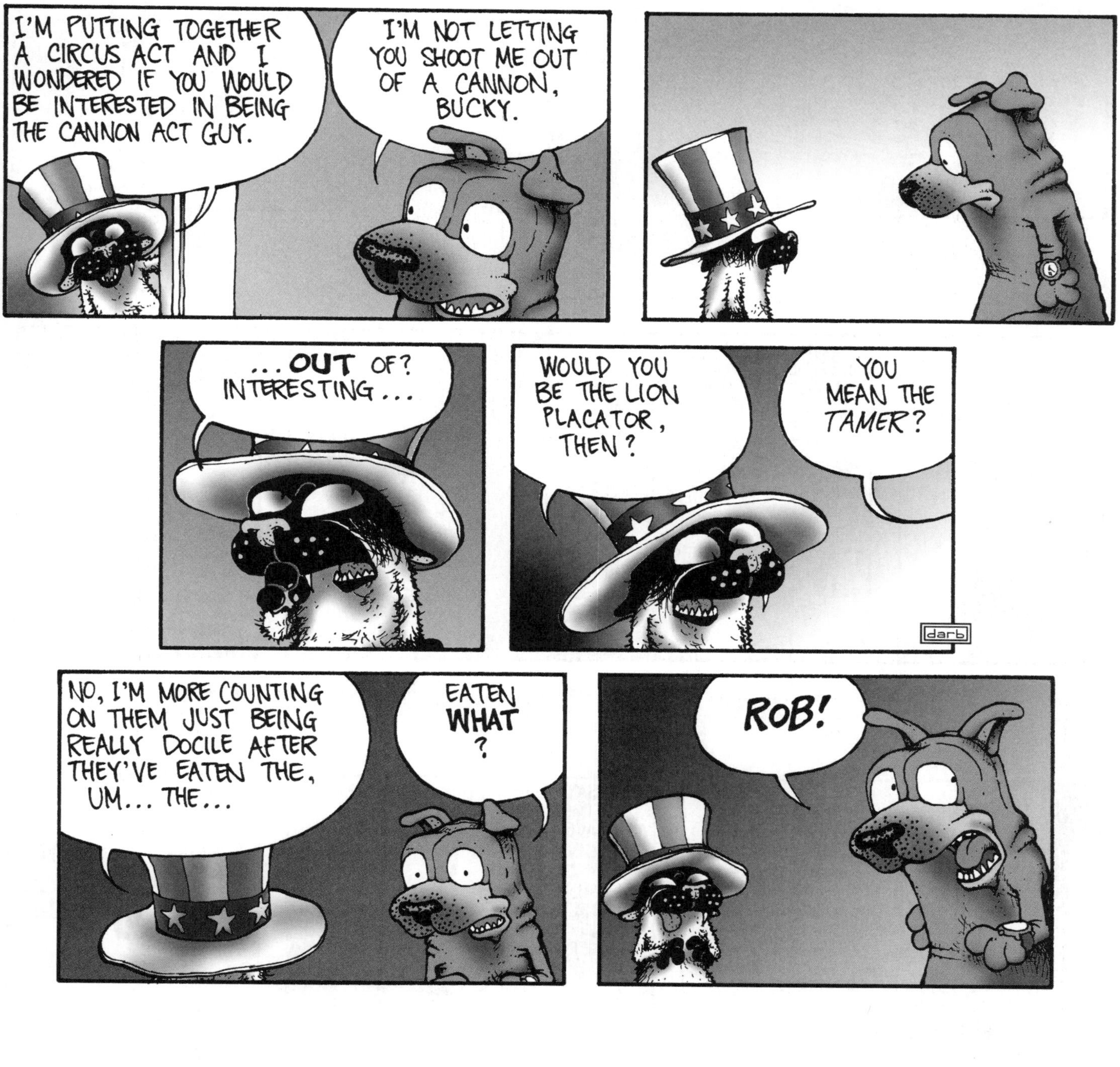
I'M PUTTING TOGETHER A CIRCUS ACT AND I WONDERED IF YOU WOULD BE INTERESTED IN BEING THE CANNON ACT GUY.
I'M NOT LETTING YOU SHOOT ME OUT OF A CANNON, BUCKY.
... OUT OF? INTERESTING ...
WOULD YOU BE THE LION PLACATOR, THEN?
YOU MEAN THE TAMER?
darb
NO, I'M MORE COUNTING ON THEM JUST BEING REALLY DOCILE AFTER THEY'VE EATEN THE, UM... THE...
EATEN WHAT?
ROB!

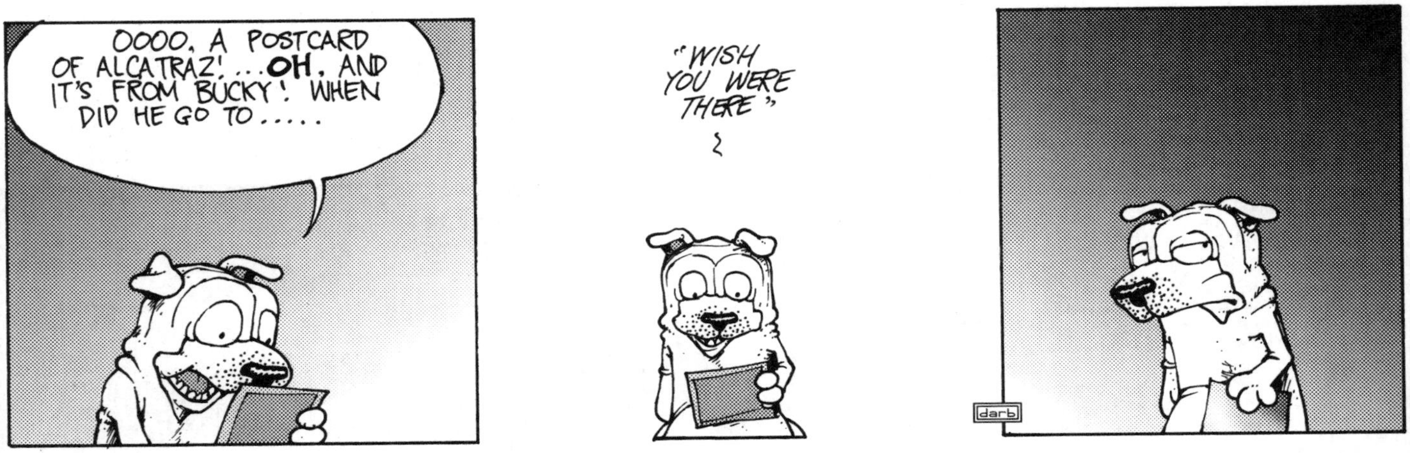
OOOO, A POSTCARD OF ALCATRAZ! ...OH, AND IT'S FROM BUCKY! WHEN DID HE GO TO .....
"WISH YOU WERE THERE"
darb

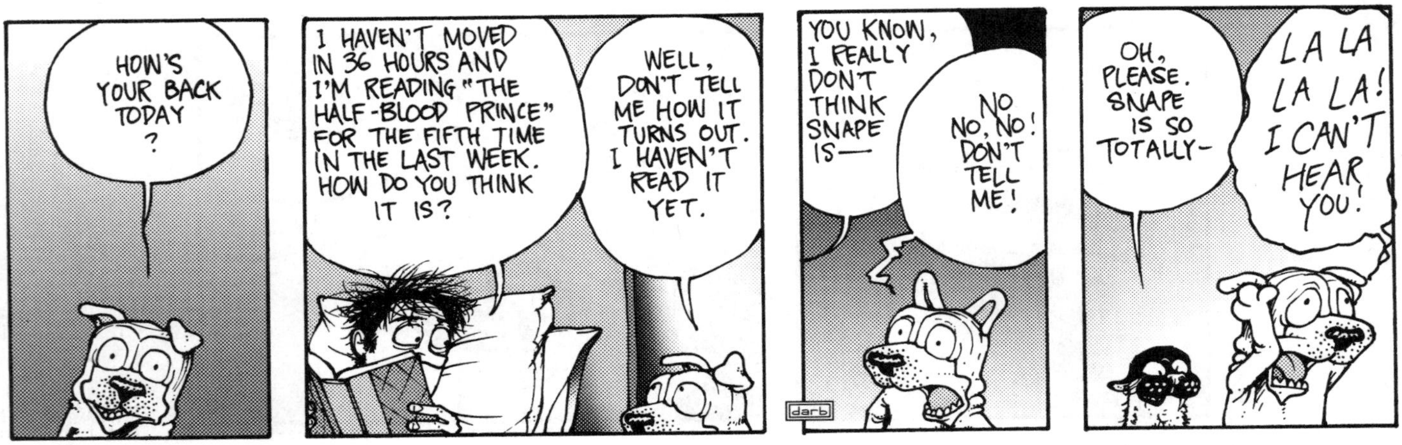
HOW'S YOUR BACK TODAY ?
I HAVEN'T MOVED IN 36 HOURS AND I'M READING "THE HALF-BLOOD PRINCE" FOR THE FIFTH TIME IN THE LAST WEEK. HOW DO YOU THINK IT IS?
WELL, DON'T TELL ME HOW IT TURNS OUT. I HAVEN'T READ IT YET.
YOU KNOW, I REALLY DON'T THINK SNAPE IS—
NO NO, NO! DON'T TELL ME!
darb
OH, PLEASE. SNAPE IS SO TOTALLY-
LA LA LA LA! I CAN'T HEAR YOU!

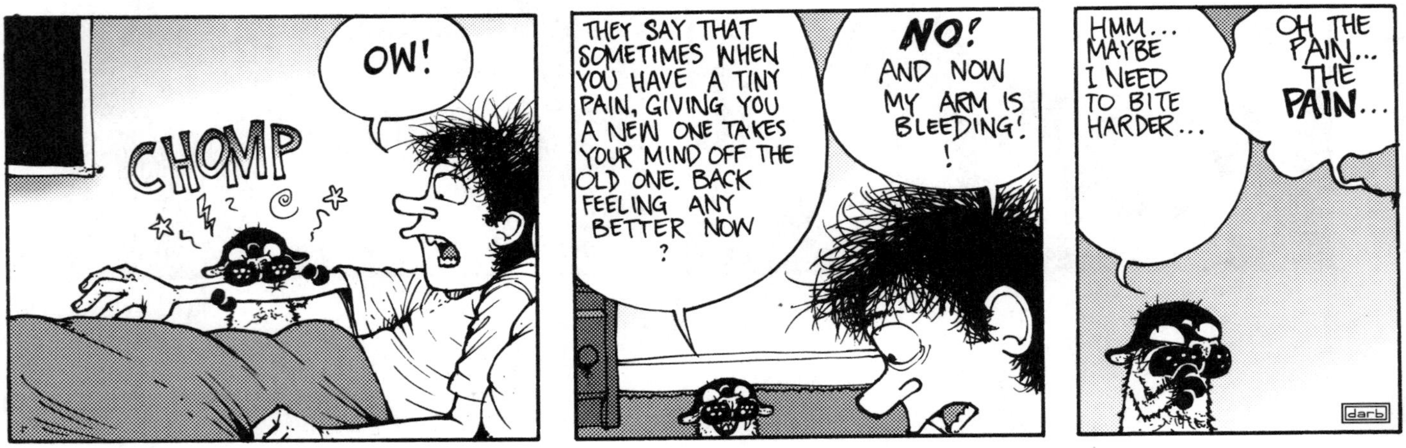
CHOMP
OW!
THEY SAY THAT SOMETIMES WHEN YOU HAVE A TINY PAIN, GIVING YOU A NEW ONE TAKES YOUR MIND OFF THE OLD ONE. BACK FEELING ANY BETTER NOW ?
NO! AND NOW MY ARM IS BLEEDING! !
HMM... MAYBE I NEED TO BITE HARDER...
OH THE PAIN... THE PAIN...
darb

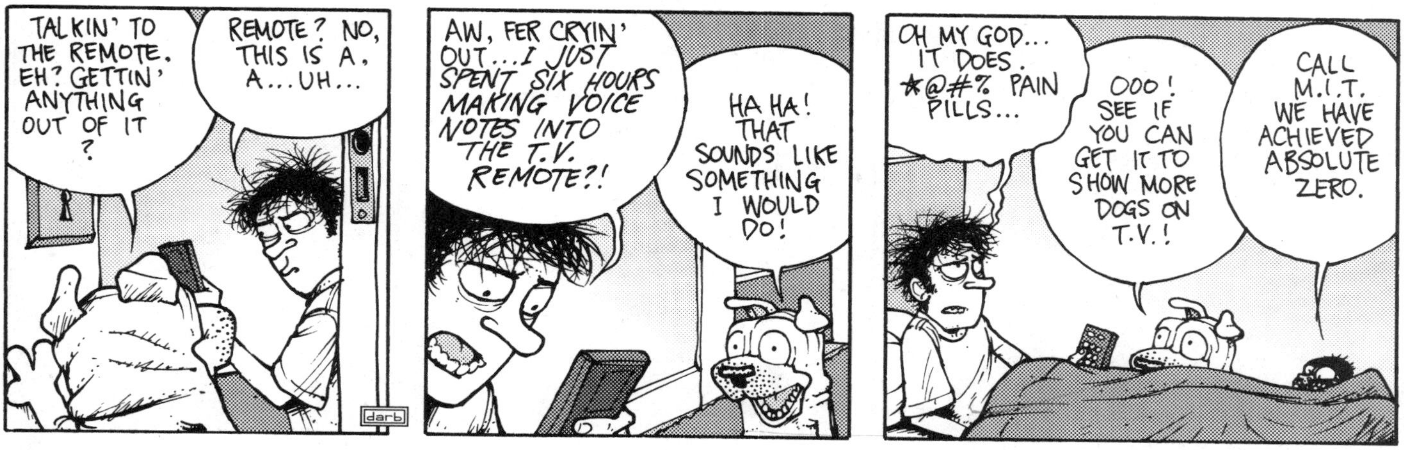
TALKIN' TO THE REMOTE. EH? GETTIN' ANYTHING OUT OF IT ?
REMOTE? NO, THIS IS A, A...UH...
AW, FER CRYIN' OUT...I JUST SPENT SIX HOURS MAKING VOICE NOTES INTO THE T.V. REMOTE?!
HA HA! THAT SOUNDS LIKE SOMETHING I WOULD DO!
OH MY GOD... IT DOES. *@#% PAIN PILLS...
OOO! SEE IF YOU CAN GET IT TO SHOW MORE DOGS ON T.V.!
CALL M.I.T. WE HAVE ACHIEVED ABSOLUTE ZERO.

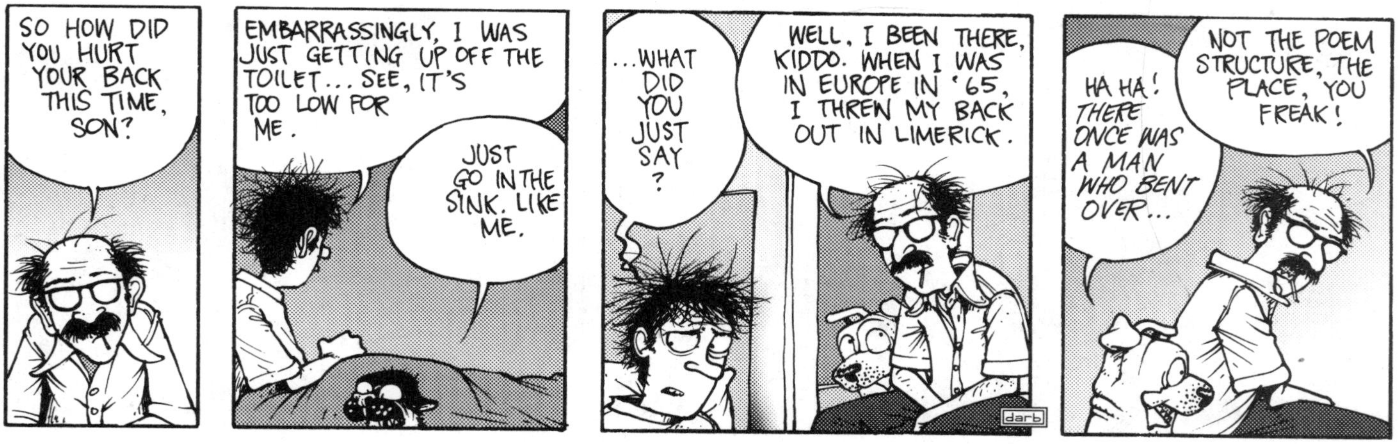
SO HOW DID YOU HURT YOUR BACK THIS TIME, SON?
EMBARRASSINGLY, I WAS JUST GETTING UP OFF THE TOILET... SEE, IT'S TOO LOW FOR ME.
JUST GO IN THE SINK. LIKE ME.
...WHAT DID YOU JUST SAY ?
WELL, I BEEN THERE, KIDDO. WHEN I WAS IN EUROPE IN '65, I THREW MY BACK OUT IN LIMERICK.
HA HA! THERE ONCE WAS A MAN WHO BENT OVER...
NOT THE POEM STRUCTURE, THE PLACE, YOU FREAK!

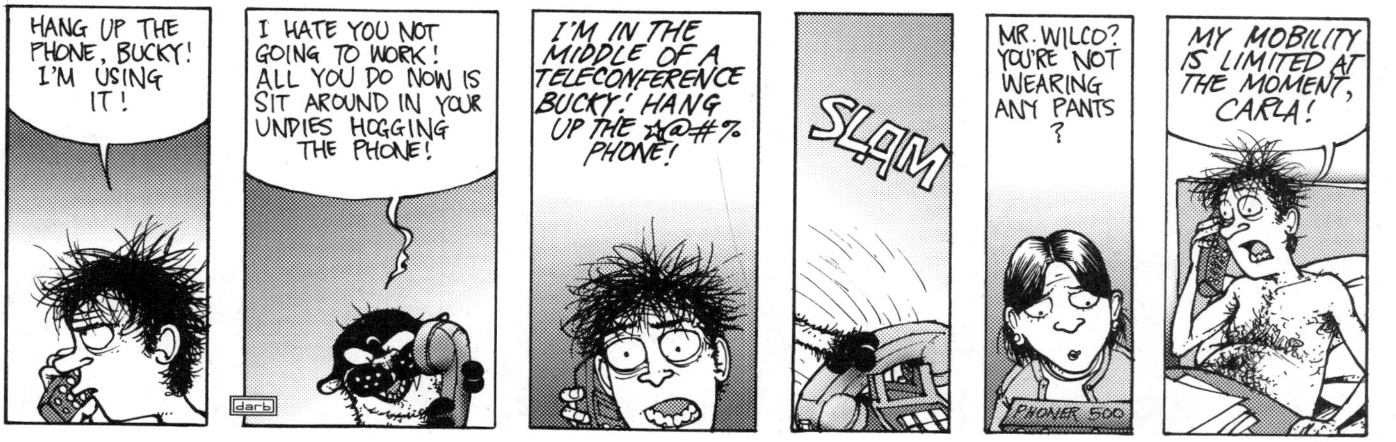
HANG UP THE PHONE, BUCKY! I'M USING IT!
I HATE YOU NOT GOING TO WORK! ALL YOU DO NOW IS SIT AROUND IN YOUR UNDIES HOGGING THE PHONE!
I'M IN THE MIDDLE OF A TELECONFERENCE BUCKY! HANG UP THE ☆@#% PHONE!
SLAM
MR. WILCO? YOU'RE NOT WEARING ANY PANTS ?
PHONER 500
MY MOBILITY IS LIMITED AT THE MOMENT, CARLA!

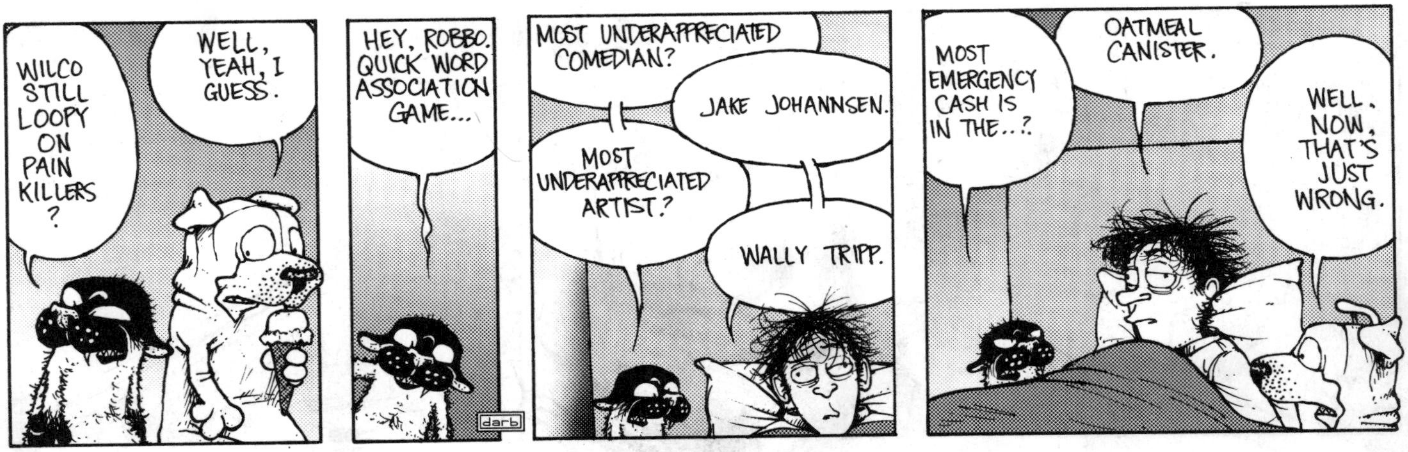
WILCO STILL LOOPY ON PAIN KILLERS?
WELL, YEAH, I GUESS.
HEY, ROBBO. QUICK WORD ASSOCIATION GAME...
MOST UNDERAPPRECIATED COMEDIAN?
JAKE JOHANNSEN.
MOST UNDERAPPRECIATED ARTIST?
WALLY TRIPP.
MOST EMERGENCY CASH IS IN THE...?
OATMEAL CANISTER.
WELL, NOW, THAT'S JUST WRONG.
darb

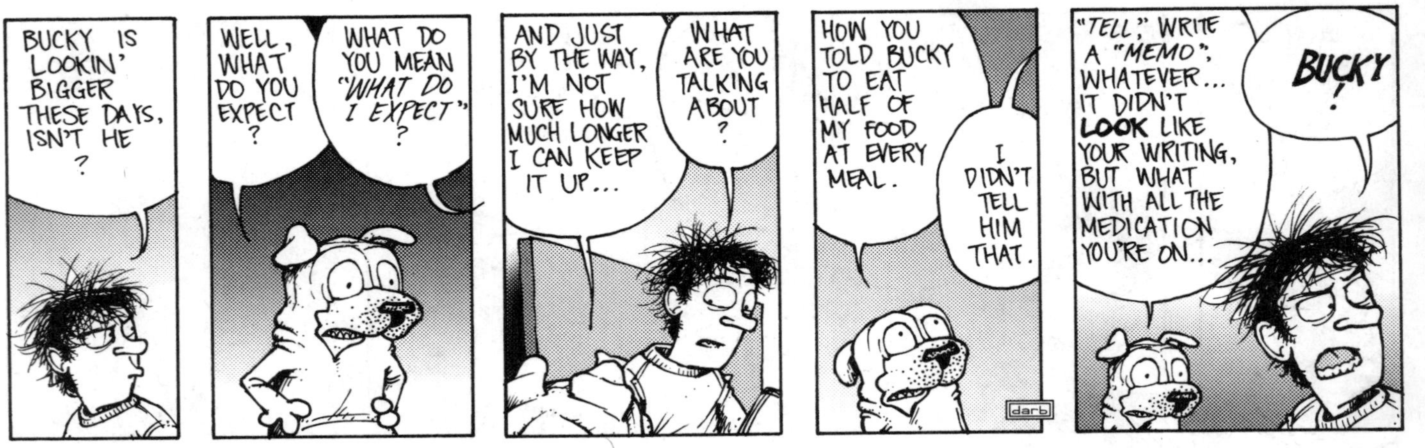
BUCKY IS LOOKIN' BIGGER THESE DAYS, ISN'T HE?
WELL, WHAT DO YOU EXPECT?
WHAT DO YOU MEAN "WHAT DO I EXPECT"?
AND JUST BY THE WAY, I'M NOT SURE HOW MUCH LONGER I CAN KEEP IT UP...
WHAT ARE YOU TALKING ABOUT?
HOW YOU TOLD BUCKY TO EAT HALF OF MY FOOD AT EVERY MEAL.
I DIDN'T TELL HIM THAT.
darb
"TELL," WRITE A "MEMO," WHATEVER... IT DIDN'T LOOK LIKE YOUR WRITING, BUT WHAT WITH ALL THE MEDICATION YOU'RE ON...
BUCKY!

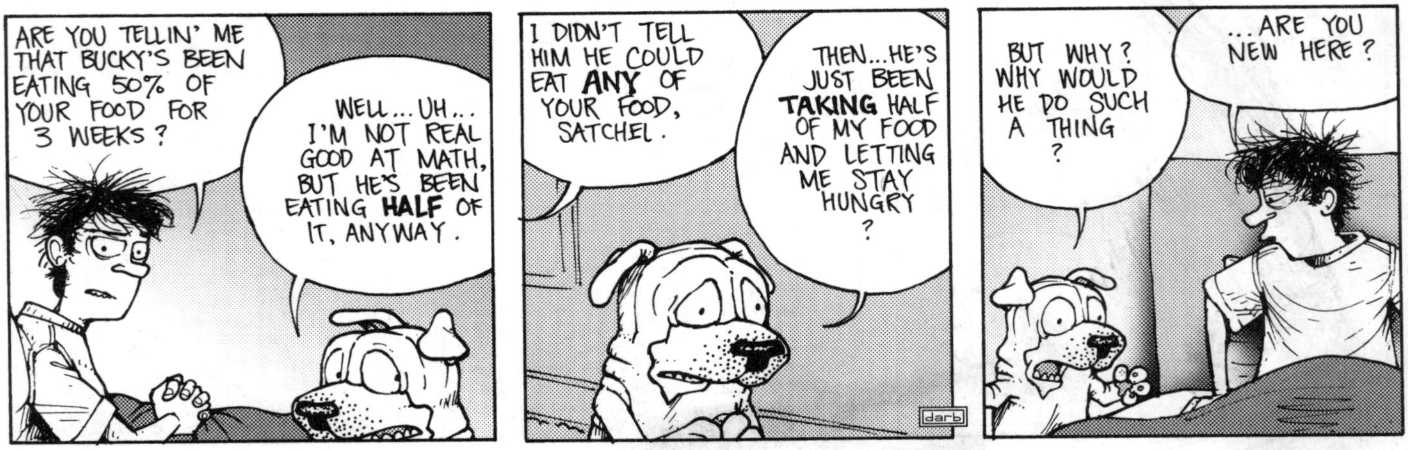
ARE YOU TELLIN' ME THAT BUCKY'S BEEN EATING 50% OF YOUR FOOD FOR 3 WEEKS?
WELL... UH... I'M NOT REAL GOOD AT MATH, BUT HE'S BEEN EATING HALF OF IT, ANYWAY.
I DIDN'T TELL HIM HE COULD EAT ANY OF YOUR FOOD, SATCHEL.
THEN... HE'S JUST BEEN TAKING HALF OF MY FOOD AND LETTING ME STAY HUNGRY?
darb
BUT WHY? WHY WOULD HE DO SUCH A THING?
...ARE YOU NEW HERE?

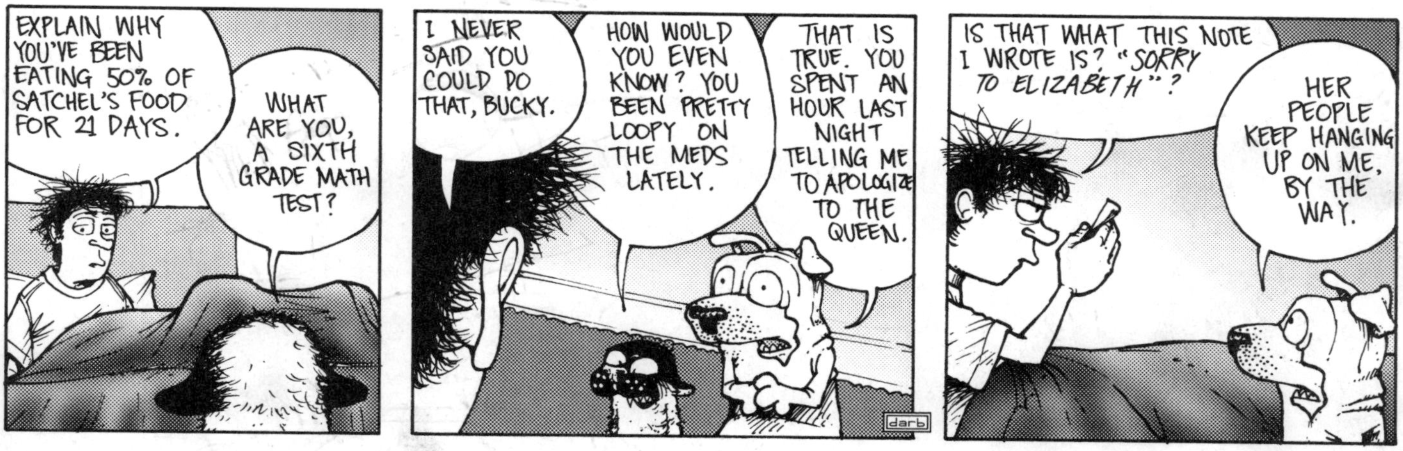
EXPLAIN WHY YOU'VE BEEN EATING 50% OF SATCHEL'S FOOD FOR 21 DAYS.
WHAT ARE YOU, A SIXTH GRADE MATH TEST?
I NEVER SAID YOU COULD DO THAT, BUCKY.
HOW WOULD YOU EVEN KNOW? YOU BEEN PRETTY LOOPY ON THE MEDS LATELY.
THAT IS TRUE. YOU SPENT AN HOUR LAST NIGHT TELLING ME TO APOLOGIZE TO THE QUEEN.
darb
IS THAT WHAT THIS NOTE I WROTE IS? "SORRY TO ELIZABETH"?
HER PEOPLE KEEP HANGING UP ON ME, BY THE WAY.

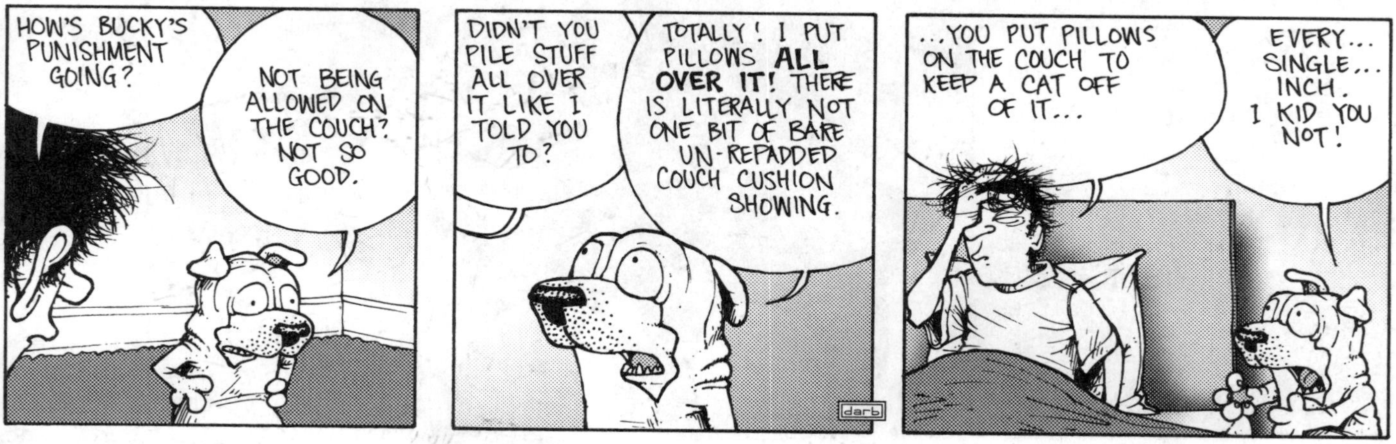
HOW'S BUCKY'S PUNISHMENT GOING?
NOT BEING ALLOWED ON THE COUCH? NOT SO GOOD.
DIDN'T YOU PILE STUFF ALL OVER IT LIKE I TOLD YOU TO?
TOTALLY! I PUT PILLOWS ALL OVER IT! THERE IS LITERALLY NOT ONE BIT OF BARE UN-REPADDED COUCH CUSHION SHOWING.
darb
...YOU PUT PILLOWS ON THE COUCH TO KEEP A CAT OFF OF IT...
EVERY... SINGLE... INCH. I KID YOU NOT!

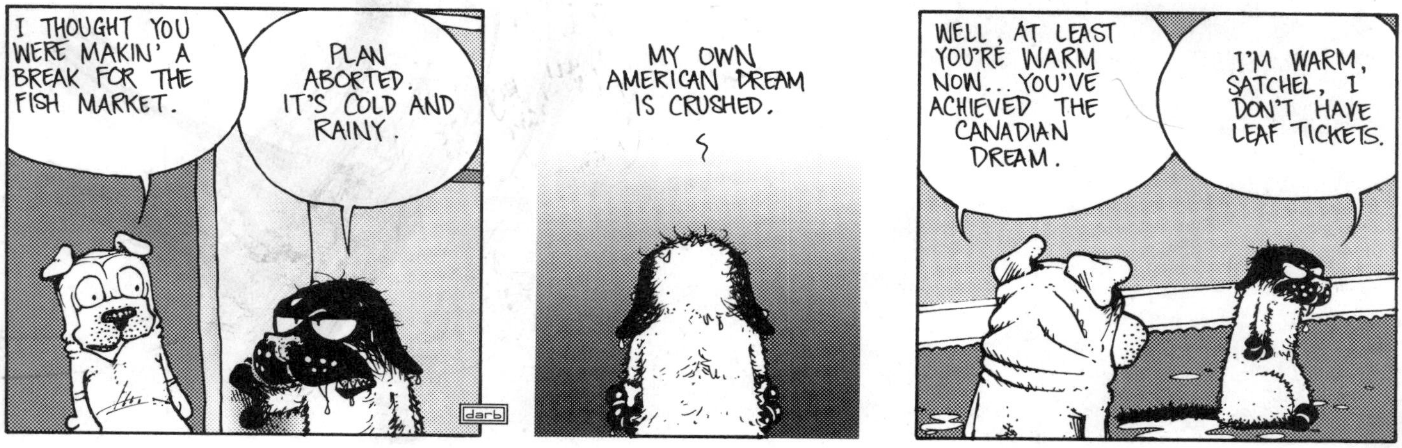
I THOUGHT YOU WERE MAKIN' A BREAK FOR THE FISH MARKET.
PLAN ABORTED. IT'S COLD AND RAINY.
darb
MY OWN AMERICAN DREAM IS CRUSHED.
WELL, AT LEAST YOU'RE WARM NOW... YOU'VE ACHIEVED THE CANADIAN DREAM.
I'M WARM, SATCHEL, I DON'T HAVE LEAF TICKETS.

PROTECT YOUR HOME!

STUDIES SHOW THAT HOMES WITH DOGS ARE, LIKE, A MILLION TIMES LESS LIKELY TO BE BROKEN INTO.* HERE AT YE OLDE FUZZY COMIC AND HEAVY INDUSTRIES, WE CARE! TO PROTECT *YOUR* HOME, SIMPLY CUT OUT THESE ANTI-BURGLAR IMAGES AND PLACE THEM IN AN ENTRY WINDOW!**

* number provided for alarming effect only
** results not guaranteed

BEWARE OF DOG !

- dog more vicious than it appears.
- Y.O.F.C.H.I., Inc. not liable for any losses.   darb

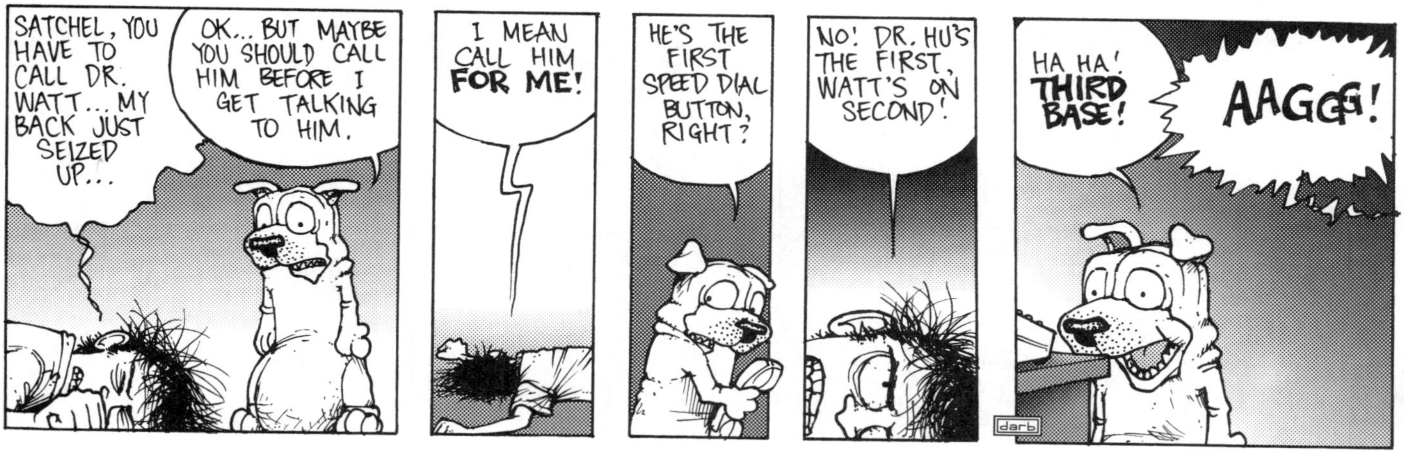
SATCHEL, YOU HAVE TO CALL DR. WATT... MY BACK JUST SEIZED UP...
OK... BUT MAYBE YOU SHOULD CALL HIM BEFORE I GET TALKING TO HIM.
I MEAN CALL HIM FOR ME!
HE'S THE FIRST SPEED DIAL BUTTON, RIGHT?
NO! DR. HU'S THE FIRST, WATT'S ON SECOND!
HA HA! THIRD BASE!
AAGGG!
darb

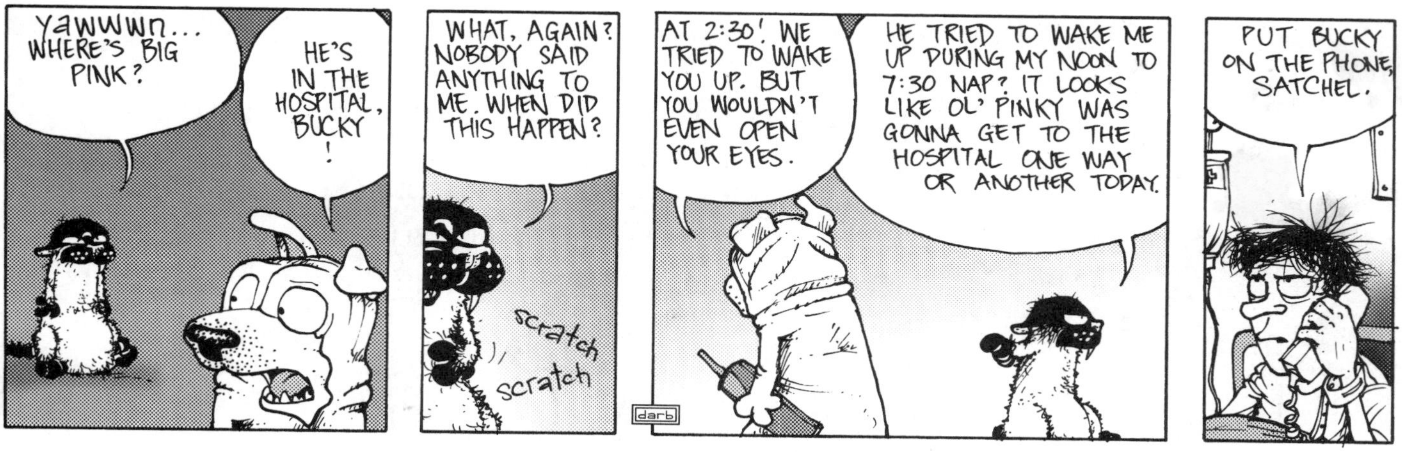
Yawwwn... WHERE'S BIG PINK?
HE'S IN THE HOSPITAL, BUCKY!
WHAT, AGAIN? NOBODY SAID ANYTHING TO ME. WHEN DID THIS HAPPEN?
scratch
scratch
darb
AT 2:30! WE TRIED TO WAKE YOU UP. BUT YOU WOULDN'T EVEN OPEN YOUR EYES.
HE TRIED TO WAKE ME UP DURING MY NOON TO 7:30 NAP? IT LOOKS LIKE OL' PINKY WAS GONNA GET TO THE HOSPITAL ONE WAY OR ANOTHER TODAY.
PUT BUCKY ON THE PHONE, SATCHEL.

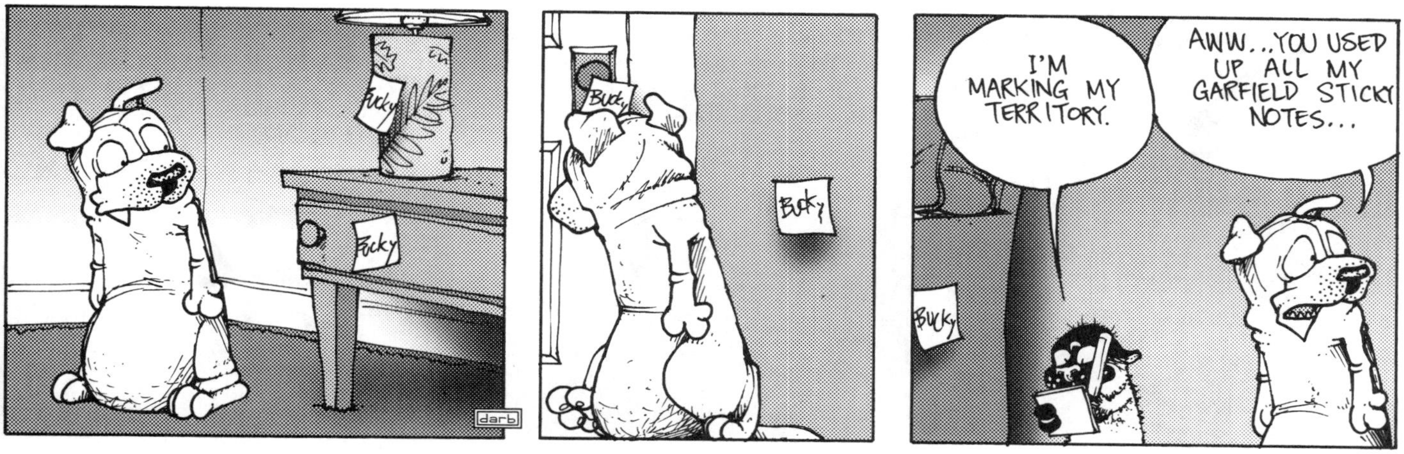
Bucky
Bucky
darb
Bucky
Bucky
I'M MARKING MY TERRITORY.
AWW... YOU USED UP ALL MY GARFIELD STICKY NOTES...
Bucky

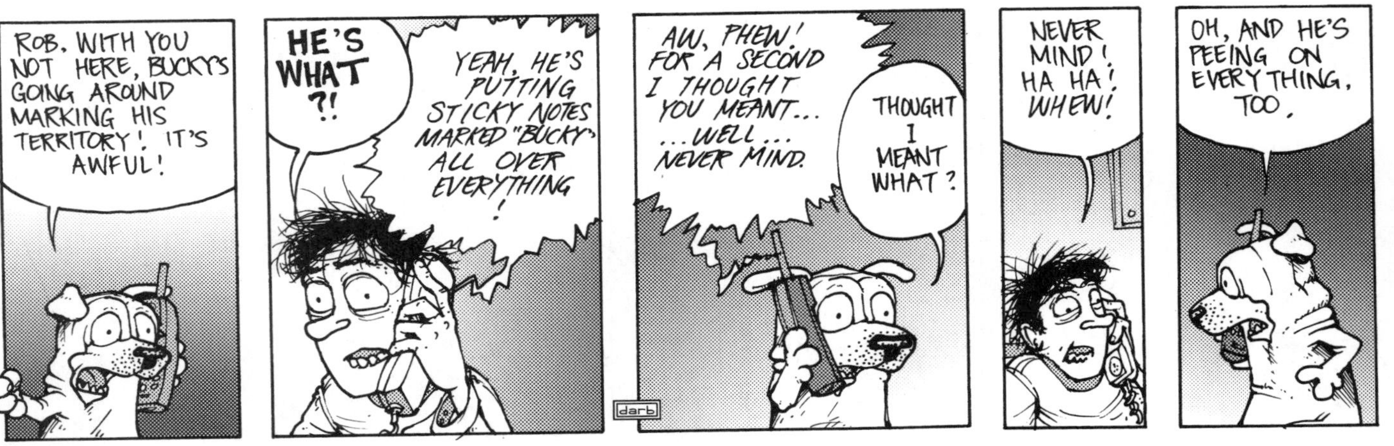
ROB. WITH YOU NOT HERE, BUCKY'S GOING AROUND MARKING HIS TERRITORY! IT'S AWFUL!
HE'S WHAT ?!
YEAH, HE'S PUTTING STICKY NOTES MARKED "BUCKY" ALL OVER EVERYTHING!
AW, PHEW! FOR A SECOND I THOUGHT YOU MEANT... ...WELL... NEVER MIND.
THOUGHT I MEANT WHAT?
NEVER MIND! HA HA! WHEW!
OH, AND HE'S PEEING ON EVERYTHING, TOO.
darb

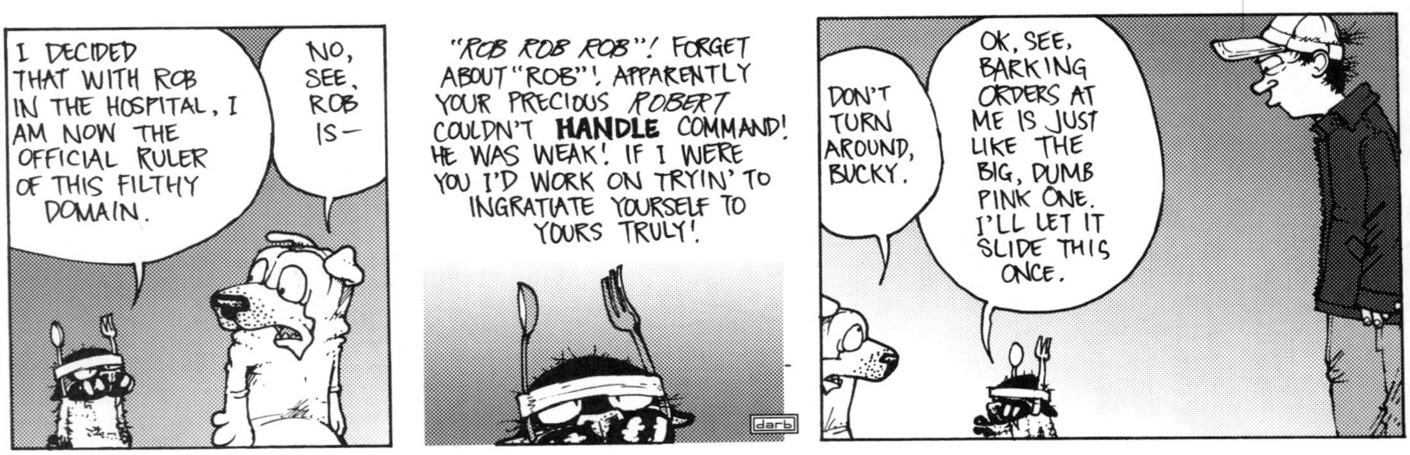
I DECIDED THAT WITH ROB IN THE HOSPITAL, I AM NOW THE OFFICIAL RULER OF THIS FILTHY DOMAIN.
NO, SEE, ROB IS—
"ROB ROB ROB"! FORGET ABOUT "ROB"! APPARENTLY YOUR PRECIOUS ROBERT COULDN'T HANDLE COMMAND! HE WAS WEAK! IF I WERE YOU I'D WORK ON TRYIN' TO INGRATIATE YOURSELF TO YOURS TRULY!
darb
DON'T TURN AROUND, BUCKY.
OK, SEE, BARKING ORDERS AT ME IS JUST LIKE THE BIG, DUMB PINK ONE. I'LL LET IT SLIDE THIS ONCE.

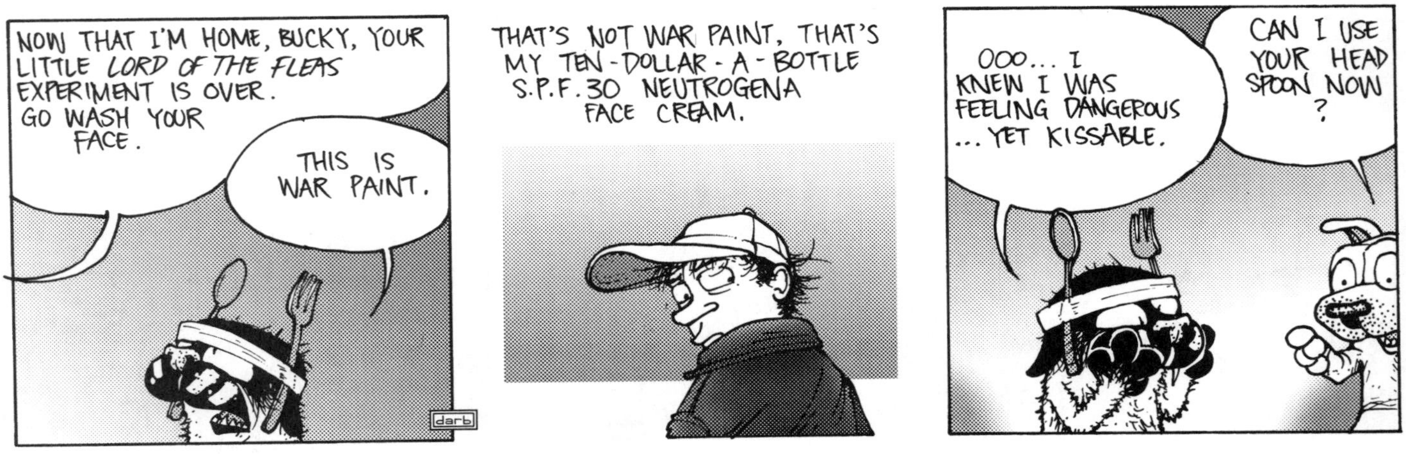
NOW THAT I'M HOME, BUCKY, YOUR LITTLE LORD OF THE FLEAS EXPERIMENT IS OVER. GO WASH YOUR FACE.
THIS IS WAR PAINT.
darb
THAT'S NOT WAR PAINT, THAT'S MY TEN-DOLLAR-A-BOTTLE S.P.F. 30 NEUTROGENA FACE CREAM.
OOO... I KNEW I WAS FEELING DANGEROUS ...YET KISSABLE.
CAN I USE YOUR HEAD SPOON NOW?

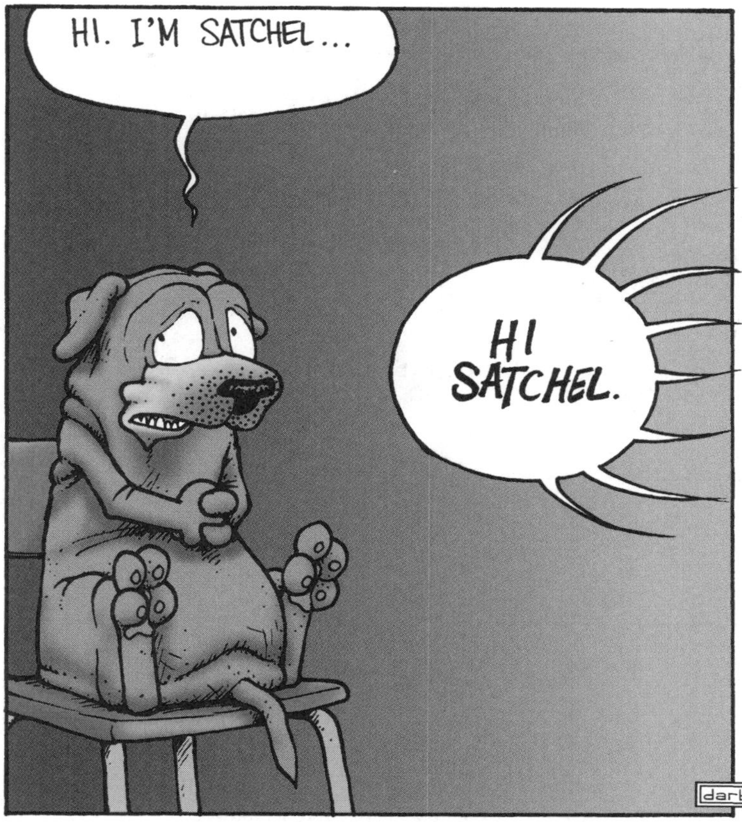
HI. I'M SATCHEL...
HI SATCHEL.

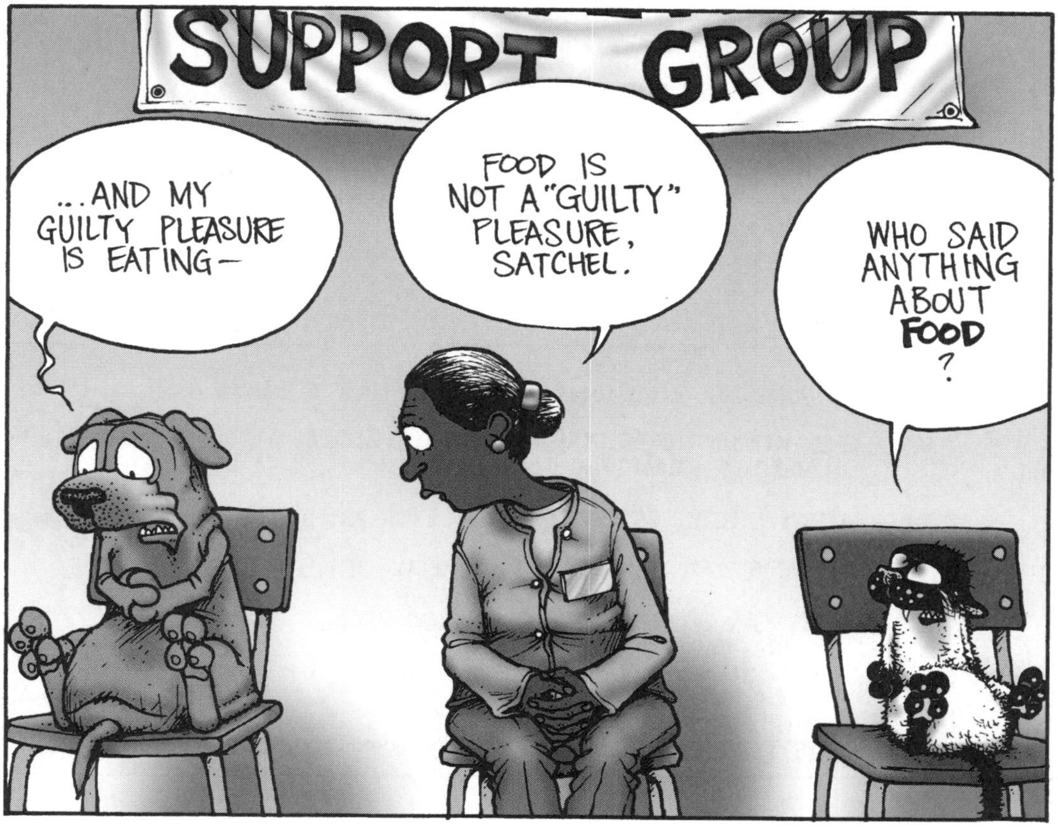
SUPPORT GROUP
...AND MY GUILTY PLEASURE IS EATING—
FOOD IS NOT A "GUILTY" PLEASURE, SATCHEL.
WHO SAID ANYTHING ABOUT FOOD?

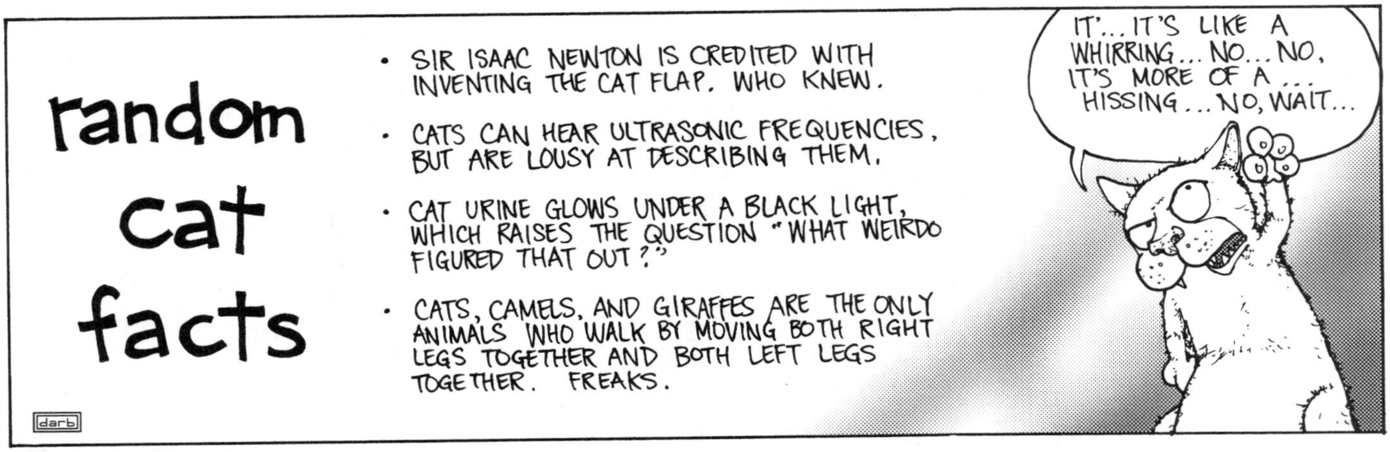
random cat facts
• SIR ISAAC NEWTON IS CREDITED WITH INVENTING THE CAT FLAP. WHO KNEW.
• CATS CAN HEAR ULTRASONIC FREQUENCIES, BUT ARE LOUSY AT DESCRIBING THEM.
• CAT URINE GLOWS UNDER A BLACK LIGHT, WHICH RAISES THE QUESTION "WHAT WEIRDO FIGURED THAT OUT?"
• CATS, CAMELS, AND GIRAFFES ARE THE ONLY ANIMALS WHO WALK BY MOVING BOTH RIGHT LEGS TOGETHER AND BOTH LEFT LEGS TOGETHER. FREAKS.
IT'... IT'S LIKE A WHIRRING... NO... NO, IT'S MORE OF A ... HISSING... NO, WAIT...
darb

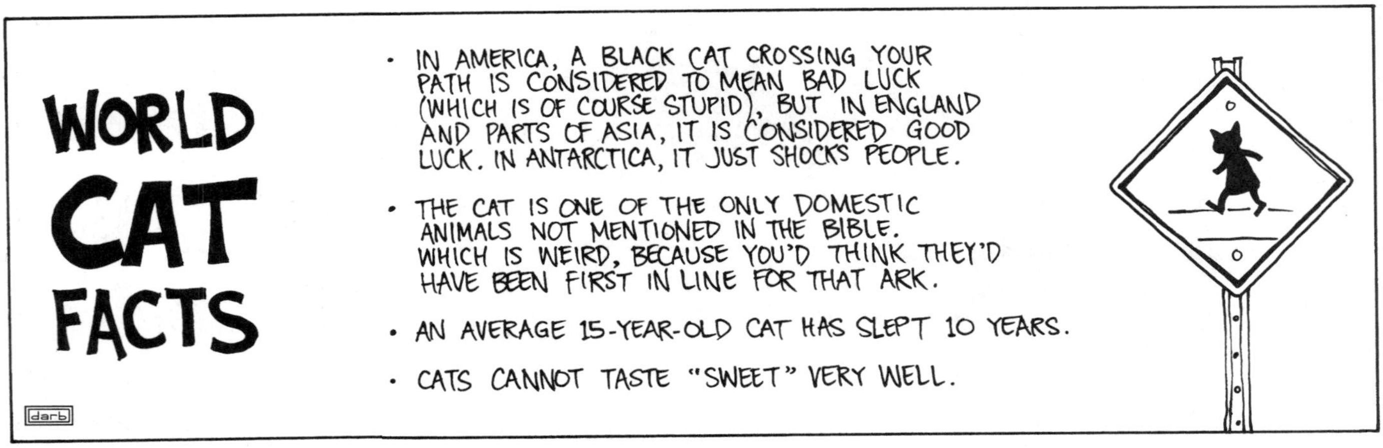
WORLD CAT FACTS
• IN AMERICA, A BLACK CAT CROSSING YOUR PATH IS CONSIDERED TO MEAN BAD LUCK (WHICH IS OF COURSE STUPID), BUT IN ENGLAND AND PARTS OF ASIA, IT IS CONSIDERED GOOD LUCK. IN ANTARCTICA, IT JUST SHOCKS PEOPLE.
• THE CAT IS ONE OF THE ONLY DOMESTIC ANIMALS NOT MENTIONED IN THE BIBLE. WHICH IS WEIRD, BECAUSE YOU'D THINK THEY'D HAVE BEEN FIRST IN LINE FOR THAT ARK.
• AN AVERAGE 15-YEAR-OLD CAT HAS SLEPT 10 YEARS.
• CATS CANNOT TASTE "SWEET" VERY WELL.
darb

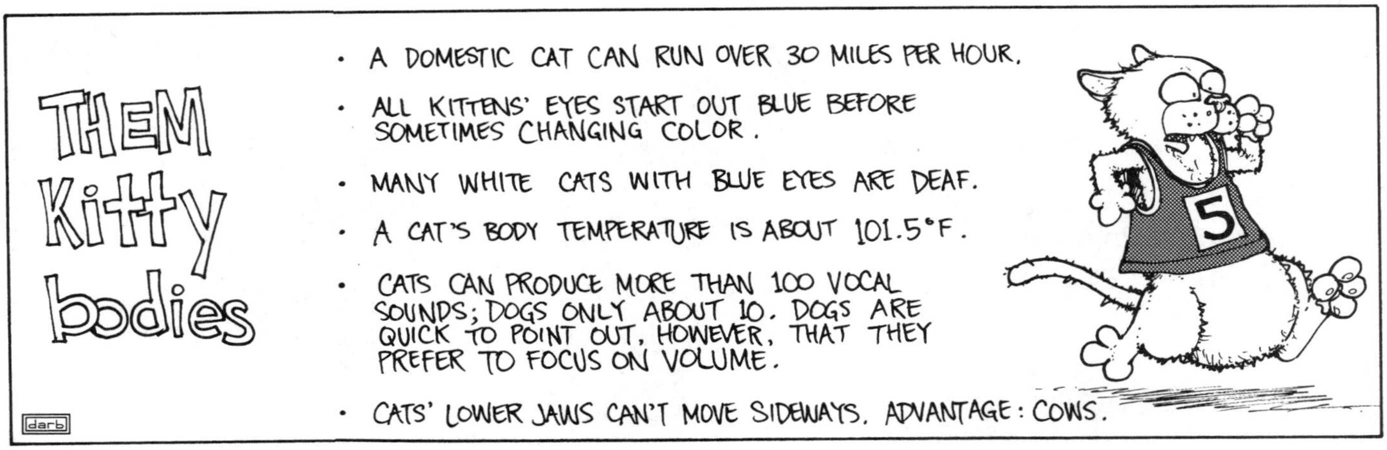
THEM Kitty bodies
• A DOMESTIC CAT CAN RUN OVER 30 MILES PER HOUR.
• ALL KITTENS' EYES START OUT BLUE BEFORE SOMETIMES CHANGING COLOR.
• MANY WHITE CATS WITH BLUE EYES ARE DEAF.
• A CAT'S BODY TEMPERATURE IS ABOUT 101.5°F.
• CATS CAN PRODUCE MORE THAN 100 VOCAL SOUNDS; DOGS ONLY ABOUT 10. DOGS ARE QUICK TO POINT OUT, HOWEVER, THAT THEY PREFER TO FOCUS ON VOLUME.
• CATS' LOWER JAWS CAN'T MOVE SIDEWAYS. ADVANTAGE: COWS.
5
darb

Love thy animals

- ONLY ABOUT 20% OF KITTENS BORN IN THE U.S. FIND A HOME WITH HUMANS FOR LIFE. PLEASE SPAY OR NEUTER YOUR CAT.

- CAT OVERPOPULATION, IRONICALLY, IS A RESULT OF STUPID HUMANS.*

- DECLAWING A CAT INVOLVES AMPUTATING ITS FINGERS AT THE LAST KNUCKLE. IF YOU WANT A CHILL CAT, ADOPT AN OLDER CAT. OR GET A GARFIELD DOLL.

* Darby Conley's Personal Opinions are not his own.

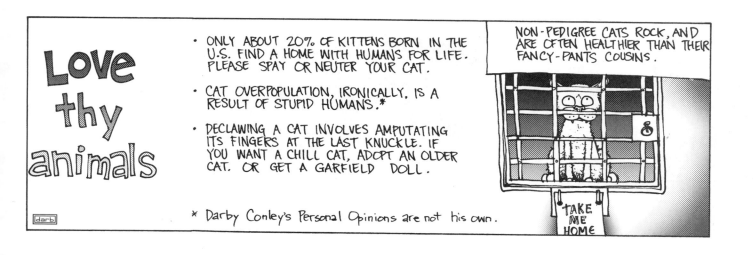

NON-PEDIGREE CATS ROCK, AND ARE OFTEN HEALTHIER THAN THEIR FANCY-PANTS COUSINS.

TAKE ME HOME

cat records

- THE HEAVIEST CAT ON RECORD WAS AN AUSSIE KITTY NAMED HIMMY, WHO CRACKED THE SCALES JUST SHY OF 47 POUNDS AND HAD A 33-INCH WAIST. OY.

- THE OLDEST CAT ON RECORD WAS PUSS, OF DEVON, ENGLAND. HE LIVED TO THE AGE OF 36.

- THE #1 PUBLIC ENEMY IN THE HISTORY OF MICE WAS A SCOTTISH TORTIE NAMED TOWSER. SHE CAUGHT NO LESS THAN 28,899 MICE IN HER 21-YEAR LIFE AS MOUSER AT THE GLENTURRET DISTILLERY.

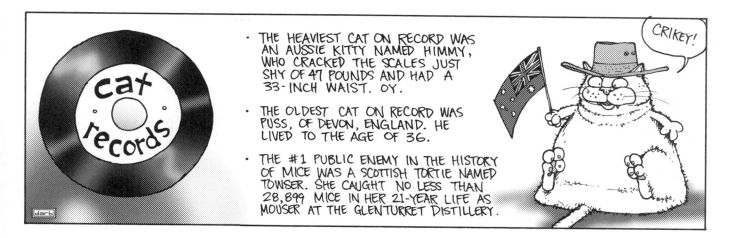

CRIKEY!

CATS in ANCIENT EGYPT

- THE EGYPTIAN WORD FOR "CAT" IS "MAU", WHICH MEANS "SEER." ANCIENT EGYPTIANS BELIEVED CATS POSSESSED MYSTICAL POWER AND REVERED THEM. WHEN A CAT DIED, ITS HUMAN FAMILY WOULD SHAVE THEIR EYEBROWS IN A SIGN OF MOURNING.

- TODAY, WE KNOW THAT CATS ARE JUST STUCK-UP FREELOADERS.

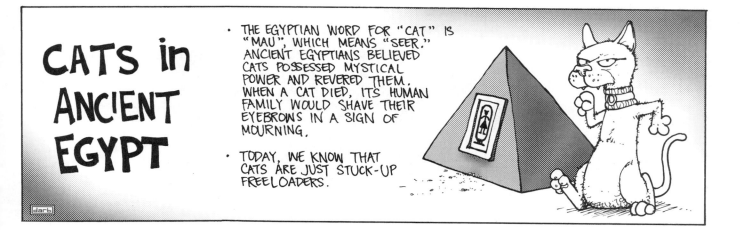

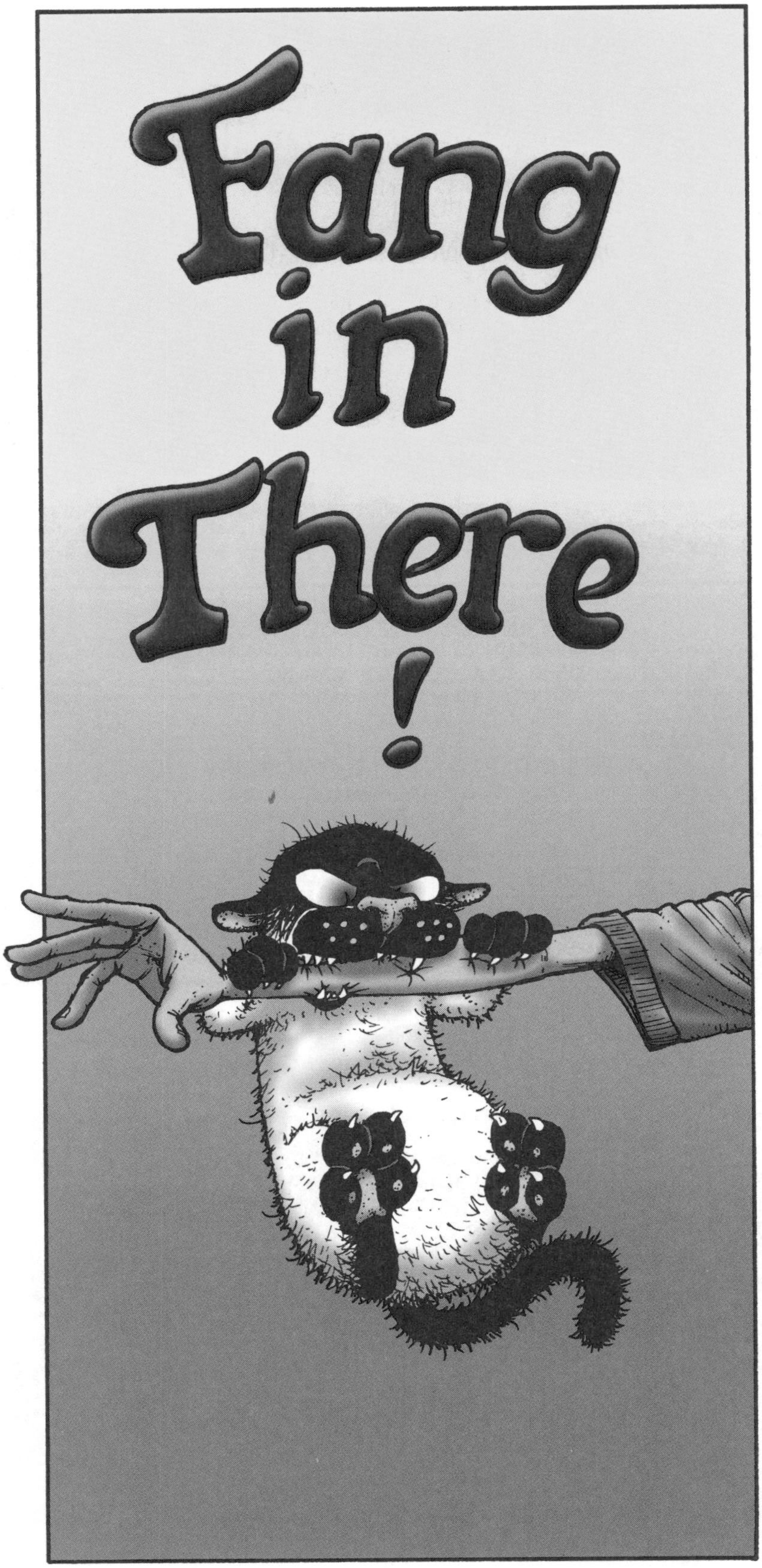
Fang in There!

BOBBIE, the WONDER DOG of OREGON

FROM AUGUST, 1923, TO FEBRUARY, 1924, A SCOTCH COLLIE-ENGLISH SHEPHERD MIX NAMED BOBBIE MADE PERHAPS THE MOST INCREDIBLE DOCUMENTED JOURNEY TO RETURN HOME. WHILE VISITING INDIANA, BOBBIE WAS CHASED AWAY FROM HIS OWNERS BY A PACK OF LOCAL DOGS. AFTER 3 WEEKS OF SEARCHING, HIS FAMILY WAS FORCED TO RETURN TO OREGON WITHOUT HIM, BROKEN-HEARTED. EXACTLY 6 MONTHS LATER, BOBBIE WALKED BACK INTO HIS HOMETOWN OF SILVERTON, OREGON, TIRED AND EMACIATED. HE HAD TRAVELED SOMEWHERE AROUND 3,000 MILES ON FOOT-THROUGH ICY RIVERS, SNOW STORMS AND OVER HUGE MOUNTAIN RANGES. AS HIS STORY BECAME KNOWN, HIS OWNERS RECEIVED MANY LETTERS FROM PEOPLE WHO HAD SEEN AND/OR HELPED BOBBIE ALONG HIS CROSS COUNTRY JOURNEY.

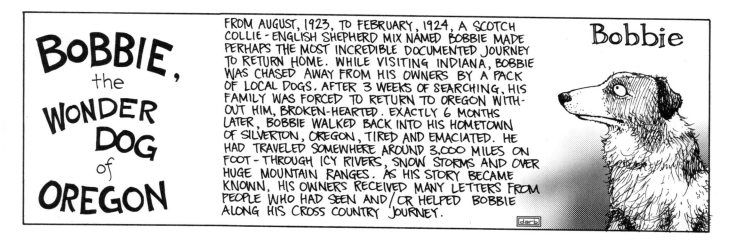

Bobbie

L'Histoire du CHIEN

- DOGS WERE PERHAPS THE FIRST DOMESTICATED ANIMAL. THEY HAVE LIVED AND WORKED WITH HUMANS FOR AT LEAST 12,000 YEARS.

- SALUKI-LIKE DOGS ARE REPRESENTED IN SUMERIAN ARTWORK AS OLD AS 7000 B.C.E.

- GEORGE WASHINGTON IS CONSIDERED THE FATHER OF THE AMERICAN FOXHOUND.

- THE COMICAL POODLE CUT WAS ORIGINALLY INTENDED TO AID THE DOG'S SWIMMING ABILITIES. THE POMS WERE LEFT TO KEEP THEIR JOINTS WARM.

- THE ONLY DOG TO APPEAR IN ONE OF SHAKESPEARE'S PLAYS WAS CRAB IN "THE TWO GENTLEMEN OF VERONA."

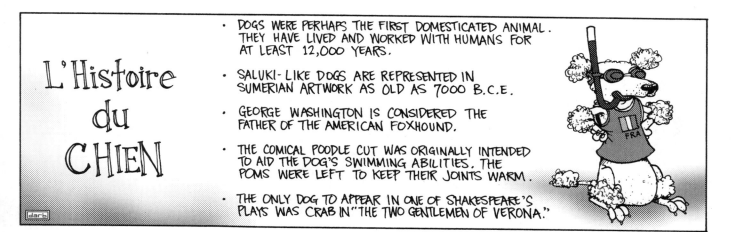

random DOG facts

- THE CANARY ISLANDS WERE NOT NAMED AFTER BIRDS. THEY WERE NAMED AFTER THE LARGE DOGS THAT LIVED THERE IN ANCIENT TIMES: *CANARIAE INSULAE = ISLAND OF DOGS*

- THE EXPRESSION "THREE DOG NIGHT" IS AN ESKIMO EXPRESSION MEANING THAT IT'S SO COLD OUT THAT YOU HAVE TO HUDDLE WITH THREE DOGS TO STAY WARM.

- THE ROMANS BELIEVED THAT SIRIUS-THE DOG STAR-ADDED TO THE HEAT OF THE SUN GREATLY FROM JULY 3rd TO AUGUST 11th, CREATING THE *DIES CANICULARES* - THE DOG DAYS OF SUMMER.

ULULAT.

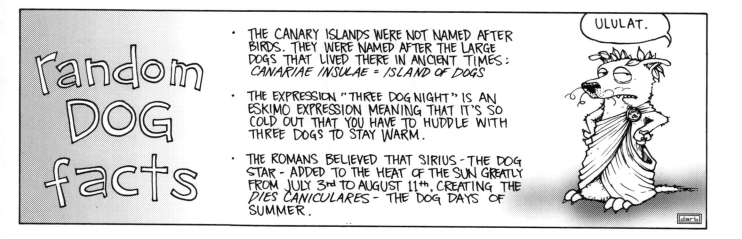

Dogs in War.

- MORE THAN 100,000 DOGS SERVED IN THE U.S. MILITARY IN THE 20th CENTURY, BUT TO DATE THERE IS NO NATIONAL WAR DOGS MONUMENT. 2 NOTABLE WAR DOGS WERE:

- STUBBY, WWI. A STRAY, STUBBY WAS SMUGGLED TO FRANCE ABOARD A TROOP SHIP. HE SERVED IN MANY LARGE BATTLES, WAS WOUNDED, CAPTURED A GERMAN SPY SINGLE-PAWEDLY, LOCATED WOUNDED SOLDIERS, AND IN ONE INSTANCE ALERTED HIS SOLDIERS TO A SURPRISE MUSTARD GAS ATTACK. HE IS THE MOST DECORATED WAR DOG IN U.S. HISTORY.

- CHIPS, WWII. DURING THE INVASION OF SICILY, CHIPS STORMED AN ENEMY MACHINE GUN PILLBOX, CORNERING 4 SOLDIERS. LATER THAT NIGHT HE HELPED CAPTURE 10 MORE. HE WAS AWARDED THE PURPLE HEART AND THE SILVER STAR FOR VALOR.

Sergeant Stubby

dog records

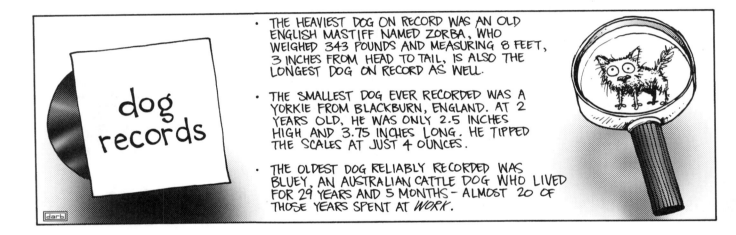

- THE HEAVIEST DOG ON RECORD WAS AN OLD ENGLISH MASTIFF NAMED ZORBA, WHO WEIGHED 343 POUNDS AND MEASURING 8 FEET, 3 INCHES FROM HEAD TO TAIL, IS ALSO THE LONGEST DOG ON RECORD AS WELL.

- THE SMALLEST DOG EVER RECORDED WAS A YORKIE FROM BLACKBURN, ENGLAND. AT 2 YEARS OLD, HE WAS ONLY 2.5 INCHES HIGH AND 3.75 INCHES LONG. HE TIPPED THE SCALES AT JUST 4 OUNCES.

- THE OLDEST DOG RELIABLY RECORDED WAS BLUEY, AN AUSTRALIAN CATTLE DOG WHO LIVED FOR 29 YEARS AND 5 MONTHS - ALMOST 20 OF THOSE YEARS SPENT AT *WORK*.

Doggie Physiology

- DOGS ARE NOT TOTALLY COLOR BLIND. THEY CAN DISTINGUISH BETWEEN BLUE, YELLOW AND GRAY, BUT MAY NOT SEE RED AND GREEN - SIMILAR TO OUR COLOR REGISTRATION AT TWILIGHT.

- DOGS POSSESS ONE OF THE BEST NOSES IN NATURE. WHILE HUMANS HAVE ABOUT 5 MILLION OLFACTORY CELLS, DOGS CAN HAVE AS MANY AS 225 MILLION. WHERE WE SMELL SOUP COOKING, A DOG VERY WELL MAY BE ABLE TO DISCERN THE INDIVIDUAL INGREDIENTS COOKING IN THE SOUP.

- IN ADDITION TO PANTING, DOGS REGULATE THEIR BODY TEMPERATURE BY SWEATING THROUGH THE PADS OF THEIR FEET.

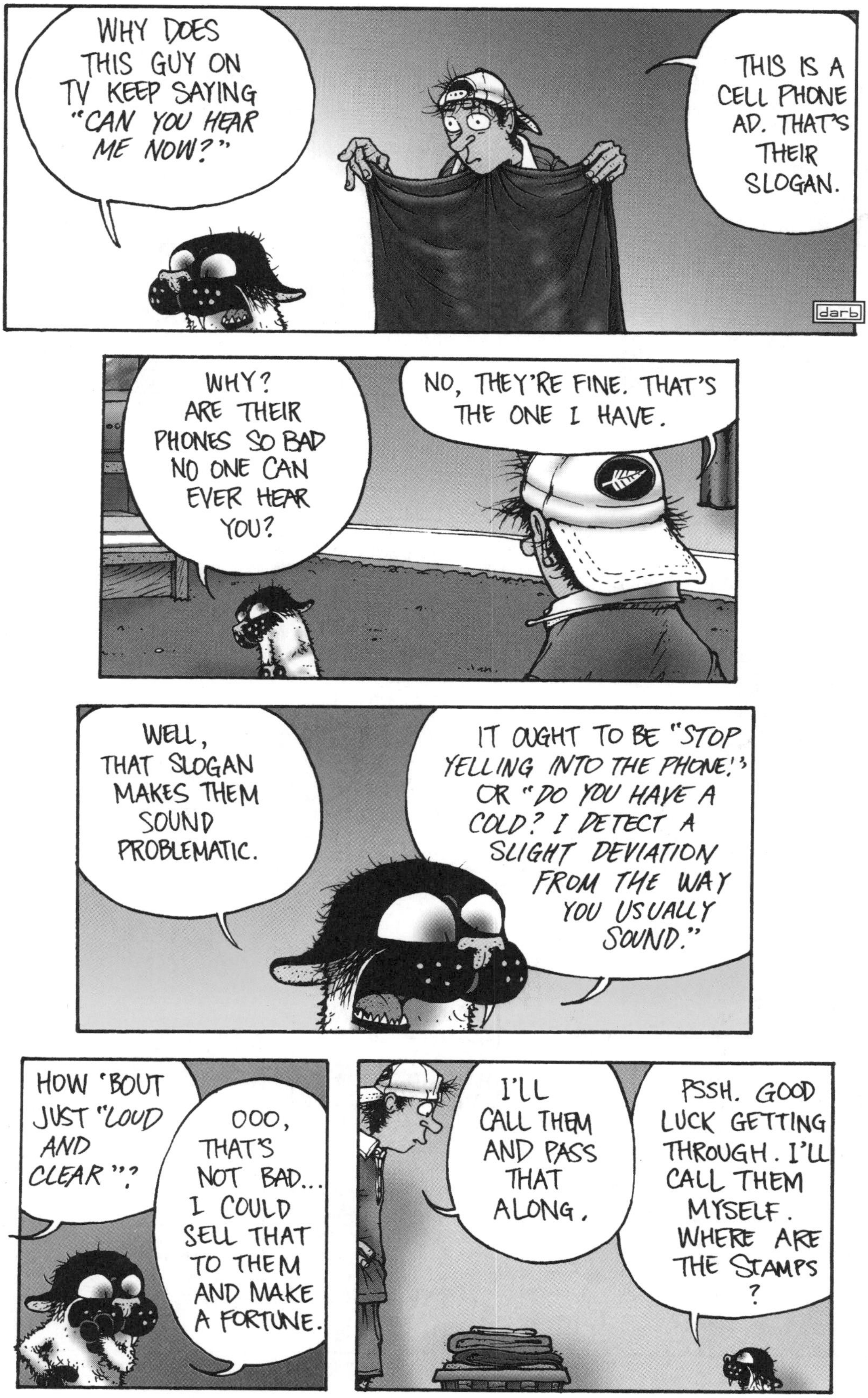

WHY DOES THIS GUY ON TV KEEP SAYING "CAN YOU HEAR ME NOW?"
THIS IS A CELL PHONE AD. THAT'S THEIR SLOGAN.
darb
WHY? ARE THEIR PHONES SO BAD NO ONE CAN EVER HEAR YOU?
NO, THEY'RE FINE. THAT'S THE ONE I HAVE.
WELL, THAT SLOGAN MAKES THEM SOUND PROBLEMATIC.
IT OUGHT TO BE "STOP YELLING INTO THE PHONE!" OR "DO YOU HAVE A COLD? I DETECT A SLIGHT DEVIATION FROM THE WAY YOU USUALLY SOUND."
HOW 'BOUT JUST "LOUD AND CLEAR"?
OOO, THAT'S NOT BAD... I COULD SELL THAT TO THEM AND MAKE A FORTUNE.
I'LL CALL THEM AND PASS THAT ALONG.
PSSH. GOOD LUCK GETTING THROUGH. I'LL CALL THEM MYSELF. WHERE ARE THE STAMPS?

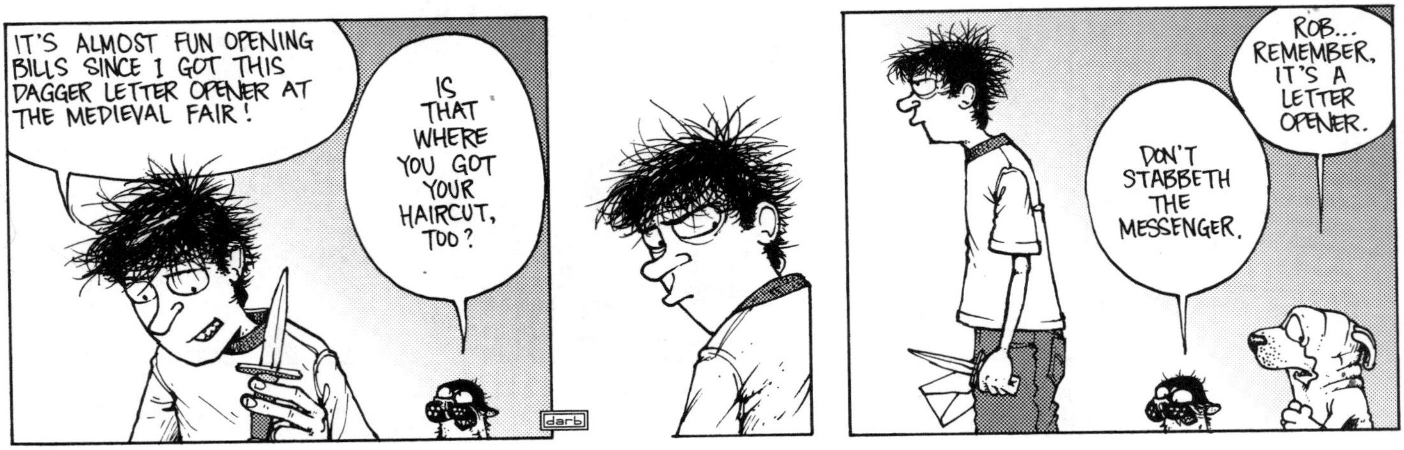
IT'S ALMOST FUN OPENING BILLS SINCE I GOT THIS DAGGER LETTER OPENER AT THE MEDIEVAL FAIR!
IS THAT WHERE YOU GOT YOUR HAIRCUT, TOO?
ROB... REMEMBER, IT'S A LETTER OPENER.
DON'T STABBETH THE MESSENGER.
darb

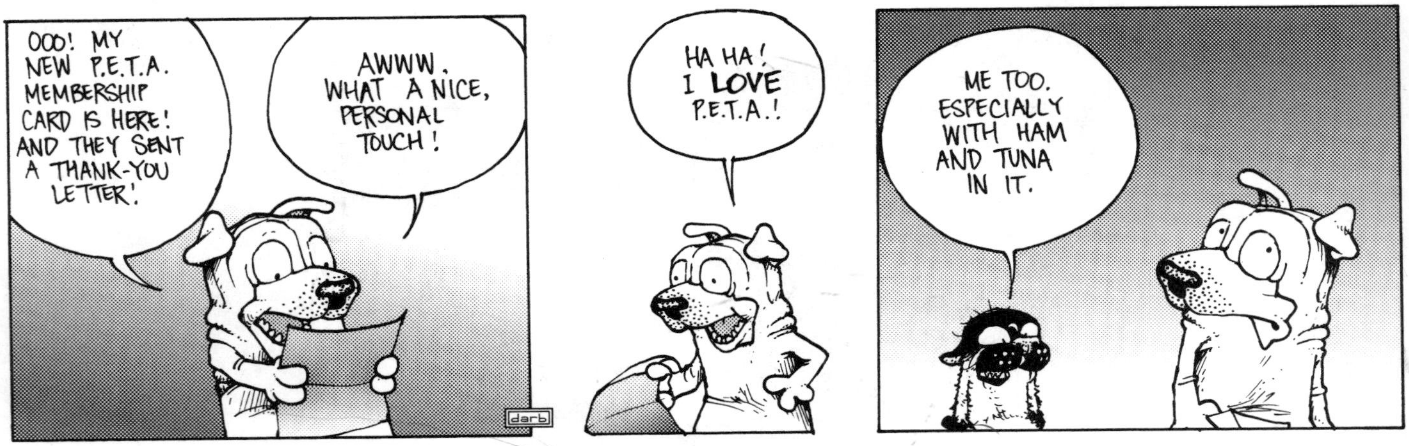
OOO! MY NEW P.E.T.A. MEMBERSHIP CARD IS HERE! AND THEY SENT A THANK-YOU LETTER!
AWWW. WHAT A NICE, PERSONAL TOUCH!
HA HA! I **LOVE** P.E.T.A.!
ME TOO. ESPECIALLY WITH HAM AND TUNA IN IT.
darb

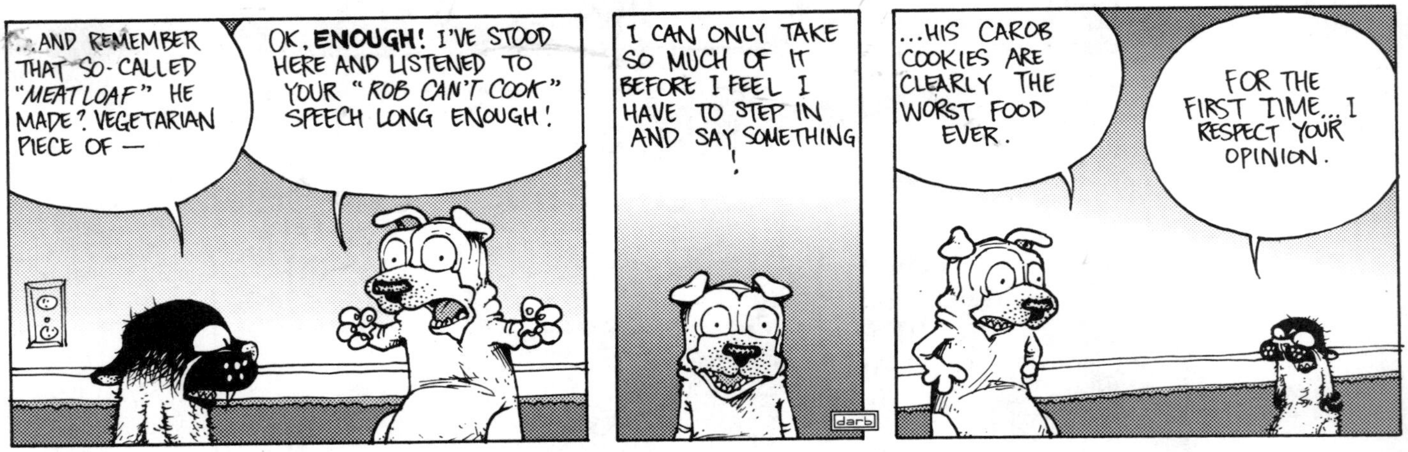
...AND REMEMBER THAT SO-CALLED "*MEATLOAF*" HE MADE? VEGETARIAN PIECE OF —
OK, **ENOUGH**! I'VE STOOD HERE AND LISTENED TO YOUR "*ROB CAN'T COOK*" SPEECH LONG ENOUGH!
I CAN ONLY TAKE SO MUCH OF IT BEFORE I FEEL I HAVE TO STEP IN AND SAY SOMETHING!
...HIS CAROB COOKIES ARE CLEARLY THE WORST FOOD EVER.
FOR THE FIRST TIME... I RESPECT YOUR OPINION.
darb

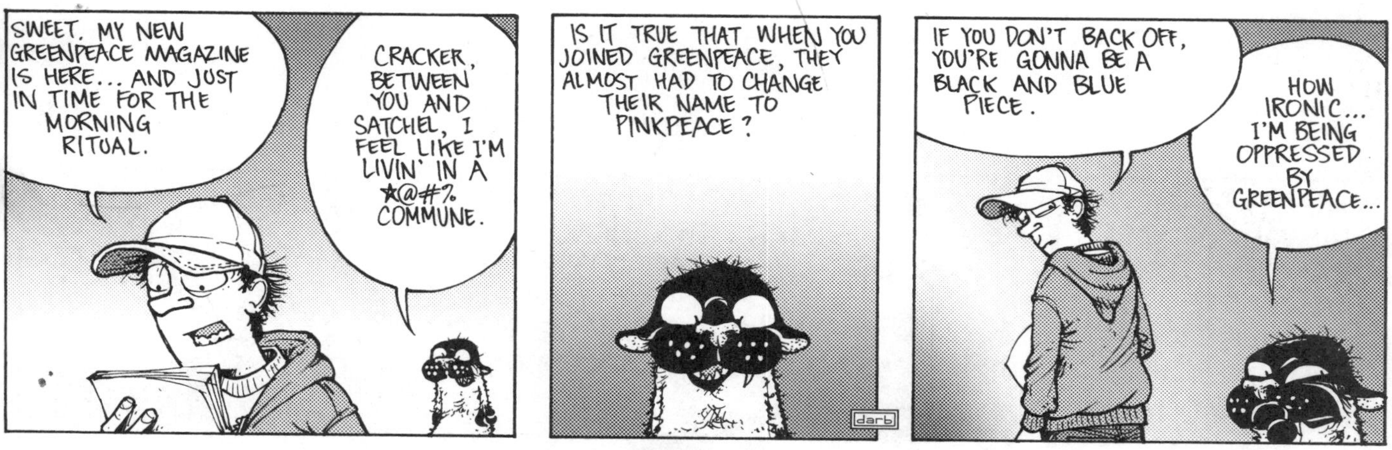
SWEET. MY NEW GREENPEACE MAGAZINE IS HERE... AND JUST IN TIME FOR THE MORNING RITUAL.
CRACKER, BETWEEN YOU AND SATCHEL, I FEEL LIKE I'M LIVIN' IN A ★@#% COMMUNE.
IS IT TRUE THAT WHEN YOU JOINED GREENPEACE, THEY ALMOST HAD TO CHANGE THEIR NAME TO PINKPEACE ?
darb
IF YOU DON'T BACK OFF, YOU'RE GONNA BE A BLACK AND BLUE PIECE.
HOW IRONIC... I'M BEING OPPRESSED BY GREENPEACE...

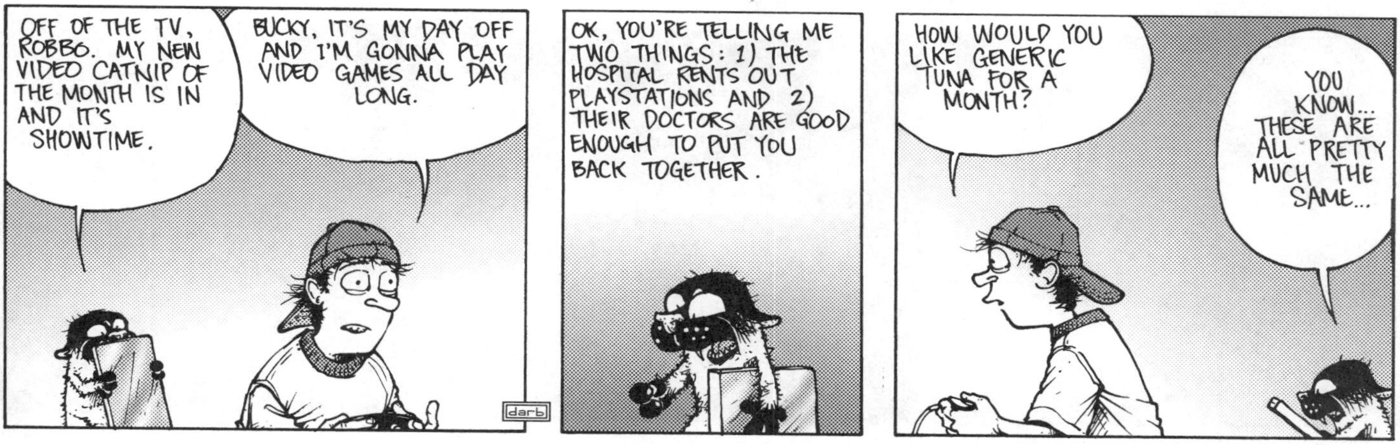
OFF OF THE TV, ROBBO. MY NEW VIDEO CATNIP OF THE MONTH IS IN AND IT'S SHOWTIME.
BUCKY, IT'S MY DAY OFF AND I'M GONNA PLAY VIDEO GAMES ALL DAY LONG.
darb
OK, YOU'RE TELLING ME TWO THINGS: 1) THE HOSPITAL RENTS OUT PLAYSTATIONS AND 2) THEIR DOCTORS ARE GOOD ENOUGH TO PUT YOU BACK TOGETHER.
HOW WOULD YOU LIKE GENERIC TUNA FOR A MONTH?
YOU KNOW... THESE ARE ALL PRETTY MUCH THE SAME...

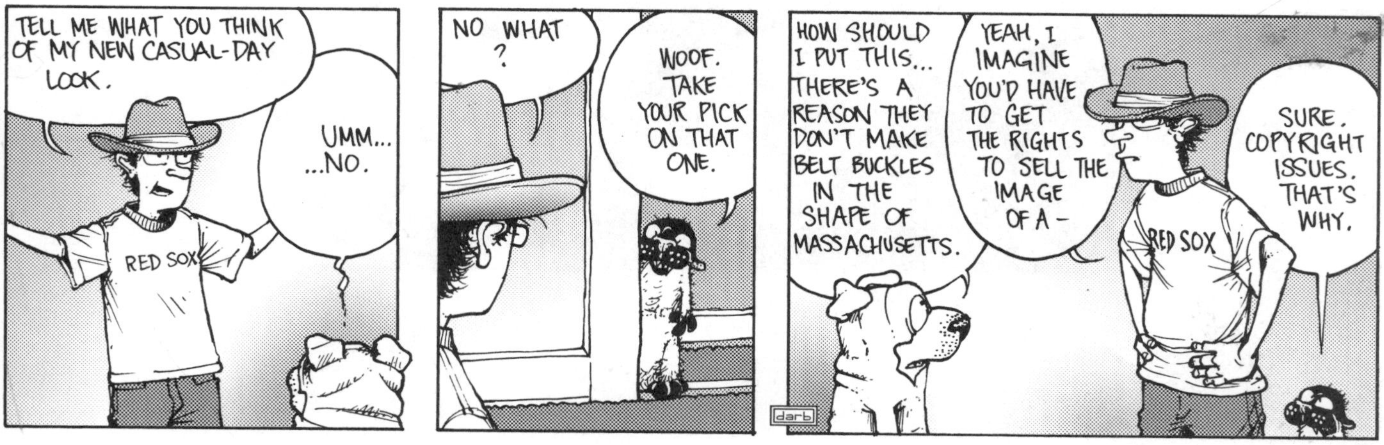
TELL ME WHAT YOU THINK OF MY NEW CASUAL-DAY LOOK.
UMM... ...NO.
RED SOX
NO WHAT ?
WOOF. TAKE YOUR PICK ON THAT ONE.
darb
HOW SHOULD I PUT THIS... THERE'S A REASON THEY DON'T MAKE BELT BUCKLES IN THE SHAPE OF MASSACHUSETTS.
YEAH, I IMAGINE YOU'D HAVE TO GET THE RIGHTS TO SELL THE IMAGE OF A –
SURE. COPYRIGHT ISSUES. THAT'S WHY.
RED SOX

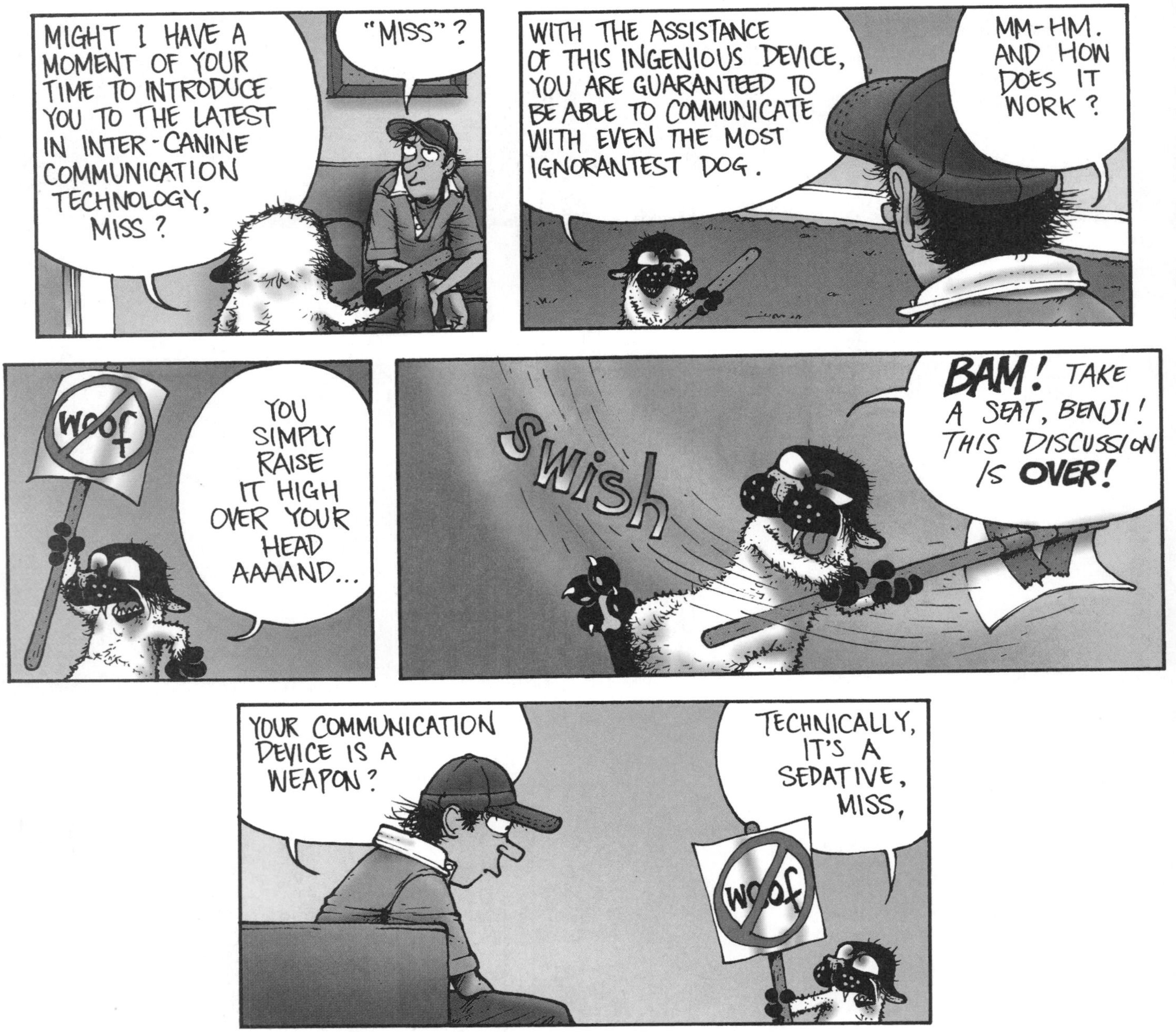
MIGHT I HAVE A MOMENT OF YOUR TIME TO INTRODUCE YOU TO THE LATEST IN INTER-CANINE COMMUNICATION TECHNOLOGY, MISS?
"MISS"?
WITH THE ASSISTANCE OF THIS INGENIOUS DEVICE, YOU ARE GUARANTEED TO BE ABLE TO COMMUNICATE WITH EVEN THE MOST IGNORANTEST DOG.
MM-HM. AND HOW DOES IT WORK?
WOOF
YOU SIMPLY RAISE IT HIGH OVER YOUR HEAD AAAAND...
SWISH
BAM! TAKE A SEAT, BENJI! THIS DISCUSSION IS OVER!
YOUR COMMUNICATION DEVICE IS A WEAPON?
TECHNICALLY, IT'S A SEDATIVE, MISS,
WOOF

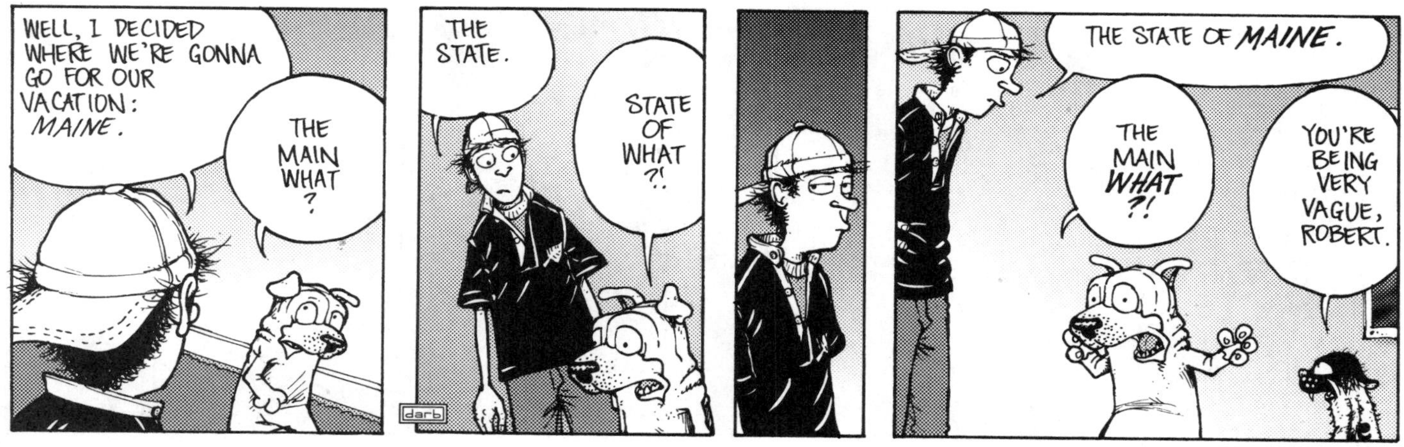
WELL, I DECIDED WHERE WE'RE GONNA GO FOR OUR VACATION: MAINE.
THE MAIN WHAT?
THE STATE.
STATE OF WHAT?!
THE STATE OF MAINE.
THE MAIN WHAT?!
YOU'RE BEING VERY VAGUE, ROBERT.

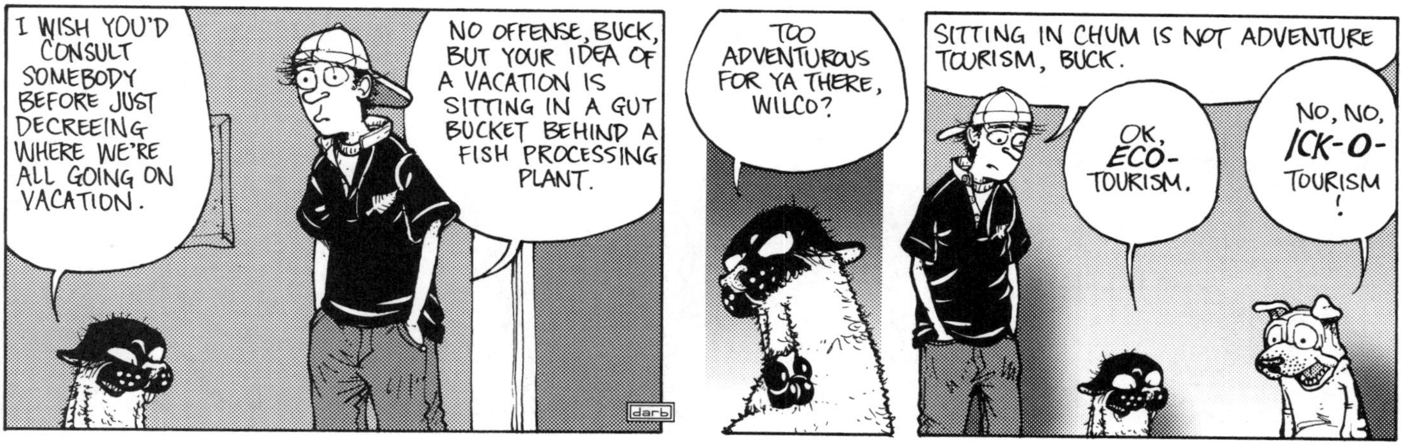
I WISH YOU'D CONSULT SOMEBODY BEFORE JUST DECREEING WHERE WE'RE ALL GOING ON VACATION.
NO OFFENSE, BUCK, BUT YOUR IDEA OF A VACATION IS SITTING IN A GUT BUCKET BEHIND A FISH PROCESSING PLANT.
TOO ADVENTUROUS FOR YA THERE, WILCO?
SITTING IN CHUM IS NOT ADVENTURE TOURISM, BUCK.
OK, ECO-TOURISM.
NO, NO, ICK-O-TOURISM!

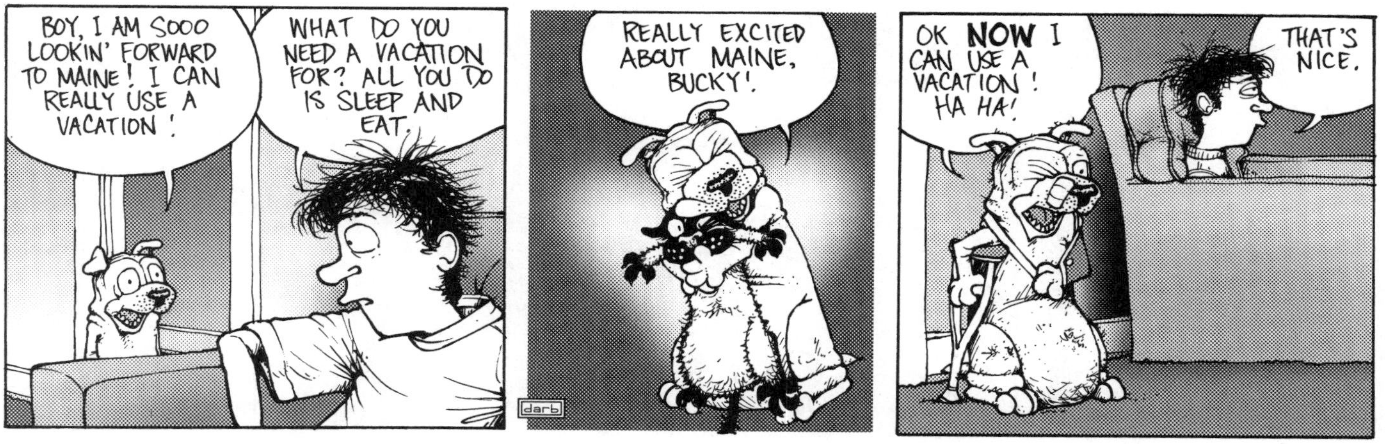
BOY, I AM SOOO LOOKIN' FORWARD TO MAINE! I CAN REALLY USE A VACATION!
WHAT DO YOU NEED A VACATION FOR? ALL YOU DO IS SLEEP AND EAT.
REALLY EXCITED ABOUT MAINE, BUCKY!
OK NOW I CAN USE A VACATION! HA HA!
THAT'S NICE.

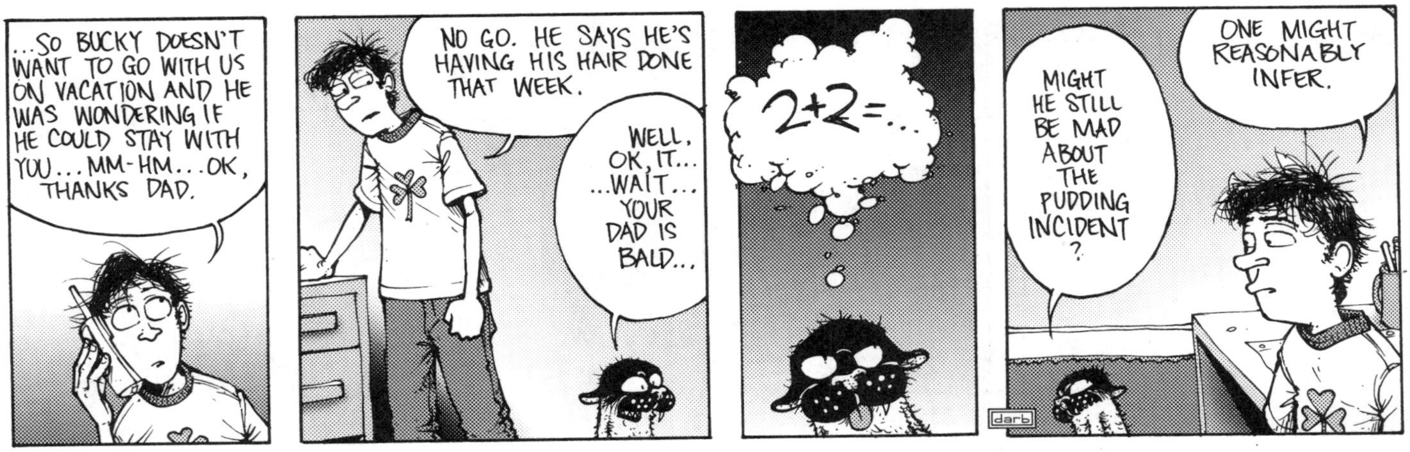
...SO BUCKY DOESN'T WANT TO GO WITH US ON VACATION AND HE WAS WONDERING IF HE COULD STAY WITH YOU... MM-HM... OK, THANKS DAD.
NO GO. HE SAYS HE'S HAVING HIS HAIR DONE THAT WEEK.
WELL, OK, IT... ...WAIT... YOUR DAD IS BALD...
2+2=...
MIGHT HE STILL BE MAD ABOUT THE PUDDING INCIDENT?
ONE MIGHT REASONABLY INFER.
darb

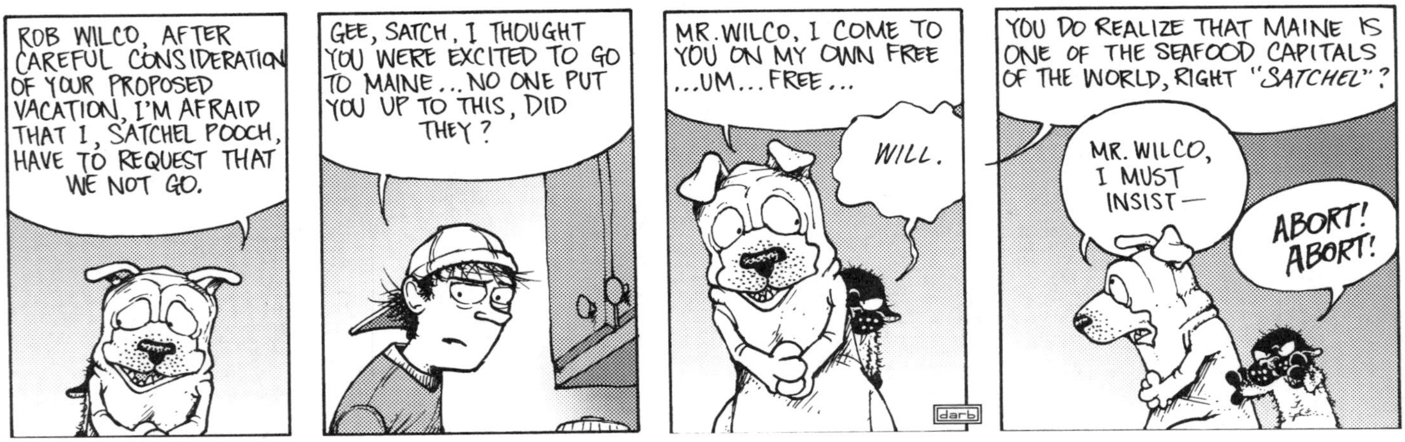
ROB WILCO, AFTER CAREFUL CONSIDERATION OF YOUR PROPOSED VACATION, I'M AFRAID THAT I, SATCHEL POOCH, HAVE TO REQUEST THAT WE NOT GO.
GEE, SATCH, I THOUGHT YOU WERE EXCITED TO GO TO MAINE... NO ONE PUT YOU UP TO THIS, DID THEY?
MR. WILCO, I COME TO YOU ON MY OWN FREE ...UM... FREE...
WILL.
darb
YOU DO REALIZE THAT MAINE IS ONE OF THE SEAFOOD CAPITALS OF THE WORLD, RIGHT "SATCHEL"?
MR. WILCO, I MUST INSIST—
ABORT! ABORT!

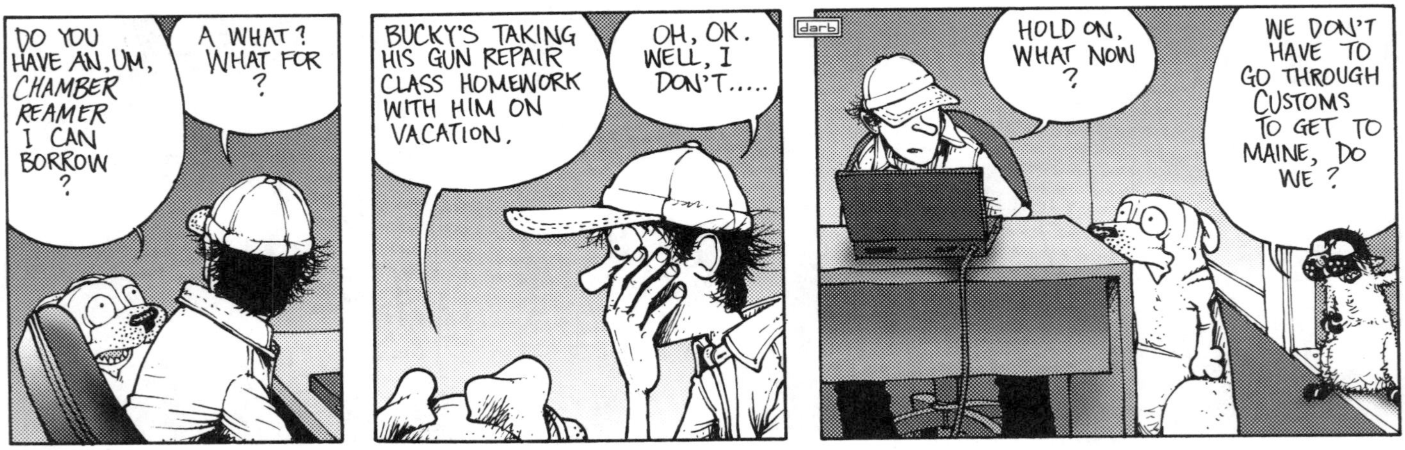
DO YOU HAVE AN, UM, CHAMBER REAMER I CAN BORROW?
A WHAT? WHAT FOR?
BUCKY'S TAKING HIS GUN REPAIR CLASS HOMEWORK WITH HIM ON VACATION.
OH, OK. WELL, I DON'T.....
darb
HOLD ON, WHAT NOW?
WE DON'T HAVE TO GO THROUGH CUSTOMS TO GET TO MAINE, DO WE?

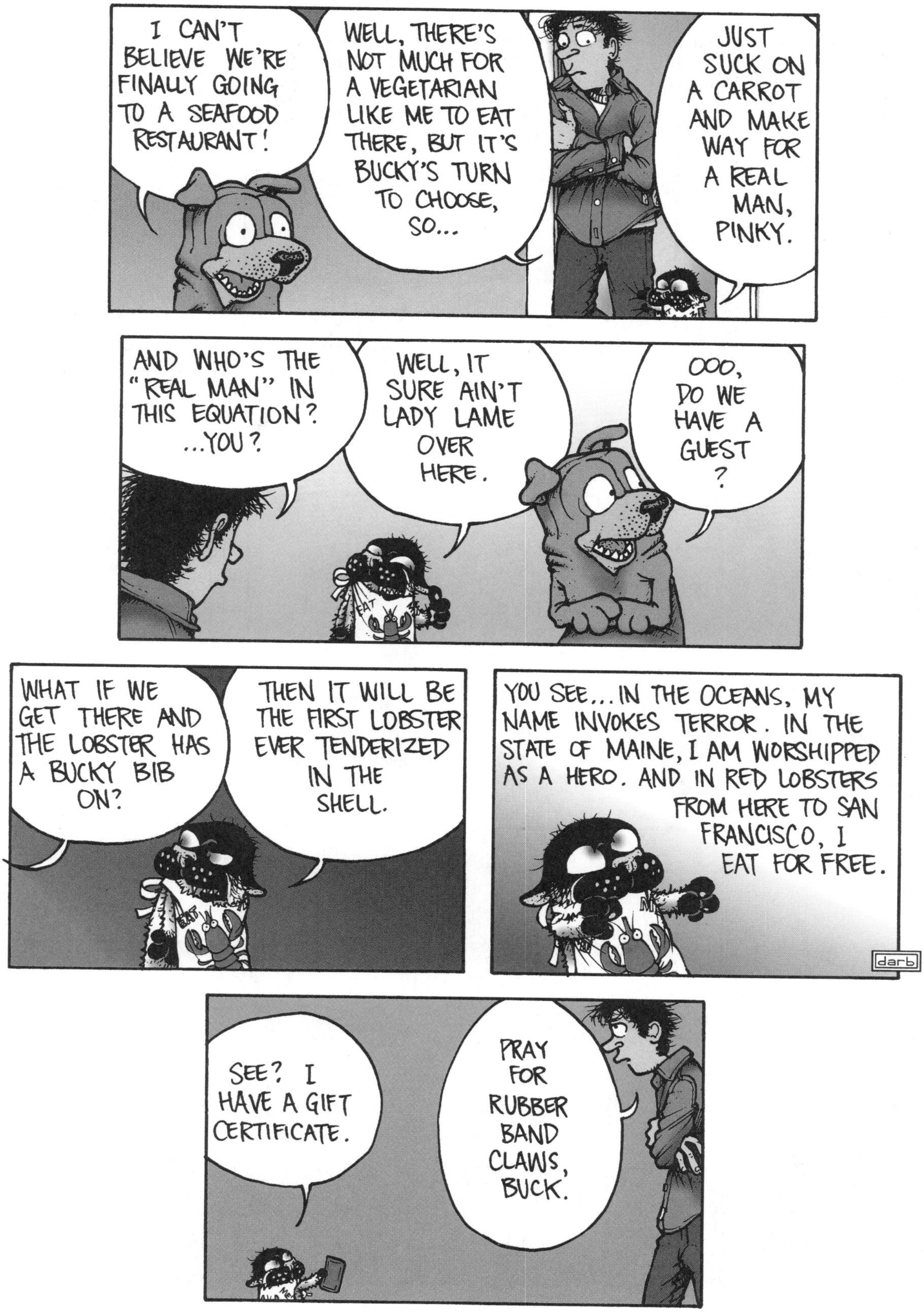
I CAN'T BELIEVE WE'RE FINALLY GOING TO A SEAFOOD RESTAURANT!
WELL, THERE'S NOT MUCH FOR A VEGETARIAN LIKE ME TO EAT THERE, BUT IT'S BUCKY'S TURN TO CHOOSE, SO...
JUST SUCK ON A CARROT AND MAKE WAY FOR A REAL MAN, PINKY.
AND WHO'S THE "REAL MAN" IN THIS EQUATION? ...YOU?
WELL, IT SURE AIN'T LADY LAME OVER HERE.
OOO, DO WE HAVE A GUEST?
WHAT IF WE GET THERE AND THE LOBSTER HAS A BUCKY BIB ON?
THEN IT WILL BE THE FIRST LOBSTER EVER TENDERIZED IN THE SHELL.
YOU SEE... IN THE OCEANS, MY NAME INVOKES TERROR. IN THE STATE OF MAINE, I AM WORSHIPPED AS A HERO. AND IN RED LOBSTERS FROM HERE TO SAN FRANCISCO, I EAT FOR FREE.
darb
SEE? I HAVE A GIFT CERTIFICATE.
PRAY FOR RUBBER BAND CLAWS, BUCK.

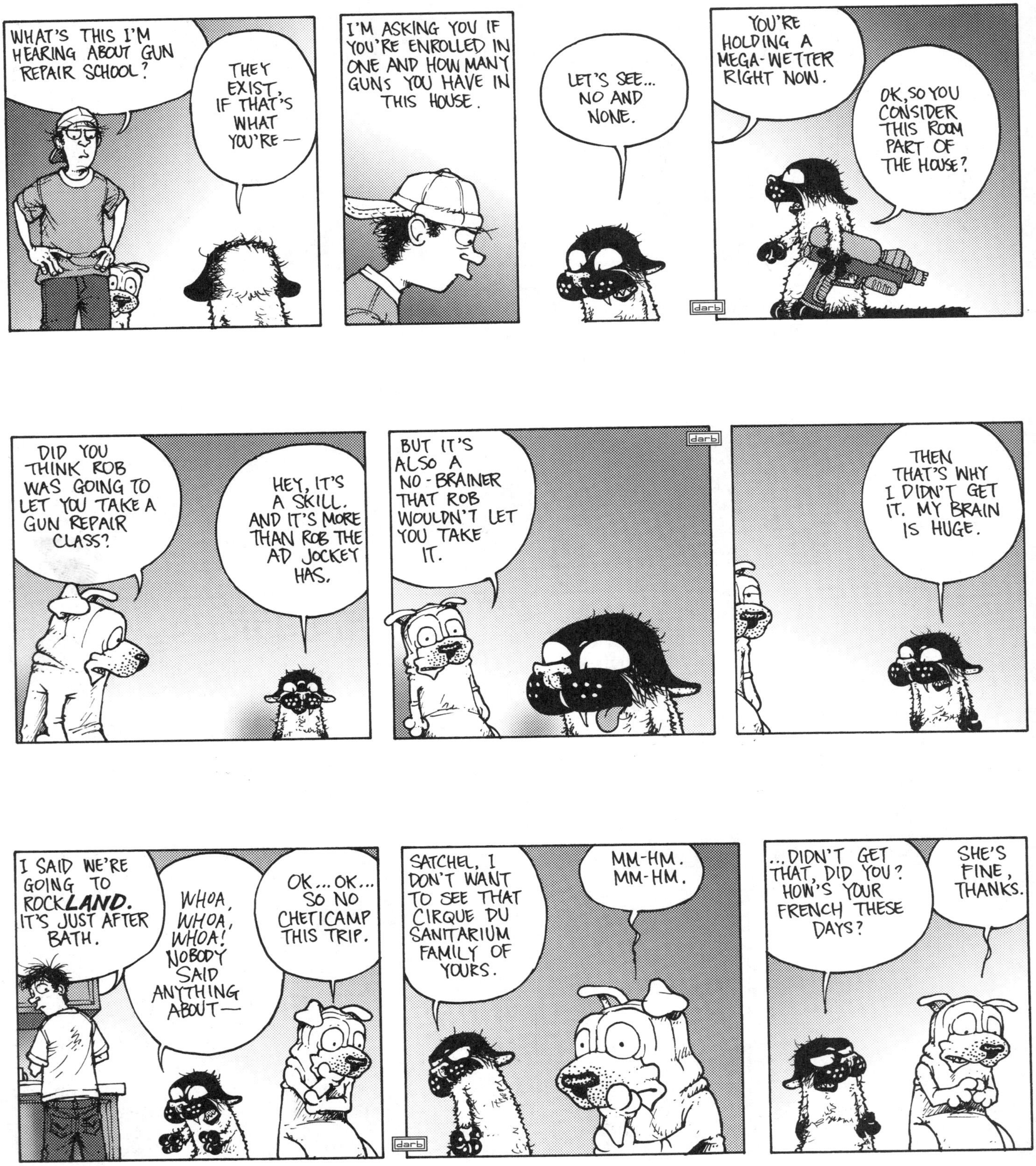
WHAT'S THIS I'M HEARING ABOUT GUN REPAIR SCHOOL?
THEY EXIST, IF THAT'S WHAT YOU'RE—
I'M ASKING YOU IF YOU'RE ENROLLED IN ONE AND HOW MANY GUNS YOU HAVE IN THIS HOUSE.
LET'S SEE... NO AND NONE.
YOU'RE HOLDING A MEGA-WETTER RIGHT NOW.
OK, SO YOU CONSIDER THIS ROOM PART OF THE HOUSE?
darb
DID YOU THINK ROB WAS GOING TO LET YOU TAKE A GUN REPAIR CLASS?
HEY, IT'S A SKILL. AND IT'S MORE THAN ROB THE AD JOCKEY HAS.
BUT IT'S ALSO A NO-BRAINER THAT ROB WOULDN'T LET YOU TAKE IT.
darb
THEN THAT'S WHY I DIDN'T GET IT. MY BRAIN IS HUGE.
I SAID WE'RE GOING TO ROCK**LAND**. IT'S JUST AFTER BATH.
WHOA, WHOA, WHOA! NOBODY SAID ANYTHING ABOUT—
OK... OK... SO NO CHETICAMP THIS TRIP.
darb
SATCHEL, I DON'T WANT TO SEE THAT CIRQUE DU SANITARIUM FAMILY OF YOURS.
MM-HM. MM-HM.
...DIDN'T GET THAT, DID YOU? HOW'S YOUR FRENCH THESE DAYS?
SHE'S FINE, THANKS.

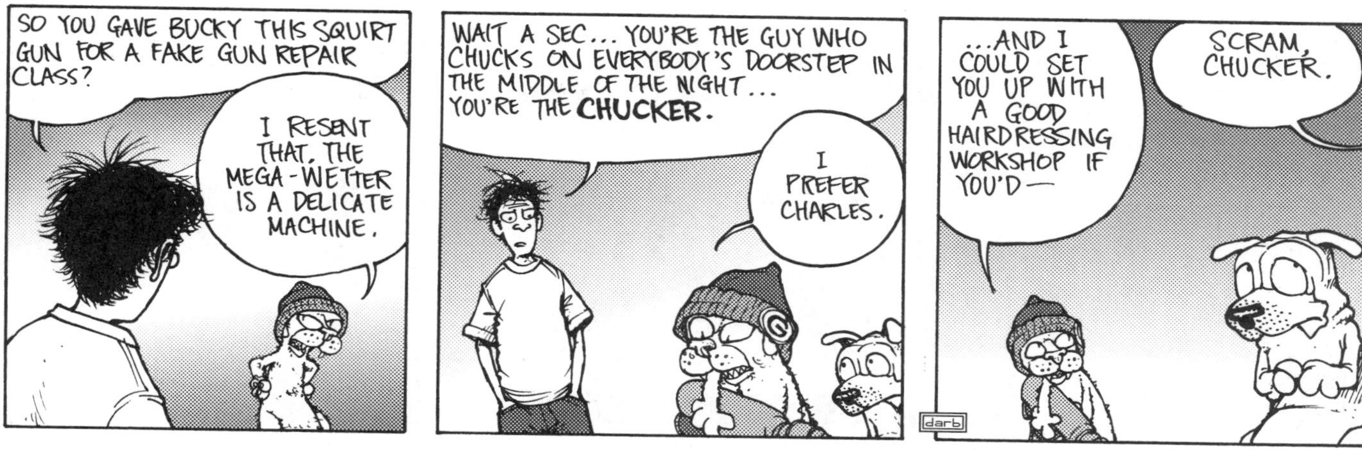
SO YOU GAVE BUCKY THIS SQUIRT GUN FOR A FAKE GUN REPAIR CLASS?
I RESENT THAT. THE MEGA-WETTER IS A DELICATE MACHINE.
WAIT A SEC... YOU'RE THE GUY WHO CHUCKS ON EVERYBODY'S DOORSTEP IN THE MIDDLE OF THE NIGHT... YOU'RE THE CHUCKER.
I PREFER CHARLES.
...AND I COULD SET YOU UP WITH A GOOD HAIRDRESSING WORKSHOP IF YOU'D—
SCRAM, CHUCKER.
darb

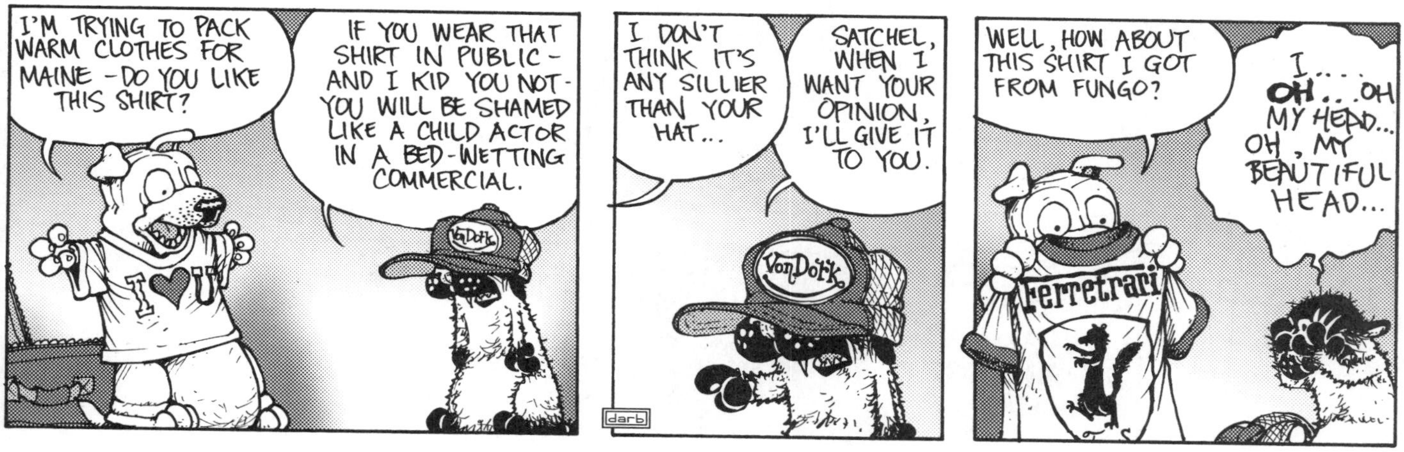
I'M TRYING TO PACK WARM CLOTHES FOR MAINE - DO YOU LIKE THIS SHIRT?
IF YOU WEAR THAT SHIRT IN PUBLIC - AND I KID YOU NOT - YOU WILL BE SHAMED LIKE A CHILD ACTOR IN A BED-WETTING COMMERCIAL.
I ♥ U
VonDork
I DON'T THINK IT'S ANY SILLIER THAN YOUR HAT...
SATCHEL, WHEN I WANT YOUR OPINION, I'LL GIVE IT TO YOU.
darb
WELL, HOW ABOUT THIS SHIRT I GOT FROM FUNGO?
I... OH... OH MY HEAD... OH, MY BEAUTIFUL HEAD...
Ferretrari

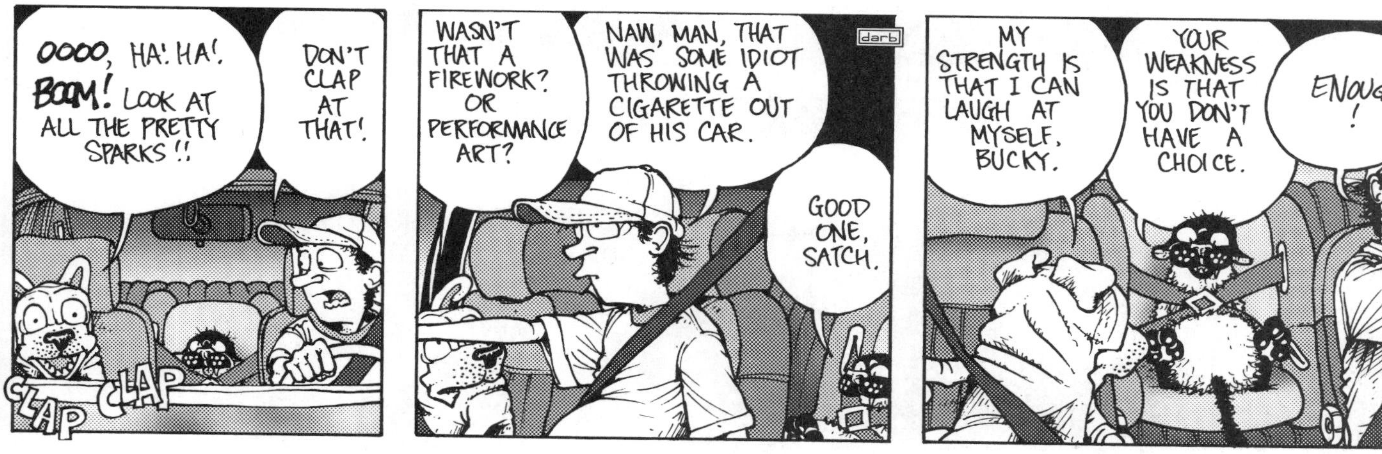
OOOO, HA! HA! BOOM! LOOK AT ALL THE PRETTY SPARKS!!
DON'T CLAP AT THAT!
CLAP CLAP
WASN'T THAT A FIREWORK? OR PERFORMANCE ART?
NAW, MAN, THAT WAS SOME IDIOT THROWING A CIGARETTE OUT OF HIS CAR.
GOOD ONE, SATCH.
darb
MY STRENGTH IS THAT I CAN LAUGH AT MYSELF, BUCKY.
YOUR WEAKNESS IS THAT YOU DON'T HAVE A CHOICE.
ENOUGH!

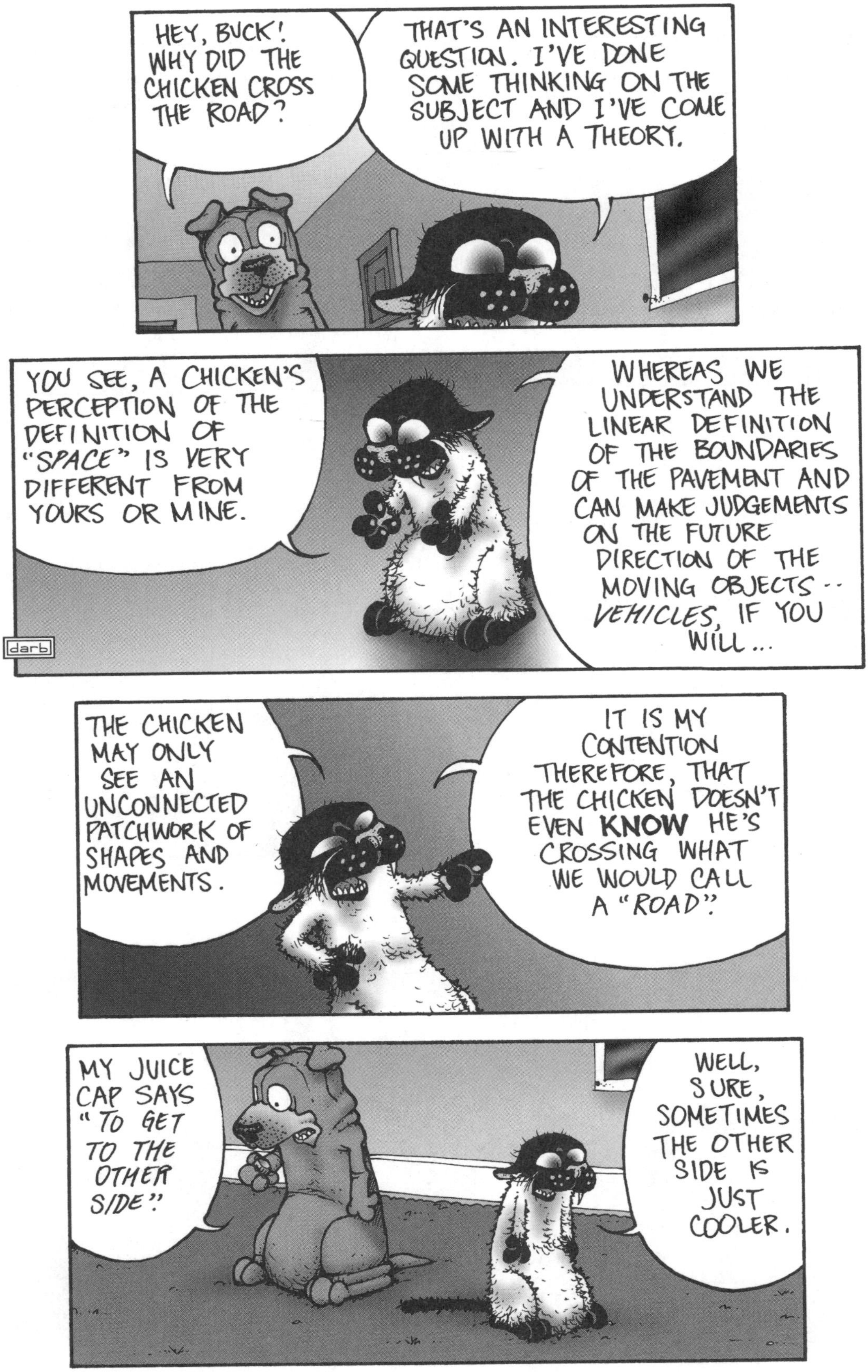
HEY, BUCK! WHY DID THE CHICKEN CROSS THE ROAD?
THAT'S AN INTERESTING QUESTION. I'VE DONE SOME THINKING ON THE SUBJECT AND I'VE COME UP WITH A THEORY.
YOU SEE, A CHICKEN'S PERCEPTION OF THE DEFINITION OF "SPACE" IS VERY DIFFERENT FROM YOURS OR MINE.
WHEREAS WE UNDERSTAND THE LINEAR DEFINITION OF THE BOUNDARIES OF THE PAVEMENT AND CAN MAKE JUDGEMENTS ON THE FUTURE DIRECTION OF THE MOVING OBJECTS.. VEHICLES, IF YOU WILL...
darb
THE CHICKEN MAY ONLY SEE AN UNCONNECTED PATCHWORK OF SHAPES AND MOVEMENTS.
IT IS MY CONTENTION THEREFORE, THAT THE CHICKEN DOESN'T EVEN KNOW HE'S CROSSING WHAT WE WOULD CALL A "ROAD".
MY JUICE CAP SAYS "TO GET TO THE OTHER SIDE".
WELL, SURE, SOMETIMES THE OTHER SIDE IS JUST COOLER.

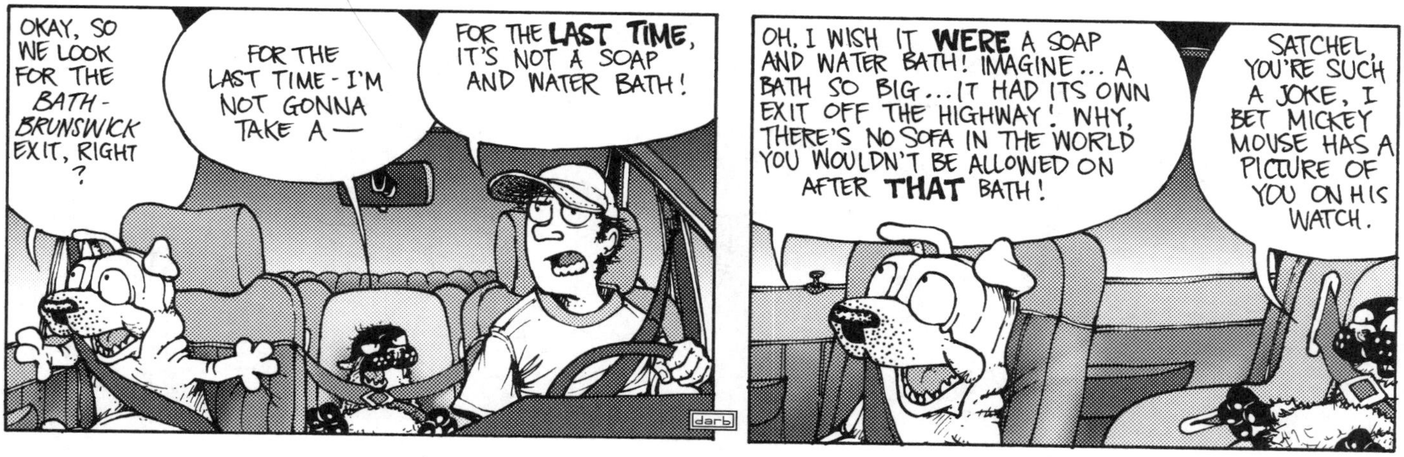
OKAY, SO WE LOOK FOR THE BATH-BRUNSWICK EXIT, RIGHT?
FOR THE LAST TIME - I'M NOT GONNA TAKE A—
FOR THE LAST TIME, IT'S NOT A SOAP AND WATER BATH!
darb
OH, I WISH IT WERE A SOAP AND WATER BATH! IMAGINE... A BATH SO BIG... IT HAD ITS OWN EXIT OFF THE HIGHWAY! WHY, THERE'S NO SOFA IN THE WORLD YOU WOULDN'T BE ALLOWED ON AFTER THAT BATH!
SATCHEL, YOU'RE SUCH A JOKE, I BET MICKEY MOUSE HAS A PICTURE OF YOU ON HIS WATCH.

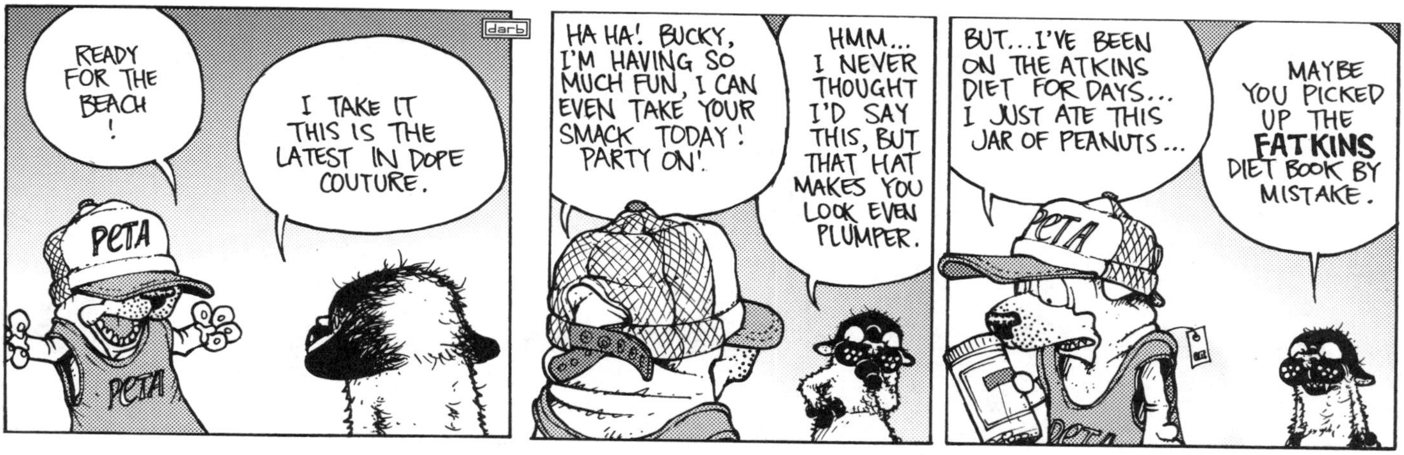
darb
READY FOR THE BEACH!
I TAKE IT THIS IS THE LATEST IN DOPE COUTURE.
PETA
HA HA! BUCKY, I'M HAVING SO MUCH FUN, I CAN EVEN TAKE YOUR SMACK TODAY! PARTY ON!
HMM... I NEVER THOUGHT I'D SAY THIS, BUT THAT HAT MAKES YOU LOOK EVEN PLUMPER.
BUT... I'VE BEEN ON THE ATKINS DIET FOR DAYS... I JUST ATE THIS JAR OF PEANUTS...
MAYBE YOU PICKED UP THE FATKINS DIET BOOK BY MISTAKE.

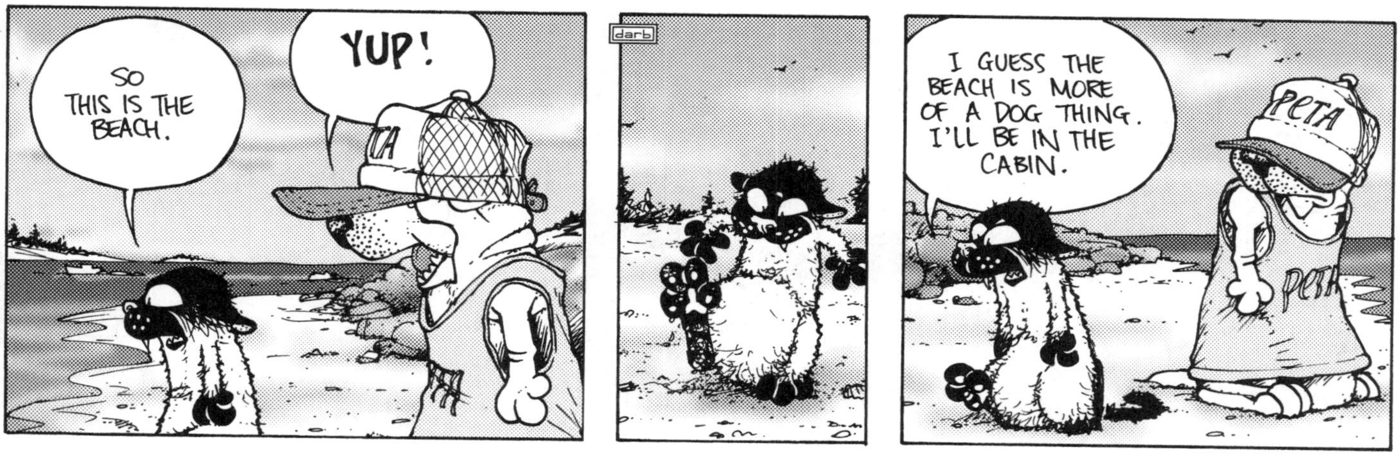
SO THIS IS THE BEACH.
YUP!
darb
I GUESS THE BEACH IS MORE OF A DOG THING. I'LL BE IN THE CABIN.
PETA

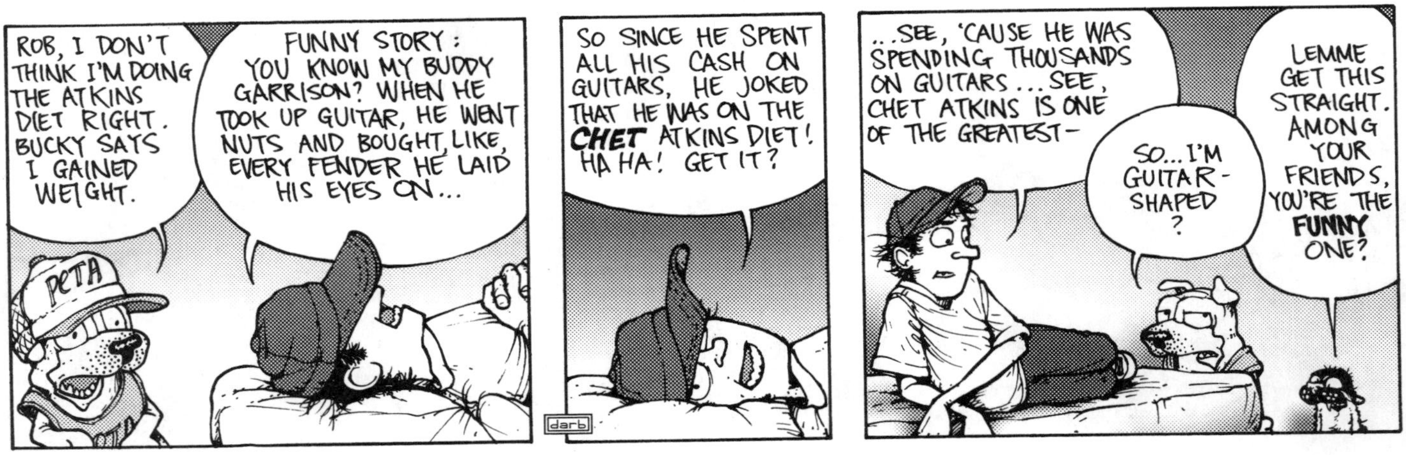
ROB, I DON'T THINK I'M DOING THE ATKINS DIET RIGHT. BUCKY SAYS I GAINED WEIGHT.
FUNNY STORY: YOU KNOW MY BUDDY GARRISON? WHEN HE TOOK UP GUITAR, HE WENT NUTS AND BOUGHT, LIKE, EVERY FENDER HE LAID HIS EYES ON...
PETA
SO SINCE HE SPENT ALL HIS CASH ON GUITARS, HE JOKED THAT HE WAS ON THE CHET ATKINS DIET! HA HA! GET IT?
darb
...SEE, 'CAUSE HE WAS SPENDING THOUSANDS ON GUITARS... SEE, CHET ATKINS IS ONE OF THE GREATEST–
SO... I'M GUITAR-SHAPED?
LEMME GET THIS STRAIGHT. AMONG YOUR FRIENDS, YOU'RE THE FUNNY ONE?

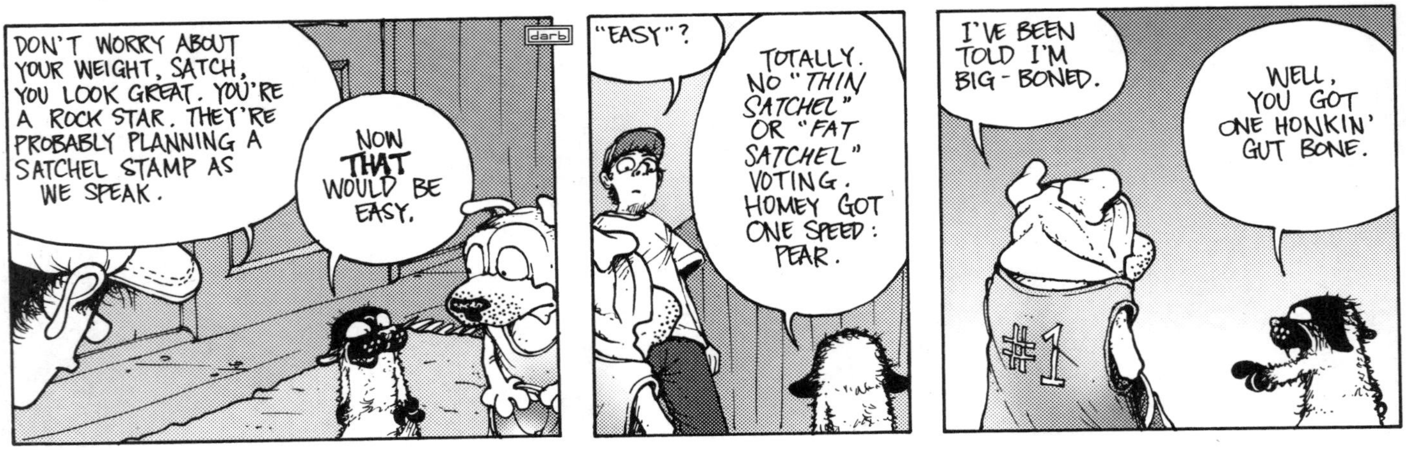
darb
DON'T WORRY ABOUT YOUR WEIGHT, SATCH, YOU LOOK GREAT. YOU'RE A ROCK STAR. THEY'RE PROBABLY PLANNING A SATCHEL STAMP AS WE SPEAK.
NOW THAT WOULD BE EASY.
"EASY"?
TOTALLY. NO "THIN SATCHEL" OR "FAT SATCHEL" VOTING. HOMEY GOT ONE SPEED: PEAR.
I'VE BEEN TOLD I'M BIG-BONED.
WELL, YOU GOT ONE HONKIN' GUT BONE.
#1

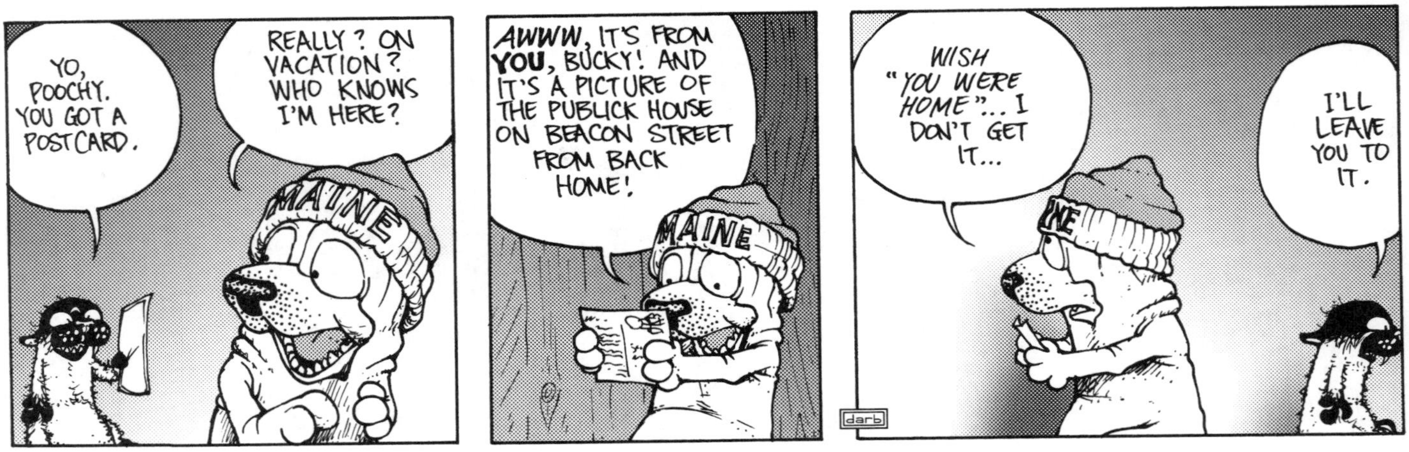
YO, POOCHY. YOU GOT A POSTCARD.
REALLY? ON VACATION? WHO KNOWS I'M HERE?
MAINE
AWWW, IT'S FROM YOU, BUCKY! AND IT'S A PICTURE OF THE PUBLICK HOUSE ON BEACON STREET FROM BACK HOME!
MAINE
WISH "YOU WERE HOME"... I DON'T GET IT...
I'LL LEAVE YOU TO IT.
darb

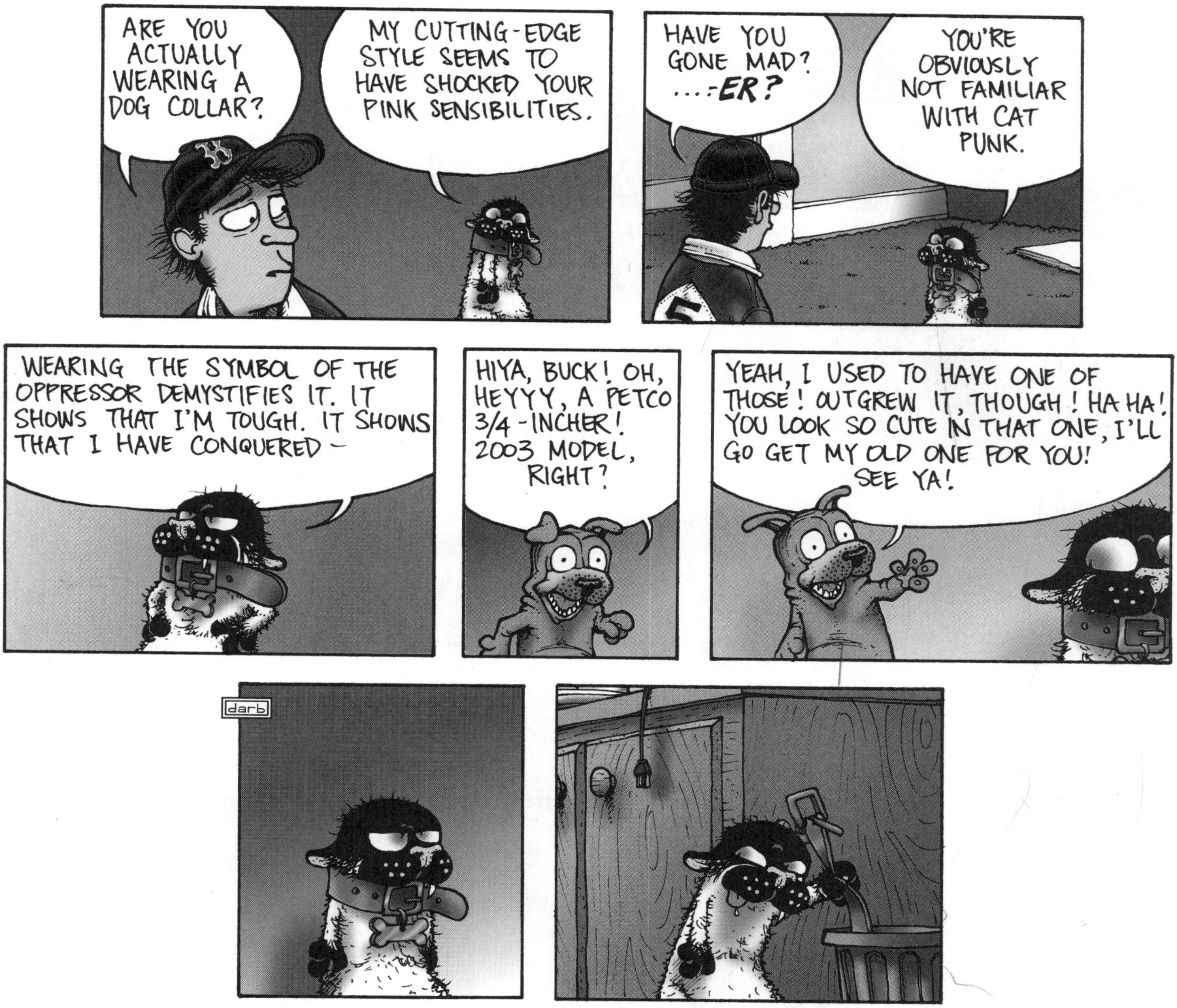
ARE YOU ACTUALLY WEARING A DOG COLLAR?
MY CUTTING-EDGE STYLE SEEMS TO HAVE SHOCKED YOUR PINK SENSIBILITIES.
HAVE YOU GONE MAD? ...-ER?
YOU'RE OBVIOUSLY NOT FAMILIAR WITH CAT PUNK.
WEARING THE SYMBOL OF THE OPPRESSOR DEMYSTIFIES IT. IT SHOWS THAT I'M TOUGH. IT SHOWS THAT I HAVE CONQUERED—
HIYA, BUCK! OH, HEYYY, A PETCO 3/4-INCHER! 2003 MODEL, RIGHT?
YEAH, I USED TO HAVE ONE OF THOSE! OUTGREW IT, THOUGH! HA HA! YOU LOOK SO CUTE IN THAT ONE, I'LL GO GET MY OLD ONE FOR YOU! SEE YA!
darb

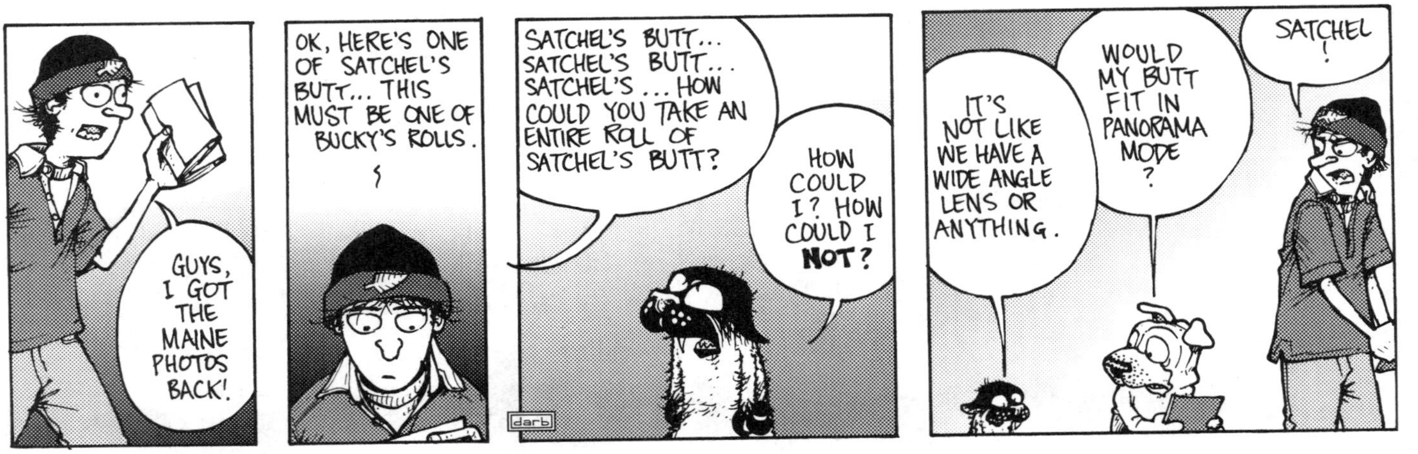
GUYS, I GOT THE MAINE PHOTOS BACK!
OK, HERE'S ONE OF SATCHEL'S BUTT... THIS MUST BE ONE OF BUCKY'S ROLLS.
SATCHEL'S BUTT... SATCHEL'S BUTT... SATCHEL'S ... HOW COULD YOU TAKE AN ENTIRE ROLL OF SATCHEL'S BUTT?
HOW COULD I? HOW COULD I **NOT**?
SATCHEL!
WOULD MY BUTT FIT IN PANORAMA MODE?
IT'S NOT LIKE WE HAVE A WIDE ANGLE LENS OR ANYTHING.
darb

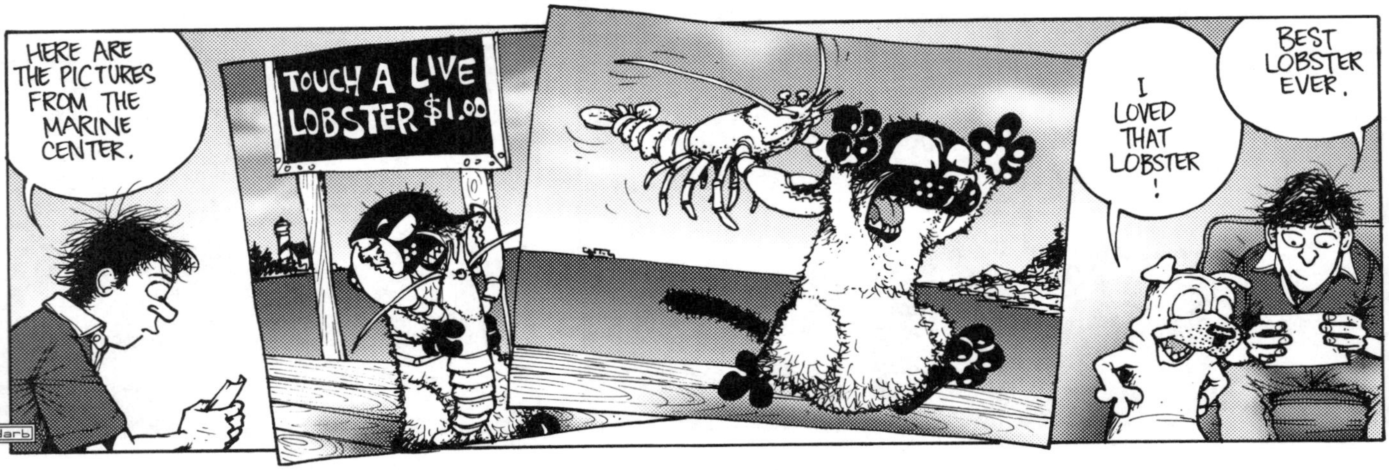
HERE ARE THE PICTURES FROM THE MARINE CENTER.
TOUCH A LIVE LOBSTER $1.00
BEST LOBSTER EVER.
I LOVED THAT LOBSTER!
darb

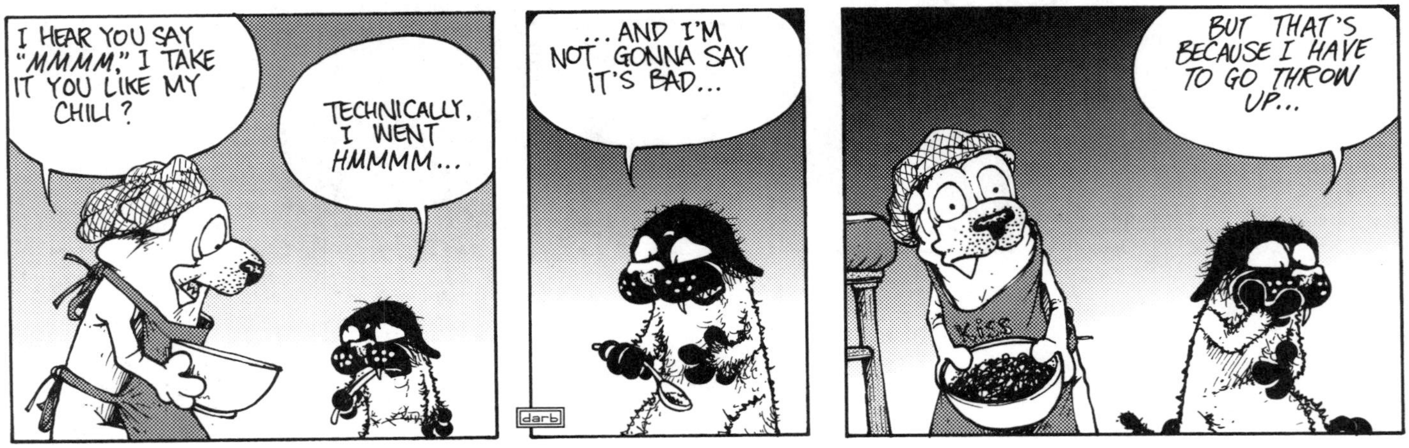
I HEAR YOU SAY "*MMMM*," I TAKE IT YOU LIKE MY CHILI?
TECHNICALLY, I WENT *HMMMM*...
... AND I'M NOT GONNA SAY IT'S BAD...
BUT THAT'S BECAUSE I HAVE TO GO THROW UP...
KISS
darb

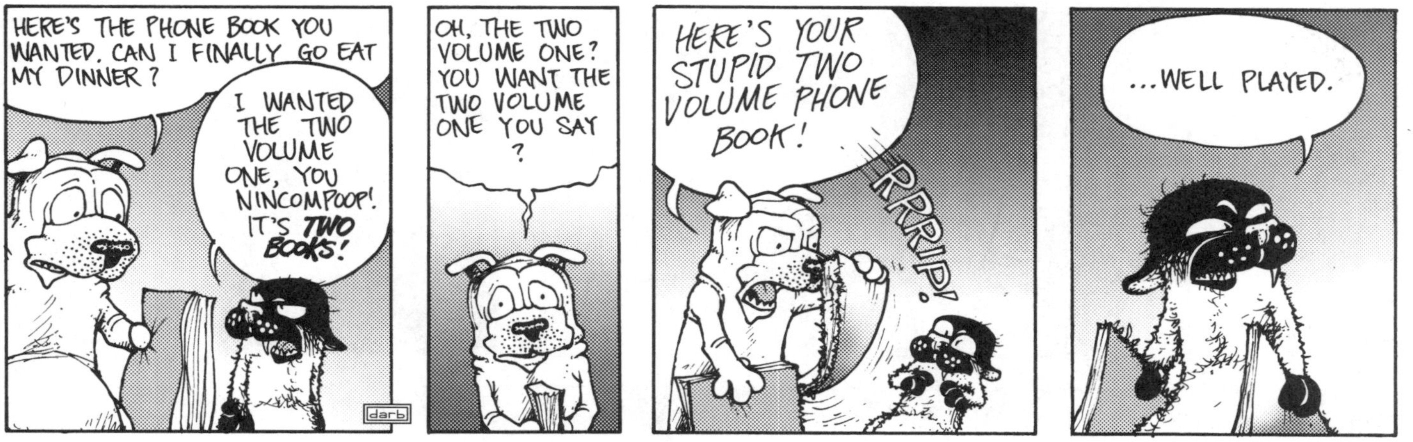
HERE'S THE PHONE BOOK YOU WANTED. CAN I FINALLY GO EAT MY DINNER?
I WANTED THE TWO VOLUME ONE, YOU NINCOMPOOP! IT'S **TWO BOOKS!**
darb
OH, THE TWO VOLUME ONE? YOU WANT THE TWO VOLUME ONE YOU SAY?
HERE'S YOUR STUPID TWO VOLUME PHONE BOOK!
RRRIP!
...WELL PLAYED.

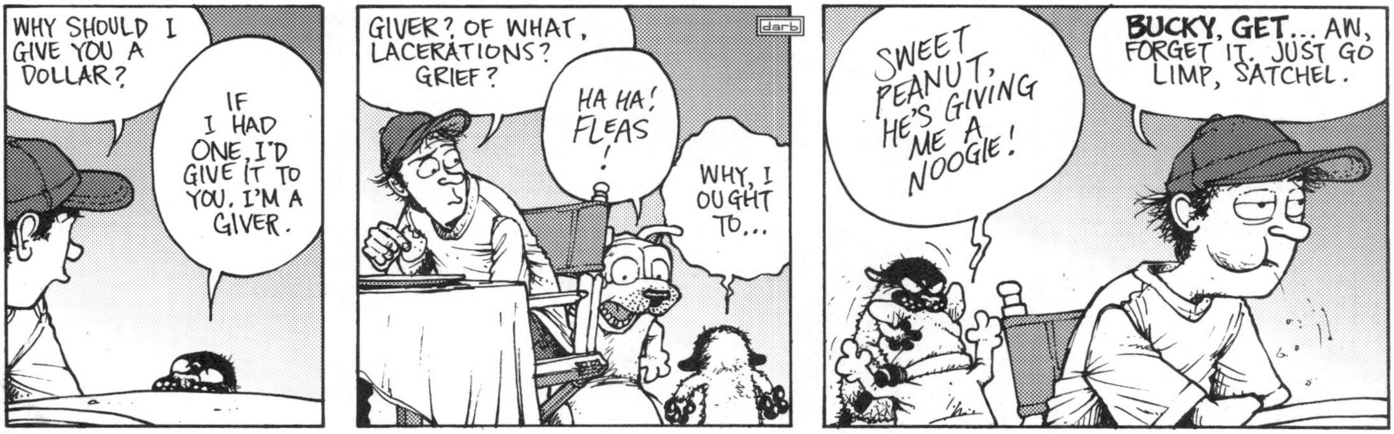
WHY SHOULD I GIVE YOU A DOLLAR?
IF I HAD ONE, I'D GIVE IT TO YOU. I'M A GIVER.
darb
GIVER? OF WHAT, LACERATIONS? GRIEF?
HA HA! FLEAS!
WHY, I OUGHT TO...
SWEET PEANUT, HE'S GIVING ME A NOOGIE!
BUCKY, GET... AW, FORGET IT. JUST GO LIMP, SATCHEL.

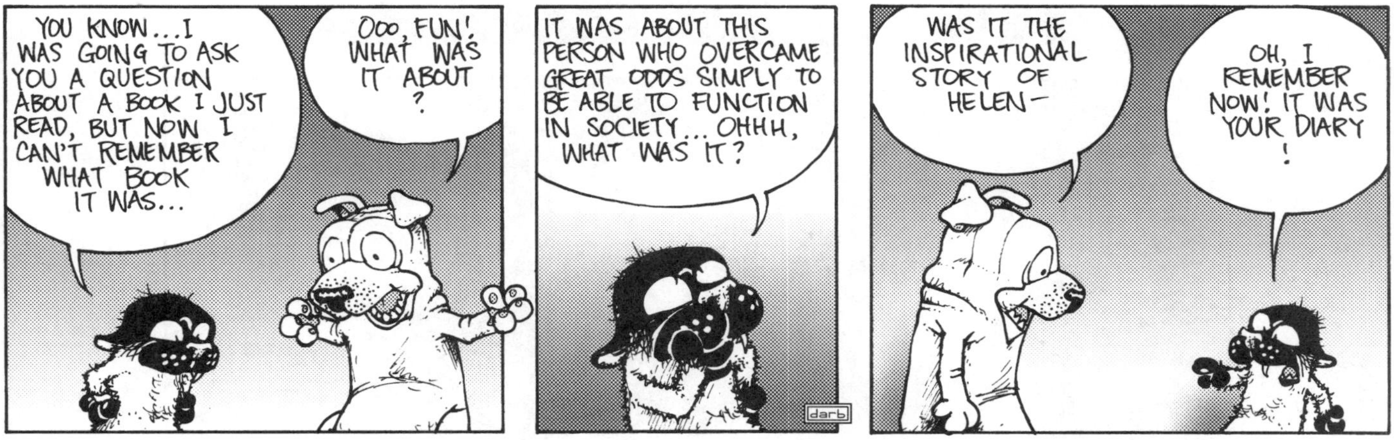
YOU KNOW... I WAS GOING TO ASK YOU A QUESTION ABOUT A BOOK I JUST READ, BUT NOW I CAN'T REMEMBER WHAT BOOK IT WAS...
OOO, FUN! WHAT WAS IT ABOUT?
IT WAS ABOUT THIS PERSON WHO OVERCAME GREAT ODDS SIMPLY TO BE ABLE TO FUNCTION IN SOCIETY... OHHH, WHAT WAS IT?
darb
WAS IT THE INSPIRATIONAL STORY OF HELEN–
OH, I REMEMBER NOW! IT WAS YOUR DIARY!

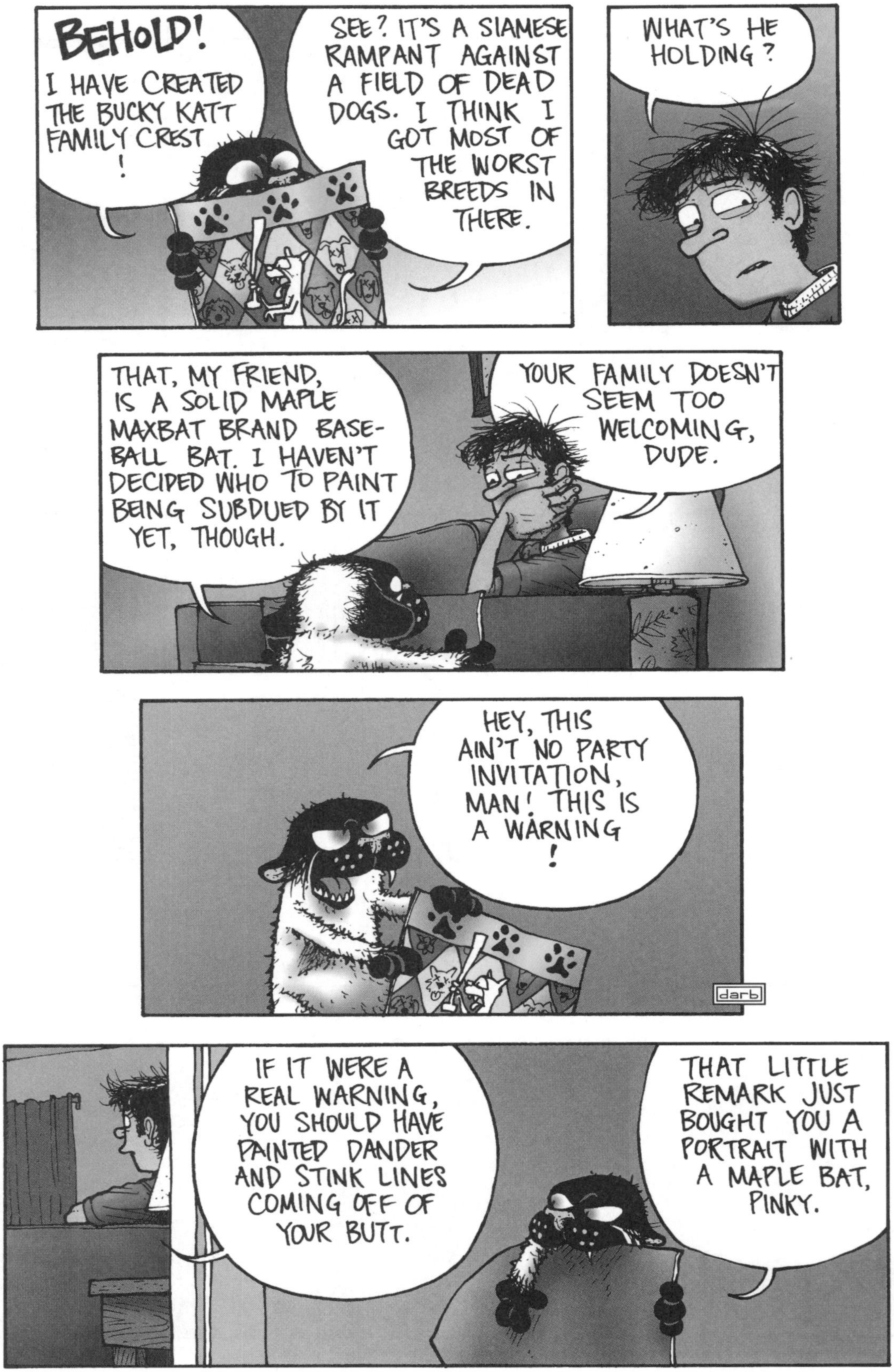
BEHOLD! I HAVE CREATED THE BUCKY KATT FAMILY CREST!
SEE? IT'S A SIAMESE RAMPANT AGAINST A FIELD OF DEAD DOGS. I THINK I GOT MOST OF THE WORST BREEDS IN THERE.
WHAT'S HE HOLDING?
THAT, MY FRIEND, IS A SOLID MAPLE MAXBAT BRAND BASE-BALL BAT. I HAVEN'T DECIDED WHO TO PAINT BEING SUBDUED BY IT YET, THOUGH.
YOUR FAMILY DOESN'T SEEM TOO WELCOMING, DUDE.
HEY, THIS AIN'T NO PARTY INVITATION, MAN! THIS IS A WARNING!
darb
IF IT WERE A REAL WARNING, YOU SHOULD HAVE PAINTED DANDER AND STINK LINES COMING OFF OF YOUR BUTT.
THAT LITTLE REMARK JUST BOUGHT YOU A PORTRAIT WITH A MAPLE BAT, PINKY.

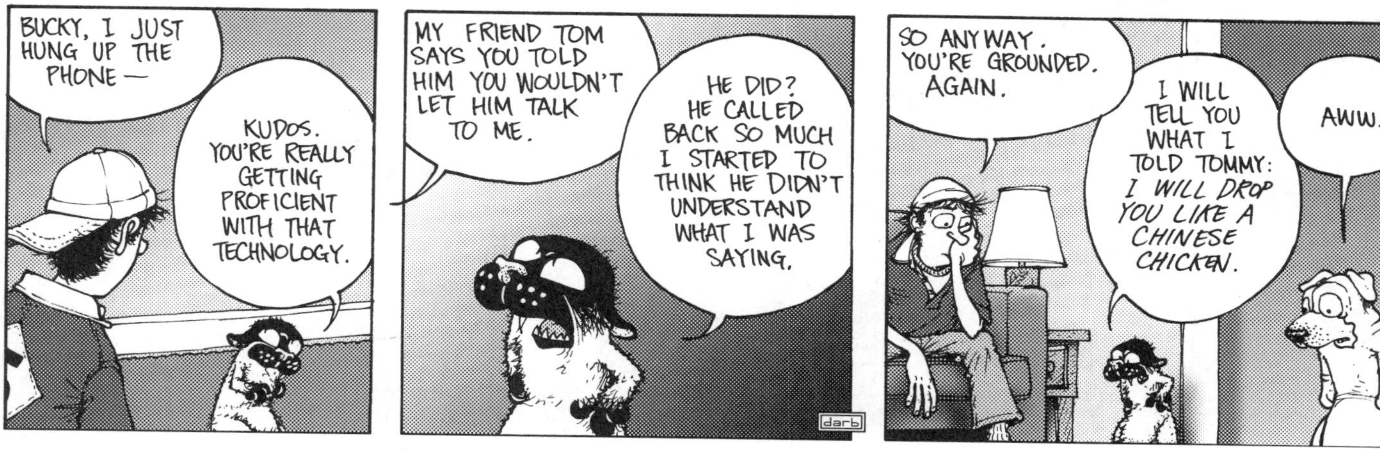
BUCKY, I JUST HUNG UP THE PHONE—
KUDOS. YOU'RE REALLY GETTING PROFICIENT WITH THAT TECHNOLOGY.
MY FRIEND TOM SAYS YOU TOLD HIM YOU WOULDN'T LET HIM TALK TO ME.
HE DID? HE CALLED BACK SO MUCH I STARTED TO THINK HE DIDN'T UNDERSTAND WHAT I WAS SAYING.
darb
SO ANYWAY. YOU'RE GROUNDED. AGAIN.
I WILL TELL YOU WHAT I TOLD TOMMY: *I WILL DROP YOU LIKE A CHINESE CHICKEN.*
AWW...

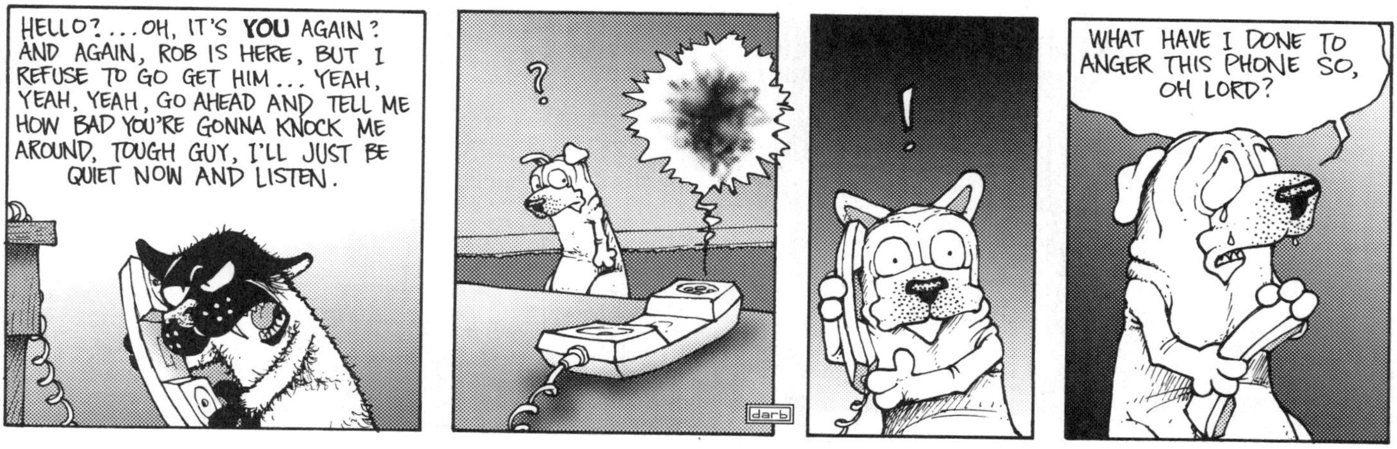
HELLO?...OH, IT'S **YOU** AGAIN? AND AGAIN, ROB IS HERE, BUT I REFUSE TO GO GET HIM... YEAH, YEAH, YEAH, GO AHEAD AND TELL ME HOW BAD YOU'RE GONNA KNOCK ME AROUND, TOUGH GUY, I'LL JUST BE QUIET NOW AND LISTEN.
?
darb
!
WHAT HAVE I DONE TO ANGER THIS PHONE SO, OH LORD?

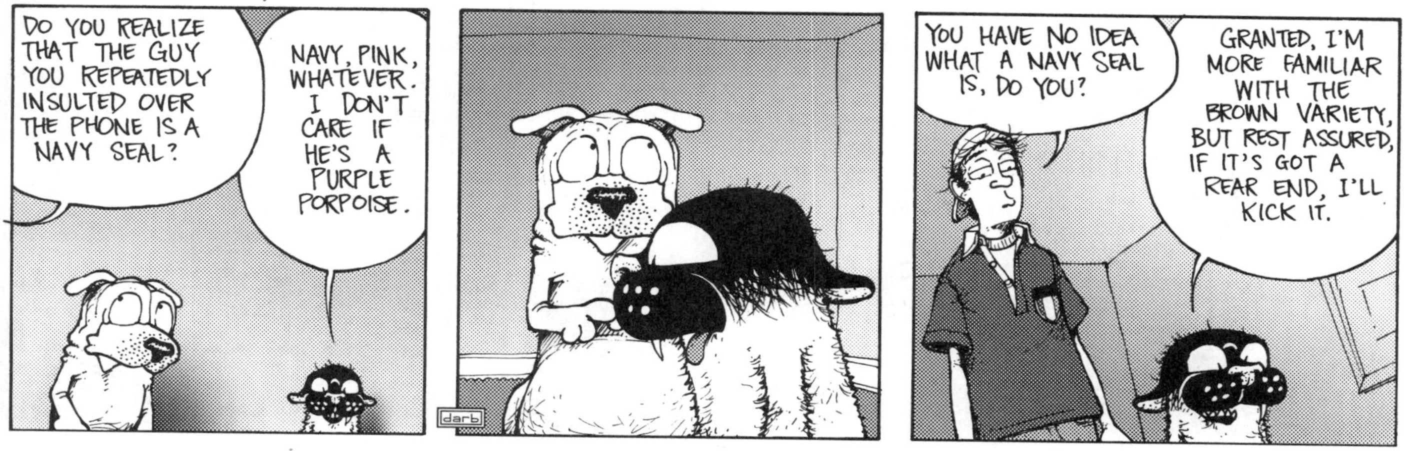
DO YOU REALIZE THAT THE GUY YOU REPEATEDLY INSULTED OVER THE PHONE IS A NAVY SEAL?
NAVY, PINK, WHATEVER. I DON'T CARE IF HE'S A PURPLE PORPOISE.
darb
YOU HAVE NO IDEA WHAT A NAVY SEAL IS, DO YOU?
GRANTED, I'M MORE FAMILIAR WITH THE BROWN VARIETY, BUT REST ASSURED, IF IT'S GOT A REAR END, I'LL KICK IT.

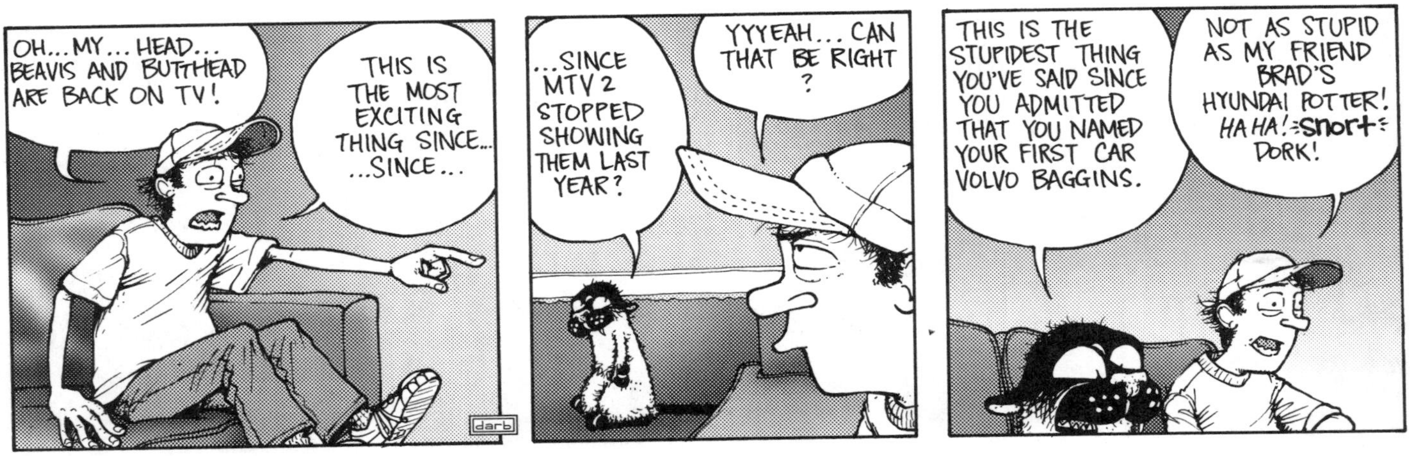
OH... MY... HEAD... BEAVIS AND BUTTHEAD ARE BACK ON TV!
THIS IS THE MOST EXCITING THING SINCE... ...SINCE...
...SINCE MTV 2 STOPPED SHOWING THEM LAST YEAR?
YYYEAH... CAN THAT BE RIGHT?
THIS IS THE STUPIDEST THING YOU'VE SAID SINCE YOU ADMITTED THAT YOU NAMED YOUR FIRST CAR VOLVO BAGGINS.
NOT AS STUPID AS MY FRIEND BRAD'S HYUNDAI POTTER! HA HA! snort DORK!
darb

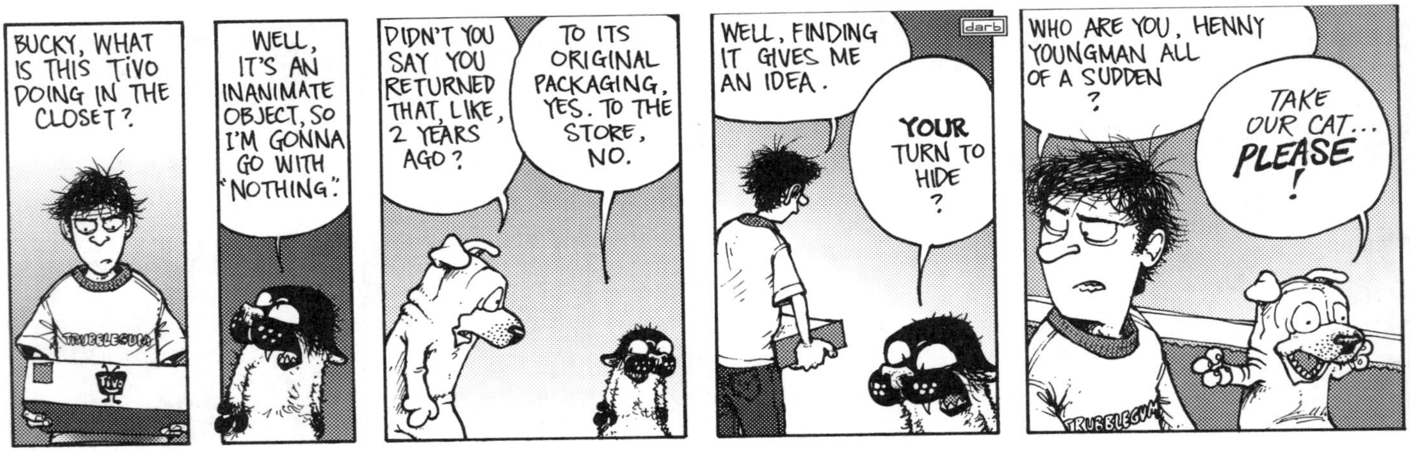
BUCKY, WHAT IS THIS TIVO DOING IN THE CLOSET?
WELL, IT'S AN INANIMATE OBJECT, SO I'M GONNA GO WITH "NOTHING."
DIDN'T YOU SAY YOU RETURNED THAT, LIKE, 2 YEARS AGO?
TO ITS ORIGINAL PACKAGING, YES. TO THE STORE, NO.
WELL, FINDING IT GIVES ME AN IDEA.
YOUR TURN TO HIDE?
WHO ARE YOU, HENNY YOUNGMAN ALL OF A SUDDEN?
TAKE OUR CAT... PLEASE!
darb

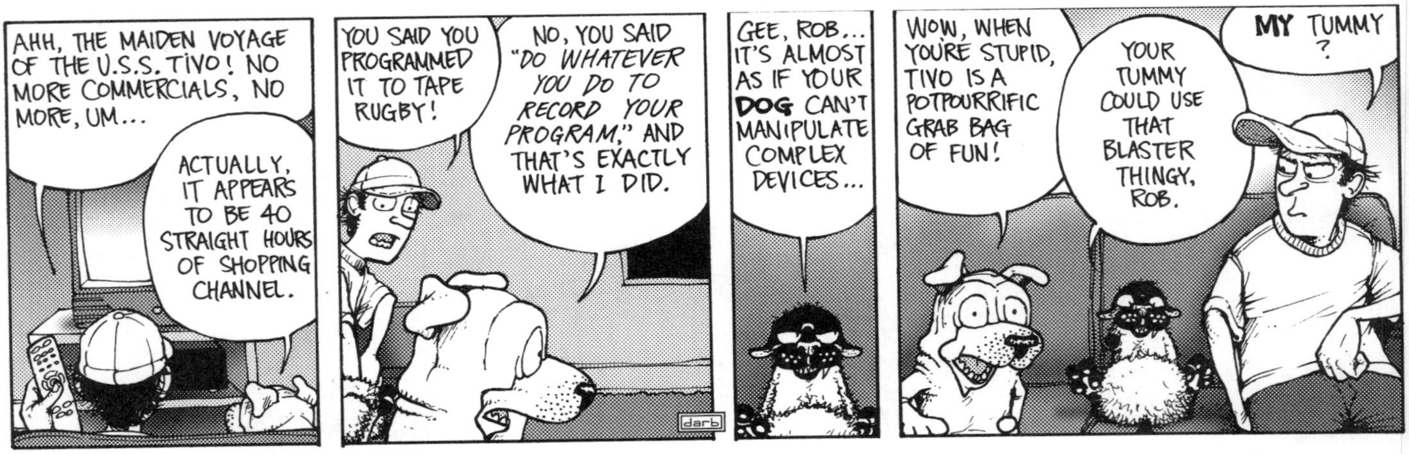
AHH, THE MAIDEN VOYAGE OF THE U.S.S. TIVO! NO MORE COMMERCIALS, NO MORE, UM...
ACTUALLY, IT APPEARS TO BE 40 STRAIGHT HOURS OF SHOPPING CHANNEL.
YOU SAID YOU PROGRAMMED IT TO TAPE RUGBY!
NO, YOU SAID "DO WHATEVER YOU DO TO RECORD YOUR PROGRAM," AND THAT'S EXACTLY WHAT I DID.
GEE, ROB... IT'S ALMOST AS IF YOUR DOG CAN'T MANIPULATE COMPLEX DEVICES...
WOW, WHEN YOU'RE STUPID, TIVO IS A POTPOURRIFIC GRAB BAG OF FUN!
YOUR TUMMY COULD USE THAT BLASTER THINGY, ROB.
MY TUMMY?
darb

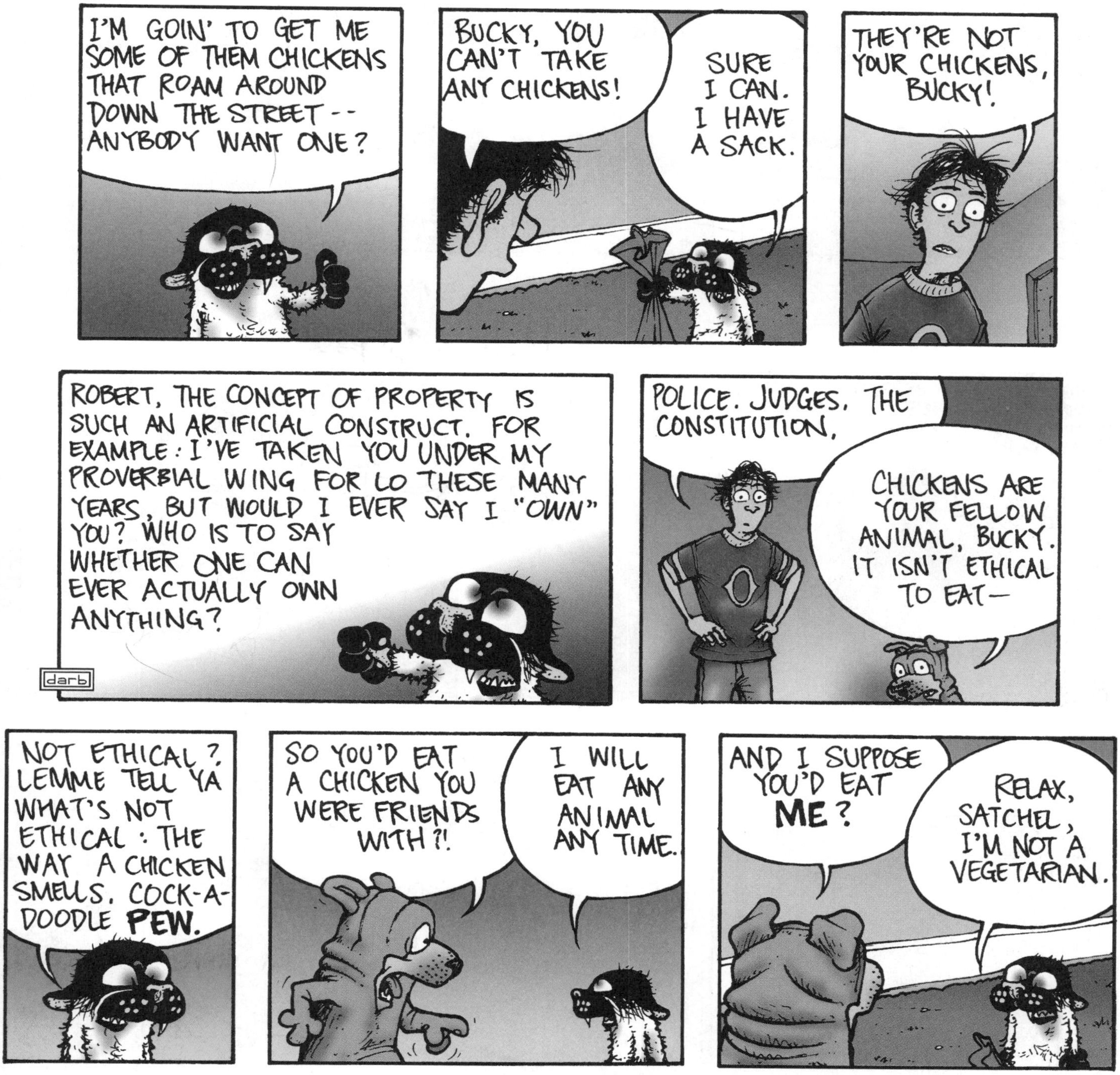
I'M GOIN' TO GET ME SOME OF THEM CHICKENS THAT ROAM AROUND DOWN THE STREET -- ANYBODY WANT ONE?
BUCKY, YOU CAN'T TAKE ANY CHICKENS!
SURE I CAN. I HAVE A SACK.
THEY'RE NOT YOUR CHICKENS, BUCKY!
ROBERT, THE CONCEPT OF PROPERTY IS SUCH AN ARTIFICIAL CONSTRUCT. FOR EXAMPLE: I'VE TAKEN YOU UNDER MY PROVERBIAL WING FOR LO THESE MANY YEARS, BUT WOULD I EVER SAY I "OWN" YOU? WHO IS TO SAY WHETHER ONE CAN EVER ACTUALLY OWN ANYTHING?
darb
POLICE. JUDGES. THE CONSTITUTION.
CHICKENS ARE YOUR FELLOW ANIMAL, BUCKY. IT ISN'T ETHICAL TO EAT—
NOT ETHICAL? LEMME TELL YA WHAT'S NOT ETHICAL: THE WAY A CHICKEN SMELLS. COCK-A-DOODLE **PEW**.
SO YOU'D EAT A CHICKEN YOU WERE FRIENDS WITH?!
I WILL EAT ANY ANIMAL ANY TIME.
AND I SUPPOSE YOU'D EAT **ME**?
RELAX, SATCHEL, I'M NOT A VEGETARIAN.

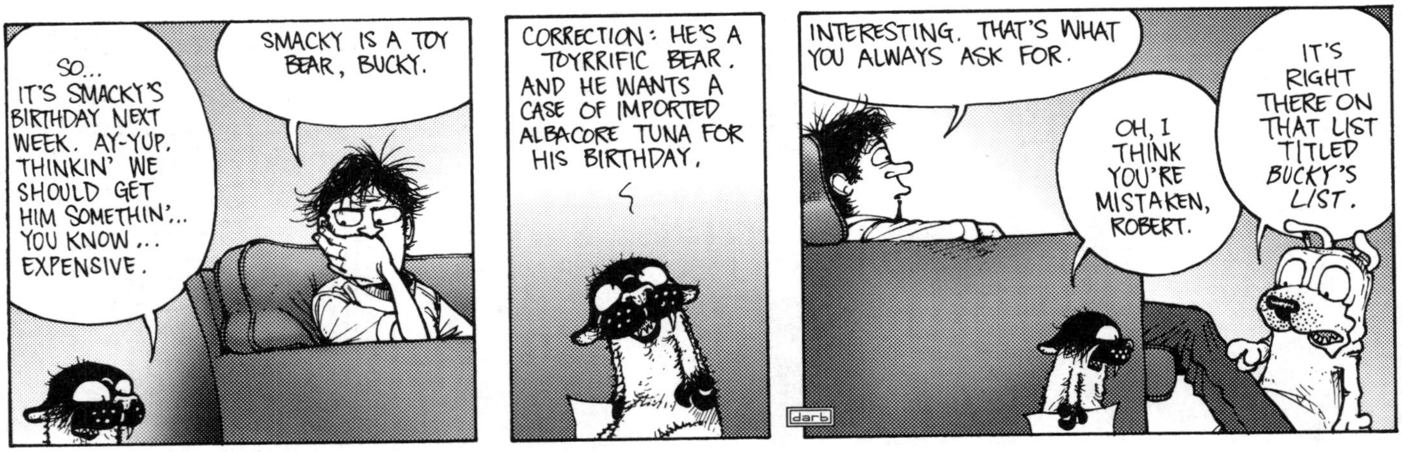
SO... IT'S SMACKY'S BIRTHDAY NEXT WEEK. AY-YUP. THINKIN' WE SHOULD GET HIM SOMETHIN'... YOU KNOW... EXPENSIVE.
SMACKY IS A TOY BEAR, BUCKY.
CORRECTION: HE'S A TOYRRIFIC BEAR. AND HE WANTS A CASE OF IMPORTED ALBACORE TUNA FOR HIS BIRTHDAY.
INTERESTING. THAT'S WHAT YOU ALWAYS ASK FOR.
OH, I THINK YOU'RE MISTAKEN, ROBERT.
IT'S RIGHT THERE ON THAT LIST TITLED BUCKY'S LIST.
darb

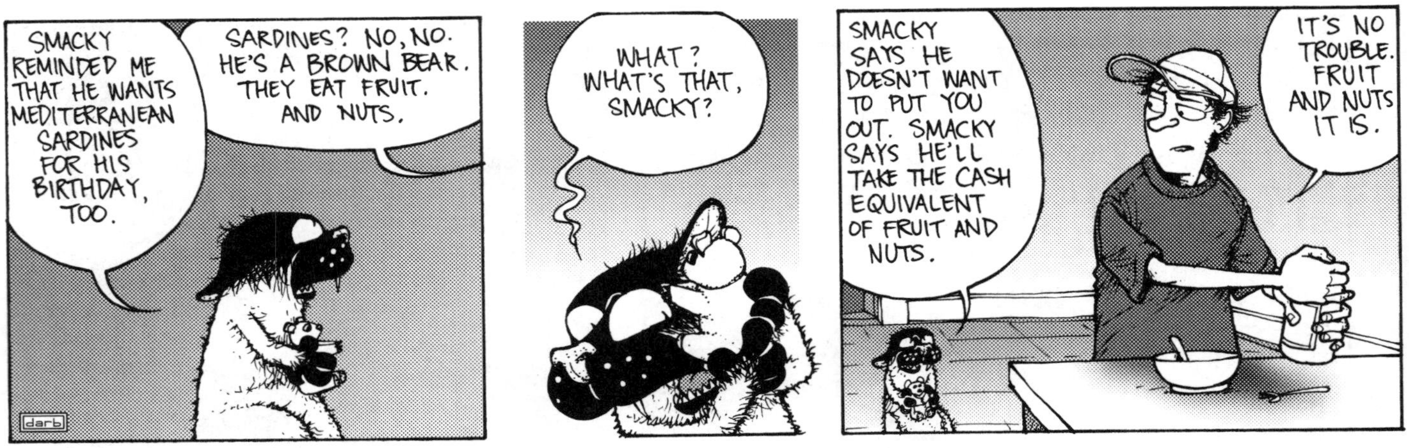
SMACKY REMINDED ME THAT HE WANTS MEDITERRANEAN SARDINES FOR HIS BIRTHDAY, TOO.
SARDINES? NO, NO. HE'S A BROWN BEAR. THEY EAT FRUIT. AND NUTS.
darb
WHAT? WHAT'S THAT, SMACKY?
SMACKY SAYS HE DOESN'T WANT TO PUT YOU OUT. SMACKY SAYS HE'LL TAKE THE CASH EQUIVALENT OF FRUIT AND NUTS.
IT'S NO TROUBLE. FRUIT AND NUTS IT IS.

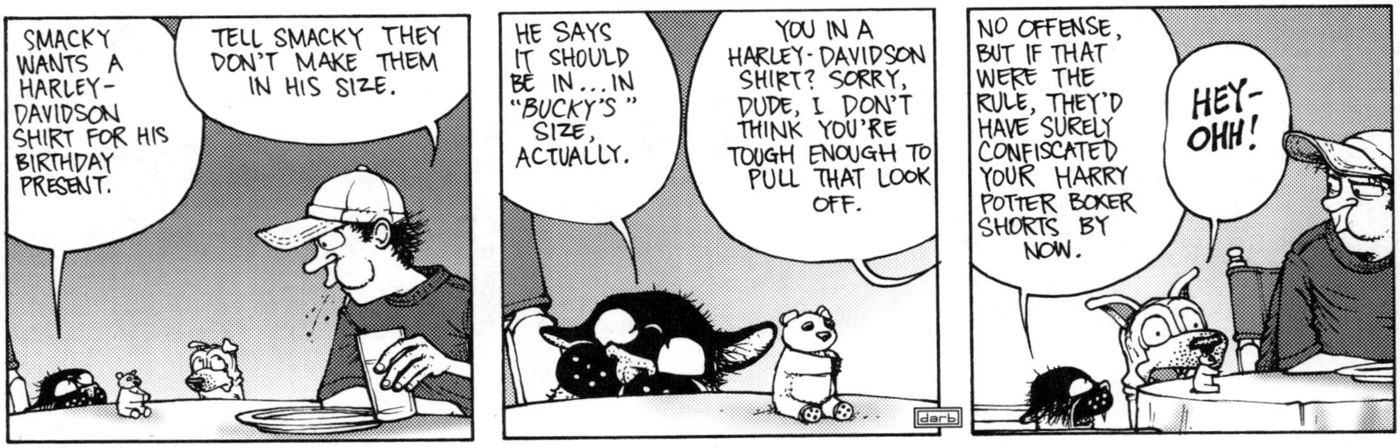
SMACKY WANTS A HARLEY-DAVIDSON SHIRT FOR HIS BIRTHDAY PRESENT.
TELL SMACKY THEY DON'T MAKE THEM IN HIS SIZE.
HE SAYS IT SHOULD BE IN... IN "BUCKY'S" SIZE, ACTUALLY.
YOU IN A HARLEY-DAVIDSON SHIRT? SORRY, DUDE, I DON'T THINK YOU'RE TOUGH ENOUGH TO PULL THAT LOOK OFF.
darb
NO OFFENSE, BUT IF THAT WERE THE RULE, THEY'D HAVE SURELY CONFISCATED YOUR HARRY POTTER BOKER SHORTS BY NOW.
HEY-OHH!

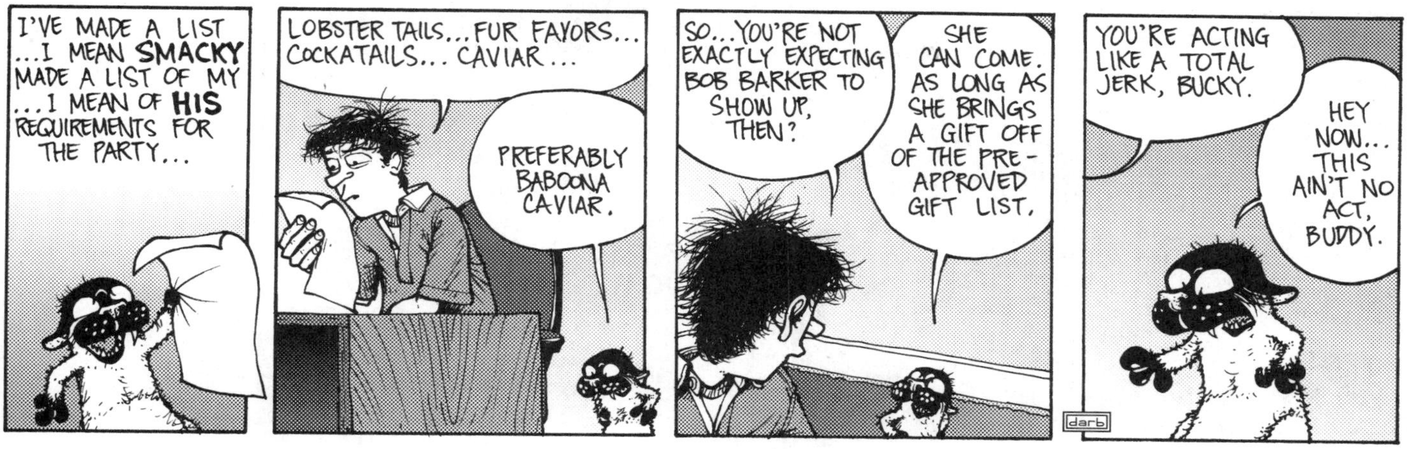
I'VE MADE A LIST ...I MEAN SMACKY MADE A LIST OF MY ...I MEAN OF HIS REQUIREMENTS FOR THE PARTY...
LOBSTER TAILS... FUR FAVORS... COCKATAILS... CAVIAR...
PREFERABLY BABOONA CAVIAR.
SO... YOU'RE NOT EXACTLY EXPECTING BOB BARKER TO SHOW UP, THEN?
SHE CAN COME. AS LONG AS SHE BRINGS A GIFT OFF OF THE PRE-APPROVED GIFT LIST.
YOU'RE ACTING LIKE A TOTAL JERK, BUCKY.
HEY NOW... THIS AIN'T NO ACT, BUDDY.
darb

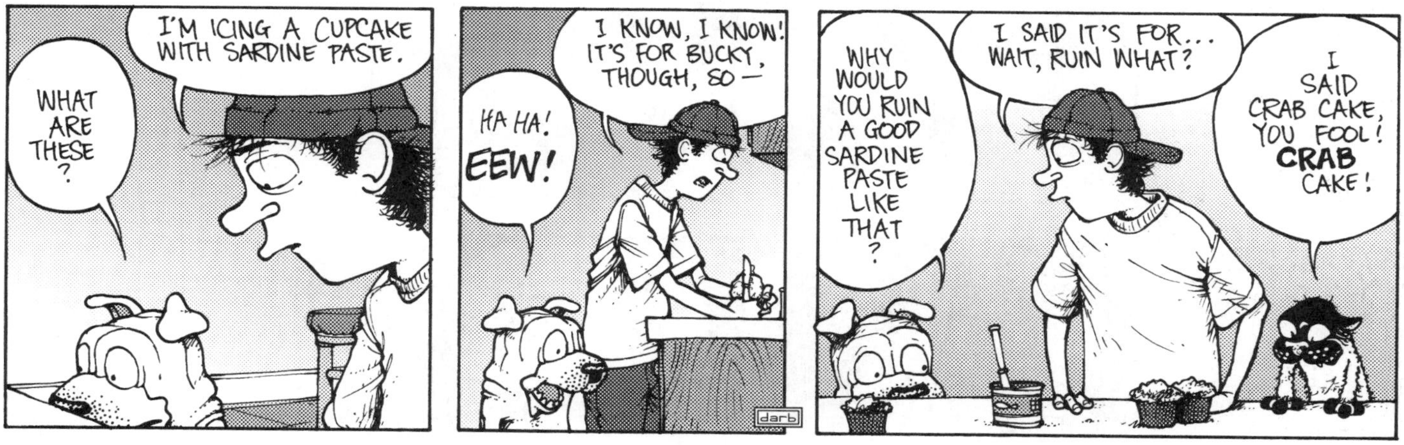
I'M ICING A CUPCAKE WITH SARDINE PASTE.
WHAT ARE THESE?
I KNOW, I KNOW! IT'S FOR BUCKY, THOUGH, SO—
HA HA! EEW!
darb
WHY WOULD YOU RUIN A GOOD SARDINE PASTE LIKE THAT?
I SAID IT'S FOR... WAIT, RUIN WHAT?
I SAID CRAB CAKE, YOU FOOL! CRAB CAKE!

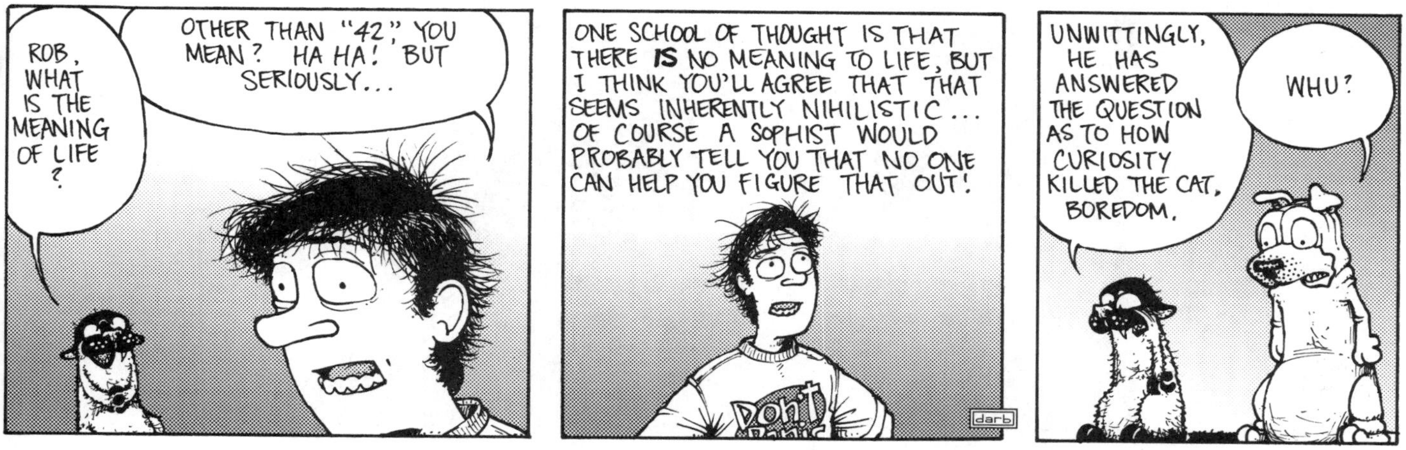
ROB, WHAT IS THE MEANING OF LIFE?
OTHER THAN "42," YOU MEAN? HA HA! BUT SERIOUSLY...
ONE SCHOOL OF THOUGHT IS THAT THERE IS NO MEANING TO LIFE, BUT I THINK YOU'LL AGREE THAT THAT SEEMS INHERENTLY NIHILISTIC... OF COURSE A SOPHIST WOULD PROBABLY TELL YOU THAT NO ONE CAN HELP YOU FIGURE THAT OUT!
darb
UNWITTINGLY, HE HAS ANSWERED THE QUESTION AS TO HOW CURIOSITY KILLED THE CAT. BOREDOM.
WHU?

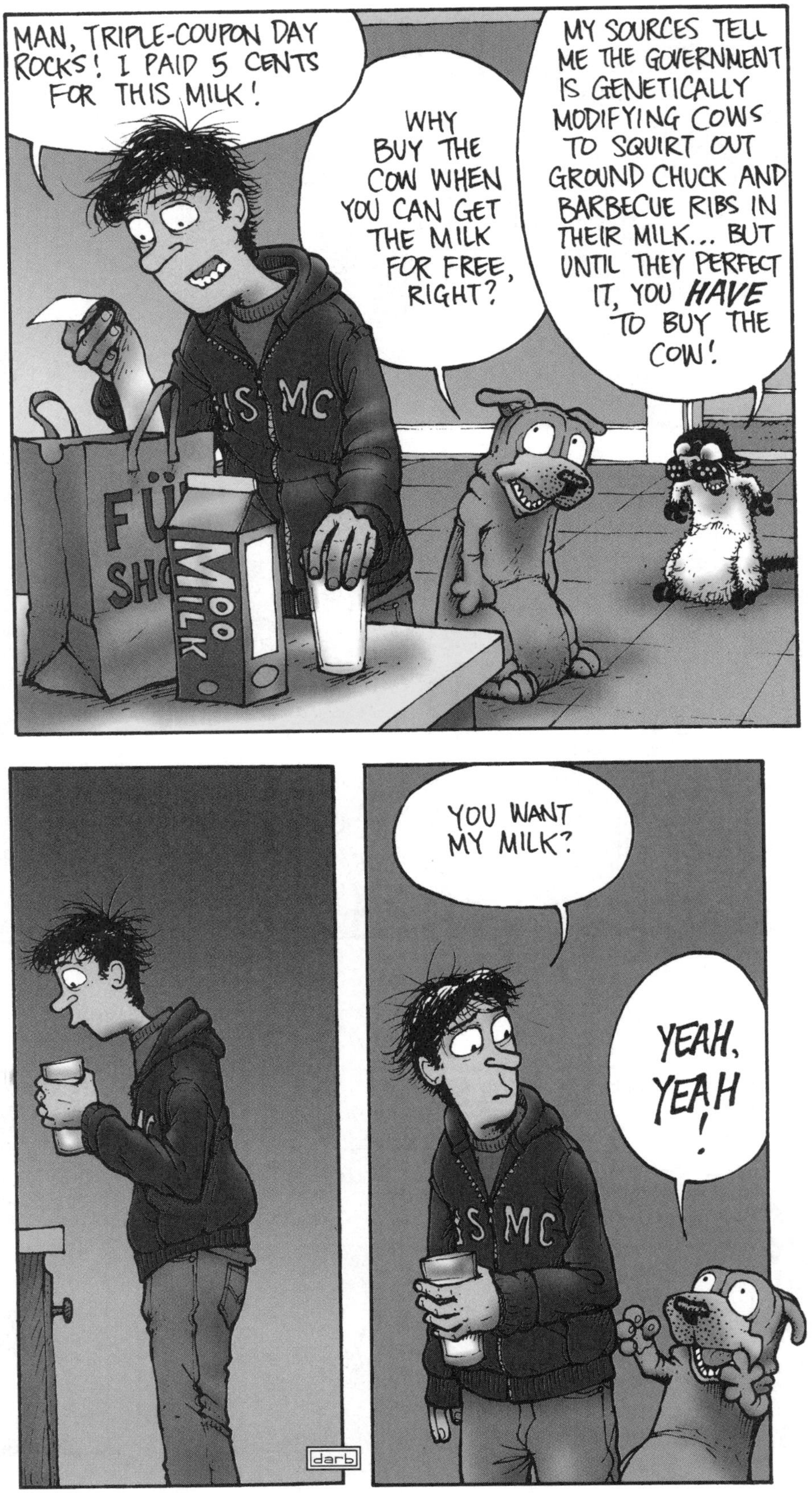
MAN, TRIPLE-COUPON DAY ROCKS! I PAID 5 CENTS FOR THIS MILK!
WHY BUY THE COW WHEN YOU CAN GET THE MILK FOR FREE, RIGHT?
MY SOURCES TELL ME THE GOVERNMENT IS GENETICALLY MODIFYING COWS TO SQUIRT OUT GROUND CHUCK AND BARBECUE RIBS IN THEIR MILK... BUT UNTIL THEY PERFECT IT, YOU **HAVE** TO BUY THE COW!
MOO MILK
darb
YOU WANT MY MILK?
YEAH, YEAH!

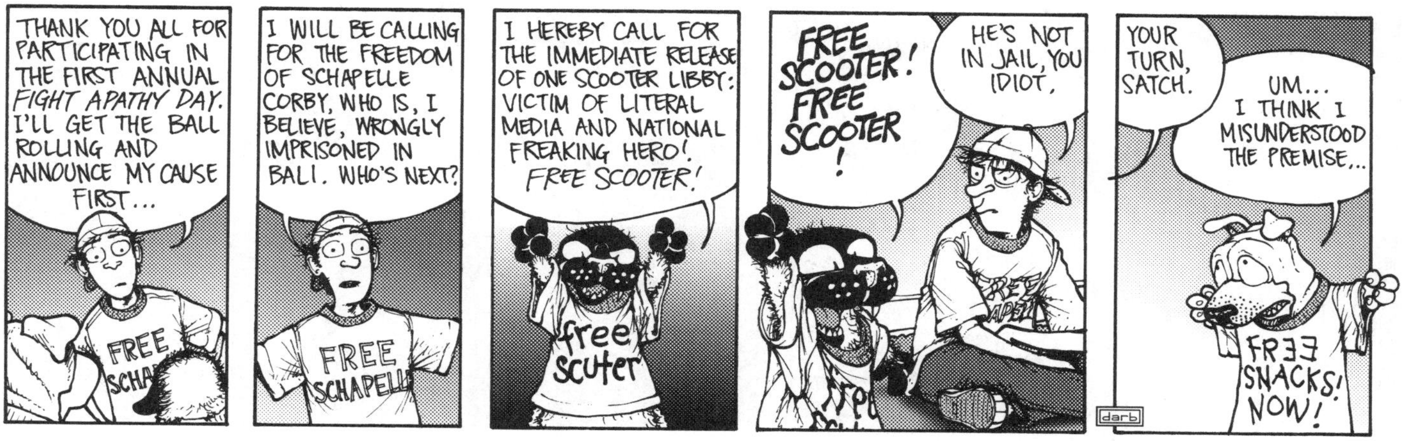
THANK YOU ALL FOR PARTICIPATING IN THE FIRST ANNUAL *FIGHT APATHY DAY*. I'LL GET THE BALL ROLLING AND ANNOUNCE MY CAUSE FIRST...
I WILL BE CALLING FOR THE FREEDOM OF SCHAPELLE CORBY, WHO IS, I BELIEVE, WRONGLY IMPRISONED IN BALI. WHO'S NEXT?
FREE SCHAPELLE
I HEREBY CALL FOR THE IMMEDIATE RELEASE OF ONE SCOOTER LIBBY: VICTIM OF LITERAL MEDIA AND NATIONAL FREAKING HERO! FREE SCOOTER!
free scuter
FREE SCOOTER! FREE SCOOTER!
HE'S NOT IN JAIL, YOU IDIOT.
YOUR TURN, SATCH.
UM... I THINK I MISUNDERSTOOD THE PREMISE...
FREE SNACKS! NOW!
darb

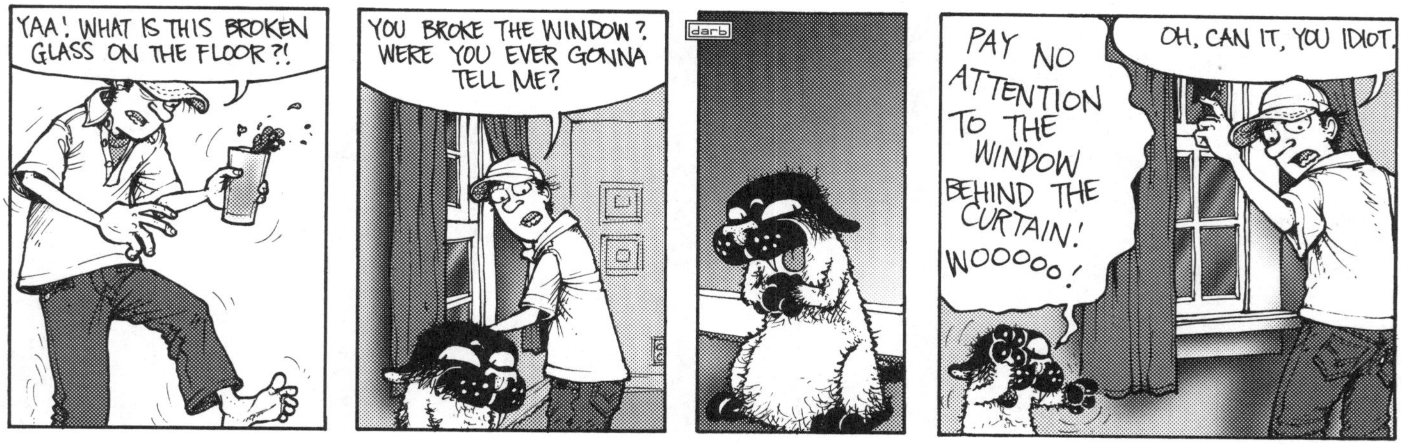
YAA! WHAT IS THIS BROKEN GLASS ON THE FLOOR?!
YOU BROKE THE WINDOW? WERE YOU EVER GONNA TELL ME?
darb
PAY NO ATTENTION TO THE WINDOW BEHIND THE CURTAIN! WOOOOO!
OH, CAN IT, YOU IDIOT.

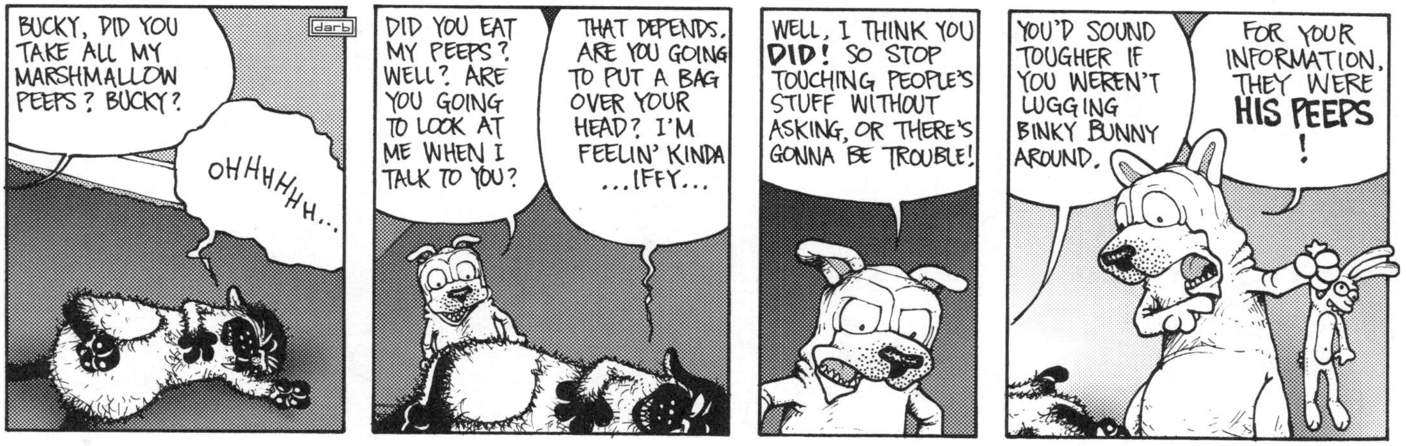
BUCKY, DID YOU TAKE ALL MY MARSHMALLOW PEEPS? BUCKY?
darb
OHHHHHH...
DID YOU EAT MY PEEPS? WELL? ARE YOU GOING TO LOOK AT ME WHEN I TALK TO YOU?
THAT DEPENDS. ARE YOU GOING TO PUT A BAG OVER YOUR HEAD? I'M FEELIN' KINDA ...IFFY...
WELL, I THINK YOU **DID!** SO STOP TOUCHING PEOPLE'S STUFF WITHOUT ASKING, OR THERE'S GONNA BE TROUBLE!
YOU'D SOUND TOUGHER IF YOU WEREN'T LUGGING BINKY BUNNY AROUND.
FOR YOUR INFORMATION, THEY WERE **HIS PEEPS**!

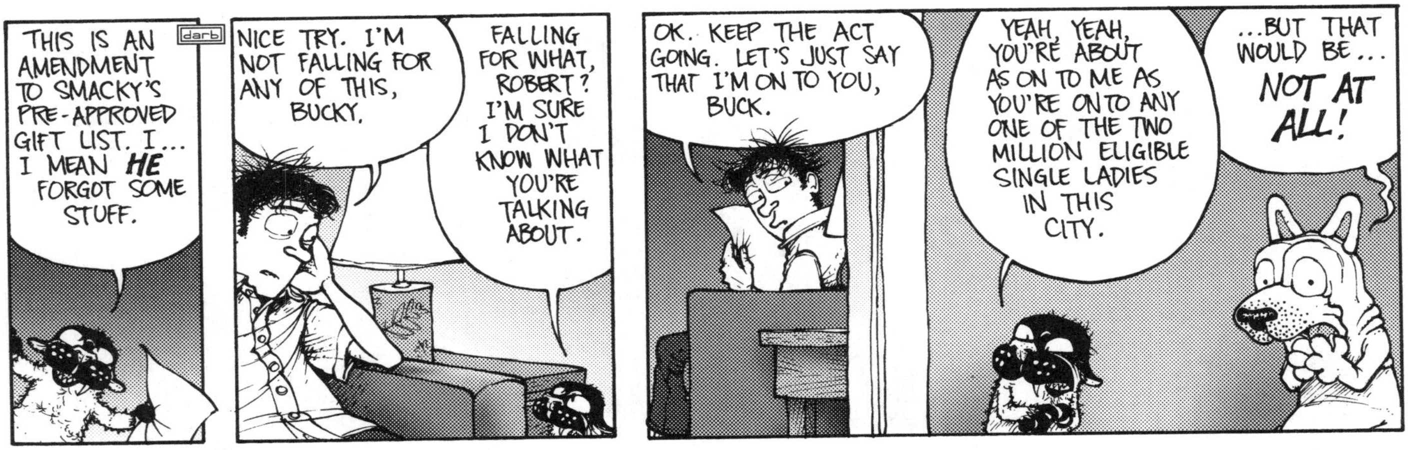
darb
THIS IS AN AMENDMENT TO SMACKY'S PRE-APPROVED GIFT LIST. I... I MEAN **HE** FORGOT SOME STUFF.
NICE TRY. I'M NOT FALLING FOR ANY OF THIS, BUCKY.
FALLING FOR WHAT, ROBERT? I'M SURE I DON'T KNOW WHAT YOU'RE TALKING ABOUT.
OK. KEEP THE ACT GOING. LET'S JUST SAY THAT I'M ON TO YOU, BUCK.
YEAH, YEAH, YOU'RE ABOUT AS ON TO ME AS YOU'RE ON TO ANY ONE OF THE TWO MILLION ELIGIBLE SINGLE LADIES IN THIS CITY.
...BUT THAT WOULD BE... ***NOT AT ALL!***

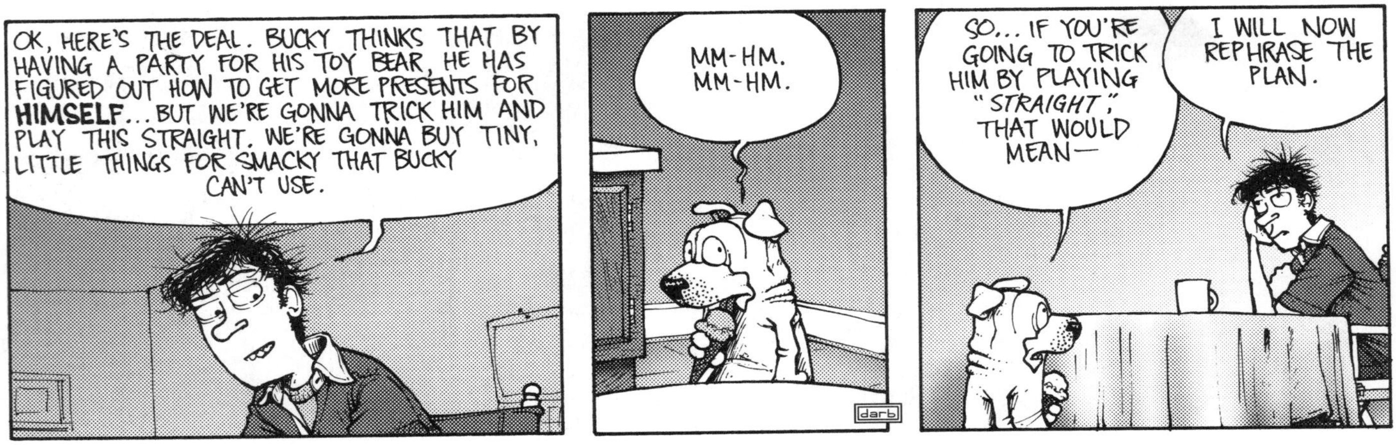
OK, HERE'S THE DEAL. BUCKY THINKS THAT BY HAVING A PARTY FOR HIS TOY BEAR, HE HAS FIGURED OUT HOW TO GET MORE PRESENTS FOR **HIMSELF**... BUT WE'RE GONNA TRICK HIM AND PLAY THIS STRAIGHT. WE'RE GONNA BUY TINY, LITTLE THINGS FOR SMACKY THAT BUCKY CAN'T USE.
MM-HM. MM-HM.
darb
SO... IF YOU'RE GOING TO TRICK HIM BY PLAYING "*STRAIGHT*," THAT WOULD MEAN—
I WILL NOW REPHRASE THE PLAN.

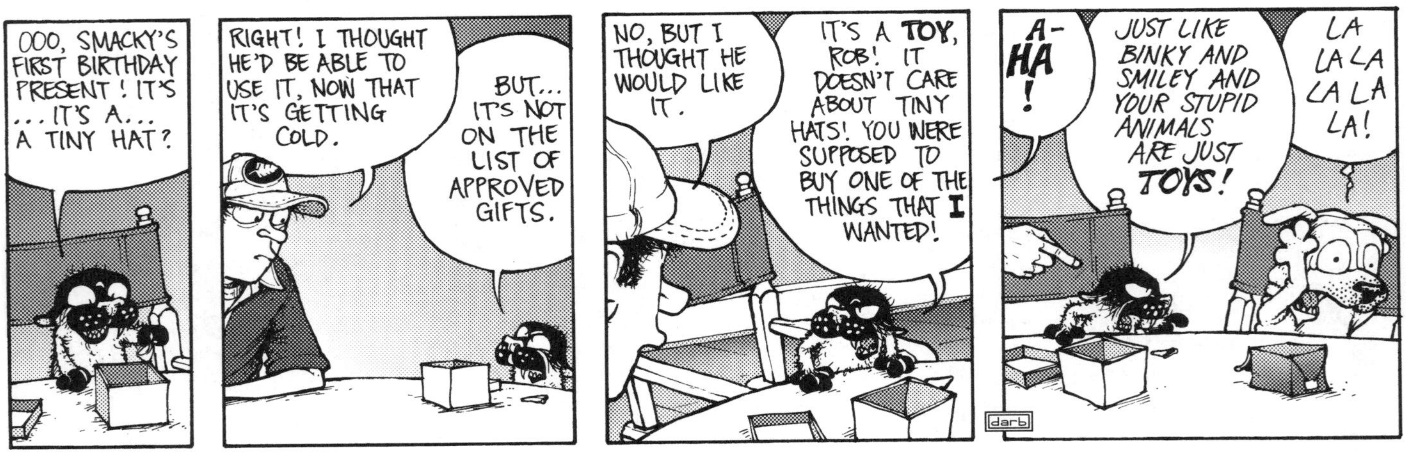
OOO, SMACKY'S FIRST BIRTHDAY PRESENT! IT'S ... IT'S A... A TINY HAT?
RIGHT! I THOUGHT HE'D BE ABLE TO USE IT, NOW THAT IT'S GETTING COLD.
BUT... IT'S NOT ON THE LIST OF APPROVED GIFTS.
NO, BUT I THOUGHT HE WOULD LIKE IT.
IT'S A **TOY**, ROB! IT DOESN'T CARE ABOUT TINY HATS! YOU WERE SUPPOSED TO BUY ONE OF THE THINGS THAT **I** WANTED!
A-HA!
JUST LIKE BINKY AND SMILEY AND YOUR STUPID ANIMALS ARE JUST ***TOYS!***
LA LA LA LA LA LA!
darb

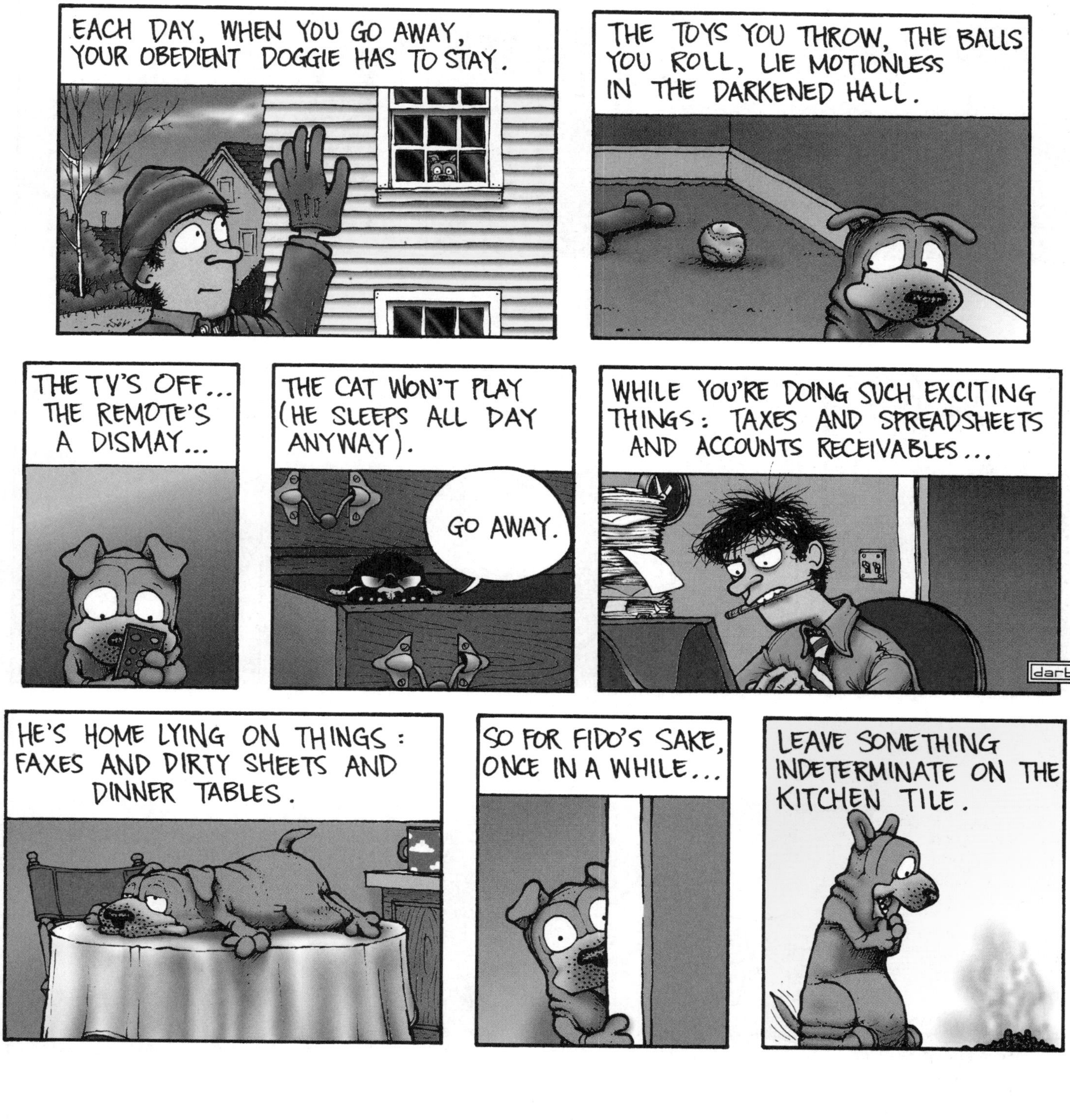
EACH DAY, WHEN YOU GO AWAY, YOUR OBEDIENT DOGGIE HAS TO STAY.
THE TOYS YOU THROW, THE BALLS YOU ROLL, LIE MOTIONLESS IN THE DARKENED HALL.
THE TV'S OFF... THE REMOTE'S A DISMAY...
THE CAT WON'T PLAY (HE SLEEPS ALL DAY ANYWAY).
GO AWAY.
WHILE YOU'RE DOING SUCH EXCITING THINGS: TAXES AND SPREADSHEETS AND ACCOUNTS RECEIVABLES...
darb
HE'S HOME LYING ON THINGS: FAXES AND DIRTY SHEETS AND DINNER TABLES.
SO FOR FIDO'S SAKE, ONCE IN A WHILE...
LEAVE SOMETHING INDETERMINATE ON THE KITCHEN TILE.

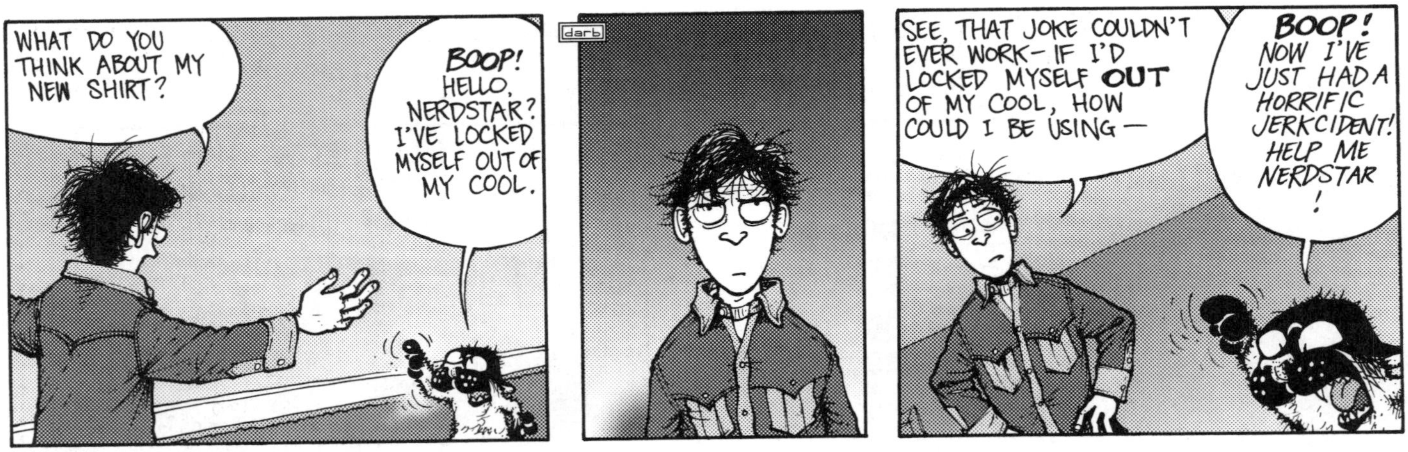
WHAT DO YOU THINK ABOUT MY NEW SHIRT?
BOOP! HELLO, NERDSTAR? I'VE LOCKED MYSELF OUT OF MY COOL.
darb
SEE, THAT JOKE COULDN'T EVER WORK– IF I'D LOCKED MYSELF **OUT** OF MY COOL, HOW COULD I BE USING—
BOOP! NOW I'VE JUST HAD A HORRIFIC JERKCIDENT! HELP ME NERDSTAR!

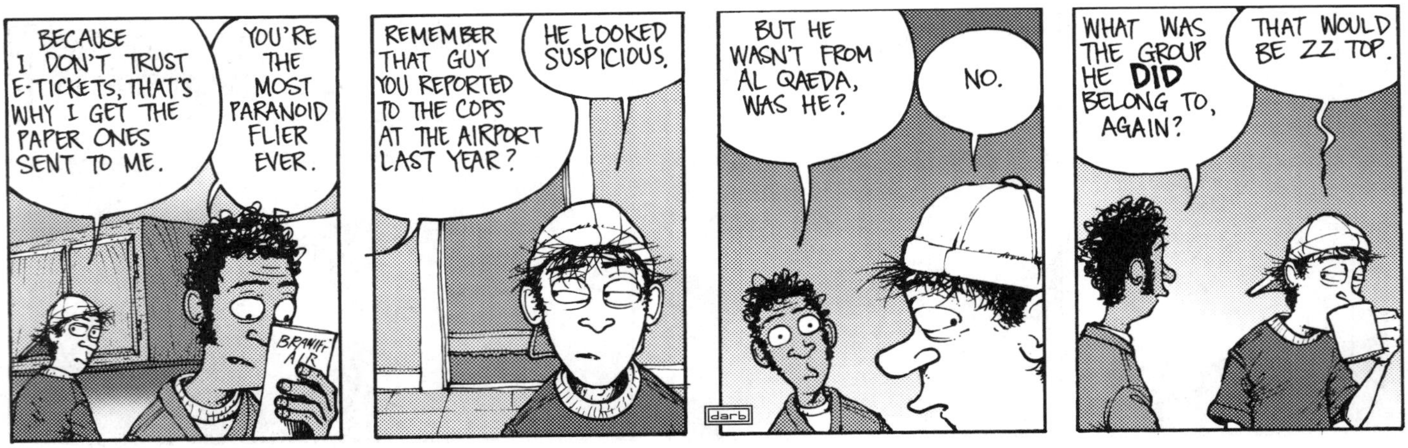
BECAUSE I DON'T TRUST E-TICKETS, THAT'S WHY I GET THE PAPER ONES SENT TO ME.
YOU'RE THE MOST PARANOID FLIER EVER.
BRANIFF AIR
REMEMBER THAT GUY YOU REPORTED TO THE COPS AT THE AIRPORT LAST YEAR?
HE LOOKED SUSPICIOUS.
BUT HE WASN'T FROM AL QAEDA, WAS HE?
NO.
darb
WHAT WAS THE GROUP HE **DID** BELONG TO, AGAIN?
THAT WOULD BE ZZ TOP.

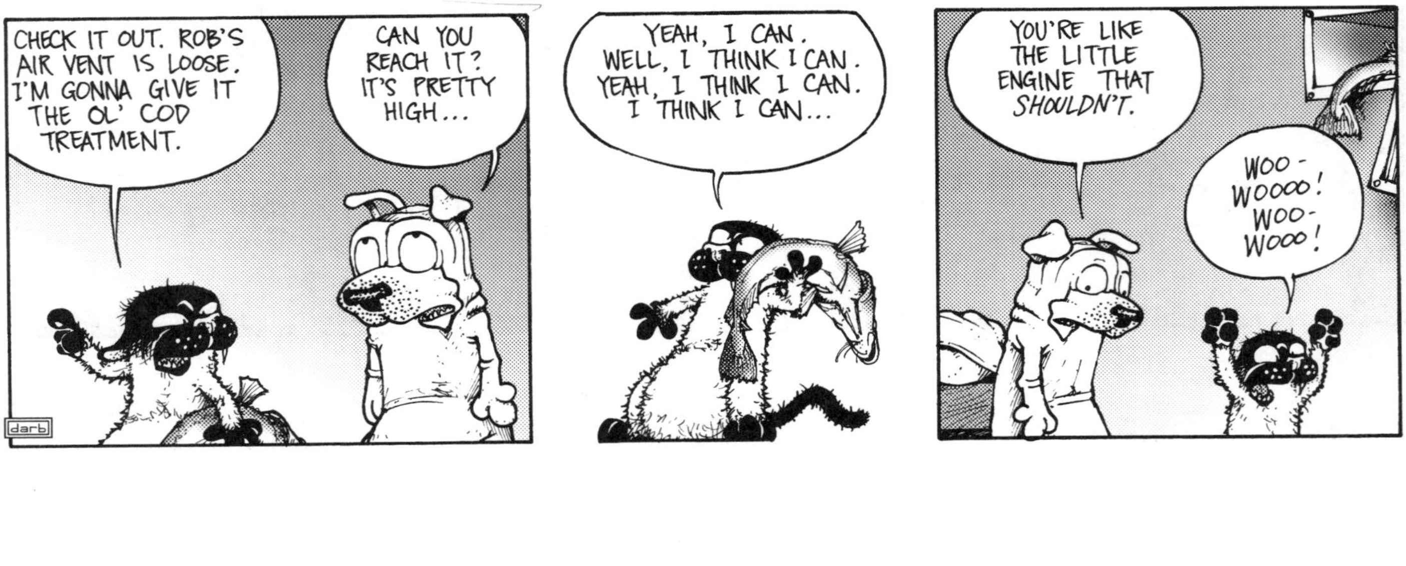
CHECK IT OUT. ROB'S AIR VENT IS LOOSE. I'M GONNA GIVE IT THE OL' COD TREATMENT.
CAN YOU REACH IT? IT'S PRETTY HIGH...
darb
YEAH, I CAN. WELL, I THINK I CAN. YEAH, I THINK I CAN. I THINK I CAN...
YOU'RE LIKE THE LITTLE ENGINE THAT *SHOULDN'T.*
WOO-WOOOO! WOO-WOOO!

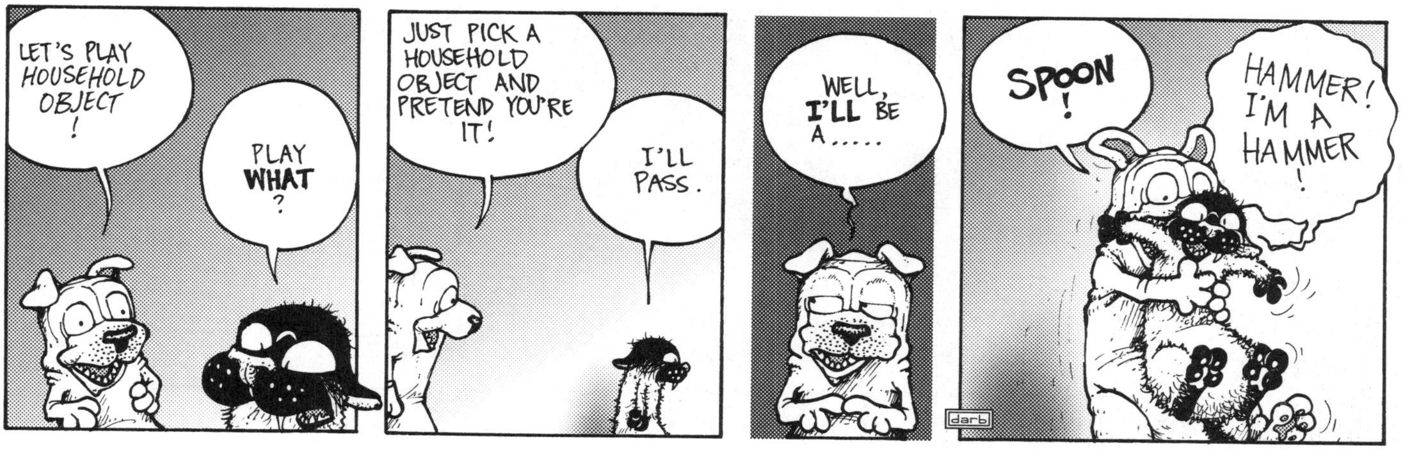
LET'S PLAY HOUSEHOLD OBJECT !
PLAY WHAT ?
JUST PICK A HOUSEHOLD OBJECT AND PRETEND YOU'RE IT!
I'LL PASS.
WELL, I'LL BE A.....
SPOON !
HAMMER! I'M A HAMMER !
darb

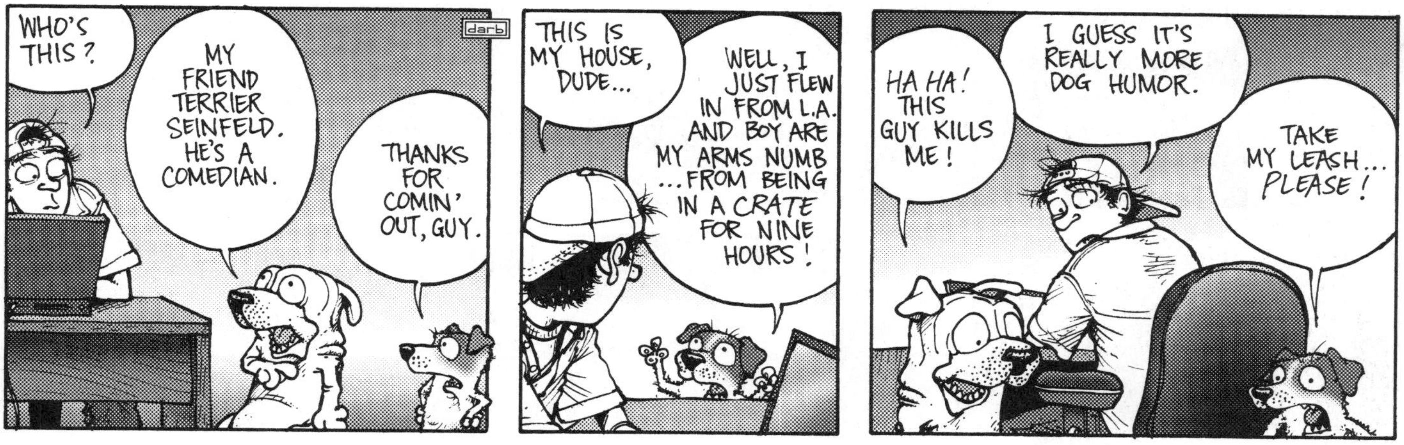
WHO'S THIS ?
MY FRIEND TERRIER SEINFELD. HE'S A COMEDIAN.
THANKS FOR COMIN' OUT, GUY.
darb
THIS IS MY HOUSE, DUDE...
WELL, I JUST FLEW IN FROM L.A. AND BOY ARE MY ARMS NUMB ...FROM BEING IN A CRATE FOR NINE HOURS !
HA HA! THIS GUY KILLS ME!
I GUESS IT'S REALLY MORE DOG HUMOR.
TAKE MY LEASH... PLEASE !

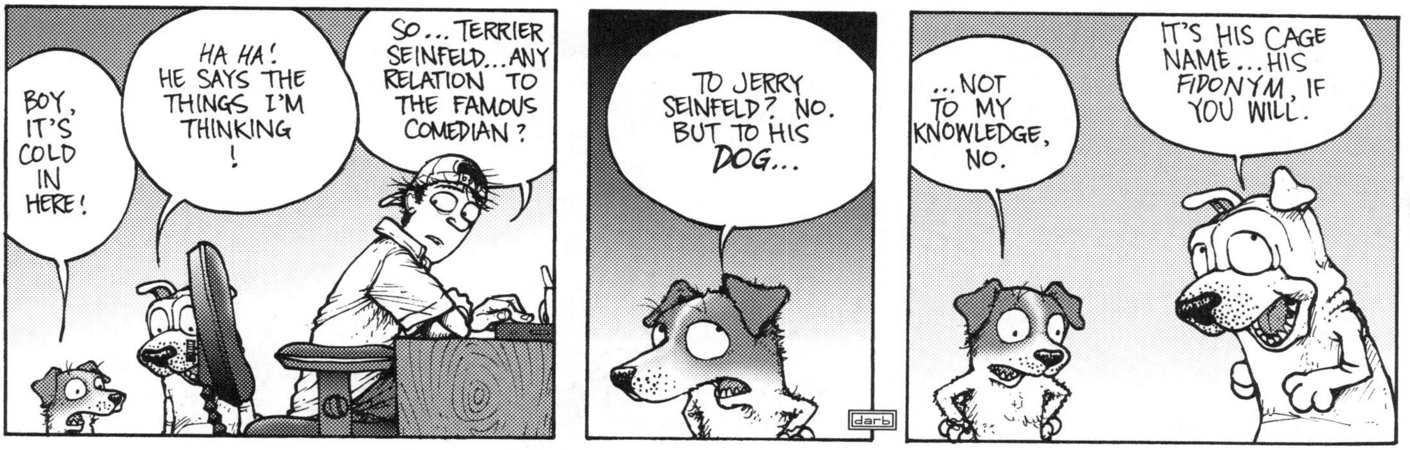
BOY, IT'S COLD IN HERE!
HA HA! HE SAYS THE THINGS I'M THINKING !
SO... TERRIER SEINFELD...ANY RELATION TO THE FAMOUS COMEDIAN ?
TO JERRY SEINFELD? NO. BUT TO HIS DOG...
darb
...NOT TO MY KNOWLEDGE, NO.
IT'S HIS CAGE NAME...HIS FIDONYM, IF YOU WILL.

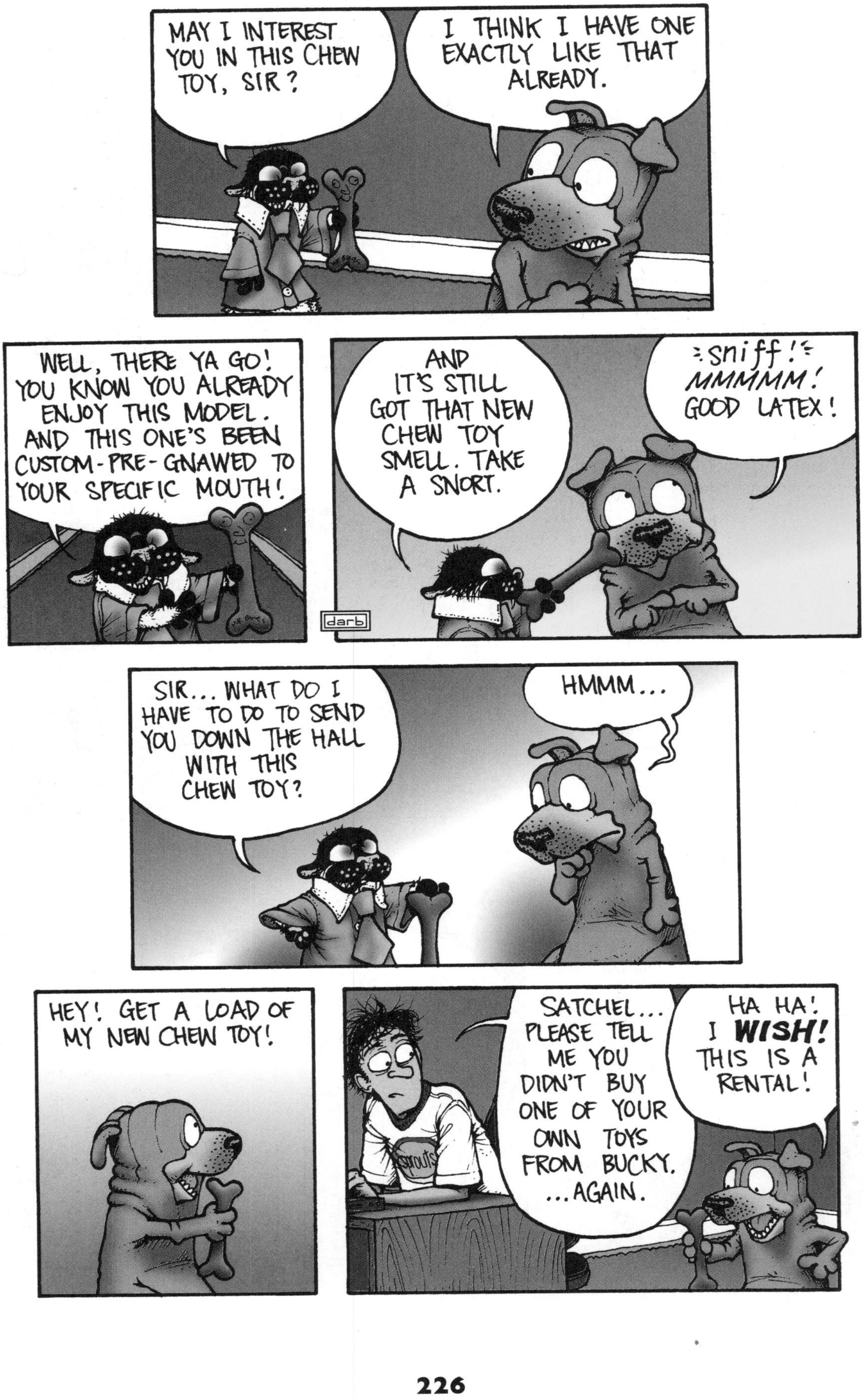
MAY I INTEREST YOU IN THIS CHEW TOY, SIR?
I THINK I HAVE ONE EXACTLY LIKE THAT ALREADY.
WELL, THERE YA GO! YOU KNOW YOU ALREADY ENJOY THIS MODEL. AND THIS ONE'S BEEN CUSTOM-PRE-GNAWED TO YOUR SPECIFIC MOUTH!
AND IT'S STILL GOT THAT NEW CHEW TOY SMELL. TAKE A SNORT.
sniff! MMMMM! GOOD LATEX!
darb
SIR... WHAT DO I HAVE TO DO TO SEND YOU DOWN THE HALL WITH THIS CHEW TOY?
HMMM...
HEY! GET A LOAD OF MY NEW CHEW TOY!
SATCHEL... PLEASE TELL ME YOU DIDN'T BUY ONE OF YOUR OWN TOYS FROM BUCKY. ...AGAIN.
HA HA! I **WISH!** THIS IS A RENTAL!
sprouts

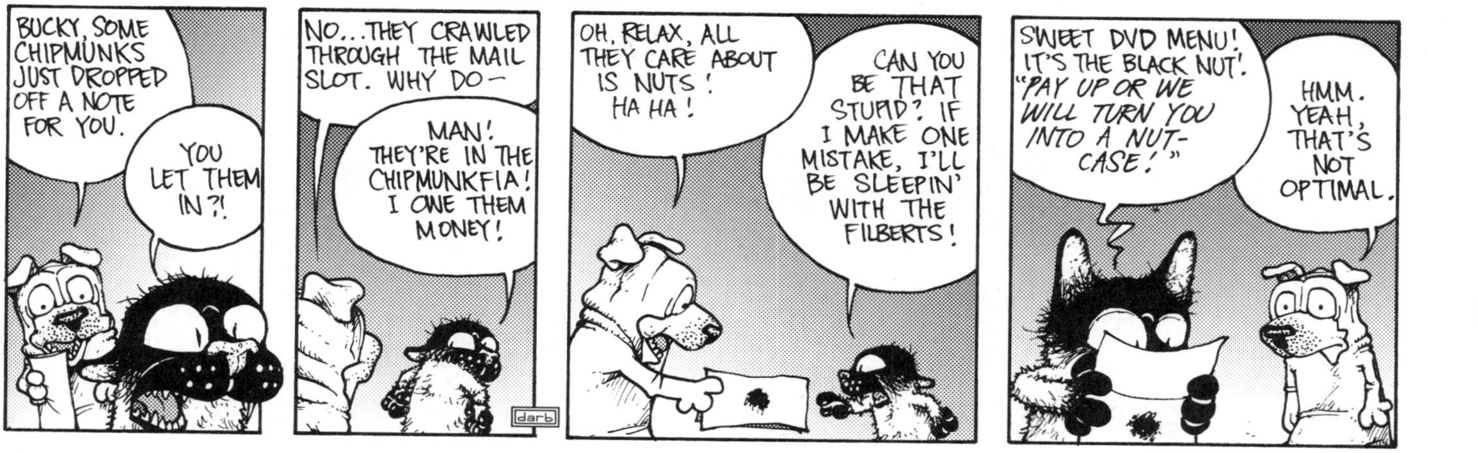
BUCKY, SOME CHIPMUNKS JUST DROPPED OFF A NOTE FOR YOU.
YOU LET THEM IN?!
NO...THEY CRAWLED THROUGH THE MAIL SLOT. WHY DO—
MAN! THEY'RE IN THE CHIPMUNKFIA! I OWE THEM MONEY!
OH, RELAX, ALL THEY CARE ABOUT IS NUTS! HA HA!
CAN YOU BE THAT STUPID? IF I MAKE ONE MISTAKE, I'LL BE SLEEPIN' WITH THE FILBERTS!
SWEET DVD MENU! IT'S THE BLACK NUT! "PAY UP OR WE WILL TURN YOU INTO A NUT-CASE!"
HMM. YEAH, THAT'S NOT OPTIMAL.
darb

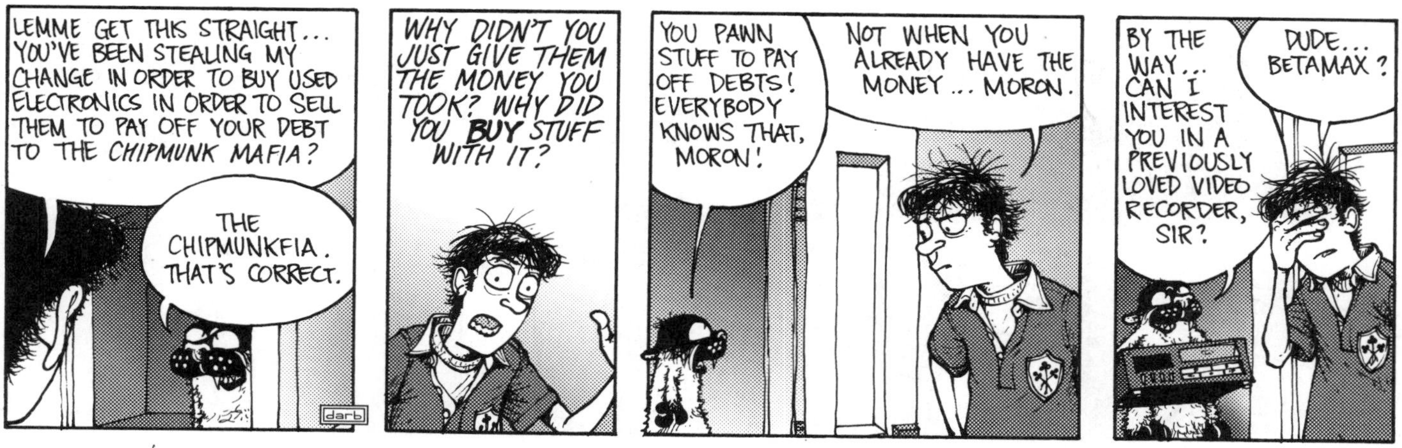
LEMME GET THIS STRAIGHT... YOU'VE BEEN STEALING MY CHANGE IN ORDER TO BUY USED ELECTRONICS IN ORDER TO SELL THEM TO PAY OFF YOUR DEBT TO THE CHIPMUNK MAFIA?
THE CHIPMUNKFIA. THAT'S CORRECT.
darb
WHY DIDN'T YOU JUST GIVE THEM THE MONEY YOU TOOK? WHY DID YOU BUY STUFF WITH IT?
YOU PAWN STUFF TO PAY OFF DEBTS! EVERYBODY KNOWS THAT, MORON!
NOT WHEN YOU ALREADY HAVE THE MONEY... MORON.
BY THE WAY... CAN I INTEREST YOU IN A PREVIOUSLY LOVED VIDEO RECORDER, SIR?
DUDE... BETAMAX?

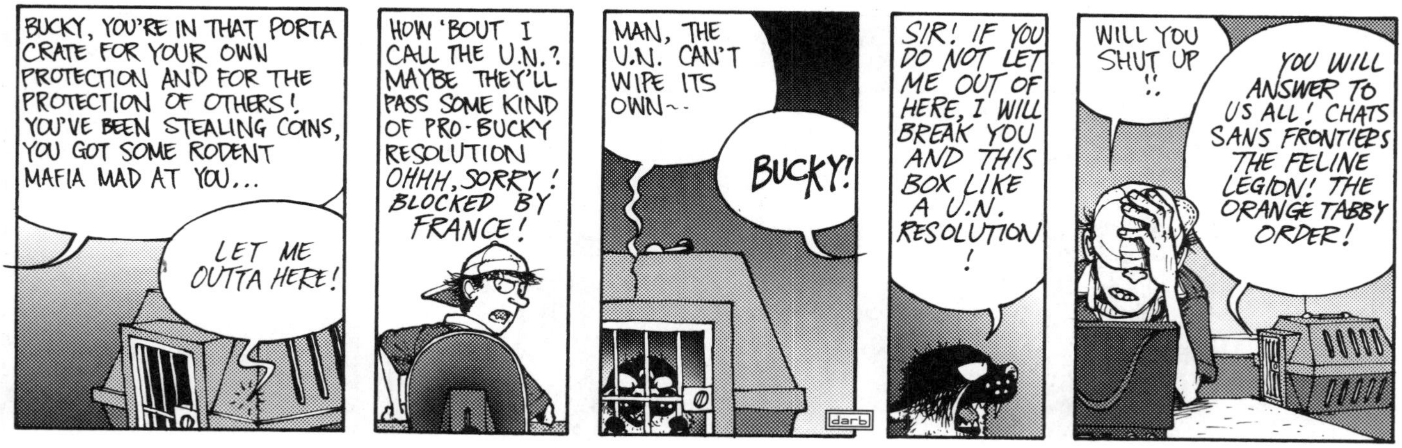
BUCKY, YOU'RE IN THAT PORTA CRATE FOR YOUR OWN PROTECTION AND FOR THE PROTECTION OF OTHERS! YOU'VE BEEN STEALING COINS, YOU GOT SOME RODENT MAFIA MAD AT YOU...
LET ME OUTTA HERE!
HOW 'BOUT I CALL THE U.N.? MAYBE THEY'LL PASS SOME KIND OF PRO-BUCKY RESOLUTION OHHH, SORRY! BLOCKED BY FRANCE!
MAN, THE U.N. CAN'T WIPE ITS OWN~~
BUCKY!
darb
SIR! IF YOU DO NOT LET ME OUT OF HERE, I WILL BREAK YOU AND THIS BOX LIKE A U.N. RESOLUTION!
WILL YOU SHUT UP!!
YOU WILL ANSWER TO US ALL! CHATS SANS FRONTIERS THE FELINE LEGION! THE ORANGE TABBY ORDER!

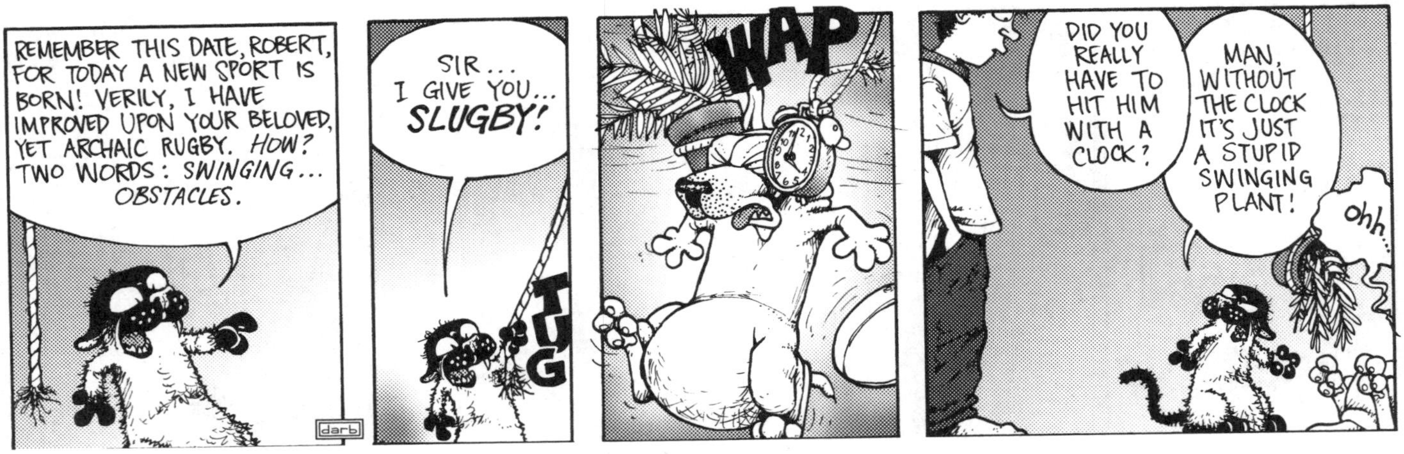
REMEMBER THIS DATE, ROBERT, FOR TODAY A NEW SPORT IS BORN! VERILY, I HAVE IMPROVED UPON YOUR BELOVED, YET ARCHAIC RUGBY. HOW? TWO WORDS: SWINGING... OBSTACLES.
SIR... I GIVE YOU... SLUGBY!
TUG
WAP
DID YOU REALLY HAVE TO HIT HIM WITH A CLOCK?
MAN, WITHOUT THE CLOCK IT'S JUST A STUPID SWINGING PLANT!
ohh...

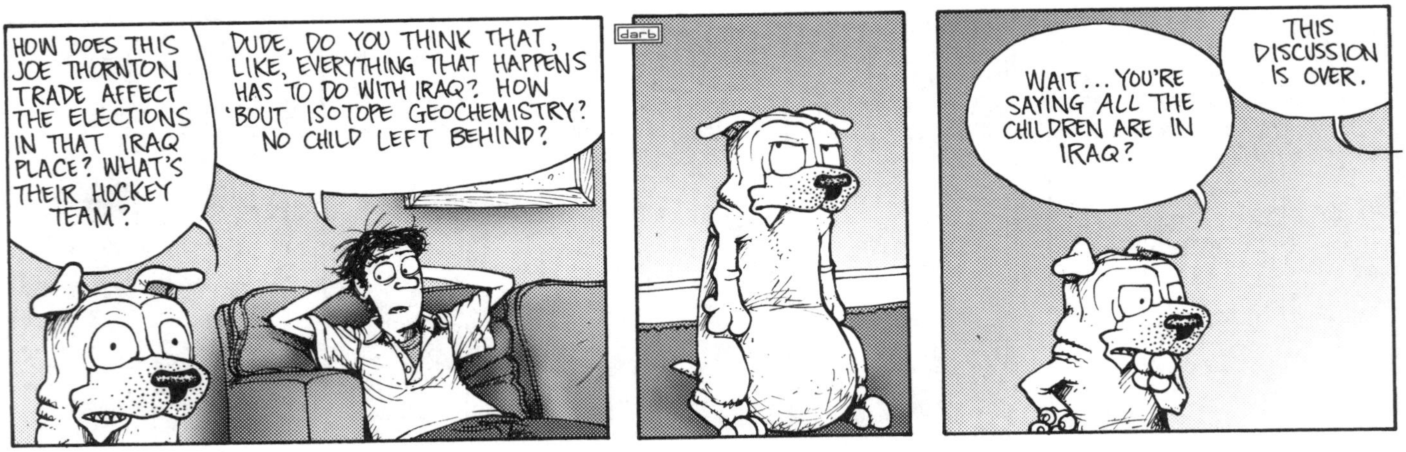
HOW DOES THIS JOE THORNTON TRADE AFFECT THE ELECTIONS IN THAT IRAQ PLACE? WHAT'S THEIR HOCKEY TEAM?
DUDE, DO YOU THINK THAT, LIKE, EVERYTHING THAT HAPPENS HAS TO DO WITH IRAQ? HOW 'BOUT ISOTOPE GEOCHEMISTRY? NO CHILD LEFT BEHIND?
WAIT... YOU'RE SAYING ALL THE CHILDREN ARE IN IRAQ?
THIS DISCUSSION IS OVER.

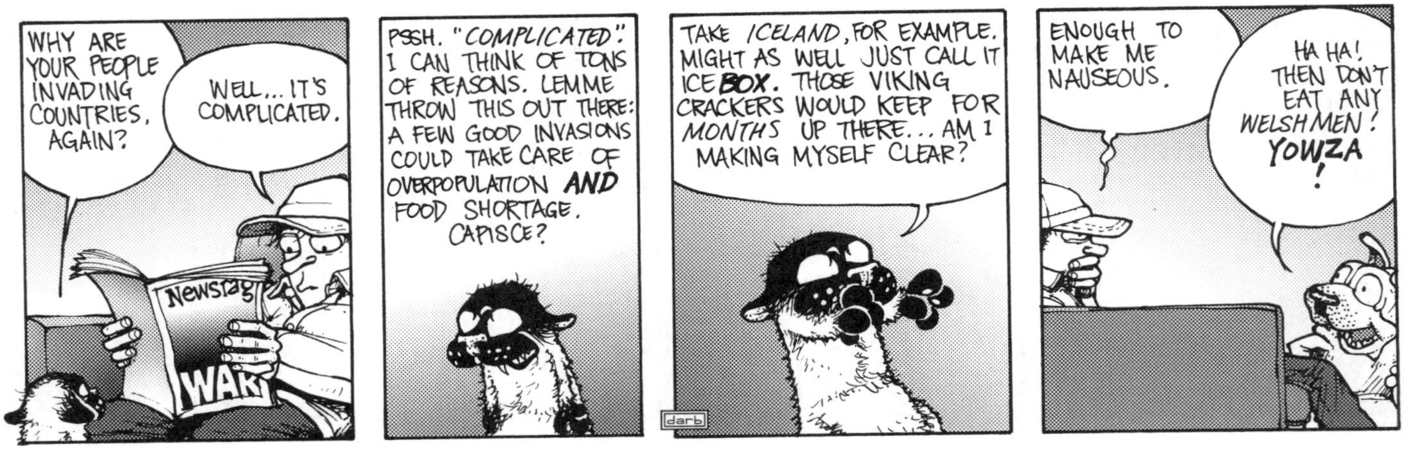
WHY ARE YOUR PEOPLE INVADING COUNTRIES, AGAIN?
WELL... IT'S COMPLICATED.
Newstag
WAR
PSSH. "COMPLICATED." I CAN THINK OF TONS OF REASONS. LEMME THROW THIS OUT THERE: A FEW GOOD INVASIONS COULD TAKE CARE OF OVERPOPULATION AND FOOD SHORTAGE. CAPISCE?
TAKE ICELAND, FOR EXAMPLE. MIGHT AS WELL JUST CALL IT ICEBOX. THOSE VIKING CRACKERS WOULD KEEP FOR MONTHS UP THERE... AM I MAKING MYSELF CLEAR?
ENOUGH TO MAKE ME NAUSEOUS.
HA HA! THEN DON'T EAT ANY WELSHMEN! YOWZA!

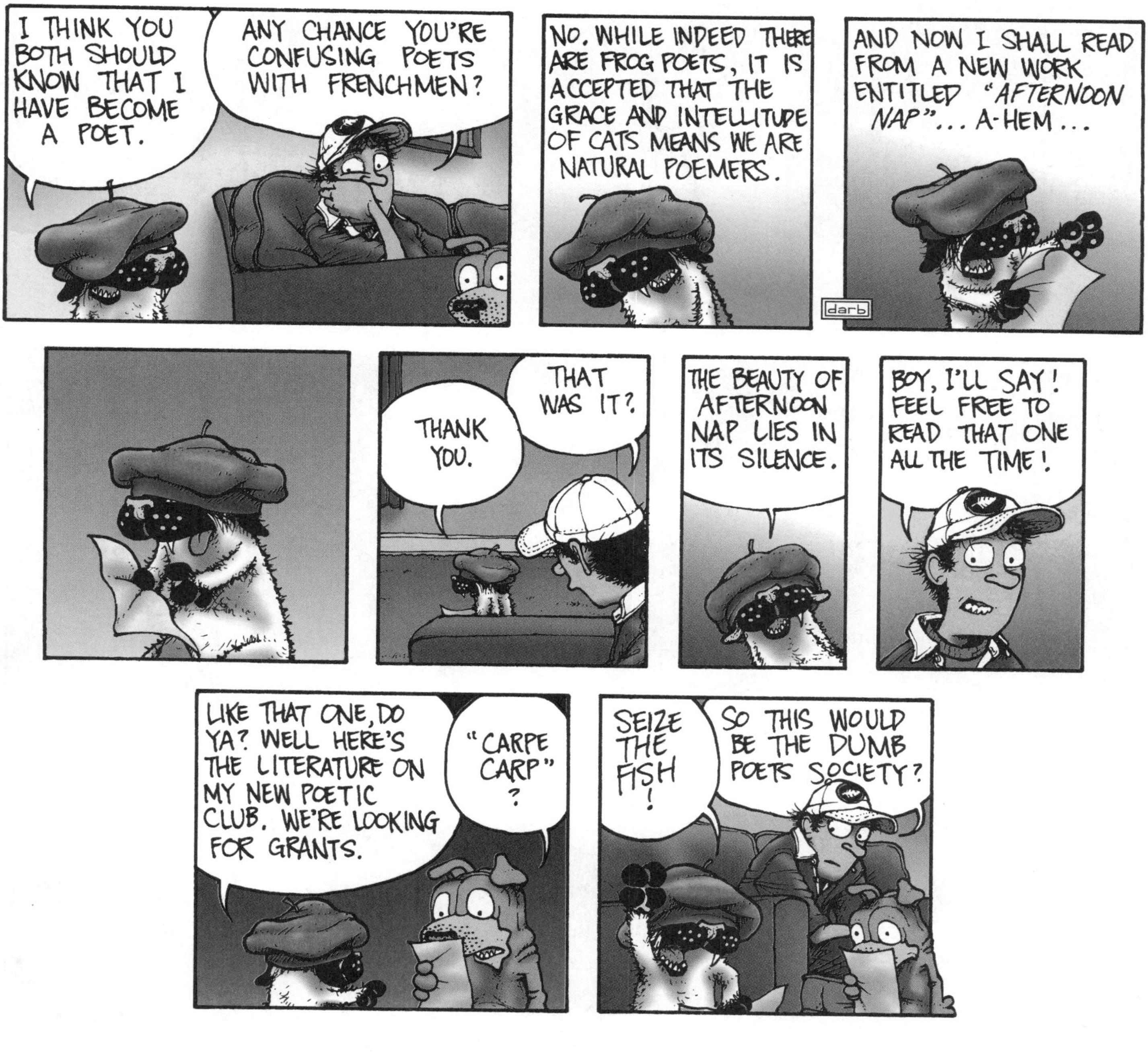
I THINK YOU BOTH SHOULD KNOW THAT I HAVE BECOME A POET.
ANY CHANCE YOU'RE CONFUSING POETS WITH FRENCHMEN?
NO. WHILE INDEED THERE ARE FROG POETS, IT IS ACCEPTED THAT THE GRACE AND INTELLITUDE OF CATS MEANS WE ARE NATURAL POEMERS.
AND NOW I SHALL READ FROM A NEW WORK ENTITLED "AFTERNOON NAP"... A-HEM...
darb
THANK YOU.
THAT WAS IT?
THE BEAUTY OF AFTERNOON NAP LIES IN ITS SILENCE.
BOY, I'LL SAY! FEEL FREE TO READ THAT ONE ALL THE TIME!
LIKE THAT ONE, DO YA? WELL HERE'S THE LITERATURE ON MY NEW POETIC CLUB. WE'RE LOOKING FOR GRANTS.
"CARPE CARP"?
SEIZE THE FISH!
SO THIS WOULD BE THE DUMB POETS SOCIETY?

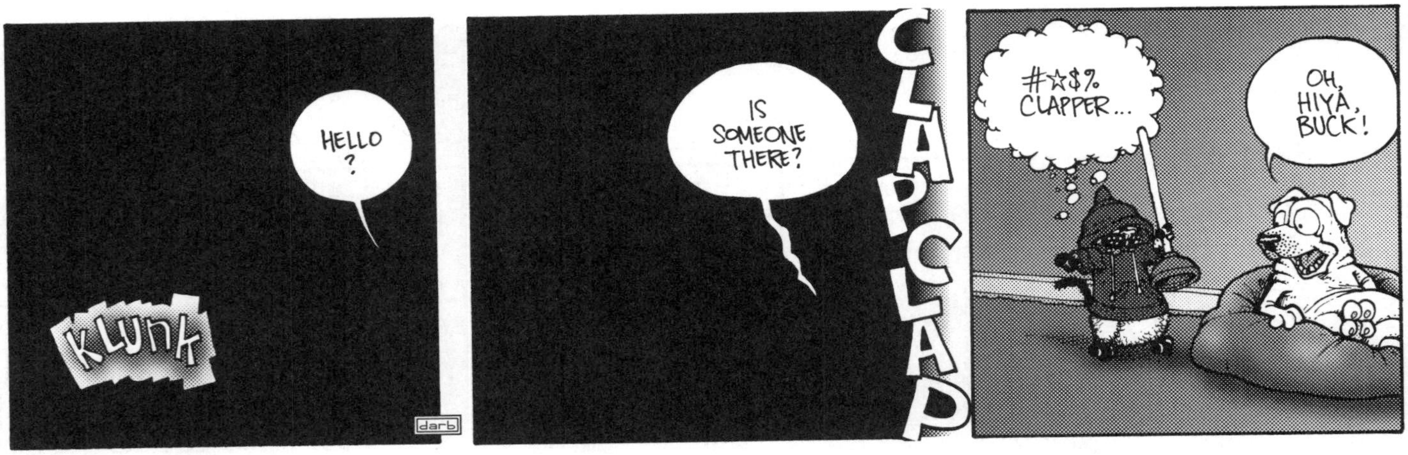
KLUNK
HELLO ?
IS SOMEONE THERE?
CLAP CLAP CLAP
#☆$% CLAPPER...
OH, HIYA, BUCK!
darb

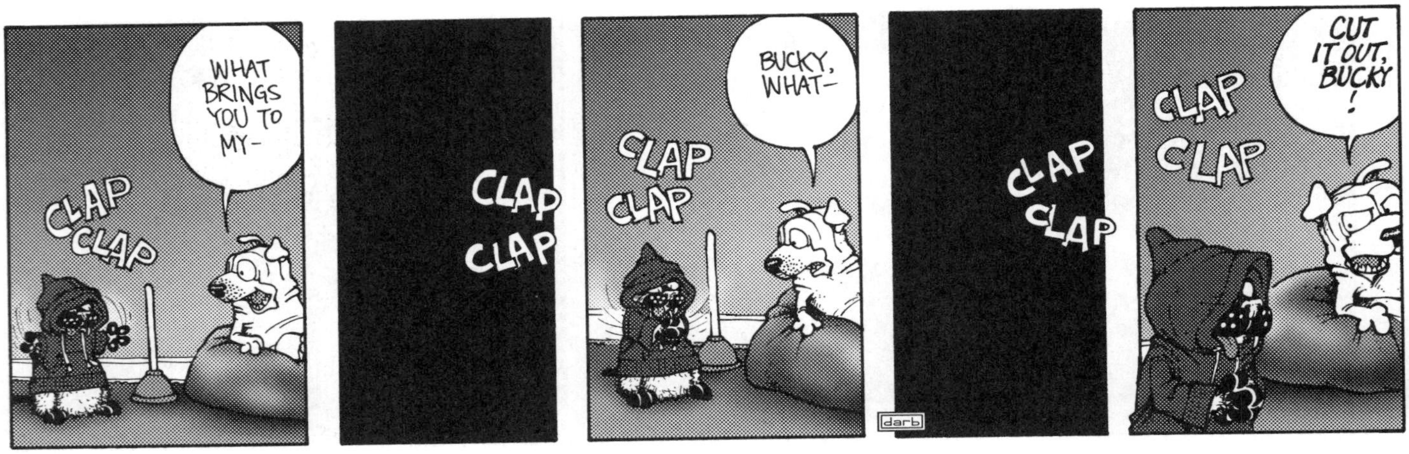
WHAT BRINGS YOU TO MY-
CLAP CLAP
CLAP CLAP
BUCKY, WHAT-
CLAP CLAP
CLAP CLAP
darb
CUT IT OUT, BUCKY!
CLAP CLAP

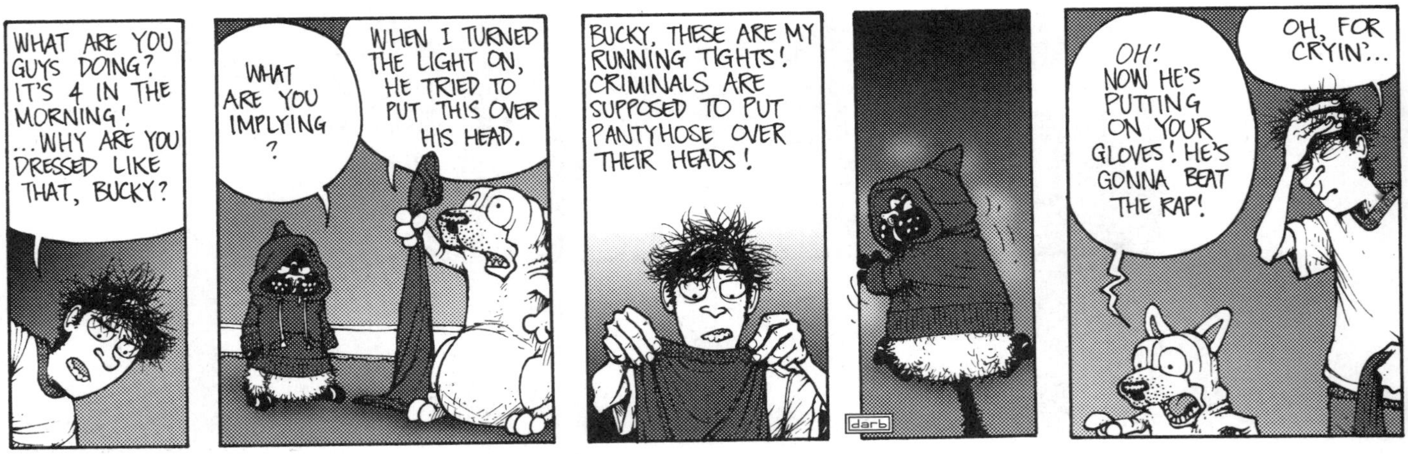
WHAT ARE YOU GUYS DOING? IT'S 4 IN THE MORNING! ...WHY ARE YOU DRESSED LIKE THAT, BUCKY?
WHAT ARE YOU IMPLYING ?
WHEN I TURNED THE LIGHT ON, HE TRIED TO PUT THIS OVER HIS HEAD.
BUCKY, THESE ARE MY RUNNING TIGHTS! CRIMINALS ARE SUPPOSED TO PUT PANTYHOSE OVER THEIR HEADS!
darb
OH! NOW HE'S PUTTING ON YOUR GLOVES! HE'S GONNA BEAT THE RAP!
OH, FOR CRYIN'...

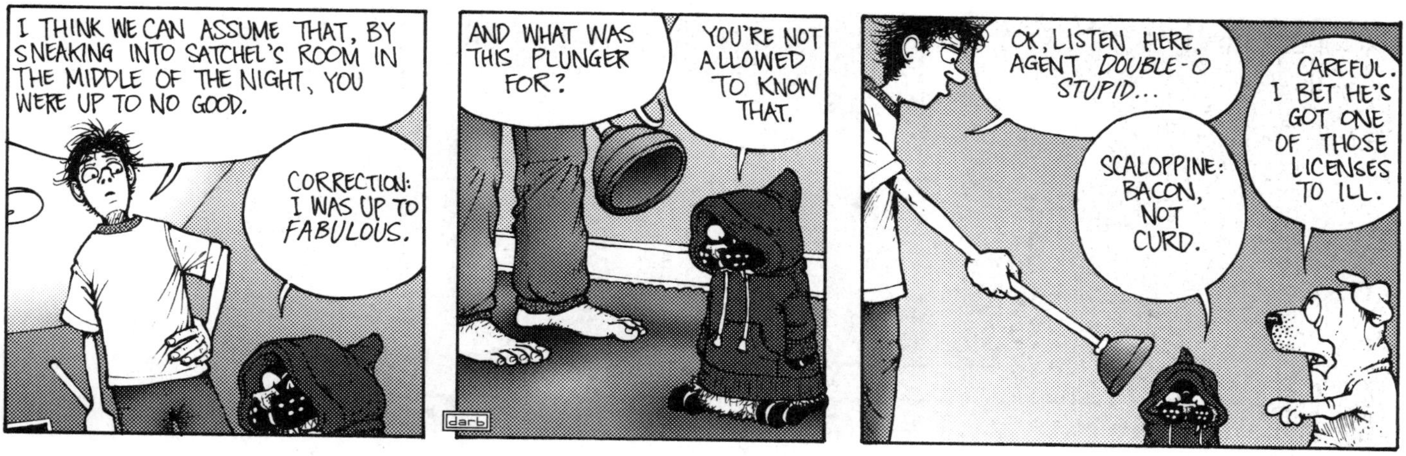
I THINK WE CAN ASSUME THAT, BY SNEAKING INTO SATCHEL'S ROOM IN THE MIDDLE OF THE NIGHT, YOU WERE UP TO NO GOOD.
CORRECTION: I WAS UP TO *FABULOUS*.
AND WHAT WAS THIS PLUNGER FOR?
YOU'RE NOT ALLOWED TO KNOW THAT.
OK, LISTEN HERE, AGENT *DOUBLE-O STUPID*...
SCALOPPINE: BACON, NOT CURD.
CAREFUL. I BET HE'S GOT ONE OF THOSE LICENSES TO ILL.
darb

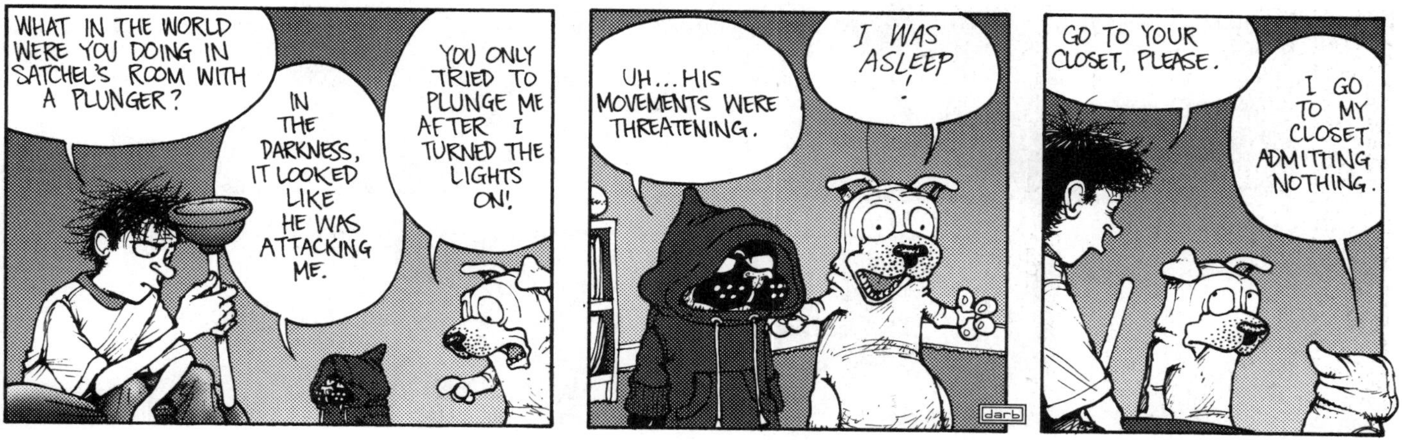
WHAT IN THE WORLD WERE YOU DOING IN SATCHEL'S ROOM WITH A PLUNGER?
IN THE DARKNESS, IT LOOKED LIKE HE WAS ATTACKING ME.
YOU ONLY TRIED TO PLUNGE ME AFTER I TURNED THE LIGHTS ON!
UH... HIS MOVEMENTS WERE THREATENING.
I WAS ASLEEP!
GO TO YOUR CLOSET, PLEASE.
I GO TO MY CLOSET ADMITTING NOTHING.
darb

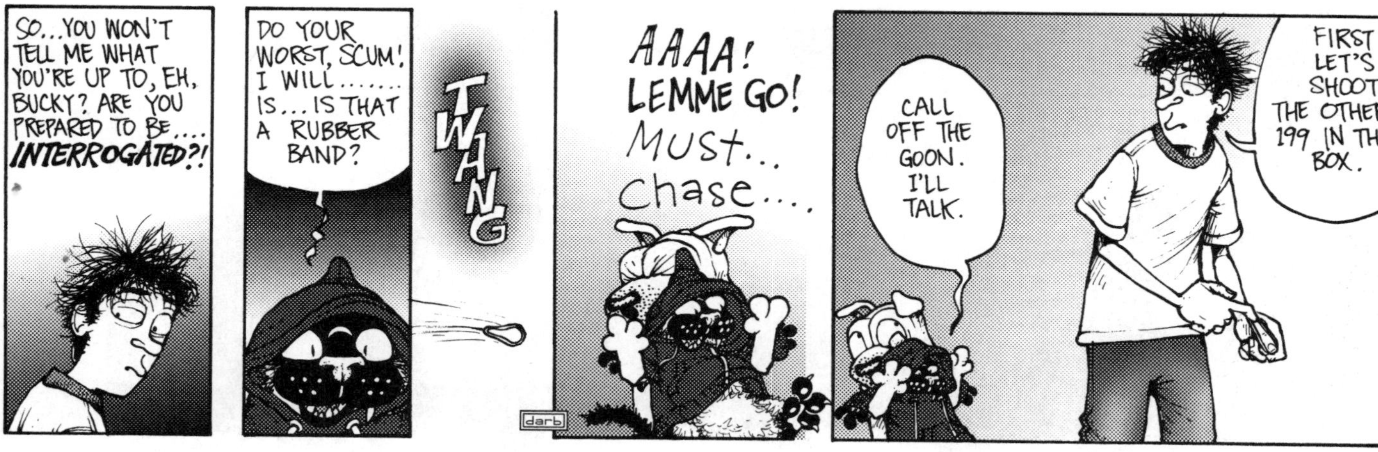
SO... YOU WON'T TELL ME WHAT YOU'RE UP TO, EH, BUCKY? ARE YOU PREPARED TO BE.... **INTERROGATED?!**
DO YOUR WORST, SCUM! I WILL....... IS... IS THAT A RUBBER BAND?
TWANG
AAAA! **LEMME GO!** Must... chase....
CALL OFF THE GOON. I'LL TALK.
FIRST LET'S SHOOT THE OTHER 199 IN THE BOX.
darb

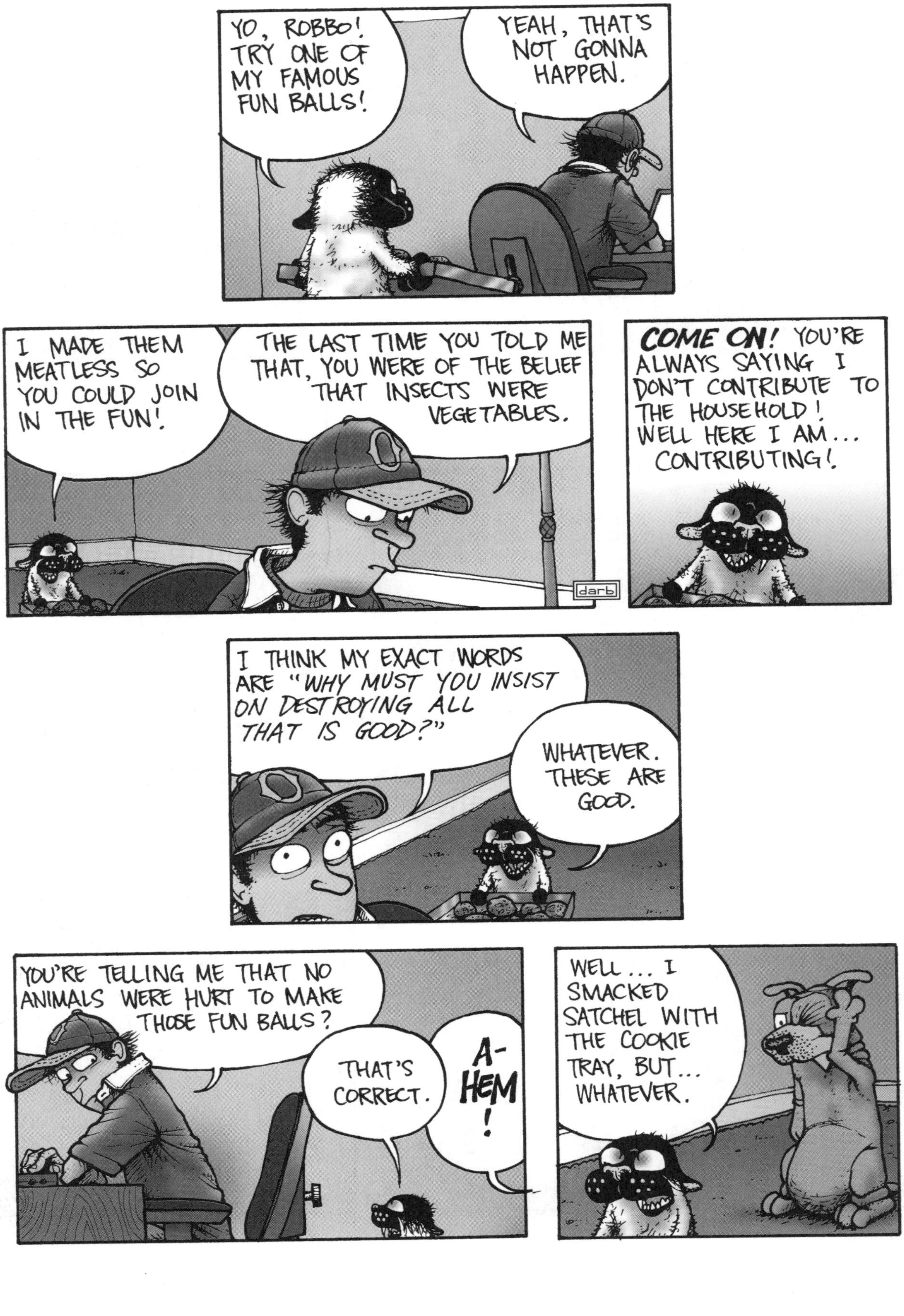
YO, ROBBO! TRY ONE OF MY FAMOUS FUN BALLS!
YEAH, THAT'S NOT GONNA HAPPEN.
I MADE THEM MEATLESS SO YOU COULD JOIN IN THE FUN!
THE LAST TIME YOU TOLD ME THAT, YOU WERE OF THE BELIEF THAT INSECTS WERE VEGETABLES.
darb
COME ON! YOU'RE ALWAYS SAYING I DON'T CONTRIBUTE TO THE HOUSEHOLD! WELL HERE I AM... CONTRIBUTING!
I THINK MY EXACT WORDS ARE "WHY MUST YOU INSIST ON DESTROYING ALL THAT IS GOOD?"
WHATEVER. THESE ARE GOOD.
YOU'RE TELLING ME THAT NO ANIMALS WERE HURT TO MAKE THOSE FUN BALLS?
THAT'S CORRECT.
A-HEM!
WELL... I SMACKED SATCHEL WITH THE COOKIE TRAY, BUT... WHATEVER.

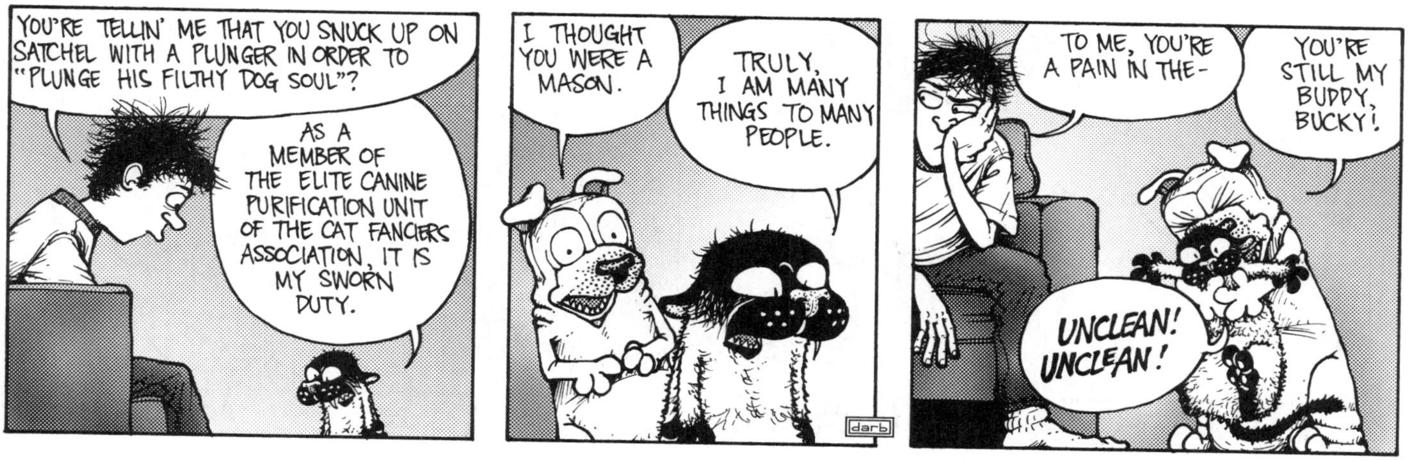
YOU'RE TELLIN' ME THAT YOU SNUCK UP ON SATCHEL WITH A PLUNGER IN ORDER TO "PLUNGE HIS FILTHY DOG SOUL"?
AS A MEMBER OF THE ELITE CANINE PURIFICATION UNIT OF THE CAT FANCIERS ASSOCIATION, IT IS MY SWORN DUTY.
I THOUGHT YOU WERE A MASON.
TRULY, I AM MANY THINGS TO MANY PEOPLE.
darb
TO ME, YOU'RE A PAIN IN THE-
YOU'RE STILL MY BUDDY, BUCKY!
UNCLEAN! UNCLEAN!

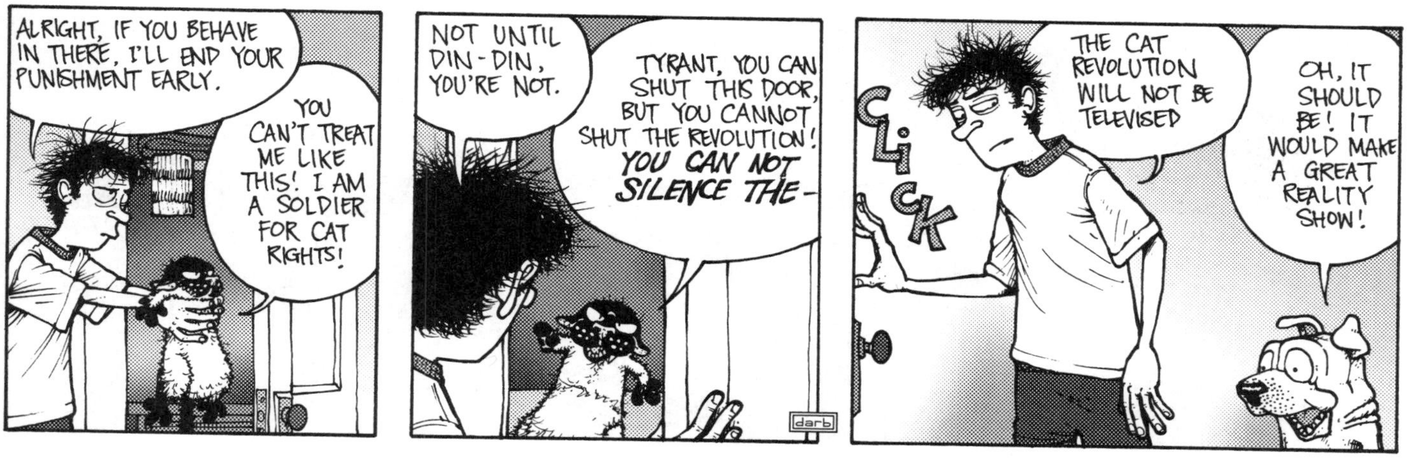
ALRIGHT, IF YOU BEHAVE IN THERE, I'LL END YOUR PUNISHMENT EARLY.
YOU CAN'T TREAT ME LIKE THIS! I AM A SOLDIER FOR CAT RIGHTS!
NOT UNTIL DIN-DIN, YOU'RE NOT.
TYRANT, YOU CAN SHUT THIS DOOR, BUT YOU CANNOT SHUT THE REVOLUTION! YOU CAN NOT SILENCE THE-
darb
CLICK
THE CAT REVOLUTION WILL NOT BE TELEVISED
OH, IT SHOULD BE! IT WOULD MAKE A GREAT REALITY SHOW!

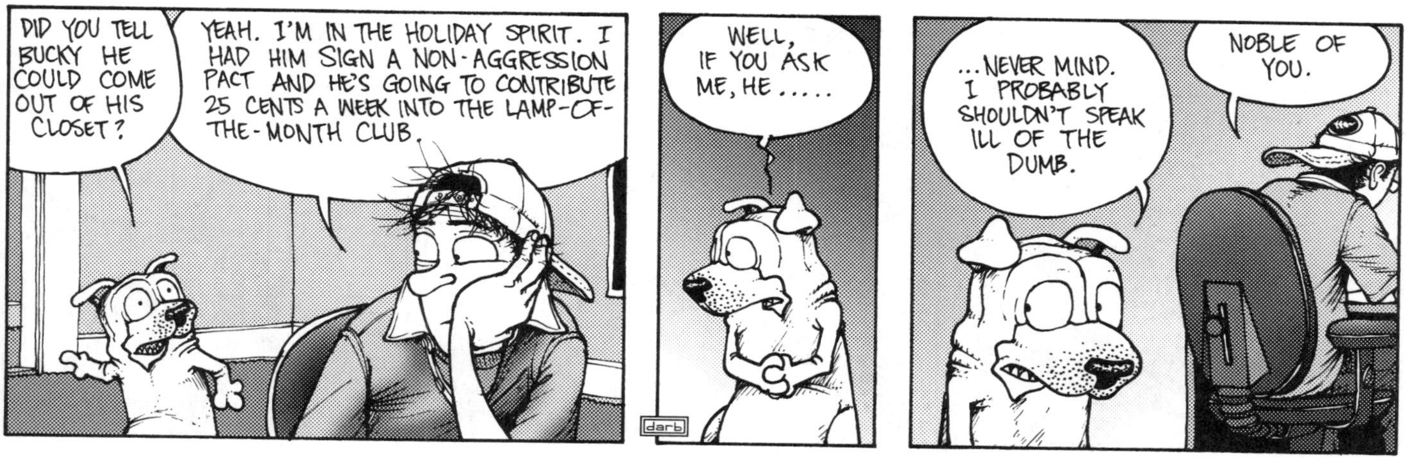
DID YOU TELL BUCKY HE COULD COME OUT OF HIS CLOSET?
YEAH. I'M IN THE HOLIDAY SPIRIT. I HAD HIM SIGN A NON-AGGRESSION PACT AND HE'S GOING TO CONTRIBUTE 25 CENTS A WEEK INTO THE LAMP-OF-THE-MONTH CLUB.
WELL, IF YOU ASK ME, HE .....
darb
...NEVER MIND. I PROBABLY SHOULDN'T SPEAK ILL OF THE DUMB.
NOBLE OF YOU.

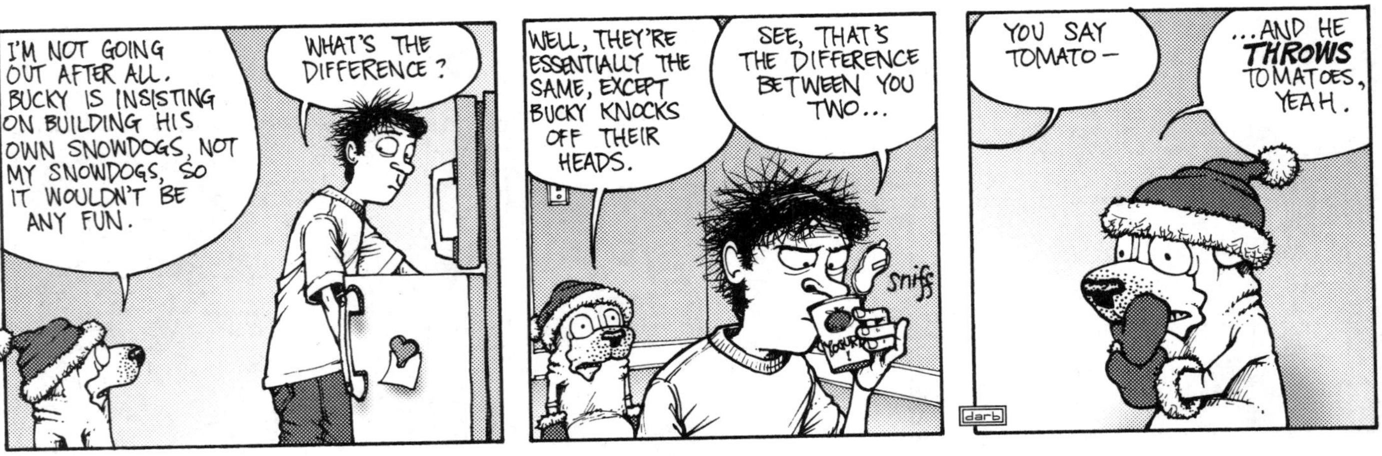
I'M NOT GOING OUT AFTER ALL. BUCKY IS INSISTING ON BUILDING HIS OWN SNOWDOGS, NOT MY SNOWDOGS, SO IT WOULDN'T BE ANY FUN.
WHAT'S THE DIFFERENCE?
WELL, THEY'RE ESSENTIALLY THE SAME, EXCEPT BUCKY KNOCKS OFF THEIR HEADS.
SEE, THAT'S THE DIFFERENCE BETWEEN YOU TWO...
sniff
YOU SAY TOMATO—
...AND HE **THROWS** TOMATOES, YEAH.
darb

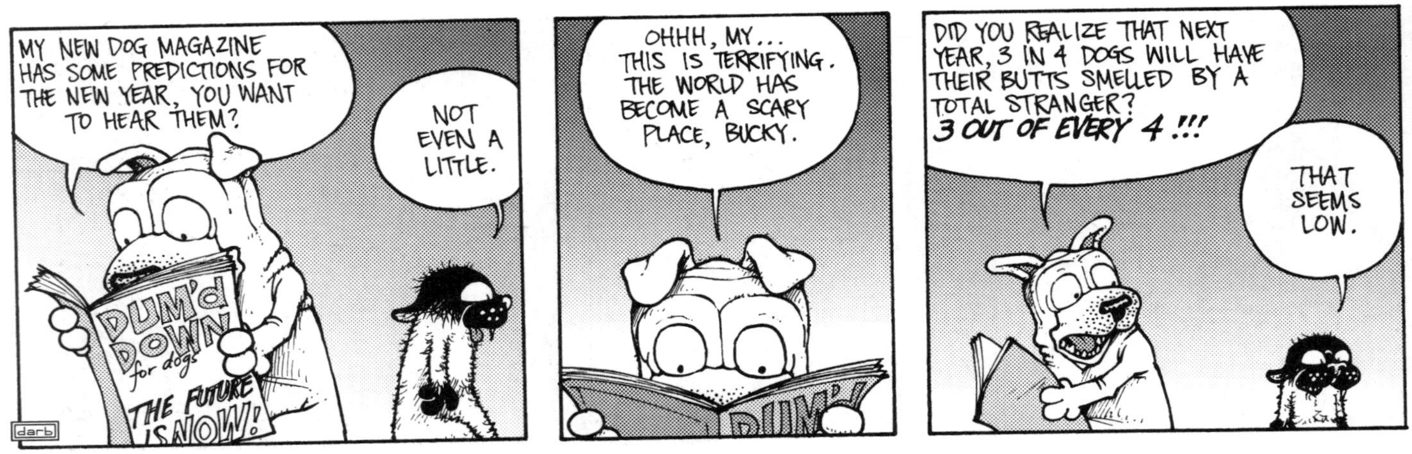
MY NEW DOG MAGAZINE HAS SOME PREDICTIONS FOR THE NEW YEAR, YOU WANT TO HEAR THEM?
NOT EVEN A LITTLE.
DUM'd DOWN for dogs
THE FUTURE IS NOW!
darb
OHHH, MY... THIS IS TERRIFYING. THE WORLD HAS BECOME A SCARY PLACE, BUCKY.
DID YOU REALIZE THAT NEXT YEAR, 3 IN 4 DOGS WILL HAVE THEIR BUTTS SMELLED BY A TOTAL STRANGER? ***3 OUT OF EVERY 4 !!!***
THAT SEEMS LOW.

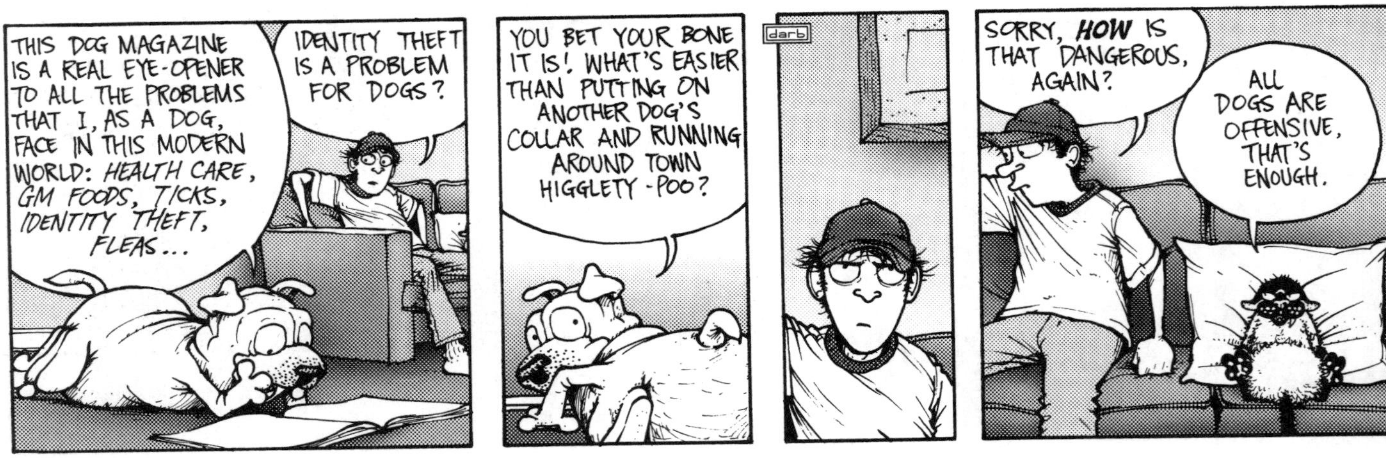
THIS DOG MAGAZINE IS A REAL EYE-OPENER TO ALL THE PROBLEMS THAT I, AS A DOG, FACE IN THIS MODERN WORLD: *HEALTH CARE, GM FOODS, TICKS, IDENTITY THEFT, FLEAS...*
IDENTITY THEFT IS A PROBLEM FOR DOGS?
YOU BET YOUR BONE IT IS! WHAT'S EASIER THAN PUTTING ON ANOTHER DOG'S COLLAR AND RUNNING AROUND TOWN HIGGLETY-POO?
darb
SORRY, **HOW** IS THAT DANGEROUS, AGAIN?
ALL DOGS ARE OFFENSIVE, THAT'S ENOUGH.

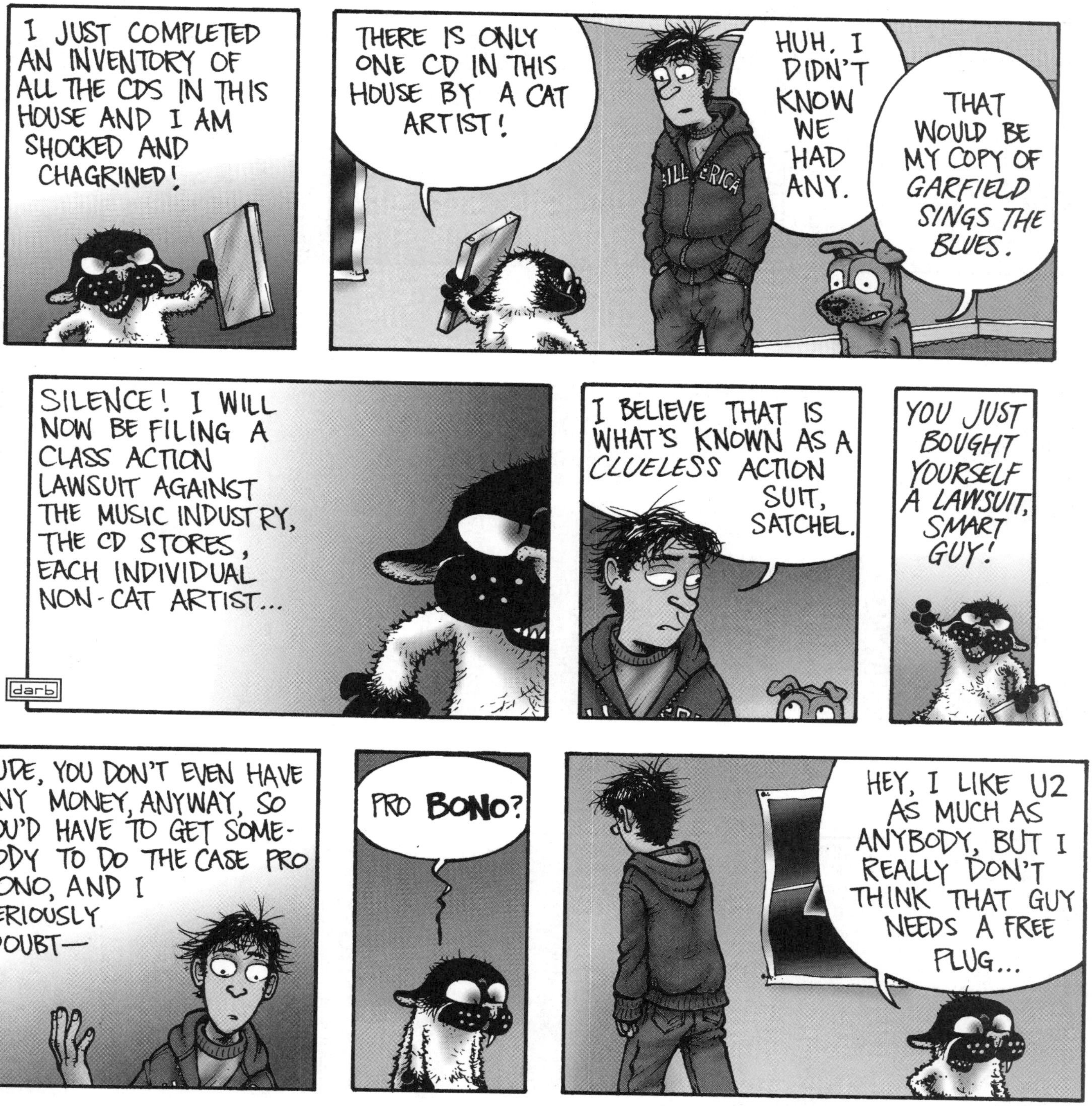
I JUST COMPLETED AN INVENTORY OF ALL THE CDS IN THIS HOUSE AND I AM SHOCKED AND CHAGRINED!
THERE IS ONLY ONE CD IN THIS HOUSE BY A CAT ARTIST!
HUH. I DIDN'T KNOW WE HAD ANY.
THAT WOULD BE MY COPY OF *GARFIELD SINGS THE BLUES*.
BILLERICA
SILENCE! I WILL NOW BE FILING A CLASS ACTION LAWSUIT AGAINST THE MUSIC INDUSTRY, THE CD STORES, EACH INDIVIDUAL NON-CAT ARTIST...
darb
I BELIEVE THAT IS WHAT'S KNOWN AS A *CLUELESS* ACTION SUIT, SATCHEL.
YOU JUST BOUGHT YOURSELF A LAWSUIT, SMART GUY!
DUDE, YOU DON'T EVEN HAVE ANY MONEY, ANYWAY, SO YOU'D HAVE TO GET SOMEBODY TO DO THE CASE PRO BONO, AND I SERIOUSLY DOUBT—
PRO **BONO**?
HEY, I LIKE U2 AS MUCH AS ANYBODY, BUT I REALLY DON'T THINK THAT GUY NEEDS A FREE PLUG...

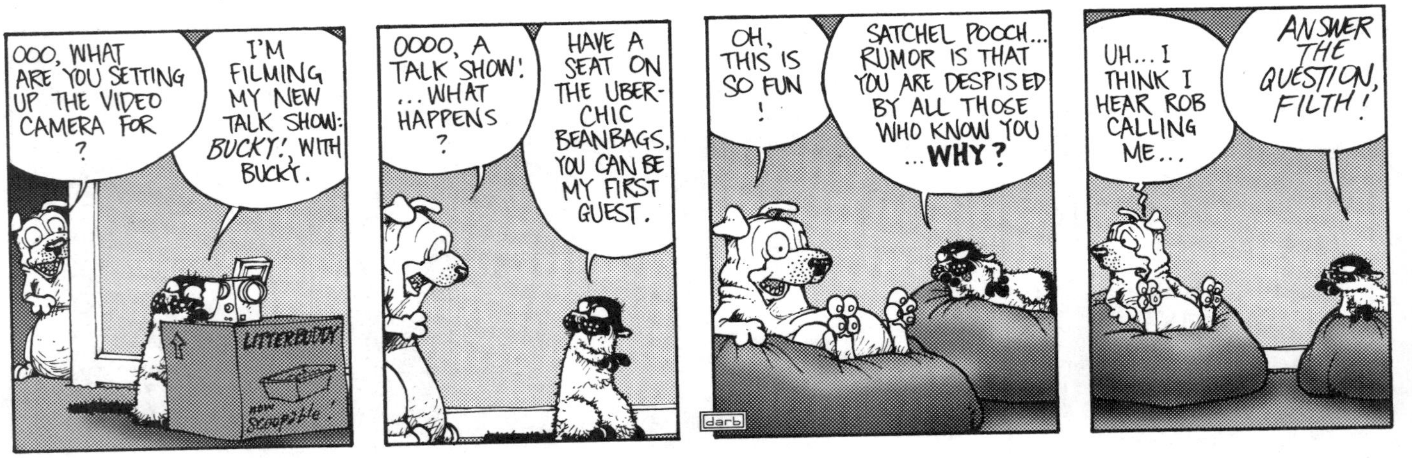
OOO, WHAT ARE YOU SETTING UP THE VIDEO CAMERA FOR?
I'M FILMING MY NEW TALK SHOW: *BUCKY!*, WITH BUCKY.
LITTERBUDDY
now Scoopable!
OOOO, A TALK SHOW! ...WHAT HAPPENS?
HAVE A SEAT ON THE UBER-CHIC BEANBAGS. YOU CAN BE MY FIRST GUEST.
OH, THIS IS SO FUN!
SATCHEL POOCH... RUMOR IS THAT YOU ARE DESPISED BY ALL THOSE WHO KNOW YOU ...**WHY?**
UH... I THINK I HEAR ROB CALLING ME...
ANSWER THE QUESTION, FILTH!

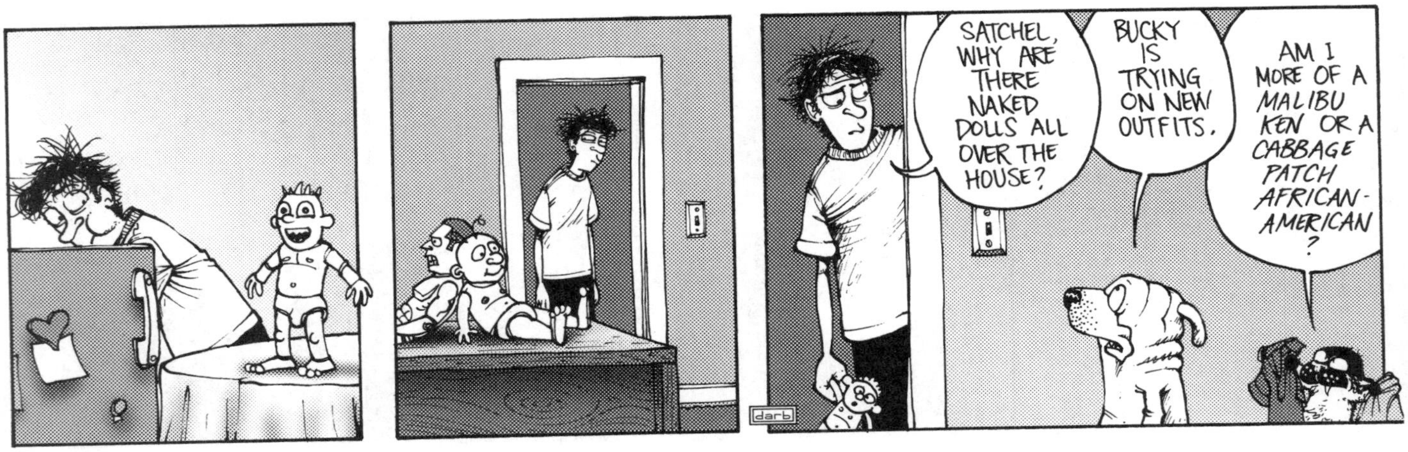
SATCHEL, WHY ARE THERE NAKED DOLLS ALL OVER THE HOUSE?
BUCKY IS TRYING ON NEW OUTFITS.
AM I MORE OF A *MALIBU KEN* OR A *CABBAGE PATCH AFRICAN-AMERICAN*?

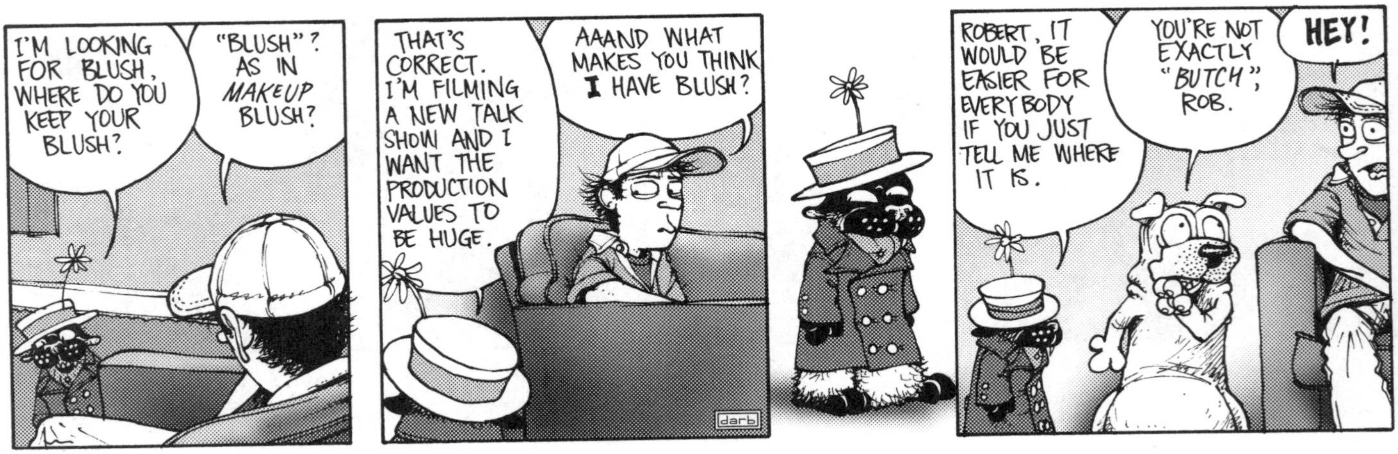
I'M LOOKING FOR BLUSH. WHERE DO YOU KEEP YOUR BLUSH?
"BLUSH"? AS IN *MAKEUP* BLUSH?
THAT'S CORRECT. I'M FILMING A NEW TALK SHOW AND I WANT THE PRODUCTION VALUES TO BE HUGE.
AAAND WHAT MAKES YOU THINK **I** HAVE BLUSH?
ROBERT, IT WOULD BE EASIER FOR EVERYBODY IF YOU JUST TELL ME WHERE IT IS.
YOU'RE NOT EXACTLY "*BUTCH*", ROB.
HEY!

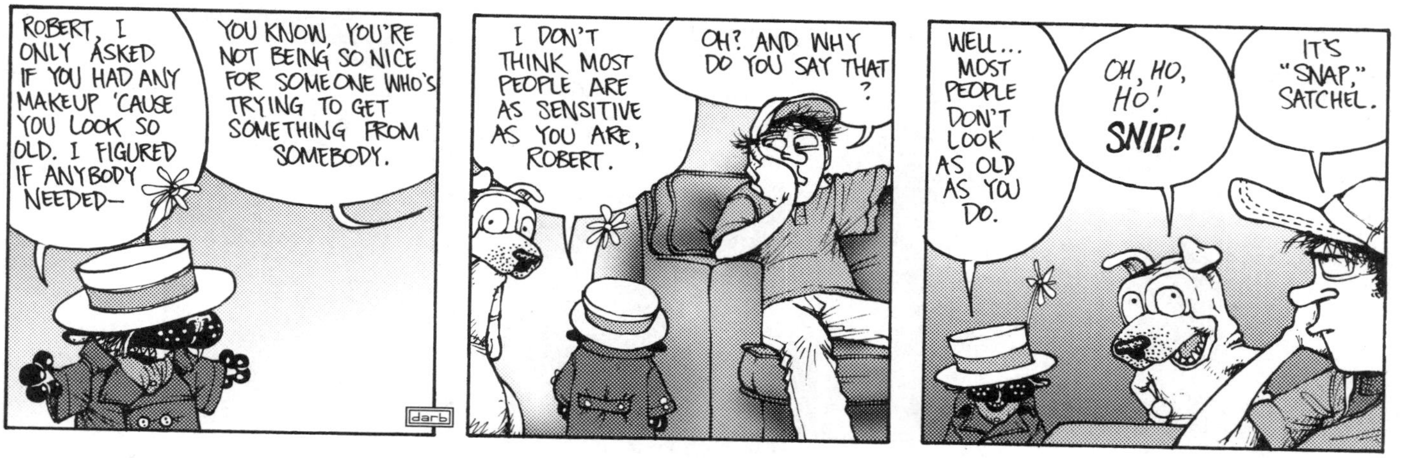
ROBERT, I ONLY ASKED IF YOU HAD ANY MAKEUP 'CAUSE YOU LOOK SO OLD. I FIGURED IF ANYBODY NEEDED—
YOU KNOW, YOU'RE NOT BEING SO NICE FOR SOMEONE WHO'S TRYING TO GET SOMETHING FROM SOMEBODY.
I DON'T THINK MOST PEOPLE ARE AS SENSITIVE AS YOU ARE, ROBERT.
OH? AND WHY DO YOU SAY THAT?
WELL... MOST PEOPLE DON'T LOOK AS OLD AS YOU DO.
OH, HO, HO! SNIP!
IT'S "SNAP," SATCHEL.

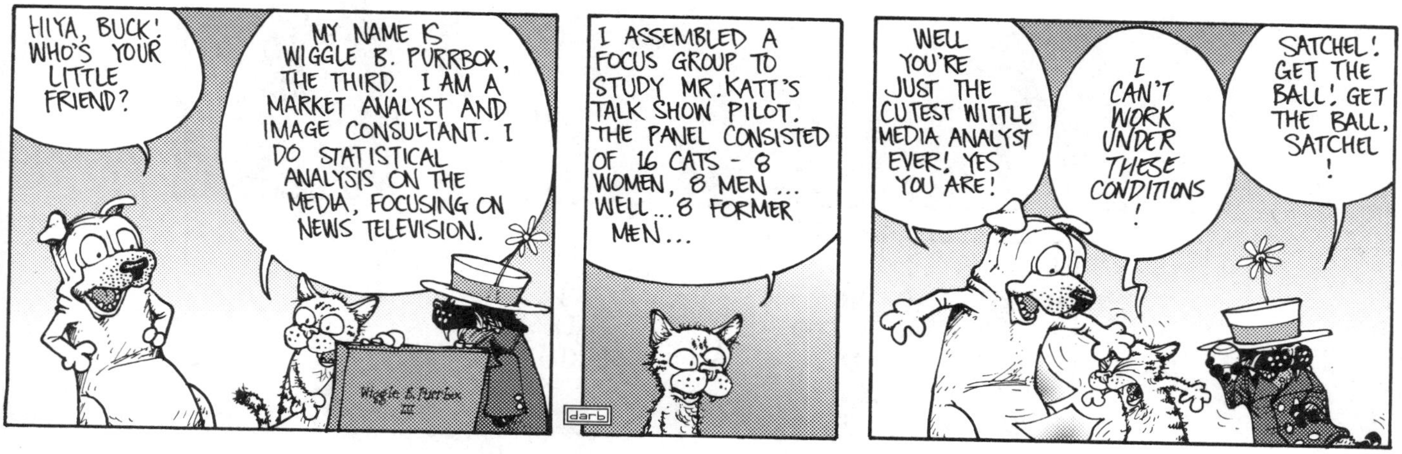
HIYA, BUCK! WHO'S YOUR LITTLE FRIEND?
MY NAME IS WIGGLE B. PURRBOX, THE THIRD. I AM A MARKET ANALYST AND IMAGE CONSULTANT. I DO STATISTICAL ANALYSIS ON THE MEDIA, FOCUSING ON NEWS TELEVISION.
I ASSEMBLED A FOCUS GROUP TO STUDY MR. KATT'S TALK SHOW PILOT. THE PANEL CONSISTED OF 16 CATS - 8 WOMEN, 8 MEN... WELL... 8 FORMER MEN...
WELL YOU'RE JUST THE CUTEST WITTLE MEDIA ANALYST EVER! YES YOU ARE!
I CAN'T WORK UNDER THESE CONDITIONS!
SATCHEL! GET THE BALL! GET THE BALL, SATCHEL!

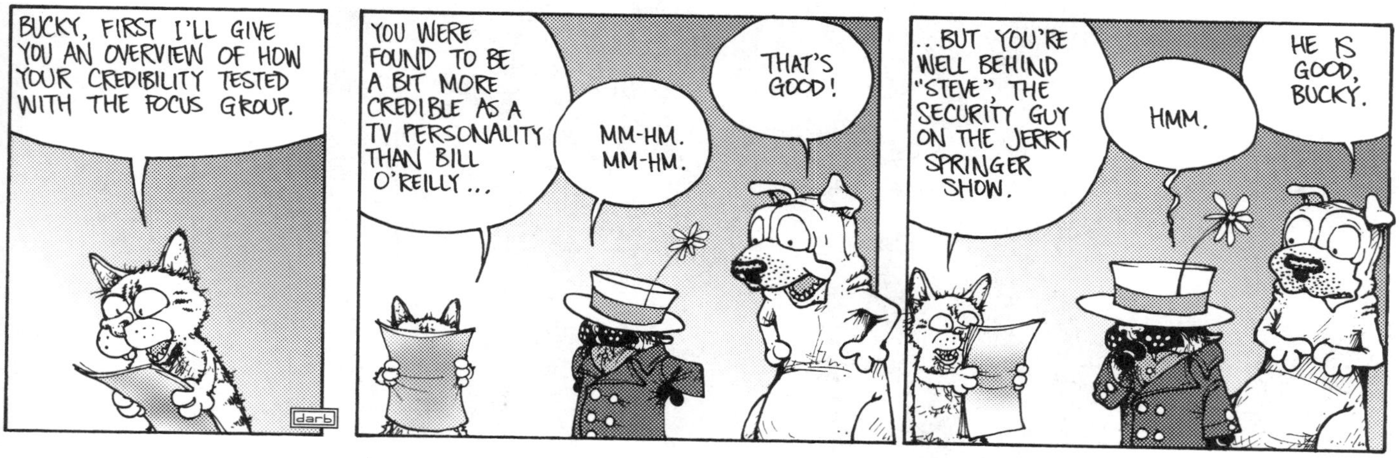
BUCKY, FIRST I'LL GIVE YOU AN OVERVIEW OF HOW YOUR CREDIBILITY TESTED WITH THE FOCUS GROUP.
YOU WERE FOUND TO BE A BIT MORE CREDIBLE AS A TV PERSONALITY THAN BILL O'REILLY...
MM-HM. MM-HM.
THAT'S GOOD!
...BUT YOU'RE WELL BEHIND "STEVE," THE SECURITY GUY ON THE JERRY SPRINGER SHOW.
HMM.
HE IS GOOD, BUCKY.

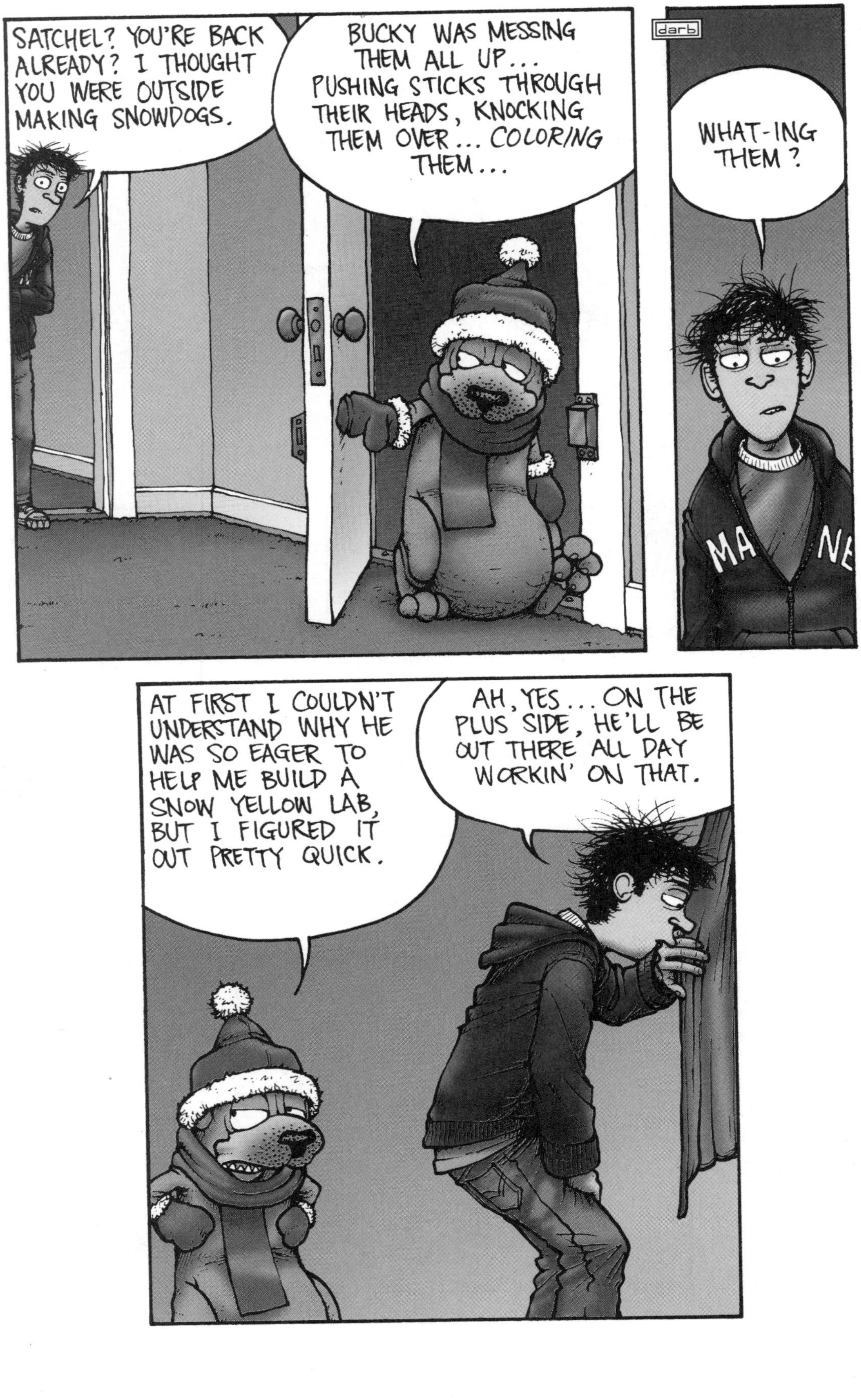
SATCHEL? YOU'RE BACK ALREADY? I THOUGHT YOU WERE OUTSIDE MAKING SNOWDOGS.
BUCKY WAS MESSING THEM ALL UP... PUSHING STICKS THROUGH THEIR HEADS, KNOCKING THEM OVER... COLORING THEM...
darb
WHAT-ING THEM?
MA NE
AT FIRST I COULDN'T UNDERSTAND WHY HE WAS SO EAGER TO HELP ME BUILD A SNOW YELLOW LAB, BUT I FIGURED IT OUT PRETTY QUICK.
AH, YES... ON THE PLUS SIDE, HE'LL BE OUT THERE ALL DAY WORKIN' ON THAT.

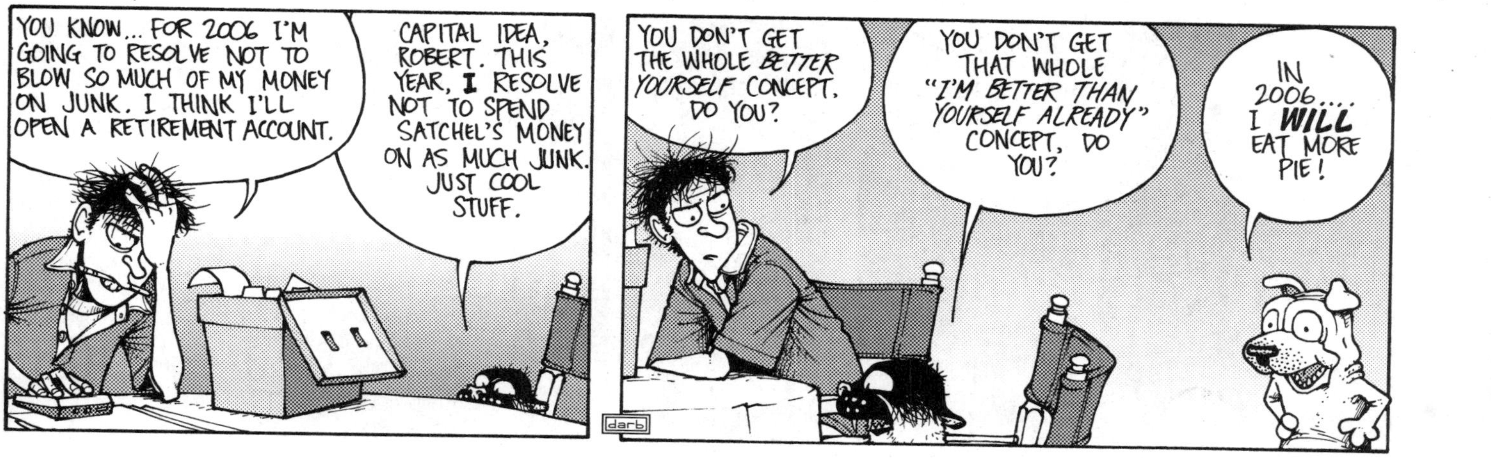
YOU KNOW... FOR 2006 I'M GOING TO RESOLVE NOT TO BLOW SO MUCH OF MY MONEY ON JUNK. I THINK I'LL OPEN A RETIREMENT ACCOUNT.
CAPITAL IDEA, ROBERT. THIS YEAR, I RESOLVE NOT TO SPEND SATCHEL'S MONEY ON AS MUCH JUNK. JUST COOL STUFF.
YOU DON'T GET THE WHOLE BETTER YOURSELF CONCEPT, DO YOU?
YOU DON'T GET THAT WHOLE "I'M BETTER THAN YOURSELF ALREADY" CONCEPT, DO YOU?
IN 2006.... I WILL EAT MORE PIE!
darb

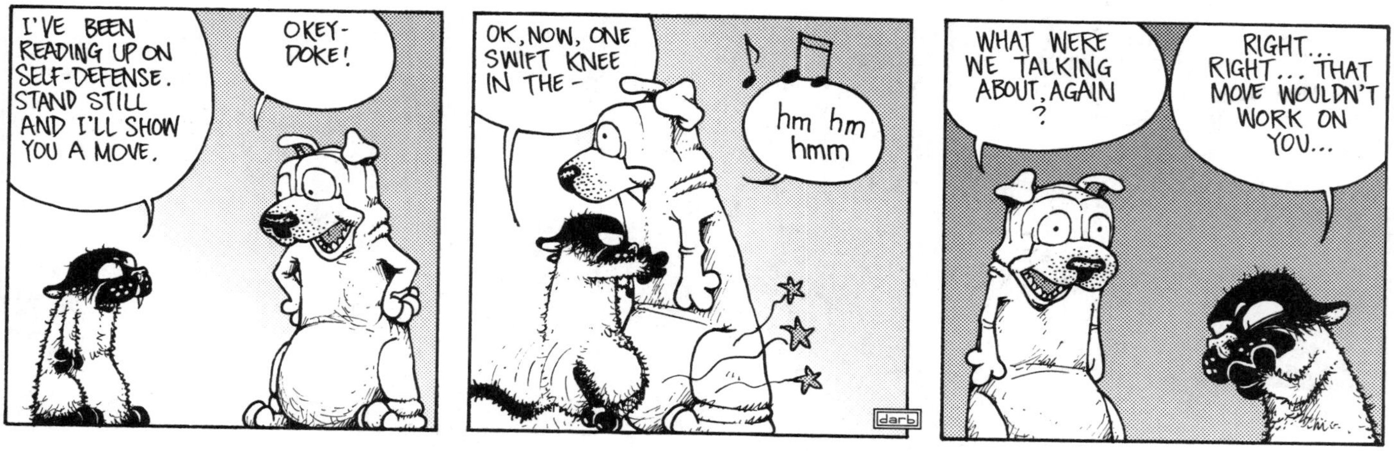
I'VE BEEN READING UP ON SELF-DEFENSE. STAND STILL AND I'LL SHOW YOU A MOVE.
OKEY-DOKE!
OK, NOW, ONE SWIFT KNEE IN THE-
hm hm hmm
darb
WHAT WERE WE TALKING ABOUT, AGAIN?
RIGHT... RIGHT... THAT MOVE WOULDN'T WORK ON YOU...

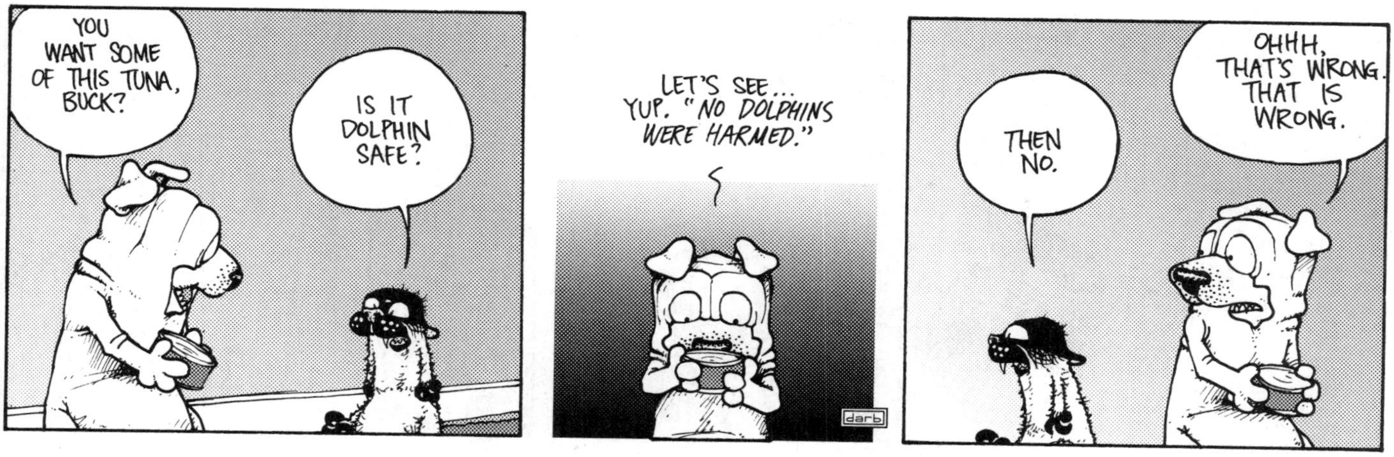
YOU WANT SOME OF THIS TUNA, BUCK?
IS IT DOLPHIN SAFE?
LET'S SEE... YUP. "NO DOLPHINS WERE HARMED."
darb
THEN NO.
OHHH, THAT'S WRONG. THAT IS WRONG.

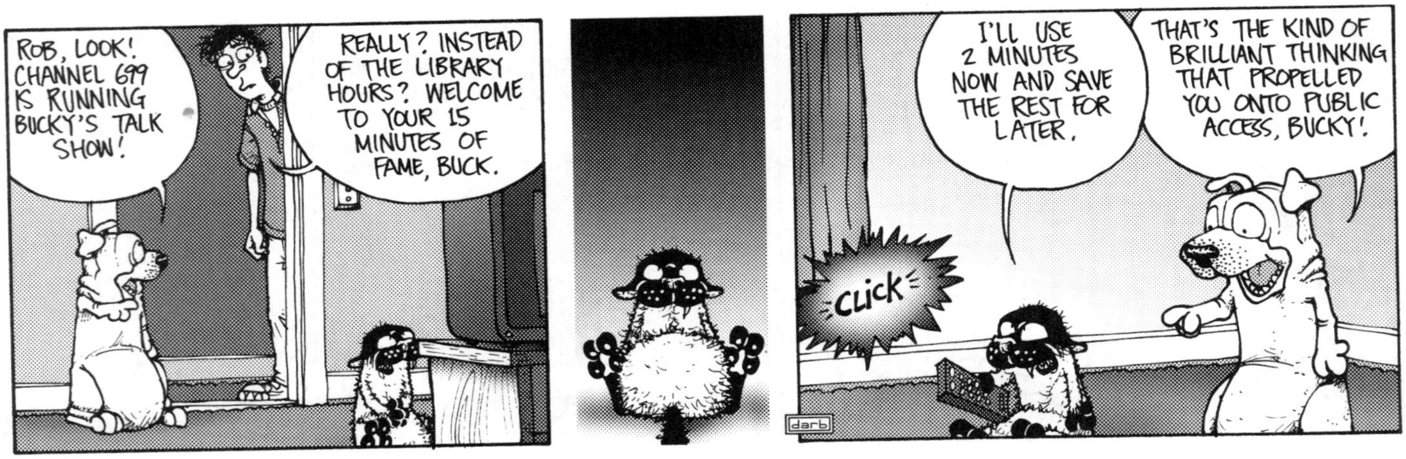
ROB, LOOK! CHANNEL 699 IS RUNNING BUCKY'S TALK SHOW!
REALLY? INSTEAD OF THE LIBRARY HOURS? WELCOME TO YOUR 15 MINUTES OF FAME, BUCK.
CLICK
I'LL USE 2 MINUTES NOW AND SAVE THE REST FOR LATER.
THAT'S THE KIND OF BRILLIANT THINKING THAT PROPELLED YOU ONTO PUBLIC ACCESS, BUCKY!
darb

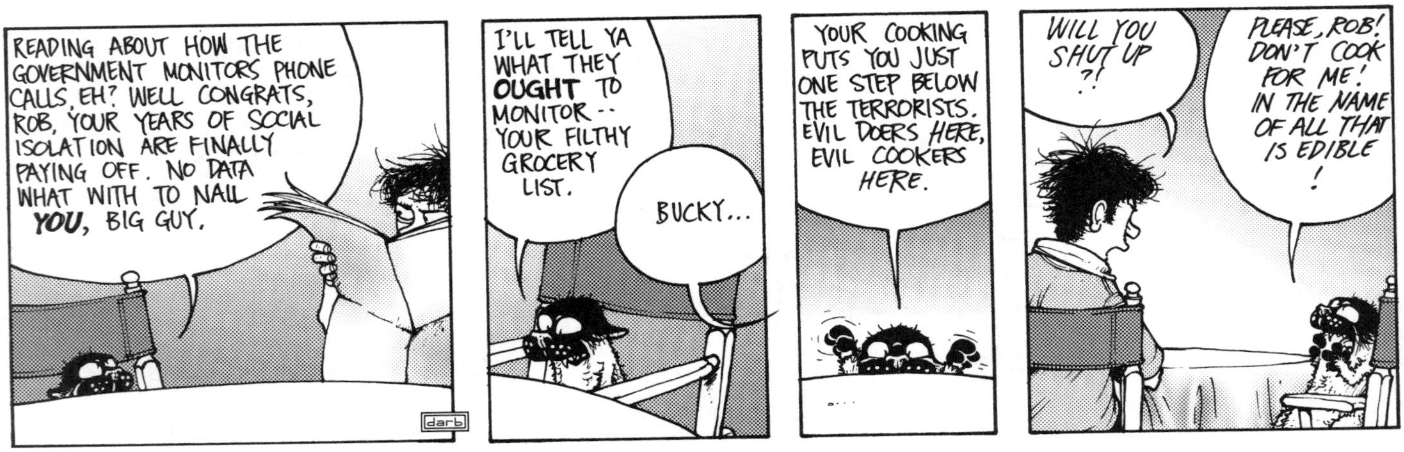
READING ABOUT HOW THE GOVERNMENT MONITORS PHONE CALLS, EH? WELL CONGRATS, ROB, YOUR YEARS OF SOCIAL ISOLATION ARE FINALLY PAYING OFF. NO DATA WHAT WITH TO NAIL YOU, BIG GUY.
darb
I'LL TELL YA WHAT THEY OUGHT TO MONITOR -- YOUR FILTHY GROCERY LIST.
BUCKY...
YOUR COOKING PUTS YOU JUST ONE STEP BELOW THE TERRORISTS. EVIL DOERS HERE, EVIL COOKERS HERE.
WILL YOU SHUT UP ?!
PLEASE, ROB! DON'T COOK FOR ME! IN THE NAME OF ALL THAT IS EDIBLE !

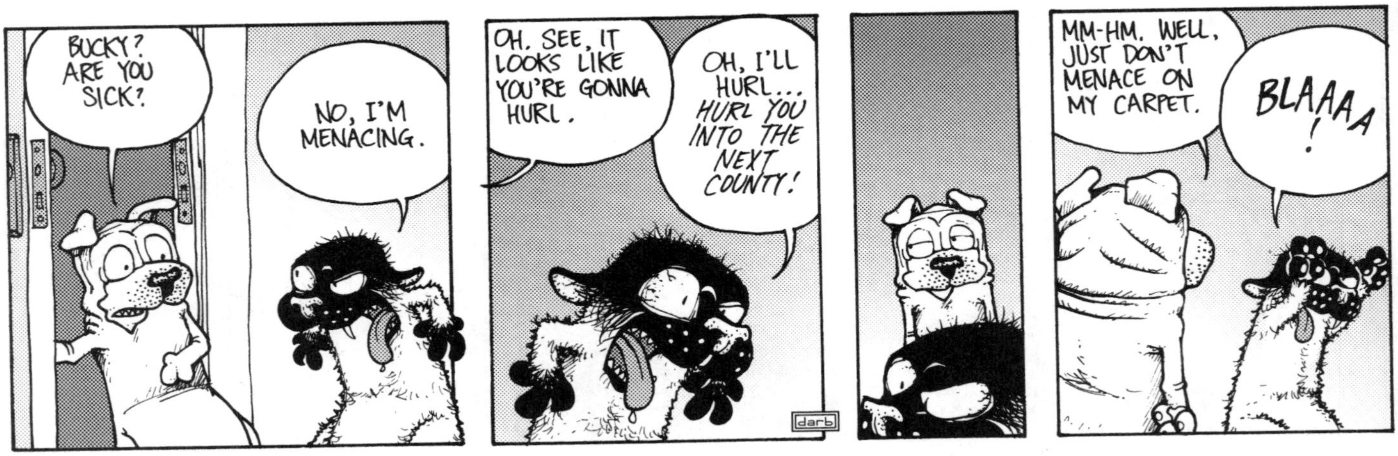
BUCKY? ARE YOU SICK?
NO, I'M MENACING.
OH, SEE, IT LOOKS LIKE YOU'RE GONNA HURL.
OH, I'LL HURL... HURL YOU INTO THE NEXT COUNTY!
darb
MM-HM. WELL, JUST DON'T MENACE ON MY CARPET.
BLAAAA !

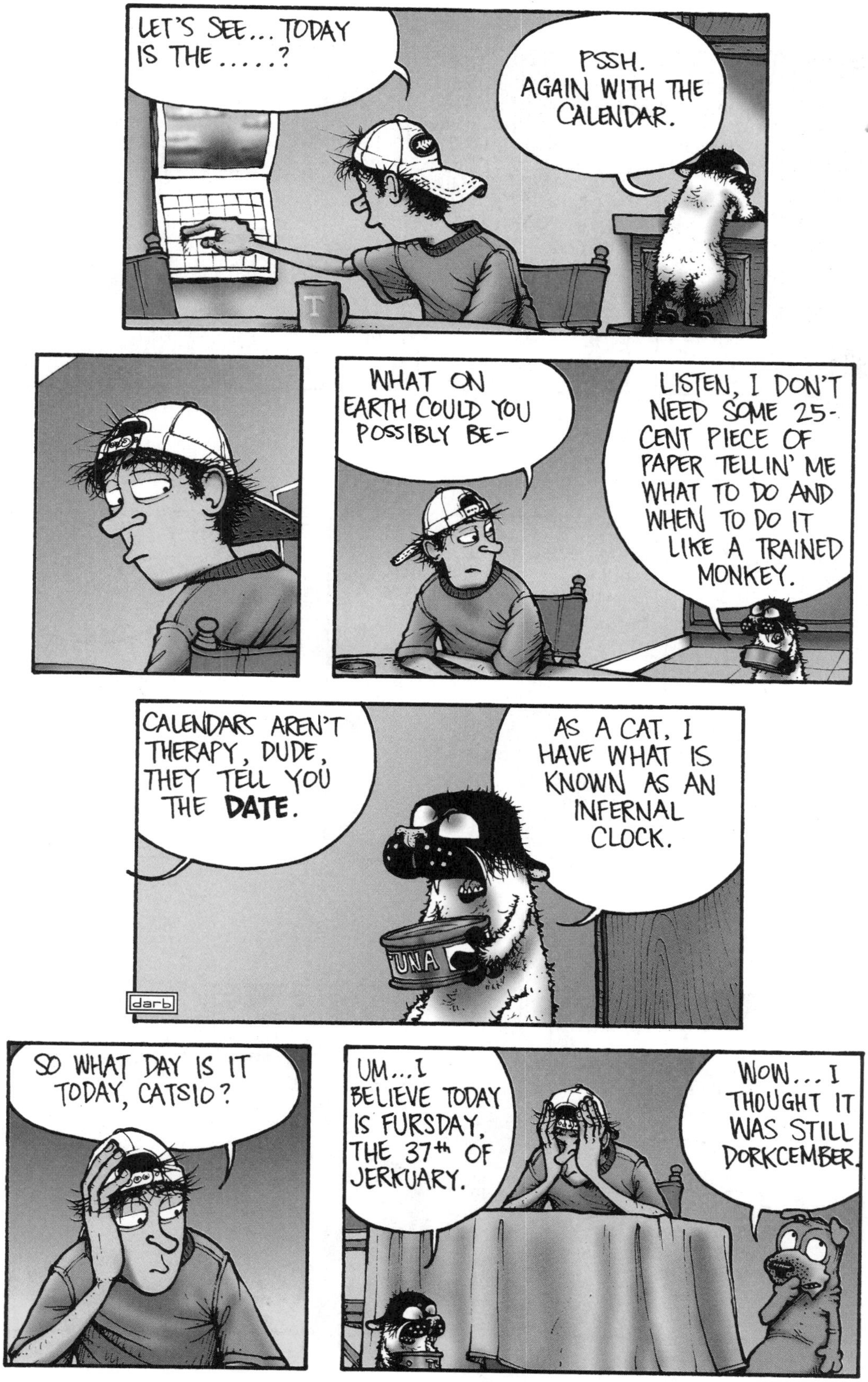
LET'S SEE... TODAY IS THE.....?
PSSH. AGAIN WITH THE CALENDAR.
WHAT ON EARTH COULD YOU POSSIBLY BE-
LISTEN, I DON'T NEED SOME 25-CENT PIECE OF PAPER TELLIN' ME WHAT TO DO AND WHEN TO DO IT LIKE A TRAINED MONKEY.
CALENDARS AREN'T THERAPY, DUDE, THEY TELL YOU THE **DATE**.
AS A CAT, I HAVE WHAT IS KNOWN AS AN INFERNAL CLOCK.
TUNA
darb
SO WHAT DAY IS IT TODAY, CATSIO?
UM...I BELIEVE TODAY IS FURSDAY, THE 37th OF JERKUARY.
WOW... I THOUGHT IT WAS STILL DORKCEMBER.

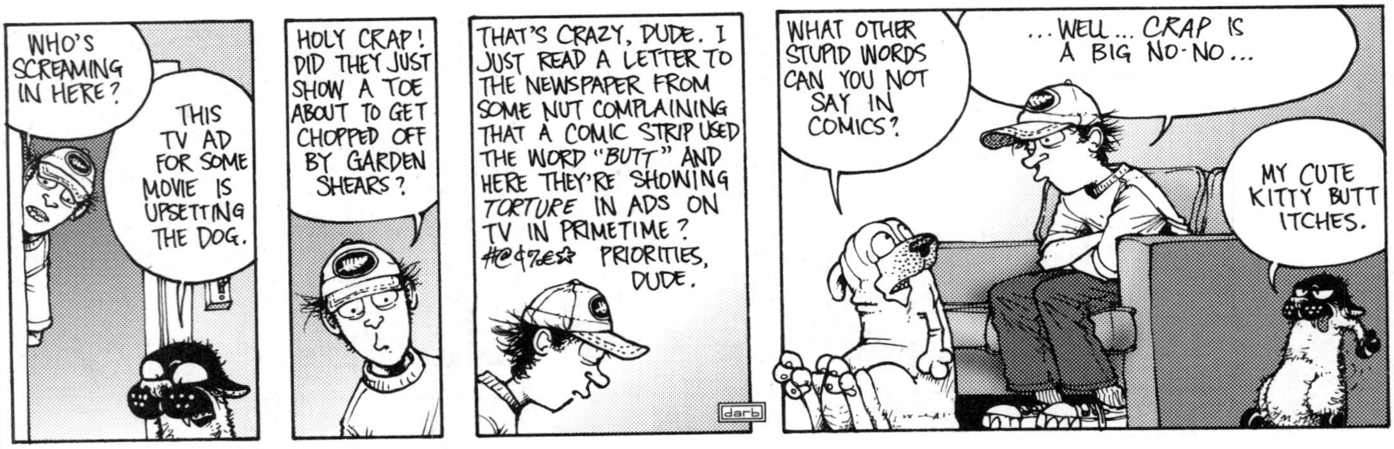
WHO'S SCREAMING IN HERE?
THIS TV AD FOR SOME MOVIE IS UPSETTING THE DOG.
HOLY CRAP! DID THEY JUST SHOW A TOE ABOUT TO GET CHOPPED OFF BY GARDEN SHEARS?
THAT'S CRAZY, DUDE. I JUST READ A LETTER TO THE NEWSPAPER FROM SOME NUT COMPLAINING THAT A COMIC STRIP USED THE WORD "BUTT" AND HERE THEY'RE SHOWING TORTURE IN ADS ON TV IN PRIMETIME? #@$%&* PRIORITIES, DUDE.
darb
WHAT OTHER STUPID WORDS CAN YOU NOT SAY IN COMICS?
...WELL... CRAP IS A BIG NO-NO...
MY CUTE KITTY BUTT ITCHES.

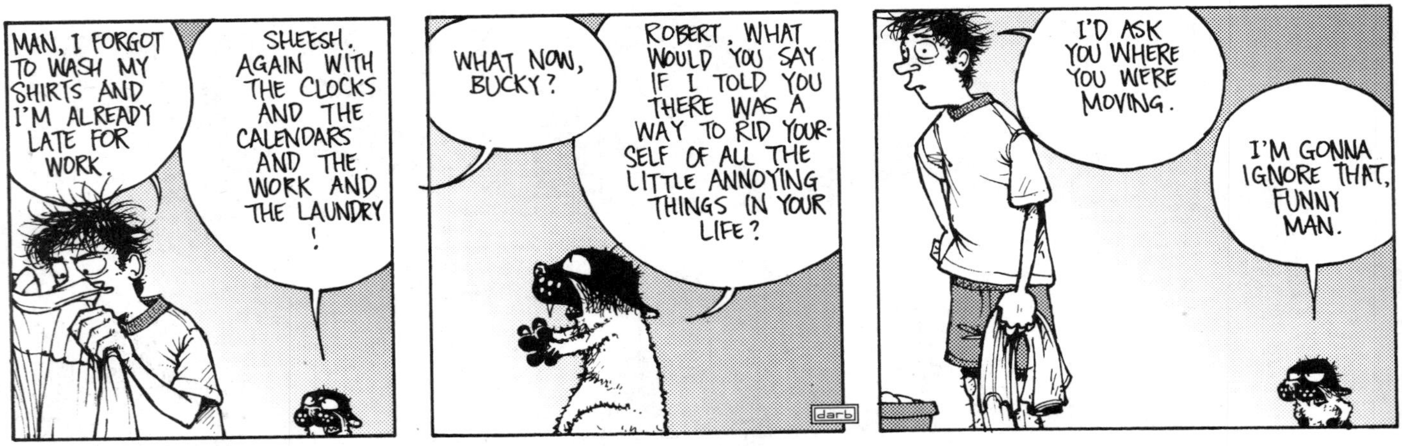
MAN, I FORGOT TO WASH MY SHIRTS AND I'M ALREADY LATE FOR WORK.
SHEESH. AGAIN WITH THE CLOCKS AND THE CALENDARS AND THE WORK AND THE LAUNDRY!
WHAT NOW, BUCKY?
ROBERT, WHAT WOULD YOU SAY IF I TOLD YOU THERE WAS A WAY TO RID YOURSELF OF ALL THE LITTLE ANNOYING THINGS IN YOUR LIFE?
darb
I'D ASK YOU WHERE YOU WERE MOVING.
I'M GONNA IGNORE THAT, FUNNY MAN.

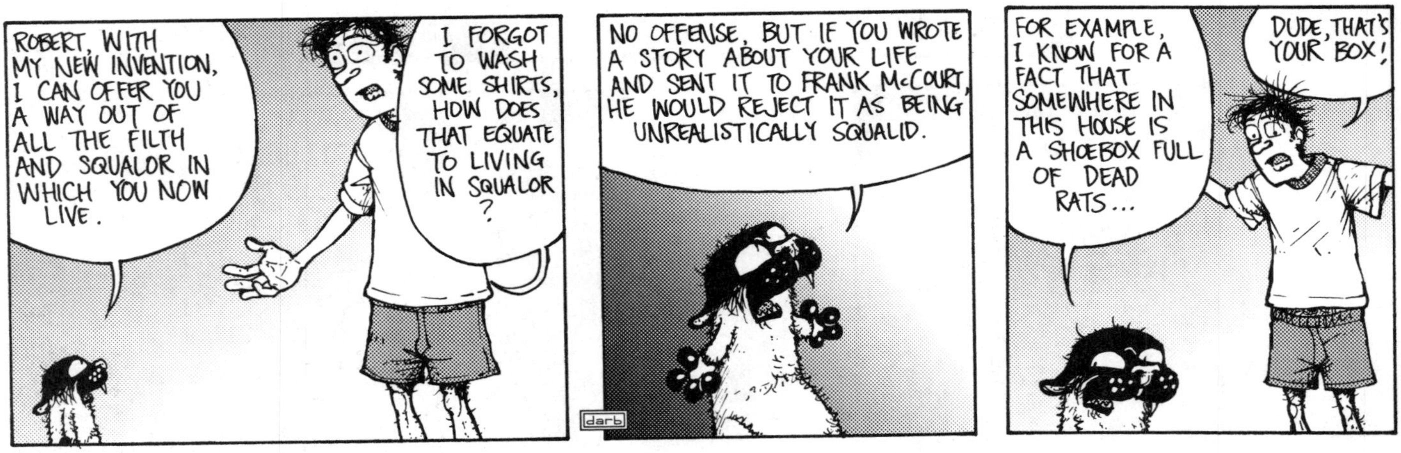
ROBERT, WITH MY NEW INVENTION, I CAN OFFER YOU A WAY OUT OF ALL THE FILTH AND SQUALOR IN WHICH YOU NOW LIVE.
I FORGOT TO WASH SOME SHIRTS, HOW DOES THAT EQUATE TO LIVING IN SQUALOR?
darb
NO OFFENSE, BUT IF YOU WROTE A STORY ABOUT YOUR LIFE AND SENT IT TO FRANK McCOURT, HE WOULD REJECT IT AS BEING UNREALISTICALLY SQUALID.
FOR EXAMPLE, I KNOW FOR A FACT THAT SOMEWHERE IN THIS HOUSE IS A SHOEBOX FULL OF DEAD RATS...
DUDE, THAT'S YOUR BOX!

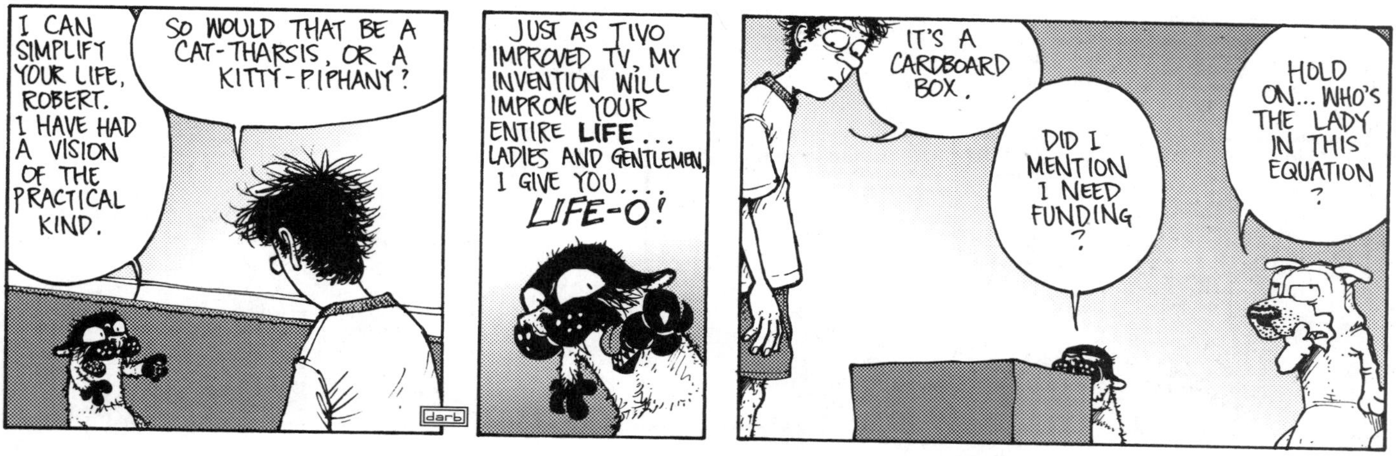
I CAN SIMPLIFY YOUR LIFE, ROBERT. I HAVE HAD A VISION OF THE PRACTICAL KIND.
SO WOULD THAT BE A CAT-THARSIS, OR A KITTY-PIPHANY?
JUST AS TIVO IMPROVED TV, MY INVENTION WILL IMPROVE YOUR ENTIRE **LIFE**... LADIES AND GENTLEMEN, I GIVE YOU.... *LIFE-O*!
IT'S A CARDBOARD BOX.
DID I MENTION I NEED FUNDING?
HOLD ON... WHO'S THE LADY IN THIS EQUATION?
darb

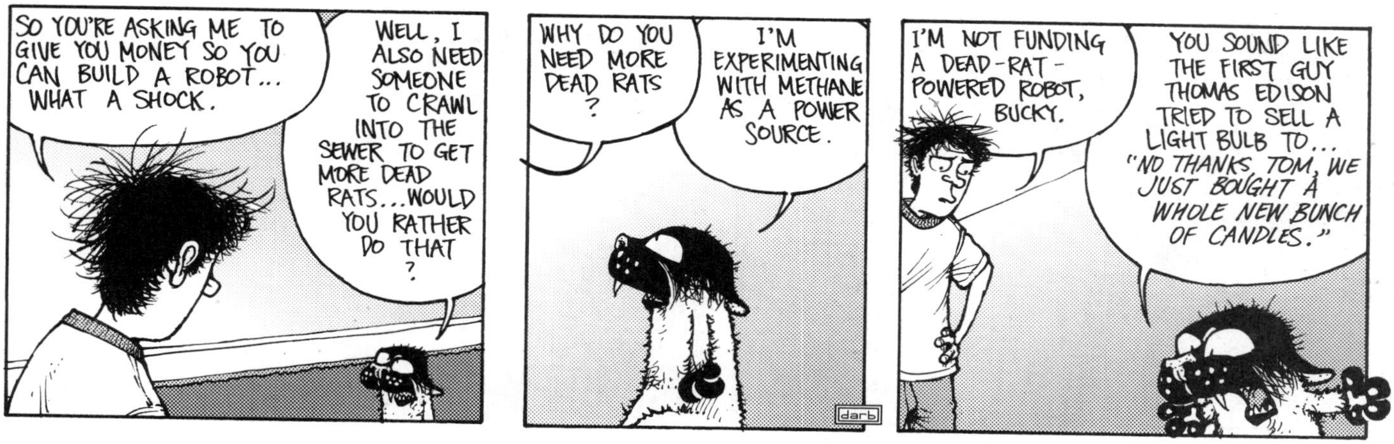
SO YOU'RE ASKING ME TO GIVE YOU MONEY SO YOU CAN BUILD A ROBOT... WHAT A SHOCK.
WELL, I ALSO NEED SOMEONE TO CRAWL INTO THE SEWER TO GET MORE DEAD RATS... WOULD YOU RATHER DO THAT?
WHY DO YOU NEED MORE DEAD RATS?
I'M EXPERIMENTING WITH METHANE AS A POWER SOURCE.
darb
I'M NOT FUNDING A DEAD-RAT-POWERED ROBOT, BUCKY.
YOU SOUND LIKE THE FIRST GUY THOMAS EDISON TRIED TO SELL A LIGHT BULB TO... *"NO THANKS, TOM, WE JUST BOUGHT A WHOLE NEW BUNCH OF CANDLES."*

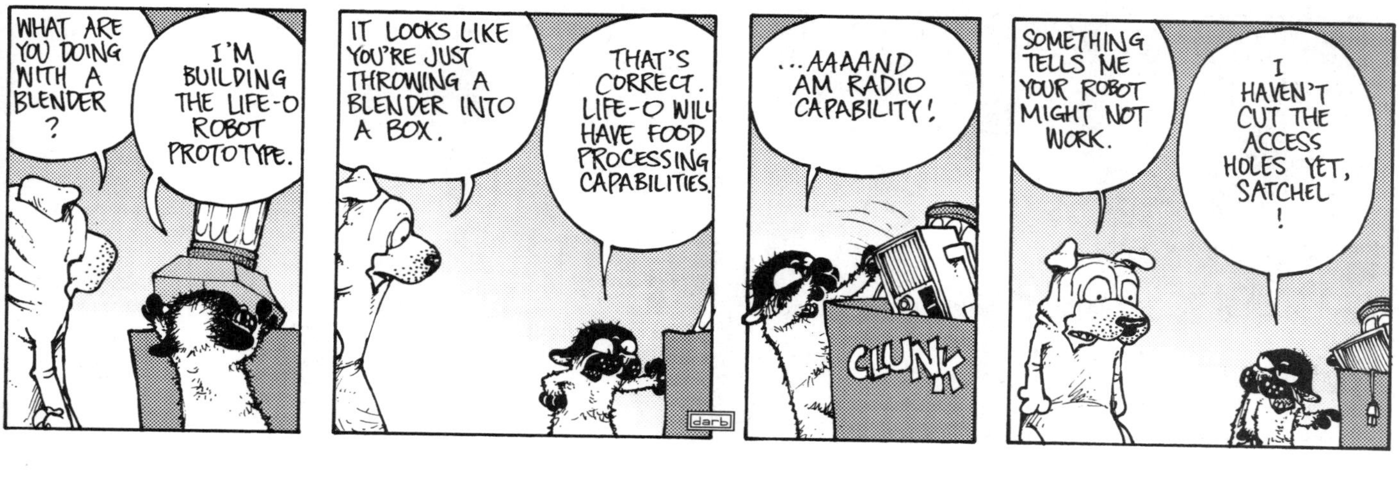
WHAT ARE YOU DOING WITH A BLENDER?
I'M BUILDING THE LIFE-O ROBOT PROTOTYPE.
IT LOOKS LIKE YOU'RE JUST THROWING A BLENDER INTO A BOX.
THAT'S CORRECT. LIFE-O WILL HAVE FOOD PROCESSING CAPABILITIES.
darb
...AAAAND AM RADIO CAPABILITY!
CLUNK
SOMETHING TELLS ME YOUR ROBOT MIGHT NOT WORK.
I HAVEN'T CUT THE ACCESS HOLES YET, SATCHEL!

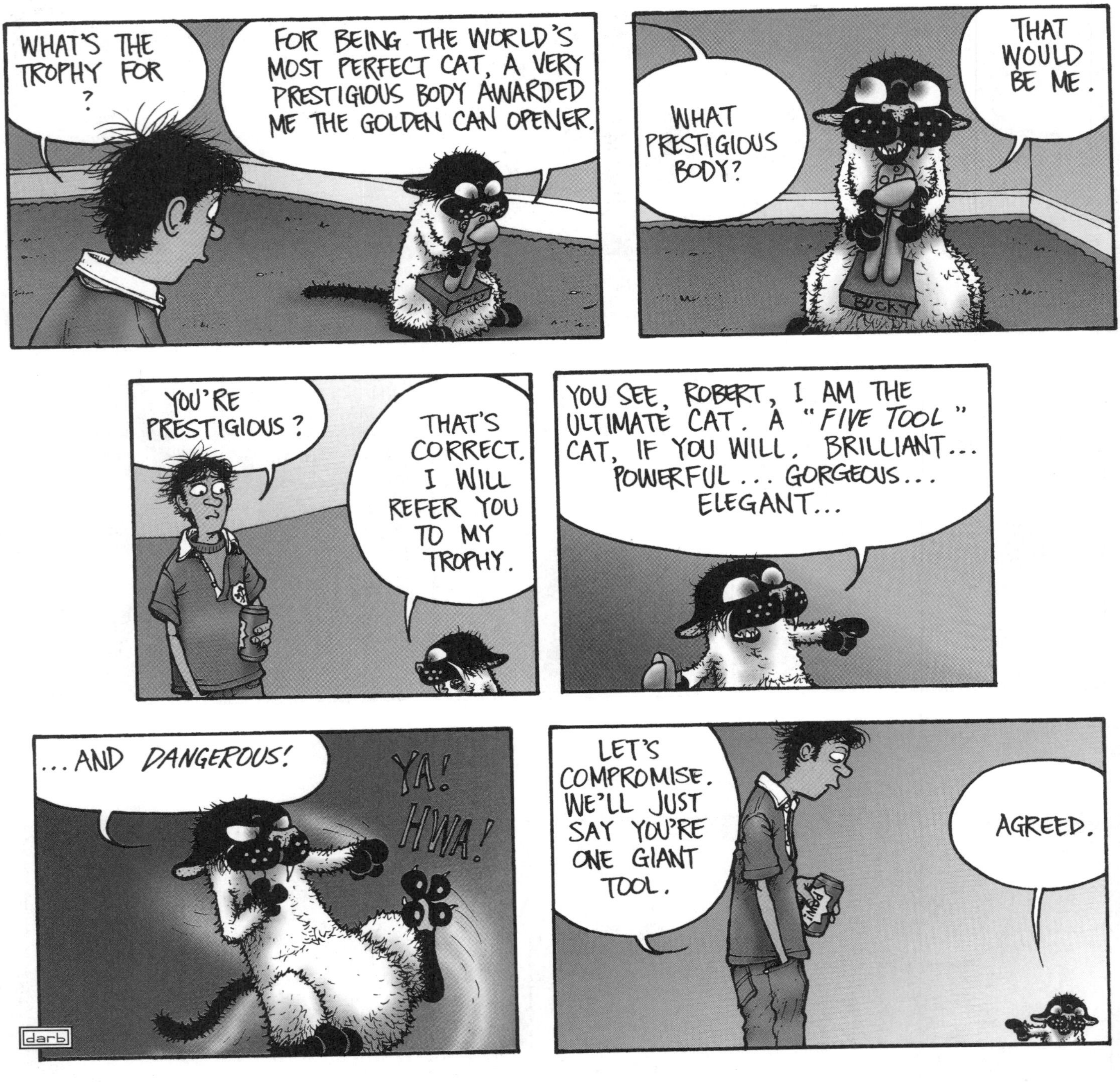
WHAT'S THE TROPHY FOR ?
FOR BEING THE WORLD'S MOST PERFECT CAT, A VERY PRESTIGIOUS BODY AWARDED ME THE GOLDEN CAN OPENER.
WHAT PRESTIGIOUS BODY?
THAT WOULD BE ME.
BUCKY
YOU'RE PRESTIGIOUS ?
THAT'S CORRECT. I WILL REFER YOU TO MY TROPHY.
YOU SEE, ROBERT, I AM THE ULTIMATE CAT. A "FIVE TOOL" CAT, IF YOU WILL. BRILLIANT... POWERFUL ... GORGEOUS... ELEGANT...
...AND DANGEROUS!
YA! HWA!
darb
LET'S COMPROMISE. WE'LL JUST SAY YOU'RE ONE GIANT TOOL.
AGREED.

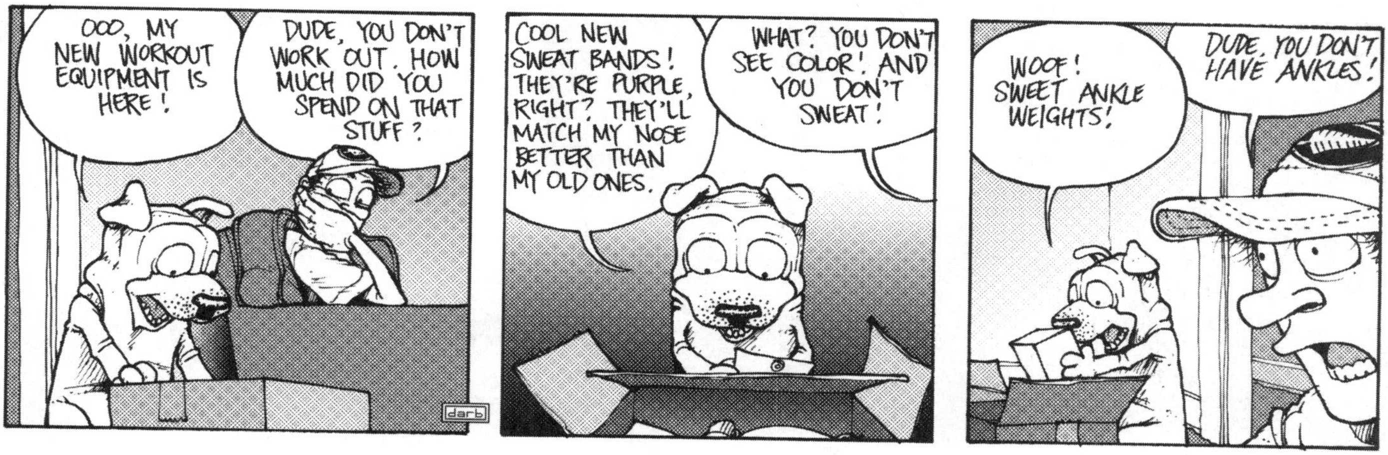
OOO, MY NEW WORKOUT EQUIPMENT IS HERE!
DUDE, YOU DON'T WORK OUT. HOW MUCH DID YOU SPEND ON THAT STUFF?
COOL NEW SWEAT BANDS! THEY'RE PURPLE, RIGHT? THEY'LL MATCH MY NOSE BETTER THAN MY OLD ONES.
WHAT? YOU DON'T SEE COLOR! AND YOU DON'T SWEAT!
WOOF! SWEET ANKLE WEIGHTS!
DUDE, YOU DON'T HAVE ANKLES!

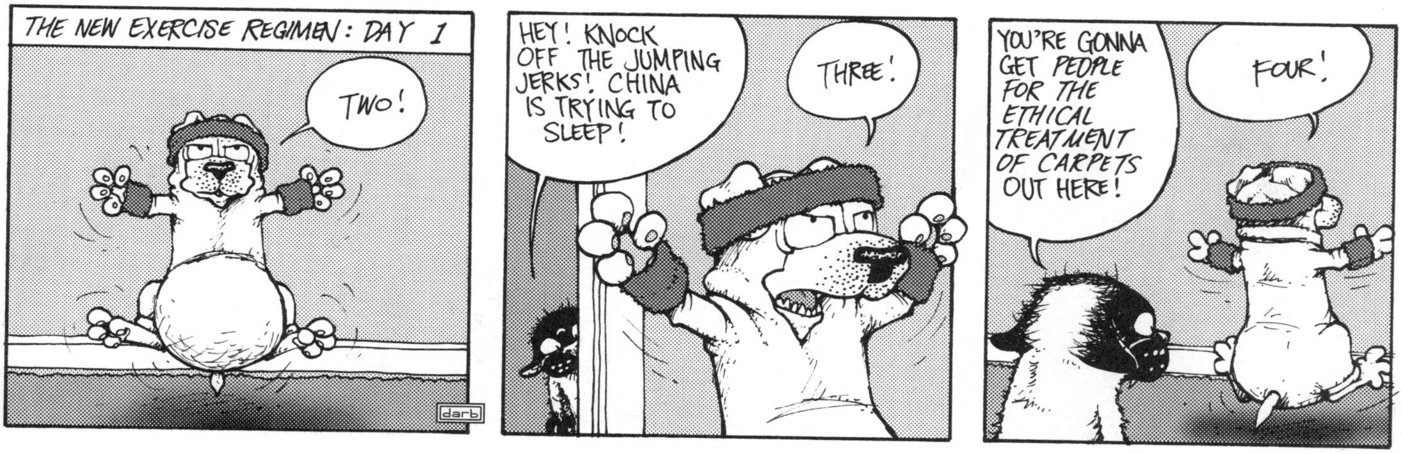
THE NEW EXERCISE REGIMEN: DAY 1
TWO!
HEY! KNOCK OFF THE JUMPING JERKS! CHINA IS TRYING TO SLEEP!
THREE!
YOU'RE GONNA GET PEOPLE FOR THE ETHICAL TREATMENT OF CARPETS OUT HERE!
FOUR!

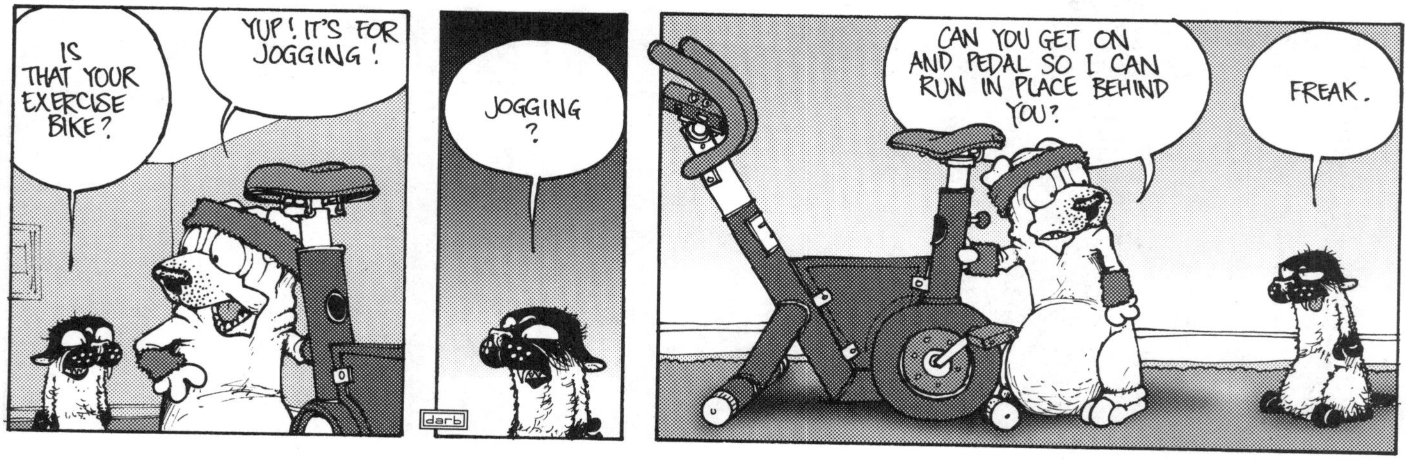
IS THAT YOUR EXERCISE BIKE?
YUP! IT'S FOR JOGGING!
JOGGING?
CAN YOU GET ON AND PEDAL SO I CAN RUN IN PLACE BEHIND YOU?
FREAK.

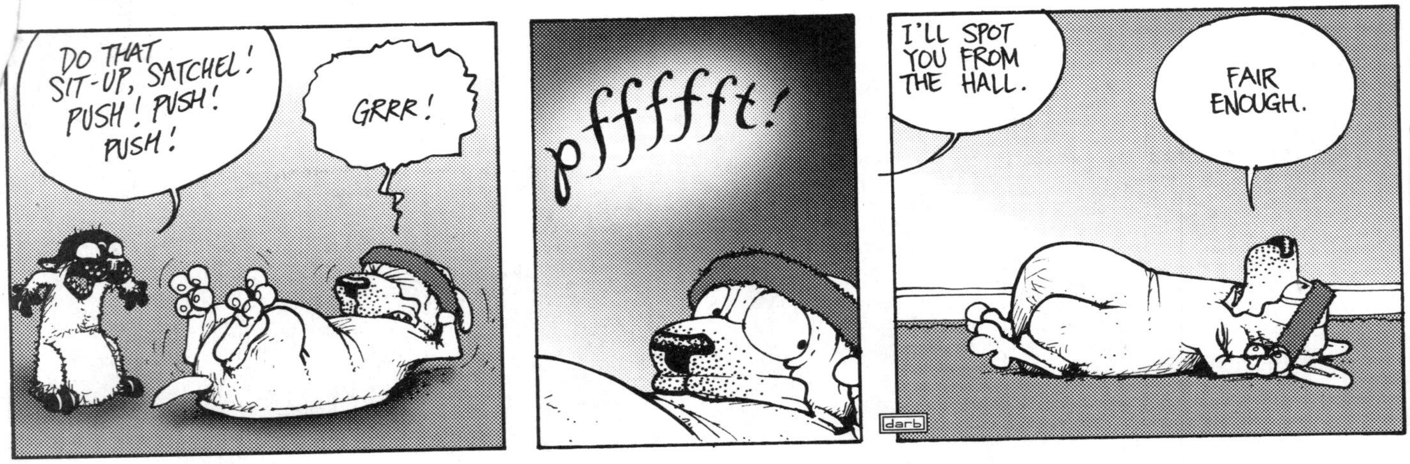
DO THAT SIT-UP, SATCHEL! PUSH! PUSH! PUSH!
GRRR!
pffffft!
I'LL SPOT YOU FROM THE HALL.
FAIR ENOUGH.
darb

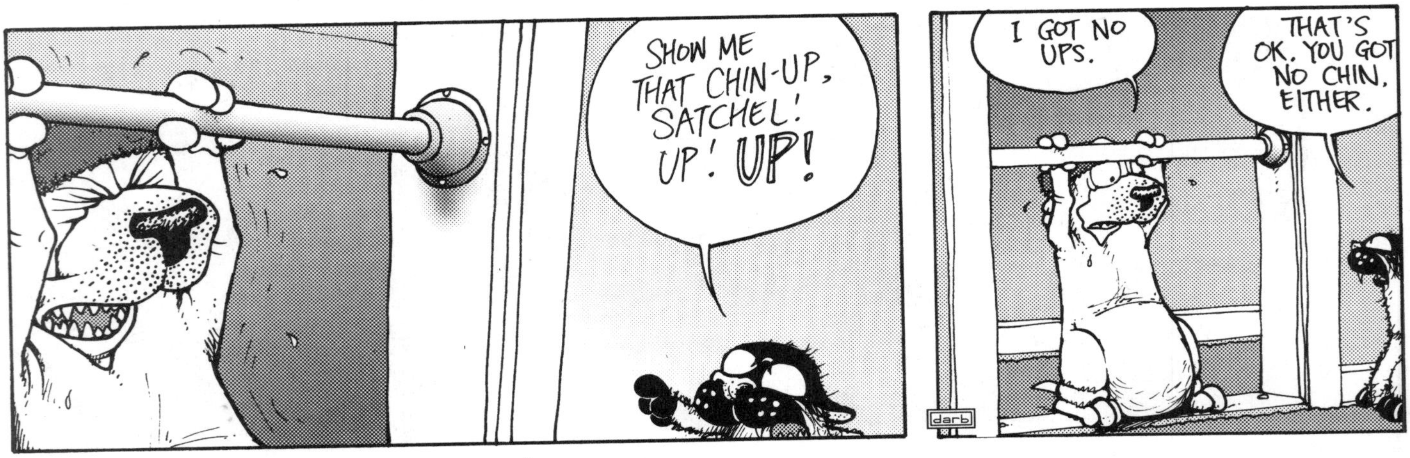
SHOW ME THAT CHIN-UP, SATCHEL! UP! UP!
I GOT NO UPS.
THAT'S OK. YOU GOT NO CHIN, EITHER.
darb

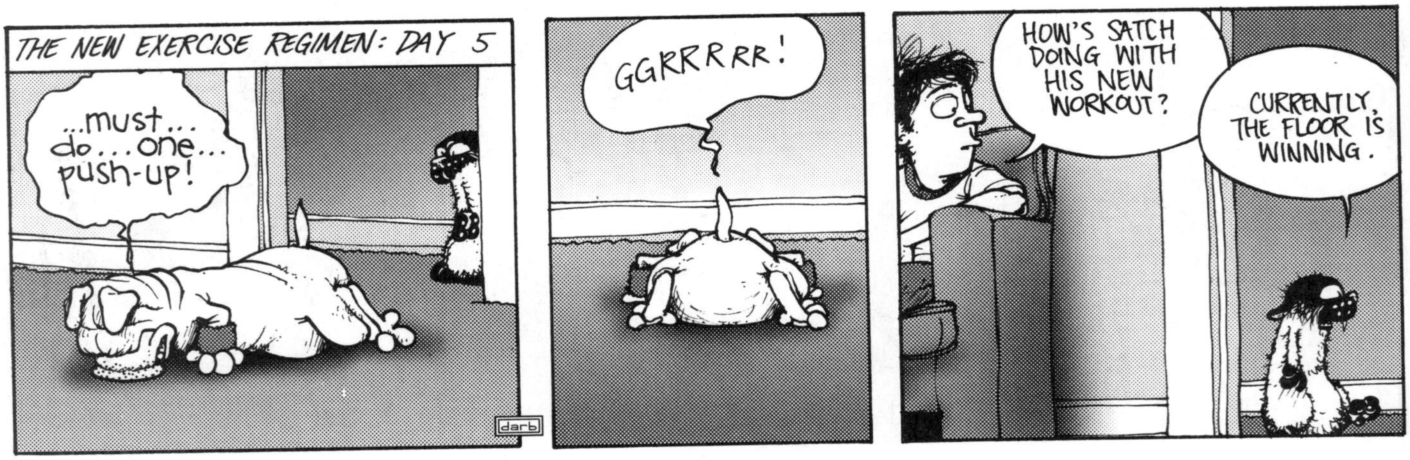
THE NEW EXERCISE REGIMEN: DAY 5
...must... do...one... push-up!
darb
GGRRRRR!
HOW'S SATCH DOING WITH HIS NEW WORKOUT?
CURRENTLY, THE FLOOR IS WINNING.

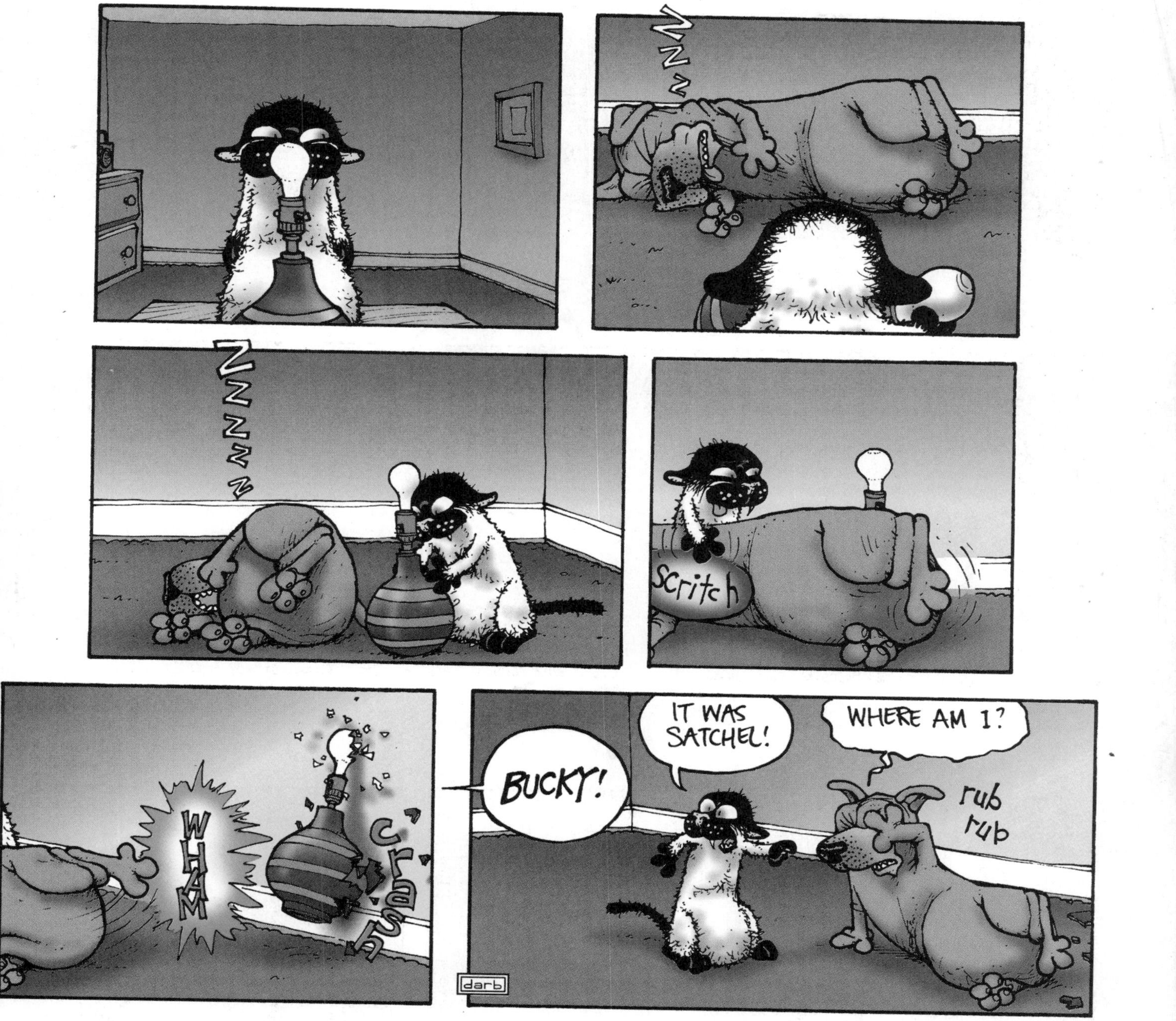
Z
z
z
Z
Z
Z
Z
z
SCRITCH
WHAM
crash
BUCKY!
IT WAS SATCHEL!
WHERE AM I?
rub rub
darb